THE NEW AFRICAN DIASPORA

THE NEW AFRICAN DIASPORA

Edited by   ISIDORE OKPEWHO

and   NKIRU NZEGWU

INDIANA UNIVERSITY PRESS

Bloomington and Indianapolis

This book is a publication of
Indiana University Press
601 North Morton Street
Bloomington, IN 47404-3797 USA

http://iupress.indiana.edu

Telephone orders 800-842-6796
Fax orders 812-855-7931
Orders by e-mail iuporder@indiana.edu

The paper used in this publication meets the minimum requirements
of American National Standard for Information Sciences—Permanence
of Paper for Printed Library Materials, ANSI Z39.48-1984.

Manufactured in the United States of America

Library of Congress Cataloging-in-Publication Data

The new African disapora / edited by Isidore Okpewho and Nkiru
Nzegwu.
    p. cm.
  Includes bibliographical references and index.
  ISBN 978-0-253-35337-5 (cloth : alk. paper) — ISBN 978-0-253-22095-0
(pbk. : alk. paper) 1. Africans—Migrations. 2. Blacks—Migrations.
3. African diaspora. 4. Africans—United States—Social conditions.
5. Immigrants—United States—Social conditions. 6. Africans—
Canada—Social conditions. 7. Immigrants—Canada—Social
conditions. 8. Africa—Emigration and immigration. 9. United
States—Emigration and immigration. 10. Canada—Emigration
and immigration. I. Okpewho, Isidore. II. Nzegwu, Nkiru.
  DT16.5.N495 2009
  305.896—dc22

                                                        2009005961

1 2 3 4 5 14 13 12 11 10 09

CONTENTS

PREFACE AND ACKNOWLEDGMENTS

This volume of essays has emerged from a symposium held on April 7–8, 2006, by the Department of Africana Studies at Binghamton University. The meeting marked the tenth anniversary of a conference, held by the department in April 1996, which gave rise to a volume titled *The African Diaspora: African Origins and New World Identities,* also published by Indiana University Press (1999). Whereas the earlier volume concentrated its attention on the fate of Africans forcibly relocated to the Americas and the Caribbean by enslavement, the present volume deals exclusively with the voluntary movements and relocations of Africans and peoples of African descent between the home continent and various parts of the western Atlantic. Whatever may be the common grounds between the old and the new diasporas, there are increasing signs of a global outlook in international relations today that needed to be addressed in the context of a conversation on the black experience across space and time.

We would like to acknowledge the contributions of several individuals and units of Binghamton University toward our efforts in hosting the symposium from which this volume arose. The offices of the provost and of the dean of Harpur College of Arts and Sciences, as well as the university's Convocations Committee, offered funds that enabled us to subsidize the participation of scholars from far and wide at the symposium. We are deeply grateful for their help. Our departmental secretary, Barbara Kumiega, put a great deal of effort into ensuring the promptness and smoothness of various services provided by the department: accommodation, transportation, meals, equipment, meetings, etc. Barbara has now retired, and we offer her not only gratitude for some dozen years of outstanding service to the department but also our wishes for a restful and healthy retirement. We are also grateful to the following students for their help in making the symposium a success: Adeolu Ademoyo, Carlie Ferrera, Andrea Frohne, and Azuka Nzegwu. And we thank AfricaResource.com for hosting a website for the conference.

PART ONE
OVERVIEWS

1 INTRODUCTION: CAN WE "GO HOME AGAIN"?

Isidore Okpewho

I am using, as my point of reference here, the forced migration of Africans to the Americas that took place—in Vincent Thompson's reckoning (*Making of the African Diaspora* 78, 82)—from about the middle of the fifteenth century to about the middle of the nineteenth AD (though the Arab trade in Africans had started much earlier than this). One of the classic testimonies of this migration is Olaudah Equiano's *Interesting Narrative,* which records the experiences of a young boy of about ten who, despite Vincent Carretta's recent contestation, was captured from somewhere in southeastern Nigeria and sold into slavery first in the West Indies, then in North America, and finally in England. His experiences took him through a range of domestic and mercantile forms of servitude in these three regions, during which he was exposed to varying levels of kindness and abuse, until he was able ultimately to achieve considerable prominence, even respectability, within British society. Early enough in his sojourn in this society, he had the opportunity to be given some Christian education by two young ladies in whose service he had been placed. But by dint of his industry and resourcefulness he gradually supplemented this with wide reading in the humane letters of the time, much of which formed the basis of arguments subtending the agitation for the abolition of slavery by many enlightened men and women in Britain late in the eighteenth century.

Along with several elements in British society—indigenous citizens and Africans who had, like himself, gained their freedom from slavery—Equiano put his literacy to the service of this agitation, which eventually led to the abolition of the infernal institution. Equiano never lived to see abolition, of course, and though he played a prominent role in preparations for the establishment of a settlement in Sierra Leone to which freed Africans and others were repatriated, differences with the organizers of the project denied him the opportunity of joining in the return to Africa. But to the end of his life Equiano seems to have clung to his African sensi-

bility despite the passage of time and the intervention of a European outlook on life. His narrative periodically invokes images of his long-lost Igbo
family, and despite a memory much frayed by time and misadventure his
reminiscences of his native land and its ways of life are impressively close
to the reality of things. To the end of his narrative he continues to refer
to himself as an "African" though he was, at the material time, firmly
British in terms of both residential and cultural identity. One can only
imagine how far he would have gone, had he actually landed in Sierra Leone with the African mission, in reintegrating himself with the land of
his origins if not exactly his native community.

It is pertinent to raise such a question, because it does matter how
much of one's culture is lost when one has been forced to live far away
from one's native home for a considerable length of time: in other words,
to what extent does *diaspora,* as the subject of reflection and study, represent a shift in orientation and outlook as against a change in zone of
residence—or is the question irrelevant? Equiano's experience does in fact
come into play here, because it has been used by those who question the
concept of a diaspora and urge—if I may borrow the title of a recent book
by Clarence Walker, one of the most prominent anti-diasporists—that
"we can't go home again." In a rather skewed reading of the *Interesting
Narrative,* Walker argues that Equiano's self-awareness suffered nothing
short of a paradigm shift simply because "he received a new name, learned
English, and became a Christian. His resistance to everything but the
name change was minimal" (62). Yet, as I indicated above, it is significant that Equiano continued to stress his "African" identity long after
he achieved integration into certain respectable cadres of British society.
True, his adoption of Christian values influenced his denunciation of the
slave system. But for him slavery was not simply an instance of man's in-
humanity to man; like Frederick Douglass in the generation after him,
Equiano felt a deep racial empathy for the victims of the system, whom
he often called "my African brethren" in his book. In other words, Africa
continued to live deep in his consciousness long after he had lost a clear,
unmediated grasp of what his native society looked like.

Of course, Equiano could not "go home again," thanks to a conspiracy
of British capitalist interests against his responsibility as "Commissary
of Provisions and Stores for the Black Poor to Sierra Leona" (Equiano 227).
There was, nonetheless, an equally valid reason why he could not return
to anything like his native home, assuming he could trace his way there;
but I am not sure that this consideration weighed much on his mind as he
did his best to find his berth in the British society he learned to call home.
When Olaudah Equiano was captured from his Igbo village, he was a mere
boy of about ten years of age. In attempting to recreate life as he knew it
in the village, he inevitably seeks to turn the tables on those who derogate
his people as unaccountable savages, by making the *Interesting Narrative*

into something of an *apologia pro gente sua* that paints enslavement—as Equiano's American contemporary Phillis Wheatley was to do in her own writing—as a cruel and heartless violation of an idyllic existence.[1] In his narrative, Equiano gives an account of the practice of slave-catching to which he and sister finally fall victim; but he portrays it pretty much as the occupation of the time, and one he never dreamed would affect him until it did. So we do not find Equiano reflecting, in his autobiography, upon what would happen to him were he to return someday to the paradise he had left behind. He had committed so much faith to a project of repatriation that promised some dignity for himself and his brethren, as well as promotion of Britain's industrial economy, that he hardly stopped to reflect that the dangers that led to his enslavement might still be alive. In his subconscious mind those dangers may well have remained intact; in planning for resettling himself and his fellow blacks in Sierra Leone, however, other considerations dominated his conscious mind. Yet these are the considerations we must bring to the fore if we are to fully understand the relations between the old and the new African diaspora.

We might begin to understand these relations by characterizing the older diaspora as *precolonial* and the more recent one as *postcolonial,* or by using the demarcation Ali Mazrui has drawn between what he calls the diaspora of enslavement and the diaspora of imperialism ("The African Diaspora and Globalization"). In the latter, the slave trade had been abolished and replaced by the establishment of Western European colonization over African nations and the exploitation of their natural resources, a process that had in fact begun, by his own admission, in Equiano's day even before slavery had been pronounced statutorily illegal by the British parliament in 1807. Africans of the precolonial diaspora had been mostly forced out of their societies into bondage, so they had no choice in their relocation to the Western world. Many of them, like Equiano himself, may have retained nostalgic memories of their native lands; the children born to them in their captivity may, under the influence of idealist accounts related to them by their parents, have embraced a "romance of Africa"—to borrow a phrase from Martin Kilson and Adelaide Hill—framed by the halo of their parents' fading memories. But there was hopelessly little they could do for the land of their origins in the circumscribed conditions of their lives. A few enslaved Africans eventually found their way back to Africa after they had gained their freedom. But even when they returned to what may be assumed to be their original "nation," as did those who joined resettlement programs in Sierra Leone and Liberia and others who retraced their lineages from Brazil to Nigeria, or when their descendants accompanied Christian or colonial missions to various African countries, the societies they encountered had been dramatically altered by new systems of control that not only bore little relation to romantic notions they may have formed about the Africa of the past but constrained whatever contributions they may have pledged themselves to make to uplift the land. The fate of Africa was now, sadly, entirely out of the hands either of themselves or of the resident population.[2]

If Olaudah Equiano had returned to his native Igbo village, he probably would have come face-to-face with what he was too young to recognize when he was captured into slavery, which is the same truth that the black sharecropper Nate Shaw, as Clarence Walker reminds us, recognized in a rather different context late in the nineteenth century: that "all God's dangers ain't a white man" (Walker 83). For was it not Equiano's own people who made it possible for the white enslavers to take him away into bondage? As we proceed to consider the new, or postcolonial, African diaspora in which many Africans like myself live today in America and elsewhere, we should perhaps ask whether the conditions that caused us to leave our homes in Africa are strikingly different from what forced the likes of Equiano out of their native communities. One of my friends once reminded me, rather cannily, that we are essentially migrant laborers. The closest equivalent to this condition in the past might be the plight of indentured laborers, which, if history is any guide, was hardly more comfortable than bondage. Uncharitable as the comparison may seem, it at least suggests something of the discomfort that attends those who forgo the security that home, whatever its inadequacies, essentially guarantees.

It would not be wrong to lay the blame for our flight from Africa at the feet of the postcolonial condition—that is, primarily at least, the state of disequilibrium in African societies brought about by the intervention of European colonization. Ngugi wa Thiong'o is certainly right in charging that the roots of Africa's disorientation lie in a system that replaced our indigenous tongues, and consequently our time-honored patterns of thinking, with foreign ones (*Decolonizing the Mind*). Once the colonizers got firmly entrenched in their respective African territories, they lost no time setting into place the social and other structures that would secure them the freedom they needed for pursuing the principal goal of their adventure, which was the exploitation of the natural resources of the colonies in the interest of their nations' industrialization programs. On the one hand, they destroyed, or at least set aside, the indigenous systems of leadership and control in favor of a political structure that put the ultimate power in the hands of an imperial metropolis far away from the colony. On the other hand, they exploited the ethnic and religious rivalries between segments of the nations they had created, so that while these rival groups fought among themselves their natural wealth was being steadily drained from their lands. Over time, of course, the Western-educated sons of the land rose to challenge colonization and, in the end, won political independence for the new nation. But the structures established by the departing colonizers had ensured that the goal of true unity would for a long time elude the nation, paving the way for a neocolonial dispensation whereby the resources of Africa continued to be appropriated by the former colonizers working in corrupt collusion with the indigenous political leadership. The result has been an abysmal lack of commitment to a unified political vision and a perennial crisis of leadership in many African nations, culminating in military coups and, in not a few cases, civil wars and genocidal conflicts. Those who have been lucky enough to escape with their lives, or have simply decided that they needed to carry on their careers in less threatening conditions, have opted to flee the land and live in exile. The expatriation has only gotten worse in the four decades that African nations have been free from colonization; hence the *New York Times* could report, on February 21, 2005, that "Since 1990, according to immigration figures, more [Africans] have arrived voluntarily than the total who disembarked in chains before the United States outlawed international slave trafficking in 1807" (Roberts).

The picture I have painted above should be familiar to those who have observed the crises in African nations including South Africa, the Congo, Nigeria, Rwanda, Liberia, Sierra Leone, and several others. In these nations, colonization may be held responsible for, on the one hand, an explosion of inter-group rivalries to a colossal scale, and on the other, the collapse of structures that could have guaranteed the proper exploitation of the wealth of the land in the people's interest. So, far be it from me to contradict anyone who lays the blame for Africa's failures at the feet of the foreign intruder.

But, for how long shall we fail to see the fingers pointing in the other direction, which is toward ourselves? Having studied the oral traditions of Africa for some time, I may be allowed some insights that could help us address the issue from a slightly different perspective. I refer, first, to some of the traditional folk poetry by which intra-ethnic and inter-ethnic groups lampoon each other and stake their claims within the power dynamics governing their relationships. Anthropologists have used the term "joking relationships" for this exchange of abuse between groups, but there has always been the inherent risk of aggravation.[3] A more serious potential for trouble may be seen in heroic traditions such as praise poems and epics glorifying great leaders of the past. However useful we may find these works as proof that, contrary to European prejudice, Africa has had its proud artistic and intellectual heritage, the fact remains that the traditions—in which the heroes are often credited with absolute power over the life and death of their subjects—appear to be the model of behavior for many an African leader today. When, for instance, a leader presumes the right, without consultation with anyone, to announce who should rule his nation after him—as we see Moussa Tounkara, the King of Mema, do in the legend of Sunjata (Niane 37), and as only in the mid-1990s President Gnassingbé Eyadéma did in Togo—how can we honestly blame colonialism for such blatant horrors of leadership?

The toll of these horrors is too long, and I will spare you further enumeration of them. I will also spare you details of the failure of the present-day African leadership in social and economic spheres of life. I will simply choose one instance of my personal experience as a university teacher in Nigeria to illustrate why some of us decided to leave our country and go where we might continue to make whatever difference we still could. In 1978, the senate of my university in Nigeria announced it would offer a block of grants for research projects across disciplines. I applied and was awarded one of these grants, which enabled me to conduct the fieldwork and library-based research on African mythology that resulted in my book *Myth in Africa* (1983). A few years later, another round of senate research grants was offered, and I again applied, in the hope of getting support for a more general study of African oral literature. This time, unfortunately, my application never went beyond the local committee that cleared candidates in the Faculty of Arts for the larger university committee. When I enquired why my application failed, I was told by one of the committee members, "Well, you are a full professor now, what are you still researching?"

That question was not an acknowledgment that I had worked hard to attain my position of full professor and a recommendation that I should ease the stress on myself, or give some junior faculty member the same chance I had had to rise to the top. It was prompted, instead, by a sense that having achieved the professorship, I owed no one any more labors; I should simply recline and savor the power and privilege the professorship gave me over less-appointed colleagues. Please do not conclude that I left my country just because I could not get another senate research grant. I cite this experience only as a symptom of a more serious problem of orientation in a postcolonial society that needed all the effort it could afford to set itself on a proper path of growth and self-realization. But how can anything be set right when a nation has lost its sense of mission in its blind pursuit of power and privilege: When the government abandons its responsibility to provide the resources for quality education in its schools and universities and instead diverts them to grandiose, meaningless schemes both inside and outside the country? When the nation's leaders fund private research initiatives in the United States—thus opening up avenues for siphoning public money into their private accounts abroad—rather than situate the same initiatives in institutions inside their own country? When writers, scholars, and journalists are thrown into jail or relieved of their appointments simply because they dared to criticize political leaders and their misguided acts? When, indeed, a journalist could lose his life for exposing the abuses of leaders, and no efforts are made to apprehend or locate the culprits? So, what intellectual would want to remain in a country where the honest pursuit of truth is either derided or discouraged? The questions raised by these experiences are too numerous to be tackled in this essay, but we should be honest enough to admit they have far less to do with colonialism than with that attitude to power and privilege epitomized by two leaders I cited above: one from folk legend (Moussa Tounkara), the other from recent history (Gnassingbé Eyadéma).

Because of their excellent qualifications, many skilled Africans—and African-descended peoples, I might add—who have relocated to the U.S. in the last few decades have had little trouble settling into good positions and securing permanent residency statuses. Unfortunately, for the vast majority of immigrants in the new diaspora, the picture is far from pretty. In fact, many have been forced to leave their countries under conditions that are hardly better than what the generation of Olaudah Equiano went through. Boat-loads of Haitians and Cubans struggling to evade the U.S. coast guard and perishing in the merciless waves of the sea are nearly as painful to watch on television as the horrors of the Middle Passage are horrible to contemplate. But how about young African boys who hide themselves in the luggage compartments and tail sections of airplanes, hoping that once they make it to the other side they may be able to prevail on the authorities to take pity on them? Luckily, we have so far been spared the photographs of their mangled corpses as they are removed from the planes. For the large numbers of immigrants who manage to evade security at the ports of entry, the perennial nightmare of immigration checks has made the long journey hardly worth the trouble.

For the new African diaspora, the experience of exile has been both beneficial and troubling. Whether we arrived here as highly skilled professionals or struggling students, many of us have been able to realize the goals of our voluntary expatriation in ways that have both benefited the host society—in the arts and sciences, technology, sports, and so forth—and improved the fate of relatives we left back home in our native lands. But these benefits have come at huge social and psychological costs that are not so easy to appreciate, and I would like to conclude this section by raising two questions that are rather closely bound with the decision we made to leave our countries and live abroad.

First, to reverse the tone of Clarence Walker's book title, we may ask: *Can we go home again?* Whether we take the question in the literal sense or in the more or less metaphorical sense Walker had in mind, the question is not at all easy to answer. True, unlike Olaudah Equiano, who was forcibly removed from his village and taken through an uncharted path he could not retrace even if he had a chance to, most of us do visit home again and again, and a few have been known to return to settle upon retirement from foreign employment. There is some truth to the statement that James Baldwin made upon his return to America after a long exile in

Europe. "I am not certain," he wrote in the *Washington Star* of January 1978, "that anyone ever leaves home. When 'home' drops below the horizon, it rises in one's breast and acquires the overwhelming power of menaced love." Hence even those who do not finally return from exile to settle home to rest continue to feel the pull to visit home again and again, so as to keep alive the umbilical cord connecting them to the earth of their ancestors. But therein lies the problem. Those who are reduced to making these tentative returns have become victims of a schizophrenia that is ultimately the price they pay for taking the decision to separate themselves from their home.

Let us be fair to ourselves. If conditions at home deteriorate to such an extent that you can no longer guarantee to yourself and your family the basic needs of life: when the water does not run for weeks, so that conditions in both the kitchen and bathroom become hazardous; when toilet facilities in the grade schools break down completely so that, in their dire need to relieve themselves, your children pick up diseases floating freely in the severely endangered environment; when the clinics can no longer provide prescribed medications because their budgets have been deeply slashed or suspended, and families are left to buy unregulated drugs from open shelves, thus putting their lives at risk; when salaries are not paid for months, so that parents cannot afford even the unregulated drugs, let alone sufficient food for the table; now who, under these conditions, would resist the urge to seek employment outside the country just so the family can at least stay alive?

Unfortunately, expatriation is never simply a physical matter; it also takes a psychological toll on the emigrants. However much they yearn to reconnect with the homeland, an extended removal from the familiar environment inevitably weakens their bonds with it and, conversely, increases their commitment to the land that now offers some nourishment to the body if not the spirit. We may not go as far as Clarence Walker in seeing Equiano's consciousness as so thoroughly dissociated from Africa. But Equiano had committed so much of his time to concretizing his place in British society, with all he comforts and securities this brought, that his thoughts of Africa, about which he knew too little anyway, inevitably suffered some reduction. Some of us who brought our families to live in America may continue to insist, against all countervailing evidence, that we are still Africans to the core. But what about our children, who, delighted to be exchanging the depressing physical conditions in Africa for a life of ease and comfort in America, have a weaker grasp than we do of the deeper losses that expatriation brings? In time, of course, living in America reduces the romance of the place for them, and they may come to see—thanks to the moral deficit of America's conduct under some of its leaders—that there is something to be said, after all, for the Africa they left behind. But their appreciation of that Africa and its values are now filtered through eyes that are no longer indigenously African, conditioned as they now are, to some extent at least, by the comforts and securities of their new environment. In the final analysis, there is something about them that may not so easily "go home again."

This brings me, finally, to a second question that is tied to our decision to leave our native homes and live in exile: What are the conditions of our affiliation with the new land? Of course, if we respect the established immigration rules and processes, we may soon achieve permanent residency. In time, too, professionals among us may realize that carrying the American passport reduces the limitations of travel abroad, and be persuaded to compromise some of our sentimental commitment to our land of origin. So we eventually naturalize as Americans. Now how does everyone, including ourselves, feel about this situation that signifies we have come to America to stay?

This is no doubt the touchiest part of expatriation, and there is no need to quibble about its implications. Anyone who expects members of the new diaspora, naturalized or not, to feel an unqualified elation about expatriation is being rather uncharitable. There is some trauma involved in the separation that will take some time to heal. But what is even more painful is the way we are received by the new society. Some details of the pain may need to await our autobiographies, if we choose to write them. But a few will do here. For a start, we are black people, and however qualified or competent we are in our fields of endeavor, some whites who judge everything in human relations by Manichean principles have not hesitated to put us in the same place they have reserved for African Americans throughout their history. It does not take long for us to be shocked by a rude curtailment of that old self-assurance that we could get anywhere we had a mind to. Some of us may eventually attain our goals; the rest are broken by despair. Those who succeed are never entirely spared the feeling that they owe their success to someone else's token nod, not the strength of their own hard work.

But how do our own black kin perceive us? In declaring that African Americans cannot "go home again," Clarence Walker is expressing an all-too-familiar sentiment. If you have any illusions about some emotional ties that bind the black race, do not forget that they have frequently been qualified throughout the history of enslavement: Africans in the homeland sold other Africans to white traders; when he was making his way up the social and economic ladder in the Western world, Olaudah Equiano himself participated in the trade, despite the tears he frequently sheds in his narrative about the plight of his "brethren"; and in Charles Johnson's award-winning novel, *Middle Passage,* the black rogue Rutherford Calhoun joins in an expedition that brings from Africa not only slaves but their local "god." Time, it seems, discourages us from expecting any miracles in human relations between black peoples. Hence it should come as no surprise when an African American writer such as Keith Richburg admits, in his book *Out of America,* that he felt more at home with whites than with blacks in apartheid South Africa: "I am terrified of Africa," he says. "I don't want to be from this place. In my darkest heart here on this pitch black African night, I am quietly celebrating the passage of my ancestors who made it out" (223).[4]

So let us put no undue pressures on our black brothers and sisters. Things are hard enough as they are.

However, some of the reasons for which they are cautious in their relations with us do hurt. I am not worried about the charge that our ancestors sold their ancestors into slavery; as I have indicated above, any black man in those days, whether here or over there, did the same if he had the chance to make a buck. What really bothers me is the animosity that has been generated by competition in the racially determined American meritocracy. In a *New York Times* report about the surge in African emigration to the U.S. since the 1990s, the Columbia University historian Eric Foner is reported to have said, "Historically, every immigrant group has jumped over American-born blacks. The final irony would be if African immigrants did, too" (Roberts). The real irony, if I may say so, is that African Americans would rather be outnumbered by Europeans and others than by Africans, who would only improve the black demographic profile in American society. To be honest, this whole argument—to borrow a very American way with words—"sticks in my craw."

There has been, as we know, some other recent controversy about foreign black students outnumbering American-born blacks in higher institutions. In the *San Francisco Chronicle* of February 22, 2005, Nathan Hare, who pioneered the establishment of black studies in the late 1960s, was quoted as saying, "I have nothing against immigrants, but there are sociological realities we have to look at . . . We are the ex-slaves and inhabitants of the slums. They (immigrants) are coming in without that (baggage)" (Johnson). I do not wish to be drawn into a comparison of the fates of Africans under colonial bondage and chattel slavery, but there is an erroneous assumption in the above statement—which has indeed been echoed often in this debate—that immigrant African children generally arrive better prepared for college than their African American counterparts. If the situation I reported above, of the depressing plight of the average Nigerian school, does not sufficiently belie Hare's assumption, perhaps I should also mention that before I relocated to the U.S. with my family in the early 1990s, not one of us had ever seen a computer, let alone used one, and I was a professor in the first and best-established university in the country (Ibadan). Even if we were given computers, how much use would they be in a place where power could fail for as long as four weeks? And if universities had no computers, what would we honestly expect of the schools and the candidates they prepared for college?

Sometime in 2004, an American network interviewed Oprah Winfrey in the midst of poor, diseased children in South Africa whom she had come to help. The journalist wanted to know why Oprah was doing this in South Africa rather than the U.S., which had its share of such children. "You don't know poor," I recall Oprah saying, with a touch of sadness, "until you've been here." But Nathan Hare would have you believe our children had no such baggage to deal with!

It would, indeed, be useful to compare the condition of recent/postcolonial African migrants with that of a much earlier generation that left Africa for the United States and Europe (including the UK): I refer here to the generation of Nnamdi Azikiwe of Nigeria, Kwame Nkrumah of (then) Gold Coast, and Leopold S. Senghor of Senegal. Living in developed Western societies, some of which held their countries in colonial bondage, they were so offended by the gross injustice of the colonial dispensation that they were determined to return home after their studies and join in the liberation struggles of their people. These Africans obviously enjoyed considerable harmony with blacks in these Western societies because each group saw itself as embroiled in the same struggle for liberation and self-affirmation as the other; it was thus convenient for the expatriate blacks to form organs and ideologies (Pan-Africanism, Negritude, etc.) that united them with their kin in Western societies in this struggle. Perhaps the absence of such a unifying agenda has severely weakened chances of real solidarity between the two groups and left the foreign blacks with the feeling of living in the kind of limbo Said has spoken about.

In choosing to live in exile we have, as you can imagine, been charged by many compatriots of jumping ship, selling out, and several other shades of bad faith. And here in exile, we are viewed with distrust even by our own black kin. So where do we belong? Earlier on, I cited James Baldwin's statement that no one ever really "leaves home," and I admitted that the trauma of separation was still too fresh for us to forget our home of origin. Edward Said once spoke, in one of his BBC Reith Lectures of 1993, of a kind of exile that "exists in a median state, neither completely at one with the new setting nor fully disencumbered of the old" (49). Honestly, I admit that many of us first-generation immigrants of the new African diaspora fit that description, and I doubt that the kinds of coding often conceived for us are likely to put us at ease. For a start, many African Americans are unwilling that we should be classified with them, because we (and our children) arc not descendants of slaves who finally won their fight for a place in this land. For their part many Africans, whether reacting to this rejection or else prompted by a lingering loyalty to ancestral ties, have suggested other modes of classification for themselves. In a recent paper, Ali Mazrui has proposed a reversal of the double coding adopted for American-born blacks, so that new diaspora Africans might be better called "American Africans." More recently, some new diaspora Africans have felt that "African" in the old double coding is too broad to reflect their specific national origins in the old world, and have offered instead to be coded as Kenyan Americans, Senegalese Americans, Namibian Americans, and so on.

I must confess I have no idea why the U.S. set up the present system of racial classification. Whether it was aimed at giving the country an accurate picture of its plural composition to ensure proper social and political engineering, or whether it was a ploy to keep the minorities perennially divided for effective control, is a question I would rather have social scientists ponder. There may be something to be said for the proposals from new diaspora Africans I have cited above. But would they not create more problems than they were meant to solve? If they were adopted, would they not intensify the antipathies between foreign- and American-born blacks? Even worse, would they not give a fresh and perhaps more dangerous twist, here in the diaspora, to geographic and political divisions already existing between Africans on their continent?

African Americans, American Africans, Nigerian Americans, South African Americans, whatever—the common denominator in all these classificatory styles is the word *American:* a name "to die for" that everybody wants to hang on to, so much so that pregnant African women would fly to the U.S. on visitors' visas just to have their babies and secure them American passports. I hope the U.S. is happy with this imperial image. But I also hope it will be bold and honest enough to realize how little is gained by these divisions it has encouraged between its plural constituencies. I hope that in time the need for these modes of classification will cease to exist, and the U.S. government will give everyone living here two choices: you are either an American pure and simple, or you are some other nationality. More pertinently, we of the new African diaspora wish our more established neighbors—white, black, and others—would only reflect that if things were well in Africa, none of us would leave our homes for a strange land. Of course there are some undesirable ones among us; Africa does not have a monopoly on them, anyway. But most of us, true professionals any nation would die for, are here to make an honest life for our families, not to deny anyone a chance to realize their American dream.

THE ESSAYS IN THIS VOLUME

The idea of "going home again" is inevitably tied to the logic of exile in the new African diaspora. Most emigrants have chosen to step aside from the traumas they faced in their countries so as to reorder their lives, in the hope that they might possibly return home and spend their last days on the earth that nurtured them; as the saying goes, one should grow old where one grew up. If you have lived long enough in a place to form an emotional attachment to it, there is always some sadness in the heart as you prepare to take a long leave of it; you never hope that that long look you are taking, as the vehicle carries you away, is the last one. You might well make a good life for yourself when you settle down where you are going. For the moment, though, expatriation remains only an uncertain fate, for you have no firm guarantee of what awaits you in that place.

The essays collected here take us through this uncharted field. Our conference was summoned on the premise that it would offer us a forum for assessing how well or poorly peoples of African descent have fared in their efforts to realize the hopes and expectations they had in leaving their native homes for foreign lands in pursuit of a better fate for their families as well as themselves. Since the expatriation has been more often than not a self-elected one, we can understand why that long, wistful look backward would be more of an *au revoir* for them than it could have been for the Africans of the old diaspora.

The essays in this book have been grouped under four major themes—somewhat different from the ones we used in organizing the sessions of the conference, but certainly more relevant to the evaluative agenda we essentially set ourselves. Here in part 1, in a truly magisterial survey of the diaspora both as site and as experience, Paul Zeleza not only explores the nature and dynamics of engagement between Africa and its historic and new diasporas but also demonstrates that the connections between the homeland and its outreaches have been far deeper and more diverse than is generally acknowledged.

Zeleza's essay provides a convenient point of departure for the essays in parts 2 and 3, which relate the harsh processes of expatriation and relocation by the immigrants. Part 2 begins with (often) chilling tales of flight from home by Adzele Kitissou Jones (Togo) and Georges Fouron (Haiti). Anyone who has read in the international media of West African boys (especially from Senegal) risking their lives in fishing boats on a trip to Europe,[5] or seen similar scenes on American television of desperate Caribbean refugees in rough-rigged craft trying to evade the U.S. Coast Guard, can easily empathize with the accounts offered by Jones and Fouron. In his chapter, Jacky Kaba expands on the circumstances driving the refugees from their homes, which are essentially the symptoms of the failed states of the Third World: political struggle, resulting in the collapse of civic structures and social security, and even in civil war; the deterioration of economic life as a result of structural adjustment programs imposed by international lending organizations and the resultant inflationary trends; the decline in the quality of life, leading to disease and the death of many; and consequently the despair of those who could have made an honest difference by the force of their skills. Kaba's essay presents a compelling tally of statistical data to back the case he establishes about the "brain drain" of such experts from Africa especially to Western Europe and North America.

For many, unfortunately, landing in the "New World" is only the beginning of the harsh odyssey. Once you have abandoned the familiar (though hardly comfortable) world of the homeland, you have essentially surrendered yourself to whatever hand fate deals you in the world on which you have staked your hopes. The same modernity that was engendered by the dreaded transatlantic trade and the imperial structures it set in place has, in time, guaranteed a system of opportunities even for those displaced by these structures from their familiar world to foreign ones. But, as Michael Gomez has pointed out in his introduction to a recent volume of essays, African peoples coming to live in the New World automatically walk into a climate of enshrined prejudices that place them in an inferior position, making it harder for them than for other races to integrate into the social order. "For a multiplicity of reasons," he says, "and notably in contrast to the experiences of Europeans in the New World, the cultural and social transformations of transported Africans tend to invite a quality of critique unique in its level of elevated scrutiny, emphasizing distance and lacunae in the substance and circumstances separating Africa and the Americas" (*Diasporic Africa* 2).

This statement—which is as good for the new diaspora as for the old— suggests, at some level, that whatever the quality of brains and skills black immigrants bring with them to the American meritocracy, they are hardly judged good enough and often have to work twice as hard to prove they are qualified to share the hallowed space occupied by white and other peoples in the New World society. Most of the essays in the next section reflect the struggles that black immigrants wage with various arms of the system to earn a decent place for themselves and their families, or simply to cope with the challenges of daily life. In part 3, James Burns highlights the "Western supercultural stereotypes" of the image of Africa and Africans that Ghanaian music and dance experts confront in trying to teach their African skills to white students in the West. Helena Anin-Boateng presents the enormous efforts Ghanaian immigrants in Britain make to offer the bereaved among them the measures of solace and support they could have had in their homeland but which have no place in British reckonings with life and death. From her ongoing research, Florence Margai reports on investigations comparing health experiences of blacks from Africa and the Caribbean with those of African Americans, which reveal that while immigrant blacks enter the U.S. with "excellent health outcomes," these outcomes "deteriorate with increasing stay and acculturation in the dominant host society"; hence, providing health care for them becomes "an epidemiological paradox" that is influenced by a variety of social factors beyond their choice or control.

The essays by Obiora Okafor, Cassandra Veney, and John Arthur offer telling portraits of the fates of black immigrants under immigration laws and systems of justice in North America. Okafor paints the picture of a Canadian system of immigration laws and law enforcement effectively designed to frustrate the efforts by African immigrants not only to achieve a stable berth in the Canadian work force, however well-qualified they are for available positions, but to obtain the documentation needed for their spouses and children in Africa to reunite with them in Canada. The immigrants are subjected to all manner of stereotyping ("accent discrimination," for one); are denied basic benefits enjoyed by the regular Canadian taxpayer (e.g., tax credits for remittances sent to take care of elderly or dependent relatives abroad); and not only is there no fair system for recognizing foreign professional qualifications, but the law appears silent and even complicit in the neglect.[6]

Veney's essay highlights the unfair, discriminatory tactics used by various official organs in the U.S., especially against black immigrants from Africa, the Caribbean, and Latin America. Despite efforts by African American legislators over the years to promote fair immigration laws, these immigrants are often subjected to harsh penalties (e.g., detention, summary deportation, and loss of lawfully acquired property) upon conviction for even minor offenses. Veney draws attention to the rather severe implications for women and children left behind when the male parent, the family's principal provider, is jailed or deported. Toward the end of the chapter, Veney makes an important comparison between the marginalization and dispossession of these immigrants and the more recent plight of the (mostly black) victims of Hurricane Katrina in New Orleans, who were "resettled in the same states and cities where African refugees and immigrants of color reside." She ends with a moving plea:

> African Americans, whether they are the descendants of the four million slaves or descendants of immigrants who came from the Caribbean in the 1950s, 1960s, and 1970s, cannot afford to sit back and watch, falsely believing that now for the first time they can breathe a little easier because the targets are "foreigners." As we witnessed in the pre-9/11 and post-9/11 eras and during the Katrina debacle, the claim to citizenship has been rendered tenuous for all people of color, regardless of their residence or immigration status.

In his discussion of black immigrants under the American judicial system, Arthur is also led into a similar comparison of them with native-born black Americans. Although most black foreigners come from countries where their blackness was not a major issue, "some of the immigrants are faced with the denigration and marginalization of peoples of black African ancestry in the U.S." As they pursue their goals of upward mobility in American society, they frequently come into confrontation with law enforcement organs. The more successful among them may be inclined to take a more positive view of the law and to adopt a more conservative attitude toward the system than the less successful and especially the youth among them, who are more often the targets of law enforcement. Nonetheless, on the whole, black immigrants find themselves in an ambivalent position where, while they see themselves united with native African Americans in terms of racial discrimination and especially their relation to the American system of justice, "they also remain aware that they are outsiders, foreign, alien. Above all, their identity as blacks marks them as second- and third-class citizens who will never achieve racial equality in the white-dominant society."[7]

These comparative insights offered by Veney and Arthur bring us finally to an issue that is at the heart of the rest of the chapters in part 3: now that you have opted to resettle in a foreign society, how do you expect to be defined, identified, or classified in relation to the rest of the society? Indeed, in her essay on the health of black immigrant peoples earlier discussed, Florence Margai tells us: "Since most minorities in the United States have never fully integrated into the dominant host society, researchers have argued that studies that seek to address the health effects of this transformative process must focus on acculturation and not assimilation." The evidence presented in her chapter indicates that the statement is truer of recent immigrants than of other, native-born minorities.

If there is one thing that unites the chapters here by Baffour Takyi, Msia Kibona Clark, and Jill Humphries, it is this sense of a subtle distinction between acculturation and assimilation, of a hesitation by recent, first-generation black immigrants to abandon the ancestral base of their identity and throw in their lot fully with their racial kith and kin in the new home. In an interesting discussion supported by impressive statistical data, Takyi reveals the residential patterns of African immigrants across the United States. He demonstrates how West Africans in particular (mostly Ghanaians and Nigerians) have in many ways integrated themselves into the American demographic and even political landscape and are thus "quietly changing the dynamics of intra-racial relations in many American cities that are home to the nation's largest share of African Americans," but reveals that the new immigrants "are more transnational and transcultural in nature, with some migrants having multiple ties and identities, attributes that could help fuel tensions between the various African-descended peoples." In other words, they do not immediately identify themselves as African Americans, like native-born blacks of the old African diaspora.

The tensions, or (to be more specific) crises, of identity are the focus of interest in the essays by Clark and Humphries. Clark is uniquely positioned to assess these tensions. Born in Tanzania to African and African

American parents, brought to live in the U.S. at a very young age, and now teaching at the nation's premier historically black college in Washington, D.C., she takes us through the stages of her early rejection by and gradual integration into the African American community, to her current researches into identity conflicts between African Americans and Africans (first-generation immigrants and their offspring). Focusing on the offspring's ambivalence as they weigh their commitments to one culture or the other and the general American society, she is nonetheless convinced of the inescapable contribution of recent African immigration to a redefinition of African American identity and culture.

Humphries's chapter is also based on ongoing research into the dynamics of intra-racial relations between African immigrants and their native-born African American counterparts. Building on her work with action groups in the southern California region, Humphries focuses especially on the immigrants' continuing transnational linkages with initiatives back in their African homelands and the problems these create for efforts to organize a unified black platform on America's policy toward Africa. For the immigrants, ethnic or national identity is a preferable basis of political action to racial affiliation, an attitude their African American counterparts have found regrettable in their confrontation with the white-dominated American political machine. In matters of political mobilization, African immigrants are satisfied that they are a distinct enough group to pursue an agenda based on their shared identity as Africans, and need not be grouped with anyone else on issues relating to their continent.[8]

It is not so hard to understand this resistance, by more recent African immigrants, to assimilation into the native-born African American world. For a start, there is evidence enough—from some of the essays in this volume alone—of uneasiness among African Americans toward the progeny of those who are thought to have sold their forebears into slavery, and who have now come to contest their scarce sources of livelihood. In turn the immigrants, who are hardly blameless in their perceptions of African American lifeways, may have chosen to build a cocoon to shield themselves from the inhospitable gaze of their kith and kin.

But there are other cogent considerations. A history of social formations in their colonial history has evidently disposed African emigrants toward building parochial communities in foreign environments. At a lower level, villagers who came to live and work in faraway urban centers of the colonial administration sought each other out and formed "hometown associations" to ensure their collective security, mutual aid in various kinds of endeavor, and protection of their cultural heritage from the corrosive influence of the urban melting pots of the colony. A classic example of this kind of association is the Umuofia Progressive Union of Chinua Achebe's *No Longer at Ease.* At a higher level is the (pan-)ethnic union formed to project the interests of those across the nation who share the same language and culture, the idea being to ensure that, whatever political structure is adopted in administering the country, their stakes in the determination of power and resources—in the "sharing of the national cake," as the idiom goes—are fully protected. Needless to say, the latter phenomenon has been the bane of political engineering in not a few postcolonial African societies.[9]

African emigrants are, therefore, transferring to a transnational framework an old habit formed in their long history of incorporation within social and political contexts that force them to reconfigure their identity and interests. In time, these migrants are suitably adjusted to their new homes, so that the enterprising ones among them find space to do what they know best and contribute to various areas of life there. Although born in the U.S., Barack Obama offers perhaps the most illustrious example. The son of a Kenyan father (who had come to the U.S. on a study-abroad scholarship) and a white American mother, Obama lived from age two with his mother and maternal grandparents after his father left the family. With a stellar educational record (which included presidency of the Harvard Law Review), he has gone on to set an exemplary mark in American politics at both state (Illinois) and federal levels with an agenda that, thanks to his diverse national origins, stresses inclusiveness against polarization, and with a personal charm that has drawn a wider spectrum of the American public than ever before—young and old as well as men and women of all races—to take active interest in issues of national concern. His election to the presidency of the United States was warmly celebrated by Africans both in and outside Africa who, though disqualified by the U.S. constitution from such aspirations, were nonetheless excited that Obama had not only enhanced the profile of blacks in the world but indeed opened the doors of limitless possibilities to children born in the U.S. to African immigrants.

New diaspora Africans have also distinguished themselves in other fields. Sports stars including Cameroonian Yannick Noah in tennis (France) and Nigerian Hakeem Olajuwon—as well as Noah's son Joakim—in basketball (U.S.) have an immediate popular appeal. Among writers, Ngugi wa Thiong'o of Kenya, Chinua Achebe of Nigeria, Maryse Conde of Guadeloupe, and Caryl Phillips of St. Kitts are luminaries who have lived mostly in the U.S.; Nobel laureates in literature Wole Soyinka of Nigeria and Derek Walcott of St. Lucia have also lived in the U.S. for considerable stints on a more or less transnational basis. In music there is Angelique Kidjo of the Republic of Benin (in France), and in film Chiwetel Ejiofor of Nigeria (in the UK). Some of these had achieved prominence in their fields well before they relocated abroad, but their presence in the new diaspora has made their expertise available to their hosts on a more direct basis than when they were living in their countries of origin.

Not so well advertised, however, are contributions in science and technology. In September 2006, the U.S.-based Nigerian supercomputer specialist Philip Emeagwali—called "one of the great minds of the information age" by President Clinton—gave a talk at the University of Alberta, Canada, in which he urged Africa to invest in its abundant intellectual capital rather than borrow endlessly from foreign financial institutions. The following extract from the lecture tells how he borrowed from the wisdom of the Arab mathematician Al-Khwarizmi—as contained in the sage's tale of the seventeen camels—to solve a problem in computer science:

> Prime numbers are to whole numbers what the laws of physics are to physics. Twenty years ago, I used an Al-Khwarizmi approach to solve a notoriously difficult problem in physics. I added inertia force, which enabled me to reformulate Newton's Second Law of Motion first as 18 equations and algorithms, and then as 24 million algebraic equations. Finally, I programmed 65,000 "electronic brains" called processors to work as one to solve those 24 million equations at a speed of 3.1 billion calculations per second.
>
> Like Al-Khwarizmi, I derived my 18 equations through out-of-the-box thinking in an in-the-box world, adding my metaphorical camel: inertia force. In other words, I applied wisdom to known knowledge to generate intellectual capital.
>
> Unless Africa significantly increases its intellectual capital, the continent will remain irrelevant in the 21st century and even beyond . . . Africa's fate lies in the hands of Africans and the solution to poverty must come from its people.[10]

The chapters in part 4 reveal the successes of African-descended immigrants in various fields. Nkiru Nzegwu presents a group of immigrant female artists who, using their lives' experiences, are redrawing the artistic landscape of the regions of the United States in which they have settled. Jacob Olupona and Regina Gemignani explore the formation of recent immigrant religious communities—Muslim, indigenous African, and Christian (especially Pentecostal). The chapter also examines the ways in which these communities serve as focal points for the cultural and political lives of their members, as well as create networks of social relations for them and for the wider community of Americans within their fold. Donald Cosentino's essay offers an insight into how well-entrenched traditions that have accompanied the successive flows of Africans to the Americas have become, so much so that the term "diaspora" may justly be extended to include cultural ideas as much as the people who carry them. His subject is an Argentinean-born worshipper in a traditional African religion, "a white magus, who finds in Yoruba cosmology the perfect completion of his own complex spiritual history." As citizens of present-day New World societies explore alternative sources of spiritual fulfillment because the old ideologies no longer address their needs, it no longer matters whether the purveyors of the new options are black or white, African or otherwise.[11] Using the case of Africaresource.com, Azuka Nzegwu describes how new African immigrants in the U.S. are using web-based technologies to create intellectual communities that challenge the dominant narratives and structures of knowledge production on Africa and about Africans, in the process changing how Africa is perceived or understood.

What all this means is that the world is truly becoming one global village. Thanks to the growing sophistication of information technology, there is such a free flow of ideas that the two regions of the world traditionally separated by the Atlantic may all the more easily now be linked together as much by imaginative as by physical travel. This interflow has implications, in turn, for power configurations in the international order, as we can deduce from demands by Emeagwali above and Ademoyo (in part 5) that Africans take their destiny in their own hands and rewrite modern history in their own terms. Africans, in other words, have an opportunity now to abandon their old status as objects of imperial gaze and control, and to assume the position of subjects defining the world and their place in it from their own perspective.

The essays in part 5 discuss efforts by peoples of African descent to transcend the divisions between "homeland" and "diaspora" and build bridges that would reconfigure disparate African worlds along political and cultural lines. The Nigerian films discussed by Folu Ogundimu and Akin Adesokan are, indeed, produced by Nigerians in Nigeria, though with some technical collaboration from experts living outside the country. But they are of tremendous appeal as much to Africans living abroad as to those on the continent, in effect redefining the concept of the diaspora more in terms of transnational cultural flows than of a rigid separation of "home" from "abroad." The two authors are just as concerned with the political dimensions of the production and reception of these films. Ogundimu examines them in the context of globalization and transborder flows of communication, with a view to determining whether the genres of African cultural production are anti-imperial or pro-imperial caricatures. Adesokan is equally concerned that despite their appeal in (mostly) North America, "Nollywood" films remain marginal as commercial products. Discussing two such films with enormous international appeal in light of critiques of commodification by Fredric Jameson, Manthia Diawara, and others, he simultaneously examines the degree to which continental African realities impinge on the identity choices of African immigrants and proposes a productive, "multifocal" frame for the reception of the video-films.

The term "Afro-diasporic literature" would be a proper description of works by writers from Africa or the diaspora who, having lived or traveled in different regions of the black world, have chosen to explore the intersection of the lives and experiences of black peoples in those places in creative ways. Such a term might even be stretched to include works by black writers from any of those regions who may never have left their home base but have seen fit to exploit ideas and images available to them in some open-access medium for creative purposes—something that is entirely possible with help from the new media technology. Few writers, of course, would want to tackle a topic to which they had no firsthand exposure. But it is a sign of the interflow of ideas and images in our increasingly transnational culture and in the present state of political awareness that black artists, wherever they are, are increasingly inclined to assume responsibility—to borrow a thought from Ademoyo—for reordering black history by exploring the issues that unite or separate them across time and space.[12]

The essays here by Joseph McLaren and Odun Balogun discuss the works of African writers who have lived or are living in the diaspora and have set some of their work in situations where black people from different regions confront each other. In his essay, McLaren examines works by writers including Armah, Emecheta, Awoonor, and others and asks to what extent they have, on the one hand, retained an awareness of political and cultural issues in their homelands, and on the other hand, succeeded in authenticating the African diaspora through representations of the consciousness, lifeways, and even the speech habits of their diasporan characters. In his comparative analysis of works written from the diaspora by the Ghanaian Meri Nana-Ama Danquah (in the U.S.) and Nigerian author Buchi Emecheta (in the U.K.), Balogun examines how living in the diaspora might have influenced their handling of central concerns in their writing—in Emecheta, female domination and abuse by men; in Danquah, personal experiences of depression—and how the different cultural orientations of the U.K. and U.S. have affected their writing.

One element that most prominently defines the transnational character of the new African diaspora is travel. I must confess I am not particularly enamored of those studies of transnationalism that look only or predominantly at movement of persons from the "Third World" societies to developed countries (for whatever reasons) and, in a somewhat celebratory spirit, see this as evidence of the demise of the nation-state; Arjun Appadurai (e.g., *Modernity at Large*) is especially guilty of this line of thinking. Others, such as Michael Kearney, are more inclined to see transnationalism in the more aggressive light of nation-states disrupting the integrity of one another by the constant movement of their citizens ("The Local and the Global"). These theories seem to ignore the simple fact that people do love and *want* to move about on their own terms and with no more aggressive reason than that they want to free their (creative) spirits. Even when conditions in their countries make things hard for them and their work, they carry their nationalities in their hearts as they move elsewhere and continue to touch base with the old places in many ways; in their works, they give solid proof of this. Besides, transnationalism may also work in the other direction, with citizens of developed nations feeling such a strong spiritual bond with places they visit that they leave a piece of their hearts there as they return to their homes.

In her study of the transnational art of the much-traveled Ethiopian artist Wosene Kosrof, Andrea Frohne draws attention to the way his paintings link together his land of origin (from which he was displaced by the 1974 revolution) and the U.S., where he has settled, and puts considerable focus on Kosrof's visual interconnections of space, nation, and culture as well as the political and spiritual dimensions of his representations. African American novelist Sandra Jackson-Opoku has traveled extensively and repeatedly in Africa and the Caribbean, and her works (*The River Where Blood Is Born; Hot Johnny [and the Women Who Loved Him]*) evince a commitment to linking these various regions with the intimate threads of history and myth, so that she conjures a vision of the intense spirituality of the black experience across space and time. In her chapter here, she reveals how the diasporic imagination negotiates memory, ignorance, shame, and pride in its writing of Africa, and how in her own fiction she continually endeavors to interrogate, reinvent, and reclaim Africa.

Perry Mars's essay presents a good instance of new African emigrants from the Caribbean who still carry their nations of origin in their hearts. The postwar period (1989 to date) has seen the deterioration of political conflict in Guyana into both criminalized and extreme state-repressive violence involving deadly dimensions of narco-gangsterism, combined with selective ethnic targeting. The Guyana diaspora especially in North America has been engaged in actual and potential contributions toward a resolution of this crisis in the homeland. On the one hand, by sending home material resources they are helping to reduce poverty levels that feed criminalized violence and political conflict; on the other hand, prominent Guyanese individuals and organizations abroad participate in mediating the conflict situation at higher political levels in Guyana.

Finally, Adeolu Ademoyo places the argument of relations between Africa and the diaspora in a *radical* philosophical terrain. Rejecting the counsels of despair inherent in the project of Black Atlanticism—that dismiss any recourse to ancestral Africa as vain and romantic "essentialism" and enshrine the Du Boisian "double consciousness" as an inevitable fate of Africans locked in a world defined by European modernity—Ademoyo insists that a recuperation of the ontological foundations of the African world is the best guarantee the new emigrants and their children have of escaping the fractal mind-set urged by the Atlanticists. This, Ademoyo adds, is the new diaspora's best hope not only of living an ethically rewarding existence in their new abode but indeed of fashioning modern history on their own terms, just as emigrants from the Jewish, European, and other worlds have done.

"Home is where the heart is," it has been said. I also recall two proverbs about "home" from the part of Nigeria—Asaba, in Delta State—where I spent the early years of my youth. One says, "At the end of his outing, the masquerade goes home," while the other says, "Home is where you mend your roof."

Now, each of these two sayings raises an odd problem. The one about the masquerade is slightly qualified by recent developments. Asaba started off as a small town (or a village, depending on whom you talk to), but is now a state capital. In the past these masquerades, representing the spirit of the departed elder now being sent off to join the ancestors, were free to cover as much of the town as they wished in their outings. As a state capital, however, Asaba is now populated by a very large number of non-citizens whose freedom of movement needs to be protected from the sometimes violent displays of the masquerades. Consequently, the masquerades' outings are nowadays often limited to the immediate neighborhood of the departed elder, thus severely constricting the once-proud universe that defined the "home" of the masquerade. The second proverb is even more problematic. The roof you mend may be not of the family house where you were born or raised, but of the house you have built for yourself and your nuclear family, if you have one; and this may be in the town or country where you live and work, a very long way from your hometown!

In the early years of my teaching at Ibadan University, my wife and I used to take our very young children on some holidays to our family homes far away in Delta State, hoping to spend about a week or two there. Within about a couple of days of our getting there, our children would begin to get restless and tell us, "Let's go home." "But we *are* home," we would say, and they would return, "No, to Ibadan," their more familiar universe. Now that we live in the U.S., and they are fully grown and pursuing their professional careers, they are even further away from what we once tried to convince them was *home*. Of course, like many other children who relocated to the U.S. with their parents, they have nationalistic feelings about Nigeria that manifest themselves at moments when, for some reason or other, they are challenged to affirm their origins. But it is increasingly clear to us that they have fewer of the atavistic feelings about roots that my wife and I frequently reveal. Can they—"go home again"?

Adzele Jones ends her chapter in this volume by stressing that we must continue to hold the present African political leadership to account "if we ever hope to go home for good one day." In light of the picture painted above by Perry Mars, one wonders where "home" really is: is it the place where you now live and which guarantees you the peace to take care of yourself and your immediate family, as well as bring needed help and comfort to those you have left behind; or is it, rather, the land you left behind and may never return to settle permanently in, only because a handful of people are so determined in their perverse pursuit of power and privilege that they will never make an honest effort to correct the mess they have put the nation in?

On July 10, 2007, the British newspaper *The Guardian* published a speech by Ban Ki-moon, the new Secretary-General of the United Nations, urging us to "welcome the dawn of the migration age." The speech essentially celebrates the benefits of migration, especially in raising the level of income earned by developing countries from emigrants who remit money home partly to ease the poverty of relatives they left behind and partly to contribute to developmental and entrepreneurial projects. Although Ban admits there are problems involved in migration, obviously in terms of the relationships between developing countries and their developed counterparts to which the migrants flee, the thrust of the speech is squarely on the economic gains of migration: "The freer movement of people oils the global economy."

There is no question that migration brings the world increasingly closer to being the large global village everyone hopes will eventually erase the walls separating peoples and ensure they respect one another. I wish, however, that the United Nations would put greater emphasis on forcing governments across the world to respect the rule of law and pursue the honest governance that would guarantee the welfare of their citizens. In this way, a healthy global economy would help in achieving a truly transnational culture that ensured no society was more desirable than another and rendered it needless for anyone to feel the urge to "go home again."

NOTES

1. Equiano's idyllic portrait of his African society extends to a comparison of indigenous African slavery with the more demonic variety he was subjected to in Western slave-holding societies: see *Interesting Narrative* 51–53. Compare this with Inikori's differentiation of the two systems in "Slaves or Serfs?" Phillis Wheatley may seem to some readers to have ambivalent feelings about her African roots. A few of her writings, however, reveal an attachment and affirmation clearly bold for the times: for instance, her poem "To S.M., a Young African Painter" evinces some African nationalism. See Gates's *Trials* 71–74 for a recent statement on Wheatley's positions on issues of the times.

2. The sad saga of the West African prince Ibrahima Abduhl Rahahman, who after some forty years of bondage in Natchez, Mississippi, was returned to Liberia but died—sick, broken, and despondent—on the eve of his repatriation to his native community, has been presented by Terry Alford in *Prince among Slaves*. In

his *Victorian Lagos,* Michael Echeruo gives us the picture of a colonial Nigerian elite whose lifestyle was orchestrated by the entrenched British mores of the day.

3. In 1977 I recorded a pre-narrative song performance in Igbuzo (Ibusa), Midwestern Nigeria, by a young lady who portrayed the differences between her community and neighboring ones such as Asaba and Onitsha in terms of their characteristic staple foods: Asaba people feed on maggots found inside fish, the Onitsha settle for insects that grow from the maggots, but her Igbuzo people feed on the fish itself! There are numerous such songs in traditional African poetry.

4. There are, however, African American writers who have expressed a different sentiment from Richburg's upon visiting Africa. Lynne Duke's *Mandela, Mobutu, and Me* is one of many examples.

5. Gruesome accounts of African youth drowning in their boats en route to Europe were given by the Associated Press on June 1, 2006, and by the *Guardian* (UK) on September 8 and October 5, 2006. In the Associated Press report, "the migrants' rusty boat drifted off course and carried them to their deaths as it crossed the Atlantic Ocean and wound up near the Caribbean islands of Barbados. By the time a fisherman found the boat [which had embarked on Christmas eve] on April 30, the bodies of 11 young men were virtually mummified by the sun and salt spray."

6. Okafor's insights in this essay complement those of Patience Elabor-Idemudia's study of African immigrant women in the Canadian labor force ("Gender and the New African Diaspora").

7. I recently saw Wyclef Jean, the Haitian-born reggae/hip-hop artist, doing a revealing music video (featuring Mary J. Blige) in which he frantically appeals, "someone please call 911," evidently to save him from the desperate state his woman has left him in. When the police finally arrive at the scene, he is shown being pursued by them though *he* was the one who called for their help! The young (immigrant) black's view of the law enforcement system is quite obvious from such a presentation.

8. In their essay here, Olupona and Gemignani report testimonies from African immigrant Muslims who have set up their own institutions because "We do not want our children to become Americans in their thinking," stressing the importance for these children to be "grounded in our history, where we came from and where we will eventually go back to settle."

9. Nigeria provides ample illustration of each of these phenomena. For hometown associations see Coleman, "The Role of Tribal Associations," Honey and Okafor, *Hometown Associations,* and Abbott, "Nigerians in North America." For ethnic unions and their effect on contemporary Nigerian politics, see Osaghae, *Crippled Giant* 25–26, and Okpewho, *Once upon a Kingdom* 182–191.

10. The story of the seventeen camels is contained in Emeagwali's lecture: www.emeagwali.com/speeches/africa/where-is-africa-going-wrong.html (accessed 2006).

11. There is abundant and growing work on African traditional religions in the New World. In addition to studies by Jacob Olupona, Donald Cosentino, and others, the following are some recent titles: Ayorinde, *Afro-Cuban Religiosity;* Wedel, *Santeria Healing;* Daniel, *Dancing Wisdom;* Matory, *Black Atlantic Religion;* Bellegarde-Smith and Michel, *Haitian Vodou;* Cros Sandoval, *Worldview, the*

Orichas, and Santeria; Long, *A New Orleans Voudou Priestess;* and Clark, *Santería.* For more recent manifestations of Afro-Cuban Santería, see Tere Figueras Ne-grete's report in the *Miami Herald* of December 2006.

12. There is growing scholarship on the phenomenon of travel and migration, by black subjects, between the various regions of the black world to the effect that Afro-diasporic literature becomes an exploration of the interfaces and uni-ties in black culture. Three of the trend-setting publications in this area are Da-vies, *Black Women, Writing, and Identity,* the volume *Atlantic Cross-Currents,* edited by Andrade and others, and Walters, *At Home in Diaspora.*

REFERENCES

Abbott, Charles W. "Nigerians in North America: New Frontiers, Old Associa-tions?" In *The New African Diaspora in North America,* ed. Kwado Konadu Agyemang, Baffour K. Takyi, and John A. Arthur. Lanham, Md.: Lexington, 2006. 141–165.

Achebe, Chinua. *No Longer at Ease.* London: Heinemann, 1960.

Alford, Terry. *Prince among Slaves.* 1977. Reprint, New York: Oxford University Press, 1986.

Andrade, Susan Z., Eileen Julien, Micheline Rice-Maximim, and Aliko Songolo, eds. *Atlantic Cross-Currents: Transatlantiques.* Trenton, N.J.: Africa World Press, 2001.

Appadurai, Arjun. *Modernity at Large: Cultural Dimensions of Globalization.* Minneapolis: University of Minnesota Press, 1996.

Ayorinde, Christine. *Afro-Cuban Religiosity, Revolution, and National Identity.* Gainesville: University Press of Florida, 2004.

Bellegarde-Smith, Patrick, and Claudine Michel, eds. *Haitian Vodou: Spirit, Myth, and Reality.* Bloomington: Indiana University Press, 2006.

Carretta, Vincent. *Equiano the African: Autobiography of a Self-Made Man.* New York: Penguin, 2005.

Clark, Mary Ann. *Santeria: Correcting the Myths and Uncovering the Realities of a Growing Religion.* Westport, Conn.: Praeger, 2007.

Coleman, James. "The Role of Tribal Associations in Nigeria." In *Nationalism and Development in Africa: Selected Essays,* ed. Richard L. Sklar. Berkeley: University of California Press, 1994. 15–19.

Cros Sandoval, Mercedes. *Worldview, the Orichas, and Santeria: Africa to Cuba and Beyond.* Gainesville: University Press of Florida, 2006.

Daniel, Yvonne. *Dancing Wisdom: Embodied Knowledge in Haitian Vodou, Cu-ban Yoruba, and Bahian Candomble.* Urbana: University of Illinois Press, 2005.

Davies, Carole Boyce. *Black Women, Writing, and Identity: Migrations of the Sub-ject.* New York: Routledge, 1994.

Douglass, Frederick. *Narrative of the Life of Frederick Douglass, An American Slave,* ed. Deborah E. McDowell. New York: Oxford University Press, 1999.

Duke, Lynne. *Mandela, Mobutu, and Me: A Newswoman's African Journey.* New York: Doubleday, 2003.

Echeruo, Michael J. C. *Victorian Lagos: Aspects of Nineteenth Century Lagos Life.* London: Macmillan, 1977.

Elabor-Idemudia, Patience. "Gender and the New African Diaspora: African Immigrant Women in the Canadian Labor Force." *The African Diaspora: African Origins and New World Identities,* ed. Isidore Okpewho, Carole B. Davies, and Ali A. Mazrui. Bloomington: Indiana University Press, 1999. 234–253.

Emeagwali, Philip. "Where Is Africa Going Wrong?" Lecture delivered at the University of Alberta, Canada, September 2006. www.emeagwali.com/speeches/africa/where-is-africa-going-wrong.html.

Equiano, Olaudah. *The Interesting Narrative and Other Writings,* ed. Vincent Carretta. New York: Penguin, 1995.

Figueras Negrete, Tere. "Santeria's Reach Goes Global via the Web." *Miami Herald,* December 6, 2006.

Gates, Henry Louis. *The Trials of Phillis Wheatley: America's First Black Poet and Her Encounters with the Founding Fathers.* New York: Basic Civitas, 2003.

Gomez, Michael, ed. *Diasporic Africa: A Reader.* New York: New York University Press, 2007.

Guardian (UK). "Senegal to Canary Islands: Sorrow and Death." September 8, 2006.

———. "Twenty Migrants Drown en route to Spain." October 5, 2006.

Honey, Rex, and Stanley Okafor, eds. *Hometown Associations: Indigenous Knowledge and Development in Nigeria.* London: Intermediate Technology, 1998.

Inikori, Joseph E. "Slaves or Serfs? A Comparative Study of Slavery and Serfdom in Europe and Africa." In *The African Diaspora: African Origins and New World Identities,* ed. Isidore Okpewho, Carole B. Davies, and Ali A.Mazrui. Bloomington: Indiana University Press, 1999. 49–75.

Johnson, Charles. *Middle Passage.* New York: Simon and Schuster, 1990.

Johnson, Jason B. "Shades of Gray in Black Enrollment: Immigrants' Rising Numbers a Concern to Some Activists." *San Francisco Chronicle,* February 22, 2005.

Kearney, Michael. "The Local and the Global: The Anthropology of Globalization and Transnationalism." *Annual Review of Anthropology* 24 (1995): 547–565.

Kilson, Martin, and Adelaide C. Hill, eds. *Apropos of Africa: Afro-Americans and the Romance of Africa.* Garden City, N.Y.: Anchor, 1971.

Long, Carolyn Morrow. *A New Orleans Voudou Priestess: The Legend and Reality of Marie Laveau.* Gainesville: University Press of Florida, 2006.

Matory, James Lorand. *Black Atlantic Religion: Tradition, Transnationality, and Matriarchy in the Afro-Brazilian Candomble.* Princeton, N.J.: Princeton University Press, 2005.

Mazrui, Ali A. "The African Diaspora and Globalization." Unpublished paper, presented at the conference "The African Diaspora: African Origins and New World Self-Fashioning." Binghamton University, Binghamton, N.Y., April 11–13, 1996.

Ngugi wa Thiong'o. *Decolonizing the Mind: The Politics of Language in African Literature.* Portsmouth, N.H.: Heinemann, 1986.

Niane, D. T. *Sundiata: An Epic of Old Mali,* trans. G. D. Pickett. London: Longman, 1965.

Okpewho, Isidore. *African Oral Literature: Backgrounds, Character, and Continuity.* Bloomington: Indiana University Press, 1992.

———. *Myth in Africa: A Study of Its Aesthetic and Cultural Relevance.* Cambridge: Cambridge University Press, 1983.

———. *Once upon a Kingdom: Myth, Hegemony, and Identity.* Bloomington: Indiana University Press, 1998.

Osaghae, Eghosa. *Crippled Giant: Nigeria since Independence.* Bloomington: Indiana University Press, 1998.

Richburg, Keith B. *Out of America: A Black Man Confronts Africa.* New York: Basic Books, 1997.

Roberts, Sam. "More Africans Enter U.S. Than in Days of Slavery." *New York Times,* February 21, 2005.

Said, Edward W. *Representations of the Intellectual: The 1993 Reith Lectures.* New York: Pantheon, 1994.

Thompson, Vincent Bakpetu. *The Making of the African Diaspora, 1441–1900.* Harlow: Longman UK, 1987.

Walker, Clarence E. *We Can't Go Home Again: An Argument about Afrocentrism.* New York: Oxford University Press, 2001.

Walters, Wendy W. *At Home in Diaspora: Black International Writing.* Minneapolis: University of Minnesota Press, 2005.

Washington Star. January 1, 1978.

Wedel, Johan. *Santeria Healing: A Journey into the Afro-Cuban World of Divinities, Spirits, and Sorcery.* Gainesville: University Press of Florida.

Wheatley, Phillis. "To S.M., a Young African Painter, on Seeing His Works." In *The Prentice Hall Anthology of African American Literature,* ed. Rochelle Smith and Sharon L. Jones. Upper Saddle River, N.J.: Prentice Hall, 1999. 21–22.

2

DIASPORA DIALOGUES: ENGAGEMENTS BETWEEN AFRICA AND ITS DIASPORAS

Paul Tiyambe Zeleza

In an essay such as this, it is tempting to start by asking some basic questions, to clear the theoretical underbrush, as it were. What does the term "diaspora" mean? What is the African diaspora? Who qualifies to be considered part of the African diaspora? How have African diasporas been formed and changed over time? How have they produced and reproduced themselves and their identities? How have they engaged Africa? How do the histories of African diasporas affect the way we think about diasporas, theorize diaspora? In this chapter I would like to explore some of these questions, obviously not in any detail given the constraints of space, but rather in offering possible analytical frameworks.

The chapter is divided into four parts. The first part seeks to define the meanings of the terms "diaspora" and "Africa(n)" as a prelude to suggesting the simple but critical point that African diasporas in the Atlantic world—certainly in the United States, the primary focus of the chapter—are multilayered, composed of multiple communities, different waves of migration and diasporization. This means that African diasporas are confronted with the challenge of how they relate not only to their hostlands and homelands but also to each other. The second part attempts to outline and explain recent African migration to the U.S., the wellspring of the new diasporas. The third part examines the relations between the historic and contemporary diasporas. The final part offers a possible analytical framework that might be useful in untangling the complex histories and dynamics of engagements between Africa and its diasporas.

DEFINING DIASPORA AND AFRICA

As George Shepperson (44) has reminded us, the term "African diaspora" did not emerge until the 1950s and 1960s. None of the major intellectual forerunners of African diaspora studies, from Edward Blyden to W. E. B.

Du Bois to the Negritude writers, used the term. Prior to the fifties and sixties, African peoples were mobilized using other terms, such as "Pan-Africanism." Today, the term "African diaspora" enjoys pride of place in the increasingly crowded pantheon of diaspora studies. Yet, despite the proliferation of the literature, conceptual difficulties remain in defining what we mean by the terms "diaspora" and "African diaspora." Contemporary theorizations tend to be preoccupied with problematizing the relationship between diaspora and nation and the dualities or multiplicities of diasporic identity or subjectivity, and they are inclined to be condemnatory or celebratory of transnational mobility and hybridity.[1]

In many cases, the term "diaspora" is used in a fuzzy and uncritical manner in which all manner of movements and migrations between countries and even within countries are gathered to its generous conceptual bosom, and no adequate attention is paid to the historical conditions and experiences that produce diasporic communities and consciousness, or lack thereof. I say "lack thereof" because not all dispersals result in the formation of diasporas. In other words, dispersal does not automatically create a diaspora, and once formed, a diaspora does not live in perpetuity. Some diasporas disappear; some dispersals turn into diasporas long after the original dispersals.

"Diaspora," I would suggest, simultaneously refers to a process, a condition, a space, and a discourse: the continuous processes by which a diaspora is made, unmade, and remade; the changing conditions in which it lives and expresses itself; the places where it is molded and imagined; and the contentious ways in which it is studied and discussed. It entails a culture and a consciousness, sometimes diffuse and sometimes concentrated in a "here" separate from a "there," a "here" that is often characterized by a regime of marginalization and a "there" that is invoked as a rhetoric of self-affirmation, of belonging to "here" differently. The emotional and experiential investment in "here" and "there" and the points in between, indeed in the very configurations and imaginings of "here" and "there" and their complex intersections, obviously changes in response to the shifting materialities, mentalities, and moralities of social existence.

Diaspora is simultaneously a state of being and a process of becoming, a kind of voyage that encompasses the possibility of never arriving or returning, a navigation of multiple belongings, of networks of affiliation. W. E. B. Du Bois in *The Souls of Black Folk* talked of the "double consciousness" of African Americans, the "sense of always looking at one's self through the eyes of others," this peculiar sensation of "twoness—an America, a negro; two warring souls, two thoughts, two unreconciled strivings; two warring ideals in one dark body, whose dogged strength alone keeps it from being torn asunder" (11). For many diaspora scholars in the anglophone tradition Du Bois's double consciousness is paradigmatic of diaspora consciousness; for those from the Latin American tradition, where blackness has been a moving target, simultaneously segmented, denied, and reluctantly embraced, a diasporic identity often transcends double consciousness (Vinson). It may be more apt, then, to refer to multiple consciousness—in its "racial," "national" and "transnational" intersections—as emblematic of a diaspora consciousness. It is a mode of naming, remembering, living, and feeling group identity molded out of experiences, positionings, struggles, and imaginings of the past and the present, and at times the unfolding, unpredictable future, which are shared or seen to be shared across the boundaries of time and space that frame "indigenous" identities in the contested and constructed locations of "there" and "here" and the passages and points in between.

In a broad sense, a diasporic identity implies a form of group consciousness constituted historically through expressive culture, politics, thought, and tradition, in which experiential and representational resources are mobilized, in varied measures, from the imaginaries of both the old and the new worlds. Diasporas are complex social and cultural communities created out of real and imagined genealogies and geographies (cultural, racial, ethnic, national, continental, transnational) of belonging, displacement, and recreation, constructed and conceived at multiple temporal and spatial scales, at different moments and distances from the putative homeland. A diaspora is fashioned as much in the fluid and messy contexts of social experience, differentiation, and struggle, and through the transnational circuits of exchange of diasporic resources and repertoires of power, as in the discourses of the intellectuals and political elites.

This is to suggest that intellectuals sometimes discover diasporas, even when the communities concerned may not think of themselves in diasporic terms. In other words, quite often diaspora identities, or rather cultural codes and representations deemed diasporic, are sharpened, mobilized, deployed, and circulated by intellectuals and other elites for careerist and political projects that may have little bearing on the diaspora communities themselves. As an intellectual project, a research paradigm, the question is: how do we best study African diasporas, capture their complex histories, their connections and disconnections, and compare their experiences?

This raises the questions of what is Africa and who are the Africans that constitute, when dispersed and reconstituted, African diasporas. The idea of "Africa" is an exceedingly complex one, with multiple genealogies and meanings that make any extrapolations of "African" culture and identity, in the singular or plural, any explorations for African "authenticity," quite slippery, as these notions tend to swing unsteadily between the poles of essentialism and contingency. Describing and defining "Africa" and all tropes prefixed by its problematic commandments entails engaging discourses about "Africa," the intellectual paradigms and ideological politics through which the idea of "Africa" has been constructed and consumed, and sometimes celebrated and condemned.

Elsewhere I have argued that Africa is as much a reality as it is a

construct whose boundaries—geographical, historical, and cultural—
have shifted according to the prevailing conceptions and configurations
of global racial identities and power as well as African nationalism, including Pan-Africanism (Zeleza, "Rewriting"). At the beginning of the
twenty-first century, the maps and meanings of "Africa" and "Africanness" are being reconfigured by both the processes of contemporary globalization and the project of African integration. One common approach is
to distinguish between Eurocentric and Afrocentric paradigms, between
ideas and conceptions of what constitutes "Africa" and "Africanness" derived from "European" and "African" perspectives. The difficulty with
this method is that it inscribes an epistemic division between two approaches that are otherwise deeply implicated with each other.

A more prosaic framing that avoids this rigid binarism would suggest
that there are at least four main constructions of Africa: Africa as biology,
as space, as memory, and as representation—that is, African identities
and cultures are mapped in racial, geographical, historical, or discursive
terms. As with the highly ideological Eurocentric-Afrocentric dichotomy,
there are no discursive Chinese walls separating the four typologies, but
they do have heuristic value. I work from the assumption that Africa is a
material and imagined place, a historical geography, the constellation of
the places and peoples embedded in its cartographic and conceptual imagining. It is an invention as much as "Asia" or "Europe" or "the West" and
all such civilizational spaces, but it has a physical, political, paradigmatic,
and psychic reality for the peoples who live within or who are from its
cartographic, cultural, and cognitive boundaries, themselves subject to
shifts.

As we all know, the name "Africa" is not African; it originally referred to the Roman province in present-day Tunisia, and only later was
it extended to the whole continent, and much later still did the various
peoples of the continent come to be referred to, or to refer to themselves,
as Africans; some still do not. Thus, exclusive claims to Africa based on
the sands of the Sahara or doses of melanin represent spatializations and
racializations of African identity that are historically spurious. My Africa
is the Africa of the African Union (AU), which has recognized the diaspora
as Africa's sixth region. How legitimate is it to project this Africa back-
wards? My answer is that, almost invariably, history is filtered through
the lenses of the present, and the Africa of the Pan-Africanist founders
of the Organization of African Unity (OAU), the predecessor of the AU,
is no less handy than, and indeed preferable to, the racist epistemic car-
tography of Africa invented by European imperialism that divided Africa
into two, North Africa and sub-Saharan Africa—the "Africa proper" of
G. W. F. Hegel (91–93) and his Eurocentric descendants.

This means, quite simply, that African diasporas include all those
peoples dispersed from the continent in historic and contemporary times

who have constituted themselves into diasporas. The key phrase is "historic times." As Colin Palmer has noted, there are at least six major migrations: three in prehistoric and ancient times (beginning with the great exodus that began about 100,000 years ago from the continent to other continents), and three in modern times, including those associated with connections with Asia, the Atlantic slave trade to the Americas, and the contemporary movement of Africans and peoples of African descent to various parts of the globe. While the prehistoric dispersals are a useful reminder of our common origins and humanity, they stretch the notion of African diaspora too far beyond analytical recognition to be terribly useful.

At a technical workshop in which I participated, convened by the African Union in Trinidad in 2004, the following definition of diaspora was adopted:

> The African Union has committed itself to providing representation to the African Diaspora in its policy process. For this purpose, we recommend that the definition of African Diaspora refer to the geographic dispersal of peoples whose ancestors, within historical memory, originally came from Africa, but who are currently domiciled, or claim residence or citizenship, outside the continent of Africa. This definition recognizes both dispersal and subsequent reconstitution of African Diaspora identities in new locations as equally important elements. Therefore, such peoples are committed to the advancement of continental African and Diaspora communities worldwide. (African Union 15)

This merely points to the complexities of the African diasporas and underscores Butler's point that "conceptualizations of diaspora must be able to accommodate the reality of multiple identities and phases of diasporization over time." She offers a simple but useful schema for diasporan study, divided into five dimensions: "(1) reasons for, and conditions of, the dispersal; (2) relationship with homeland; (3) relationship with hostlands; (4) interrelationships within diasporan groups; (5) comparative study of different diasporas" (127). For Darlene Clark Hine, black diaspora studies, as she calls the field, needs to have three features: a transatlantic framework, an interdisciplinary methodology, and a comparative perspective. I would agree with the last two, and revise the first to suggest that African diaspora studies needs to have a global framework.

THE MAKING OF THE CONTEMPORARY AFRICAN DIASPORAS

In the Americas we can distinguish between two major diaspora formations, what I call the historic diasporas and the contemporary diasporas. The term "historic diasporas" refers to the old diasporas formed before the construction of colonial and postcolonial states, which have profoundly altered the territorial identifications of Africans on the continent since the late nineteenth century. African migrants since then have had to contend with the imperative of the modern nation-state, which often frames the political and cultural itineraries of their travel and transnational networks. It is in this sense, then, that I use the term "contemporary diasporas," to refer to diasporas formed since the late nineteenth century. In this context, I distinguish among three main waves: the diasporas of colonization, decolonization, and the era of structural adjustment that emerged out of the disruptions and dispositions of colonial conquest, the struggles for independence, and the "lost decades" of structural adjustment programs (SAPs), respectively.

The diasporas of colonization would include the students who went to study abroad and stayed, seamen who became settlers, and many others who could migrate and become citizens according to the prevailing immigration regimes in the host countries. The diasporas of decolonization include, besides the so-called indigenous Africans, European and Asian settlers who relocated overseas during the struggles for independence and immediately after. The diasporas of structural adjustment have been formed since the 1980s out of the migrations engendered by economic, political, and social crises and the destabilizations of SAPs. They include professional elites, traders, refugees, and students.

African migrations are of course part of a much larger story of complex global migrations. The late twentieth century has in fact been characterized as "the age of migration" (Castles and Miller). However, the available evidence indicates that while the volume of international migrants has indeed grown significantly in absolute numbers since the 1960s and there have been significant changes in the character and direction of international migration, the percentage of people who have left and remained outside their countries of origin has remained remarkably steady and small: in 2005 a mere 3 percent (191 million out of 6.5 billion) of the world's people lived outside the countries of their birth, up from 2.5 percent in 1960 (75 million out of 3 billion). Africa's migrant population has been growing gradually.[2] In 2005, Africa's migrant stock was 10 percent of the world's total, compared to Europe (33.6 percent), Asia (28 percent), Northern America (23.3 percent), Latin America and the Caribbean (3.5 percent), and Oceania (2.4 percent). Between 2000 and 2005 Africa lost 455,000 more people annually to migration than it gained, compared to annual losses of 804,000 for Latin America and the Caribbean and 1,297,000 for Asia, which translate into annual net migration rates of –0.3 percent, –0.5 percent, and –1.5 percent, respectively. During the same period, the highest net gains in international migration were claimed by Northern America (1.4 million annually), followed by Europe (1.1 million annually)

and Oceania, which includes Australia and New Zealand (103,000 annually).

While the majority of African migrants stay within the continent,
a growing number have been finding their way to the global North, including Europe and the United States. The United States is the leading
destination for international migrants: in 2005 one in five lived there.
Prior to the twentieth century, African migrations to the Americas were
dominated by slavery. After the staggered abolitions of the European and
American slave trades and the end of African forced migration, only small
numbers of Africans left the continent to settle in North America, as
compared to other immigrant groups. A systematic analysis of American census data covering the period 1850 to 2000 shows that the number
of African-born migrants in the U.S. population rose from 551 in 1850 to
2,538 in 1900, climbing to 18,326 in 1930, 35,355 in 1960, 199,723 in 1980,
363,819 in 1990, and 881,000 in 2000. In 2005 there were more than a
million. As rapid as this rise may seem, Africans accounted for a small
proportion of immigrants to the United States, 3 percent of the nearly
33 million foreign-born residents in 2005, up from 0.4 percent in 1960 and
1.9 percent in 1990 (Grieco; Dixon; U.S. Census).

The bulk of the African immigrants came in the 1980s and 1990s,
during which 192,000 and 383,000 entered the country, respectively. In
the years 2000–2004 an additional 229,000 arrived. The relatively low
rates and levels of voluntary emigration from Africa to the U.S. until
the 1960s can be attributed both to restrictive U.S. policies against non-
European immigration and to the reluctance and inability of colonized
African populations to migrate in any significant numbers outside the
continent (Logan). It is instructive to note that the largest numbers of
African immigrants to the U.S. in 1960 came from Egypt and South Africa. Both countries had relatively advanced economies and had been sov-
ereign for many years, and their migrants were, in the case of South Africa, largely white, or in the case of Egypt, considered as white under U.S.
immigration law. From 1980 Western Africa overtook Northern Africa,
which dropped to third place after Eastern Africa, ahead of Southern Africa. What accounts for the patterns of this African migration to the U.S.
and elsewhere in the world that has contributed to the emergence of new
African diasporas?

Changes in Africa—the political conflicts, economic hardships, and
social disruptions—are obviously important; so are the transformations
in the U.S. political economy and cultural ecology, primarily related to
the civil rights struggles. Quite literally, many Africans who migrated
from Africa to the U.S. from the mid-1960s owed their fortunes to the
doors opened by African American struggles. The Congressional Black
Caucus played a pivotal role in broadening immigration law to accommo-

date immigrants from Africa and the Caribbean (Eissa). In the literature on the causes, courses, and consequences of international migration there are several theories, each employing radically different concepts, assumptions, and frames of reference, that seek to explain the factors which both initiate and perpetuate international migration and that attempt to assess the effects of international migration on both the sending and receiving countries. Some emphasize economic factors and motivations; others offer political or sociological perspectives and propositions.

The economic theories can be grouped into four.[3] In the neoclassical economic model, international migration is seen, at a macro level, as the result of wage differentials and employment conditions between countries which, at a micro level, propel individuals as rational actors making cost-benefit calculations to migrate in pursuit of income maximization (Massey et al., "Theories"; Todaro). In contrast, the "new economics of migration" attributes migration decisions to households, not simply isolated individuals, seeking both to maximize income absolutely and relative to other households and to minimize risks associated with a variety of economic failures in addition to those in the labor market (Stark, *Migration*; Wallace et al.). As is common in much neoclassical economics, these theories tend to reify migration, ignoring the historical, institutional, and structural contexts in which it occurs. Often neglected in the neoclassical economics literature is the role of the state in regulating migration flows through its control over borders.

Proponents of the dual labor market theory argue that international migration is caused not by push factors in the sending countries but by pull factors in the receiving countries, by the structural requirements of the modern industrial economies for low-wage and low-status jobs in labor markets that are segmented and where the traditional sources of entry-level workers—women and teenagers—have progressively shrunk (Salt). In contrast, the world system theorists see international migration not as the result of recent processes of market segmentation in particular industrial economies, let alone wage rate or employment differentials between countries, but as the natural outcome of the capitalist economic expansion that began in the sixteenth century. Besides internal capitalist transformations and thickening external ties of trade, financial transactions, transportation, and communications, capitalist globalization also generates ideological and cultural linkages, constantly reinforced by mass communication and advertising campaigns, which foster popular and seductive consumerist images of the global North that stoke the engines of international migration (Sassen; Hamilton and Chinchilla).

These theories need not be mutually exclusive. International migration is such a complex process that it cannot but be the result of equally complex forces operating at various levels in space and time. There can be little doubt that international migration flows are determined by conditions in both the sending and receiving countries, including the state of the economy, political stability and freedoms, and immigration law, all of which are affected by broader forces in the global political economy. Whatever might initiate migration, the factors and forces that perpetuate it can be quite different. Several theories have been developed to account for the rise of new conditions that emerge in the course of international migration, that sustain it and function as independent causes for further migration.

The first is network theory, according to which the networks that arise in the course of migration and that link migrants, former migrants, and non-immigrants in countries of origin and destination through kinship, friendship, and community ties constitute an expanding pool of social and cultural capital, which lowers the costs and risks and raises the benefits of movement, and therefore increases the likelihood of international migration (Portes, "Contemporary"; Buechler and Buechler; Boyd; Heisler).[4] The second is institutional theory, which argues that, as migration expands, profit-seeking and humanitarian institutions, organizations, and entrepreneurs develop to service both legal and illegal migrants, especially as restrictive immigration policies are adopted by the receiving countries, and serve to institutionalize and promote international migration irrespective of the causes that originally started it. The third theory, cumulative causation, maintains that migration brings about changed social, economic, and cultural contexts which affect subsequent migrations. In other words, each migration decision is influenced by previous migrations, which alter the regional distribution of income, land, and human capital, the organization of productive activities, and the cultural and social meanings of migration and work. In the sending countries migration can become an esteemed rite of passage, while in the receiving countries occupations dominated by immigrants can become culturally labeled "immigrant jobs" and therefore shunned by native workers, thereby reinforcing the structural demand for immigrants (Massey et al., *World in Motion*; Stark et al., "Remittances"; Taylor; Stark and Taylor).

Once again, there is little that is intrinsically incompatible among the three theories. Each explains an important dynamic and dimension of the migration process. It stands to reason that migration involves both social networks and enabling institutions and is a cumulative process. The interplay between these factors obviously varies in specific contexts. Increasingly, international migration has come to be seen as an integral part of globalization, or the phenomenon known as "transnationalism," a social process in which migrants establish social fields that cross geographic, cultural, and political borders. Viewing international migration from the transnational perspective has serious implications for how immigrants should be viewed by both sending and receiving countries and how migration is analyzed (Glick Schiller et al.).

As might be expected, there is no agreement on the consequences
of migration for the migrants themselves as well as for their countries
of origin and their countries of immigration. How do African migrants
fare and adapt in their new countries of settlement? What is the impact
of their migration on their home and host countries? Much of the literature has focused on the economic dimensions of these questions. A
variety of models seek to explain the performance of migrants. One is
human capital theory, according to which education and training are important determinants of income and occupation. Some studies inspired
by this theory make claims of immigrant superiority, that immigrants,
even if they are not always "the best and the brightest" of migration folklore, tend to be self-selective and highly motivated, qualities that are invaluable for adaptation and success. Others emphasize that immigrants
arrive in the host country with many handicaps, including sometimes
lack of language skills as well as limited knowledge of the job market,
local customs, cultural values, and the social structure, which impedes
their assimilation or adaptation (Chiswick et al.; Borjas). Human capital
theory tends to assume that economic discrimination is irrational and
exogenous.

Other theories take labor market discrimination as a given and seek
to explain it. One explanatory model sees it in terms of job segregation
or closure by dominant groups who limit the eligibility of new members for high-rewarding occupations. The split labor market thesis postulates that the market is divided along racial, gender, and other hierar-
chized lines along which rewards are unequally distributed. Immigrants
are positioned accordingly. The succession model predicts that a group
that arrives last occupies the bottom position in economic rankings as
previous groups progressively move up the occupational hierarchy. A version of this model, the queue theory, suggests that employer preferences
often determine rankings on the labor queue, which may result in some
groups being selected for jobs that may be high-paying. The rankings are
often determined by ethnic and racial characteristics (Waldinger). Many
studies show that there is a cost to being a racial or ethnic minority in
the Northern countries (Amissah 31–42). From these perspectives, African
migrants can be expected to suffer triple subordination: as immigrants, as
people who arrived recently, and as people many of whom are black.

Space does not allow for a detailed analysis of how successive waves
of African immigrants in the United States have fared. One school argues that the African immigrants compare extremely well with the host
American population and other immigrant populations. But there are studies which show that the mean earnings of African immigrants are lower
than their relatively high levels of education would suggest (according
to the 2000 U.S. census, 49.8 percent had a college education compared
to 25.4 percent of all other immigrants, and 25.6 percent of native-born

Americans).[5] If this is correct, it would seem that in addition to a racial tax, African immigrants pay a cultural tax, the devaluation of their human capital in a society where things African are routinely negatively stereotyped and despised.[6] One more reason why the African immigrants cannot escape Africa and have to be concerned about its development: its shadows of underdevelopment cast a pall over how they are perceived and perform overseas.

A critical question raised by the literature on African immigrants and diasporas is the connection between the two—immigration and diasporization. In other words, when do new immigrants become part of the diaspora? Given the rapidity of transnational movements today, the compression of time and space spawned by the information and communication technologies of contemporary globalization, the unprecedented possibilities of traversing and maintaining links across national and regional boundaries, at what point and in what ways do Africa's recent emigrants become new diasporas? I would suggest that not every migrant turns into a diasporan. Many Africans who have come to the United States, for example, since the end of the Second World War, have done so for temporary periods as workers, expatriate professionals, business people, students, and tourists, and often go back after the realization of their objectives. It does not seem to make much sense to regard such *temporary* migrants as members of the new diaspora. But temporary migrants can, and often do, become permanent migrants even if they maintain connections with home through periodic visits. A precondition for the transition from a migrant into a diasporan is *prolonged* settlement, followed by *permanent* resettlement in a new host country. Neither condition need be planned, of course; indeed, many African migrants abroad do not always anticipate staying long or settling permanently, but often end up doing so.

At issue, then, is not *intention*, but the *duration* of stay, the separation of the there of the home country and the here of the host country. It is the offspring of such migrants who complete the transition from migration to diasporization for their families and communities. Thus the diasporization process is a cumulative one beginning with migration, followed by resettlement, and reproduced through the offspring of the migrants. Using this schema, I would distinguish between African migrants, diasporized Africans, and African diasporas. In this context, long-term African-born residents of the United States would be considered diasporized Africans, while their offspring turn into African diasporas, more fully socialized into the experiences and identities of the historic diaspora. It can be argued, then, that temporality defines diasporization as much as spatiality. In other words, the process of diasporization has spatial and temporal dimensions: African diasporas refer to Africans and their offspring resettled outside the continent. The historic diasporas are those whose resettlement occurred in the past, while the new diasporas are those formed from the waves of more recent migrants. The past is of course a moving location. It might be useful to distinguish the two in generational terms, to confine the new diasporas, broadly, to the diasporized Africans and their first-generation offspring; subsequent generations often become absorbed into and indistinguishable from the historic diaspora formed out of much earlier waves of migration.

RELATIONS BETWEEN THE HISTORIC AND CONTEMPORARY DIASPORAS

In the United States, there are at least four waves of African diasporas: first, the historic communities of African Americans, themselves formed out of complex internal and external migrations over several hundred years; second, migrant communities from other diasporic locations, such as the Caribbean, that have maintained or invoke, when necessary or convenient, national identities as Jamaicans, Puerto Ricans, Cubans, and so on; third, the recent immigrants from the indigenous communities of Africa, some of whom share racialized affinity with the two groups; and finally, African migrants who are themselves diasporas from Asia or Europe, such as the East African Asians or South African whites. Each of these diasporas, broadly speaking, has its own connections and commitments to Africa, its own memories and imaginations of Africa, and its own conceptions of the diasporic condition and identity. The third group is sometimes divided by the racialized codifications of whiteness and blackness that are sanctified in the colonial cartographies of North Africa and sub-Saharan Africa and by U.S. immigration law, under which North Africans are classified as white.

Given the complexity and diversity of the African diasporas in the U.S., it stands to reason that relations between the various groups are exceedingly difficult to map out. There is a growing body of literature focusing on different aspects of the complicated relationship between the new and old African diasporas in the country (Arthur; Ogbaa; Copeland-Carson; Mwakikagile). What I would like to suggest is a possible analytical schema containing three elements that structure these relations: first, the contexts of engagement; second, the constructs of engagement; and third, the character of the engagements. By "context" I refer to the social arenas in which the different diasporas interact; by "constructs" I mean the dynamics that mediate their interactions; and "character" entails the content and processes of interactions.

The contexts in which the historic and contemporary diasporas interact with each other are both private and public and often varying degrees of both. The private or privatized spheres include family and interpersonal relations. In the case of families, we can think of inter-diasporan marriages and partnerships as well as intra-family generations of diasporization. Marriages and partnerships between African migrants and African Americans have been growing, although there are important differentiations of gender, class, religion, and what Florence Margai, in this volume, calls "settlement geographies." For example, some studies seem to suggest that more African men marry African American women than African American men marry African women, which can be attributed to the gender imbalances in the composition of college graduates and professionals in the African American community, and constructions of beauty.

But even in families in which the parents are from the same African country, culture, or community, challenges of intra-diasporan relations arise between the parents and their American-born children and their grandchildren, who are progressively acculturated into not only American society, but African American society. All of us who are parents have experienced this—I know I have: the constant negotiations over socialization that are framed in the idioms of age and diasporization in which the cultural and cognitive authority of parenthood in the original homeland and the new hostland are pitted against each other, and that the increasingly Americanized children sometimes contest, both overtly and covertly, subtly and defiantly. There is a class dimension to these dynamics: the fears, real and imagined, of professional class reproduction, insofar as most African migrants are middle-class and African Americans are routinely pathologized in America's racial imaginary, although the majority, too, are middle-class.

The public contexts of intra-diasporan engagements are obviously even more multidimensional. I have identified seven in terms of their social weight and explanatory possibilities. They are: (1) educational institutions (composition of students and faculty in K–12 and tertiary institutions, curricula representations of Africa and African America, and membership of sororities and fraternities); (2) labor market (access to employment, workplace culture, and workers' organizations); (3) religious practices (Christianity, Islam, and the African-derived religions); (4) leisure activities (sports, entertainment, media, and festivals); (5) business enterprises (size, location, ownership, and employment patterns); (6) political process (citizenship, voting patterns, leadership roles, lobbying activities, and involvement in public protests); and (7) community life (neighborhoods, activities, and organizations).

There can be little doubt that the encounters within and across the various social domains are complex, contradictory, and always changing. For example, Jill Humphries has noted the challenges of political coalition building among what she calls the "neo-diaspora" and the historic diaspora over, on the one hand, U.S. foreign policy toward African countries, and on the other, public policy in the U.S. toward black communities, as each group makes proprietary claims. And as academics we are all aware of the tensions between African and African American students and fac-

ulty in schools and universities, engendered by struggles over identity in America's highly racialized imaginary, over access to resources, and over the limited social capital of affirmative action, which was originally intended to mitigate the centuries-long deprivations of slavery and segregation that the historic African American diaspora experienced, but which has greatly benefited recent professional African immigrants and their children, as well as other racial and ethnic minorities and white women.[7] It is not a secret that sometimes university committees prefer to hire African immigrants to fulfill affirmative action mandates and thus to save themselves from combative race relations with African Americans, among whom memories of racial terror and bigotry are deeply ingrained.

The connections and disconnections among the different diasporas are conditioned by four sets of factors: namely, institutional, ideological, identity, and individual dynamics. Different sectors and organizations have specific institutional cultures that set the broad parameters of intra-diasporan interactions, just as the push and pull of ideological affiliations—left-wing or right-wing, conservative or liberal, Afrocentric or Eurocentric, nationalist or internationalist, sexist or feminist politics—affect the tenor and possibilities of cooperation, accommodation, or conflict within specific or between different diaspora groups. The nature and formation of collective identity and individual subjectivity, which are constructed through the prevailing practices of socialization, spatialization, and representation, also help structure these dynamics. Insofar as all communities have multiple identities, inter-group relations are partly affected by the intersections of some of these identities and interests.

The social and historical geography of new immigrant and diasporic identities involves the fluid and sometimes competing claims constructed around ethnic, national, subregional, linguistic, Pan-African, and transnational identities. Some of these intersect with the identities of the historic diasporas, while others do not, which can provide the basis for cooperation or conflict. A person who prizes his or her ethnic identity may find it hard to forge a Pan-African identity. This is to suggest that first-generation African migrants who already have trouble dealing with people from other ethnic groups in their countries of origin may have difficulties dealing with African Americans.

How can we conceptualize the content and character of the intra-diasporan engagements? We can identify five dimensions that may or may not denote cumulative phases of acculturation mediated by the length of stay in the U.S. for the new diasporas, their social and spatial locations, their respective connections to Africa and America, and the attitudes—hospitality or hostility—of the historic diasporas. On the whole, the revolution in telecommunications and travel, which has compressed the spatial and temporal distances between home and abroad, as well as the reflexivities of globalization, offer the contemporary diasporas unprecedented opportunities to be transnational and transcultural, to be people of multiple worlds and focalities perpetually translocated, physically and culturally, between several countries or several continents. They are able to retain ties to Africa in ways that were not possible to earlier generations of the diaspora.

The relations between the old and new diasporas can be characterized by antagonism, ambivalence, acceptance, adaptation, and assimilation. Antagonism is engendered by stereotypes and poor communication on both sides. Several studies have recorded the negative stereotypes the two groups hold about each other. African American stereotypes of Africans evoke negative bodily images while African stereotypes of African Americans evoke negative behavioral images. The bodies of African blacks are despised for their color and alleged ugliness, while African Americans are detested for their alleged propensity to violence and criminality. African Americans blame Africans for having sold them into slavery and see them as embodiments of cultural and economic backwardness, while Africans accuse African Americans of laziness and not taking advantage of their country's enormous resources. And both groups sometimes see each other as arrogant.

These stereotypes are rooted in the sensational media representations of both groups, as well as selective experiences with each other both in the United States and in Africa. However, antagonism is only one facet of the relationship. We need to investigate more systematically the other dimensions, the dynamics that tilt the relationship toward assimilation. Historically, this is what has happened as successive waves of new arrivals have been integrated, over time, into the African American community. Our challenge as researchers in the field of African diaspora studies is to map out these processes and promote mutual understanding through education and communication, to encourage a strategic solidarity among our communities that comes from respect for each other's histories and struggles and from a clear understanding of the ties that bind us as we seek to recover from the ravages of the past and build new futures in our more globalized world. Indeed, the connections between Africa and its diasporas—both historic and contemporary—have been far deeper and more diverse than is generally acknowledged.

LINKAGES BETWEEN AFRICA AND ITS DIASPORAS

One critical measure of the diaspora condition as a self-conscious identity lies in remembering, imagining, and engaging the original homeland, whose own identity is in part constituted by and in turn helps constitute the diaspora. This dialectic in the inscriptions and representations of the homeland in the diaspora and of the diaspora in the homeland is the thread that weaves the histories of the diaspora and the homeland together. Two critical questions can be raised. First, how do the different African diasporas remember, imagine, and engage Africa, and which Africa—in temporal and spatial terms? Second, how does Africa, or rather, how do the different Africas—in their temporal and spatial framings—remember, imagine, and engage their diasporas? Given the complex ebbs and flows of history, for Africa itself and the various regional hostlands of the African diasporas, it stands to reason that the engagements between Africa and its diasporas have been built and shaped by continuities, changes, and ruptures.

Created out of movement—dispersal from a homeland—the diaspora is sometimes affirmed through another movement—engagement with the homeland. Movement, it could be argued, then, in its literal and metaphorical senses, is at the heart of the diasporic condition, beginning with the dispersal itself and culminating in reunification, which is often perpetually postponed. The spaces in between are marked by multiple forms of engagement between the diaspora and the homeland, of movement, of travel between a "here" and a "there" in terms of both time and space. The fluidity of these engagements is best captured by the notion of flow: flows of several kinds and levels of intensity characterize the linkages between the homeland and the diaspora. The diaspora or the homeland can serve as a signifier for the other, subject to strategic manipulation. The flows include people, cultural practices, productive resources, organizations and movements, ideologies and ideas, images and representations. In short, we can isolate six major flows: demographic flows, cultural flows, economic flows, political flows, ideological flows, and iconographic flows.[8]

Much of the scholarly attention has gone toward the political flows, as manifested, for example, in the role that the transatlantic Pan-Africanist movement played in engendering territorial nationalisms across Africa and in the way continental nationalism and the Civil Rights Movement in the United States reinforced each other, and in how in postcolonial times the various diasporas have engaged political processes and projects from conflict to democratization. In studies of the historic diasporas, there has been an analytical tendency to privilege the political connections represented by the Pan-Africanist movement, while in studies of the contemporary diasporas focus concentrates on the economic impact—flows of remittances and investment. Economics is, of course, at the heart of the diasporic condition for both the historic and contemporary diasporas, insofar as both were engendered by labor imperatives, one involving demand for forced slave labor and the other supply of free wage labor.

Ideological flows refer to the flows of ideas and ideologies that can be embodied in social and cultural movements and discursive paradigms, ranging from visionary philosophies and projects to transnational feminisms to literary movements in the African and black worlds. For example, there has been what Abiola Irele calls the "cycle of reciprocities" between the literary movements of Africa and the diaspora, most significantly the Harlem Renaissance and the Negritude movement, whose echoes found resonances in the Black Arts and the Black Aesthetic movements in the U.S. and the cultural nationalist and the nativistic critical movement in Africa in the 1960s and 1970s.

Iconographic flows refer to images and visual representations of Africa, Africanness, and blackness that are created, circulated, and consumed through art works and the media. As Nkiru Nzegwu has demonstrated, transatlantic artistic dialogue has been continuous and intensified over the last half-century, sustained and reproduced by the travels of artists, a shared visual language, and invocations of cultural memories and artistic motifs. "Because the socio-economic conditions under which these artists create activate psychic vortices," she writes, "art-making becomes a ritual in which cultural genealogy is revitalized, new realities are constructed, and new identities are announced" (Nzegwu, "Memory Lines"). African American iconographic constructions of diasporan identity and black modernity have been particularly influential, thanks in part to the global tentacles of the American state and capital, on whose corporate media and imperial wings they have been exported to the rest of the world. Examples of this influence include appropriations of African American cultural identity by British blacks during World War II, and of political blackness by the oppressed peoples of South Africa in the late 1960s. For their part, the new African diasporas have been simultaneously recycling old and inventing new iconographies of Africa and Africanness. Examples include the Senegalese traders selling the monolithic Africa of Afrocentricity, and the imports of Nollywood films by new African diasporas hungry for modernist self-representation.

The demographic flows are self-evident. Almost from the beginning to the present, the traffic of people from Africa to the Americas has never been one-way; some have returned from the diaspora to the continent, whether permanently or temporarily, and through them contacts and memories between the diasporas and the continent have been kept alive, and vibrant cultural exchanges maintained. Thus, Africa and the Americas have been permanently connected since the sixteenth century by the continuous flows of people in both directions. It is well to remember that the slave trade was not a one-time event, but a continuous process that lasted four centuries, from the mid-fifteenth century to the mid-nineteenth century. We all know about the resettlement schemes in Sierra Leone and Liberia. Up to the end of the nineteenth century, the quintessential sojourners of these transoceanic voyages were sailors, and to a lesser extent soldiers, but there were also traders, students and scholars, political leaders and rebels, religious seers and proselytizers, and ordinary

men and women seeking personal and collective salvation from the dep-
redations of their times and circumstances.

Over the centuries cultures in both continental Africa and diaspora
Africa changed and influenced each other, to varying degrees across time
and space. This was a dynamic and dialogic exchange, not simply a de-
rivative one between a primordial, static Africa and a modern, vibrant diaspora. This is to suggest the need for an analytical methodology that is
historically grounded, one that recognizes the enduring connections between Africa and its diasporas, that the cultures of Africa and the diaspora
have all been subject to change, innovation, borrowing, and reconstruction, that they are all "hybrid," and that the cultural encounters between
them have been and will continue to be multiple and multidimensional.
We need to transcend the question of African cultural retentions and sur-
vivals in the Americas, to examine not only the traffic of cultural practices from the Atlantic diasporas to various parts of Africa, but also the
complex patterns and processes of current cultural exchanges through the
media of contemporary globalization, from television and cinema to video
and the internet.

This is not always acknowledged in studies that examine the development of expressive cultures among the diaspora communities and the
cultural traffic between the diasporas and Africa. Gerhard Kubik provides a useful typology that divides the interpretive schemes of diaspora
cultures into six categories, what he calls, first, biological reductionism;
second, socio-psychological determinism; third, pseudo-historical reductionism; fourth, historical particularism; fifth, cultural materialism; and
sixth, cultural diffusionism. It stands to reason that all these elements—
the imagined ontologies of blackness, constructions of racial hierarchies,
selective appropriations of African memories and alterity, material imperatives of cultural change, and the diffusionist trails of cultural transfer—have played a role in the development of diaspora cultures as distinctive cultures marked by similarities, differences, parallels, connections,
and exchanges with the numerous cultures of continental Africa. The
communication and circulation of cultural practices and paradigms between Africa and its diasporas have encompassed religion, education, literature, art, and music, to mention a few. These flows have constituted,
I would argue, an essential part of Africa's modernities, globalization,
transnationalism, and cosmopolitanism.

Religion has been one of the most important elements of cultural exchange. The traffic in religious ideas, institutions, and iconography has
been particularly intense and an important aspect of the African diasporic experience, identity, struggle, agency, and linkages with Africa. Africans dispersed from the continent brought religious beliefs, rituals, and
values into their new lands of settlement and resettlement, just as diasporan Africans who subsequently returned or established connections with

the continent came with reinvented religious practices or were sometimes proselytizers of the world religions, especially Christianity. Also, religious institutions and fervor mediated relations between Africans within and outside the continent in settings that sometimes had little to do with religion per se. Like all markers of identity, the nature and role of religion ebbed and flowed, changing over time, depending on local and international contexts as well as the shifting configuration of the religious ideas, institutions, and interlocutors themselves.

The historic diasporas brought with them two major religious traditions: first, those often referred to as "traditional" or "indigenous" religions, which developed into what have come to be called "African-derived religions" (ADRs); and second, Islam. The latter was as African as the former. The tendency to treat Islam as non-African is based on essentialist notions of African cultural and religious authenticity or purity that are unsustainable on historical or experiential grounds: for African Muslims, their identity as Muslims and Africans is indivisible; one does not invalidate the other. And if Jacob Olupona, a leading authority on African religions, is to be believed, there were Christians among the enslaved Africans from the Congo, thanks to conversions during the early period of Congolese-Portuguese contact (personal communication). There is also the intriguing suggestion by Walter Isaac that the enslaved people from Western Africa included some African Jews. Further research on these two religious traditions promises to be a fruitful area.

The ADRs are widely distributed throughout the Americas and have survived, even thrived, and played an important historical role despite a long history of repression, ridicule, vilification, and violence against them. The transnational circulation of Afro-American religious ideas and iconographies in the Black Atlantic world accelerated during the course of the twentieth century, thanks to increased migration of people and circulation of religious signs facilitated by modern communication technologies. In the process, many of these gradually became decoupled from exclusive territorial ontologies and adopted indigenizing discursive moves intended to stress their Africanness.

The Islamic dimension of the diasporan experience is not always appreciated. Many of the enslaved Africans were Muslims. Estimates vary, ranging from 10–15 percent to at least a third. In her fascinating study, Sylviane Diouf suggests a figure of between 2.25 and 3 million Muslims sold, of whom 15 to 20 percent were women (*Servants of Allah* 48). She insists that the experience of enslavement seems to have deepened the religious fervor of the Muslims, who went to great lengths to preserve their belief systems, ritual practices, social customs, modes of dress, and literacy. It has been suggested that the influence of the Muslims was probably much greater than their numbers. Thanks to their spiritual, intellectual, and martial fortitude, Islam became a critical resource for cultural

and political resistance. Muslims provided critical leadership to many of
the slave revolts in the Americas, including the Haitian Revolution and
the numerous uprisings in Bahia, such as the Malês Rebellion of 1835.

The pressures for religious conversion or syncretism were high, and
many of the descendants of the Muslims, Michael Gomez (1994) contends
in the case of the United States, lost their faith, although he offers tan-
talizing suggestions that some elements of Islam were incorporated into
African American Christianity, and more remarkably, that many of the
founders of the Nation of Islam may have been descendants of Muslims
and that the new religion tapped into the Islamic practice of their ancestors. In the twentieth century, orthodox Islam reemerged in the United
States, rekindled by the arrival of new Muslim communities. Among these
were members of the new African diasporas, who established a series of
organizations that helped to spread and consolidate the Islamic presence
in the country, and who found themselves having to negotiate their relations with Muslims of the historic diaspora as well as with Muslim immigrants from other parts of the world, and their identity as Muslims with
their old and new identities of nationality, race, ethnicity, gender, and
even class and sexuality.

Christianity has had an equally complex history in the relations between Africa and its diasporas. For much of the nineteenth and twentieth centuries, from the diaspora came the proselytizers of Christianity
and from the continent went the propagators of traditional religions; Islamic influences flowed in both directions. The diasporan missionaries
were, simultaneously, among the most committed to African repatriation
and redemption and also among the most ethnocentric, with negative and
contemptuous views of indigenous African peoples and cultures. They de-
fended the humanity of Africans but derided the historicity of Africa, so
that they were often concurrently critics and collaborators of European
colonialism, although they faced numerous restrictions imposed by colonial governments.

In the course of the twentieth century, Christians from Africa increasingly flocked in the opposite direction, toward Europe and the Americas.
Three forms of Christianity came. First were missionaries and followers
from the conventional Christian denominations, both Catholic and Prot-
estant. Particularly remarkable has been the Pentecostal upsurge among
the new African immigrants (Olupona). Second were members of the independent African churches that had emerged in opposition to European
missionary Christianity in colonial and postcolonial Africa. Third were
followers of Africa's ancient Christian traditions belonging to the Egyptian Coptic Church and the Ethiopian Orthodox Church. We need to know
more about the impact of the different forms of Christianity brought by
the contemporary African diasporas and their linkages to those developed
by the historic African diasporas across both the diaspora and Africa.

Music has been one of the primary media of communication in the Pan-African world, through which cultural influences, ideas, images, instruments, institutions, and identities have continuously circulated, in the process creating new modes of cultural expression both within Africa itself and in the diaspora. This traffic in expressive culture is multidimensional and dynamic, affecting and transforming all it touches. Rooted in the dispersals and displacements of African peoples, it has been facilitated by persistent demographic flows and ever-changing communication technologies and has involved exchanges—that are simultaneously transcontinental, transnational, and translational—of artistic products, aesthetic codes, and conceptual matrixes. The musical linkages are governed as much by the impulses of cultural ecology as by the imperatives of political economy, and our understanding of them is, in turn, filtered through the paradigmatic lenses of changing scholarly preoccupations and perceptions.

There is a vast body of literature on the development and global impact of the music produced by various African diaspora communities, especially in the Americas, and there has been extensive debate on the African roots of these musics, but far less systematic attention has been paid to the musical flows between Africa and its diasporas. Studies written from the diasporic perspective tend to oscillate between two poles: those that emphasize the rootedness of diaspora musics in African musical traditions and those that see these musics as inventions of the diasporic experience itself, with no underlying African dynamic or essence. In reality, insofar as African music is itself complex, always changing, and difficult to categorize, attempts to capture some static African essence in diasporan music may be futile. A more comprehensive historical analysis of Atlantic diaspora cultures and musics shows that, first, African musics have been influenced by and are intricately connected to diaspora musics; second, diaspora musics emerged out of specific mixtures, borrowings, experimentations, inventions, and circulations within the diaspora itself; and third, during the twentieth century the cross-fertilization created new African musics, making music on the continent more diasporic and music in the diaspora more African, a fusion that in all its fluidity has produced African-derived musics of extraordinary creative energies and immense global power and popularity.

Another cultural sphere in which linkages between Africa and its diasporas have been important is education. Records show diasporan Africans coming to the continent for formal and informal education, although our knowledge of the patterns and magnitude of this trend remains poor. When Fourah Bay College in Sierra Leone and Liberia College in Liberia opened in 1827 and 1862, respectively, they served as Pan-Africanist institutions that attracted students and faculty from across West Africa especially, many of whom were themselves of diasporan origin, such as

Edward Blyden. More common were flows from Africa to the United States, where the black colleges and universities (HBCUs) that mushroomed in the late nineteenth century served both as a magnet for African students and as a model for higher education in Africa itself.

It was in these colleges that the African and African American elites encountered and engaged each other most intimately and that Africa was imagined with an intensity peculiar to a besieged intelligentsia. Until desegregation in the 1950s and 1960s, the HBCUs remained the main centers of African higher education in the U.S. It was there that the serious and systematic study of Africa was pioneered, courses on African peoples were established, and monographs and journals were published long before the historically white universities, in pursuit of national security, disciplinary excitement, or belated multiculturalism, discovered African studies or diaspora studies. Thus, these institutions were in the forefront of producing knowledge and personnel, counter-hegemonic discourses, and developmental capacities for the diaspora itself and Africa (Zeleza, "The African Academic Diaspora").

*   *   *

As we can see, engagements between Africa and its diasporas have been characterized by flows and counterflows of various magnitude. The flows include people, cultural practices, productive resources, remittances and investments, organizations and movements, ideologies and ideas, and images and representations. Individually and collectively, these flows and the complex linkages they entail have produced varied impacts on social groups, communities, and nation-states in the diaspora and on the continent itself. They have helped shape identities, representations, and self-perceptions among Africans and diasporan Africans. So dense have some of the flows and counter-flows been that in some domains, continental and diasporic issues are often difficult to disentangle. Indeed, perspectives and debates on national or Pan-African issues may be predominantly shaped by one or the other, as circumstances change. The emergence of independent nation-states in Africa from the 1950s onward and the Civil Rights Movement in the U.S. brought about significant changes in the nature of the engagements between the continent and its diaspora in the United States. So too did the subsequent transformation and intensification of the flows between them.

With the growth of global African migrations and the accompanying expansion of contemporary diasporas, diasporic networks have come to encompass and impact more communities, countries, and even families as their members increasingly straddle multiple locations. Consequently, national and regional politics as well as day-to-day family matters and decision-making often involve interactions among people living on different continents. Through the new diasporas, Africa's presence among the historic diasporas has been acquiring a new intensity and intimacy, which is helping to reshape and reinforce the historic engagements between Africa and its diasporas, and in the process recasting the trajectories of Pan-Africanism. As Thandika Mkandawire has argued, "in Africa, as elsewhere, diasporas have played an important role in the reinvention and revitalization of the 'home country's' identity and sense of itself. And today, with the capacity to participate in the political life of their homelands, there can be no doubt that diasporic groups will be even more immediate in the rethinking of a new Africa" (2). The interconnections between diasporic communities, the flows which they generate with Africa, and the processes of globalization with which they are implicated are critical questions to investigate. There can be little doubt that current diasporic processes, linkages, and flows are part of the contemporary processes of globalization. Clearly, African diasporas are crucial, indeed indispensable, for Africa's globalization and the Africanization of globalization.

NOTES

1. Part of this section draws on Zeleza, "Rewriting."

2. For a succinct study of migration trends between the 1960s and 1990s see Hania Zlotnik, "Trends of International Migration Since 1965."

3. There is of course a vast literature on international migration in general and African migration in particular that cannot be adequately addressed here. For a sample of this literature see Zeleza, "African Labor and Intellectual Migrations to the North" and "Contemporary African Migrations in a Global Context."

4. James Fawcett proposes twelve types of linkages in migrations systems and discusses their applicability to various systems of international migration. The linkages are classified into four categories and three types. The four categories are state-state relations, mass culture connections, family and personal connections, and migration agency activities. The three types are tangible linkages, regulatory linkages, and relational linkages.

5. Portes and Zhou attribute the low earnings of Nigerian and Iranian immigrants in the United States, among the most highly educated immigrants, "to their recency in the country, outside discrimination, and small numbers that, by 1980 at least, precluded the emergence of a protective ethnic community." The creation of ethnic enclaves is seen as necessary for the emergence of vibrant entrepreneurial communities, and beneficial for the immigrants.

6. Comparisons are often drawn between African Americans and immigrant Africans and Afro-Caribbeans. Unfortunately, they are sometimes used to support right-wing attacks against African Americans, to bolster claims that the latter's problems have less to do with racism than with cultural pathology. For example, Thomas Sowell used the positive income gap between Caribbean immigrants and African Americans as evidence that "color alone, or racism alone, is clearly not a sufficient explanation of the disparities within the black population or between the black and white populations" (41). Yanki Djamba continues this dangerous assault: "Compared to native blacks, black and white African immigrants are more

educated, less likely to be on welfare . . . more likely to be married, and more em-
ployable" (211). The reality is far more complex. Employers sometimes show preference for foreign-born blacks because as well as being free from the baggage of
"historical victims of discrimination, their numbers can be used to fill Affirmative Action quotas leaving many victims of historical discrimination in America
unassisted by the Affirmative Action system" (Hawk 30). Kristin Butcher shows
that the income differentials between the American population and immigrants
are not confined to blacks: "native-born *white* men also earn less than the corre-
sponding group of *white* immigrants" (267). More importantly, when African and
Caribbean immigrants are compared to what she calls "native black movers," that
is, African Americans who reside in a state other than their state of birth, and who
therefore have the allegedly positive characteristics of migrants, albeit as internal
migrants, the picture is different: "Native movers earn 35% higher wages than native non-movers . . . Even black immigrants in the highest income earnings group
earn substantially less than the native black movers." The fact remains that all
these groups, "the native black movers, native black non-movers, and all black
immigrant groups are worse off than both native whites and immigrant whites"
(Butcher 272).

7. See the debate about the overrepresentation of Africans and Afro-Caribbeans
in the Ivy League colleges as reported by the *New York Times* (Rimer and Arenson), and the critique by Belinda Edmondson.

8. Each of these flows is discussed at length in its own chapter in the book I
am currently working on (*Africa and Its Diasporas*) on the subject of linkages between Africa and its diasporas. Each chapter contains an exhaustive list of references which I do not think it necessary to catalogue for these brief notes.

REFERENCES

African Union. General Report. Technical Workshop on the Relationship with the
    Diaspora. June 2–5, 2004, Port of Spain, Trinidad and Tobago. http://www
    .democracy-africa.org/Reports/AUTWreport.pdf (accessed March 25, 2006).
Amissah, Charles K. "The Socio-Economic Achievement of Sub-Saharan African
    Immigrants in the United States." Ph.D. diss., University of Illinois at Chi-
    cago, 1994.
Apraku, Kofi K. *African Emigres in the United States: A Missing Link in Africa's
    Social and Economic Development.* New York: Praeger, 1991.
Arthur, John A. *Invisible Sojourners: African Immigrant Diaspora in the United
    States.* Westport, Conn.: Praeger, 2000.
Borjas, George J. "Economic Theory and International Migration." *International
    Migration Review* 23, no. 3 (1989): 457–485.
Boyd, Monica. "Family and Personal Networks in International Migration: Re-
    cent Developments and New Agendas." *International Migration Review* 23,
    no. 3 (1989): 638–670.
Buechler, Hans Christian, and Judith Maria Buechler, eds. *Migration in Europe:
    The Role of Family, Labor and Politics.* New York: Greenwood, 1987.
Butcher, Kristin F. "Black Immigrants in the United States: A Comparison with
    Native Blacks and Other Immigrants." *Industrial and Labour Relations Re-
    view* 47, no. 2 (1994): 265–284.

Butler, Kim. "From Black History to Diasporan History: Brazilian Abolition in Afro-Atlantic Context." *African Studies Review* 43, no. 1 (2000): 125–139.

Castles, Stephen, and Mark J. Miller. *The Age of Migration: International Population Movements in the Modern World.* 3rd ed. New York: Guilford, 2003.

———. *The Age of Migration: International Population Movements in the Modern World.* 2nd ed. London: Macmillan, 1998.

Chiswick, Barry R., Carmel U. Chiswick, and Paul W. Miller. "Are Immigrants and Natives Perfect Substitutes in Production?" *International Migration Review* 19, no. 4 (1985): 674–685.

Copeland-Carson, Jacqueline. *Creating Africa in America: Translocal Identity in an Emerging World City.* Philadelphia: University of Pennsylvania Press, 2004.

Diouf, Sylviane. *Servants of Allah: African Muslims Enslaved in the Americas.* New York: New York University Press, 1998.

Dixon, David. "Characteristics of the African Born in the United States." Migration Information Source, January 2006. http://www.migrationinformation .org/USfocus/display.cfm?ID=366 (accessed March 25, 2006).

Djamba, Yanki K. "African Immigrants in the United States: A Socio-Demographic Profile in Comparison to Native Blacks." *Journal of Asian and African Studies* 34, no. 2 (1999): 210–215.

Du Bois, W. E. B. *The Souls of Black Folk,* ed. Henry Louis Gates and Terry Hume Oliver. New York: Norton, 1999.

Edmondson, Belinda. "The Myth of Black Immigrant Privilege." *Anthurium: A Caribbean Studies Journal* 4, no. 1 (2006). http://anthurium.miami.edu/volume_ 4/issue_1/edmondson-themyth.html (accessed March 26, 2006).

Eissa, Salih Omar. "Diversity and Transformation: African Americans and African Immigration to the United States." Immigration Policy Brief (2005). http://www.ailf.org/diversityandtransformationprint.asp.

Fawcett, James T. "Networks, Linkages, and Migration Systems." *International Migration Review* 23, no. 3 (1989): 671–680.

Glick Schiller, N., L. Basch, and C. Blanc-Szanton, eds. *Towards a Transnational Perspective on Migration. Race, Class, Ethnicity, and Nationalism Reconsidered.* New York: New York Academy of Sciences, 1992.

Gomez, Michael. "Muslims in Early America." *The Journal of Southern History* 60, no. 4 (1994): 671–710.

Grieco, Elizabeth. "The African Born in the United States." Migration Information Source http://www.migrationinformation.org/USFocus/display.cfm?ID=250.

Hamilton, Nora, and Norma S. Chinchilla. "Global Economic Restructuring and International Migration." *International Migration* 34, no. 2 (1996): 195–227.

Hawk, Beverly G. *Africans and the 1965 U. S. Immigration Law.* Ph.D. diss., University of Wisconsin, Madison, 1988.

Hegel, G. W. F. *The Philosophy of History.* New York: Dover, 1956.

Heisler, Barbara S. "The Future of Immigrant Incorporation: Which Models? Which Concepts?" *International Migration Review* 26, no. 2 (1992): 623–645.

Hine, Darlene Clark. "Frontiers in Black Diaspora Studies and Comparative Black History: Enhanced Knowledge of Our Complex Past." *The Negro Educational Review* 52, no. 3 (2001): 101–108.

Humphries, Jill. "Resisting 'Race': Organizing African Transnational Identities in the United States." Paper presented at the Conference on "The New African Diaspora: Assessing the Pains and Gains of Exile." Organized by the Department of Africana Studies, Binghamton University, April 7–9, 2006.

Irele, Abiola. "Dimensions of African Discourse." In Kostas Myrsiades and Jerry McGuire, eds. *Order and Partialities: Theory, Pedagogy, and the 'Postcolonial.'* Albany: State University of New York Press, 1995, 15–34.

Isaac, Walter. "Locating Afro-American Judaism: A Critique of White Normativity." In Lewis R. Gordon and Jane Anna Gordon, eds. *A Companion to African-American Studies.* Malden, Mass.: Blackwell, 2006, 512–542. http://www.h-net.msu.edu/reviews/showrev.cgi?path=14761911341962—note2.

Kritz, Mary M., Lin L. Lim, and Hania Zlotnik, eds. *International Migration: A Global Approach.* Oxford: Clarendon, 1992.

Kubik, Gerhard. "Analogies and Differences in African American Musical Cultures Across the Hemisphere: Interpretive Models and Research Strategies." *Black Music Research Journal* 18, no. 1/2 (1998): 203–227.

Logan, Bernard I. "The Reverse Transfer of Technology from Sub-Saharan Africa to the United States." *Journal of Modern African Studies* 25, no. 4 (1987), 597–612.

Margai, Florence. "Acculturation, Assimilation and the Health of Black Immigrant Families in the United States." Paper presented at the Conference on "The New African Diaspora: Assessing the Pains and Gains of Exile." Organized by the Department of Africana Studies, Binghamton University, April 7–9, 2006.

Massey, Douglas S. "International Migration at the Dawn of the Twenty-First Century: The Role of the State." *Population and Development Review* 25, no. 2 (1999): 303–322.

Massey, Douglas S., Joaquim Arango, Graeme Hugo, Ali Kouaouci, Adela Pellegrino, and J. Edward Taylor. "Theories of International Migration: A Review and Appraisal." *Population Review and Development* 19, no. 3 (1993): 431–466.

———. *World in Motion: Understanding International Migration at the End of the Millennium.* Oxford: Oxford University Press, 1998.

Mkandawire, Thandika. "Rethinking Panafricanism." Paper presented at the First Conference of Intellectuals from Africa and the Diaspora (CIAD), African Union, October 7 to 9, 2004, Dakar, Senegal.

Mwakikagile, Godfrey. *Relations Between Africans and African Americans: Misconceptions, Myths and Realities.* Grand Rapids, Mich.: National Academic Press, 2005.

Nzegwu, Nkiru. "Memory Lines: Art in the Pan-African World." *Ijele: Art eJournal of the African World* 1, no. 2 (2000). http://www.ijele.com/vol1.2/nzegwu2.html.

Ogbaa, Kalu. *The Nigerian Americans.* Westport, Conn.: Greenwood, 2003.

Olupona, Jacob, ed. *African Immigrant Religions in America* (forthcoming).

Palmer, Colin. "The African Diaspora." *Black Scholar* 30, no. 3/4 (2000): 56–59.

Portes, Alejandro. "Contemporary Immigration: Theoretical Perspectives on Its Determinants and Modes of Incorporation." *International Migration Review* 23, no. 3 (1989): 606–630.

Portes, Alejandro, and Min Zhou. "Divergent Destinies: Immigration, Poverty, and Entrepreneurship in the United States." Program in Comparative International Development, Johns Hopkins University, Working Paper 8, 1992. http://www.jhu.edu/-soc/pcid/papers/8 (accessed 6/26/99).

Rimer, Sara, and Karen W. Arenson. "Top Colleges Take More Blacks, but Which Ones?" *The New York Times,* Thursday, June 24, 2004.

Salt, John. "A Comparative Overview of International Trends and Types, 1950–80." *International Migration Review* 23, no. 3 (1989): 431–456.

Sassen, Saskia. *The Mobility of Labor and Capital: A Study in International Investment and Labor Flow.* Cambridge: Cambridge University Press, 1988.

Shepperson, George. "African Diaspora: Concept and Context." In Joseph E. Harris, ed. *Global Dimensions of the African Diaspora.* 2nd ed. Washington, D.C.: Howard University Press, 1993, 41–49.

Sowell, Thomas. "Three Black Histories." *Essays and Data on American Ethnic Groups.* Washington, D.C.: Urban Institute, 1978.

Stark, Oded. *The Migration of Labor.* Cambridge, Mass.: Basil Blackwell, 1991.

Stark, Oded, and J. Edward Taylor. "Relative Deprivation and International Migration." *Demography* 26 (1989): 1–14.

Stark, Oded, J. Edward Taylor, and S. Yitzhaki. "Remittances and Inequality." *The Economic Journal* 96 (1986): 722–740.

Taylor, J. Edward. "The New Economics of Labor Migration and the Role of Remittances in the Migration Process." *International Migration* 37, no. 1 (1999): 63–86.

Todaro, Michael P. *International Migration in Developing Countries.* Geneva: International Labor Office, 1976.

United Nations. *International Migration 2006.* New York: United Nations, Department of Economic and Social Affairs, Population Division, 2006. http://www.un.org/esa/population/publications/2006Migration_Chart/2006IttMig_chart.htm.

U.S. Census. Statistical Abstract of the United States 2006, p. 11. http://www.census.gov/prod/2005pubs/06statab/pop.pdf.

Vinson, Ben. "African (Black) Diaspora History, Latin American History." *The Americas* 63, no. 1 (2006): 1–18.

Waldinger, Roger. *Still The Promised City? African-Americans and New Immigrants in Postindustrial New York.* Cambridge, Mass.: Harvard University Press, 1996.

Wallace, Suzanne B., Charles D. Delorme, and David R. Kamerschen. "Migration as a Consumption Activity." *International Migration* 35, no. 1 (1997): 37–56.

Zeleza, Paul Tiyambe. "Africa: The Changing Meanings of 'African' Culture and Identity." In Elisabeth Abiri and Håkan Thörn, eds., *Horizons: Perspectives on a Global Africa.* Göteborg, Sweden: National Museum of World Cultures and Göteborg University, 2005, 31–72.

———. *Africa and Its Diasporas: Dispersals and Linkages* (forthcoming).

———. "The African Academic Diaspora in the United States and Africa: The Challenges of Productive Engagement." *Comparative Studies of South Asia, Africa, and the Middle East* 24, no. 1 (2004): 265–278.

———. "African Labor and Intellectual Migrations to the North: Building New

Transatlantic Bridges." Paper presented at the African Studies Research Seminar, Center for African Studies, University of Illinois at Urbana-Champaign, February 10, 2000.

——. "Contemporary African Migrations in a Global Context: Towards Building the Black Atlantic." Paper presented at the 10th CODESRIA General Assembly, Kampala, Uganda, December 8–12, 2002.

——. "Rewriting the African Diaspora: Beyond the Black Atlantic." *African Affairs* 104, no. 1 (2005): 35–68.

Zlotnik, Hania. "Trends of International Migration Since 1965: What Existing Data Reveal," *International Migration* 37, no. 1 (1999): 21–59.

PART TWO
LEAVING HOME

3   TOGO ON MY MIND

Adzele K. Jones

"THREE DAYS OF FEAR": A PERSONAL ACCOUNT

*January 5th, 1994. It was 6:00 PM. . . . Gunshots were heard. First,
we did not pay attention to the noise because, since August 1990, the
strange music had punctuated people's daily lives through the country,
particularly in Lomé, the capital of Togo. We continued to do our home-
work, only to realize a few minutes later that the gunshots were increasing and getting closer and closer. We quickly packed our things,
closed the windows, and locked the doors. Then we lay down on the
floor, planning, thinking, praying for a better tomorrow. That was how
we spent the night.*

*Around midnight, we heard a heavy gunfight in our neighborhood,
probably in front of the post office about 300 meters from our house.
We remained on the floor with the hope that the following day, things
would calm down. That was a false hope. The gunshots continued
until dawn. When things calmed down in the morning, we slowly put
our noses outside the house to see what was going on. It was a disas-
ter. Some said there were dead bodies on the streets. The rumor was
that the opposition's aggressors came from the neighboring republic of
Ghana. They were supposedly trained by the Togolese opposition and
their goal was to overthrow the ruling regime of President Gnassingbé
Eyadéma.*

*Near the house and close to the post office was the official border
between Ghana and Togo. We could observe movements of tanks, ar-
mored cars, and other military equipment. Our entire neighborhood
was occupied by the government troops of Togo.*

*Around noon on January 6, 1994, the intensity of gunshots de-
creased, but two hours later, there was another attack. We could hear
bullets hitting the roof of our house. Once again, everybody lay down
flat on the floor until the following morning. On the third day, a Satur-
day, one could get out to take a look at the streets again. The dead bod-*

*ies had been removed. Some people were picking up bullets from the
streets, walls and yards of their homes.*

*These three days of heavy gun fighting were awful for everybody. It
was estimated that more than 1,500 people lost their lives. The political
problems continue in Togo, up to the present . . .*

A HISTORY OF POLITICAL UNREST

In 1960, Togo gained independence from colonial France. In 1963 its first
president, Sylvanus Olympio, was assassinated and replaced by Nicolas
Grunitzky, a former prime minister from the colonial era. In 1967, Ser-
geant Etienne Eyadéma seized power after a coup and dissolved all political parties. From 1967 until his death on February 5, 2005, President
Eyadéma, soon to become General Gnassingbé Eyadéma, ruled in a dictatorship that lasted thirty-eight years. After his death, contrary to the provisions of the Togo constitution, the military inaugurated his son, Faure
Gnassingbé, as president. This provoked domestic and international con-
demnation. After pressures from the international community, the African Union, and internal opposition groups, a new presidential election
took place on April 24, 2005. In the end, Faure Gnassingbé was declared
the winner and took presidential office in Togo. However, this election
triggered several days of intense civil unrest.

Judging from my experience and from the reports of international
news agencies and nonprofit organizations, elections in Togo have been
followed by riots and violence since Gnassingbé Eyadéma declared himself the president in 1967. The table below documents the key political
events in Togo along with reported human right violations.

Togolese have endured more than four decades of human rights violations since the dictatorial rule of Gnassingbé Eyadéma began. In 2000,
Amnesty International (AI) requested an investigation of the regime's actions. It reported that civilians and soldiers alike were arrested, tortured,
killed, or disappeared. In particular, AI demanded justice for the killings
of the "1991 Bé lagoon massacre in which at least 28 non-violent demonstrators were killed by the army and the January, 1993, killing of more
than 20 people by the Togolese armed forces during a peaceful demonstration in the capital, Lomé" ("Togo: Truth and Justice" 1). Amnesty International noted that "the Togolese government is yet to open an independent,
impartial and effective inquiry to shed light on past abuses, especially
the massacres of 1991, 1993, 1994 and 1998" ("Human Rights" 1). In addition, AI alleged that "hundreds of people had been killed by the security
forces around the time of the June 1998 elections and that bodies had been
dumped at sea by military aircraft" ("Togo: Rule of Terror," 25). Amnesty
International and a special United Nations commission also reported that
"literally hundreds of bodies, all obviously murdered, had washed ashore

Table 3.1. Togo Timeline with Human Right Violations

Year	Event	Year	Event
1979	Eyadéma, standing as sole candidate, elected as president in first parliamentary and presidential polls since 1967.	1998*	Eyadéma re-elected.
1985	Series of bombings in Lomé. Coup attempt, French troops come to government's assistance.	2000	UN-OAU begins inquiry into Amnesty International allegations that the country's armed forces summarily executed hundreds of people during the run-up to the presidential election in 1998.
1986	Eyadéma re-elected.	2001	**February**—International inquiry into allegations of summary executions and torture in Togo concludes there were systematic violations of human rights after 1998 presidential election. **August**—Demonstrators take to the streets.
1991*	Strikes, demonstrations. (AI: leading to hundred of reported deaths)	2002	Parliament alters the constitution, removing a clause which would have barred President Eyadéma from seeking a third term in 2003.
1992	New constitution approved by referendum	2003	Eyadéma re-elected
1993–1994*	Eyadéma dissolves government, sparking protests and fatal clashes with military forces and police. Hundreds of thousands flee to neighboring states.	2005*	**February**—President Gnassingbé Eyadéma dies at age 69. The military appoints his son Faure as president in a move condemned as a coup. **April**—Faure Gnassingbé wins presidential elections which the opposition condemns as rigged. Deadly street violence followed. The UN later estimates that 800 people were killed.

*Amnesty International reported violence and human right violations during the years marked with asterisk in the chart above.
Data Source: BBC News, "Timeline: Togo: A Chronology of Key Events," ca. 2005, http://news.bbc.co.uk/2/hi/africa/country_profiles/1067813.stm (accessed March 17, 2006).

Table 3.2. Togolese Refugees

Year	Number of Refugees	
	Benin	Ghana
1993–1994	N/A	240,000
1996	10,000	20,000
2005	23,221	15,000

Data Source: Afrol News, "Refugee Numbers from Togo Still Increasing," May 13, 2005, www.afrol.com/articles/16329 (accessed March 15, 2006).

along the coast" (LeVine and Seely 2). Afrol News reported that before, during, and after the 2005 election, 811 people were killed and 4,500 were injured ("Refugee Numbers" 1). The table above shows documented numbers of refugees from Togo to Benin and Ghana for the years of reported massacres.

These events in Togo—political unrest, murder, torture, and ultimately human rights violations as defined by Amnesty International—only worsen the living conditions of its people and indirectly force them to seek better opportunities outside the country. Political unrest produces unfavorable conditions for economic growth, and, as is the case with Togo, it also negatively impacts the economy of some of the surrounding countries, such as Burkina Faso, Mali, and Niger (IRIN, "Togo: Gnassingbe Sworn In" 3).

MY PERSONAL TOGO TIMELINE, 1990–1994

Before I became aware of the political situation in Togo, my life was pleasant. We attended school and celebrated each joyous occasion, sang, danced, shopped in the market, and traveled to other parts of the country for summer vacation. Like most children, I dreamed about the future and what I would be when I grew up. Needless to say, I did not dream about living in a foreign country and my nightmares did not contain images of soldiers with guns.

My life started to change in October of 1990. A riot started at the courthouse where the government had put some students on trial for handing out anti-government pamphlets. In retaliation, the soldiers opened fire on the demonstrators and took to the streets. On that afternoon, I heard gunshots as we were released from school. The streets were almost empty. The only people I saw were running for their lives with armed soldiers close by. Luckily, my home was not so far from the school and I managed to get there safely. Unrest continued and the following days and months were marked by anti-government demonstrations and violent standoffs between soldiers and civilians. In the following days, gunshots were heard, soldiers patrolled the streets, and in spite of the fear that was present among the people, some still took to the streets to demonstrate. On one particular day, after a period of gunshots, we ventured outside and saw bullet holes in the wall of our house. I remember someone from the neighborhood going around collecting bullets as souvenirs. The routine for the years to come was to run and seek refuge once you heard gunshots.

In 1991 a conference, La Conference National Souveraine, was organized in an attempt to address and resolve the political difficulties of the country, particularly the issue of power-sharing between the president and the government. I remember how the students and some of my relatives talked about this conference: this was going to be the end of our problems. President Eyadéma was going to yield some of his exorbitant power, and social affairs would be better with the choice of Kokou Joseph Koffigoh, a member of the opposition, as prime minister.

As the country soon discovered, this sharing was a challenge to implement since President Eyadéma was resistant to the change. This resulted in further demonstrations and violence. Later in 1991, many leading opponents who had returned to the country to take part in the conference paid the price for daring to challenge him. Hundreds of people, including allegedly "disloyal" bureaucrats, professionals, and military personnel, were imprisoned, tortured, and summarily executed. Since then, Togo has been under European as well as U.S. sanctions for what the EU calls a "democratic deficit" (LeVine and Seely 2).

From the age of twelve, I had become aware of the sad reality of the country I was living in. There were soldiers everywhere. Rumors about the president constantly circulated around the country. Some people questioned his position in the French colonial army; others questioned his education. School administrators used to interrupt classes and send us to line up on streets to salute, sing, and dance as the president's car passed by. At one point, the running joke was that in a televised speech, the president used the expression "n'est-ce pas" (loosely translated to "isn't it?") forty-five times. Though we sometimes laughed, most of the time we were afraid. We would only whisper our political opinions to trusted family members and friends, because we feared being the next victims of the ubiquitous informants and the forces of repression. One of my brothers had a telescope, but he was told not to use it anymore because the government might think he was spying on them with it. My friends and I used to sit and make up strategies of defense and survival against the soldiers if they happened to come to our homes. One day, a medical doctor from our neighborhood was taken away by soldiers because he was treating the government's opponents.

In 1992, a strike was called by the opposition because the interim legislative body had been held hostage by the presidential army for twenty-four hours. The opposition called for a two-week strike: we were not to go to school or to work. Two weeks later, the strike had not ended; it continued for months and resulted in severe economic damage to the country. I remember having to go to typing school at some point, since the regular schools were closed. After that, I was sent to a friend's hair salon as an apprentice. Some schools later reopened, but most of us were too afraid to attend. We believed the schools were for Eyadéma's supporters, and, after all, we were supposed to be on strike.

Eventually, we attended for the sake of our education. Needless to say, we learned very little; it was more like a daylong recess. Most of us lost that year of our education as the demonstrations and riots continued. Those who participated were severely beaten and arrested by the soldiers. As one of my brothers recalls, soldiers were throwing demonstrators on burning tires that served as barricades. It was not uncommon for soldiers to torture, beat, and burn people, dead or alive. It was even rumored that one of the president's sons had a torture camp in the north of the country.

In January 1993, President Eyadéma called an end to the transitional government and took control once again. On January 15, the French Co-operation Minister and the German Minister of Foreign Affairs were visiting Togo and the opposition took this opportunity to call for a large-scale demonstration. Everyone, young and old, was participating in the march. In the early afternoon of that day, I saw a crowd pass by my house as they marched to the center of the capital. Our family urged us not to join them and to stay inside, but my oldest brother decided to join the march.

This was an important event since we finally had the chance to make our plea before the international community. However, during this demonstration, attended by an estimated 300,000 unarmed civilians, the soldiers were given orders to open fire on the crowd. Those that survived this massacre, including my brother, said that the police were hidden in the trees and in covered trucks. They drove over the crowd and fired on people from different angles. They started burning and senselessly killing people. The demonstrators were surrounded; children, men, and women, young and old, were witnesses to and victims of this massacre. It was reported that about 100,000 people were brutally murdered. Some were burned, raped, and thrown in the river. I remember quietly waiting with my family, too afraid to say anything, as my father went out to look for my brother. I would take a quick look outside and see people here and there, some wounded, some crying and also searching for their loved ones. I remember a child passing in front of us, with tears in his eyes and blood on his clothes. I remember my father returning without my brother, and for a while I wondered if he was hurt, or worse, killed. Fortunately, my brother finally returned home in the middle of the night. He had managed to hide until things calmed down and had slowly made his way home. I was relieved, but more afraid than ever. Some around him were not so lucky.

After this ordeal, I was one of the 200,000 Togolese refugees who crossed the border to Ghana. As we were approaching the border, there were crowds of people, most of whom were carrying their belonging on their heads. Naturally, the soldiers were also present, asking for bribes as fees to cross the border. I remember taking a breath of relief once we were clearly into Ghana.

My family was separated as our father took us to separate relatives' homes in Ghana, where we stayed for six months. My time as a refugee was easier than that of most people. I was lucky enough to stay with a family and not in a refugee camp. Sometimes we joined the UN food line to get some rice to support ourselves and the family that opened their home to us.

Since Ghana's colonial language was English and ours was French, we were not able to join their schools. Some of the opposition personnel set up a station for the youth to attend school. We carried our own school desks to and from the designated area, since it was just an open field with sand at our feet. It was then I learned that the conditions in which you learn have nothing to do with the knowledge and wisdom you gain.

After six months we returned to Togo, where the situation had calmed down. A six o'clock curfew was instituted; the streets were often deserted and oddly quiet. Most of my friends and family did not return from exile. Other refugees returned much later and only for a short while. Some continued on to France, Germany, Spain, and elsewhere in Europe. Some came to the United States, while others who could not travel abroad remained with family in Ghana, Benin, or other neighboring countries.

Then in 1994, my last year in Togo, we lived through three more days of fighting as described above, an account I have reconstructed from a diary I kept at the time. I left my country in September 1994, a few months after the events took place.

During those four years (1990–1994), some of us condemned the French because we believed they were supporting Eyadéma, which was why his actions remained unpunished by the international community. We believed that, in the first place, he had been put in power because the first Togolese president had not been in agreement with General de Gaulle, the French president at the time. Even though we had received our independence from them, the French still kept control of the few economic assets of the country. One of the theories was that Eyadéma was just their puppet, a mere figurehead, and the French were running the government. Some people even asked for the Germans to come in and take over once

again, since they had been the first to colonize the country prior to World
War I. Needless to say, neither Eyadéma nor the French liked that idea.
Victor T. LeVine and Jennifer Seely write that

> One would have thought that the excesses of Eyadéma's regime should
> have evoked loud international condemnation. There was a good deal of
> hand-wringing, denunciation and some mild punishment, but not so much
> else . . . What prevented more vigorous action against Eyadéma were his
> close ties to the French government and the protection afforded by his in-
> volvement in the informal African "reseaux" (networks) of influence and
> economic clout operated through the Elysée Palace (the French presidency),
> French businesses and politicians with African interests and compliant
> African leaders.

Unfortunately, this is a situation common to many African leaders.
Despotic and corrupt, they are known to hold millions of their countries' money in Swiss bank accounts while their people live in poverty.
At the same time, the countries often find themselves under heavy economic sanctions as a result of human rights violations. Because of the
very premium put on money and power, some of these leaders are willing
to compromise people's lives, kill communities, and destroy the future of
their own people for the sake of material possessions. Consequently, their
people are left to struggle to find new opportunities elsewhere.

Political unrest and violence are part of my past and present. Now, as
an immigrant in the United States, I continue to seek opportunities and
continually struggle to reconcile my Togolese past with my present experience. I was able to come to the United States because my father had
a teaching position at one of the universities in the U.S., so my younger
brother and I made the journey. In so doing, we were like many Togolese,
like many Africans, and like many others pushed out of our homes and
pulled to other places by opportunity.

WHY DO WE EMIGRATE?

It is perhaps best explained in this statement from a Togolese: "We have
lived badly all our lives and now I have sacrificed my future. The best
thing is to seek a new life elsewhere" (IRIN, "Benin-Togo" 3). There are
many reasons why one leaves one's home in search of other opportunities.
I left because I had the chance to, and there was nothing else to work for
at home. We had to seek new opportunities elsewhere: education and a
chance for a future. Due to globalization, the need for labor and the speed
of travel have transcended national borders. According to April Gordon,
some of the factors contributing to migration in general are globalization
and the integration of the world economy. She explains that Africans migrate to the U.S. because of the latter's immigration and refugee policies,

as well as the economic and development failures of Africa (85). Research shows that two-thirds of Africa's population lives in absolute poverty. In addition, political instability is linked to the poor economic performance on the continent. Two-thirds of the world's victims of war during the 1980s were African. In 1991 alone, military conflict affected one-third of Africa's nations. As of 1994, Africa had surpassed Asia as the region with the most refugees (Gordon 85).

According to Baffour Takyi, "push and pull theorists suggest that people migrate because they are pushed out of their former location by such factors as the lack of employment, poverty, civil unrest, and lack of food, with the absence of these attributes acting as a pull to the prospective migrants" (2). Political unrest does not only produce negative social results, such as human rights violations. It also has a negative impact on the country's economic development. As a result, the living standard of the country falls, inflation rates increase, and the national income declines. In most developing countries, economic growth is already at a low point, and political unrest only puts the country further in debt. If the country borrows through international loans, which usually come with such sanctions as a structural adjustment program, the population is left fighting for survival and seeking new opportunities elsewhere. For those that have the opportunity, the most common option is to migrate. As Gordon puts it, "all the countries producing the largest number of immigrants have been experiencing economic and political problems but countries with the highest increase in immigration from 1975 to 1995 experienced ruinous, recent civil wars or other political crises along with severe economic deterioration" (94).

IMMIGRATION TO THE U.S.: A TWO-WAY DEAL

Although most Africans migrate to Europe, mainly because of lasting colonial ties, recent records have shown a great trend of African migration to the United States. This trend is especially true for Togo. In the past, since Togo's official language is French, most Togolese traveled primarily to France and to other French-speaking countries. Others sought opportunities in Germany, the earlier colonial power. There was a relatively small number of Togolese immigrants in the United States. But this number has shown a substantial increase since the late 1990s. The graph below shows the scale of deviation from the average for Togolese and African immigrants to the U.S. from 1995 to 2004. It indicates that, in more recent years, there has been a relatively greater increase in Togolese immigrants than in those from the general African population.

Although migrants may leave their homeland in search of better opportunities elsewhere, the country in which they settle also benefits from

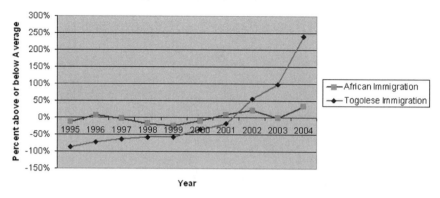

FIGURE 3.1.
African and Togolese Immigrants to U.S. Data Source: United States
Dept. of Homeland Security, Office of Immigration Statistics, Yearbook
of Immigration Statistics: 2004, December 2006.

their presence. In fact, many countries campaign and employ strategies to
attract them. As Gumisai Mutume states, industrial countries need migrants because they often face labor shortages in highly skilled areas such
as information technology and health services, as well as for trade jobs in
agriculture, manufacturing, and construction (Mutume 15). On the whole,
Africans who immigrate to the U.S. or Europe are usually well-educated
or skilled professionals.

   According to Rotimi Sankore, the U.S. Diversity Visa Program re-
cruits skilled and educated Africans (4). It is estimated that 30 percent of
sub-Saharan Africa's highly skilled workers and professionals left their
countries for Europe and the United States between the years of 1960
and 1989. In addition, a third of all college graduates left the continent.
As Gordon points out, 20–50 percent of skilled and professional Africans
leave the continent, while the less skilled migrate to neighboring countries (86). It is reported by Hal Kane that there are more Togolese doctors
in France than in Togo (39).

   Africans enter the United States in many ways. Besides the regular
applicant groups such as students, visitors, and sponsored relatives, immigrants have the opportunity to come to the U.S. through the lottery
and diversity programs offered by the government. These programs are
designed to recruit immigrants with professional skills and education so
they contribute to the advancement of their targeted communities. The
diversity program in 1995 gave 20,200 visas to Africans. This was about
37 percent of all available visas. This increase coincided with Africa's de-

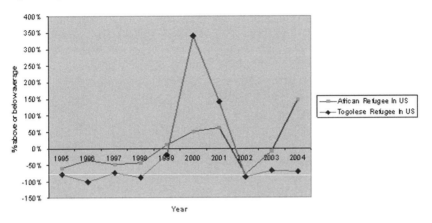

Figure 3.2.
African and Togolese Refugees in U.S. Data Source: U.S. Committee for
Refugees and Immigrants, "World Refugee Survey 1997: Togo," 1997.

teriorating economic and political conditions (Gordon 89). For example,
the years of greater increase in Togolese immigration to the United States
coincide with the years of greater political unrest in the country. The
graph below illustrates the percentage deviation from the average for Togolese and African refugees coming to the U.S. between 1995 and 2004. It
also shows a more than 300 percent deviation above the average of Togolese refugees between 1998 and 1999. This profile matches the years Amnesty International reported political unrest and massacres in Togo.

SETTLING IN THE U.S.

African immigrants clearly have an added drive to succeed because they
have made many sacrifices to seek these new opportunities. It is calculated that African immigrants have spent a longer time on their education and hold higher-level degrees than the average European immigrants
and U.S. natives (Sankore 7). As Gordon puts it, "the average African immigrant continues to have 15.7 years of education, and a higher proportion of Africans than any other group in the U.S. (including white natives
and white immigrants) have college degrees" (91). Africans and Asians
are also more likely than any other immigrant groups to be highly skilled
professional and technical workers. According to the census bureau data
of 1990, 64 percent of foreign-born Nigerians aged twenty-five and above
have at least a four-year degree.

From the fifteen interviews I was able to conduct with Togolese migrants who live in the United States, I discerned that some were hoping to apply the knowledge and education they gained in the U.S. to the improvement of their native country. Others were concentrating on their own survival and the survival of their family members. Regardless of their motivation for success in the United States, one common spirit among African immigrants and Togolese alike is that failure is not an option. With new life in the U.S comes a new commitment. Of the 252,397 Africans who became U.S. citizens in 1997–2003, Togolese accounted for 571 (U.S. Dept. of Justice, "Person Naturalized" 1).

African immigrants are significantly enriching not only the culture but also the economy of the U.S. African lifestyles are slowly merging with mainstream American culture. In his article on an African restaurant opened by refugee women from Sudan, Terry Farish notes that in Maine, where there are more than 10,000 African refugees, the state's former attorney general James Tierney admits that "Maine sees immigrants as an opportunity" (1). African immigrants also impact agricultural activity by growing ethnic food, which makes up $25 billion in the specialty food industry. According to the National Association of Specialty Food, sales of ethnic foods jumped to 16 percent of all specialty foods between 2002 and 2004 (Paley 2). The chart below shows the contribution to the U.S. economy by Togolese immigrants who were naturalized between the years 1993 and 2004. The "unknown" and "no occupation" data might account for children, students, or homemakers.

NAVIGATING THE DIALECTIC: AFRICAN EMIGRATION OUTCOMES

As Sankore points out, between 20 and 50 percent of the African skilled and professional population lives outside the continent. He continues by stating that "if a key factor for anticipating the future development and productivity of any modern society is the number of intellectual thinkers, visionaries, professionals and skilled workers it produces, then Africa had better beware" (2). For example, the U.S. green card lottery is designed to award visas to educated and skilled professionals. In 2005, six African nations were in the top ten of those nations with the greatest number of green card lottery winners: Nigeria (6,725), Egypt (6,070), Ethiopia (6,060), Morocco (5,298), Ghana (3,974), and Kenya (3,168). Africans totaled 31,295 and non-Africans 23,044 (Sankore 3). On one hand, African immigrants have the intellectual and academic credentials for achieving success and contributing greatly to the U.S. economy, culture, and life. On the other hand, the contributions that these educated and skilled Africans could be making to their nations of origin are priceless. Unfortunately, as the

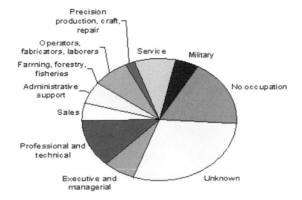

FIGURE 3.3.
Occupation of U.S. Naturalized Togolese. Data Source:
U.S. Department of Justice, Immigration and Naturaliza-
tion Service, "Person Naturalized Fiscal Year 2004: Sta-
tistical Yearbook of the Immigration and Naturalization
Service," April 2005.

social, economic, and political crises in many African countries (Togo,
Nigeria, etc.) continue, the impact that these contributions could make
continues to be postponed. Revitalized by study and work abroad, many
African emigrants, including Togolese, return home to visit, while others
attempt to build a new life back in their native countries with the skills
and knowledge they have gained abroad. In some cases these attempts
fail, and these migrants return to immigrant life in the diaspora. In the
case of Togo, political unrest continues with no avenue for advancement
or opportunity for investment, unless the proper networks with the ruling party are established.

Although most emigrants are unable to contribute directly to the development of their homelands, they transfer substantial resources to their
country of origin. Despite the brain drain effect of emigration, it is important to recognize that "migration can be positive for those who move,
for the societies they move to and for the societies they leave behind"
(Mutume 17). One manifestation of this positive effect is through remittance, which has become a source of global development, especially in
the poorer countries (Bridi 2). A World Bank report indicates that emigrants remit about $75 billion a year. In 1995, remittances amounted to
10 to 50 percent of GNP in Africa; remittance from Europe to Africa was
estimated at $2.6 billion (World Bank 172). Some emigrants invest in the

trading business, and in construction of schools; others invest in housing and consumer goods. Remittance reduces poverty levels by contributing to food, clothing, education, medical expenses, and housing. According to Haleh Bridi, remittance provides a "stable resource without liabilities," it "finances education, and public infrastructure," and it "funds consumption or investment which generate multiplier effects" (11). Mutume reports that, in Uganda, remittance reduced the poverty level by 11 percent (16). In sub-Saharan Africa, distribution of remittance for the years 2001–2003 was as follows: $3.9 billion (2001); $4.1 billion (2002); and $5.1 billion (2003) with an increase of 3.5 percent from 2001 to 2003 (World Bank 170). Remittance is certainly making an impact on Africa, but its effectiveness is severely reduced by the failure of most African governments to provide a market for investment that is transparent or free of corruption.

I had difficulty getting Togolese to answer survey questions for this research. Their honest response was that they were afraid; they wanted to know why I was writing this essay and who was going to read it. This was even after I had assured them that their comments would be anonymous. In an interview conducted by Chris Riemenschneider, a Togolese musician now living in the U.S. explained that "they [fellow Togolese] have spent so many years under dictatorship that they are afraid that if they organize and socialize here, it might get back to Togo and to their families there and make people suspicious of them." This may explain why, although African immigrants make up only 3 percent of all immigrants in the United States, they have the highest rate of naturalization (Gordon 97). They hope that foreign citizenship will provide a cover of security for whatever nationalist agitation they may have done abroad. As this Togolese states, "with this government in place, I can't return to Togo." Political unrest indeed creates an unfavorable atmosphere where emigrants are too afraid to be involved when it comes to the political situation in their home country. Even more ominously, it creates a situation where investors stay clear of the African market because of widespread political instability and corruption. It also deters African emigrants who are in a position to invest in their native land (Gordon 97).

African governments clearly need to provide an environment that is friendly to private investment and entrepreneurship and to initiate policies that can draw on the skills of their citizens in the diaspora (Takyi 7). Mutume suggests that African governments can curtail the urge to migrate by creating more job opportunities (16). African governments also need to maximize remittance legally by offering tax incentives, unifying the official and black market exchange rates, and negotiating with foreign agencies for lower charges on remittance. Also, greater access to banks in rural areas and a compatible electronic transfer system would help increase the flow of remittance into the country (Bridi 14–17). Most importantly, African governments need to create a transparent investment climate. It is only through this process that remittance and investment will greatly impact the economic development of the area.

* * *

As immigrants, we struggle to balance our push and pull factors, as well as the dialectic between the past and the present. At the same time, we are trying to ensure a successful future in our new home country. Our sense of community is redefined. In this whole process, we strive not to lose sight of our personal identities and the stories that ground us amid the flux of statistics that define our status as migrants. As Filmon Mebrahtu, an African filmmaker in Philadelphia, has stated, "I think what happens is a lot of times when we go through statistics, whether it's African immigrants or other immigrants, how many are there, education, how are they successful here . . . the people get lost in the numbers. And for me, it's just a chance to meet a person, a story, and through those stories you see the issues around their lives, issues that new immigrants face" (quoted in Dragan 2). It is a way to make sure that we relate our past to our children, raise awareness, educate, and hopefully assist in the rebuilding of our continent, Africa.

As an immigrant in the United States, I had a chance to contemplate these issues in both contexts: at home in Togo and in the U.S. I decided to take advantage of the opportunities in the U.S., especially those concerning learning and education. A good number of African immigrants in the U.S. and Europe have joined the ranks of scholars specializing in African issues. They contribute to the future of the continent by first educating themselves and then educating others, teaching our children, building communities, and raising awareness about Africa.

Due to lack of job opportunities and stable incomes, and the ever-increasing inflation, more and more Togolese are emigrating. Those who do not have the opportunity to leave remain and struggle to make a living while hoping for political and social justice under the new president, Faure Gnassingbé. We emigrants need to do our part and make a critical difference. When asked whether the Togolese emigrants think of home and contribute to the improvement of the conditions in their home country, one of my interviewees in Togo wrote, "The immigrants help Togo by sending money to their families, and that helps to feed numerous families and meet their health and education needs. Without the diaspora many families in this country would be poorer" (Anonymous, personal interview).

It is significant that this Togolese says nothing about the political situation. Despite the obstacles we face in intervening in issues of human rights, good governance, transparency, and accountability of the political leadership, we must never leave them unaccounted for if we ever hope to go home for good one day.

REFERENCES

Afrol News. "Refugee Numbers from Togo Still Increasing." May 13, 2005. www
.afrol.com/articles/16329 (accessed March 15, 2006).

Amnesty International. "Human Rights Manifesto for Togo." December 1, 2001.
http://web.amnesty.org/library/Index/ENGAFR570152001?open&of=ENG-TGO
(accessed March 17, 2006).

———. "Togo: Truth and Justice Demanded for Victims." June 9, 2000. http://web
.amnesty.org/library/Index/ENGAFR570072000?open&of=ENG-TGO (accessed
March 17, 2006).

———. "Togo: Rule of Terror." May 5, 1999. AI Index AFR 7/001/1999.

Anonymous. E-mail interview. March 22, 2006.

BBC News. "Timeline: Togo: A Chronology of Key Events." http://news.bbc.co.uk/
2/hi/africa/country_profiles/1067813.stm (accessed March 17, 2006).

Bridi, Haleh. "Consequences of Labour Migration for the Developing Countries:
Management of Remittances." World Bank Brussels Office. Presentation to
Conference on Labour Migration, February 26, 2005. http://siteresources.
worldbank.org/INTBELGIUM/Resources/HalehBridiRemittances.pdf (accessed
March 15, 2006).

Dragan, Oksana. "African-Born Filmmaker Documents African Immigrants'
Lives." *Voice of America*, July 11, 2005. http://www.voanews.com/english/
archive/2005-07/2005-07-11-voa32.cfm (accessed March 15, 2006).

Farish, Terry. "Letter from Portland, Maine: A Restaurant from Portland Links
African Refugees to Their Past and Maine to Its Future." *Regional Review*
Q2 (2003): 31–33.

Gordon, April. "The New Diaspora—African Immigrants to the United States."
Journal of Third World Studies (Spring 1998): 79.

IRIN (Integrated Regional Information Networks). "Benin-Togo: Refugees from
Togo Still Trickling across the Border." IRINnews.org, July 6, 2005. http://
www.irinnews.org/Report.aspx?ReportId=55322 (accessed March 15, 2006).

———. "Togo: Gnassingbé Sworn In, Opposition Left with Limited Options."
IRINnews.org, May 4, 2005. http://www.irinnews.org/Report.aspx?ReportId=
54240 (accessed March 15, 2006).

Kane, Hal. " The Hour of Departure: Forces That Create Refugees and Migrants."
Worldwatch Paper 125, Worldwatch Institute. June 1, 1995. http://www
.worldwatch.org/node/865 (accessed March 15, 2006).

LeVine, Victor T., and Jennifer Seely. "Close Ties with France Let Dictator Flourish." *St. Louis Post-Dispatch*, February 27, 2005, sec. B4.

Mutume, Gumisai. "African Migration: From Tensions to Solutions." *Africa Re-
newal* 19, no. 4 (Jan. 2006). http://www.un.org/ecosocdev/geninfo/afrec/vol19no4/
194migration.html (accessed March 15, 2006).

Paley, Amit R. "Hunting for a New Cash Crop: As Immigrant Populations Grow,
Small Farms Turn to Ethnic Foods." *Washington Post*, September 12, 2005.
http://pqasb.pqarchiver.com/washingtonpost/search.html (accessed March 15,
2006).

Riemenschnieder, Chris. "African Musicians Find a New Home in Twin Cities."

Minneapolis Star-Tribune, March 14, 2003. http://www.startribune.com/ dynamic/mobile_story.php?story=3740822 (accessed March 15, 2006).

Sankore, Rotimi. "Killing Us Softly." *New African* 445, no. 8 (Nov. 2005): 8.

Takyi, Baffour K. "The Making of the Second Diaspora: On the Recent African Immigrant Community in the United States of America." *Western Journal of Black Studies* 26, no. 1 (Spring 2002): 32.

U.S. Committee for Refugees and Immigrants. "World Refugee Survey 1997: Togo." 1997. http://www.refugees.org/countryreports.aspx (accessed March 15, 2006).

——. "World Refugee Survey 1998: Togo." 1998. http://www.refugees.org/ countryreports.aspx (accessed March 15, 2006).

U.S. Department of Homeland Security, Office of Immigration Statistics. *Yearbook of Immigration Statistics: 2004.* December 2006. http://www.dhs.gov/ ximgtn/statistics/publications/YrBk04Im.shtm (accessed March 15, 2006).

U.S. Department of Justice, Immigration and Naturalization Service. *1999 Statistical Yearbook of the Immigration and Naturalization Service.* March 2002. http://www.dhs.gov/xlibrary/assets/statistics/yearbook/1999/FY99Yearbook.pdf (accessed March 15, 2006).

——. "Persons Naturalized Fiscal Year 2004: Statistical Yearbook of the Immigration and Naturalization Service." April 2005. http://www.dhs.gov/ximgtn/ statistics/data/DSNat04c.shtm (accessed March 15, 2006).

World Bank. "Appendix A: Enhancing the Devolvement Effect of Workers' Remittances to Developing Countries." In *Global Development Finance: Harnessing Cyclical Gains for Development.* Washington, D.C.: The World Bank, 2004. 169–173. http://siteresources.worldbank.org/GDFINT2004/Home/20177154/ GDF_2004%20pdf.pdf (accessed 15 March 2006).

4 "I, TOO, WANT TO BE A BIG MAN": THE MAKING OF A HAITIAN "BOAT PEOPLE"

Georges E. Fouron

During the early 1960s, Haiti began losing a substantial portion of its population through migration. At that time, the country was reeling under a brutal, authoritarian regime headed by Dr. François Duvalier, a dictator who had been ruling the country with an iron fist since 1957. The strength of his government was invested in a non-salaried paramilitary civilian militia known as the *Tonton Makout* (Uncle Knapsack). Staffed by informers, spies, bullies, neighborhood bosses, and extortionists, the Makout freely used extreme violence, terror, and intimidation to cow the population out of all illusions of destabilizing the regime.

Local opposition to Duvalier's autocratic rule, timid at first, became more daring when President Kennedy publicly denounced the regime's brutality and lent his full support to Haitian exiles who had sought refuge in the United States and were plotting to overthrow the dictator. Next, to cripple the Haitian regime and orchestrate its fall, Kennedy discontinued all forms of non-emergency financial and military assistance to Duvalier (Ferguson). However, instead of buckling under Kennedy's pressures, Duvalier exploited the cold war polarization to his advantage and successfully blackmailed Washington into supporting him, instead.[1]

Soon after President Kennedy's assassination on November 22, 1963, his successor, Lyndon Johnson, more preoccupied with Castro than with Duvalier, reconciled with the Haitian dictator and reversed his predecessor's policy.[2] Assured of Washington's support, on April 1, 1964, Duvalier organized openly fraudulent "elections" that proclaimed him president-for-life. To the dismay of the Haitian population, instead of condemning these sham elections, on April 8, 1964, President Johnson met with André Théard, the Haitian ambassador to Washington, asking him to convey his congratulations to Duvalier and stating that the American government was looking "forward to close cooperation and solidarity with the government of Haiti" (Heinl and Heinl 608). On the day of Duvalier's investiture as president-for-life on May 22, 1964, the U.S. ambassador to Haiti, Benson E. L. Timmons III, went to the Haitian presidential palace to convey the U.S. government's congratulations to Duvalier.

The first opportunity Duvalier had to test the strength of the new ties he had established with the United States occurred on August 5, 1964, when a group of thirteen young leftist idealist exiles calling themselves *Jeune Haiti* (Young Haiti) invaded Haiti's southwestern peninsula with the intention of starting a guerrilla war à la Castro to topple Duvalier. The day after Duvalier's forces had defeated the invasion and summarily executed the invaders, "staff officers representing the Assistant Secretary of Defense for International Security Affairs (ASD/ISA), the Chief of Naval Operation (CNO), and the Commandant of the Marine Corps (CMC)" called an emergency meeting to investigate the ways in which the United States could shore up his regime. They met at the Pentagon and resolved to fund a military mission "with teeth in it" to "assist in strengthening [Haiti's] internal security forces" which were being *"threatened by communism"* (Williamson 21; emphasis in original). Soon after this high-level meeting had taken place, the United States and Haiti "agreed to expand the existing US Naval Mission, which had long been working with the G-Cd'H (Guardes-Côtes d'Haiti). The plan was to augment it with US Navy and Marine Corps officers and noncommissioned officers who would work with Duvalier's newly designated FAd'H (Forces Armées d'Haïti)" (Williamson 32). In addition to the U.S. military missions that were dispatched to assist Duvalier, the United States delivered an arsenal of weapons to the dictator and refitted Haiti's bedraggled air force with jet fighters, while the Pentagon sponsored many Haitian military officers to study at the School of the Americas (SOA),[3] where they learned procedures in crowd control, spying techniques, and interrogation methods and strategies.

Subsequently, the United States Agency for International Development (USAID) and the Inter-American Development Bank (IADB) reviewed Kennedy's ban on financial aid to the Duvalier regime and reinstated it. And although the regime's international financial backers knew that the aid money was being pilfered by Duvalier and his associates, between 1964 and 1968, in addition to many loans the regime received from many U.S. and international financial lending institutions, Duvalier received more than $15 million in "grants" from various U.S. institutions, and Haiti was allowed once more to benefit from the U.S. foreign aid program. Finally, to send a clear message to other exile groups and to discourage them from following Jeune Haiti's example, the United States Navy sent its ships to make courtesy calls to Port-au-Prince and Cap-Haïtien, Haiti's second city (Plummer).

Feeling unassailable because he had the United States' support, endorsement, and protection, during the second half of the 1960s Duvalier

lowered his guard ever so slightly, but perceptibly, and more and more—
since he could now afford it—cultivated an air of reasonableness, the better to impress foreigners and international agencies. By now, too, he had
worn down the morally outraged; Americans, leaders of the Organization
of American States, and representatives of the United Nations accepted the
fait accompli. (Rothberg 248)

From that moment on, to justify his excesses, it sufficed for Duvalier to
append a "communist" label to those he did not particularly like or trust.
And although in many instances Washington denounced the regime's brutality, Duvalier was the least troubled by these criticisms; he knew that as
long as he continued to profess his anticommunism, his regime was safe.

At the end of the 1960s, Duvalier unleashed his wrath on the Haitian
population with full force. First, he decimated the ranks of the upper-class
mulatto merchant and emasculated the Haitian army. Next, he attacked
the Catholic and Anglican churches. Finally, he preyed upon the black
intellectuals who were vying for political change in Haiti. In the end,
to consolidate his rule over the population, Duvalier imprisoned, murdered, or exiled the most dynamic members of Haitian society. However,
cold war realpolitik led the United States, instead of dissociating itself
from the Haitian dictator, to put its perceived national interests ahead of
the Haitians' human rights. Gratified that Duvalier was an avowed anticommunist, Washington turned a blind eye to the dictator's venality and
brazen peculation and continued to collaborate with him.

To justify its closeness to the dictatorial regime, Washington argued
that the assistance it was providing to Duvalier was only meant to institute law and order in Haiti, to protect the region from communist in-
filtrations, and to assuage the suffering of the Haitian masses in order
to stop illegal migration from Haiti. However, Washington's embrace of
the Haitian regime disheartened the majority of the Haitian population.
Added to that, the impunity the members of the Makout force enjoyed and
the brazenness the devotees of the regime displayed significantly shrank
the arena for political debates and left no space for a public discourse of
change.

PATTERNS OF HAITIAN MIGRATION

Feeling insecure in that volatile and dangerous atmosphere, members of
the intellectual and financial elites began leaving Haiti. While the latter
groups used their own financial resources and personal contacts to emigrate, the former groups relied on the initiatives of international organizations such as the United Nations and the Organization of American States
and countries such as Canada and France to escape from the regime's grip.

These foreign interventions initiated a brain drain that systematically de-
pleted the small Haitian cadre. Indeed, by 1970, there were

> more Haitian physicians in either Montréal or New York than Haiti. Mon-
> tréal had ten times more Haitian psychiatrists than Port-au-Prince. Of 246
> medical school graduates from 1959 to 1969 from the University of Haiti,
> only three could be found in practice in the country in 1969. Some public-
> health nurses, trained by the United States, were all lost to Africa. The
> Organization of the American States and the UN had more Haitian econo-
> mists on their payrolls than the government of Haiti. (Heinl and Heinl 612)

In the end, Washington's endorsement of the dictatorship and the departure of the best-educated cadres and the economic elite conspired to fuel
the Haitians' initial migratory endeavors. This massive exodus produced a
migratory domino effect that enticed Haitians of all social classes to seek
all possible means to leave their homeland.

In 1971, when Duvalier died, many expected the regime to collapse.
Instead, he was succeeded by Jean-Claude Duvalier, his nineteen-year-
old son, also as president-for-life. The smooth and uneventful transfer of
power from Duvalier to his son caused a general sense of foreboding to
grip the Haitian population. And when Jean-Claude Duvalier reneged on
the promise he had made at the time of his investiture to discontinue his
father's legacy of brutality and impunity and to instead concentrate his
efforts on the economic development of the country, Haiti experienced
a dramatic rise in the number of people who went searching for ways
to leave. By that time, securing a visa had become nearly impossible for
those who did not have relatives living abroad to sponsor them. And since
the majority of the prospective new emigrants did not have the financial
resources, social capital, and professional credentials to leave through the
normal channels, many were forced to leave by boat. These clandestine
routes represented the only way they could leave Haiti.

Facing a bleak future in Haiti and undeterred by tales of emigrant
hardship, the potential refugees preferred to put their lives in the hands of
human traffickers and smugglers rather than stay in Haiti and be subjected
to the regime's atrocities. The risks they took were very dangerous, because they involved taking a 700-mile long-distance sea journey in poorly
fitted vessels threading dangerously through the treacherous waters of
the Caribbean Sea. Known as "boat people," participants in this new migration phase were of lower urban and peasant extractions and came from
villages and towns scattered around Haiti. To pay for their passage, they
sold all their possessions. If they owned land, they heavily mortgaged or
sold their small plots. If they had relatives and friends who resided abroad,
they appealed to them to secure the cost of their passage.

During the 1970s and 1980s, excluding those who perished at sea, an estimated 50,000 to 80,000 of these clandestine migrants landed on Florida's shores (Fass). These figures are just estimates, however. According to the U.S. Immigration and Naturalization Service (INS), because as many as half of the arrivals escaped detection, the actual number of boat people may have exceeded 100,000 (U.S. Library of Congress).

Between 1986 and 1991, subsequent to Jean-Claude Duvalier's overthrow and up to the election of Jean-Bertrand Aristide as president in 1990, few instances of clandestine escapes were recorded.[4] However, the momentum was renewed in 1991 soon after President Aristide had been overthrown by the Haitian army after only seven months in office, allegedly with the help of the CIA. It again subsided in 1994, after Aristide had been returned to power by 20,000 U.S. troops (Farmer). According to Amnesty International, between 1991 and 1994 the remainder of the Makout forces, the Haitian army, and affiliates of a CIA-sponsored right-wing militia known by its French acronym, FRAPH, used force, intimidation, assassination, rape, and many other forms of terror upon the population.[5] In addition, they summarily executed hundreds if not thousands of Aristide's supporters. To escape from that dangerous situation, "over 100,000 Haitians were believed to have crossed to the Dominican border to the east; tens of thousands left the country by sea" seeking refugee status in the United States and the Bahamas (Farmer 190).

The rest of this essay represents the experiences of a sixteen-year-old teenager named Jonas—a pseudonym—who left Haiti for Miami in 1981. I interviewed Jonas in Miami, Florida, in April of 2006. While Jonas's story reflects, to some significant degree, the common experiences of many boat people, it does not pretend to represent the saga of them all.

THE HAITIAN BOAT PEOPLE PHENOMENON

From the early 1970s to the present, the U.S. government has maintained that grinding poverty and not political persecution is alone responsible for the migratory debacle that has been ferrying a substantial number of lower-class dark-skinned Haitian refugees to the United States. Therefore, except in some rare cases, the refugees' requests for political asylum have always been denied. Yet although the Haitian boat people are poorer and have fewer credentials than those Haitians who left their country during the first migratory waves, they are not among the poorest in Haiti. Many among these emigrants are skilled and literate and have access to some financial resources in Haiti or abroad which have allowed them to access the necessary funds to pay for their passage (Stepick, *Pride against Prejudice*).

To better understand the characteristics of this massive movement by which a significant portion of the Haitian population have left their country through irregular and unconventional means during the last three decades, it is necessary to appraise the Haitian population's attitude vis-à-vis migration. In effect, the massive exodus of Haiti's best-educated cadres and members of the business sector marked a turning point in the Haitians' traditional normative thinking processes, which, for a long time, considered permanent migration out of Haiti as anathema.

Indeed, during the nineteenth century and the first half of the twentieth, except for seasonal labor migration to the Dominican Republic and the neighboring Caribbean islands, Haitians were not represented in significant numbers in the mass permanent migration of the world's population in search of improved economic, social, and political conditions. Although Haiti was a very poor country and the Haitians' life conditions were very difficult, instead of exposing themselves to the stings of racism by migrating, Haitians preferred to remain in their country. As early as 1873, a prominent Haitian intellectual warned those Haitians who would contemplate leaving their country to settle in white-dominated societies that to do so would not only entail the loss of their dignity, but would also constitute an affront to their national identity. In a heartfelt appeal to the Haitians to stay home, he reported that in Europe and in the United States,

> Black people are forced to live like the Jews lived in the Middle Ages, tolerated but persecuted. Like the Moors lived in Spain after the overthrow of the kingdom of Grenada, reduced to bow down with humility and live in fear . . . to migrate would mean to abdicate your sovereignty and betray the nation. (Delorme 127)

As late as the end of the 1960s, the same sentiment prevailed in Haiti. For example, Duvalier, the instigator of the Haitian migratory debacle, characterized those whom he forced out of Haiti or who left on their own as *apatrides*—i.e., traitors, scum, and enemies of the nation. The opposition to Duvalier also accused the emigrants of deserting and abandoning the Haitian population by leaving it at the mercy of a brutal and predatory regime, instead of staying home to lend their support to the resistance movement against Duvalier. Aristide, the firebrand and militant opposition leader who led the national rebellion that resulted in the regime's collapse, appealed to the migrants to return home in the following terms:

> My generation is running away from Haiti, with its dark corners and byways. I want to call them back before they begin their fruitless travels. . . . I say to them come back and make a new Haiti. Spurn comfort. Come back, live in misery, and build a new way. (Aristide 8)

To shame the emigrants into returning home, he accused them of lacking in dignity because, like roaches, they were shamelessly and subserviently waiting patiently under the tables of white racist capitalists for crumbs. Because they "accepted" being treated with that level of scorn and disdain in the host societies, Aristide accused them of betraying Haiti's heroic and glorious past, of profaning its name, and of sullying the memory of its founding leaders, who, against all odds, led the only successful slave revolt in modern times, defeated the mighty French army, and proclaimed the establishment of the first black independent nation in the world in 1804.

However, despite the negative political rhetoric that sought to create a wedge between Haitians living abroad and those in Haiti, the first Haitian emigrants did not forsake their homeland. To the contrary, even after they had acquired foreign citizenship, their identification with the place of settlement did not preclude or supersede their identification with Haiti and they remained, for the most part, connected with the sedentary populations. They even took important initiatives to help improve life conditions in Haiti.

With the passing of time, the linkages the first Haitian migrants had forged across the boundaries of the communities in which they had settled with Haitians in Haiti brought all Haitians, regardless of their place of residence, to evolve in the same social and political terrain. Through this rapprochement, migration began to be no longer viewed as a desertion of the homeland, a betrayal of the epic spirit of the nation, and an abandonment of its population. Instead, the first Haitian migrants helped institutionalize a "culture of migration" that has led many Haitians to firmly believe that, for them, the best and surest way of achieving social and economic mobility *in Haiti* is to leave for foreign lands.

The first Haitian emigrants' attitude toward Haiti and its population challenges the widely accepted notion which asserts that, once they leave, migrants break off ties with their homeland after a certain period of time. Rather, similar to the strategy other migrant groups from around the world have been utilizing, Haitian emigrants have established strong, vibrant, and enduring transborder linkages that have kept them connected with various groups, communities, and associations in their homeland. These transnational linkages create overarching webs of sustained symbolic, affective, and effective ties, the contents of which can be found in multiple nation-states. Through these transnational linkages, Haitian migrants and the sedentary populations use the same nationalist discourse, mediate similar desires and expectations, and act as political actors driven by the same goals and motivations. The prerequisites for the construction of these durable transnational communities are as follows:

> Regular and sustained long-distance communication and travel, contentious minority politics in the countries of emigration, perceived discrimina-

tion on the part of the migrants in the countries of immigration, helped by the absence of forced assimilation and perhaps even generous multi-cultural policies. (Faist, *Volume and Dynamics* 198)

Migration scholars have respectively labeled these transnational networks as a third space (Bhabha), transnational social formations (Smith and Guarnizo), transnational social fields (Basch et al.), transnational circuits (Rouse), and transnational social spaces (Faist; Faist and Özveren).

The Visiting Migrants, the Sedentary Populations, and Migration

The impetuses to migrate tend to grow exponentially when the visiting migrants' unrealistic and exaggerated tales of boundless opportunities in their place of settlement clash with the situations of near total destitution and bleak futures that often pervade the life of most Haitians. And as Haiti's socioeconomic and political conditions have continued to decline during the past half-century, these often largely inaccurate feedbacks and unrealistic expectations have served to persuade the sedentary populations that the remedies to their problems reside abroad, causing an incessant flow of migration out of Haiti. Reflecting on the tall tales the visiting Haitian migrants recount to their compatriots in Haiti, Jonas stated,

> In spite of what the visiting immigrants often tell their compatriots in Haiti, being black in America is a curse and a calamity. This is something that immigrants who return to visit choose not to tell those who reside in Haiti. When Haitian immigrants visit their homeland, they often lie about their life realities abroad. They are forced to lie because if they tell the truth, people may think that they do not want them to come to the United States to be like them, because most Haitians believe that the United States is a very liberal and rich country where it is easy to make money and get rich quickly. As for me, had I known that aspect of life in the United States, maybe I would have hesitated to come here.

The prospective migrants are also greatly impressed by the relative wealth the emigrants unabashedly display when they visit their homeland. During these visits, they exude images of success, well-being, and confidence in a secure future. As prospects for a bright future in the homeland grow bleaker, with local and international politics rendering life more and more dangerous and uncertain; and as the pressures of economic globalization widen the economic disparities that already exist between the developed world and their country's economy, the natives' interaction with these visitors becomes so powerful and tempting that it tends to destabilize their normative value systems and increase significantly the enticement to leave. At that moment, for the most dynamic sectors of Haitian society, especially the young, migration "becomes the rite of passage, and those who do not attempt to elevate their status through international movement are considered lazy, unenterprising, and undesirable" (Joshua S. Reichert, quoted in Massey 46).

Human Rights and Migration

Haitian migration is also accelerated by the tales of democratic practices the visiting emigrants claim to be normative in their places of settlement. According to the returning migrants, in these countries people have natural and constitutional rights, and their governments, which function only with the consent of the governed, respect these rights. These renditions of the quality of life abroad have a special appeal to those who were bullied by the dictatorship and to those who have been victimized by successive Haitian regimes and their allies. In the end, the prospects of living in a society where people's rights are respected and guaranteed constitute a very enticing proposition for the sedentary populations even when they know that, very often, the law is not applied equally and fairly in all sectors of these societies.

Long-Distance Nationalism and Migration

Moreover, the homeland governments often appeal to the emigrants' sense of patriotism and encourage them to play important roles in national and local projects and programs geared at building the country's infrastructure, even when they have taken the citizenship of the place of settlement. In turn, to better respond to their government's calls for help, the migrants create organizations called "hometown or regional associations," which "represent perhaps the most significant institutions of civil society" the migrants rely upon to attend to the needs of the left-behind populations (Honey and Okafor 9). As change agents, these associations play multiple and important roles in the immigrants' homelands. They

> provide immigrants with legitimate institutions to pursue their own interests; they mobilize the [immigrant] community to raise money, lobby, and educate the population on political as well as social issues; and they encourage the maintenance of cultural ties with the home country. Through linkage associations that are established in their home country, immigrants create platforms on which they can influence local politics and raise money for projects. (Pierre-Louis 14)

The hometown associations are called "shadow states" because they often furnish important services to their homeland communities and assume responsibilities that are the obligations of the state. Through their activities and projects in the homeland, they introduce the native populations to modernity, they assume important civic responsibility through their involvement in the affairs of the local populations, and they seek to reform the political landscape of the native land by pressuring their government into being responsive to the needs of their constituents.

Many Haitian diaspora-connected towns and communities subsist mainly because their expatriates, through their hometown associations, regularly contribute to important civic and development projects that their central government often fails to support and/or finance. Through the conduit they create, the emigrants' hometown associations often deliver more and better public services than the Haitian government does. For example, they help build schools, telephone networks, public roads, and hospitals; they provide electricity and water distribution systems to their home communities; they make banking services and credit more widely available to the left-behind populations; and they closely monitor and publicly denounce instances of waste, violations of rights, and corruption in the homeland.

The contributions the emigrants make to their homeland's evolution through the hometown organizations stand as concrete examples of the ways in which migration can provide the homeland and its population with a pathway to modernity, democracy, and development. And although in many cases these initiatives are undertaken more for prestige than for true development, they nevertheless tend to offer the homeland populations an alternative to total dependency on their governments. Also, the presence of the hometown associations in the homeland communities often leads the sedentary populations to visualize the migrants as providers of services and to envision migration itself as the only hope their country has for a better future. In this context, the emigrants are seen as successful individuals who must be emulated.

Transnationalism and Migration

Finally, the left-behind population often makes claims upon the emigrants by treating them as loyal members of the nation, even after they have acquired the nationality of the host society. These renewals and continued maintenance of kinship ties make it easy for those who would be reluctant to leave the homeland to do so. In this case, the potential migrants can anticipate that if life becomes insufferable in the host society, they can always return "home" to find solace from the emotional distresses and economic difficulties they often experience there, because they are still considered members of the homeland's polity. Therefore, the angst accompanied with migrating is somewhat abated and may even dissipate totally.

For example, Jonas believes that Haitian emigrants who have taken other nationalities remain Haitians and therefore can legitimately participate in nationalist projects in Haiti. He interprets the emigrants' initiatives to take the nationality of the place of settlement as utilitarian and pragmatic acts rather than as evidence that they have abandoned the homeland and its population. He explained his position in the following manner:

> *People change their nationality for many reasons. You know, the U.S. passport carries high prestige wherever you go. If you keep your Haitian passport and you want to go on a vacation in Europe, for example, you may not be able to do it because some countries do not give Haitians visas. Not only that, if you want to send for your relatives to come join you in the United States, it is easier when you have U.S. citizenship. When you retire and you go back to Haiti to live, you are protected as a U.S. citizen.*
>
> *To me, however, a Haitian is a Haitian until you die. There is no way you can stop being a Haitian. Therefore, for me, this is not a big problem if, after they changed their nationality, they want to help rebuild the nation.*

As for the individuals who benefit from or witness the migrants' largess, they often want to become players in the game as well. They are completely sold on the idea that migration will solve all their problems, fulfill all their dreams, and give them an opportunity to help save the homeland from political tyranny and economic decadence. And although the decision to migrate may be fraught with many apprehensions, dangers, and doubts, the prospective migrants may brush them aside to realize their goals.

MIGRATION, A COMPLEX PHENOMENON

The incorporation of the homeland populations into the networks of exchange of goods and capital; the expansion of the transnational networks the migrants and the sedentary populations create and sustain; the maintenance of ties between the home and host communities, which both the homeland and diaspora communities encourage; the settlement societies' democratic image, and the ideology of multiculturalism they claim to practice—these factors encourage the left-behind populations to become active participants in the emigration process. And as these ties are strengthened, the urge to leave becomes firmly embedded in the homeland populations' normative dispositions—this, in spite of whatever opportunities may exist in the homeland, the uncertainties of life in a foreign country, and, in the case of the boat people, the dangers entailed in the crossing. At the moment, migration is seen by many in the homeland communities as the most promising path to a secure future and the best way to elevate their status.

In Haiti's case, many factors have contributed to the making of the massive exodus of people the country has been experiencing during the last forty years. Among the most influential factors, we can cite the United States' callous indifference toward the plight of the Haitians in the context of the Duvalier regime's egregious violations of their human rights; the day-to-day effects that Haiti's political insecurity, pervasive poverty, and worsening environmental degradations have been having upon the most vulnerable sectors of the Haitian population; the transnational connections the emigrants have established between their places of settlement and their homeland; and the impact that visiting migrants' tales of advantages, benefits, and protection have been having on the psyche of the sedentary populations. But more importantly, those who put their lives in great danger by taking the sea routes to reach the United States and the Bahamas have despaired of any other means of avoiding the growing political chaos and economic decline that have marked and affected Haiti during the past decades.

JONAS'S PREDICAMENT

It was from these perspectives that Jonas decided to leave Haiti through a risky sea crossing to an uncertain future in the United States at a very young age, although he was not destitute and had never been personally harassed by the Makout. His decision to leave Haiti was nevertheless caused by many factors that were directly connected with the regime's policies and practices. Jonas explained his situation at the time he decided to leave as follows:

> When I was young, the political situation was going from bad to worse. Everybody was at risk, even those of us who were not directly involved with politics. For example, if you stayed in school to get an education but refused to support Duvalier, you would not be able to find work. Yet, as an educated person, if you did not support the regime, you automatically put yourself and your family at great personal risk. For a young person like me, therefore, there was no point in staying in Haiti.

Why did you want to leave Haiti? I asked.

> Why did I want to leave Haiti? My goals were to escape Duvalier's Makout forces that were daily harassing people to go to a place where I would breathe free, to taste some democracy, and to finish my studies. However, I will not lie to you, I also wanted to go, make some money, and come back to make them jealous of me.

At the time he took the decision to leave Haiti, Jonas was being supported rather comfortably by the remittances two older brothers, who had preceded him to the United States, were sending regularly to his family in Haiti. For a while, these remittances represented the only steady income the family had. However, Jonas knew that he could not rely on his brothers' support forever. He explained his fears of living in Haiti without that lifeline in these terms:

> *Rejoining my brothers in the U.S. seemed to me the only opportunity I had to have a future. Also, my mother was getting old and would reach an age where she would no longer be able to work. If I stayed in Haiti, I would not be able to help her in case my brothers stopped sending money home. But, by migrating, I could help my mother, my relatives, my friends, and my country.*

Migrant workers' remittances provide many households in the homeland societies with their most constant, important, and vital sources of income. In addition, the sums the emigrants send to their families provide their homeland governments with much-needed hard-currency inflows. In many countries, these remittances, not the national government, are the only promoters of real development, for they often "provide *more* money for investment than TNCs, Western banks, and the World Bank *combined*" (Schaeffer 142; emphasis in original). According to Richard Boudreaux,

> Today, remittances are the largest, fastest growing and most reliable source of income for developing countries. Poor nations received $167 billion from overseas workers last year, according to the World Bank, more than all foreign aid.
> This giant transfer of wealth crisscrosses the earth in millions of trickles, a few hundred dollars at a time, sent by workers who have assumed much of the burden of Third World development. Their remittances offer a rare chance to accumulate savings; invest in schooling, housing or a small business; and a rise into the middle class. (2)

In the Haitian case, remittances from the Haitian emigrants not only constitute the sole continuous and substantial income many families can count on, but the government also relies on the migrants to fund many social services it no longer delivers to its citizens (de la Garza and Lowell). It is estimated that Haitians of the diaspora send to Haiti around $1.5 billion a year. In the Haitian context, this is an awesome sum. It represents five times the money Haiti receives from foreign aid, up to three times the country's budget, and at least 20 percent of its gross domestic product (Williams 1). In addition to these transfers of cash, Haitian emigrants send ample supplies of provisions and consumer goods of all kinds to their relatives and friends in Haiti. The multiplier effects of these remittances and transfers of commodities truly keep Haiti's economy afloat.

In many cases, remittances become seed money for small businesses that the migrants' relatives set up in their communities. The profits earned from these small businesses go to complement the transfers of money received from abroad, and help alleviate the emigrants' unending burden of supporting two sets of households, one in the homeland and one in the place of settlement. They also help subsidize the income of the sedentary populations and serve as cushions when the flow of remittances is discontinued.

Jonas's mother, who had been widowed when her son was only ten years old, took the same approach to make certain that the family did not fall on hard times should these remittances dry up. Realizing that her sons' own family obligations in the United States, illness, joblessness, or other unforeseen situations could easily force them to cut their ties with the family and discontinue the flow of cash to them, she had set aside a portion of the money she was receiving from them and had invested it in a small grocery store she ran from her house. The profits she made from her small business, combined with the transfers of cash and goods she was receiving from her sons, helped improve her family's circumstances significantly.

JONAS'S TIES TO THE HAITIAN DIASPORA

Although Jonas had many close relatives who lived abroad, his only sustained contact with them was embodied in the regular remittances his two brothers, who lived in New Jersey and Miami respectively, were sending to his mother. His two siblings had left Haiti before he was born; therefore, they were total strangers to him. Although they had regularized their status in the United States, since leaving they had never been back to Haiti, preferring to use their resources to support their own families in the United States and their mother's household in Haiti rather than to spend them in buying status in Haiti.

In general, Haitian emigrants undertake regular multipurpose visits to their homeland not only to reconnect with their family members and friends, but also to recount rags-to-riches stories of how, as down-and-out immigrants, they were able to achieve their dream of wealth and success through hard work, courage, and determination. The drawback of such often-inaccurate depictions of their allegedly prosperous life conditions in the place of settlement is that the migrants often face a barrage of requests, solicitations, demands, and obligations from kith and kin to which they must respond. The extent of their largess toward that coterie of solicitors may depict them either as generous and bounteous members of the Haitian diaspora or as miserly flunkies. If they liberally distribute goods and money to these solicitors, their claims to success are substantiated, and in return, they receive the recognition they lack in the United

States. If, on the other hand, they do not respond generously to these requests, they are disparaged, depreciated, and underrated. In the end, these unnecessary outlays of capital often heavily tax the migrants' limited budgets. For these reasons, Jonas's brothers had never visited their homeland, opting instead to maintain from afar the steady flows of remittances that were the lifelines of their extended family there.

The brothers had made that difficult choice because they knew that they were expected to provide support for the family and because they had firsthand knowledge of how difficult life in Haiti was. This awareness of the suffering of those who are left behind compels action from the emigrants in the form of a "morality of obligation" that cuts across all groups and ages and links the immediate reasons for migrating to the economic situation of one's family, friends, and nation. In the end, the migrants assert their humanity by fulfilling their responsibilities. Neglecting these obligations is an indication of bad faith and a violation of trust (Glick Schiller and Fouron, *Georges Woke Up*).

For example, Lundi, a former "boat person" who left the town of St. Louis du Nord some thirty-three years ago for Miami, is a regular visitor there. Each year, on two or three occasions, he makes the pilgrimage to his hometown to renew his ties to his family and to distribute cash and goods to them and his friends. Lundi, who is not a rich person, earns his living by "working in fish markets and selling frozen food from the back of a battered Ford van" (Williams 2). When asked why he sends home at least half of what he earns in the United States to support his mother and siblings and the children he has fathered by nearly a dozen women during his visits, as well as cousins, friends, and former neighbors, he put it this way:

> God blessed me with good fortune, and I have to give it back to Haiti. If
> I have two dollars, I have to give Haiti one of them. When I visit Haiti, I
> have a lot of friends who are always saying, "Lundi, I need this" and "Lundi,
> I need that." And I give it to them if I can, because I know God will give it
> back to me. (Williams 2)

Notice that he equates helping his friends and family with helping Haiti. This sentiment is shared by many Haitian emigrants, who think that by meeting their obligations toward their kin and friends, their claims upon the nation as long-distance nationalists who love and cherish the motherland from afar are legitimized and strengthened, although they have left her, may have never been back, and may have taken the citizenship of another country. In this case, the nation is seen as an extension of the family. And since family ties are extended beyond Haiti's political boundaries to reach the place of settlement, the nation, as well, exists where the migrants dwell.[6] They may have left Haiti for more clement shores, but in reality they never intended to abandon her. Conversely, those who forsake their families by cutting their ties once they leave Haiti are considered to have abandoned the nation as well. Therefore, if the emigrants claim to love Haiti, continue to identify with Haiti, see themselves as part of Haiti, and regard Haiti as a place where they can go to find solace from the problems they face in the place of settlement or as a place to retire, they have to assist those they left behind. By assisting them, they are helping themselves, their families, their relatives, their friends, and Haiti.

Jonas had learned about life in the United States through similar regular trips many Haitian emigrants, such as Lundi, had made to their impoverished and almost destitute town of St. Louis du Nord. During these visits, he had observed the ways in which these visiting migrants liberally distributed cash and goods of all sorts to the members of the St. Louis du Nord community and had witnessed the adulation they received from the people and the special recognition the town's dignitaries bestowed upon them. He was, in some respects, jealous of the dynamic relationship that he used to witness between visiting emigrant natives of St. Louis du Nord and his city's inhabitants. He expressed his feelings regarding this dynamic in the following manner:

> When I was young, from time to time, immigrants who had settled abroad used to visit St. Louis du Nord. They came back with money and the latest fashion in clothes and jewelry. I was always impressed and jealous of them. They always looked well fed and fat, they were usually dressed nicely with fine clothes. During their stay in Haiti, everyone catered to them and they were placed on a pedestal. Like them, I thought that if I ever had the chance and opportunity of leaving Haiti, I too would come back to visit and enjoy the same special treatment during my trips to Haiti. I strongly desired to experience those kinds of feelings. At that time, whatever you told me and whatever reason you would give me, I would not have postponed my departure from Haiti. I did not care about the risk I was taking. I did not care about the adversities I would face in the United States as an immigrant and a black person from Haiti; I had to leave Haiti.

The strategy of maintaining their pre-migratory ties with the homeland populations by visiting "home" on a regular basis, by investing their earnings in cultivating their past social relations, by sending remittances, and by becoming engaged through the hometown associations' civic endeavors in the struggle to pull Haiti out of its economic and political morass helps the emigrants hedge their bets by guaranteeing them a place in the society they had left. And if one day they are forced by the vagaries of their lives abroad to return to live permanently in the homeland, they would be guaranteed a warm welcome from family members and friends. In addition, there is the dynamic of social status such contacts provide. While their immigrant life may be beset with all kinds of problems and difficulties and while they may be invisible in the place of settlement, when they visit their homeland, they are somebody and they are persons of substance (Glick Schiller and Fouron, "Terrains").

JONAS'S VOYAGE

Bearing these issues in mind, and attracted by the idea of going abroad to make a fortune and returning to impress his compatriots, one day Jonas made up his mind to leave Haiti. To plan his departure, he telephoned his brothers to explain his intention, but also to ask them to wire to him the $500 he needed to pay for the trip. Plagued by their own personal financial problems and concerned about his safety, they denied his request. In the meantime, one of his sisters, who was a year younger than he was, made the decision to leave with him. Despite his mother's objections, he chose to leave by boat because he could not secure a visa to migrate legally to the United States. Without a visa, he had no other means of reaching the U.S.

Through his own investigation, he learned from an informant that a group in Port-de-Paix, the capital of the Nord-Ouest department, was organizing a clandestine trip to Florida. He went there to inquire about the possibility of leaving with them. At Port-de-Paix, he was sent to a small island on Haiti's northern coast called Ile de la Tortue. After fifteen days of intense negotiation at la Tortue, he and his sister were accepted as passengers free of charge because of their young age and also because they engaged themselves to perform domestic services for the crew and the passengers. His passage guaranteed, he alerted his brothers of his arrival and asked them for guidance on what to do once he reached Florida.

Jonas left Haiti for Florida, together with 326 other "boat people," on a rough-and-ready, overcrowded sailboat one late July night in 1981. The passengers who were crammed into that boat had two main objectives: they were determined to reach the coast of Florida at any cost to escape the horrors of Duvalier's dictatorship, but most especially, they were eager, as Jonas put it, to "reach the promised land to enjoy the good life in the United States, to realize all our dreams, to help our families, our country and become *gwo nèg* (a person of importance) in Haiti."

To slip incognito out of Haiti, they set sail at 9:00 PM under the cover of total darkness. Laden with its cargo of desperadoes, the boat drifted in the treacherous Windward Passage and landed on the northeastern coast of Cuba, not far from where they had embarked. Once the Cubans had been informed of the boat's destination, they received them with compassion and understanding. In a sign of solidarity with the passengers, the Cubans replenished their meager resources, repaired their boat, towed them to the high seas, and pointed them in Miami's direction. A day later, again they entered Cuba's territorial waters and the same scenario was repeated.

After a few days at sea, the boat's water supply and provisions began to dwindle, the boat's sanitary conditions worsened, and infighting among the passengers began affecting everybody's morale. To manage their dwindling resources, the boat's crew imposed a very stringent rationing protocol that was to be followed by all. Subsequently, the lack of adequate food and water and the constant exposure to the hot sun took its toll on the passengers and caused some of them to hallucinate. Two days into the restricted regimen, one passenger gathered all his belongings, bid the other passengers farewell, and plunged into the sea. The next day, a minister began to have visions of Christ. Clutching his Bible close to his chest, he too jumped overboard, declaring that he was on his way to be with his savior. The boat's passengers, who had no means to rescue and save them, could only watch their comrades' suicides in horror.

A day later, they shipwrecked on the Bahamian island known as Cayo Lobos. Contrary to the reception the Haitians had received from the Cubans, the Bahamian authorities treated them with hostility and harshness. They refused to replenish their provisions and brushed off all demands for boat repairs. They did not take the passengers into custody to repatriate them to Haiti, however. Instead, they allowed them to rest for a while and soon after towed them toward the high seas. The Bahamian coastal guards monitored their activities for a while, making sure that they did not return to the island. While on the high seas, the passengers crossed paths with many vessels and tankers that ignored their calls for help and refused to stop for them. Soon, their condition became more precarious, as their water and food reserves dwindled significantly. Not knowing exactly where they were and having no idea how long it would take them to reach Florida, they adopted even more stringent rationing of water and food.

In a fit of rage, a member of the crew who felt cheated out of his ration broke up the boat's rudder and threw it into the sea. Without its rudder, the boat began to turn erratically in the high seas. At that moment, an entrepreneurial member of the crew fashioned a new rudder with cannibalized parts of the boat. However, the new rudder was too flimsy and too light to control the boat, which continued to drift aimlessly and uncontrollably. Again, they entered into Cuban territorial waters and were rescued by Cuba's coast guard. As on the two previous occasions, the Cubans allowed them to rest, replenished their water and provisions, made them a brand-new rudder, and pointed them in the direction of Florida's coast once more.

After a number of days on the high sea, they began to be visited by sea birds and at night could see the flickering of lights in the horizon. Finally, one night, a member of the crew who had climbed on top of the highest mast to scout the horizon announced that the coast of Florida was within sight. A few hours later, the boat hit a sandbar and stopped. At that moment, it was pure pandemonium on board as both passengers and crew members scrambled to reach the shores before they could be rounded up and arrested. Those who were good swimmers made land contact quickly. Others had to be helped. It had taken them a total of twenty-seven days to reach Florida, including the seven days they had spent in Cuba and the Bahamas.

Weakened by the long voyage, Jonas could barely carry himself. But he knew he had a dream, and besides, he could not abandon his sister. So, he took two empty plastic gallons he had brought with him for the occasion, tied them around his waist as floatation devices, took his sister with one arm, and swam with her to shore. In the meantime, the police arrived and took most of the boat people into custody.

U.S. POLICY VIS-À-VIS THE HAITIAN BOAT PEOPLE

Since the inception of the boat people phenomenon, the U.S. government has been criticized on many occasions for its bias against the Haitian refugees. For example, in 1980, a U.S. federal court report noted that "all the Cubans who sought political asylum were granted asylum routinely. [Yet] none of the 4,000 Haitian refugees . . . were granted asylum" (Kurzban 1). An independent blue-ribbon panel that reviewed U.S. policies vis-à-vis the Haitian refugees concluded that in the case of the Haitian boat people, "shared anticommunist objectives have taken priority over human rights considerations" (Loescher and Scanlan 314).

Subsequently, the U.S. government's policy vis-à-vis the Haitian refugees was strongly denounced by the Eleventh Circuit U.S. Court of Appeals in two landmark decisions. In the first, it declared that although the brutality of the Haitian government was widely known and although the Haitian refugees' claims for asylum were justified, the "prejudice of our government against the first substantive flight of *black* refugees has led the U.S. government to refuse to extend asylum to them" (Kurtzban 1; emphasis in original). In the second, it found "a stark pattern of discrimination" by U.S. immigration officials against the Haitians (Lehman 9). In 1980, the U.S. Civil Rights Commission declared that "the lack of minority representation and the apparent lack of sensitivity and cultural awareness on the part of some INS employees have resulted in some applicants from minority communities being treated contemptuously and presumed to be wrong until they can prove otherwise" (Lawless 126). In 1982, a federal district court judge was so outraged by the callousness of the federal government vis-à-vis the Haitian refugees, and so infuriated at the conditions in which they were being detained, that he ordered their immediate release pending adjudication of their asylum claims. The federal government ignored the court's decision and continued their incarceration (Lawless).

Throughout the 1980s, many more reports and judicial decisions faulted the INS for its blatantly invidious policies that openly and decisively discriminated against the Haitians because they were black refugees, but most especially because they were fleeing a right-wing dictatorship supported by the United States. Yet during the same period, says Stepick, "Cubans were quickly processed and released, classified as asylum applicants, while the Haitians were still classified as in exclusion proceedings. Some of the Cubans were given cash gifts by the American authorities, while the Haitians were detained in jails" (1982:187).

WELCOME TO THE UNITED STATES

In line with the U.S. government's standing policy vis-à-vis the Haitian refugees, the boat's passengers and crew members were transported to a detention center named Krome.[7] After being fingerprinted, searched, photographed, and fed, they were assigned to their barracks. The next day, through the aid of interpreters, they were interviewed to assess their claims to political asylum. Jonas, like the other passengers, refused to answer any specific questions about the trip and refused to admit that the passengers had been charged a fee for their passage. Instead, he maintained that the passengers, together with the crew, had pooled their resources to make the journey possible. Also, when asked to substantiate instances of political persecution, Jonas, fearing retaliation against his family members in Haiti, kept silent, as his brothers had advised him to do. His instruction was to immediately contact the brother who lived in Miami through the latter's wife, who worked in Krome's cafeteria and who was on the lookout for them.

Although Jonas and his sister did not obtain political asylum, they were luckier than the majority of the other boat people because of their young age and also because one of their brothers had gone to Krome to sponsor them. In contrast, in Jonas's recollection, the passengers who had no sponsor to whom they could be released were subsequently deported back to Haiti.

After spending ten days at Krome, Jonas's sister was conditionally released. The following day, he obtained his own conditional release. They were required, as a condition of their release, to report to the offices of the Immigration and Naturalization Service for further investigation of their case. However, after visiting the INS's office only once, they were discharged to the care of an agency and were given temporary work permits, because they had a sponsor and also because of their young age. In 1986, when Congress passed a general amnesty program through the Immigration Reform and Control Act (IRCA), a Miami-based Haitian refugee center helped them obtain their permanent papers. Jonas went to stay in Miami with the brother who had sponsored them, while his sister went to New Jersey to stay with the other brother.

THE HAITIAN IMMIGRANTS' IDENTITY IN THE UNITED STATES

The locality where Jonas's brother lived in Miami was a lower-class black neighborhood of mixed African American and Caribbean immigrant residents plagued with high crime, drugs, and prostitution. Jonas, who had created in his imagination an idealized picture of his brother's social conditions in the United States, was profoundly disappointed. And when he ventured out of his neighborhood, he quickly noticed the contrast between where and how blacks and whites lived. He expressed his impressions in the following terms:

> It did not take me long to realize how different the conditions of life for whites and blacks were. I also realized that the pictures my brothers used to send us did not truly represent the reality of black life in America. At that moment, I felt a deep sense of betrayal. I also felt as if black people, from the beginning of time, had been cursed. While I thought that I was going to a beautiful place to live with my brother in an ideal situation, to the contrary, I landed in a desolate place. When I asked my brother why he chose to live in a black and decrepit neighborhood, he did not like it. He angrily told me that the reason he had to live this way was because he was spending all his money supporting us in Haiti. From that moment on, I made myself a promise that I would work hard, go to school, get a good job, and move to a nice neighborhood. Unfortunately, things did not work out that way for me.

During the late 1970s and early 1980s, the Haitian immigrant populations were very disturbed by the use of blackness as a marker for lower-class location in the United States. In contrast, they had migrated with a heightened sense of pride in their own conception of blackness, which was highly valued and appreciated in Haiti. Therefore, the Haitian immigrants of the period were not too eager

to accept the type of black identity ascribed to them in the United States, since this identity was . . . used to delineate populations with limited access to the productive system, to status, and to power. To accept a black

identity in the United States would mean accepting the subordinate status
of Black Americans. (Glick Schiller and Fouron, "Everywhere" 336)

To that effect, they often spoke of not wanting to be "black twice." Instead,

> to differentiate themselves from African-Americans, many Haitian im-
> migrants stressed the French aspects of Haitian culture and cherished the
> labels "Frenchie" and "French-fried" widely assigned to them by Ameri-
> cans. Some even identified with Hispanics or West Indians. (Glick Schiller
> and Fouron, "Everywhere" 336)

Although the "Frenchie" and "French-fried" labels were tainted with ridicule, the Haitian immigrants nevertheless felt them more respectable than
the denigrated and tarnished identities the larger U.S. society had assigned
to the African American populations.

However, despite these attempts at avoiding racial stigmatization, the
Haitian immigrant population continued to be branded by U.S. society.
In 1982, unexpectedly, the U.S. Centers for Disease Control (CDC) listed
Haitians among the at-risk populations for AIDS.[8] As a result, Haitians
felt that their identity had been seriously damaged and irreparably compromised as they began to be viewed with suspicion and hostility by the
larger U.S. population. Thus, instead of embracing the United States as
their country, they yearned to return home even though Haiti remained a
poor and dangerous place.

At the same time, anti-minority and anti-immigrant discourses permeated the U.S. media and the country's political landscape. Too often, issues related to overpopulation, the browning of America, the overburden-
ing of social institutions such as the schools and the hospitals, abuses in
the welfare programs, rising native-born unemployment rates, budgetary
deficit, environmental degradation, high levels of criminal activities, the
proliferation of drugs, and inflation-unemployment syndromes were im-
puted to immigrants, especially to black and Hispanic immigrants, causing them to feel unwelcome and unwanted in their new home (Bryce-
Laporte). Also, because they were foreign blacks who often did not speak
English and were not familiar with U.S. ways, the Haitian immigrants
faced the sting of racism, the effects of social rejection and marginalization, and the pangs of neglect and discrimination more than the native-
born blacks. As a result of these profound malaises and in spite of the
cushion the immigrant enclaves provided them, the immigrants of color
often felt a deep sense of alienation, anomie, and personal disorientation
in their new country. To survive in this very complex situation, they
adopted "de-territorialized identities," splitting their loyalties between

their homeland and their place of settlement (Glick Schiller et al., "Toward a Transnational Perspective").

For these reasons, Jonas never contemplated acquiring U.S. citizenship although he knew well the advantages a U.S. passport entailed and conveyed. Declared Jonas, regarding this issue,

> I am Haitian and I will die a Haitian. I do not see the need to sell my nationality for another. The Americans do not treat Haitians well. The term "Haitian-Americans" tells you that the United States does not consider those Haitians who have become Americans as true Americans. If they are Americans why is it they are forced to keep the word Haitian on their American passport? I have also heard of Haitian-Americans who have been deported to Haiti after they had committed crimes in the United States. If the Americans truly considered them Americans, they would not have deported them to Haiti. This tells me that in the eyes of the United States, these people remain Haitians.

He continued:

> I will spend my last years in Haiti. I know that in my lifetime, Haiti will not change. Maybe many generations after me will see change in Haiti. This is not important to me. When I retire, I will return to live in Haiti totally. I may not choose to stay there permanently, but I will spend most of my time in Haiti and very little time in the United States because Haiti is my country. My blood is Haitian, my language is Haitian, and nobody can change that.

REALIZING THE DREAM

The search for a better life has taken Jonas and his sister to the United States through a perilous and arduous 700-mile sea journey. Have they realized their dreams?

For a while, things worked well for Jonas. He found a part-time job and was making plans to continue his education. Soon, however, his brother lost his job and their relationship began to sour. Lacking marketable skill and English fluency, but also because of his young age, Jonas could not get a full-time job. In addition, because his part-time job paid very little, he was unable to help his brother with the household's finances. To make matters worse, his brother stopped sending his part of the remittances to their mother, saddling Jonas with responsibilities he was not ready to shoulder. Soon after, his relationship with his brother irreparably deteriorated and he was asked to move out.

Unable to rent an apartment on his own, he went to stay with an aunt who also lived in Miami. There, things did not work out well either. Because he did not speak English and was not acclimated to U.S. culture, his aunt's children did not extend to him the respect he felt he deserved. Instead, they ridiculed and derided him for his lack of English fluency and his "Haitian ways." Distressed and depressed, he decided to risk being on his own. He moved out of his aunt's house and went to live with a young lady he had met soon after arriving in Miami.

A few months after his joining her, she was pregnant. The birth of the child added to his financial obligations. The girlfriend asked Jonas to dedicate all his earnings to their household and to let his other siblings attend to his mother's needs in Haiti. Jonas did not see things that way, however. Instead, he told her that his mother was so important to him that even if he earned only one dollar a week, he would share it with her. Beset by many financial problems, the relationship deteriorated and ended. He was forced to vacate the apartment and went to stay with another girlfriend. The same scene was repeated a number of times. When I interviewed Jonas in April 2006, he had already fathered ten children with five women through the same scenario. He had never been married, had not resumed his education as he had planned, had never had a decent and lucrative job, had never been able to move out of the same rundown neighborhood where his brother still lives, and had not had a stable life since coming to Florida in 1981.

However, in spite of his financial woes and unstable personal life situation, he has been visiting Haiti at the rate of twice to three times a year, because he feels important only in Haiti. In the United States he feels not only unimportant, but also insignificant and marginalized. His lack of English fluency and skills, his precarious financial situation, and his position as a black person in the United States make him feel like a failure. In contrast, according to Jonas,

> You see, when you visit Haiti, people don't care and do not want to hear about what you do, how you are being treated in the United States, and how you make your money. Instead, they are only interested in what you can give them. They respect and value you for what you give them. As a consequence, they treat you like a person. It is not the same here in the United States. No matter how much money or education you have, if you are a black person you are always placed beneath the whites. To tell you the truth, the day Haitians get their act together, I would leave the United States. Because Haiti, with all its problems, is sweet and lovely. I love Haiti more than any other place on earth.

*   *   *

This account—of the experiences of a sixteen-year-old Haitian who, leery about his future in a country beset by many political and economic problems, and endowed with a skewed perception of life in the United States as conveyed by the remittances that sustained him and the behavior of visiting Haitian migrants that fascinated him, decided to risk his life and that of his sister to come and experience life in the United States—tells us a great deal about the dynamics of migration. Although Jonas succeeded in his first attempt to reach the shores of Florida, his dreams have only partially materialized. As a legal resident, he has been able to support his mother. He travels regularly to Haiti to display his relative wealth and to indulge in his aspiration to be a *gwo nèg*, a man of relative substance there, despite his tenuous financial situation in the United States. Yet he did not continue his education, has failed to master a trade or a profession, has never had a stable family life, has grown bitter about life in the United States as a black Haitian immigrant, is stuck in a neglected ghetto neighborhood, and has become disenchanted about the continued deterioration of his country.

Jonas's personal life in the United States is also in shambles. At this time, after going through all the disappointments of being a black immigrant from Haiti in America, he has no other plan for the future than to wait to reach retirement age, when he can collect his Social Security check and divide his time between Haiti and the United States. His ten children and those he may have in the future, sired through unstable relationships with many women, may not have a bright future either, although he claimed to support them financially and morally. Without a stable home life and the support of parents who make sensible choices in their lives, they can expect to achieve very little themselves.

It is doubtful that Jonas's pledge to return home when he retires will ever become a reality, either. For his life and his native land are adrift, and his homeland's economy does not show any signs of recovery. In the meantime, his earnings are invested in buying in Haiti the prestige and recognition he does not have in the United States. Not only that, the resources that flow through the transnational networks in which he participates, and the sums he spends when he visits the homeland, make migration a very attractive and feasible proposition for the populations left behind. And although he expressed some reservations about the illusion of most Haitians that the United States is a Shangri-la, his behavior is encouraging more people to migrate and is helping to perpetuate the cycle of disappointment and disillusion he is experiencing in the United States.

It is true that some boat people have achieved great success in the United States. One of them even became the first black mayor of a medium-sized city in Florida. However, the landscape of migration is littered with the broken dreams of many Haitian migrants who, after risking their lives on the high seas and coming to the United States in the vain hope of living in a free world, doing honest work, and regaining their lost humanity, have become totally disillusioned with life in the United States. And after spending decades trying unsuccessfully to build new lives and reach out to the larger American society, many have discarded the idealistic dreams they nurtured before they left Haiti. As a result, many Haitian immigrants have remained intimately and integrally tied to their homeland. Indeed, many more are contemplating returning "home," although life in Haiti continues to be mired in deep political instability and economic calamity.

These migrants are caught in situations they have not chosen, but that were thrust upon them because fate has caused them to live in a society that hangs on the edge of the global economy. As in Plato's Allegory of the Cave, Haitians, like many people in the developing world, are exposed to images and promises that life at the center of the global economy creates for them. Yet, when they reach out to grab them, these promises evaporate, like mirages. Although they have moved to live in the center of globalization to escape the predicaments of life on the fringes of the global economic system, their lives continue to be fraught with many difficulties and uncertainties and they have remained, for the most part, stuck at the margins of globalization.

Worse yet, their identity is often compromised. Thus, it is very difficult for them to navigate the conflicting relationship that often emerges between "their historical experiences, . . . their cultural backgrounds, their continued ties to their home societies, and the conditions, structures, and ideologies of the dominant capitalist societies in which they have settled" (Glick Schiller and Fouron, "Everywhere" 342). In the end, the lure of the good life at the very center of globalization has proved to be an illusion and a nightmare for many, if not most, of them.

Their strong desire and blind determination to become part of modernity through migration have prevented them from grasping the true nature of the global economy. And the notion that migration can be offered as a solution to the conditions of poverty and political oppression they experienced in their homeland has impeded the emergence of a grassroots movement that could have helped them address the root causes of their tragedy. Finally, the disenchantment they experience as black immigrants in the United States may render them cynical about political activism, lessening the impetus and incentives to participate in the political discourse of rights and social justice in both homeland and host society.

NOTES

1. To twist the arm of the Kennedy administration, Duvalier opportunistically engaged Haiti in the cold war's ideological polarization by threatening to become an ally of the communist bloc if the United States continued to refuse to help his regime. On two occasions, this form of blackmail succeeded and it led the Kennedy administration to resume aid, although reluctantly, to Duvalier.

The first occasion was in 1960. As he needed money to finance a coffee port in Jacmel, a city situated in the Sud-Est department of Haiti, Duvalier delivered

a speech in that port city to the effect that "For thirty-nine months, my government and people have lived on promises, smiles, encouragements, recommendations, hesitancy, lengthy delays, and lack of understanding . . . A massive injec-
tion of money is needed . . . Haiti has to choose between the poles of attraction in
the world today to realize her needs." That same day, he received with great pomp
Aleksandr Bekier, the Polish trade representative in Haiti, to discuss the ways in
which the Warsaw Pact countries might help Haiti. That year, the Kennedy administration revised its policy toward Duvalier and American aid to Haiti was
resumed. It totaled $9.3 million, equal to 30 percent of Haiti's budget (Heinl and
Heinl 588–89; Ferguson).

   The second occasion was in 1962. Again, Duvalier needed money to build
a modern jet airport in Port-au-Prince. To get the Americans to pay for the airport, he used the instance of the OAS meeting at Punta Del Este, during which
the United States sought Cuba's expulsion from the regional organization. Again,
he successfully blackmailed the Kennedy administration into resuming aid to his
government.

   According to the historian Arthur M. Schlesinger, Jr., at the meeting the
United States could count on twelve sure votes for a hard policy vis-à-vis Cuba.
However,

> among the dissenters, were the largest countries of the hemisphere—Brazil,
> Argentina, Mexico, and Chile—as well as Bolivia and Ecuador. Uruguay and
> Haiti hung uncertainly in the middle. The foreign minister of Haiti [Rene
> Charmers], recognizing the value of his vote, calmly remarked to Rusk [U.S.
> Secretary of State] that he came from a poor country in desperate need of
> help; obviously this need would affect his vote. If the United States, which
> had been disengaging from aid to Haiti because of the Duvalier dictatorship,
> would agree to finance particular projects . . . Rusk turned away and later
> sent him a message saying that, while the United States as a matter of
> policy did not associate economic aid and political performance, now that
> Haiti itself had made the link, it had to understand that any future aid
> would be scrutinized in the light of its role at Punta del Este. (782–783)

As the United States struggled to find the two-thirds final vote to expel Cuba from
the organization, it "finally yielded to blackmail and agreed to resume our aid to
the airport at Port-au-Prince" (Schlesinger 783). Haiti's vote to expel Cuba from
the OAS cost the United States $3 million.

   Duvalier used another clever strategy to extract resources from the U.S. government. In effect, as he was proclaiming his anticommunism for all to hear,
he tolerated some members of his administration, especially the Blanchet brothers, Albert, Jules, and Paul, who in the columns of their newspaper, *The Pano-
rama*, regularly published pro-Moscow diatribes. For example, during the 1962
Cuban missile crisis, they sided with Havana and Moscow against Washington,
and Duvalier took no action against them (Heinl and Heinl 588). That maneuver
prompted the U.S. ambassador to Haiti, Benson Timmons III, to send, on April 24,
1964, a secret diplomatic memo to the U.S. State Department asking the government to support Duvalier personally. The fear was that these ideological Marxists

who were allowed to evolve in his administration unmolested could easily depose Duvalier to replace him with a procommunist regime.

2. Kennedy's assassination was a serious setback for Duvalier's opponents. In addition to causing them to lose a very good ally, it also had a very negative psychological impact upon them. Indeed, the date of Kennedy's assassination, 22, was the date on which the Haitian president made all his most important decisions. He was elected on September 22, 1957, he took office on October 22 of the same year, he began his illicit second mandate on May 22, 1961, and later on, he took office as life president on May 22, 1964. Using that fateful coincidence, Duvalier played in the Haitians' imagining by attributing Kennedy's assassination to his magical powers. In turn, the Haitian population, steeped in Vodou dogma, believed him. Not only that, even the United States Congress showed some interest in his assertions, as evidenced by the fact that the Warren Commission, which was set up to look into the assassination, took investigators to Haiti to assess Duvalier's purported role in the American president's death. For a long time, the combination of Duvalier's claim and the United States' decision to take Duvalier's words seriously had a chilling effect on all potential plotters against the regime because many Haitians became convinced, as Duvalier himself had proclaimed it, that he was "an immaterial person," that he had extraordinary extrasensory perception, and that the Vodou gods would reveal in advance to him the names of all of those who were planning to overthrow him (Heinl and Heinl 631).

3. The School of the Americas (SOA) was established in 1946, in Panama. Since its foundation, it has been frequently cited as an example of the United States' support for Latin American dictatorial regimes that have a history of employing death squads and infringing upon their citizens' human rights. In 1963, it was renamed the U.S. Army School of the Americas. In 1984, when the United States signed the treaty that turned over the Panama Canal to Panama, it was relocated to Fort Benning, Georgia.

To respond to its critics, who contended that it was instituted to groom the Latin American military in undemocratic practices, in the 1990s the school introduced an eight-hour course to its curriculum that covered democratic principles and human rights topics. Its critics, however, continued to argue that this course was only taken by a few students and that the minimum of eight hours of ethical instruction was too short to be effective. In 2000, mounting pressure upon the United States Congress to stop funding the SOA reached a high point. Subsequently, the Pentagon decided to rename it the Western Hemisphere Institute for Security Cooperation, abbreviated as WHISC or WHINSEC.

WHISC's $10 million budget is funded by the U.S. Army. The grantees' tuition is usually paid through subventions from the International Military Education and Training (IMET) or International Narcotics Control (INC) assistance programs, or through the Foreign Military Sales (FMS) program. See *Wikipedia*, s.v. "Western Hemisphere Institute for Security Cooperation," http://en.wikipedia.org/wiki/School_of_the_Americas (accessed 2006).

4. Jean-Bertrand Aristide was an activist priest who had led the opposition to Duvalier.

5. FRAPH, a French acronym that stands for Front pour l'Avancement et le Progrès d'Haïti (Front for the Advancement and Progress of Haiti), was a right-

wing paramilitary death squad that operated with total impunity, as the Tonton Makout had under Duvalier. Its members used terror, intimidation, arson, and murder to bully and cow Aristide's supporters. Jean Bertrand Aristide, a former populist priest who had energized the anti-Duvalier movement in the late 1980s, was elected president in 1991 with the support of 62 percent of the population. Only seven months into his presidency, he was deposed by the Haitian army. To undermine the growing and persistent popular resistance movement that was asking for Aristide's return to power, FRAPH was established in 1993 by Emmanuel "Toto" Constant, the son of a former army general very close to Duvalier. In a December 1995 interview he gave to the CBS program 60 Minutes, Constant revealed that he had created the organization at the suggestion of Colonel Patrick Collins, a U.S. Defense Intelligence Agency (DIA) operative attached to the U.S. embassy in Port-au-Prince, to conduct intelligence against Aristide's supporters. Toto Constant also revealed that as a CIA collaborator, he regularly reported the activities of Aristide's supporters to the embassy and Colonel Collins. Soon after the program had been aired, both the CIA and the U.S. embassy acknowledged that Toto Constant had indeed been on the CIA payroll (Heinl and Heinl).

6. When he was campaigning for the presidency Jean-Bertrand Aristide changed his views about the emigrant populations. Instead of alienating them, he brought them back to the fold of the nation by constituting them into the tenth of Haiti's nine departments. When he became president, he created the Ministry of Haitians Living Abroad, symbolizing that the Haitian state now includes the Haitian diaspora. By having this ministry, the Haitian government implies that Haitian emigrants, whatever their nationality, remain Haitian.

7. Krome Detention Center is a sprawling 580-bed former military barrack turned into a prison, located in the eastern Florida Everglades, southwest of Miami. The facility was built during the cold war era as a U.S. Air Force airbase (Chardy). In the early 1980s, as the cold war was winding down, it was decommissioned as a base and the Air Force turned it over to the U.S. Justice Department for use as a detention center to accommodate the Mariel boat people Cuba's Fidel Castro had expelled to the United States.

Krome has always been plagued with controversies. At Krome, convicted felons are incarcerated with detainees who are there for minor immigration violations, such as working without a visa and/or overstaying their visitor visas, or with asylum seekers who are awaiting a disposition of their cases. According to Jonas, the facility offers no meaningful activities for the prisoners to engage in. From 5:30 AM, when they are awoken to take a cold shower, to their 11:00 PM curfew, they spend their days in total idleness.

Krome was ordered closed by the Dade County Department of Health in 1980 because of its unsanitary conditions. The federal government, however, ignored that order and kept it open. Because 1,600 inmates were kept in Krome while the maximum capacity of the jail was 580 inmates, in July 1981 the governor of Florida sued the federal government to have the detention center closed. Once again, the U.S. federal government ignored the court decision to close the facilities.

8. The at-risk population for AIDS was known as the 4-H Club because it was comprised of four groups that were said to be responsible for the AIDS epidemic in the United States. The members of the 4-H club were as follows: Heroin addicts,

Homosexuals, Hemophiliacs, and Haitians. Haitians were the only members that earned their place in the group because of their national identity.

REFERENCES

Amnesty International. "Haiti on the Horns of a Dilemma: Military Repression or Foreign Invasion?" AMR36/33/94. 1994. www.amnesty.org/ailib/aipub/1994/ AMR/363394.AMR.txt (accessed 2007).

Aristide, Jean-Bertrand. *In the Parish of the Poor.* New York: Orbis Books, Mary-knoll, 1990.

Basch, Linda G., Nina Glick Schiller, and Cristina Blanc-Szanton. *Nations Unbound: Transnational Projects, Postcolonial Predicaments, and Deterritorialized Nation-States.* Langhorn, Pa.: Gordon and Breach, 1994.

Bhabha, Homi K. *The Location of Culture.* London: Routledge, 1994.

Boudreaux, Richard. "Mexicans' U.S. Wages Fuel Dream." *Seattle Times,* April 30, 2006.

Bryce-Laporte, Roy. "New York City and the New Caribbean Immigrant: A Contextual Statement." *International Migration Review* 13, no. 2 (1979): 214–279.

Chardy, Alphonso. "A Detainee's Life within the Walls of Krome Detention Center—Miami." *Miami Herald,* January 31, 2005.

de la Garza, Rodolfo O. and Briant Lindsay Lowell. *Sending Money Home: Hispanic Remittances and Community Development.* New York: Rowman and Littlefield, 2002.

Delorme, Demesvar. *Réflexions Diverses sur Haïti* [Various Reflections on Haiti]. Paris: F. Dentu, 1873.

Faist, Thomas. *The Volume and Dynamics of International Migration and Transnational Social Spaces.* Oxford: Clarendon, 2004.

Faist, Thomas, and Eyüp Özveren, eds. *Transnational Social Spaces, Agents, Networks, and Institutions.* Burlington, Vt.: Ashgate, 2004.

Farmer, Paul. *The Uses of Haiti.* Monroe, Maine: Common Courage, 1994.

Fass, Simon M. *Political Economy in Haiti: The Drama of Survival.* New Brunswick, N.J.: Transaction, 1990.

Ferguson, James. *Papa Doc, Baby Doc: Haiti and the Duvaliers.* Oxford: Blackwell, 1989.

Glick Schiller, Nina, Linda G. Basch, and Cristina Blanc-Szanton. "Toward a Transnational Perspective on Migration." *Annals of the New York Academy of Sciences* 645 (1992): 1–24.

Glick Schiller, Nina, and Georges E. Fouron. "'Everywhere We Go, We Are in Danger': Ti Manno and the Emergence of a Haitian Transnational Identity." *The American Ethnologist* 17, no. 2 (May 1990): 329–347.

———. *Georges Woke Up Laughing: Long-Distance Nationalism and the Search for Home.* Durham, N.C.: Duke University Press, 2001.

———. "Terrains of Blood and Nation: Haitian Transnational Social Fields." *Ethnic and Racial Studies* 22, no. 2 (1999): 340–366.

Greene, Anne. *The Catholic Church in Haiti: Social and Political Change.* East Lansing: Michigan State University Press, 1993.

Haiti Program at Trinity College. "Haiti and the USA: Neighbors Linked by History and Community." 1993. http://www.haiti-usa.org/index.php (accessed 2007).

Heinl, Robert Debs, and Nancy Gordon Heinl. *Written in Blood: The Story of the Haitian People, 1492–1995*. Rev. ed., ed. Michael Heinl. Lanham, N.Y.: University Press of America, 1996.

Honey, Rex, and Stanley Okafor, eds. *Hometown Associations: Indigenous Knowledge and Development in Nigeria*. London: Intermediate Technology Publications, 1998.

Kurzban, Ira. "Haitian Refugees: A Flight from Persecution." *Rights* 26, no. 3–4 (1980): 1, 13–15.

Lawless, Robert. *Haiti's Bad Press*. Rochester, Vt.: Schenkman Books, 1992.

Lehman, Mel. "The Journey for Haitians Is Not Over Yet." *Refugees and Human Rights Newsletter* (Summer 1983): 9–10.

Loescher, Gilburt, and John Scanlan. "Human Rights, U.S. Foreign Policy and Haitian Refugees." *Journal of American Studies and World Affairs* 26 (1984): 313–356.

Massey, Douglas S. "Why Does Immigration Occur? A Theoretical Synthesis." In *The Handbook of International Migration: The American Experience*, ed. Charles Hirschman, Philip Kasinitz, and Josh DeWind. New York: Russell Sage Foundation, 1999.

Pierre-Louis, François, Jr. *Haitians in New York City: Transnationalism and Hometown Associations*. Gainesville: University Press of Florida, 2006.

Plummer, Brenda Gayle. *Haiti and the United States: The Psychological Moment*. Athens: University of Georgia Press, 1992.

Rothberg, Robert I., with Christopher K. Clague. *Haiti, the Politics of Squalor: A Twentieth Century Fund Study*. Boston: Houghton Mifflin, 1971.

Rouse, Roger. "Mexican Migration and the Social Space of Post Modernism." *Diaspora* 1, no. 1 (1991): 8–23.

Schaeffer, Robert K. *Understanding Globalization: The Social Consequences of Political, Economic, and Environmental Change*. 2nd ed. New York: Rowman and Littlefield, 2003.

Schlesinger, Arthur M., Jr. *A Thousand Days: John F. Kennedy in the White House*. Boston: Houghton Mifflin, 1965.

Smith, Michael Peter, and Luis Eduardo Guarnizo, eds. *Transnationalism from Below*. New Brunswick, N.J.: Transaction, 1998.

Stepick, Alex. "Haitian Boat People: A Study in the Conflicting Forces Shaping U.S. Refugee Policy." *Law and Contemporary Problems* 45 (1982): 163–196.

———. *Pride against Prejudice: Haitians in the United States*. Boston: Allyn and Bacon, 1998.

Trouillot, Michel-Rolph. *Haiti, State against Nation: The Origin and Legacy of Duvalierism*. New York: Monthly Review Press, 1990.

U.S. Library of Congress. *Haiti: A Country Study*. Washington, D.C.: Foreign Area Study, The American University. U.S. Government Printing Office, 1990.

Williams, Carol. "Dozens Live on Émigré's Largess." *Seattle Times*, May 1, 2006.

Williamson, Charles T. *The U.S. Naval Mission to Haiti, 1959–1963*. Annapolis, Md.: Naval Institute Press, 1999.

5

AFRICA'S MIGRATION BRAIN DRAIN: FACTORS CONTRIBUTING TO THE MASS EMIGRATION OF AFRICA'S ELITE TO THE WEST

Amadu Jacky Kaba

It was before, during, and after World War II that the "brain drain" phenomenon began receiving significant attention internationally, when highly educated individuals in Europe were emigrating to North America and other rich nations to flee the war there. Since then, the brain drain has impacted all other parts of the world, including Africa ("Brain Drain or Overflow?" 24; Ushkalov and Malakha 80; Medawar and Pike; Zeleza; Blau 2; National Science Foundation 176; Leiman).

"Brain drain," which Oberoi and Lin characterize as "the loss of intellectual and technical personnel" (25), could be either domestic (within a nation) or international. International brain drain is the movement of the educated or economic elite from their home nations to more prosperous nations to seek a better life; Docquier and Marfouk note that "[i]n a narrow economic sense, brain drain denotes the international transfer of human resources" (3). This chapter examines the international brain drain and its impact on the continent of Africa.

The beginning of the twenty-first century is witnessing two major problems confronting the continent of Africa. They are the massive emigration to the West by the educated and economic elite of the continent and the massive deaths of Africans in countries or parts of the continent which not only have relatively high proportions of people able to at least read and write, but which have fairly strong economies. With respect to the first problem, hundreds of thousands of educated Africans have, since the 1990s, emigrated to Western Europe, North America, and Australia seeking better-paying jobs, leaving the continent without the adequate human resources needed for any real chance of economic development. Regarding the second problem, some countries and regions of Africa with relatively high proportions of Africans who can read and write—or have

high school or college education—as well as strong economies are also severely devastated by the HIV/AIDS epidemic. The ravages of this epidemic
may be found across the Southern African region as well as, for example,
Kenya and Nigeria.

This chapter focuses on Africa's emigration brain drain as a contribution to the general literature on this important issue. The chapter is divided into three sections. The first section examines the rates of emigration to the West by educated Africans, and their numbers and percentages
in these Western nations. The second section presents various examples
showing the consequences to Africa of the massive emigration of its educated and economic elite. The third presents sample reasons for such high
rates of emigration by the best minds of the continent.

MIGRATION BRAIN DRAIN FROM AFRICA

The emigration of highly skilled Africans has reached a point where it
has caused international debates and suggestions as to how to reduce its
impact on the societies left behind. In a speech at the Pan African Conference on Brain Drain in Elsah, Illinois, on October 24, 2003, the renowned Nigerian-born American computer scientist Philip Emeagwali
stated: "For 10 million African-born emigrants the world over, 'home' is
synonymous with the United States, Britain or other country outside of
Africa . . . Ten million Africans now constitute an invisible nation that
resides outside Africa." Versi notes that an estimated five million African
entrepreneurs and professionals are living in the Diaspora and that 40 percent of African professionals and higher level managers are residing outside the continent (11). Khan reports that

> Between 1960 and 1975 an estimated 27,000 highly qualified Africans left
> the continent for the West . . . This number increased to approximately
> 40,000 between 1975 and 1984, and then almost doubled by 1987, represent-
> ing 30% of the highly skilled manpower stock. Africa lost 60,000 profes-
> sionals (doctors, university lecturers, engineers, etc.) between 1985 and
> 1990. ("Population" 1)

Sautman also tells us: "By 2005, 300,000–500,000 including 30,000 doctoral degree holders, had left [Africa] and 20,000 more emigrate each year
to the U.S. or Europe" (32). Furthermore, Docquier and Marfouk state that
in 2000, 31.4 percent of African migrants outside their countries were tertiary educated, while the proportion in Africa was only 3.6 percent (22).

The *Journal of Blacks in Higher Education* noted in 2002 that in the
United Kingdom, 21 percent of black adults of African origin had uni-
versity degrees as against 14 percent of white Britons similarly educated
("News and Views"). Crush points out that between 1987 and 2001, South

Africa lost an estimated 310,000 of its citizens, including 50,000 professionals, as a result of the brain drain (147). Carrington points out that the migration rate of highly educated individuals from Ghana to the Organization for Economic Co-Operation and Development (OECD) countries was "a dramatic 26 percent; for South Africa, it is more than 8 percent; for Egypt, the Brain drain includes 2.5 percent of such individuals emigrating to the United States and another 5 percent emigrating to other OECD countries" (169).

AFRICAN BRAIN DRAIN TO THE UNITED STATES

The United States may have the largest number of educated Africans who live and work in Western nations. According to the U.S. Census Bureau, as of 2002 there were just over one million African immigrants residing in the United States (U.S. Bureau of the Census, *American Community Survey*). Just as most African slaves were brought to the United States from West Africa, so also do West Africans account for the highest proportion of all Africans emigrating to the United States. This fact might contribute to why West Africa is still underdeveloped, because for hundreds of years, that part of the continent has been losing its talented people to Western nations and other parts of the world. According to the U.S. Census Bureau, as of the year 2000, there were an estimated 884,300 African immigrants in the United States. During that year, West African immigrants numbered 326,507 (37 percent of all African immigrants), with Nigerians numbering 134,940 (41.3 percent), Ghanaians 65,572 (20.1 percent), and Sierra Leoneans 20,831 (6.4 percent) of the West African total. East African immigrants in 2000 numbered 213,299 (24.2 percent of all African immigrants), with Ethiopians accounting for 69,531 (32.6 percent) of this East African total. North African immigrants in 2000 were some 190,491 (21.6 percent of all African immigrants), with Egyptians constituting 113,396 (59.5 percent) of this total. Middle African immigrants in 2000 in the United States totaled 26,900 (3 percent of all African immigrants in the U.S.). Southern African immigrants in the United States in 2000 came to 66,496 (7.5 percent of all African immigrants in the U.S.), with South African immigrants making up 63,558 (95.6 percent) of the Southern Africa total. There were 57,607 (6.5 percent of all African immigrants) African immigrants in the United States in 2000 whose origin was not classified. The 134,940 Nigerian immigrants in the United States in 2000 comprised 15.3 percent of all African immigrants in the United States (U.S. Bureau of the Census, *Census 2000 Summary*).

    As a group, despite their relatively small population, the 700,000 African immigrants in the United States as of March 2000 not only were proportionally more highly educated than their compatriots in Africa, but also have become one of the most highly educated groups within the entire United States, at a time when the people of Africa are at the bottom of the literacy ladder of the world. According to a 2001 U.S. Census Bureau report, 94.9 percent of these African immigrants aged twenty-five and over had at least a high school diploma, compared with 87 percent of the American population. Furthermore, the proportion of the 700,000 Africans in the United States (as of March 2000) aged twenty-five and over with at least a bachelor's degree was 49.3 percent, substantially higher than the general population average of 25.6 percent, and that for other foreign-born populations in the country, such as Asians (44.9 percent) (U.S. Bureau of the Census, *Profile* 37). In a study of the comparative earnings of African American males, African immigrant males, and Caribbean immigrant males in the U.S., Dodoo presents data that showed that of the 1,973 African immigrants in the study, 58 percent of them had college degrees (534).

In a study of blacks in the United States entitled "Black Diversity in Metropolitan America," Logan and Deane claim that "Educational attainment of Africans (14.0 years) is higher than of Afro-Caribbeans (12.6 years) or African Americans (12.4 years); indeed, it is higher even than of whites and Asians. This suggests that black Africans migrate selectively to the U.S. based on their educational attainment or plans for higher education" (5).

Egyptian and Nigerian immigrants in the United States are among the most highly educated groups. For example, according to a 1998 U.S. Census Bureau publication listing over sixty-five ancestry groups, in 1990, 60.4 percent and 52.9 percent of people aged twenty-five and over of Egyptian and Nigerian descent, respectively, had at least a bachelor's degree. No other single group (English, German, Irish, Italian, Scottish, Dutch, etc.) had a 50 percent bachelor's degree attainment rate. For master's degrees, 26.3 percent of Nigerians and 25.6 percent of Egyptians aged twenty-five and over held such degrees in 1990, with Egyptians third only behind Nigerians and Iranians (26 percent) (U.S. Bureau of the Census, *Education Attainment*). In a World Bank policy research paper, Richard H. Adams, Jr., points out that in 2000, there were 90,620 Nigerian immigrants and 75,170 Egyptian immigrants aged twenty-five and older who had attained tertiary education in the United States. Adams also points out that in 2000, there were 361,773 Moroccan immigrants and 91,019 Tunisian immigrants aged twenty-five and over who had attained tertiary education in OECD countries (26). According to Leiman, "hardly any educated people are left in Sierra Leone to help a country with a literacy rate of only 15%" (675), with a high proportion of the educated living in the United States. Faye notes that in the West African nation of Senegal, over 105 lecturers and researchers have migrated, primarily to American and French universities, in recent years (1).

As a result of the large numbers of educated Africans living outside the continent, most government agencies, educational institutions, hospitals, businesses, etc., in Africa are understaffed, causing serious development problems for the continent. Let us briefly examine some of the impacts of this problem.

CONSEQUENCES OF THE AFRICAN BRAIN DRAIN

According to McAuliffe and MacLachlan (232), 10 out of 45 countries in Africa have physician-to-population ratios of fewer than 5:100,000, with a sub-Saharan African average of 17.1 doctors per 100,000. For nurses it was 89.7 per 100,000. In industrialized countries, they point out, there is an average of 303.7 doctors and 723.6 nurses per 100,000. McAuliffe and MacLachlan add that nearly half of doctors trained to work in Africa emigrate to the West or outside the continent. They claim that

> With an estimated cost of USD60,000 for training a general medial practitioner in the Southern African Development Cooperation (SADC) region, outflows from the region to more "developed" countries amount to a $500 million reverse subsidy per annum . . . UNCTAD has estimated that the United States has saved USD3.86 billion as a consequence of importing 21,000 doctors from Nigeria alone. (233)

According to Schrecker and Labonte, estimates of the vacancy rates for physicians in public health services were "26% in Namibia, 36.3% in Malawi, and 42.6% in Ghana; for nurses, vacancy rates were just 2.9% in Namibia and Malawi, but 25.5% in Ghana"; when the Kenyan government advertised 100 doctor vacancies in 2001, it received only 8 applications. Nigeria and Zimbabwe are among the Africa nations claimed to lose tens of millions of dollars as a result of training their natives who leave after graduation. The Deputy Director-General of the International Organization for Migration pointed out in 2002 that "[A]t a cost of $60,000 to train a medical doctor in the South and $12,000 for a paramedical, it may be said that the developing countries are 'subsidising' the OECD countries to the tune of some $500 million per year," which is, sadly, "largely financed by . . . development aid" (Schrecker and Labonte 410).

Clemens and Pettersson conducted a study which attempted to locate physicians and professional nurses born in Africa whose names appeared in nine receiving countries in 2000, including Australia, Belgium, Canada, France, the United Kingdom, and the United States. According to Table 1 of their study, as of 2000, there were 280,808 African physicians, with 64,941 (19 percent) of them abroad in those nine countries. For sub-Saharan Africa, there were 96,405 physicians, with 36,653 (28 percent) of them residing in those nine countries in 2000 (12). According to Table 2 of that same study, there were 758,698 African professional nurses, with 69,589 (8 percent) working in those nine countries abroad in 2000. For sub-Saharan Africa, of the 414,605 nurses, 53,298 (11 percent) were working in those nine countries in 2000 (13). There is a similar brain drain of engineers, according to Sautman (32): "Africa produces only 83 engineers per one million people annually . . . Many African engineers emigrate moreover; there are more African engineers working in the US than in all of Africa."

On the other hand, African governments and people are paying massive amounts of money to employ foreign nationals from the West to fill vacancies in Africa. An estimated 100,000 expatriates from Western nations or the developed world are employed in Africa. It costs the continent $4 billion annually to pay the salaries of those foreign expatriates (Kollehlon and Eule 1165). The World Markets Research Centre also reports: "Skilled workers emigrating from South Africa are estimated to have cost the country R67.8bn (US$7.8bn) in lost human capital since 1997 and this has retarded economic growth. . . . Currently there are no official statistics on the number of teachers who have left South Africa, but estimates put the figure at about 8,000" ("The Brain Drain"). According to the International Organization for Migration:

> Development in Africa cannot be achieved without the participation of an adequate contingent of human resources. African countries see their efforts on the way to a better health system stifled by professional migration. . . . an important part of development aid to Africa is used for the training of medical personnel, who subsequently leave to apply their skills and qualifications in developed countries. . . . The number of Beninese doctors in France now far exceeds the number in Benin. ("The Brain Drain")

The Nobel Prize–winning human rights organization Physicians for Human Rights released a report in July 2004 in which it urged rich countries in the West to reimburse African countries for the loss of health professionals who leave the continent for the West after being trained by African universities at the expense of the people of the continent. The 129-page report, entitled "An Action Plan to Prevent Brain Drain: Building Equitable Health Systems in Africa," notes: "Data from the American Medical Association (AMA) reveal that 5,334 non-federal physicians trained in African medical schools were licensed to practice medicine in the United States in 2002" (2). That same report also noted that 1,200 Ghanaian physician are in the United States (2). Leslie notes that there were 1,700 South African–trained doctors practicing in Canada alone ("Is It Wrong" 12).

Mazrui points out that Philip Emeagwali might have overstated a claim that Africa is indirectly sponsoring developed countries, but that it might be a claim that is worth considering. According to Mazrui, Emeagwali has asserted that "'One in three African university graduates lives and works outside Africa. In effect, we are operating one-third of African universities to satisfy the manpower needs of Western nations. One-third of [the] African education budget is a supplement for the American education budget. In effect, Africa is giving development assistance to the United States'" (Mazrui 86–87). Vaknin makes a similar claim:

> Poor countries invest an average of $50,000 of their painfully scarce resources in every university graduate—only to witness most of them leave for richer places. The have-nots thus end up subsidizing the haves by exporting their human capital, the prospective members of their dwindling elites and the taxes they would have paid had they stayed put. The formation of a middle class is often irreversibly halted by an all pervasive brain drain. ("Analysis: Migration and Brain Drain—II")

In a 1995 International Monetary Fund (IMF) brain drain study, Haque and Kim concluded that "human capital flight generates a permanent reduction of per capita income growth rate in the country of emigration, and that the effect of brain drain on the growth in the country of immigration varies over time with the evolution of the ratio of the average level of human capital in the two countries" (Haque and Kim 580).

FACTORS CONTRIBUTING TO THE MASS EMIGRATION OF EDUCATED AFRICANS TO THE WEST

It should be clear to those observing Africa's political history in the half-century since African nations have been free from European colonization that political instability is a principal problem in most societies on the continent. Internal dissention has often led to civil war and the resultant tally of casualties: civil wars in the Congo, Nigeria, Angola, Rwanda, Sierra Leone, and Liberia have been responsible for millions of lives lost on the continent. The climate of insecurity has inevitably driven many families to seek a better environment abroad to carry on their lives and their goals.

In this section, I am concerned with factors besides war that have been cited for the emigration of educated Africans to the West or to rich, developed nations. According to a report of the International Organization for Migration, "The main reasons for leaving are political conflicts, search for material advantages and professional dissatisfaction. These and other 'push' factors encourage people to leave their countries of origin. At the same time, many industrialized countries lack health professionals and therefore attempt to 'pull' doctors, nurses and midwives to work in their countries." In an article discussing Africa's brain drain, the World Markets Research Centre asserted that "South African teachers are tempted to go abroad as the salaries and working conditions in the UK and other developed countries are much better than they are at home."

As noted above, low salaries are a major factor for the emigration of highly skilled individuals from developing countries. As Faye observes, in the Western African country of Senegal, a university lecturer earns between $246 and $261.5 a month, while a senior professor earns "about 923 U.S. dollars." In Europe or North America, on the other hand, those same professors would earn three to five times their salaries in Senegal (Faye 1). The same discrepancies hold true across other professions. In East Africa, for example, nurses are paid from $200 to $500 a month. "I was contacted by a western placement agency and offered $1,000 for every nurse I could deliver," Leatita King, associate dean of nursing at Nairobi's Aga Khan University Hospital, is quoted as saying (Remington A3). Siringi notes that most doctors in Kenya earn less than $256 a month (307). According to the Ministry of Health in Kenya, only 10 percent of the 6,000 physicians trained every year in public hospitals remain in the country (Remington A3).

In the United States, as in other Western nations, educational attainment is an important factor in the type of occupation, the earning potential, or the potential for upward mobility of workers.[1] African immigrants in the U.S. are "heavily concentrated toward the top of the occupational hierarchy in managerial and professional specialty (MPS) occupation" (Kollehlon and Eule 1165). A 2001 U.S. Census Bureau report shows that of the 400,000 African immigrant workers aged sixteen and over in the United States in March 2000, 36.5 percent were in managerial and professional specialties (compared to 30.9 percent of native workers), the highest rank of job categories in the nation. That same 2001 U.S. Census report showed that the median income for all households in the country in 1999 was $40,816. For the 300,000 African immigrant households in the United States in 1999, the median income was $36,371, higher than the median of $36,048 for all 11.6 million foreign-born households (U.S. Bureau of the Census, *Profile* 41–45). In 2000, according to Logan and Deane, the median household income for African immigrants in the United States was $42,900 (6). Also, according to the U.S. Census Bureau statistics, with over sixty-five ethnic ancestry groups listed, the median household income for people of Egyptian descent in the U.S. in 1989 was $40,095, third behind people of Maltese ($40,552) and Israeli ($40,242) descent (U.S. Bureau of the Census, *Income and Poverty*). This high earning power of African professionals in the West is primarily responsible for the substantial increase in remittances back home to their families and friends as more and more professionals have migrated.

Remittances to the developing world by its emigrants are now reported to total more than foreign aid. In 1995 remittances to the developing world were estimated at $70 billion (Guarnizo 672). In 2003, worldwide remittances to developing countries surpassed $100 billion (Wucker 37). According to Khan, "Already, remittances (the term for migrant payments) to Africa accounts for more than donor aid flows to the Continent" (1). The IMF estimates that the African diaspora now constitutes the biggest group of foreign investors in Africa (Emeagwali). Khan also reports that "In Eritrea, for example, remittances account for 83 percent of exports. In Mali, payments from migrants account for a staggering 20 percent of gross national product" (1). Wucker (37) tells us that remittances to Somalia were $500 million annually at the time of writing in the early 2000s. The money wiring service company Western Union is reported to have claimed that "it is not atypical for an immigrant to wire $300 per month to relatives in Africa (Emeagwali). And Adams states that in 1999 remittances from Africans abroad were estimated at $2.959 billion for Egyptians, $1.772 billion for Moroccans, $1.198 billion for Nigerians, $696 million for Tunisians, and $607 million for Sudanese (23).

Frustrated career goals are frequently cited as the reason for the emigration of African professionals. Nyikuli reports: "Limited job opportunities and education facilities, a lower standard of living and security, and lack of professional recognition are among the factors that have caused many African workers, especially those with professional skills, to seek work outside the continent" (633). Docquier and Marfouk (3) present a list of emigration initiatives, including easy access to work visas in Australia, Canada, France, Germany, and the U.S., which tend to lure highly skilled workers from developing countries to emigrate to those rich nations. And in a study conducted for the International Council of Nurses (ICN), Campbell points to some of the factors contributing to the shortage of nurses in sub-Saharan Africa: "Limited career and professional opportunities resulting in frustration and the perception that health professions are undesirable" (47).

Oberoi and Lin present interview evidence of factors contributing to the brain drain from Southern Africa. They point to both endogenous and exogenous factors. The endogenous factors are "poor remuneration and wage; lack of job satisfaction; lack of further education and career development; poor working conditions; and HIV/AIDS." The exogenous factors are "lack of quality of life; high levels of crime; civil conflict and political instability; and social pressure" (29–31). In an article arguing that the brain drain from developing countries may be positively beneficial to home-land development, Patterson also notes:

Potential advantages stemming from African emigration to developed countries are so great that African governments should aid and abet such emigration. This proposition should not be considered against an ideal world wherein all African nationals can find productive work in their country of birth as they labor collectively with fellow citizens to build a prosperous society. Rather, the proposition should be considered against the real world in which African citizens are inhibited from freely contributing to national and professional development due to economic and political constraints. (1891)

POOR SOCIAL SERVICES

Social services—power, transportation, water supply, health services, etc.—have been either underdeveloped or severely stretched in many an African nation. Electricity offers a striking example. The shortage or lack of twenty-four-hour electricity in many countries is a key factor contributing to the emigration of the educated and economic elite in African nations. It is extremely difficult for scientists in any field to perform successfully without electricity. Africa has large quantities of crude oil, natural gas, and hydropower that could be harnessed for economic development, yet most African governments have grossly underestimated the relevance of these for their development needs as well as the welfare of their people. Regular power outages for many hours are common occurrences in many African countries, "even in some capital cities such as Accra, Dar es Salaam and Lagos" ("The African Internet"). Some oil-producing African nations such as Nigeria lack consistent electricity, yet they continue to sell crude oil to developed countries. In Nigeria, Jimba tells us, electricity is available to only 3 out of every 10 homes (64).

In 1999, Kenya, Tanzania, and Uganda combined had electricity production of 7.8 billion kWh, and 7.26 billion kWh of electricity consumption. For comparative purposes, during that same year, Malaysia's electricity production was 59 billion kWh, with 54.87 billion kWh of electricity consumption (Central Intelligence Agency, 2001). If African governments and businesses could provide twenty-four-hour electricity, it is possible that many of the millions of African professionals in the West would consider returning home, especially since the increased use of cell phones, the internet, and satellite radio and television on the continent has greatly enhanced the availability of one crucial factor in development: communications flow.

The Energy Information Administration (a United States government agency that compiles data on crude oil, natural gas, and other resources, and their uses around the world) reports that Africa's known crude oil reserves as of January 1, 2001, were estimated at 75 billion barrels (7 percent of the world total), and its natural gas estimates were 394.2 trillion cubic feet (7.4 percent of the world total); yet there is the potential for more crude oil and natural gas being discovered in the continent (Energy Information Administration). For instance, my investigations reveal that as of 2005, Africa had at least 126 billion barrels of proved crude oil reserves (compiled from Central Intelligence Agency, 2006).

The following African countries are reported to have had five of the world's top crude oil reserves in 2001: Libya, 29.5 billion barrels; Nigeria, 22.5 billion; Algeria, 9.2 billion; Angola, 5.4 billion; and Egypt, 2.9 billion (Energy Information Administration 2003). African countries would obviously do well to begin using their crude oil for their own development, rather than simply selling it to Western or developed countries.

*   *   *

This chapter has presented various factors explaining why millions of Africa's "talented tenth" have left and continue to leave for the West or for rich countries, seeking better opportunities. Among the factors contributing to this mass emigration of skilled and educated Africans with their families are political conflicts or civil wars; lack of economic and political freedoms; low salaries; lack of facilities and encouragement of professionals; and lack of adequate social services, especially uninterrupted electricity.

It can hardly be denied that for the well-being and survival of Africa, some policies need to be implemented by both African governments and the Western and rich nations benefiting from the brain drain, so as to arrest the trend in mass emigration. Without a doubt, the responsibility rests primarily with African nations themselves to pursue honest and determined policies to improve the conditions of life and work for their citizens. But there are also policies of a collaborative nature that need to be pursued. One such policy could be an agreement between member states of the African Union to develop a program that allowed African professionals to take three to four months off every year from their substantive employments, without any penalties, and be deployed to African nations that desperately needed their expertise. This means, for instance, that a Nigerian computer engineer would be deployed to Tanzania, where his or her skills would be needed for a concentrated period of service.

Another policy could be for Western nations such as Canada, the United Kingdom, and the United States, in collaboration with the African Union, to establish a fund to which a certain percentage (5 to 10 percent) of the annual taxes of African professionals in those countries would be transferred, to be used for development purposes all across the continent. In the United States alone, a substantial number of African professionals pay tens of thousands of dollars each year in taxes. Despite the enormous gains they bring to the American society and economy, these professionals would evidently be willing to contribute significantly to the revitalization of the societies they left behind, with which they retain deep emotional ties.

Another policy that could be implemented by the African Union or a group of African nations is to create a project whereby about 100,000 African professionals from various fields who resided abroad would be recruited, each for an agreeable sum with benefits attached, and strategically deployed to locations across the continent where their services were sorely needed. For Africa to participate with dignity in the growth of a harmonious "global village" rather than be a perpetual burden on the rest of the world, no sacrifice should be judged too costly for donor nations or too dishonorable for receiving ones.

NOTES

Some parts of this chapter are adapted from an earlier article by the author entitled "Africa's Migration Brain Drain: The Costs and Benefits to the Continent." *Chimera* 2, no. 3 (2004): 19–30. This article can be found at http://www.usaafrica .org/Chimera-FallWinter04.aspx.
    1. Consider the following report from the United States Census Bureau: "Over an adult's working life, high school graduates can expect, on average, to earn $1.2 million; those with a bachelor's degree, $2.1 million; and people with a master's degree, $2.5 million, according to a report released today by the Commerce Department's Census Bureau. People with doctoral ($3.4 million) and professional degrees ($4.4 million) do even better" (U.S. Bureau of the Census, "Census Bureau Report").

REFERENCES

Adams, Richard H., Jr. "International Migration, Remittances and the Brain Drain: A Study of 24 Labor-Exporting Countries." World Bank Policy Research Working Paper 3069. Washington, D.C.: World Bank, 2003. 1–29.
"The African Internet—A Status Report." July 2002. http://www3.sn.apc.org/ Africa (accessed January 1, 2005); see also http://www.comnet-it.org/pubs/ newsletter/issue4/afrcon.html.
Blau, John. "Trans-Atlantic Brain Drain Worries Europe's Policy Makers." *Research Technology Management* 47, no. 2 (2004): 2.
"Brain Drain or Overflow?" *The International Executive* 12, no. 3 (1970): 23–25.
Campbell, Sue. "Addressing Nursing Shortages in Sub-Saharan Africa." *Nursing Standard* 20, no. 51 (2006): 46–50.
Carrington, William J. "International Migration and the 'Brain Drain.'" *The Journal of Social, Political, and Economic Studies* 24, no. 2 (1999): 163–171.
Central Intelligence Agency. *World Factbook.* Washington, D.C.: Office of Public Affairs, 2001.
———. *World Factbook.* Washington, D.C.: Office of Public Affairs, 2006.
Clemens, Michael A., and Gunilla Pettersson. " New Data on African Health Professionals Abroad." Working paper 95. Washington, D.C.: Center for Global Development, 2006. www.cgdev.org/content/publications/detail/9267 (accessed November 20, 2008).

Crush, Jonathan. "The Global Raiders: Nationalism, Globalization and the South African Brain Drain." *Journal of International Affairs* 56, no. 1 (Fall 2002): 147–172.

Docquier, Frederic, and Abdeslam Marfouk. "Measuring the International Mobility of Skilled Workers (1990–2000)—Release 1.0." Washington, D.C.: World Bank, 2004.

Dodoo, F. Nii-Amoo. "Assimilation Differences among Africans in America." *Social Forces* 76, no. 2 (1997): 527–546.

Emeagwali, Philip. "How Do We Reverse the Brain Drain." Speech delivered at the Pan African Conference on Brain Drain, Elsah, Illinois, October 24, 2003. http://www.emeagwali.com/speeches/brain-drain/to-brain-gain/reverse-brain-drain-from-africa.html (accessed November 2008).

Energy Information Administration. "Table 8.1: World Crude Oil and Natural Gas Reserves, January 1, 2001." 2003. http://www.eia.doe.gov/emeu/iea/contents.html (accessed February 12, 2003).

Faye, Abdou. "Education: Europe, North America Tapping Africa's 'Brain Reservoir.'" *Global Information Network*, December 27, 2002, 1.

Guarnizo, Luis Eduardo. "The Economics of Transnational Living." *The International Migration Review* 37, no. 3 (2003): 666–699.

Gwynne, Peter. "'Brain Circulation' Replacing 'Brain Drain' to U.S. as Foreign-Born Scientists . . ." *Research Technology Management* 42, no. 1 (1999): 2.

Haque, Nadeem U., and Se-Jik Kim. "Human Capital Flight: Impact of Migration on Income and Growth." International Monetary Fund, staff papers. *International Monetary Fund* 42, no. 3 (1995): 577–607.

International Organization for Migration (IOM). "The Brain Drain." 2003. http://www.iom.int/mida/mida_health.shtml (accessed April 24, 2004).

Jimba, Samuel W. "Information Technology, Globalization and Africa's Information Development." *OCLC Systems and Services* 14, no. 2 (1998): 64.

Khan, Farah. "Population: African Union Courts Africans in the Diaspora." *Global Information Network*, July 14, 2003, 1.

Kollehlon, T. Konia, and Edward E. Eule. "The Socioeconomic Attainment Patterns of Africans in the United States." *International Migration Review* 37, no. 4 (2003): 1165–1190.

Leiman, Lisa. "Should the Brain Drain Be Plugged? A Behavioral Economics Approach." *Texas International Law Journal* 39, no. 4 (2004): 675–695.

Leslie, Colin. "Is It Wrong to Recruit MDs from Poor Nations?" *Medical Post* 39, no. 11 (2003): 12.

Logan, John R., and Glenn Deane. "Black Diversity in Metropolitan America." Lewis Mumford Center for Comparative Urban and Regional Research, University at Albany, August 15, 2003. http://mumford1.dyndns.org/cen2000/BlackWhite/BlackDiversityReport/Black_Diversity_final.pdf (accessed April 12, 2004).

Mazrui, Ali A. "Brain Drain between Counterterrorism and Globalization." In "The African 'Brain Drain' to the North: Pitfalls and Possibilities," special issue, *African Issues* 30, no. 1 (2002): 86–87.

McAuliffe, Eilish, and Malcolm MacLachlan. "'Turning the Ebbing Tide': Knowledge Flows and Health in Low-Income Countries." *Higher Education Policy* 18, no. 3 (2005): 231–242.

Medawar, Jean, and David Pyke. *Hitler's Gift: Scientists Who Fled Nazi Germany.* London: Judy Piatkus Publishers, 2001.

National Science Foundation, Division of Science Resources Statistics. *Women, Minorities, and Persons with Disabilities in Science and Engineering.* NSF 04-317. Arlington, Va., 2004.

"News and Views: African-Born Blacks in the United Kingdom Are Far More Likely Than Whites to Hold a College Degree." *Journal of Blacks in Higher Education,* January 31, 2002, 29.

Nyikuli, Peter K. "Unlocking Africa's Potential: Some Factors Affecting Economic Development and Investment in Sub-Saharan Africa." *Law and Policy in International Business* 30, no. 4 (1999): 623–636.

Oberoi, Sumit S., and Vivian Lin. "Brain Drain of Doctors from Southern Africa: Brain Gain for Australia." *Australian Health Review* 30, no. 1 (2006): 25–33.

Patterson, Rubin. "Transnationalism: Diaspora-Homeland Development." *Social Forces* 84, no. 4 (2006): 1891–1907.

Physicians for Human Rights. "An Action Plan to Prevent Brain Drain: Building Equitable Health Systems in Africa." Boston, 2004. http://www.phrusa.org/campaigns/aids/pdf/braindrain.pdf (accessed July 25, 2004).

Remington, Robert. 2005. "Officials Accuse West of Stealing Developing World's Nurses." *Calgary Herald,* October 30, 2005, A3.

Sautman, Barry V. "Friends and Interests: China's Distinctive Links with Africa." Working paper 12, Center on China's Transnational Relations. 2006. http://www.cctr.ust.hk/ (accessed May 2, 2007).

Schrecker, Ted, and Ronald Labonte. "Taming the Brain Drain: A Challenge for Public Health Systems in Southern Africa." *International Journal of Occupational and Environmental Health* 10, no. 4 (2004): 409–415.

Siringi, Samuel. "Kenya Government Promises to Increase Doctor's Salaries to Curb Brain Drain." *The Lancet* 358, no. 9278 (2001): 307.

U.S. Bureau of the Census. *American Community Survey Profile 2002.* Washington, D.C., September 2, 2003. http://www.census.gov/acs/www/products/Profiles/Single/2002/ACS/Tabular/010/01000U (accessed April 21, 2004).

———. "Census Bureau Report Shows 'Big Payoff' from Educational Degrees." Press release, Washington, D.C., July 18, 2002. http://www.census.gov/Press-Release/www/2002/cb02-95.html (accessed July 18, 2004).

———. *Census 2000 Summary File 3, Matrix PCT19.* Washington, D.C.: Government Printing Office, 2000.

———. *Educational Attainment for Selected Ancestry Groups 1990.* Washington, D.C., February 18, 1998. http://www.census.gov/population/socdemo/ancestry/table_01.txt (accessed April 13, 2004).

———. *Income and Poverty for Selected Ancestry Groups 1989.* Washington, D.C., February 18, 1998. http://www.census.gov/population/socdemo/ancestry/table_04.txt (accessed April 13, 2004).

———. *Profile of the Foreign-Born Population in the United States: 2000.* Washington, D.C.: Government Printing Office, 2001. http://www.census.gov/prod/2002pubs/p23-206.pdf (accessed May 2, 2007).

Ushkalov, I. G., and I. A. Malakha. "The 'Brain Drain' as a Global Phenomenon and Its Characteristics in Russia." *Russian Social Science Review* 42, no. 5 (2001): 79–95.

Vaknin, Sam. "Analysis: Migration and Brain Drain." *United Press International*, March 18, 2002. http://www.upi.com/view.cfm?StoryID=18032002-120828-5062r (accessed April 15, 2004).

——. "Analysis: Migration and Brain Drain—II." *United Press International*, March 19, 2002. http://www.upi.com/view.cfm?StoryID=18032002-5536r' (accessed July 30, 2004).

Versi, Anver. "Bring Home the Best and Brightest." *African Business* 286 (April 2003): 11.

World Markets Research Centre. "The Brain Drain—Africa's Achilles Heel." In *Africa in Focus 2002*. 2002. http://www.worldmarketsanalysis.com/ InFocus2002/articles/africa_braindrain.html (accessed April 22, 2004).

Wucker, Michele. "Remittances: The Perpetual Migration Machine." *World Policy Journal* 21, no. 2 (2004): 37–46.

Zeleza, Paul Tiyambe. "Contemporary African Migrations in a Global Context." In "The African 'Brain Drain' to the North: Pitfalls and Possibilities," special issue, *African Issues* 30, no. 1 (2002): 9–13.

PART THREE
RELOCATION AND REDEFINITION

6

"THE WEST IS COLD": EXPERIENCES OF GHANAIAN PERFORMERS IN ENGLAND AND THE UNITED STATES

James Burns

Mother, Oh Mother, your son has made a terrible journey.
Now I am stranded overseas.
Darkness has encircled me.
There can be no witness to what I endure alone.

An unsuccessful mission is a disgrace,
So how can we come home?
If you fail, no child is named after you.
Death is preferable to shame.

The cold weather gets so bitter men lose their senses.
Poverty, family problems, illness and accidents
All aggravate the stranger's sad state.
Married or single, life is not pleasant in a foreign land.[1]

In Ghana, one of the forest's most appreciated bounties is palm wine, a beverage whose source is the oil palm tree. Oil palms are legendary workhorses that retire after years of active production of palm kernels by leaning over to bear a "nutritionally" intoxicating beverage from their trunks. In the sixteenth century, the native palm trees eventually came to meet the Spanish guitar, brought by Portuguese sailors who were then exploring the West African coast (Kaye 74–75). Lutes like the guitar were not strangers in Africa; in fact, the European lute derives from an instrument, called *al oud* in Arabic, which is widely dispersed from North Africa to the Middle East.

Eventually, the guitar was adopted by the Kru, a nation of sailors and traders who were employed by the Portuguese for their valuable knowledge of sailing and navigation. The Kru were a highly mobile population that settled temporarily within enclaves throughout the coast of Western

Africa (Schmidt). Significantly, the Kru also worked on European ships, and through this they were able to experience life in the Caribbean and Americas. Returning from their overseas travels, Kru guitarists helped introduce the guitar to other African musicians throughout coastal West Africa. The guitar eventually became a part of the local "tradition" in many West African cultures in a pattern that mirrored trans-regional networks of trade, influence, and migration. In the early twentieth century, Akan musicians in what is now Ghana fused these two elements: "local" palm wine and "foreign" musical sounds into *palmwine*[2] music—a new artistic combination that was painted from a sound palette enhanced by the new styles of music that accompanied the guitar, including European religious hymns, sea-shanties, and popular music (Collins 222–223).

Since its inception, *palmwine* music has inspired poetic song texts which capture the essential truths of each generation. Comparing his music with African American music, Koo Nimo dubbed his style of *palmwine* music "Ashanti Blues." For people of Koo Nimo's generation (1950–1970s), a new subject for the blues became the difficulties faced by Ghanaians living abroad. Reflecting on his own experiences living in England in the 1950s, Koo Nimo composed the song "Aborokyiri Abrabo" (Overseas Life), quoted above. The text aptly expresses the ambivalence felt by Ghanaians who come to settle in Europe and America in search of better opportunities. The Akan term *Aborokyiri* from the title literally means "the land beyond the cornfield," and in Ghana its use signifies the world outside of Africa, and specifically the West.[3]

After years of local economic decline, Aborokyiri has become the semantic representation of a Western paradise, promising untold wealth and opportunity for those fortunate enough to get a sponsor for the visa and plane ticket. Those chosen few who make the journey become emissaries for their families, whose collective aspirations become their burden and responsibility. Most immigrants find that life "beyond the cornfield" does not lead to sufficient success to satisfy familial demands. Koo's sense of this turmoil is conveyed in the lines "An unsuccessful mission is a disgrace, / So how can we come home?" Accompanying the chill of despair is the physical discomfort of having to reside within an unnaturally cold city, made of concrete and ice blocks, away from the comfort of a warm and caring community.

Today, Ghanaian artists who have followed after Koo Nimo in pursuit of new musical and artistic opportunities in Aborokyiri continue to articulate the oral history of immigrant communities overseas. Therefore an ethnographic study of contemporary immigrant artists would illuminate the current social and artistic climate in the diaspora, as well as document ongoing processes of negotiation between immigrant musicians and the larger cultures they reside within. In this essay, I will present the experiences of two Ghanaian artists: master drummer Mohammed Alidu, and dancer/choreographer Pierrette Aboadji. Mohammed and Pierrette are both currently living overseas in pursuit of new financial and artistic opportunities.[4] Specifically, I would like to focus on the ways in which their artistic experiences reflect current cultural dynamics in the U.S. At the same time, I also wish to recognize that their music is situated within a constantly evolving local environment, and is the result of a complex interaction with local cultural and social paradigms.

SUBCULTURAL SOUNDS: CREATIVE MUSICIANS OVERSEAS

Until fairly recently, the focus of most ethnographic studies of non-Western music traditions tended to be within the music's endemic cultural context (Rasmussen, "Mainstreaming" 301–303). When musicians migrated outside of their home cultures and began to perform within diasporic communities in Europe and America, it was assumed that the process of musical innovation and retention followed a deterministic route leading to increasing formalism and ossification of the tradition, in conjunction with the eventual deterioration of musical skills due to the absence of a thriving artistic scene. This simplistic model placed the home context as the nexus of the "original tradition," and by extension musical ability and creativity, and the diaspora as a locus of artistic stagnation and deterioration.

In contrast to this approach, recent qualitative studies of music traditions in diasporic communities have rather revealed a dynamic process of innovation, adaptation, and hybridization.[5] One important facet of this process is how creative artists reinterpret their tradition within a new environment. Engaging their audiences in an aesthetic discourse, diaspora musicians introduce their products while simultaneously tempering them to meet local tastes. The resulting musical texts are important records of a particular environment: the literature of their lyrics documents and gives significance to a community of a particular generation, and their musical sounds represent a meeting between the home culture and local tastes. Representing such a complex intercultural connection requires a method for describing some of the contours of this encounter, and this task has drawn the attention of scholars working in ethnomusicology and Africana studies.

Marc Slobin has created a promising framework that seeks to describe the diverse dynamics of world music traditions that relocate to Europe and America ("Micromusics," "Music in Diaspora"). Slobin's model distinguishes between a predominant superculture and the various subcultures that reside within its sphere of influence. In this schema, Europe and America would be considered a superculture, visualized as an overarching "grid of influences within which they [diasporic music traditions]

are embedded" ("Music in Diaspora" 246). The superculture not only influences the sounds of the transplanted tradition, but also imposes certain
controls and conventions through the media, law, and consumption patterns of the majority, and by monopolizing the discourse of legitimacy and
value. Slobin employs the term "subculture" to refer to diasporic music
communities located within the supercultures of Western nations. Using
these broad zones of influence, Slobin is able to analyze the various intercultural connections between them, specifically looking at the various
ways in which the two cultures interact and affect each other.

For instance, scholars have recently observed an artistic trend prevalent
within the Euro-American advertising industry (superculture), whereby
sonic mélanges of world music styles (subcultures) are superimposed into
television and radio commercials (Taylor, "World Music"). This has the
effect of connecting the images of Western products to the sounds of an
imagined global village that are wired together in the harmonious pursuit
of commodities. Subsequently, the increased presence of these traditions
in our daily soundscape has stimulated an increased, albeit superficial,
awareness of the world through films, music, and popular culture. Slobin
aptly compares this process of cultural contact to food, which is another
"means of identification of diasporic groups, as well as local/regional subcultures" ("Music in Diaspora" 245). As Westerners begin to sample these
new foods and become active consumers, the foods become subject to homogenization and mass marketing, in the same way that Latin American salsa—a sauce of tomatoes, onions, and hot pepper—has surpassed
ketchup as the primary American condiment, and has even been marketed with a mild version to suit American tastes. In other words, salsa
negotiated its acceptance into the American superculture by addressing
diverse levels of spice tolerance. Accordingly, our understanding of diasporic musics must now take into account the ways in which both cultural
zones stimulate and affect each other.

(RE)CREATING COMMUNITIES
THROUGH MUSIC

Like salsa, Mohammed and Pierrette have also had to negotiate their acceptance within new communities in the U.S. These communities contain people from their own varied cultures, as well as significant numbers
of students and patrons from diverse backgrounds and with diverse motivations. Before we can appreciate the significance of their experiences,
however, we must address the dynamics and influence of their newfound
communities. Let us begin by considering the wider perspective of diasporic music traditions in the West, in order to identify key patterns of
intercultural connection.

A brief survey of diasporic music cultures in the U.S. reveals idiosyncratic configurations of music, community, and identity within the communities where such cultures reside (Rasmussen, "Mainstreaming" 300). In some cases, the music scene serves as a rallying point for members of a well-defined ethnic community, "linking homeland and hereland with an intricate network of sound" (Slobin, "Musics in Diaspora" 243). Particularly within subcultures at the fringes of the shared cultural network, artists may express the collective sentiments of the entire community. Averill's research among Haitian immigrant musicians in the United States notes a common belief that music must not only conjure a sense of nostalgia for Haiti; it must also address "the indignities of immigrant life and encounters with American racism and xenophobia" (254). The parochial dialect of Haitian Creole insulates their music from the superculture and even from fellow Caribbean immigrants. This Haitian méringue song, composed by a Haitian immigrant to the United States in the early twentieth century, captures this sense of alienation by using poetry eerily similar to Koo Nimo's song quoted above:

> When you are in the white's country
> There is a constant despicable cold
> And all day you have to burn charcoal
> You can't see clearly with the sky covered
> And for six months, the trees have no leaves[6]

In contrast, Su Zheng's study of Chinese music organizations in New York City ("Music and Migration," "Music Making") reveals a complex interrelationship between subculture and the superculture. Within the Chinese community, international networks of Chinese families link amateur musicians with professional musicians who come to tour or settle in New York (Gargan). They have founded community social service organizations that act as intermediaries between the subcultural Chinese community and the surrounding New York community, including state and regional governmental bodies. This has allowed them to draw on government funds to support cultural festivals and activities in Chinatown, which are now attended by both Chinese and white American audiences. By overt support of these activities, the government is able to tout its support of multiculturalism. Zheng describes this as a triangular relationship between the subcultural group, the homeland, and the host country (Zheng, "Music Making" 280–281).

Both of these aforementioned studies have looked at groups of ethnically homogenous people, who share a common homeland and cultural identity. However, subcultural musics may also arise from within minority groups who share other sources of common interest. Velez ("Eya Aranla") looks at the community of Santería worshippers in the United States. The Santería religion, although traceable back to Yoruba-speaking peoples in Nigeria, has been rearticulated by Afro-Cubans, who are responsible for bringing the religion to the United States. In the United States, the religion has been adopted by other Latin Americans as well as by African Americans and Anglo-Americans, with each group bringing their own cultural agenda to the theory and practice of the religion. Furthermore, the religious dance-drumming tradition that normally accompanies rituals has now become folkloricized in Cuba, with state-sponsored performing groups bringing Santería music to the tourists (Hagedorn, *Divine Utterances*). This has subjected it to the influence of the superculture of concert promotion, which, Velez argues, "domesticates" the tradition, "forcing groups to make adaptations in order to comply with the standardized format of presentation" (301). This influences aspects of the music such as song length, costume, and stage choreography. Yet the artists within these ensembles, many of whom are also practitioners of the religion, believe that the transformative power of the music transcends any concessions made in folkloric performance settings. For these Cuban artists, the barriers of the superculture can be permeated by sacred music; perhaps they are right, given the unprecedented growth of Santería converts in the U.S. Certainly, these musicians are not passive victims of the system, but are rather expert negotiators, introducing their art and religion to overseas tourists with conscientious detail and dignity.

Mohammed and Pierrette also find themselves within a unique musical environment. As experts in traditional music, they struggled back home to make a living because an increasing number of Ghanaians no longer enjoy traditional music. I have written extensively on this cultural divide, which is based primarily on religion (Burns, "The Beard Cannot Tell Stories," *Our Music*). Essentially, Christian evangelists have stigmatized traditional music as being rooted in the worship of traditional religion, and therefore consider it satanic. Moreover, the histories of Ghanaian popular musics such as Highlife have been intertwined with European culture, including Christianity, romantic love, and modernity. Therefore Ghanaians are increasingly embracing an attitude toward dance-drumming as being antiquated at best, and paganistic at worst. Overseas, Mohammed and Pierrette have fared much better, for their music is gradually being accorded respect as an "African" art form. Pierrette's dance classes, for example, now attract a heterogeneous community of white, African American, Chinese, Korean, Pilipino, and Latino students who form an invented community of African music enthusiasts, much in the same way Santería communities organize around shared religious beliefs. This unique environment transcends simple dichotomies between insider and outsider, and even the connection between music and ethnicity. Let us now observe some important interactions that have occurred during the course of my research.

AFRICAN MUSICIANS OVERSEAS

Judging by the myriad of Ghanaian musicians I have worked with and interviewed in London and America over the past ten years, the experiences and ordeals of Mohammed and Pierrette felicitously illuminate the larger perspective of Ghanaian musicians in the West. Although I will be concentrating on these artists, I will continue to include the perspectives of other artists from Ghana and Africa in order to expand the scope of the discussion. Allow me to now introduce these two performers and discuss the ways in which their artistry has adapted to and been affected by the supercultures of America and England.

Mohammed Alidu is a thirty-four-year-old drummer who comes from the Dagomba ethnic group in northern Ghana. Mohammed's family are *lungsi*, a caste of griots who maintain the history and oral literature of the society through the mediums of speech, song, and the hourglass talking-drum known as *lunga*.[7] Mohammed's family trace their lineage back to the originator of the lungsi caste, a drummer/praise singer named Bizung. Bizung lived nearly six hundred years ago, and was the son of Dagomba paramount chief Naa Nyagsi. Since the time of Bizung, Dagomba lungsi and their chiefly patrons have formed a mutually beneficial network, whereby lungsi depend on the support of the chief, who in turn receives a permanent place in the annals of Dagomba history. Most of Mohammed's male relatives continue to be engaged in praise drumming/singing and derive a substantial portion of their livelihood from music. Mohammed grew up within this musical environment, but left as a teenager to settle with relatives in the Ghanaian capital, Accra. He subsequently auditioned for the Ghana Dance Ensemble (GDE), and was accepted as a drummer in 1995. During his three-year tenure with the GDE, he studied drum rhythms from most of the ethnic groups in Ghana, as well as their songs and dance steps. Mohammed joined at a time when the ensemble was facing reduced government support due to the prevailing climate of privatization brought by mandated World Bank structural adjustment programs. Despite the unique artistic environment at the GDE, the ensemble faced a rapid exodus of artists, who jumped at any opportunity to work in the West.

In 1998, Mohammed was given the opportunity to travel to London, where he began performing and giving workshops with a local Ghanaian dance company. A few years later he joined Adzido, an internationally renowned dance company that specialized in African dances from many regions of the continent. Adzido was formed in 1984 by former GDE member George Dzikunu, who was able to secure funding for the group from the Arts Council England (ACE), a governmental organization that supports a variety of artistic endeavors with public and National Lottery money (Austin, "ACE Withdraws"). With ACE support, Adzido was able to employ twenty full-time artists, who received work visas, salaried contracts, and pensions. Like the Chinese music associations in New York, Adzido was able to benefit from state sponsorship while simultaneously contributing a visual testament of the government's multicultural policies. Having chosen the path of government support, Adzido had to face the responsibilities incurred in maintaining a legitimate organization worthy of public funding. The group was not able to adapt to this requirement, and by the 1990s it was running annual deficits, despite increased funding from the ACE which rose to a level of £1 million per year. The creative environment suffered the effects of these financial pressures, and many performers departed from the group. The ACE finally decided to withdraw its funding of Adzido in 2004, and the remaining members lost their government work contracts.

Although I knew Mohammed in Ghana, having studied Dagomba drumming with his older brother in Tamale, we were never close until I moved to London in 2001 to pursue my PhD in ethnomusicology and consequently entered the local African music scene as a performer-researcher. By that time Mohammed had already become disillusioned with Adzido, which was beginning its decline. Fearing its imminent demise, Mohammed had joined other Ghanaian group members in seeking odd jobs such as cleaning, shop-keeping, and petty trading. Mohammed and I eventually formed a small performing group made up of Ghanaian and white musicians who had been to Ghana and learned drumming. We were able to give occasional performances at universities, parties, festivals, and neighborhood council events, which worked to supplement our meager incomes.

Mohammed left Adzido in 2004 and joined Drum Café, a company that facilitates drumming workshops for schools, companies, and events. By this time, Mohammed had become proficient in many styles of African drumming, including Djembe music, which is currently the most popular style of African drumming in Europe and the U.S. (Charry, "Guide"). Meanwhile, he had married an American girl and was given a visa to stay in America. Before moving to the U.S., the new couple resided for a year in Madagascar, where Mohammed's wife had found a job. This brief period was a source of great creative activity, as Mohammed was able to secure steady work teaching African music in an American school, while also entering into the thriving popular music scene. Originally he was playing percussion in several local groups, but eventually he began to sing, and he composed six songs that were eventually recorded with local African musicians playing the backing instruments. The sound and production of the recordings evoke an eclectic mix of Afro-pop styles, including the Senegalese *mbalax* of Youssou N'Dour and the Afro-beat grooves of the late Nigerian rebel Fela Kuti. Mohammed readily acknowledges these influences, citing a formative experience of working with N'Dour and Peter Gabriel while he was in England. Like N'Dour, Mohammed creates arrangements that feature combinations of African drums, xylophones, and flutes with conventional pop instruments including keyboard, guitar, bass, and drum set. The resulting sound evokes the possibility of a more harmonious blending of African culture with the emerging global super-culture.

Lyrically, Mohammed sings in both English and his native Dagbani, producing a unique vocal sound that distinguishes his music from the multitude of offerings released by similar groups each year. The opening track on the disc, "Land of Fire," is a passionate plea for Africa to recognize its inherent beauty and stop fighting. It opens with a chorus of female singers intoning a refrain that evokes the image of fire to symbolize the warfare that besets Africa. The verses of the song are arranged in call and response format, with Mohammed introducing a feature of Africa's natural beauty, and the female chorus singers elaborating the image of Africa as paradise:

Refrain:
Africa, Africa, land of fire, I love my country!

Verse:

Call	*Response*
Look at the sky that surrounds us,	look at the beauty and the majesty!
Look at the trees and the mountains,	look at the rivers and the rain fall ah!
Look at the land that surrounds us,	look at the beauty and the majesty!

Analyzing the theme of this song, a particular artistic vision emerges that reflects Mohammed's greater consciousness of a pan-African identity as distinct from his Ghanaian identity. This raises a complex issue in regard to the notion of Africa, which has come under critical scrutiny by scholars who recognize that the concept of Africa is bound with Western paradigms of ordering knowledge (Mudimbe, *The Invention of Africa*). Mohammed has also absorbed the common misperception in America that Africa is a country, and not a continent, as is evident from the text of the refrain. Yet the notion of African unity, however imagined or invented, is certainly a sympathetic ideal, and represents the continued struggle to articulate a pan-African consciousness begun by African leaders including Nkrumah, Touré, Lumumba, and Nyerere.

The song "Salbee" presents a fusion of Dagomba lyrics with a musical background from Senegal. Mohammed based the music on a song by

Senegalese singer Cheikh Lô that he had heard in London (he did not remember the name of the original song). Mohammed replaced the original
Wolof lyrics with a panegyric epithet drawn from the lungsi drum language repertory. Dagomba praise poetry (*salima*) is composed in the form
of proverbial statements, which reflect upon bravery, wisdom, and social
existence. Here, Mohammed selects a rather jeremiad text whose meaning (fear human beings) is a common theme in Ghana, and represents the
local view that man is the source of his own suffering, as opposed to God
or the ancestors. The imagery of loving someone with the face is also a
common proverb encountered in speech, song, and drum language, usually with the additional line "but the stomach is different," indicating a
rupture between one's inner feelings and outer demeanor.[8] I would argue
that the juxtaposition of Dagomba wisdom with a Senegalese mbalax beat
further reflects the integration of Mohammed's artistic and social identity
into the larger pan-African community.

<Cheikh Lo beat>

Refrain (×2): Lai lai lai bi yuri ti lai ninni	They only love us in their faces.
Verse: Gbugginli be mogguni o ka taali,	The lion in the bush presents no problem,
Zomia ninsala	But you have to fear human beings.
Refrain (×2): Lai lai lai bi yuri ti lai ninni	They only love us in their faces.

<Change to N'Dour beat>

La la la la ah nawoe nawoe nawoe na.	(non-lexical syllables)
Chant (××3): Sala mbongo la, sala mbongo la, sala mbongo la, sali be.	That is human being, that is how people are.

In 2005, Mohammed and his wife settled in Colorado, where he formed
his own group, called Mohammed Alidu and the Bizung Family. The Bizung Family is a mixed group of African and American musicians who
were selected by Mohammed to perform the compositions he had recorded
on the CD produced in Madagascar. Mohammed described his new focus on Afro-pop as both artistic and commercially based. Throughout
his travels, he has noticed the success of Afro-pop groups that mix traditional instruments within a conventional pop format established by African popular music pioneers such as the aforementioned N'Dour, along
with Salif Keita, Fela Kuti, Thomas Mapfumo, and Manu Dibango. Afro-
pop is not only more palatable for Euro-American audiences, it is also
more patronized by Africans living in the diaspora, many of whom enjoy

groups from outside their homelands, suggesting that Afro-pop music provides some of the affinity functions that Haitian music brings to Haitian-Americans (Averill). Indeed, Afro-pop concerts in the U.S. bring together Africans from many regions, often congregating together and sporting traditional dress. As we will learn below, Mohammed struggled to make a living playing traditional music due to the restrictive vision of traditional music in the West. By shifting his focus to popular music, Mohammed feels he is keeping his music relevant to Africans as well as his newfound American audience.

Pierrette Aboadji is a thirty-three-year-old dancer who also got her start in the GDE. She was born in Ghana to Ewe parents, one from the Ghanaian side of Eweland, and the other from the Togolese side. She moved around quite a bit as a child, living for periods in Accra and in her mother's village in Togo. Eventually, she was introduced to traditional dancing through a neighborhood community group, based at her church, who hired a teacher to instruct them in Borborbor, a neo-traditional dance that has become part of Ewe Christian worship. Noticing her aptitude for dance, the teacher selected her to join his youth group, based in a nearby neighborhood. After six years in this group, Pierrette auditioned for and was accepted into the GDE in 1995, around the same time as Mohammed. Unlike Mohammed's, Pierrette's immediate relatives are all Christians, and they had no experience or interest in traditional music. Some of her extended family and ancestors, however, were members of traditional religious shrines, and were talented drummers and singers. Pierrette has therefore had to negotiate two competing systems of belief in her life. On one hand, her membership in a Pentecostal Church in Accra has brought her into contact with a class of people who view traditional music and culture as backward and satanic, and therefore discourage members from even remotely participating in these events. In her view, however, God has given her a talent for dancing, and through it she earns a living for herself and her two sons. Therefore, Pierrette has learned to distinguish between the folkloric versions of the dances as enacted by the GDE, and the actual realizations of these dances in their cultural context by native exponents.

In 2005, I made arrangements for Pierrette to join the Department of Theatre at Binghamton University as an adjunct lecturer in African dance. I had already started a regular drum class, and wanted to enrich the diversity of music and dance at Binghamton by forming a dance-drumming ensemble that not only would provide classroom instruction but would also give high-quality performances in the local and regional area. Pierrette joined the Theatre Department in August 2006, and started teaching beginning and advanced sections of African dance during the fall semester. Our new ensemble, christened *Nukporfe* (seeing is believing), began performing immediately; selecting students from the advanced class, we performed the Gahu dance after only two weeks of classes on September 9, 2006, at a conference of the New York State Association of College Music Programs (NYSACMP).

The highlight of the fall semester was a concert given at Anderson Center, the main performance venue at Binghamton University, on November 19, 2006. This concert represented a collaboration between Nukporfe and the three university chorus groups. Pierrette worked extensively with the Women's Chorus and the Harpur Chorale to teach them how to sing in harmony for the Ewe dances Gahu and Borborbor, and it was her first experience working with a group of classically trained musicians. The first rehearsal we had with the Harpur Chorale provides a poignant example of the way in which diasporic musicians such as Pierrette can actually enrich the superculture by increasing knowledge and awareness of other performing styles and practices. To illustrate this, let me describe the experience Harpur Chorale had in learning the Ewe song "Míawoe míegbona afegã me" from Pierrette.

The song has two sections, A and B, which may be freely juxtaposed in any order, and is set in call-and-response format, with Pierrette singing the lead part, and the Chorale responding. One of the most interesting junctures was when we reached the end of a section. The Harpur Chorale, working off a fixed score, anticipated proceeding to section B from section A, and to section A from the end of section B based on the notated scores I transcribed for them, and also based upon their expectation of a linear structure where sections are repeated a set number of times before directly leading to the next section. Pierrette, however, began singing the songs as she was accustomed to, by freely negotiating the different sections. Sometimes she would sing section A twice before going to section B; other times she would sing section A four times. At the end of section B, she would often go back to the beginning of the section, rather than moving to section A.

After a few confused attempts to get through the song, the director and students suggested that we set a certain number of repeats for each section and follow that convention every time we sing the song. Pierrette, however, refused to circumscribe her singing style, and suggested to the students to listen to which line she led with, and respond with the appropriate text. Thus, if she led with "Míawoe míegbona" (section A) the Chorale should respond with "Míawoe míegbona," and if she led with "Alelele" (section B) they should respond with "Midzra nuawo do." Following her suggestion, the Chorale was able to keep up with her extemporaneous renditions of the song. By teaching them the essence of Ewe antiphonal singing, Pierrette increased the musical knowledge and ability of the Harpur Chorale members. The experience reveals how diasporic musicians like Pierrette can affect the superculture by increasing knowledge and awareness of important world music traditions, while simulta-

Table 6.1.

A		Leader:	Míawoe míegbǫna	We are coming
			Afegã me	To the mansions.
				Noble people,
	Afegãmetǫwo			
			Nedzra nuawo dǫ	Get everything ready.
		Chorus:	Míawoe míegbǫna	We are coming
			Afegã me	To the mansions.
				Noble people,
	Afegãmetǫwo			
			Nedzra nuawo dǫ	Get everything ready.

B	L: Alelele	Oh!
	C: Midzra nuawo dǫ	Get everything ready.
	L: Abǫbǫbǫ	Oh!
	C: Midzra nuawo dǫ	Get everything ready.
	Míawoe míegbǫna	We are coming
	Afegã me	To the mansions.
	Afegãmetǫwo	Noble people,
	Nedzra nuawo dǫ	Get everything ready.

neously improving musicianship and critical introspection toward their own music traditions.

Pierrette's experience in the West has been quite different from Mohammed's because rather than a performance setting she has been based in an academic setting, where she has been able to simultaneously pursue traditional music. Among her fellow Ghanaian expatriate musicians, she is envied for her stable work environment, where she gets a regular salary and health insurance for teaching African dance. Most of her Ghanaian colleagues have to mix occasional classes at local dance studios with regular jobs as cleaners, hospice nurses, or other low-income occupations.

Within the university community, however, Pierrette has become aware of the disparities in the perception of African dance versus ballet, jazz, and other Western dance styles. Her daily classes blast African drumming through the halls of the music building, which is not accustomed to the sustained presence of non-Western music in its soundscape. This represents a clear example of how the superculture of Western academia, which publicly encourages diversity but privately seeks to contain its "disturbing" influence, restricts the flow of foreign music styles by delegitimizing their sounds as being too "exotic" or "monotonous" to merit serious consideration. Nevertheless, the fact that these dance classes exist and are reshaping the local soundscape constitutes an important record of how subcultural musics such as Ghanaian dance-drumming gradually sensitize

the superculture to new sounds, and can positively shape the consciousness of students in both the Music and the Theatre/Dance departments. A
measure of her success can be gleaned from the interest her music generated with the graduate student director of the Women's Chorus, who subsequently joined the African Music Ensemble at Binghamton.

The stories of Pierrette and Mohammed in England and America reveal how they must negotiate a complex cultural environment. Lack of
support from their own community denies them the respect and financial
support enjoyed by Zheng's Chinese musicians. In response, Mohammed
has changed his genre to popular music in hopes of finding greater commercial success and community appreciation. Pierrette, while having a
stable avenue to pursue traditional music, finds herself in a climate that
places her art on the periphery, and therefore is denied appropriate resources and respect for her substantial efforts to bring African music to
upstate New York. Having discussed the routes by which they settled
overseas, and aspects of their experience, I would like to now focus on
some of the ways in which the supercultural environments of London
and New York have tried to reshape Mohammed and Pierrette's artistic
visions.

STRANGE FACES

What I've achieved might be considered threatening by traditionalists, but
western musicians I've worked with have mastered the music better than many
Zimbabweans. If the guitar has a place in African music, why can't a westerner
master the mbira? Some people tell me I can't be the leader with whites in my
band, but I think the mix of people adds to my music. Sponsors disagree with
me. I went to the University of Bologna to run seminars twice, and then they
invited me to come play a concert. We agreed on fees and terms, but when they
got the list of band members they cancelled the concert, saying they *wanted to
book Africans to play African music.* Some venues in Britain only book me as a
soloist, but won't book my band. It is the sound that makes the spirits come, not
the person.
                                   —Dutiro and Howard, *Zimbabwean Mbira Music* 5 (emphasis mine)

This quotation aptly expresses one of the most significant intrusions
of the Western superculture on African subcultural musics: its attempt
to restrict the performance of African music to Africans (or at least black
people) dressed in tribal outfits. The musician who provided the quotation, Chartwell Dutiro, is a Shona *mbira*[9] player from Zimbabwe who
has been teaching in England for over ten years. Like the Ghanaian musicians introduced above, Chartwell has discovered that Zimbabweans
have little interest in learning to play traditional instruments such as the
mbira; therefore the majority of his students and audience are white. Implicit in the actions of the club owners and University of Bologna concert planners is the power to control the visual aspect of African perfor-

mance. In other words, they were not concerned with the musical abilities of Chartwell's group; presumably, he could have hired "Shona look-alikes" that could not actually play, and they would not have noticed. The real issue is that African music must conform to the conventions of the super-culture.[10] And yet, if Chartwell and his hypothetical group of "Africans" came to perform in tuxedos, they would be criticized for not wearing "authentic" dress!

A similar tribulation occurred when Mohammed and I were working together in London. He had gotten a gig at a university to perform some African music to commemorate a visit by a noted African scholar. The invitation came about through one of his drumming students, who was an undergraduate music major at the institution and suggested Mohammed to the department chair. The performance was to take place after the guest speaker had finished his presentation, during the follow-up reception. Mohammed called several of his drum contacts, including me, to try and line up enough people to do the event. On the day of the event, two of his friends were not able to get out of their work commitments, leaving only Mohammed and Cudjoe Wuashie from Ghana, and myself. I suggested another common friend, a talented white American, and a white Englishmen who was a student of mine and was also very good. When we arrived at the event carrying our drums (and in appropriate African garb), the representative from the music department came to meet Mohammed to show us where to set up; upon looking at Mohammed and Cudjoe, he frantically asked, "Oh, where are the rest of your group members? We need you to start in about five minutes!" Mohammed pointed to us and said we were part of the group (and not simply drum carriers). I will never forget the reply: "[*disappointedly*] Oh, hmm, we were expecting an African group!"

What is at stake in these two examples is the ability of African musicians to make creative decisions about their music and their performance practice. African musicians such as Mohammed find themselves in a difficult quandary because the societies where they have come to reside have accepted a vision of African music which is limited to drumming by black bodies with bare chests. This paradigm often impacts the reception of Africans who play popular music. At a recent concert held at Binghamton University, the Royal Drummers of Burundi came to perform along with a group playing a style of popular music from Kenya known as *taarab*, led by the female vocalist Zuhura Swaleh. The taarab group opened the performance, featuring Swaleh on vocals accompanied by an electric bass player, a percussionist, and a keyboard player. I had assigned students from my undergraduate African music course to attend the concert and do a write-up of the event. Most of them indicated they were troubled by the first group, because they did not conform to the advertisements, which featured the bare-chested drummers of Burundi. They simply could not accept Africans playing an electric bass and keyboard. Not surprisingly, when the Drummers of Burundi finally came on, many students wrote comments to the effect that "then the real African music finally began."

Reacting against Western stereotypes toward what constitutes African music, the Beninese pop singer Angelique Kidjo was famously quoted in the world music magazine *The Beat* as saying:

> I won't do my music different to please some people who want to see something very traditional. The music I write is me. It's how I feel. If you want to see traditional music and exoticism, take a plane to Africa. They play that music on the streets. I'm not going to play traditional drums and dress like bush people. I'm not going to show my ass for any fucking white man. If they want to see it, they can go outside. I'm not here for that. I don't ask Americans to play country music (quoted in Wentz, "No Kid Stuff" 43)

Pierrette was also deeply affected by a series of events that occurred at Binghamton University during the weeks preceding the November 2006 performance. During the short time that she had been residing in America, she had already noted the ways in which Africa and Africans were (mis) represented in the media. In a discussion we had one evening, she asked why television programs, magazines, and newspaper articles about Africa always featured scenes of starvation, nakedness, and war. She was disturbed to think that this was the way Americans perceived Africa. Confirming her observations, I assured her that we in academia were trying to redress this perception in our courses, publications, and events. The following week, however, an exhibit opened at the University Art Gallery featuring a series of photographs taken by Hector Acebes, a Colombian amateur photographer who traveled in Africa in the 1940s. The photographs selected for the exhibit featured several young girls completely naked, without any contextualizing or assurance that they had consented to being photographed. While there was an immediate outcry from several faculty members as well as the African student community, the curator refused to close the exhibit. In this climate, Pierrette's artistic vision must continually engage with spirits from the superculture in (re)articulating the local collective image of Africa.

*   *   *

Throughout this chapter we have encountered different experiences of artists who leave their homelands to reside in the West. One of the main themes of the conference that gave rise to this collection of essays was how these individual experiences articulate the dynamics of diasporic life. Mohammed and Pierrette's experiences within the new environments of England and America portray the multifarious pathways of influence and interaction between their subcultural sounds and the surrounding superculture. Issues that emerge from these experiences include fluctuating notions of identity and community, as well as processes of negotiation between subcultural arts and the mainstream.

In many ways, their music continues to actively benefit their local communities. In the tradition of Mohammed's griot ancestors, his new Afro-pop lyrics memorialize the present, while drawing in new audiences who reexperience Africa through his music. Pierrette has traded state support in Ghana for state support in New York, where she has been given the opportunity to counterbalance alternative visions of Africa with a vision of extended communities of sound. As artists they challenge "orthodox" views of Africa in their work, Mohammed through his embrace of Afro-pop, which counters notions of African music as being constricted to drums and acoustic instruments, and Pierrette with her efforts to educate music students about the intricacies of Ghanaian music.

Both have struggled to work within a limiting paradigm of African music that continuously attempts to regulate the visual and cultural impact of their music. Exhibits like the Acebes photographs further delineate a sphere of acceptability for the "African" subculture in the West, which is conceived of as tribal, one-dimensional, and naked. Consequently, both Mohammed and Pierrette have become more conscious of their imposed African identity through living in the West and interacting with local paradigms about Africa. Their creative artistry has allowed them some degree of success, and they have strategically learned to negotiate the complex cultural landscape to their benefit. Representing the hopes of their families in Ghana, they continue to endure the cold with the hope of one day returning to Ghana with the resources to develop something more meaningful and permanent. I think they would both agree that despite it all, hope must continue, echoing the fight song of their hometown football club, Accra Hearts of Oak:

"Never say die—until the bones are rotten!"

NOTES

1. Quoted from the song "Aborokyiri Abrabo" (Overseas Life) by Koo Nimo, transcribed and translated by Latham, "Ashanti Ballads."

2. In this essay I italicize *palmwine* to distinguish it as a genre of music versus the actual beverage, palm wine.

3. I acknowledge the shortcomings of the conception of "Africa" and "the West." These terms have come to shape discourse in both societies. For example, the Akan conception of *Aborokyiri* is bound within the history of their encounters with outsiders. As a term it is equally vacuous, referring to Europe and America, but certainly encompassing other areas of the world. "Overseas" is therefore perhaps a better representation; however, as the setting of this essay happens to be Europe and the U.S., "the West" is certainly an acceptable compromise.

4. This chapter is based on informal interviews and shared experiences with

Mohammed Alidu and Pierrette Aboadji. I have known and worked with both
of these artists in Ghana and in Europe and America over the course of the past
ten years. Additional Ghanaian musicians whose experiences contributed to this
study are Kwasi Amankwah, Cudjoe Wuashie, George Addotey, Mary Boatemma,
Emmanuel Quashie, and Victoria Dzivenu.

5. See studies by Dutiro and Howard; Rasmussen ("'An Evening'"); Hammarlund; Velez; and Zheng ("Music Making").

6. Quoted from the song "Souvenir d'Haiti" (Memory of Haiti), in Averill,
255–256.

7. Locke and Lunna, and Chernoff, provide more detailed ethnographic information about Dagbomba music in its home context.

8. In my upcoming work on Ewe female musicians (Burns, *Our Music*), this
theme forms one of the topoi for understanding and analyzing Ewe social life.

9. The mbira is a twenty-two-key lamellophone, often referred to as "thumb
piano," a term that has gained acceptance in Zimbabwe and among lay Western
audiences, but which has been thoroughly critiqued by ethnomusicologists, who
are concerned about the history of colonial denigration toward African instruments that is encompassed in the term (see Berliner 8–9).

10. See Rasmussen ("'An Evening'") for a description of a similar phenomenon
in Middle Eastern music. In this case, the image of the bare-chested drummer is
replaced by the equally "exotic" image of the belly dancer.

REFERENCES

Austin, Jeremy. "ACE withdraws 1 million from Adzido." *The Stage News*, Oc-
     tober 5, 2004. http://www.thestage.co.uk/news/newsstory.php/4499 (accessed
     March 5, 2007).
Averill, Gage. "'Mezanmi, Kouman Nou Ye? My Friends, How Are You?': Mu-
     sical Constructions of the Haitian Transnation." *Diaspora* 3, no. 3 (1994):
     253–271.
Berliner, Paul F. *The Soul of Mbira: Music and Traditions of the Shona People of
     Zimbabwe.* Chicago: University of Chicago Press, 1981.
Burns, James M. "The Beard Cannot Tell Stories to the Eyelash: Creative Trans-
     formation in an Ewe Funeral Dance-Drumming Tradition." Ph.D. diss., Uni-
     versity of London, School of Oriental and African Studies, 2005.
———. *Our Music Has Become a Divine Spirit: Female Voices from an Ewe Dance-
     Drumming Community in Ghana.* In publication, 2007.
Charry, Eric. "A Guide to the Jembe." *Percussive Notes* 34, no. 2 (1996): 66–72.
Chernoff, John Miller. *African Rhythm and African Sensibility: Aesthetics and
     Social Action in African Musical Idioms.* Chicago: University of Chicago
     Press, 1979.
Collins, John. "The Early History of West African Highlife Music." *Popular Music*
     8, no. 3 (1989): 221–230.
Dutiro, Chartwell, and Keith Howard. *Zimbabwean Mbira Music on an Interna-
     tional Stage: Chartwell Dutiro's Life in Music.* London: Ashgate, 2007.
Gargan, Edward A. "Trading Fame for Freedom: Chinese Opera Stars Find Haven,
     Hardship, in U.S." *New York Times*, June 21, 1998, 25, 28.

Hagedorn, Katherine J. *Divine Utterances: The Performance of Afro-Cuban Santería.* Washington: Smithsonian Institution, 2001.

Hammarlund, Anders. "Migrancy and Syncretism: A Turkish Musician in Stockholm." *Diaspora* 3, no. 3 (1994): 305–323.

Kaye, Andrew L. "The Guitar in Africa." In *Garland Encyclopedia of World Music.* Vol. 1: Africa, ed. Ruth M. Stone. New York: Garland, 1997. 74–93.

Latham, Joe L. "Ashanti Ballads." 1986. http://homepage.ntlworld.com/latham/koonimo/ashball.htm (accessed February 15, 2007).

Locke, David, and Abubakari Lunna. *Drum Damba: Talking Drum Lessons.* Crown Point, Ind.: White Cliffs Media, 1990.

Monson, Ingrid T. "Forced Migration, Asymmetrical Power Relations and Africa-American Music: Reformulation of Cultural Meaning and Musical Form." *The World of Music* 32, no. 3 (1990): 22–45.

Mudimbe, V. Y. *The Invention of Africa: Gnosis, Philosophy, and the Order of Knowledge.* Bloomington: Indiana University Press, 1988.

Rasmussen, Anne K. "'An Evening in the Orient': The Middle Eastern Nightclub in America." *Asian Music* 23, no. 2 (1992): 63–88.

———. "Mainstreaming American Multiculturalism." *American Music* 22, no. 2 (2004): 296–309.

Schmidt, Cynthia. "Kru mariners and migrants of the West African coast." In *Garland Handbook of African Music,* ed. Ruth M. Stone. New York: Garland, 2000. 94–106.

Slobin, Mark. "Micromusics of the West: A Comparative Approach." *Ethnomusicology* 36 (1992): 1–87.

———. "Music in Diaspora: The View from Euro-America." *Diaspora* 3, no. 3 (1994): 243–251.

Taylor, Timothy D. "World Music in Television Ads." *American Music* 18, no. 2 (2000): 162–192.

Velez, María Teresa. "Eya Aranla, Overlapping Perspectives on a Santería Group." *Diaspora* 3, no. 3 (1994): 289–303.

Wentz, Brooke. "No Kid Stuff." *The Beat* 12, no. 5 (1993): 42–45.

Zheng, Su. "Music and Migration: Chinese American Traditional Music in New York City." *The World of Music* 32, no. 3 (1990): 48–66.

———. "Music Making in Cultural Displacement: The Chinese-American Odyssey." *Diaspora* 3, no. 3 (1994): 273–288.

7 MIGRATION AND BEREAVEMENT: HOW GHANAIAN MIGRANTS COPE IN THE UNITED KINGDOM

Helena Anin-Boateng

This chapter attempts to share some of my research on a significant aspect of cultural life that sustains Ghanaian migrants in the UK in moments of bereavement and tragedy.

Within the Ghanaian community in the UK, communal bonding, shared grief, and ceremonies of burial have been crucial in helping the bereaved to cope with the trauma of death. The strength of these social networks and the psychological impact they have may be explained by the specific nature of the new migrations that brought Africans to the United Kingdom in the mid-twentieth century. Unlike the earlier migrations that forced millions of enslaved Africans into the Caribbean and the Americas between the fifteenth and nineteenth centuries, these contemporary migrations are freely chosen acts and are still ongoing. Though there were Ghanaian migrants among the influx of seamen to the UK during the Second World War, the bulk of Ghanaian migration to the UK really began after the war and continued throughout the postwar years. Between the mid-1940s and the present moment, the volume of migration has increased to such an extent that we can now identify at least three generations of Ghanaian migrants in the UK. The UK Census of 1991 put the number of Africans in the UK at 32,000. But more than a decade and a half after this census, the figure could be more than double the 1991 figure.

This migratory movement, though relatively small in volume, presents interesting sociological angles on migration and settlement that are of general significance. Unlike the earlier forced migrations of Africans to the Americas, this new diaspora is far from a total displacement. Continuous channels of communication between home and migrant locations ensure that individual migrants are not completely displaced. The history of this migration reveals a number of varied reasons why migrants came to the UK, stayed on as workers, and later became UK residents and citizens. Most of these postwar migrants came to the UK to study for university and professional qualifications, and were originally drawn to the UK by old colonial ties and a general familiarity with the UK system of education. They did not set out as emigrants. Most maintained links with their families and communities back home and harbored plans of eventually returning home, even when this possibility seemed to recede with the passage of time. In the 1970s, the political instability in Ghana and the near-collapse of the Ghanaian economy sparked a new surge in different groups of migrants—mostly economic migrants, less skilled and less educated. As migrants, their main aim was to raise money to improve the lives of their families back home. They also ended up living and working in the UK, eventually settling down as part of the Ghanaian migrant community in the UK.

In the late twentieth century, the presence of other ex-colonial migrants and the emergence of a new breed of migrant scholars willing to challenge the notion of a white monocultural Britain paved the way for Britain's own redefinition of itself as a multicultural society. The ethos of a multicultural Britain created a sense of inclusiveness that made it possible for Ghanaian migrants to stake their futures as Ghanaian Britons. As a result, a sizeable number of Ghanaian professionals in the UK are now fully assimilated in the UK professions as doctors, nurses, teachers, engineers, lawyers, accountants, architects, secretaries and media personnel. Several other Ghanaian migrants now operate their own businesses, while a still greater number of migrants work in lower-paid jobs as care assistants, office cleaners, and construction workers.

One common link that binds these Ghanaian migrants, whatever their professional standing, is that as black Africans they experience common prejudices about Africans and have similar difficulties in establishing new community networks to replace those lost through their displacement. The proliferation of ethnic associations, village organizations, past student associations, church groups, and professional associations in the UK is a testimony to the desire of migrants to recreate a sense of community that would both link them to communities back home and root them more positively in their new place.

For most of these migrants, it is in times of life-threatening illnesses and bereavement that the need for a supportive community is felt most. Bereavement and grief are a basic part of human existence, but they are experienced in different ways in different cultures and communities. Cultural conditions and social norms play a major part in the ways in which death and loss are experienced and internalized. West African communities express grief and sorrow openly and verbally. News of death attracts large crowds of sympathizers and is marked by the release of intense emotion, public wailing, and the singing and performance of funeral dirges. In mainstream Britain, however, grief is expressed with some emotional reserve and stoicism. As Walter observes, the English do not wear their emotions on their sleeves and are unlikely to approve of funerals that challenge their emotional reserve. In fact, they have often criticized Irish funerals for being wild and sentimental.

For the Ghanaian migrant, used to a different understanding of and response to death, the loss of a loved one in this wider social environment of emotional reserve may lead to a sense of isolation and perhaps even trigger a deep depression. Religion and faith may provide succor in these moments, but they may not give the same social and emotional support as the familiar ceremonies and community presence of the ordinary Ghanaian funeral. There have been cases of tragic breakdowns and mental illnesses of migrants in the UK that ordinary mainstream counseling has proved inadequate to redress. Such incidents suggest that contrary to De Witte's suggestion that traditional ritual centered on the extended family and belief about ancestors will decrease in importance with increased globalization and individualization (33), migrants still feel a need for such cultural and social support and may continue to recreate old forms and systems in their new locations. On the other hand, it can be argued that Ghanaian migrants live their daily lives in a new migrant location and social world that impacts on their personalities and attitudes, and they are continually moved to negotiate their Old and New World ideas and beliefs. It would be of immense significance to our understanding of the implications of contemporary diasporas if we could examine the nature and importance of these cultural intersections and adjustments. What do they suggest about the resilience of old cultures and the impact of a different, new environment? What do they reveal about the sociology of the new Ghanaian (and West African) diaspora in the UK?

It is in relation to such questions that my research on how Ghanaian migrants cope with bereavement might yield interesting sociological insights, in spite of its primary contextualization within a health science and counseling enquiry. The original aim of the research was to use multicultural knowledge and skills creatively in a counseling program that would help people to live and survive satisfactorily in a changing migrant environment. Multicultural[1] counseling is based on an assumption that each client, counselor, presenting problem, and counseling environment is shaped by culturally defined relationships. This fundamental assumption is often overlooked, particularly in counseling regimes that take their references from Western psychology (Ata). Parkes has argued persuasively that the systematic exploration of the causes and consequences of cultural differences in reaction to death and bereavement is an important task that will add much to our understanding of migrant psychology and cultural adjustment.

My research situated itself in this literature on multicultural bereavement care but moved beyond its frames of reference to focus specifically on the experiences of first-generation Ghanaians[2] who have lost close family members since moving to England. My original objectives were to examine the effect that grief reaction has on the health of Ghanaians, to explore the Ghanaian experience of emotional and social support during bereavement, to investigate the kinds of strengths that these revealed about the Ghanaian migrant community, and to explore the perceptions that Ghanaians hold on the potential role of counseling in coping with bereavement. Framing my objectives in this way left room for other, related observations which, though not directly within the ambit of my study, are (as I hope to demonstrate) of significance to the cultural adjustments and transformations of generations of Ghanaian migrants in the UK.

The choice of a hermeneutic phenomenological approach to my research proved a most useful way not only of assessing the value and efficiency of interventions carried out by healthcare professionals but also of estimating the strength and value of such community-based support systems in dealing with feelings of isolation and exclusion. The framework also helped me to move beyond the mere description of the phenomenon of bereavement away from home to an exploration of the hidden meanings of the stories elicited from bereaved migrants. Thus, on one hand, the research focused on each Ghanaian respondent's experience of bereavement, and on the other, arranged these lived meanings into discernible themes that suggested further questions: what meanings did the Ghanaian migrants themselves place on these experiences, and how did their meanings relate to the original ways in which they perceived reality?

Schutz underlines the value of such modes of perceiving reality when he argues that

> Man finds himself at any moment in his daily life in a biographically determined situation, that is, in a physical and sociocultural environment as defined by him, within which he has his position, not merely his position in terms of physical space and outer time or of his status and role within the social system but also his moral and ideological positions. (73)

In line with this phenomenological perspective, the research began with the assumption that the Ghanaian migrants who participated in the study possessed an inner awareness and knowledge of what it was like to lose a close family member while living away from an original home; that such an understanding was part of their sociocultural, moral, and ideological makeup and could be uncovered from their personal accounts.

To this end, the research analyzed data on the experiences of first-generation migrants aged between 28 and 71, as shown in table 7.1.

My approach to the interview was to ask the selected participants

Table 7.1. Participants' history

Names	Age	No of years living in UK	Relationship	Time lapsed since death	Where the death occurred	Where buried	Travelled to Ghana at time of death	Awareness of Counseling at time of bereavement	Experience of Counseling at time of bereavement
Augustina	62	23	Husband	2 years	England	Ghana	Yes	Yes	No
Maame Yaa	51	15	Brother	8 months	England	England	No	No	No
Comfort	49	31	Father	2 years 4 months	Ghana	Ghana	Yes	Yes	No
Ruth	28	7	Daughter (baby)	5 years	England	England	No	No	No
Alice	60	35	Brother	10 months	England	England	No	Yes	No
Paul	52	20	Sister in Law	2 years 6 months	Ghana	Ghana	Yes	No	No
Frank	50	25	Mother	1 year	Ghana	Ghana	No	Yes	Yes*
Dora	41	25	Father	8 years	Ghana	Ghana	Yes	Yes	Yes*
James	35	18	Sister	3 years 4 months	England	Ghana	Yes	No	No
Patrick	60	32	Wife	2 years 6 months	England	Ghana	No	No	No
Grace	48	5	Brother	4 years	England	England	No	Yes	No
Peter	38	21	Grandmother	8 years 6 months	England	England	No	No	No
Alex	55	30	Mother	6 years	Ghana	Ghana	No	No	No
Patience	56	32	Sister	11 months	Ghana	Ghana	Yes	Yes	Yes
Mary	44	19	Teenage son	1 year 7 months	England	England	No	Yes	Yes
Katie	71	41	Husband	10 months	England	Ghana	Yes	No	No
Hannah	57	11	Daughter	2 years 8 months	England	England	No	Yes	Yes*
Ken	36	12	Wife	3 years	England	England	No	No	No
Brenda	54	31	Mother	5 years	Ghana	Ghana	Yes	Yes	Yes*
Cudjo	48	20	Brother	4 years	England	Ghana	Yes	No	No

* Pastoral counseling

to talk generally about their experiences and feelings of being bereaved while away from home. From their responses I identified emerging themes in order to give form to structures of experience from which I could make generalizations. Four specific and sometimes overlapping themes emerged from the participants' responses. First was a sense of shock, helplessness, and stupor that I have characterized as a *feeling of being unable.* This psychosomatic sense of paralysis extended into many domains and functions. Respondents described it as "a wrenching of the gut," a feeling of being lost and shattered in a strange land.

The participant, Ruth, who had lost a daughter in England, recalled her experiences vividly:

> *I remembered screaming oh my God no! no! No! . . . it was like I was in a stupor or something [pause] the room was spinning and I could feel myself sinking, sinking. It's been five years and I still feel unable to pick myself up.*

Ruth was planning to take her baby to Ghana to meet the grandparents. She added that after the event of her baby's death, the thought of going home always made her "freeze." Mary, whose teenage son died of leukemia, conveyed this theme by stating:

> *I felt unable to think, eat, feel, or sleep. Like I wasn't really there. I had a feeling that part of me was not there, like being in another world. Some days . . . like yesterday I felt like I was just going through the motions. Nothing made sense, everything was in a blur. The strange thing was, I wanted to remain like that.*

Hannah felt like "a zombie" and as though she was living in "a cocoon." For her life would never be the same. "I had plans . . . the best laid plans . . . all for nothing." Her daughter was her "future." She explained that she had made plans to leave her house in London for her daughter and settle back home.

Varying types and degrees of inability expressed by the bereaved spouses included "being at loose ends" and unable to "believe." Both Augustina and Ken noted the inability to believe the reality of the death, even when the deaths had been long-anticipated. They did not deny that death had occurred but found the absolute finality of death the most difficult fact to acknowledge. The sense of disbelief and denial was significant in their accounts:

> *I knew he was dying. He was terminally ill with cancer . . . oh it was awful—but I saw him every day, if you know what I mean, I thought so long as he was alive there was hope. You can cope with almost every challenge in life, but death is so final. . . .*

Augustina felt as if she was in a "cinema," a world of "make-belief." Her experience of not being able to believe meant not letting go. She alleged she would rather "die" first than accept her loss. Her husband's illness lasted for eighteen months and she had time to be prepared but was never "really" ready. Likewise Ken, father of two young children, believed in many things but the absence of his wife was not one of them. He mentioned that people had told him "it gets easier" with time, but he had to be convinced first. Katie, who was recently bereaved, gave this sorrowful account:

> You know at my age—[pause] I ought to know different, you know all these feelings . . . they don't know how I feel inside . . . it's hard, I can't . . . I hope somebody would tell me it's not true, it's kind of unreal. I wonder . . . its sort of like I'm waiting for him to come back.

The sense of loss and isolation that the respondents felt was compounded by the keen sense they felt of being in a foreign land and of being abandoned, alone, and desolate. The experience of the respondent Grace touches the very nerve of the theme in a profound and powerful way.

> The death of my twenty-two-year-old brother four years ago was the most dramatic experience of my time in the UK . . . After the first shock of the news, I felt totally alone and desolate. I was in a strange and different land. I had only been in the country for nine months, and I was at a loss, what to do and where to begin from. In Ghana, no one faces the news of death alone. You are either amongst your wider clan or your closest relatives. Preparations for the rituals of death and burial begin at once, leaving you with no room to brood alone with your thoughts. With my news four years ago, I could not help feeling "guilty" for my younger brother's death. I could not help feeling "alone," and I was assailed by thoughts of "guilt," "sorrow," "desolation." . . . "Had I done enough to protect and help him," what could I have done to save his life. Assailed by all these terrible thoughts, I could not even cry or fall asleep.

Grace's story is particularly significant because it shows the extent to which grief, loneliness, and isolation may be intensified when bereavement occurs in a foreign land. Whereas in Ghana such extreme grief and desolation may be contained through open public grieving and rituals, no such outlets were available to the bereaved in the totally different environment of the UK. To make up for this trauma some respondents spoke of conjuring images of past bereavement ceremonies in Ghana to help them cope with the terrible fate of burying a loved one in the cold, snow-drenched terrain of Britain.

Yet it also emerged, from the responses of the participants, that traveling back to Ghana to bury the dead or carrying a dead body all the way to Ghana for funeral rites and burial may be equally traumatic, and may in fact appear like a journey to another foreign land. Comfort's experience of traveling home for a burial gives some insight into the difficulties of managing bereavement from two different places. For instance, she had to travel twice for the same funeral. The family back home needed a longer time to prepare for the funeral in accordance with Ghanaian traditions, since her dead father was a chief and a man of prominence. As a result Comfort had to travel twice to Ghana and spent a fortune on fares traveling back and forth. Comfort also discovered, to her disappointment, that funeral traditions back home had acquired a new kind of materialistic outlook. She had to "shop" extensively for "made in Britain" goods as the family preferred "foreign" products to those manufactured locally. The shopping list, Comfort recalled, went on and on. "Because you lived in London everyone at home thought you had loads and loads of money." Because the bereaved migrant is often confused, totally dependent on the wider clan for the rituals that would finally bury their loved ones, they go on spending and spending.

Other respondents recalled similar feelings of strangeness and difference. For instance, Brenda commented that although she quite enjoyed meeting all her extended family, she felt kind of "lost." In affirmation, Cudjo, another correspondent, confessed that he felt "mesmerized" by the changes he met in Ghana when he attended his brother's funeral four years ago. He reflected during his conversation, saying that he used to want to be buried in Britain until he attended the burial service of one of his colleagues. He characterized his experiences by saying:

> I was shocked . . . as if he never existed, the whole thing was over so quickly. Then when I went to Ghana . . . I felt "completely lost" and that was when it hit me how much my own life had changed. It didn't matter any more. Don't get me wrong, my heart cries out for Ghana, but I feel in-between now.

Many of the individuals who shared their stories reported having "mixed feelings" about settling back home and revealed that their bereavement experience in Ghana was like "being in a foreign land." The majority of the bereaved conveyed a sense of "fear of the unknown" in their interview, which was related to "losing touch" with the cultural ceremonies of their past environment.

It is possible to surmise that the trauma of having to cope with a different culture of death in England as well as a subtle estrangement from the developing attitudes to funerals back home in Ghana have been instrumental in the creation of a distinctive mourning culture and ceremonies of burial within the Ghanaian migrant community in the UK. The mixture of church ceremonies, social gatherings, and new rituals of burial created among Ghanaian migrants reveals new and different contexts in which the migrants live, their present and future expectations, and their special spiritual and cultural needs as a migrant community. It is clear from the personal stories of the respondents that Ghanaian migrants have sought to introduce and rework African cultural elements, such as funeral songs, in an attempt to create a "place to feel at home." All the participants in the investigation sought and tapped the memory of those who knew how things should be done, firstly, in accordance with Ghanaian bereavement practices, and secondly, in relation to compliance with the socially prescribed norms of the new society.

Within the context of rapid social and cultural change and the "Africanization" of some areas of London, Ghanaian funeral practices are becoming more established, and the ritual center is gradually moving from Ghana to the United Kingdom. Consequently, the meanings and practices which surround death are, increasingly, becoming the products of a particular social, cultural, and historical circumstance. Gardner has observed a similar transformation in the cultural and social fabric among Asian migrants in some parts of East London. Some of the participants would have preferred a simpler burial and mourning ceremony, which is in keeping with twenty-first-century Britain. This is because of the high spending and the cost involved in conducting Ghanaian funerals. Conforming to British social norms means that the law of their new environment does not permit bodies to be kept or laid in state at home. As a result, jobs which in Ghana would have been carried out by lineage men and women, as in the case of those who were buried in the homeland, were in England done by undertakers. Some of the participants were distressed by the image of "austere-looking" undertakers rather than their close family members carrying the loved one's coffin. It seemed also that in contrast to the open expression of grief illustrated by their parents in this enquiry, the British-born Ghanaians bore their sorrow in silence, the English way. The key themes selected to illustrate what happened in confronting death and loss while living away in a new society showed how migrants have evolved to deal with their situation when a loved one dies in the British Isles.

Issues that were highlighted in the theme *being with people* were recurrent throughout all the bereavement accounts. Ways of "being with people" were related to "strength and support," "compassion," "comfort," "prayers," and "help." Particular references to people in numbers, special groups of people, time spent with people, and space for people were made in the conversations. However, some of the bereaved reported negative experiences with regard to the length of time spent with visitors. On the whole, it would seem that the participants in general experienced positive relationships with people. The nature of the special moments that Dora spent in the company of her two non-Ghanaian friends became a familiar feature of all the accounts. Dora explained that her friends had just entered the house when she received a telephone call informing her of the death of her father. She recounted:

> I found it very helpful the way in which I was allowed to express my grief amidst much wailing. As I was wailing I broke into a dirge, which might have seemed a little bit over the top, but I found it quite therapeutic and it did a lot, I think, to desiccate those awful feelings . . . and though it might have sounded strange to them, the understanding and the compassion was there. They sang it all with their eyes.

In the same vein, Peter's colleague who went to fetch him home from the hospital where his grandmother died did not have to say much. Peter described that moment in this way:

> I felt his hand, then his arm, and I realized that he had arrived. We stood there holding on to each other. We struggled to find words to explain the inexplicable, the unknown. He couldn't talk because there was nothing to say. Just being there was more than words could say.

The news of his grandmother's death had spread quickly among the Ghanaian community, and people had started coming to the house even before they reached home. Peter elaborated, saying:

> I don't know, but everybody seemed to have known about it. Relatives and friends came in their numbers and soon the place was crammed with sympathizers. The next day, and I mean, as you've probably guessed, more people visited, consoled, and comforted.

The importance that the bereaved placed on "being with people" was further illustrated by Alice, who explained that her brother had returned briefly to Manchester to seek medical attention following his illness in Ghana. She recalled:

> In Manchester itself the support was even greater. Tom died at 4 PM. By 8 PM that evening the news had broken in the close-knit Ghanaian community. Friends, neighbors, colleagues all came to the house to offer their sympathy and condolences to Anne and the children.

Paul was another participant who found "strength and comfort" in the "wonderful support" of his friends and family when his sister-in-law died. He indicated that his experiences of multiple losses two and a half years previously had brought family and friends "rallying" around him, and he provided this explanation:

> *I just couldn't take it in. It was the most shocking thing that ever happened to me. Because right after talking to them on Saturday, come Monday the 2nd of October, my elder brother also died. I just couldn't hold myself together. Everybody came to sympathize with me. The fact that they all shared my sadness helped me.*

Apart from family and friends, some of the participants were visited by members of their local Ghanaian Welfare Association, as reported by Grace:

> *I didn't know a lot of people then as I had only been in the country for nine months. I think most of the people who were with me most of the time were members of our ethnic community welfare association in London.*

All those interviewed had pastoral support. Augustina found solace among her fellow church members, while the vicar visited and offered prayers of comfort to Cudjo and also to Brenda. Cudjo alluded to the "help" offered by the medical professionals, stating:

> *The hospital staff showed us the proper things to do. They gave us advice and made helpful suggestions.*

Augustina also commented,

> *The nurses at the respite home where my husband spent his final days were kind and helpful. They took good care of him.*

In both cases, the deaths had occurred in London but the families had decided to send the bodies to Ghana for burial. They reported that particular undertakers in North London, with experience in Ghanaian bereavement practices, had helped to ease their distress. They asserted that the undertakers were "very supportive."

As the Ghanaians discussed issues related to "being with people" in the event of bereavement, it became apparent that the length of time spent in sitting with sympathizers had, in some cases, been attributed to backache and feeling unwell. Another concern which surfaced in the conversations was related to increased disruptions in family life due to repeated visiting. Comfort described how it affected her domestic situation, with the following example:

It was a very difficult time as my children were not used to the culture. Since the death had occurred in Ghana and not here, they didn't understand what all the fuss was all about. Their life was interrupted with the constant stream of people to the house and their inability to sleep early and tiredness at college.

As these conversations continued, it became clear that the participants attached great importance to the subject of *kinship systems and customs.* Combined with these, rituals of bereavement were carried out in each of the twenty cases. Apparently, this helped in diverse ways to heal and comfort these individuals. Most of the bereaved reported a combination of Christian and traditional ceremonies as an integral part of their bereavement experience. An example provided by Grace showed this clearly:

The chairman and the executive committee had helped a number of Ghanaians to cope with such tragedies, and they had experience of how to manage our funerals and rituals in this country for as far as was possible. We discussed a combined Christian and traditional ceremony with the undertakers. . . . The next day, with two bottles of gin, we went together to the undertakers'. . . . We poured libation to the spirit of my brother and to the spirit of our ancestors. . . . called them wherever they were even from the undertakers' parlor in London. I put a ring on my brother's finger, said my goodbye and prayed.

Meanwhile, in Ghana, Paul had to officially open the funeral celebrations for his brother and sister-in-law with the support of his family and the wider clan:

We stood next to the bodies, in our black traditional mourning attire . . . there was an absolute hush, as we all bowed down our heads and prayed to the Almighty God the creator of heaven and earth. . . . We thanked the Lord for their lives, for the deliverance of their souls. Then, we poured libation, prayed for their spirits and the spirits of our ancestors. Then the viewing commenced. The whole atmosphere was loaded with emotion.

When asked if it made any difference to the way they felt whether the rituals were conducted in the UK or in Ghana, Grace replied:

The only difference was that it was the austere-looking undertakers who carried my young brother's coffin in their formal, businesslike way, instead of my relations as it would have been back home. But at the burial, we were able to pour a second libation. We were able to do some of the traditional libation ceremonies that we would at home. We sprinkled earth on the coffin just as we would at home.

With the exception of Patrick, all the participants spoke of "wonderful" church services and claimed that it did not matter where they were held. Augustina pointed out that there was a church service in the UK for her husband before his body was flown out of the country, and afterward in Ghana. "They sang his favorite hymn, which was very moving" and there were "traditional funeral songs, testimonies, poems, and tributes" Nevertheless, the participants affirmed that the customs and the rituals that they experienced when they were bereaved helped to comfort and sooth their pain, but did not remove it.

It was evident from the conversations that, with the exception of Grace, all the participants had relatives living in the UK when they were bereaved. However, some highlighted distance as an issue and asserted that, even if key family members were in Britain, close and regular contact between different areas of London or England was hard to maintain, and obviously not the same as being in the same town or village in Ghana. In spite of what they said, it would seem that in the event of death these distances were overcome. Participants' homes were "jam-packed" and "crammed" with people. During the discussions on kinship systems and bereavement practices, it emerged that the relatives not only "rallied" round the bereaved in times of tragedy but also brought with them material and spiritual comfort. James provided a good example with this statement:

> *Family and friends gave enormous support . . . visited home. Offered prayers, consoled and comforted us. They also brought drinks, food, gifts of money, traditional mourning clothes, and undertook errands.*

Alice recalled that in Manchester, the support was even greater:

> *Those who arrived early went home to fetch drinks so that we could offer refreshment to the later guests. Others brought food so that we could serve those who had traveled from London. A number of young women volunteered to cook and serve refreshment on the day of the funeral. Many young men offered to drive guests who had no cars to the church service and from there to the funeral. There were donations of money and drinks.*

Participants who traveled to Ghana felt equally supported. Patience stated:

> *People were really very generous in Ghana. We received gifts of monies to help defray some of the cost, we received much prayer, offers of accommodation and transportation; people offered to pay for the music, the traditional singers and the dancers. The painter who painted the family home did not charge us.*

Ruth remarked that when her baby girl died, an older relative moved in with her, cooked, washed, ironed, and basically looked after her for three whole months. Likewise, Comfort had the ticket for her second journey to Ghana paid for by a close friend. Dora, too, claimed that a friend had bought a ticket so that she could accompany Dora and her sisters to Ghana.

Nevertheless, some of the bereaved interviewed reported instances that were perceived as upsetting. These related to the authoritative and hierarchical nature of the kinship system—in particular, the decision of when and where to bury the deceased. Dora provided an example with the following report:

> The fact that I was so far away in London did not help. It then had to be quite a few weeks before we could actually go to Ghana. And by that—I mean about three weeks. The head of the family together with the elders had to get together and decide when my father could be buried.

In support of Dora's statement, Katie commented, "People here, we can't decide without the consent of the head of the family." She added that the ultimate desire to have her husband buried in "the land of his birth" meant that the closest kin—children and grandchildren—had been denied the opportunity to visit his grave. This aspect of the kinship system appeared to have caused distress not only to these two participants, but also to Maame Yaa as well as Augustina, who had problems securing extra time off work. In listening to their stories, it became transparent that instead of bringing comfort and the healing, kinship systems and customs, in some cases, failed to have the desired effect. The participants also concluded that the relative isolation and lack of support seemed to be experienced when the bereavement event was over.

One participant related his worries to the "natural stresses and strains" of life, but was still at pains to point to what he called his "bereavement legacy." The death of his brother had left him "in charge" of the extended family together with the family lands and other properties. This, he alleged, had given him a "real headache" due to the disagreements and conflicts that exist within the family. Alex revealed that he identified with such a situation, since his mother's death had left him with "unimaginable problems." Alternatively, Maame Yaa reported that she had been given some tablets by her doctor for "bouts of depression" which seemed to have occurred since her bereavement. The remaining fifteen participants seemed to have experienced different levels of physical, emotional, and psychological stresses which they claimed were no more than what one would expect in circumstances of bereavement.

The fourth theme which was evident from the various bereavement accounts pertained to *being able to communicate* with people. For the participants, this involved contacting immediate and distant relatives with the news of the death; informing family members, friends, colleagues, and the Ghanaian community at large about the funeral arrangements; communicating feelings through the use of metaphors, dirges, and prayers; and seeking comfort and advice through talking to relatives and members of the Ghanaian community and professional people. For most of the study group, this involved therapeutic dialogue with members of their family, the clergy, and in two cases health professionals.

All of the bereaved agreed that the family (nuclear or extended) became an indispensable source of support and a necessary arena for healing in their bereavement experience. Some of them stated that they were given "counseling advice" by the family. In addition, four of the participants said that they received pastoral counseling, and a further two reported that they were counseled by professionals from a mainstream bereavement agency.

Two of the bereaved provided examples of announcing the death and keeping relatives informed of the funeral arrangements. Augustina explained the difficulties involved in contacting the head of the family to announce the death of her husband in London. She stated,

> *Even the communication was a big problem because the head of the family was in the village and there was no telephone in the house. We had to send a messenger from Accra, the city . . . and he had to wait for the head of the family to come back from the farm.*

However, the rest of the bereaved were able to contact relatives easily in Ghana. When asked how she received the news of her father's death, Dora replied,

> *It was in the late afternoon; by the evening I rang Ghana to speak to my stepmother to find out how she was feeling . . . and that was a great source of comfort to me at that time . . . just to speak to her and find out what she was doing and what daddy died from and so forth.*

One of the participants, who had only been in the country for nine months prior to her loss, explained that "they put me in touch with the chairman and the executive committee . . . After a brief conversation with the chairman, we set a date for a kind of family meeting. I could at last now see my way through my tragedy." From these illustrations, it would seem that the ability to reach out and talk to people when the participants first heard the news helped. After the initial "shock" of the news, all the Ghanaians stated, they were expected to maintain a free-flowing dialogue between families in Britain and in Ghana. The following excerpt demonstrates the series of conversations that Paul had with his family, both in the UK and in Ghana:

> *Researcher: Tell me more about keeping everybody informed.*
> *Paul: To start with, first, when the news of my sister-in-law's death came, I had to make numerous telephone calls to all the extended family here in London and in America and elsewhere. The telephoning went on for days. Decisions had to be made on who would be going to Ghana for the funeral. Then we all met in this house and had a family discussion.*
> *Researcher: Uh-huh.*
> *Paul: We had to inform people about the preparations here and in Ghana too. Everybody needed to know what was going on. The sort of shopping to be done, ongoing discussions with family members at home. Some big people to be contacted and so on.*
> *Researcher: Uh-huh.*
> *Paul: You see, people come to mourn with you and listen to what arrangements you have made. On my return from Ghana I had to contact people all over again.*
> *Researcher: Then . . .*
> *Paul: We all met at my senior cousin's house in Wimbledon and watched the video I brought from Ghana . . . they saw and heard everything that went on at home for themselves.*
> *Researcher: And . . . ?*
> *Paul: And . . . hmm [pause] It was very, very sad . . . but it was worse when my cousin sang a dirge, calling the names of my brother and my sister-in-law, to express how she was feeling, that was when nearly everybody cried.*

However, some of the participants reported that they had experienced negative responses in family discussions, and even among individuals, as was evident from Augustina's situation. She explained that she had found it difficult to get through to people because of the controversy over her husband's will. She remarked:

> *It was the will . . . I couldn't get through to anybody. Instead of thinking of him, they were thinking about what he had left behind and fighting over things and I think, that . . . that in itself overshadowed my actual grieving, it somehow distracted me from actually allowing myself to grieve for my husband.*

Another participant, Peter, reported that his parents had contested his grandmother's will, and as a result "the relationship in my family had been troubled in the last years." He went on to add, "I think the best support I got was from my close friends and my partner."

From these accounts, it seemed that Ghana and Britain could not be meaningfully separated from each other. The bereaved migrants did not simply belong to home or away, but to a third space, between them, where new and altered rituals and hybrid identities and meanings must be socially constructed.

*   *   *

The data presented in this study highlight the influence of cultural identity, values, beliefs, and rituals on the way the participants responded to loss and bereavement. Under the circumstances of migration, those interviewed relied on close as well as extended family members, friends, religious communities, and members of the Ghanaian ethnic associations for support and healing. In the event of bereavement, participants were confronted with reminiscences of how things had been done back home. Some within the Ghanaian community presented themselves as protectors and transmitters of cultural knowledge. All the participants reported that the rituals of bereavement had been subjected to considerable changes due to the changed circumstances of living in the United Kingdom. These rituals and practices were central to the identities and meanings the respondents had constructed for themselves. In the new diaspora, culture is no longer confined to a particular geographical boundary but rather has its presence wherever Africans have emigrated to. Imported ancestral rituals, as constructed by the Ghanaians, can be viewed as windows that reveal the ways contemporary migrant societies see themselves and the world around them. Changes are necessarily made, which inevitably cause problems in embracing new norms.

Issues relating to the place of burial, material resources, and the relative ability of the individuals and the family members to negotiate the complexities of living in a "foreign land" had implications for healthy grief resolution. While migration had contributed to a shift in attitudes and perceptions, most of the participants were at pains to stress the degrees in which this shift had impacted on their bereavement experience. In the event of death, old as well as new migratory communities rely on bereavement rituals and strong social networks developed within the Ghanaian communities for healing and adjustment.

NOTES

1. "Multicultural" and "multicultural environment" are expressions frequently used in this essay to indicate living where different people have different beliefs, rituals, and feelings.

2. "First-generation Ghanaians" refers to people who were born in Ghana and have settled in Britain, but not to their children, grandchildren, or great-grandchildren.

REFERENCES

Ata, Abe W. *Bereavement and Health in Australia: Gender, Psychological, Religious and Cross-Cultural Issues.* Victoria, Australia: David Lovell, 1994.

De Witte, Marleen. *Long Live the Dead! Changing Funeral Celebrations in Asante, Ghana.* Amsterdam: Aksant Academic Publishers, 2001.

Gardner, Katy. "Death, Burial and Bereavement amongst Bengali Muslims in Tower Hamlets, East London." *Journal of Ethnic and Migration Studies* 24, no. 3 (1998): 507–552.

Office of Population Census. National Statistics [United Kingdom]. London, 1991.

Parkes, Colin M. "Comments on Dennis Klass' Article 'Developing a Cross Cultural Model of Grief.'" *OMEGA* 41, no. 4 (2000): 323–326.

Schutz, Alfred. *On Phenomenology and Social Relations.* Chicago: University of Chicago Press, 1970.

Walter, Tony. *On Bereavement: The Culture of Grief.* Buckingham, England: Open University Press, 1999.

8 ACCULTURATION AND THE HEALTH OF BLACK IMMIGRANTS IN THE UNITED STATES

Florence M. Margai

The health of immigrant populations in the United States is best characterized as an epidemiological enigma that is influenced by a range of factors including migration selectivity, nativity, cultural protective attributes, linguistic proficiency, and health care access. Some researchers have identified a "healthy immigrant effect" that suggests that those who immigrate initially have excellent health outcomes, with low rates of chronic and degenerative diseases and less adverse reproductive outcomes (Perez; McDonald and Kennedy). Others have identified an epidemiological paradox, with immigrants reportedly having better health outcomes than their U.S.-born counterparts, despite the difficulties they face in accessing and utilizing the health care system and other institutional barriers (Markides and Coreil; Scribner and Dwyer; Grady; Margai, "Using Geodata"; Yu et al.). There is also increasing evidence that the superior health status observed among immigrants does not remain in effect forever. Rather, it declines with resettlement and increasing acculturation in the U.S. host society (Lee et al.; Gordon-Larsen et al.).

The effects of acculturation on health have been well documented for Latino and Asian American immigrant groups; however, the trends among African-born black immigrants are still sketchy and yet to be fully discerned. Given the volume and rapidity of African immigrant flows to the U.S. in recent years, several researchers have now called for a more detailed assessment of black immigrant families by nativity to uncover any health differentials that might exist between the immigrants and their native-born counterparts (Kamya; Read et al., "Implications"). In concert with these latest efforts, the present study compares the health status of three black subgroups in the United States: U.S-born blacks, African-born black immigrants, and black immigrants from the Caribbean. The study draws on national survey data to investigate whether the relative health advantage observed among Asian and Latino immigrant populations also exists among the African black immigrants; whether this advantage varies by geographical region of nativity; and whether this advantage declines with increasing acculturation in the U.S. society. The research findings are expected to yield important implications for understanding black immigrant health and developing public health strategies that are geared toward racial/ethnic health parity in the United States.

The rest of the chapter is divided into four parts. The first section provides an overview of black health geographies in the United States, focusing on the demographic and spatial distributional patterns and the health care challenges. The second section summarizes four models of immigrant health, providing a useful context for conceptualizing and developing the research framework for this study. The third section outlines the research design, data source, and sample profiles. This is followed by a presentation of the results derived from the statistical comparison of chronic health outcomes among the three different black subgroups. An effort will be made to explain these disparate health patterns based on the geographic and socioeconomic factors as well as the varying patterns of health care access.

BLACK GEOGRAPHIES AND HEALTH DISPARITIES IN THE UNITED STATES

As of the 2000 census, black Americans constitute 13 percent of the U.S. population, or roughly 35 million people (U.S. Bureau of the Census). Several articles have articulated the demographic history and settlement geographies of this population, including the emerging patterns and health care challenges facing the group in the twenty-first century (Carter-Pokras; Geronimus; Margai, "Racial and Ethnic Disparities"). The spatial attributes of blacks have been described as predominantly urban and hypersegregated in environmentally and socioeconomically stressed neighborhoods. Historically, blacks have been faced with systemic and structural disadvantages such as residential segregation, racial discrimination, psychosocial conditions of acute and chronic stress, disrupted social support systems, and toxic environmental exposures resulting in deleterious health outcomes (Geronimus; Margai, "Health Risks"; Grady). The health differentials between black Americans and the dominant white majority have been persistent in many health domains and across all age groups (Margai, "Racial and Ethnic Disparities"). A larger proportion of blacks die of chronic health conditions such as heart disease and cancer than their white counterparts. Further, the risks of diabetes, HIV/AIDS, infant mortality, and low birth weights are significantly higher among African Americans than among other racial/ethnic communities. The reasons for these disparities are complex but linked to systemic disadvantages including poverty, discrimination, limited access to health services and utilization of these services, the late diagnoses of diseases, and treatment disparities (Williams and Collins; Williams; Gee).

Of increasing interest in the study of black health geographies is the growing diversity of the black population, and more specifically, the rapid expansion of African-born blacks in the U.S. Even though federal population statistics are aggregated by race/ethnicity, the decomposition of the data by nativity shows that about 6.3 percent of blacks now residing in the United States are foreign-born, and an additional 3.9 percent have at least one foreign-born parent. Black immigrants have historically originated from the Caribbean/West Indies, but recent statistics show an increasing number of them originating from Africa. To date, there are more than 1 million African-born immigrants in the U.S., constituting about 3 percent of the total foreign-born population. This number of documented African immigrants reflects a significant increase of 170 percent in just a little over a decade, up from 364,000 in the early 1990s (U.S. Dept. of Homeland Security).

A breakdown of the African immigrant flows by source region shows that the largest group is from Western Africa (35 percent), with Nigeria accounting for at least a third of these West African immigrants. The second-largest regional grouping is from Eastern/Central Africa (26 percent); Ethiopians constitute the largest plurality among this group. Emigrants from Northern Africa constitute 20 percent of the African-born immigrants, and within these the leading country of origin is Egypt. Finally, emigrants from Southern Africa make up 7 percent of the migrant flows, with the majority emerging from South Africa.

The diverse origins of African immigrants have contributed significantly to the demographic complexity of the black population in the U.S. Contrary to popular perception of African immigrants, these recent migrants originate from distinctive source regions, resulting in a diverse array of cultures, languages, religions, dress codes, customs, diets, value systems, health practices, and behaviors. The circumstances surrounding the arrival of African immigrants into the U.S. also vary. Only about 16 percent of these migrants arrived as refugees or asylum seekers (Eissa, "Diversity and Transformation"). The majority arrived either through professional visas (H-1B visas based on advanced degrees or specialty occupations such as nursing) or the Diversity Visa Lottery Program, which has a high school education criterion. The eligibility requirements for both of these entry programs have inherently resulted in a significant pool of human capital from Africa consisting of highly skilled and upwardly mobile professionals (Djamba; Eissa).

Overall, the increasing number of African immigrants coupled with the increasing heterogeneity of the black population in the U.S. raises several new questions about the variations between the subgroups and emerging health care challenges. For example, do recent African-born immigrants arrive with specific health advantages that, if uncovered, are likely to improve the health conditions and overall well-being of the rest of the black population? Alternatively, do these immigrants arrive with pre-existing illnesses that are likely to heighten the burden of disease among the native-born blacks and/or widen the black/white health disparities alluded to earlier? What are the effects of acculturation on the health of these new immigrants? Are there any commendable health practices or behaviors that one can learn from to help develop new public health strategies that would improve black health geographies across the nation?

MODELS OF IMMIGRANT HEALTH

Previous attempts to address the preceding questions and to evaluate the spatial patterns of population mobility, disease diffusion, and the health of immigrant families have resulted in several research frameworks: the Pre-Existing Illness Paradigm, the Healthy Immigrant Effect, the Resettlement/ Acculturative and Health Convergence Paradigm, and more recently the Racial Context of Origin Paradigm (McDonald and Kennedy; Macpherson and Gushulak; Beiser; Read and Emerson).

The Pre-Existing Illness Paradigm

The pre-existing illness paradigm is perhaps one of the oldest frameworks and provides the historical context for the formulation of immigration policies in several countries. It is based on concerns about the geographic spread of infectious diseases through relocation of migrants from source areas to their new host communities. Specifically, it is widely believed that without proper screening and regulatory controls, immigrants are likely to arrive with pre-existing illnesses such as infectious diseases or chronic non-contagious diseases that would heighten the burden of disease in their destination areas. As Beiser opines in his research paper, this assumption is probably warranted since "it was the 16th and 17th century immigration that brought measles, smallpox and syphilis to the North American continent" (6). More recently, Gushulak and Macpherson have examined the contemporary patterns of population mobility and health and suggested a range of pre-existing conditions in source areas that potentially influence the health of immigrants and their host communities. The genetic predisposition of the migrants, personal and population health characteristics of the source area, physical/environmental characteristics, disease prevalence, and limited access to health care are all cited as key determinants of immigrant health upon arrival in their host communities. Moreover, the effects of globalization and the emergence/ re-emergence of infectious diseases such as HIV/AIDS, SARS, malaria, tuberculosis, hepatitis, and other infectious diseases have all heightened concerns about migration and health.

To date, the pre-existing illness paradigm remains at the core of the U.S. immigration policy which mandates that all potential migrants undergo a comprehensive medical examination for infectious diseases prior to being granted permanent residency status in the U.S. The policy, in effect, implies that legal immigrants to the U.S. are more likely to be "pre-selected" for good health. This selection bias is arguably one possible explanation for the healthy-immigrant effect that is widely reported among immigrants, particularly Latino and Asian-American populations. Likewise, since many recent African immigrants arrived legally through diversity lottery visas and professional visas, these stringent health screening requirements have probably contributed to the selection of healthy African migrants for entry into the country.

The Healthy Immigrant Advantage

The healthy immigrant advantage has been well documented for Latino and Asian American immigrant families (Markides and Coreil; Perez; Newbold and Danforth; Yu et al.). A few studies have also reported the existence of a superior health advantage among black immigrants. For example, Lucas et al., who examined the health status and health practices of three population subgroups, confirmed that foreign black men reported substantially better health outcomes than the U.S.-born black men, and their overall health status was similar to, or slightly better than, that of the U.S.-born white men. Further, their findings underscored the epidemiological paradox, implying that despite the tough circumstances and high risk factors facing these new residents, they fared better in health than their native-born counterparts.

Beyond the immigrant health screening policies, three additional factors have been suggested for the healthy immigrant advantage. First, the self-selectivity of migrants has been credited for their superior health status. Studies have shown that typically the most highly skilled, best-educated, and healthiest individuals are the ones who choose to migrate voluntarily (Read and Emerson; Read et al.; Djamba). Such individuals are also likely to have the financial resources to travel to their new destinations, including the support systems and social networks required to survive in the new host societies. Second, the healthy immigrant advantage is believed to exist because of the under-utilization of health care services among immigrants (Leclere et al.; Yu et al.), which subsequently results in the underreporting of health incidences among these groups (McDonald and Kennedy). Third, the "salmon bias" has also been suggested based on evidence that some migrants do return to their country of origin after they retire, become seriously ill, or are close to dying (Abraido-Lanza et al.). These re-migration patterns and related health outcomes are also likely to contribute to the underreporting of health incidences among the immigrant populations.

Resettlement, Acculturation, and Convergence of Immigrant Health

The superior health advantage observed among immigrant families diminishes with increasing stay in the host communities. Studies among Latinos and Asian Americans have documented deteriorating health trends, especially in second-generation immigrant families (Gordon-Larsen et al.; Newbold and Danforth; Beiser). These trends, commonly characterized as part of the acculturative, assimilative, and convergence health paradigms, show a chronology of health events that starts out with positive health outcomes that deteriorate with increasing stay and acculturation in the dominant host society. Ultimately, the health of the immigrant not only declines with acculturation, it converges with the health of the native-born residents in the dominant host society.

Both acculturation and assimilation have been studied extensively as part of a sequential process that results in the partial or complete cultural transformation and integration of immigrants into the mainstream society (Lee et al.; Gordon-Larsen et al.; Salant and Lauderdale). Acculturation, typically viewed as the first step toward assimilation, has been described as a multi-factorial process involving behavioral and lifestyle changes as well as structural changes in neighborhood composition, institutions, and social networks. Various terms such as modernization, Westernization, or Americanization have been used to characterize this complex transformation of migrants through language, behavior, diet, dress codes, neighborhood characteristics, and social interaction with members of the mainstream society. Since most minorities in the United States have never fully integrated into the dominant host society, researchers have argued that studies that seek to address the health effects of this transformative process must focus on acculturation and not assimilation.

The analytical models that seek to assess the linkages between acculturation and health are typically based on complex lifestyle models, mental health, and stress-related/convergence paradigms. One example of the lifestyle model is drawn from a study of Hispanic immigrants in which Gordon-Larsen et al. examined the effects of acculturation on the overweight behaviors and health of adolescents. They found that with resettlement and acculturation, immigrants went through lifestyle and dietary changes that elevated their risk for poorer health outcomes. These changes included the transition to "obesegenic" environments characterized by sedentary lifestyles, lack of physical activity, greater exposure to the mass media, and diets consisting of high-fat foods and large portion sizes. Geographic factors such as current residence, duration of stay, citizenship, home ownership, and neighborhood conditions, and contextual factors such as poverty, residential segregation, unemployment, and high crime were also cited as key determinants in explaining the declining health outcomes.

Beiser, known primarily for his work on the mental health status of immigrant families, also argued that a number of psychological stressors heighten the risks for chronic diseases. Using findings from several studies, he found that mental health stressors were particularly harmful to immigrants, including pre-migration experiences and intolerable memories for those who went through traumatic conditions such as war or political or religious persecution at home, and post-migration experiences such as unemployment, racial discrimination, and other problems in the new host society. These experiences, he argued, contribute to post-traumatic stress disorders, depression, and other somatic conditions that may be life-threatening for immigrants after they resettle in their new host countries.

Another study, focusing exclusively on African immigrants, suggested the need to evaluate the health effects of acculturative changes on the African value system, a key determinant of the spiritual well-being of African immigrants (Kamya, "African Immigrants"). Using survey data, Kamya showed that African immigrants scored highly on self- esteem and hardiness scales, both of which were strongly related to their spiritual well-being and their ability to cope with stressful conditions. As with other immigrants, however, the study reported a downward trend between length of stay and spiritual well-being. Though the relationship was insignificant, Kamya (1997) confirmed a decline in spiritual well-being with increasing stay and acculturation in the host country.

Racial Context of Origin and Immigrant Health

This fourth paradigm corroborates the existence of a black immigrant health advantage but notes that the advantage varies by region of birth and health status measure. In two seminal studies, African-born blacks experienced the best health, followed by West Indians and European-born blacks (Read et al.; Read and Emerson). All of the three groups fared better than the U.S.-born blacks, with a notable health advantage among African-born blacks. In explaining these differentials, Read and Emerson (2006) confirmed the selectivity hypothesis, specifying, however, that the underlying factors of migrant selectivity were more influential with greater distance between the origin and destination areas of the migrants. Their study suggested the need for understanding black health geographies, specifically, the source regions, the racial context of origin of the immigrants, and the underlying mechanisms of race and class in those societies that worsen the health and well-being of population subgroups such as native-born black Americans. They argued that cumulative exposure to racism and other systemic problems associated with minority status played an influential role in black health outcomes beyond just the lack of exercise and poor diet. Black immigrants from "minority white" regions in Africa and South America were more likely to have superior health outcomes than their counterparts in "majority white" regions such as Europe or the United States. Specifically, when compared to their counterparts from "minority white" countries, blacks originating from "majority white" countries were more likely to have encountered problems in their racialized environments including racial discrimination, residential segregation, poverty, group inequities in education, employment, and health care, and other disadvantages. These systemic factors, they argued, were also responsible for the deteriorating health conditions of blacks within the United States.

To summarize, the four paradigms reviewed in this section provide a valuable context for evaluating the emerging health patterns and challenges facing black immigrant populations in the U.S. Concerns about pre-existing illnesses, migrant selectivity, acculturation characteristics, neighborhood conditions, and contextual attributes of the migrants are all relevant. The proposed study will incorporate several of these perspectives in assessing black health disparities and emerging concerns. However, unlike the previous studies, which used white Americans as a reference category in their analyses, this study will focus exclusively on the health status of three black population groups: U.S.-born, Caribbean-born, and African-born blacks. Further, since the research objectives are geared primarily toward the changing health circumstances of black immigrants in the U.S., the analytical research design will focus on the adult population using long-term, degenerative, and chronic health outcomes. The details, including research design and data sources, are provided below.

HEALTH SURVEY DATA AND SAMPLE PROFILES

This research relied on data collected through the National Health Interview Survey (NHIS) program (U.S. Department of Health and Human Services). The NHIS is a multipurpose survey that is conducted annually through the joint auspices of the National Center for Health Statistics (NCHS) and the Centers for Disease Control (CDC) in Atlanta, Georgia. Trained personnel from the U.S. Census Bureau conduct face-to-face interviews among members of the non-institutionalized civilian population. The participant response is typically high, as witnessed by the 73 percent response rate achieved in the 2003 survey. To ensure a nationally representative sample, the survey is based on a complex methodological design that includes stratification, clustering, and multi-stage sampling procedures. Further, a series of post-adjustment strategies are adopted to account for variability in the age, sex, and race/ethnicity of the population. The use of this data set therefore requires a full grasp of the design procedures and preprocessing of the data to include the weights that adjust for sampling and post-stratification procedures.

The present study utilized the combined adult core sample data obtained from the 2002 and 2003 surveys. These records included data gathered on 93,386 persons in 2002 and 92,148 persons in 2003, resulting in an aggregated data set of 185,534 persons. Each data record included several variables measured across a range of topics, including subject identification and geography (nativity, region of current residence, housing tenure, U.S. citizenship), health status and behaviors, health care access and utilization, and socio-demographic information. Following the preprocessing of the data, the first step was to query the records by race to extract only the individuals characterized as blacks/African Americans. A total of 26,334 cases were retained. The data were queried further by age of the respondents, to extract adults (ages eighteen and over). This resulted in 17,348 records. Next, another query was performed using the geographic region by birth, to focus on the three subregions of interest in the study. Approximately 88 percent of the respondents were United States–born blacks (denoted from here on as USB), 8.8 percent originated from the Caribbean islands and neighboring countries (denoted as CRB), and 2.3 percent were African-born blacks (denoted as AFB). To avoid over-sampling from one region, a randomized subsample of 400 cases was selected from each of the three subregions for further statistical analyses. All subsequent statistical analyses were based on the comparison of residents from these three subregions: USB, CRB, and AFB. Following is a brief overview of the sample profile, based on the major variable sets utilized in the study.

Resettlement and Acculturative Attributes

Table 8.1 provides a profile of the current residential patterns of the three population subgroups. The results underscore what is generally known about the geography of these groups, especially native blacks and Caribbean blacks, in the U.S. As expected, U.S.-born blacks are still highly concentrated in the South, a pattern that is reflective of the historical geography of the group but also the more recent reverse migration shifts to the south. Caribbean-born blacks predominate in the Northeast, with an almost equal representation in the South. African-born blacks are the most widely dispersed group, although they also appear to favor the northeastern and southern regions of the U.S.

Three variables, duration of residence in the U.S., citizenship, and home ownership, were used as proxies for characterizing the acculturative attributes of the residents. A cross-tabulation of the variables that measure duration and citizenship against geographic region of birth confirms the newcomer status of African immigrants in the U.S. Roughly 26 percent have lived in the U.S. for less than five years and another 23 percent for less than 10 years (Table 8.1). In contrast, nearly three-quarters of the CRB respondents have been in the U.S for more than 10 years, with half of the group indicating over 15 years of residency. Further evidence is provided by their citizenship status, with half of the Caribbean-born blacks being U.S. citizens, compared to only a third of all AFB respondents. Home-ownership patterns also tend to favor those who were born in the U.S. (USB) or have resided in the U.S. for a longer time period (CRB). Nearly two-thirds of the African-born blacks are renters, though an increasing number of them are now purchasing homes.

Socio-Demographic Characteristics

A comparison of the socioeconomic profiles of the three subgroups shows that the African blacks are relatively younger (mean age of 38 years) when compared to the 42.6 years for Caribbean-born blacks and 44.3 years for the resident U.S.-born population (p < 0.01). This is in concert with the typical age structures of immigrants being relatively younger than their native-born counterparts. The sex ratios differ within the subsamples, with slightly more females in the USB and CRB samples, while both sexes are equally represented in the AFB sample. A comparison of the educational attributes of the respondents also indicates marked differences among the three population groups (p < 0.01). African-born blacks are more highly educated than their U.S.-born or Caribbean counterparts. A detailed comparison of the groups based on educational attainment revealed that only 14 percent of the U.S.-born blacks and 16 percent of Caribbean-born blacks had completed four-year bachelor's or advanced degrees, whereas among the African-born blacks, more than twice as many respondents (36.8 percent) had four-year or advanced college degrees.

The high educational attainment of African-born blacks was also reflected in their employment status. Despite their shorter duration of residency in the U.S., only 20 percent of AFB respondents were unemployed last year. Caribbean-born blacks also fared better, with only 22 percent unemployed compared to 33 percent of the U.S.-born black adults. The high human capital in this foreign-born population was not, however, reflected in the annual earnings. All groups reported comparable levels of household earnings (p = 0.969). Family income levels across the three groups were also fairly consistent (p = 0.286), with approximately 30 percent of the households earning below the poverty level ($20,000).

Health Status

The health assessment of the three population subgroups was based on three sets of measures: health insurance coverage, self-reported health

Table 8.1. Settlement, Acculturative, and Socioeconomic Characteristics of Blacks Groups

Variable	Nativity: Geographic Region of Birth		
	U.S.-Born $n_1 = 400$	Caribbean-Born $n_2 = 400$	African-Born $n_3 = 400$
Settlement and Acculturative Attributes			
Current Residence (%) ***Φ = 0.35			
Northeast	14.3	46.5	32.5
Midwest	19.5	2.5	18.8
South	60.5	45.5	39.3
West	5.8	5.8	9.5
U.S Citizenship (%) *** Φ = 0.56	—	54.3	35.1
Duration of stay in U.S. *** Φ = 0.51			
Under 5 (yrs)	—	10.3	26.3
5–10	—	13.3	23.8
10–15	—	19.5	16.8
Over 15	—	57.0	33.3
Housing Tenure (%)***Φ = 0.21			
Own	54	58	30
Socio-Demographic Attributes			
Mean Age (yrs) ***	44.3	42.6	38.0
Education (%)***Φ = 0.29			
High school	25.8	24.1	9.7
High School/GED Dip.	31.5	28.3	19.6
Some College	28.4	30.7	34.2
Bachelor's degree	11.2	10.8	24.0
Master's/PhD	3.1	6.0	12.5
Unemployed (%) *** Φ = 0.13	33.2	22.4	20.5
Family Income (%) ns			
Under $20,000	28.7	23.3	26.5
Health Insurance*** Φ = 0.158			
Uninsured (%)	16.8	30.3	32.5

Significance based on Contingency Analysis using Chi-Square Statistics; ***$p < 0.01$
Φ = phi coefficient representing strength of the observed relationship.

status, and a Chronic Health Index (CHI). Health insurance coverage was a binary measure based on whether or not the respondents had access to health insurance. The analysis showed statistically significant group disparities in health care access (p < 0.01). African-born blacks faced the greatest disadvantage, with 32.5 percent having no health insurance, followed closely by the Caribbean-born blacks (30.3 percent). On the other hand, only about 16 percent of U.S.-born blacks were uninsured, the numbers being fairly consistent with previous studies (Margai, "Racial and Ethnic Disparities"). These findings confirm that African-born and Caribbean-born blacks share similar patterns to the Hispanic Americans, with more than 30 percent lacking insurance.

The documentation of self-reported health status also showed major differentials among the groups. Despite the higher portion of uninsured persons, nearly half of the AFB respondents (45.8 percent) reported excellent health outcomes, compared to 39.5 percent of CRB and 22 percent of the USB respondents. Overall, there were significantly more U.S.-born blacks in fair or poor health, nearly three times the number of African-born respondents reporting similar health (p < 0.01).

Not surprisingly, the results obtained from the self-reported health status were congruent with the Chronic Health Index computed in the study. This index was created using twelve well-documented measures of chronic health conditions and known risk factors: heart disease, stroke, hypertension, diabetes mellitus, lung/respiratory disease, cancer, depression/anxiety, obesity, nervous system disorders, digestive system disorders, urinary system disorders, and physical limitation. A reliability analysis of the index showed that it was acceptable with strong inter-item correlations (Cronbach's α = 0.81). A descriptive analysis of this measure by population subgroup showed group differences, with native-born blacks scoring slightly higher on the index compared to their foreign-born counterparts (Figure 8.1). The index also showed a statistically significant increase with increasing duration and stay in the United States (Figure 8.2).

RESULTS FROM THE LOGISTIC REGRESSION ANALYSIS

The next step in the study was to perform a logistic regression analysis, with two objectives in mind. First, in concert with the research questions posed earlier, the purpose of the logistic regression analysis was to determine whether the health status of the adult black population could be correctly explained by nativity, citizenship, and duration of residency in the United States. The second objective was to determine whether the preceding relationships would hold while controlling for the socioeconomic and demographic characteristics of these individuals.

To carry out these analytical objectives, the sample statistics derived

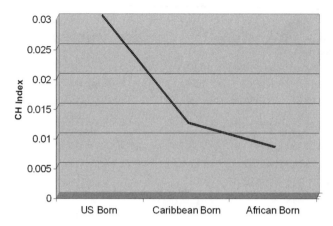

FIGURE 8.1.
Mean chronic health index by nativity.

from the Chronic Health Index were used to stratify the respondents into two groups. Those with a CHI above the mean were classified as having poor (or negative) health outcomes. Those with a CHI below the mean were placed in the second group, characterized as having positive health outcomes. Approximately 90.3 percent of the respondents fell into the latter group. Next, using the dichotomized CHI measure as the dependent variable, two separate regression models were run. The first model focused on the origin and settlement geographies of the respondents. The second model incorporated all of the other socioeconomic and demographic factors as contextual factors in explaining the observed health status of these individuals. Prior to both analyses, a series of tests were run to evaluate levels of multicollinearity among the predictor variables. The tolerance of all of these variables was above 0.10, indicating the statistical independence of these variables in the multivariate analysis.

Table 8.2 summarizes the results from the two logistic models. Model 1 confirms the relevance of the geographic region of birth (nativity) in explaining the observed differences in health. Using U.S.-born blacks as the reference category, the results show that the likelihood of a poor health status was significantly less among the Caribbean-born, and even lesser among the African-born counterparts. The analysis of the duration of residency showed that those who had lived in the U.S. for less than five years had the greatest health advantage. Consistent with other findings, this health advantage was less apparent among those who had stayed longer in the U.S. Citizenship status in the U.S., noted earlier as a proxy for acculturation, also appeared to have a negative impact on the chronic health

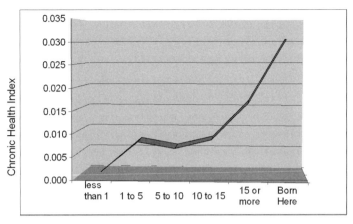

FIGURE 8.2.
Chronic health index by length of stay in the United
States.

status of the black adult population. The analysis by settlement region showed marginal differences. Using the Western states as the reference category, the results showed slightly higher but marginally significant risks for those in the Northeast, Midwest, and South, the latter being the most at-risk region for poor health. Overall, the fit of the model was good, with a Nagelkerke R^2 of 0.731.

The second logistic regression model was run using the preceding variables while adjusting for socioeconomic and other contextual factors such as age, income, marital status, employment status, housing, and availability of health insurance. Among these variables, age was positively related to the health status of the black residents ($p < 0.01$). Poverty was not statistically significant; however, those who were unemployed were nearly five times more likely to have a negative health condition. The latter relationship might be bidirectional, with the negative health status possibly accounting for the unemployment status of the individual and vice versa. The risks of poor health conditions were also greater among renters than homeowners and nearly three times higher among those without a high school diploma. Not surprising also was the fact that those without health insurance were statistically three times more likely to suffer from a chronic health condition.

The results from Model 2 showed that all but two of the geographic/settlement indicators remained key determinants of health status, while

Table 8.2. Odds Ratios and Confidence Bands (95%) Derived from Logistic Regression Analysis

	Chronic Health Index	
	Model 1	Model 2
Nativity		
US-Born (Ref)		
CR-Born	0.30 (0.18, 0.52)***	0.26 (0.12, 0.52)***
AF-Born	0.21 (0.11, 0.40)***	0.15 (0.07, 0.35)***
Current residence		
Northeast	0.54 (0.28, 1.0)*	0.22 (0.10, 0.48)***
Midwest	0.55 (0.28, 1.1)*	0.30 (0.13, 0.69)***
South	0.61 (0.35, 1.1)*	0.28 (0.14, 0.54)***
West (Ref)		
Duration of stay in U.S.		
Under 5 years	0.36 (0.15, 0.94)**	0.27 (0.1, 0.75)**
5–10	0.23 (0.08, 0.70)***	0.25 (0.07, 0.83)**
10–15	0.40 (0.16, 0.99)**	0.44 (0.16, 1.21)ns
Over 15 (ref)		
U.S. Citizenship	0.36 (0.22,0.59)***	0.14 (0.07, 0.27)***
Age (years)		1.02 (1.0, 1.03)**
Family Income		
Percent < $20,000		1.51 (0.89; 2.59)ns
Marital Status		
Married		1.20 (0.69; 2.10)ns
Employment		
Unemployed		4.75 (2.82, 7.9)***
Home Ownership		
Renter		1.1 (0.68, 1.8)ns
Educational Attainment		
Without High School Dip		2.0 (1.2, 3.4)***
Health Insurance		
With Coverage		0.36 (0.18, 0.71)***

*** denotes significance at $p < 0.01$; ** at $p < 0.05$; * at $p < 0.10$; and ns is not significant adjusting for these socioeconomic factors. The geographic region of birth was still a significant predictor of health status, with even greater health advantage among the African-born blacks. This implies that when the socioeconomic attributes are taken into account, the observed differentials between the groups widen, with foreign-born blacks enjoying even better health outcomes. The duration of residency in the U.S. also remained a strong predictor in the analysis, with the lowest risks among those who had lived between five and ten years in the U.S. When controlling for socioeconomic factors, U.S. citizenship and geographic region of current residence were no longer significant in explaining health status.

Overall, the addition of the socioeconomic and contextual factors led to a slight improvement in the fit of the model. Model 2 had a Nagelkerke R^2 of 0.80, indicating that nearly 80 percent of the observed differentials in the chronic health status of adult black residents in the U.S. had been explained by the variables included in the analysis.

RESEARCH SUMMARY AND IMPLICATIONS

Given the increasing heterogeneity of the U.S. black population, analysis of the settlement/acculturative attributes of the immigrants and the health differentials between the population subgroups is critical. The information gained from such studies is useful in debunking commonly held myths about black immigrants and race-based explanations for black/white health differentials in the U.S. More importantly, knowledge gained from such studies provides the basis for uncovering socioeconomic and health advantages among the black immigrant groups for use in promoting health parity.

This study reviewed four research paradigms on immigrant health: pre-existing illness; healthy immigrant advantage; acculturative stress; and racial context of origin. Then, using the national health survey data, the chronic health status of three black subgroups in the U.S. was analyzed as a function of the nativity, acculturation, and socioeconomic characteristics of the residents. The analysis produced a number of findings with significant implications for U.S. black health geographies. First, the analysis confirmed the existence of a healthy immigrant advantage among foreign-born blacks in the United States. African-born blacks and Caribbean-born blacks fared better than native-born blacks, based on the self-reported health measures as well as the Chronic Health Index. Second, the study provided evidence of an epidemiological paradox among African-born and Caribbean-born blacks. These two groups had better health outcomes, despite the low levels of health insurance coverage that limit their access to health care services in the U.S. Third, the positive health outcomes observed among the foreign-born blacks, particularly Africans, were most evident among those who had lived in the U.S. for less than ten years. Age and education were found to be strong predictors of these chronic health outcomes; however, these variables were not the only factors responsible for the observed differentials among the groups. These results showed that upon controlling for these socio-demographic factors, African-born blacks showed even greater health advantages over their U.S.-born counterparts.

From a paradigmatic point of view, the results provide strong evidence in favor of the healthy immigrant effect and acculturative models in explaining U.S. black health outcomes. However, as noted earlier in this chapter, several processes may be at work, including the self-selectivity of the migrants, the mandatory health screening programs, the "salmon bias" hypothesis, and the under-utilization of health care and under-reporting of health incidences due to the lack of health insurance among the immigrants. The relative contribution of these factors in explaining the observed group disparities is largely unknown, and will require a more detailed health assessment and longitudinal study of foreign blacks. For example, a health survey of African immigrant communities in major U.S. cities such as Washington, D.C., Houston, Columbus, or Cincinnati might provide explanatory leads on the cultural protective factors and other processes that account for the relative health advantage observed within the group. Such information would be highly beneficial in developing health-protective strategies aimed at reducing the prevalence gaps in chronic diseases between the native-born and foreign-born blacks, with more far-reaching goals of expanding health access among all groups and eliminating black/white health disparities.

REFERENCES

Abraido-Lanza, A. F., B. P. Dohrenwend, D. S. Ng-Mak, and J. B. Turner. "The Latino Mortality Paradox: A Test of the 'Salmon Bias' and Healthy Migrant Hypotheses." *American Journal of Public Health* 89 (1999): 1543–1548.

Beiser, M. "The Health of Immigrants and Refugees in Canada." 2004. http://www.igh.ua (accessed March 10, 2005).

Carter-Pokras, O. "Health Profile of Racial and Ethnic Minorities in the United States." *Ethnicity and Health* 4, no. 3 (1999): 117–120.

Djamba, Y. K. "African Immigrants in the United States: A Socio-Demographic Profile in Comparison to Native Blacks." *Journal of Asian and African Studies* 34, no. 2 (1999): 210–215.

Eissa, S. O. "Diversity and Transformation: African Americans and African Immigration to the United States." Immigration Policy Brief. 2005. http://www.ailf.org/ipc/diversityandtransformationprint.asp (accessed March 31, 2006).

Gee, G. C. "A Multi-Level Analysis of the Relationship between Institutional and Individual Racial Discrimination and Health Status." *American Journal of Public Health* 92, no. 4 (2002): 615–623.

Geronimus, A. T. "To Mitigate, Resist or Undo: Addressing Structural Influences on the Health of Urban Populations." *American Journal of Public Health* 90, no. 6 (2000): 867–872.

Gordon-Larsen, P., K. M. Harris, D. S. Ward, and B. M. Popkin. "Acculturation and Overweight Related Behaviors among Hispanic Immigrants to the U.S.: The National Longitudinal Study of Adolescent Health." *Social Science and Medicine* 57 (2003): 2023–2034.

Grady, S. "Low Birth Weight and the Contribution of Residential Segregation, New York City, 2000." In *Multicultural Geographies: The Changing Racial/Ethnic Patterns of the United States,* ed. J. Frazier and F. M. Margai. Binghamton, N.Y.: Global Academic, 2003. 65–75.

Gushulak, B. D., and D. W. MacPherson. "Population Mobility and Health: An Overview of the Relationships between Movement and Population Health." *Journal of Travel Medicine* 11 (2004): 171–178.

Kamya, H. A. "African Immigrants in the United States: The Challenge for Research and Practice." *Social Work* 42, no. 2 (1997): 154–165.

Leclere, F. B., L. Jensen, and A. E. Biddlecom. "Health Care Utilization, Family Context, and Adaptation among Immigrants to the United States." *Journal of Health and Social Behavior* 35, no. 4 (1994): 370–384.

Lee, S. K., J. Sobal, and E. Frongillo. "Acculturation and Health in Korean Americans." *Social Science and Medicine* 51 (2000): 159–173.

Lucas, J. D., J. Barr-Anderson, and R. S. Kington. "Health Status, Health Insurance and Health Care Utilization Patterns among Immigrant Black Men." *American Journal of Public Health* 93, no. 10 (2003): 1740–1747.

MacPherson, D. W., and B. D. Gushulak. "Human Mobility and Population Health: New Approaches in a Globalizing World." *Perspectives in Biology and Medicine* 44, no. 3 (2001): 390–401.

Margai, F. M. "Health Risks and Environmental Inequity: A Geographical Analysis of Accidental Releases of Hazardous Materials." *The Professional Geographer* 53, no. 3 (2001): 422–434.

———. "Racial and Ethnic Disparities in Health and Health Care: A Geographical Review." In *Race, Ethnicity, and Place in a Changing America,* ed. J. Frazier and E. Tettey-Fio. Binghamton, N.Y.: Global Academic, 2006.

———. "Using Geodata Techniques to Analyze Environmental Health Inequities in Minority Neighborhoods: The Case of Toxic Exposures and Low Birth Weights." In *Multicultural Geographies: Changing Racial and Ethnic Patterns in the U.S.,* ed. J. Frazier and F. M. Margai. Binghamton, N.Y.: Global Academic, 2003. 263–274.

Markides, K. S., and J. Coreil. "The Health of Hispanics in the Southwestern United States: An Epidemiological Paradox." *Public Health Reports* 101 (1986): 253–265.

McDonald, J. T., and S. Kennedy. "Insights into the 'Healthy Immigrant Effect': Health Status and Health Service Use of Immigrants to Canada." *Social Science and Medicine* 59 (2004): 1613–1627.

Newbold, K. B., and J. Danforth. "Health Status and Canada's Immigrant Populations." *Social Science and Medicine* 57, no. 10 (2003): 1981–1995.

Perez, C. "Health Status and Health Behavior among Immigrants." Supplement to *Health Reports* 13 (2002). Statistics Canada Catalog 82-003.

Read, J. G., and M. O. Emerson. "Racial Context, Black Immigration and the U.S. Black/White Health Disparity." *Social Forces* 84, no. 1 (2005): 181–199.

Read, J. G., M. O. Emerson, and A. Tarlov. "Implications of Black Immigrant Health for U.S. Racial Disparities in Health." *Journal of Immigrant Health* 7, no. 3 (2005): 205–212.

Salant, T., and D. S. Lauderdale. "Measuring Culture: A Critical Review of Acculturation and Health in Asian Immigrant Populations." *Social Science and Medicine* 57 (2003): 71–90.

Scribner, R., and J. H. Dwyer. "Acculturation and Low Birthweight among Latinos in the Hispanic HANES." *American Journal of Public Health* 79 (1989): 1263–1267.

U.S. Bureau of the Census. *The Black Population: 2000 Census of Population and Housing.* Washington, D.C.: U.S. Department of Commerce, Economics and Statistics Administration, 2000.

U.S. Department of Health and Human Services, National Center for Health Statistics. *2003 National Health Interview Survey Description: Division of Health Interview Statistics and Centers for Disease Control and Prevention.* Washington, D.C., December 2004.

U.S. Department of Homeland Security, Office of Immigration Statistics. *Yearbook of Immigration Statistics.* Washington, D.C., 2004.

Williams, D. R. "Race and Health: Basic Questions, Emerging Directions." *Annals of Epidemiology* 7 (1997): 322–333.

Williams, D. R., and C. Collins. "U.S. Socio-Economic and Racial Difference in Health." *Annual Review of Sociology* 21 (1995): 349–386.

Yu, S. M., Z. J. Huang, and G. K. Singh. "Health Status and Health Services Utilization among U.S. Chinese, Asian Indian, Filipino and other Asian/Pacific Islander Children." *Pediatrics* 113 (2004): 101–107.

9

SOCIO-LEGAL BARRIERS TO THE FULL CITIZENSHIP OF RECENT AFRICAN IMMIGRANTS IN CANADA: SOME PRELIMINARY THOUGHTS

Obiora Chinedu Okafor

The central thesis that is developed in this chapter is that notwithstanding the understandable and sometimes justified claims that are often made to the effect that we now live in a "multicultural Canada,"[1] some important aspects of Canada's immigration-related policies and practices (and other relevant and related regimes) have combined to ensure that, in reality, far too many recent African immigrants in Canada have remained significantly distant from the attainment of the full citizenship quite admirably promised by Canada's laudable aspirations to the entrenchment of a multicultural governance framework.[2] This thesis will be developed by discussing two illustrative aspects of Canada's immigration-related policies and practices that constitute some of the socio-legal obstacles to the attainment of full citizenship by most recent African immigrants. These obstacles serve to produce and/or reproduce a sense and experience of suboptimal citizenship within this immigrant population. The issues I will discuss are the problems caused by immigration processing backlogs, and the lack of a fair foreign credentials recognition system. These issues will be examined in the same order listed here.

But first, two caveats must be entered. The first is that almost all of the difficulties faced by these African immigrants are also experienced by most other "third-world" or "non–Western European" immigrant populations, such as those from the Indian subcontinent or Latin America. Thus the intention here is not really to offer an account of a *peculiarly* or *exclusively* African immigrant experience in Canada. African immigrants in Canada do not in general face much greater difficulties in the relevant respects than these other third-world immigrants. I intend, rather, to identify and show how particular policies and practices work in effect to construct recent African (and other) immigrants in Canada as less than full citizens. The second caveat is that although I am intensely aware of the difference between an immigrant and a refugee, and of the dangers of conflating the two categories, I nevertheless use the generic term "immigrant" in this chapter to include those refugees who have been granted permanent residence, and who therefore stand in substantially the same position as other recent African immigrants in Canada.

While a great deal of work has been done on "citizenship," and scholars from Hannah Arendt to Will Kymlicka and Joseph Carens have ably theorized its meaning,[3] the concept of citizenship (at least in its ideal form) that I invoke here denotes and suggests the approximately co-equal and actual enjoyment by all the formally accepted members of a society (virtually as one class) of all the rights and responsibilities attributable to membership in that polity.[4] In other words, reference to "citizenship" in this chapter suggests a substantive rather than a formalistic understanding of that concept.

IMMIGRATION PROCESSING BACKLOGS

At some point in the histories of their migration to Canada, a very high proportion of recent African immigrants in Canada will have spouses, children, and/or parents who still live in another country, usually in Africa, and whom these immigrants would quite naturally like to bring to Canada. The text of the relevant Canadian immigration laws, especially Section 3(d) (on family reunion), Section 13(1) (on the sponsorship of the family class), and Section 11 (on their right to be granted permanent resident status) of the Canadian Immigration and Refugee Protection Act (the Act), as well as Section 117 (on the definition of the family class) and Sections 130, 131, and 133 of the Canadian Immigration and Refugee Protection Regulations (the Regulations), do together recognize this imperative need for genuine family physical union or reunion. For this reason, Canadian immigration law does mandate the grant of permanent residence status to the foreign spouses, children, or parents of qualified Canadian citizens or permanent residents as long as the relevant foreign relatives are not otherwise inadmissible to Canada.[5]

A detailed discussion of the grounds on which these foreign spouses or children could be declared inadmissible and therefore excluded from uniting or reuniting with their Canadian immigrant relative is beyond the scope of this chapter.[6] So is a detailed discussion of what it means to be a "qualified" Canadian immigrant who can sponsor a spouse or child's permanent residence application.[7] Yet it is important, in the present context, to note that not every immigrant, and thus not every intending recent African immigrant in Canada, qualifies as a sponsor. In many cases there are certain income, criminality, and other such restrictions on who can sponsor a foreign relative.[8] There are also high processing/cost recovery fees that must be paid.[9] These restrictions affect recent African immigrants, a significant percentage of whom are relatively poor.

This section does not focus on such issues. It focuses on another kind of troubling barrier to sponsorship, one that has affected or can affect virtually every recent African immigrant in Canada regardless of their membership in the class of qualified sponsors. This is the issue of the highly excessive delays to spousal or other family unions or reunions that are routinely caused by heavy immigration processing backlogs, and which cause great pain for the immigrants involved and their family members. While the wait times for one type of family reunion application (i.e., spousal sponsorships) to be processed to completion are getting shorter globally, they are still quite long in absolute terms. In any case, until most recently, these wait times tended on the average to last about two years at most immigration posts in Africa (outside Pretoria, South Africa). And the processing wait times for the other kinds of family sponsorship applications have thus far not decreased significantly either.

For much of the last decade, the close foreign relatives of recent African immigrants in Canada have tended to experience far more delays than the foreign family members of most Western European immigrants. Processing times for various immigration applications submitted to Canadian missions in Africa were, generally speaking, significantly longer than in Western Europe, but were a bit shorter when compared to the collective evidence from the posts located in highly populated Asia. For example, as of April 2006, of the five immigration posts around the world listed by the Canadian government as the ones at which applications take the longest to process on average, two were in Africa.[10] What is more, those two African posts (Accra in Ghana and Abidjan in the Cote d'Ivoire) are the two slowest posts on this list of five.[11] During the relevant period, it took twenty-five months on average to process a spousal application to completion in Accra and twenty-one months in Abidjan.[12] Keep in mind that there are only five permanent resident processing posts on the entire African continent.[13] However, it must be said in contrast that, for reasons that are not all that difficult to fathom, Pretoria (South Africa) enjoys the reputation of being one of the posts at which spousal applications are most speedily processed.[14] Most instructively, no Western European visa processing post appears on the list of the five slowest spousal processing Canadian immigration missions around the world.[15]

The contrast is not as sharp when the African evidence is placed against the evidence concerning the foreign family members of other third-world immigrant populations. Nor is it as sharp when the combined evidence regarding the time it takes to process all types of permanent residence applications made in Western European immigration posts is contrasted against the African evidence. Yet, it is important to realize that on the average, 30 percent of *all types* of permanent resident applications submitted in Europe are finalized within 7 months, as opposed to 9 months in Africa. The point remains, therefore, that howsoever one slices and dices the relevant evidence, in nearly every case, the Canadian immigration posts that are located in Africa tend to appear at the top of the list of missions at which the longest visa processing delays occur.

Some of the reasons offered for this greater-than-average incidence of excessive delays in the processing of family sponsorship and other immigration applications at visa posts located in Africa are not far-fetched. While there is some truth to the reasons often attributed to the Canadian government—including the need to take time to filter out undesirable foreigners such as those who arrange marriages merely for immigration purposes, people with criminal records, people who will make bogus refugee claims when they reach Canada, or people who will not be able to support themselves financially when they get to Canada[16]—these reasons do not adequately explain the huge discrepancies between most European and most African immigration posts in the processing of spousal applications, for example. Unless it is assumed that African immigrants in Canada will tend to have *far more* fake marriages than Europeans living in Canada (an unsupported assumption if ever there was one), it is very difficult to justify the difference in processing times (as opposed to the differential refusal rates) on the basis of virtually all of the reasons offered by the Canadian government.

While other unofficial reasons of course exist, there seem to be important structural/institutional reasons for this bias against the speedier processing of the family reunion applications made by recent African immigrants in Canada. Reliance here on structural/institutional reasons as major (not total) explanations for this problem is bolstered by the significant drops in the average global processing times for spousal applications recorded between 2002 and 2005, thanks to the infusion of appreciably more resources into that aspect of permanent residence processing. For that period, there was a relatively rapid *global* rise in the proportion of applications processed to completion in six months or less, from a mere 38 percent in 2002 to a much more robust 63 percent in 2005.[17] However, these global numbers do not tell the entire story. To an appreciable extent, the African numbers still lag behind.

The institutional reasons for the structural bias against family reunion and other kinds of immigration from Africa can be found in two aspects of immigration processing: (1) the relatively small number of Canadian missions in Africa (especially vis-à-vis Europe), and the narrower scope of services provided by most them; and (2) the *inferred* lack of sufficient resources in the African posts. First of all, clear evidence of underservicing as a result of the establishment of an insufficient number of immigration processing posts in Africa exists. Only 5 out of 14 African offices (that is, Cairo, Accra, Abidjan, Nairobi, and Pretoria) provide the full range of immigration processing services, i.e., including permanent resident application processing. What is more, three of the African missions (Addis Ababa, Algiers, and Dar-es-Salaam) do not process any immigration applications at all, but refer them to other missions in Europe or Africa. In contrast, the vast majority of the posts in Europe provide a full range of services, including permanent resident application processing. Three out of eleven Canadian missions in Europe (Prague, Belgrade, and Budapest) do not process permanent resident applications. Thus, only about 27 percent of the African posts process permanent resident applications while roughly 64 percent of the European missions handle the same task. Yet the total number of spousal permanent residence applications processed in Europe is not significantly higher than the total number of applications processed in Africa. What is more, since 1997 African and Middle East processing posts have together handled more spousal and other family class applications than their European counterparts.[18] And so, with only five posts to Europe's eight, African/Middle East posts have sought to handle as many or even more such applications. No wonder the processing times were higher in Africa—much to the disadvantage (and even distress) of many of the recent African immigrants who typically sponsor such applications.

Secondly, a conclusion that can be *inferred* from the relatively small number of immigration processing posts located in Africa, the significantly longer processing times at almost all African visa posts, and the success at cutting wait times significantly that has been enjoyed by many visa posts when they have received increased allocations of human and financial resources, is the fact that the immigration processing posts in Africa do not presently possess adequate resources to deal expeditiously with the relatively large number of applications that are filed at those posts. At the very least, these posts currently lack the resources to deal with the number of applications that they receive in a fashion that would bring the wait times their "clients" experience closer to those of their seemingly better-resourced European counterparts. The relative scarcity of visa offices that provide the full range of visa services in Africa, and the longer processing times that this deficiency has helped produce, may be viewed as factors impeding the access to Canadian immigration of the close relatives of recent African immigrants in Canada. In this connection, it is worth noting that over the past ten years no African country was among the top 10–16 source countries from which permanent residents came to Canada.[19] Indeed, during 1995–2005, family class migration numbers from Africa were generally 20–30 percent lower than similar migration figures from Europe. Economic class migration to Canada from Africa was also 3–20 percent lower than from Europe. This is an empirical proxy for the "lack" that is felt by far too many recent African immigrants in Canada in relation to the fullness of their Canadian citizenship.

The highly excessive delays that have resulted from these problems of insufficient resource allocation (hence the fewer immigration posts and the longer processing times in Africa) have had important negative impacts within the recent African immigrant community in Canada. As a Canadian citizen who has waited for a long time to be reunited with her Rwandan economist/banker husband who holds a *Schengen* passport has put it, "waiting months and years to be reunited can destroy your personal life. And what business does the government have destroying my personal life?"[20] If a Canadian-born citizen who more likely than not has a family here can feel this way, how much more an already vulnerable recent African immigrant who in the vast majority of the cases has no close family in Canada? It is no wonder, then, that spousal relationships can, and sometimes have, gone awry largely as a result of long, enforced separations of spouses. Spouses, children, and parents are in effect deprived of the care and love of their close relatives, and some have even gone as far as describing their admittedly very difficult experience of family separation as unmitigated, unalloyed, "cruel and unusual punishment."[21] Just as importantly, many in the community of recent African immigrants are as a result forced to feel and experience the reality of their lack of full citizenship.

It can, of course, be argued that as these processing backlogs apply to Canadian citizen and non-citizen alike, there is no discrimination involved, and hence the latter cannot on this basis alone claim that they have been treated as suboptimal citizens. There is a grain of truth in this argument. The reality, however, is that relatively few within the wider community can or do in fact have this kind of experience. For the most part, this intensely negative experience is the preserve of third-world (including African) immigrant communities in Canada, among whom a very large number of people either have had the same experience or know many who have. Therefore, the production of negative meaning about citizenship that is associated with this experience of temporary exclusion tends to be similarly concentrated in these communities. Besides, even though citizen and non-citizen alike can experience the long separations and negative effects thereof that are caused by excessive immigration delays, the already secure sense of belonging of most Canadian-born citizens is much less liable to be shaken, destabilized, and pushed in negative directions by the experience of enforced separation from their spouses, children, or parents.

My claim here, then, is that the excessive delays in the physical union or reunion of recent African immigrants in Canada and their spouses, children, parents, and other close relatives, which result from the significantly larger immigration backlogs and fewer immigration processing posts in Africa (especially as compared to Western European processing posts), cause much pain in the personal and other lives of far too many such immigrants. The unavoidable effect of these conditions is a real sense and experience of suboptimal citizenship within this community.

AN UNFAIR CREDENTIALS RECOGNITION SYSTEM

For many years now, there has been growing recognition within Canada, and even within the highest echelons of government, of the relative unfairness of many of the processes and systems put in place by the various professional bodies in most provinces to assess and recognize the credentials of foreign-trained (and therefore mostly foreign-born) professionals such as doctors, nurses, and engineers.[22] This has made it hard for far too many immigrants to find a job that is appropriate to their level of training and education.[23] Canada's former Liberal Party government paid some attention, however belated, to this problem when it announced its foreign credentials recognition (FCR) program in April 2005.[24] The current Conservative government has also recognized this problem and has pledged to address it.[25]

Much of the public discourse on this FCR problem has, however, centered on the fact that while Canada is in the throes of a doctor shortage, a large number of mostly third-world-trained immigrant doctors have been forced by the non-recognition of their credentials to take up taxi-driving or janitorial jobs in their adopted country. In many cases, such doctors have been forced to drive these taxis even when they have already passed their Canadian re-qualifying exams. The problem for the most part has been the requirement that most third-world doctors undertake internships after passing their written qualifying exams. This is a problem in Canada because of the serious dearth of such internship positions relative to the number of qualified foreign-trained doctors. Since it is the issue of "foreign-trained doctors as taxi drivers" that has dominated Canadian discussions of the FCR problem, this section will focus on the situation of these doctors as illustrative of the difficulties posed by often unfair or inadequate credentials recognition systems—systems which continue to deny far too many recent African immigrants the attainment of full integration into Canadian professional life and thus a secure sense of citizenship in the country.

This particular (though still allegorical) foreign-trained doctor problem will be illustrated through a discussion of a fairly recent Canadian human rights law case on the issue. In *Bitonti v. College of Physicians and Surgeons of British Columbia*,[26] the Human Rights Tribunal of the Province of British Columbia was faced with a human rights challenge that had been launched against the credentials recognition system established by that province's College of Physicians and Surgeons. Although this case did not involve any African immigrants, it demonstrates some of the very same problems faced by them when they seek to have their foreign credentials recognized in Canada, especially in the professional medical fields. This case was brought by five immigrant doctors from around the world, two of whom were, interestingly, Italian. Their names are Rosa Bitonti and Gabriele Salvadori (from Italy), Adina Alexescu (from Romania), Teofilo Goyengko (from the Phillipines), and Raminder Singh Randhawa (from India). They alleged that the FCR system that applied to immigrant doctors who wanted to practice medicine in British Columbia discriminated against them on the basis of their country of origin and thus prevented them from obtaining internships required as a part of the professional licensing system for people from certain countries. At the relevant time, the B.C. College of Physicians and Surgeons distinguished between two categories of physicians: Category I included graduates of medical schools in Canada, the United States, Great Britain, Ireland, Australia, New Zealand, or South Africa, while Category II included graduates of medical schools anywhere else in the world. Applicants from Category II had to complete a hospital internship, while foreign-trained doctors from Category I were allowed to bypass the internship requirement after passing the evaluating exam and to immediately begin their practice. The tribunal found in their favor, holding that this scheme did discriminate against the applicants on the basis of their place of origin. The tribunal therefore ordered the College to negotiate a resolution with the doctors. In particular, the tribunal noted that it was

> particularly troubling that, while graduates of Category I medical schools were assumed to be qualified because they had done one year of post-graduate training in one of those countries, those from Category II schools were not assumed to be qualified even if they had done two years of post-graduate training in those countries. Moreover, there was no mechanism in place by which those graduates from Category II schools could demonstrate that their training met the standards demanded of Canadian doctors.[27]

Although this system is no longer in place in British Columbia, there continue to be serious obstacles to the recognition of the credentials of even excellent foreign doctors in that province. The most serious obstacle remains access to internship positions. For instance, in 2006, only eighteen such positions were available in that province.[28] This means that no matter how well a foreign doctor performs, if she does not rank in the top eighteen, she will be forced to continue working as a janitor or in some other position that underutilizes her skills. This is clearly not fair to bright immigrants, most of whom come to Canada with the reasonable expectation of improving, and not lowering, their professional, social, and economic status. The situation in Ontario, Canada's largest, most populated, and most diverse province, is not all that different.[29]

It could, of course, be argued by some that the College of Physicians and Surgeons was justified in discriminating in this way against foreign-trained doctors from everywhere else except the five anglophone and mostly "white Commonwealth" countries noted above. It could be said in favor of this argument that doctors from these countries tend to speak the same English language as most Canadians, and tend to speak it with fairly similar accents. Yet, it is unclear what scientific value there is to a similarity of accents. After all, the essential objective is to cure the patient! Clearly, almost all the immigrant doctors who have passed the highly demanding written qualifying exams and who live here speak the English language well enough. It could be said, in the college's favor, that it was right to be cautious about the qualifications of third-world-trained doctors and to require more training from these doctors than from doctors trained in Britain or Australia. Again, this argument is unconvincing. Whatever power this argument might have is neutralized by the fact that the doctors in question have already passed the rigorous written qualifying exams set by the same College. To hinge final certification on a successful internship in an atmosphere where such doctors virtually never secure such internship positions is to effectively deny these foreign-trained doctors an *opportunity* to demonstrate their competence. They are denied certification not because they are incompetent, but because they have not been given any opportunity to show that they are competent.

While scholarly debate continues to rage as to the exact effect on recent immigrants to Canada of failure to recognize and utilize their skills in the labor market, there is near unanimity among serious scholars that this has had some negative impact on the immigrant experience of these newcomers to Canada.[30] The severely negative effects of the difficulties faced by new immigrant professionals (including recent African immigrants) in securing the recognition of their skills and in gaining employment in their fields of training are fully acknowledged even by the Canadian government. As Canada's new Conservative prime minister, Stephen Harper, has acknowledged, "The biggest barrier to new Canadians [that is immigrants] is the frequent failure to recognize legitimate foreign credentials. Whenever this happens, not only are *the dreams of individuals and families shattered*, but Canada as a whole is deprived of all they have to offer."[31] Indeed, the Paul Martin–led Liberal Party government that preceded the current Stephen Harper–led Conservative regime also recognized these negative effects. For instance, the then–Canadian Minister of Human Resources and Skills Development, Lucienne Robillard, was convinced that the FCR program she initiated to attempt to fix this problem was "crucial to enhancing the cultural vibrancy of our society and maintaining our country's commitment to *equality of opportunity* so that *prosperity can be shared by all Canadians*."[32]

The shattered dreams of individuals and families that the Government itself has recognized, the denial of equal opportunity this situation has fostered, and the frustrations in the daily lives of these immigrants and their families combine to produce the impression and reality of sub-optimal citizenship among many recent immigrants, including the African community in Canada.

Happily, work has already begun and efforts are currently being made, however modestly, to fix this serious problem. As I have noted above, in 2005 the Liberal Party government established its FCR Program. This program was intended to address this problem by providing $68 million to improve the integration of immigrants and foreign-trained Canadians into the work force by funding "stakeholder organizations" such as the Canadian Council of Professional Engineers and the Canadian Tourism Human Resource Council in their efforts to tackle the problem.[33] The then–Minister of Health, Ujjal Dosanjh, had also announced a $75 million program to speed up the assessment and integration into the Canadian workforce of up to 1,000 physicians, 800 nurses, and 500 other regulated health care professionals.[34] It is not clear to what extent these objectives were achieved before the Liberal government lost power early in 2006.

Recognizing for its own part that Canada "owes it to new Canadians to fix this [credentials recognition] problem," the governing Conservative Party of Canada initially indicated an intention to create a special agency for recognition of foreign qualifications and to cooperate with provincial authorities and professional associations in the process.[35] At first the Harper-led government appeared to set aside funds for the creation of the new foreign credentials recognition agency.[36] However, the agency was never established in the originally promised form. In its stead, the Government has promised to create a foreign credential *referral* agency.

*   *   *

This chapter has tried to establish that by operating unduly lengthy immigration processing backlogs and an unfair foreign credentials recognition system, among other impediments, the Canadian immigration policy and practice have tended to produce a sense and experience of sub-optimal citizenship among recent African immigrants in Canada. To demonstrate this point, I have not only exposed the nature of these backlogs but have also identified and analyzed the institutional and structural reasons for their persistence, as well as highlighted the resultant human costs thereof. In addition, I have illustrated the unfairness of the foreign credentials recognition system in most parts of Canada by drawing attention to the situation of foreign-trained medical doctors in the province of British Columbia and pointed to the effects of this system on the lives of recent African (and other) immigrant doctors and their families. I also noted the incipient efforts of the Canadian federal government to redress this credentials recognition problem. If recent African immigrants in Canada are to fully realize and enjoy the lofty promise of formal Canadian citizenship, the kinds of policies and practices discussed in this chapter—which help to produce widespread dissatisfaction and skepticism among these newcomers about their full acceptance within Canadian society—ought to be reformed and reoriented in ways that would minimize if not eliminate their unfairness.

NOTES

Some of the data and insights discussed in this chapter rely on a research memorandum written to me by Sasha Baglay, who was at the time a doctoral candidate at Osgoode Hall Law School and one of my research assistants. I am grateful to her for her excellent work in this regard. I should also express my gratitude to Shannon Kampf for her assistance in researching some aspects of the chapter.

1. See Harper, "Statement on Multiculturalism Day." This is at least implied in the work of the Multiculturalism Office in the Department of Canadian Heritage. See Department of Canadian Heritage, *Annual Report* iv, 3.

2. This framework is in part broadly outlined in the *Canadian Multiculturalism Act*.

3. For example, see Arendt; Sklar; Habermas; Taylor; Kymlicka and Norman; Kymlicka; and Carens.

4. This definition has been adapted from T. H. Marshall's work on the subject. See Marshall 58.

5. See Section 12 of the Act.

6. See Sections 33–40 of the Act.

7. See Sections 130, 131, and 133 of the Regulations.

8. For an excellent account of these restrictions and their effects, see Canadian Council for Refugees, *Non-Citizens in Canada, Equally Human, Equally Entitled to Rights* 2–5.

9. Ibid. 5.

10. See Citizenship and Immigration Canada, *Statistical Information: Applications Processed at Canadian Visa Offices* (on file with the author).

11. Ibid.

12. Ibid.

13. For a list of these posts and their mandates, see http://www.cic.gc.ca/english/offices/missions.html (accessed December 6, 2006).

14. See Citizenship and Immigration Canada, *Statistical Information*, supra note 10.

15. Ibid.

16. See *Montreal Gazette*, April 2, 2006.

17. For instance, see http://www.tbs-sct.gc.ca/dpr-rmr/0506/CI-CI/ci-cio5_e .asp#4_15 (accessed December 6, 2006).

18. See Citizenship and Immigration Canada, *Facts and Figures 2004— Immigration Overview: Permanent Residents* (on file with the author).

19. Ibid.

20. See *Montreal Gazette*, April 2, 2006.

21. Ibid.

22. See Standing Committee of the House of Commons on Citizenship and Immigration (Canada), *A Sense of Belonging—"Feeling at Home"* (June 2003); Bauder; Reitz; Wayland 24; MOSAIC.

23. See Campbell Cohen, "Foreign Credentials Recognized in a Conservative Canada."

24. See Human Resources and Skills Development (Canada), press release, April 25, 2005 (on file with the author).

25. See *Globe and Mail*, February 25, 2006.

26. *Bitonti v. College of Physicians and Surgeons of British Columbia* [1999] B.C.H.R.T.D. no. 60.

27. Ibid., paragraph 178.

28. See http://www.IMG-Canada.ca (accessed April 5, 2006).

29. Ibid.

30. Contrast Bauder, who argues that it is one of the main causes of the significantly lower income of highly educated recent immigrants vis-à-vis their Canadian-born and educated counterparts, and Picot and Sweetman, who do not seem to attribute as much significance to the lack of recognition of foreign credentials in explaining the differential in the income of recent immigrants to Canada.

31. See "Address by the Hon. Stephen Harper, P.C., M.P., Leader of the Conservative Party of Canada," January 4, 2006 (on file with the author), 1; emphasis added.

32. See *Foreign Credentials Recognition Program—Immigrants, Foreign-Trained Canadians to Benefit from Government of Canada Investments*, April 25, 2005 (on file with the author). Emphasis added.

33. Ibid.

34. See "Health Minister Dosanjh Announces $75 Million Initiative to Bring More Internationally Educated Professionals into [the] Health Care System," April 25, 2005 (on file with the author).

35. See "Address by Stephen Harper," supra note 28 at 2.

36. See Harper, "Promoting Opportunity for New Canadians."

REFERENCES

Arendt, H. *Origins of Totalitarianism.* London: George Allen and Unwin, 1967.

Bauder, H. "'Brain Abuse,' or the Devaluation of Immigrant Labour in Canada." *Antipode* 35, no. 4 (2003): 699–717.

Bitonti v. College of Physicians and Surgeons of British Columbia [1999] B.C.H.R.T.D. no. 60.

Campbell Cohen. "Foreign Credentials Recognized in a Conservative Canada." http://www.canadavisa.com/foreign-credentials-recognized-in-a-conservative-canada.htm (accessed February 27, 2006).

Canadian Council for Refugees. *Non-Citizens in Canada, Equally Human, Equally Entitled to Rights.* March 2006. http://www.web.ca/ccr/CESCRsubmission.pdf (accessed March 21, 2006).

Canadian Multiculturalism Act. Revised Statutes of Canada 1985, c. 24, s. 4.

Carens, J. *Culture, Citizenship and Community: A Contextual Exploration of Justice as Evenhandedness.* Oxford: Oxford University Press, 2000.

Department of Canadian Heritage. *Annual Report on the Operation of the Canadian Multiculturalism Act, 2003–2004.* http://www.canadianheritage.gc.ca/progs/multi/reports/ann2003-2004/multi-ann-2003-2004_e.pdf (accessed April 5, 2006).

Globe and Mail, February 25, 2006.

Habermas, J. "Citizenship and National Identity: Some Reflection on the Future of Europe." *Praxis International* 12, no. 1 (1999): 1–19.

Harper, Stephen. "Promoting Opportunity for New Canadians." Address given in Mississauga, Ontario, May 12, 2006. http://www.pm.gc.ca/eng/media.asp?id=1159 (accessed December 6, 2006).

Harper, Stephen. "Statement on Multiculturalism Day." June 27, 2006. http://www.pm.gc.ca/eng/media.asp?id=1225 (accessed December 6, 2006).

Kymlicka, W. *Multicultural Citizenship.* Oxford: Clarendon Press, 1995.

Kymlicka, W., and W. Norman. "Return of the Citizen: A Survey of Recent Work on Citizenship Theory." *Ethics* 104 (1994): 352–381.

Marshall, T. H. *Citizenship and Social Class and Other Essays.* Cambridge: Cambridge University Press, 2000.

Montreal Gazette, April 2, 2006.

MOSAIC. *Improving Access to Licensure: A Report on the Access to Licensure in Regulated Professions for Internationally Trained Professionals in British Columbia.* Vancouver: MOSAIC, 2006.

Picot, G., and A. Sweetman. *The Deteriorating Economic Welfare of Immigrants and Possible Causes: Update 2005.* Report for Statistics Canada, Catalogue No. 11F0019 No. 262, 2005.

Reitz, J. G. "Tapping Immigrants' Skills." *Choices* 11, no. 1 (2005): 1–18.

Sklar, J. N. *American Citizenship: The Quest for Inclusion.* Cambridge, Mass.: Harvard University Press, 1991.

Taylor, C. "The Liberal-Communitarian Debate." In *Liberalism and Moral Life,* ed. N. Rosenblum. Cambridge, Mass.: Harvard University Press, 1989. 178.

Wayland, S. V. *Unsettled: Legal and Policy Barriers for Newcomers to Canada.* Report for the Law Commission of Canada and the Community Foundations of Canada, 2006.

10 THE EFFECTS OF IMMIGRATION AND REFUGEE POLICIES ON AFRICANS IN THE UNITED STATES: FROM THE CIVIL RIGHTS MOVEMENT TO THE WAR ON TERRORISM

Cassandra R. Veney

People from Africa and people of African descent have been coming to the United States for hundreds of years. Some of the migrations have been voluntary while others have been involuntary or forced. While we often think of the historic African diaspora as those individuals who are the descendents of the four million slaves emancipated in 1865, it is important to point out that the first Africans brought to the early British colonies in what later become the United States were not slaves but indentured servants. Migrants from Cape Verde came to the United States, mainly Massachusetts, in the latter part of the nineteenth century to work in the whaling industry, in the textile mills, and later in the cranberry bogs, while a small number of Africans traveled to the United States for educational and political reasons (Frazier). However, it was not until late in the twentieth century that large numbers of African immigrants began to resettle permanently in the country with the passage of the Hart-Cellar Immigration Act in 1965, "which ushered in sweeping changes to immigration policy by abolishing the national origins quota system as the basis for immigration and replacing it with a seven-category preference system for the allocation of immigrant visas" (Jernegan).

Eissa argues that the "drafting and passing of the Act is widely considered to have been spawned by the ideology of the Civil Rights Movement." The possibility of applying for refugee status was basically non-existent until "Congress codified and strengthened the United States' historic policy of aiding individuals fleeing persecution in their homelands. The Refugee Act of 1980 provided a formal definition of 'refugee,' which is virtually identical to the definition in the 1967 United Nations Protocol Relating to the Status of Refugees" (U.S. Office of Refugee Resettlement).[1]

Furthermore, "the definition of 'asylee' followed the new definition of 'refugee'" (Leibowitz 168). Both refugees and asylees had to prove that they had a well-founded fear of persecution based on their membership in a particular race, religion, nationality, social class, or political opinion and that they were unwilling or unable to return to their countries of origin (Leibowitz). Finally, the Immigration Reform and Control Act (IRCA) of 1986 allowed undocumented immigrants to regularize their stay in the country and enacted mandatory employer sanctions that made it a crime to employ a person who was not legally allowed to work in the country (American Friends Service Committee).

Individuals who had entered the country illegally or who had entered legally but let their visas expire could now become permanent residents and later apply for citizenship—several thousand African immigrants took advantage of the legislation. Therefore, African refugees and immigrants are a recent phenomenon. African refugees and immigrants came to the United States and continue to come at a time when the media, politicians, and citizens are preoccupied with welfare reform that is in essence a "new" war on poverty and an extension of the war on drugs. The more recent war on terrorism completes the trinity. In addition, many individuals from various sectors of society grappling with the political, economic, and social fallout from Hurricane Katrina as American-born citizens, albeit African American, Latino, and poor whites, have been characterized as refugees—stripped of their citizenship simply because they were unable or unwilling to evacuate New Orleans before the onslaught of the hurricane.

This chapter has three goals. First, it will situate the admissions of refugees and immigrants from Africa within the context of the Civil Rights Movement. Second, it will examine various public policies prior to September 11, 2001, and examine how they affected African refugee and immigrant men, women, and children in an effort to provide the gender dynamics of being an African refugee, immigrant, or asylum seeker in the pre–9/11 and post–9/11 eras. Third, it will examine those same policies following the 2001 terrorist attacks, to argue that the current war on terrorism is not new and is not just waged against Middle Eastern, South Asian, and North African refugees, asylum seekers, and immigrants; instead, Africans throughout the continent and those seeking to enter the U.S. have been adversely affected. The restrictions have made it increasingly difficult for them to enter the country and have deprived them of their rights once they have entered (Chishti).

CIVIL RIGHTS AND AFRICAN REFUGEES

Many commentators, academics, and policy makers are quick to point out that immigration has affected, and will negatively affect, African Americans in terms of jobs, housing, affirmative action, and social services and that African Americans harbor anti-immigrant sentiments that extend to refugees. What they fail to recognize and acknowledge is the role of African Americans in immigration and refugee reform legislation that is situated within the context of gains made by African Americans as part of the Civil Rights Movement, and how those gains were translated into political demands for more equitable immigration and refugee policies that allowed thousands of previously excluded Africans to resettle in the United States. The Civil Rights Movement was not meant to bring about equality, freedom, democracy, and social justice just for African Americans with a long experience of human rights violations and terrorist attacks by the government and private citizens; the gains of the movement were intended to be inclusive (Eissa). Therefore, when more African Americans were elected to Congress as a result of the Voting Rights Act of 1965 and the creation of majority-minority districts, these legislators used their positions on various House of Representatives committees and subcommittees, as well as their national reputations, to advocate fairer immigration and refugee policies.

These political developments undergirded the establishment of the Congressional Black Caucus (CBC), created in 1971 after nine African Americans were elected to the House of Representatives. The Senate remains predominately white and male. Members of the CBC openly characterized the U.S. refugee admissions policy as racist and lobbied to increase the ceiling for African refugees (Pojmann). The 1980 Refugee Act, supported by the CBC, allowed for the admission of more refugees from the Caribbean and Latin America (many of them of African descent) who fled from civil wars, political violence, and human rights abuses. But their numbers were not equal to those of refugees coming from Southeast Asia and later the Soviet Union, its Eastern European bloc, and Cuba—these large numbers reflected U.S. relations with the refugee-generating countries, which were all communist.

The bulk of refugees admitted to the United States from the 1970s to the 1990s were from the Soviet Union and Southeast Asia—approximately three-quarters (Ryan). The Refugee Act of 1980 allowed refugees from Africa to be admitted to the United States for the first time; however, the majority of African refugees were Ethiopian and Eritrean (Woldemikael 1996). Subsequently, beginning in the 1980s, the numbers of African refugees who applied for political asylum and were resettled in the United States slowly began to increase. For example, the ceiling for African refugees for fiscal year 1980 was only 2,000, and in 1981 4,200 African refugees were admitted; ten years later, in 1990, the ceiling had only increased to 7,000, and by fiscal years 2005 and 2006, the number had increased to 20,000. These refugees were mainly from the Horn of Africa (Ethiopia and Somalia), which represented a contested space in the superpower rivalry between the United States and the Soviet Union. It is no wonder that between 1980 and 2002, 35,000 Ethiopian and 40,000 Somali refugees were resettled in the United States (Emergency Committee for African Refugees; U.S. Department of State).

The IRCA, which had its critics, was also supported by the CBC in terms of it allowing undocumented immigrants who had been in the country since 1982 to legalize their status and remain in the country. There were thousands of African immigrants who benefited from this legislation. TransAfrica, the major lobbying group for African issues, the CBC, the National Association for the Advancement of Colored People (NAACP), and ordinary African Americans kept up with events in Ethiopia, Somalia, South Africa, and other African countries that experienced political violence during the 1980s, and did not necessarily view the admissions of these refugees as displacing them from their homes, communities, and jobs. The late congresswoman Shirley Chisholm illustrated this position when she stated, "We must not be tempted by those who use immigrants and refugees as scapegoats for the economic plight of black Americans. We must be willing to advocate for the protection of black refugees" (24). Members of the CBC including William Gray, Walter Fauntroy, Mervyn Dymally, Harold Ford, Sr., Julian Dixon, and Shirley Chisholm supported legislation to reinstate Extended Voluntary Departure (EVD) status—later changed to Temporary Protected Status (TPS)—for Ethiopians, which the Reagan administration had revoked in 1981 under the pretext that Ethiopians did not qualify for such protection because they had come before or soon after the ouster of Emperor Haile Selassie in 1974. By the early 1980s, the political climate in the country was safe enough for them to return (according to the Reagan administration), despite representations by Ethiopians in the U.S. (including students and professors) that vast segments of the Ethiopian population suffered from the Red Terror campaign and other human rights abuses (Emergency Committee for African Refugees; Veney).

Advocacy for African refugees was manifested in the work of the NAACP. For example, the late Benjamin Hooks, who served as the NAACP's executive director during the 1980s, was also in the forefront of the fight to reinstate the EVD status that the Carter administration had granted to Ethiopian refugees in 1977. Hooks, representing the NAACP, openly called the revocation racist (Lapchick, Hooks, and Williams). In sum, these politicians, individuals, and organizations represented members of a community that for hundreds of years had fought for basic citizenship rights, a struggle in which thousands of lives had been sacrificed along the way. Their main focus could have been on the myriad of problems and issues that plagued African Americans who had been politically, socially, educationally, and economically disfranchised. Instead, they championed African causes (including the plight of refugees) in Congress, in the media, and in public forums and lobbied over the years to raise the ceiling for African refugees.

These organizations have continued to use various tactics and strategies to bring to the attention of U.S. policy makers, the media, and ordinary American citizens the atrocities of the former apartheid regime in South Africa, along with the civil wars and unrest in Sudan, Liberia, Rwanda, Burundi, Sierra Leone, the Democratic Republic of Congo, Kenya, Cote d'Ivoire, and other African countries that have led thousands to flee their homelands in search of sanctuary. Again, the CBC was in the forefront of efforts to extend TPS to Liberians, and when the Clinton and second Bush administrations moved to rescind the designation on the grounds that conditions in the country had improved and Liberians were then safe to return home, they worked against such a reversal in policy. However, the political climate in the U.S. shifted more to the right, and the Democrat President Clinton had to contend with a Republican, conservative majority in the House and Senate. This development, coupled with the first terrorist attack on the World Trade Center (1993) as well as other attacks in Yemen and Beirut, did not bode well for less restrictive refugee and immigration policies.

IMMIGRATION POLICIES IN THE PRE-9/11 ERA

Prior to the September 11, 2001, terrorist attacks on the World Trade Center, the Pentagon, and an airplane in Shanksville, Pennsylvania, U.S. domestic and foreign policy makers, the media, and the American public had been already preoccupied with identifying, rounding up, apprehending, detaining, and deporting those who were deemed to be foreign, alien, undocumented, and therefore illegal as part of the agenda to win the war on terrorism and to secure American borders. Those in the "foreign" category could even include legal, documented residents. Two events triggered this—the 1993 terrorist attack on the World Trade Center and the 1995 Oklahoma City bombing (Parker). It must be pointed out that the individuals involved in the Oklahoma City bombing were American-born and had no links to foreign terrorist groups. The passage of the Illegal Immigration Reform and Immigrant Responsibility Act (IIRIRA), signed into law by President Clinton in 1996, served as a clear indication of future public policies that would have an adverse effect on African refugees and immigrants. According to Handmaker and Singh, "the passage of the Illegal Immigration Reform and Immigrant Responsibility Act of 1996 (IIRIRA) radically altered United States asylum law. Significantly, there are three aspects to IIRIRA that have increased the barriers to gaining refugee status and radically affected the rights of asylum seekers in the United States" (12). The act allowed for the detention and deportation of legal immigrants with green cards if they were convicted of offenses that included shoplifting, assault, selling marijuana, vandalism, drunk driving, and tax evasion (Parker).

More serious crimes that came under the aggravated felony category also resulted in individuals being detained and removed; however, this immigration law, unlike criminal law, allowed for a wide variety of crimes to be considered aggravated felonies. The law is also retroactive, which means that legal residents and immigrants can be detained and removed for crimes they committed in the past that were not considered aggravated felonies at the time (National Immigration Forum).

It is interesting to note that the year 1996 ushered in the era of welfare reform as demonstrated by the Personal Responsibility and Work Opportunity Reconciliation Act (PRWORA), also signed into law by Clinton. The clampdown on immigrants both legal and illegal coincided with a new war on poverty that focused on getting the welfare queen, who was mainly portrayed in the media as African American and Latina, into the workforce. In addition, the war on drugs was still being mounted against communities of color, including immigrant communities with African American, African, Caribbean, Latin American, and Asian residents. Anti-immigration developments in the post–9/11 phase were simply a continuation of those prior to 9/11. On one hand, the war on terrorism has targeted people who have their origins in the Middle East and South Asia (Ahmad). On the other hand, September 11 is directly connected to the increased concern, anxiety, and efforts to make our borders (especially the Mexican border) safe from those who attempt to cross illegally on a daily basis. September 11 has also served to keep our ports of entry, especially airports, closed to African refugees, immigrants, and asylum seekers.

Before we can understand current immigration and refugee policies, it is important for us to fundamentally understand that the decision to let people into the country legally and then give them the opportunity to regularize their status means that they eventually can become citizens. Each time Congress attempts to reform immigration laws to allow illegal immigrants to remain in the country and to adjust their status, there is much public outcry. Moreover, citizenship has always been racialized and gendered because it was viewed as an entitlement and a privilege. It was never intended to confer equality nor to eradicate the racial and gender hierarchy that continues to plague America. Citizenship was first granted to white males who owned property; later it was extended to white women, and then to Native Americans, African Americans, Asian Americans, and Latinos. Even American-born white women at one time lost their citizenship, through congressional acts, by marrying foreigners. This was an effort to maintain the racial and gender hierarchy by punishing women who married foreign men who were unable to become citizens. A woman took on the citizenship or immigrant status of her husband, along with his ethnicity. If he was a citizen, she would not lose her status; if he was not or could not become a citizen through naturalization, then she lost her American citizenship (Nicolosi). The 1790 Naturalization Act allowed only whites to become citizens through naturalization. Leslye Orloff argues convincingly: "Early United States immigration law incorporated the concept of coverture, which was a legislative enactment of the common law theory that the husband is the head of the household. Under it, the very being or legal existence of the woman was suspended during the marriage, or at least incorporated and consolidated into that of the husband, under whose wing, protection, and cover, she performs everything" (50).

Immigration scholar Timothy H. Edgar also argues that "immigrants in the United States face greater challenges than ever, and not only as a result of an unfortunate backlash against immigrants after the terrorist attacks of Sept. 11, 2001. Even before those attacks, immigrants in the U.S. were suffering the effects of punitive anti-immigration legislation passed in 1996" (171). The onslaught on the rights of citizens, legal residents, and the undocumented began in the pre-9/11 era with three particular pieces of legislation, although ten years earlier "undocumented immigrants who secured status under . . . (IRCA) generally were barred from major federal public assistance programs for five years after legalizing" (Blazer 1). First, the PRWORA made it more difficult for legal immigrants to survive in the country after initially being denied federal welfare benefits that included Supplemental Security Income (SSI), food stamps, Medicaid, Temporary Assistance to Needy Families (TANF), child health insurance, and public housing (Ewing; Edgar). After much outcry from immigration advocacy groups, Congress lessened its draconian policy and "restored SSI eligibility for most legal immigrants present in the country prior to the law's enactment. In 1998, Congress also restored food-stamp eligibility to immigrant children and those elderly or disabled immigrants present before the law's enactment" (Ewing). PRWORA was particularly harmful to women immigrants and their children (some were U.S.-born citizens), including African women in violent/abusive relationships and marriages in which they were dependent on their male partners for sponsorship and financial support.

It is well documented in the literature that immigrant households are viewed as being headed by men, and wives and children obtain their sponsorship through them. Many women remain in abusive partnerships because they fear they will be deported, their husbands will be deported, or they will not be able to adjust their status without their husbands. Moreover, "until a non-citizen has legal status, they can be deported at any time and cannot obtain permission to work legally" (Haynes). Welfare reform legislation that targeted immigrant women has served to keep women in abusive relationships due to these fears. The legislation made an exception for immigrant women who were battered and could prove that their battering was linked to their need for public assistance—which has made this provision fairly useless, as more and more immigrants (even those with documentation) are reluctant to reveal themselves to any U.S. authorities for fear they will be deported (Edgar). The same can be said for immigrant women who were supposed to benefit from the IIRIRA. Battered immigrant women were allowed to access public benefits that included public housing, the Special Supplemental Nutrition Program for Women, Infants, and Children (WIC), TANF, Medicaid, school lunch programs, and food banks. However, given the anti-immigrant sentiment and crackdown against legal and illegal individuals in the country, many immigrant women were afraid to ask for help, which meant that their children and other dependents suffered as they struggled to secure food, health care, housing, job training, and language skills.

Those who were undocumented were not entitled to receive any benefits under the new legislation. The gender and racial dimension of the legislation cannot be ignored. We know that the "American" targets of the legislation were primarily African American women who were viewed as lazy, unwilling to work, and having too many babies out of wedlock, followed by Latinas and then white women. The "foreign" targets of the legislation were women who, according to Timothy Edgar, "are far more likely than their male counterparts to receive public assistance" (174). These "foreign" targets included African refugees, asylees, and immigrants. Again, we do not see the white immigrants, either from the Caribbean (Cubans) or from Europe and Canada, who received welfare benefits; some of these African and black immigrant women were disabled, some were pregnant or had just given birth, some were underage, elderly, taking care of small children and elderly and sick family members, or simply unable to secure employment that was enough to meet individual or family needs.

PRE–9/11 LEGISLATION AND THE DETENTION OF IMMIGRANTS AND ASYLUM SEEKERS

The Illegal Immigration Reform and Immigrant Responsibility Act may have allowed battered immigrant women to receive benefits, but it wreaked havoc in other areas of their lives, along with the Anti-Terrorism and Effective Death Penalty Act (AEDPA), which " made it easier to arrest, detain, and deport non-citizens" (Jernegan). The American Friends Service Committee and other immigration advocacy groups reported that this legislation "authorized the use of secret evidence against noncitizens in certain types of legal proceedings. It also subjected immigrants—even legal permanent residents—to deportation for relatively minor offenses, even if they were committed in the past" (American Friends Service Committee). The AEDPA and IIRAIRA "produced an explosive increase in the number of people incarcerated in detention facilities," prompting the Immigration and Naturalization Service (INS)—later changed in 2003 to the Bureau of Citizenship and Immigration Services, under the Department of Homeland Security—"to lease space in county jails and private detention centers around the country" (American Friends Service Committee). For example, thanks to these two pieces of legislation, there were 5,532 people in INS detention in 1994 and 19,533 in fiscal year 2001, and their stays are getting longer (American Friends Service Committee).

THE DETENTION OF LEGAL AND ILLEGAL IMMIGRANTS AND ASYLUM SEEKERS: POST-9/11

The racial and gendered dynamics of mandatory detention deserve some discussion. In the post–9/11 era, we are led to believe that the detainees are all of Middle Eastern, North African, and South Asian descent, and that certainly all are terrorists who entered the country illegally. The truth of the matter is that the detainees include Russians, Poles, Irish, Ukrainians, Chinese, Western Europeans, Jamaicans, Dominicans, Cambodians, Vietnamese, Koreans, Africans, and others. Africans who have been detained come from a variety of countries that include the Democratic Republic of Congo, Sierra Leone, Liberia, Mali, Somalia, Cote d'Ivoire, Kenya, Zimbabwe, and so forth. Due to legislation passed before 9/11, legal immigrants are detained who have been convicted of a crime, sometimes a minor one. Furthermore, legal permanent residents can be detained for minor crimes committed in the past (even if they did not serve any time in jail for the offenses), whether their sentences were suspended or they were put on parole. They become part of the prison industry complex that is an extension of the government's war on drugs, which aims, with societal approval, to remove and make invisible those who are a drain on and a danger to society—primarily black and Latino men and teenagers. This detained population includes a wide variety of individuals—ranging from African Americans to Jamaicans, Dominicans, Colombians, Guyanese, Trinidadians, and Haitians. All of these people are criminalized when they are detained in private, local, state, county, and federal jails and prisons.

It is an open secret that the passage of harsher and stricter immigration legislation coincided with welfare reform that left many states and localities desperate for new ways to increase their budgets, as the role of the federal government in the provision of social services was rolled back and states scrambled to meet the social service needs of both citizens and non-citizens. The detention of legal immigrants, illegal immigrants, and asylum seekers pumped much-needed money into states and communities that were struggling to survive. In other words, "the detention of resident aliens and refugees in the United States has become a money making operation for local jails and prison corporations . . . resulting in a small fortune to many local governments who are able to sell empty beds in their county jails to the INS" (Handmaker and Singh 13–14). The detention of immigrants, asylum seekers, and legal residents is now the responsibility of Immigration and Customs Enforcement (ICE), which is under the Department of Homeland Security (DHS). New detention measures implemented after 9/11 allowed mandatory, indefinite detention in which people were removed from family and housed alongside criminals without the right to a lawyer or to a public arraignment, the knowledge of what they were being accused of, or what evidence was being used against them (United Nations High Commissioner for Refugees; Human Rights First).

For example, under Operation Liberty Shield, which went into effect in March 2003, "asylum applicants from nations where al-Qaeda, al-Qaeda sympathizers and other terrorist groups are known to have operated will be detained for the duration of their processing" (White House, "Fact Sheet: Operation Liberty Shield"). In other words, they are presumed guilty until proven innocent, but they are not given the opportunity or means to prove their innocence. Furthermore, they can be moved around the country without their family knowing and without having access to counsel, let alone translators for those who do not speak English. This policy is clearly directed at Arab and Muslim immigrant men of a certain age and has had a harmful effect on African asylum seekers, especially those from Somalia and Sudan, but we need to bear in mind that Muslim and Arab immigrants and refugees from Africa can come from many countries on the continent (Chishti).

The intersection of the perception and treatment of Hurricane Katrina victims and the treatment of African immigrants and asylum seekers is important. The largely African American, Latino, and poor victims of the hurricane were presumed guilty by the media and politicians and not given the opportunity to prove their innocence before they were shipped off to other states. Immigrants and asylum seekers are criminalized when they are detained; Katrina victims were, too, when they were accused of looting, killing, and raping. This is merely an extension of how the African American and Latino communities are viewed: full of violence and in need of law and order that only a militarized police state can provide—a thinking characteristic of the prison complex where African American and Latino men are disproportionately represented. In addition, African immigrants and asylum seekers are treated in a manner that reflects how the government and larger society view African Americans: they are subjected to verbal and physical assaults, overcrowded conditions, strip searches, solitary confinement that isolates them from the larger prison population, lack of medial care, and mental abuse—all of them violations of human rights.

At the same time, large portions of federal and state budgets are devoted to policing borders that have become increasingly militarized (by both the government and private citizens) and to meeting mandatory detentions, while social services for citizens and immigrants have been reduced. The immigrants serve their time and are then deported. Yet they are often subjected to heavy fines. For some, even removal is difficult, because their home governments (as in Mali, Somalia, and Cote d'Ivoire) will not accept them back. We often think of these detainees as male, and a lot of them are, which brings up the question of what happens to the women and children in their lives. When the men are detained, their spouses/partners, children, and other dependents both in the U.S. and back home are deprived of their income, emotional support, and other resources. Sometimes the man is the only one working in the home, the only one with a driver's license and a car, and the only one who speaks English.

WOMEN HELD IN DETENTION

Hundreds of women refugees, undocumented immigrants, and legal residents are held in detention and they are housed with people who have been convicted of violent and nonviolent crimes. In other words, it is not just men who are criminalized by these policies, but women as well. Many of the women asylees sought political asylum because they had a well-founded fear of persecution for being women—they had been raped or were afraid of being raped. They escaped female genital mutilation (FGM) or did not want their daughters to undergo the procedure as well as forced prostitution, marriages, and abductions. Many of them fled from war-torn countries and have physical and psychological scars that will be difficult to heal while they are held in detention under harsh conditions. The Women's Commission for Refugee Women and Children has reported that women detainees in the U.S. face the same human rights violations as refugees abroad while they are held: intrusive body searches, poor food, lack of medical care, sexual abuse (women face this more than men because they are women), physical assault, solitary confinement, verbal abuse, and overcrowded conditions (Young). Women detainees are not provided adequate sanitary supplies. This situation is common in refugee camps abroad, where funding is not adequate to cover this necessity. But we should ask why it is the same in U.S. detention facilities, which we know are a multi-million-dollar industry. Women detainees are also moved around the country and are not given access to legal representation or to their families.

However, men and women are often treated somewhat differently. In her study of women detainees in Florida, Marleine Bastien reports that "there is a double standard in the treatment of women and men asylum seekers. In Miami, men are housed mainly at Krome, an open door facility where detainees are not placed in cells or locked down. They have access to a separate cafeteria, law library, outside patio and a large recreation area, as well as better access to family visits and lawyers" (126). Men also have better access to translators and can work (without pay); this gives them something to do with their time, whereas women report that the boredom is overwhelming. Thus even in detention, women are shortchanged. Furthermore, women who are detained are unable to work, to provide for their families, and to send money back home. Philippa Strum provides a brief but telling summary when she says, "we as a nation disfavor immigrants, and among the immigrants we value the least are women" (182).

DETENTION OF UNACCOMPANIED MINORS

Men and women held in detention are receiving less and less protection, and children hardly fare better. There are thousands of children (mainly from China, Cuba, Haiti, and Central America, but there are some African children) who are held in detention without the necessary language and educational skills to understand the United States' very confusing immigration process. In 1994, before 9/11, there were ten thousand unaccompanied children held in detention (*Albion Monitor*). Children come to the U.S. for various reasons, and some are similar to those given by adults: to escape rape, FGM, forced prostitution and marriages, civil war, famine, and economic hardships. On the whole, some want to make a better life for themselves, while others come to be reunited with family members (Becker). These children also cannot depend on the federal or state governments to protect them. First, we should ask ourselves, why do we detain children who have not committed a violent crime? Hundreds of children, many of them girls, are held throughout the country in detention; some are as young as one year old! The average age is between fifteen and seventeen years old (Florence Immigrant and Refugee Rights Project). If this is about the war on terrorism, the question must be asked, how can a baby be a threat to this country's national security? Whatever the answer is, children who have not committed a violent crime should not be locked up. Indeed, doing so is against international law that prohibits the detention of children, except as a measure of last resort (Human Rights Watch).

When children arrive "illegally" with a parent or guardian, they are separated from that person and put in detention. Children who are waiting to have their asylum applications reviewed are also put in detention, although some of them have parents and legal guardians with whom they could stay while they await the outcome of their cases. Children are also housed alongside convicted felons who, though they are underage, have been convicted of rape, selling drugs, murder, assault, or robbery (Becker). The conditions in the detention facilities are not better for children than they are for adults. Children are not given access to legal representation and are expected to represent themselves if their cases make it to an immigration court (American Bar Association). They are not provided adequate medical and dental care or translators, nor are they given access to their relatives, yet they are punished for not following instructions they often cannot understand due to language barriers (Young). Some of the female children enter the facilities pregnant, while others become pregnant during their stay and must remain in detention with their children after they have been born. These conditions have led to emotional and mental problems that in some cases have caused children to commit suicide.

Due to the lack of facilities, some children are placed in privately run foster care facilities that are insecure and unsafe, and girls are put at risk for rape and other forms of sexual abuse. Human Rights Watch has reported that sexual, physical, and verbal abuse has occurred in some facilities. Many children who could be released to family members languish in detention facilities because the family members refuse to pick them up, especially if they are themselves undocumented. This is because the family member must report picking the child up to the ICE, thus putting his/her own stay in the U.S. in danger. Many of the children are in the end deported.

DEPORTATION AND EXPEDITED REMOVAL OF IMMIGRANTS AND ASYLUM SEEKERS

Language for deporting immigrants and asylum seekers was changed to "removal" in the IIRIRA, which incorporated the practice of expedited removal of asylum seekers who arrived at ports of entry but could not demonstrate a credible risk if returned to their country of origin, as well as those accused of attempting to enter the country with false documents. In other words, African asylum seekers and others had to prove at the point of entry that they had left their countries of origin because they had a well-founded fear of persecution and their lives would be in danger if they returned. From as early as 1995, there has been a substantial increase in deportations: 51,000 in 1995; 70,000 in 1996; 114,000 in 1997; 193,000 in 1998; 176,990 in 1999; 186,000 in 2000; 148,000 in 2002; 198,000 in 2004; 168,906 in 2005; and 185,431 in 2006 (Levine, U.S. Immigration and Customs Enforcement, "ICE Removes"). Most of the removals were for noncriminal charges.

It is important to point out that black immigrants within the historic African diaspora in North and South America (e.g., Jamaicans and Dominicans) are deported at higher rates than others; yet they were not implicated in the 9/11 terrorist attacks. They are deported more for criminal offenses—as many as 70 percent fit this category (Mitchell). If black immigrants are deported due to criminal records, this means that they have served their time in jail and then are deported. While the criminal ele-

ment within the African American community can be removed by imprisonment, the criminal element within the black immigrant community can be further removed, permanently, through deportation. Before
the implementation of the IIRIRA, legal immigrants could be deported
only if they were convicted of committing a felony. Under the new legislation, legal residents can be deported after serving their time, sometimes
for minor offenses. In addition, some of the deportees came to the U.S. at
a very early age; some do not speak the language of their home country,
while others leave spouses/partners and children here. When this happens, families can be permanently separated without the economic and
emotional support of the person who has been deported. Individuals who
enter the country with the intention of applying for political asylum can
also be detained and then deported, without having their cases adjudicated, under the IIRIRA (Handmaker and Singh).

Clearly, this is in violation of international law and the 1951 and 1967
UN Convention and Protocol Relating to the Status of Refugees, which
the U.S. is a signatory to; the U.S. government immediately requires the
asylum seeker to prove that she has a well-founded fear of persecution. If
she is unable to do so, she is immediately detained and deported without
consideration for the possibility that she may have left her country in a
hurry, may not have had the time to collect the proper documentation,
or may simply be unable to prove her case at that point, especially if she
is an African refugee who fled because she was raped (Edgar). Even those
who demonstrate a well-founded fear of persecution may be detained before they can have their day in court under the new legislation. Worse
still, "individuals who arrive with facially valid documents showing they
are United States citizens, permanent residents, or that they have already
been granted refugee status in the United States may be sent back without
a fair hearing and without review solely on an immigration inspector's
suspicion that the documents they present are not genuine" (Edgar 172).

Finally, the ICE's National Fugitive Operations Program, established
in February 2002, and the Return to Sender Program, established in May
2006, need to be addressed because their main goal is "to identify, locate,
arrest, or otherwise reduce the fugitive alien population in the United
States" (U.S. ICE, "National Fugitive Operations Program"). Their aim is
to make sure that those who have received final removal orders are arrested and then deported. Between May 2006 and June 2006, 2,179 persons
were arrested under the Return to Sender Program (White House, "Fact
Sheet: Basic Pilot"). A large number of these cases came from black societies in Africa and the Caribbean.

*   *   *

The goal of this chapter has not been to make comparisons between,
on the one hand, African refugees who become legal permanent residents
or asylum seekers, and African Americans on the other hand. However, in

light of public policies enacted prior to and following September 11, 2001, and the treatment and experiences of the mostly African American population that was affected by Hurricane Katrina, the precarious positions of all three groups—refugees, asylum seekers, and African American Katrina victims—need to be viewed in comparative perspective. First, as Henry Giroux points out, "Cries of desperation and help were quickly redefined as pleas of 'refugees,' a designation that suggested an alien population lacking both citizenship and legal rights had inhabited the Gulf Coast" (177). The characterization of American-born citizens as refugees, though they had not crossed an international border, put them in the same "alien" category as African refugees, immigrants, and asylum seekers, who are seen by many as a drain on society. The PRWORA solved this problem for both groups: federal welfare benefits were reduced or eliminated, and African American women went from welfare to workfare. Several thousand mostly African American victims of Hurricane Katrina in New Orleans not only were criminals, in the eyes of some politicians and media outlets, but were seen too as a drain on the city and state because they were mostly poor, on welfare, and unemployed or underemployed. As stated earlier, pre–9/11 and post–9/11 immigration laws and policies criminalized African immigrants and asylum seekers and allowed for their detention and removal from the country. Although they were not removed from the country, the African American victims of Hurricane Katrina were treated as non-citizens when they were removed from New Orleans and the state of Louisiana. This point needs to be firmly established.

Furthermore, the Katrina evacuees were resettled in the same states and cities where African refugees and immigrants of color reside, along with long-term African American residents. Asylum seekers who are successful in their application for legal residence will join them. These cities include primarily New York, Chicago, Atlanta, Washington, D.C., Phoenix, Houston, Miami, Los Angeles, and various cities in New Jersey. These are the same communities in which the war on drugs continues to be waged and toward which the new war on welfare is targeted. Moreover, in light of September 11, these are the communities where the war on terror is being fought through rounding up, detaining, and removing immigrants. Overall, these communities are marginalized, invisible, filled with disposable people, and neglected by the American government in its version of structural adjustment whereby it reduces its role in providing funding for various social services. Yet the people who live in these states and communities are not neglected when it comes to tactics used in fighting the war on terror—racial profiling, surveillance, roundups, and removals.

The issue of property is just as common to both groups. The new immigration measures that permit the detention and deportation of legal African immigrants result in the loss of property. For instance, even an immigrant who has resided in the country for years and bought property could be detained and then deported under the IIRIRA for a minor crime that was committed before the legislation was enacted. And what happens to him when he is detained? Being unemployed while in jail, he is in danger of losing his house, business, car, and other property; similarly, a person permanently removed from the country loses all of her/his property. This issue of property has been central to debates concerning how New Orleans should be rebuilt, because the area that was disproportionately affected was primarily home to a large African American community. Many of these residents owned homes, businesses, and other property regardless of how the media portrayed them. In addition, a number of churches were destroyed, and they represented property loss for African Americans. If African Americans are unable or unwilling to return to New Orleans even if their communities are rebuilt, they will have lost their property.

New Orleans was not, of course, the only area affected by the hurricane. African Americans in other parts of Louisiana, Mississippi, and Alabama were also hit hard by Katrina and lost their property. It is important to note that in 2006, the ICE targeted the above three states for the removal of criminal aliens, including Africans (U.S. ICE, "ICE Removes"). African Americans, whether they are the descendents of the four million slaves or descendents of immigrants who came from the Caribbean in the 1950s, 1960s, and 1970s, cannot afford to sit back and watch, falsely believing that now for the first time they can breathe a little easier because the targets are "foreigners." As we witnessed in the pre-9/11 and post-9/11 eras and during the Katrina debacle, the claim to citizenship has been rendered tenuous for all people of color, regardless of their residence or immigrant status.

NOTE

1. This chapter primarily focuses on individuals who applied for refugee status from the African continent and were legally admitted into the United States as part of the U.S. Refugee Resettlement Program. These individuals are required by law to apply for permanent resident status one year after entering the country. Other individuals who are classified as refugees include asylees. Asylees are individuals who applied for refugee status after entering the United States or who applied at a port of entry, e.g., airport. They are not required by law to apply for permanent resident status after being in the country for one year. However, as the climate has become more anti-immigrant, they are advised to adjust their status as soon as they are eligible to do so.

REFERENCES

Ahmad, Muneer. "Homeland Insecurities: Racial Violence the Day after September 11." *Social Text* 20, no. 3 (2002): 101–115.

Albion Monitor. "U.S. Immigration Abuses Rights of Women and Children, Groups Charge." May 7, 1997. http://www.albionmonitor.com/9705a/alientreatment.html (accessed March 15, 2006).

American Bar Association. "American Bar Association Fact Sheet Unaccompanied Immigrant Children." 2002. www.abanet.org.poladv/priorities/immigration/chidlren.pdf (accessed July 30, 2006).

American Friends Service Committee. "Immigration Law and Policy." http://www.afsc.org/ImmigrantsRights/ht/d/sp/d/ContentDetails/i/19146 (accessed November 24, 2008).

Bastien, Marleine. "Detention of Women Asylum Seekers in the United States." In *Women Immigrants in the United States,* ed. Philippa Strum and Danielle Tarantolo. Washington, D.C.: Woodrow Wilson International Center for Scholars, 2003. 117–128. http://www.wilsoncenter.org/index.cfm?topic_id=1427&fuseaction=topics.publications&group_id=21754 (accessed December 15, 2008).

Becker, Jo. "The Other Immigrant Children." Human Rights Watch, May 1, 2000. http://hrw.org/english/docs/2000/01/usdom12803.htm (accessed March 1, 2006).

Blazer, Jonathon. "Immigration Reform and Access to Public Benefits: The Return of an Uneasy Coupling." National Immigration Law Center, 2006. www.nilc.org (accessed October 20, 2006).

Chisholm, Shirley. "U.S. Policy and Black Refugees." *Issue: A Journal of Africanist Opinion* 12, nos. 1–2 (1982): 22–24.

Chishti, Muzaffar. "Immigration and Security Post–Sept. 11." Migration Policy Institute, 2002. http://www.migrationinformation.org/Usfocus/display.cfm?id=46 (accessed February 15, 2006).

Edgar, Timothy H. 2003. "Legislative Solutions to Challenges Faced by Women Immigrants and Refugees." In *Women Immigrants in the United States,* ed. Philippa Strum and Danielle Tarantolo. Washington, D.C.: Woodrow Wilson International Center for Scholars, 2003. 171–179. http://www.wilsoncenter.org/index.cfm?topic_id=1427&fuseaction=topics.publications&group_id=21754 (accessed December 15, 2008).

Eissa, Salih Omar. "Diversity and Transformation: African Americans and African Immigration to the United States." Immigration Policy Center, 2005. http://www.immigrationpolicy.org/index.php?content=pro503b (accessed November 24, 2008).

Emergency Committee for African Refugees. "U.S. Policy and the Current Refugee Crisis in Africa." *Issue: A Journal of Africanist Opinion* 12, nos. 1–2 (1982): 10–12.

Ewing, Walter A. "Not Getting What They Paid For: Limiting Immigrants' Access to Benefits Hurts Families without Reducing Healthcare Costs." Immigration Policy Center, 2003. http://www.immigrationpolicy.org/index.php?content=B030601 (accessed November 24, 2008).

Florence Immigrant and Refugee Rights Project. "Detained Immigrant and Refugee Children's Initiative." http://www.firrp.org/children.asp (accessed October 6, 2006).

Frazier, Martin. "New Dimensions—African Immigrants in the U.S." *People's Weekly World,* May 21, 2005. http://www.pww.org/article/view/7085/1/270 (accessed January 21, 2006).

Giroux, Henry A. "Reading Hurricane Katrina: Race, Class, and the Biopolitics of Disposability." *College Literature* 33, no. 3 (2006): 171–1996.

Handmaker, Jeff, and Karam Singh. "'Cross Borders': A Comparison of United States and South Africa Border Control Policies." Working paper for the Research Unit on Law and Administration (RULA), School of Law, University of Witwatersrand, Johannesburg, August 2002.

Haynes, Kimberly. "Strengthening Refugee Families and Marriages." National Conference of Catholic Bishops. http://nccbuscc.org/mrs/DomesticViolence/Info/part/doc (accessed October 18, 2006).

Human Rights First. "'Operation Liberty Shield' Turns Liberty on Its Head: Iraqi Asylum Seekers Targeted for Detention." Press release, March 18, 2003. http://www.humanrightsfirst.com/media/2003_alerts/0318b.htm (accessed October 22, 2006).

Human Rights Watch. "Slipping through the Cracks: Unaccompanied Children Detained by the U.S. Immigration and Naturalization Service." Human Rights Watch Children's Report, April 1997. http://www.hrw.org/reports/1997/uscrcks (accessed March 15, 2006).

Jernegan, Kevin. "A New Century: Immigration and the U.S." Country Profiles, Migration Information Sources, Migration Policy Institute, February 2005. http://www.migrationinformation.org/Profiles/display.cfm?ID=283 (accessed October 1, 2006).

Lapchick, Richard, Benjamin Hooks, and Franklin Williams. "Racial Implications of U.S. Immigration Policy." *Issue: A Journal of Africanist Opinion* 12, nos. 1–2 (1982): 13–15.

Leibowitz, Arnold H. "The Refugee Act of 1980: Problems and Congressional Concerns." *Annals, AAPSS* 467 (1983): 163–171.

Levine, John. "America's Internal "Gulag": The Imprisonment of Immigrants in the U.S." International Committee of the Fourth International, June 9, 2005. http://www.wsws.org/articles/2005/jun2005/immi-j09.shtml (accessed October 1, 2006).

Mitchell, Christopher. "The Impact of 9/11 on Migration Relations Between the Caribbean and the United States." The Janey Program for Latin Americans Studies and the Argentina Observatory of the Graduate Program in International Affairs Spring Conference, New School University, New York, April 2, 2004.

National Immigration Forum. "Due Process: Immigration Laws Deny Access to Justice." 2005. http://www.immigrationforum.org/DesktopDefault.aspx?tabid=174 (accessed February 27, 2005).

Nicolosi, Ann Marie. "'We Do Not Want Our Girls to Marry Foreigners': Gender, Race, and American Citizenship." *National Women's Studies Association Journal* 13, no. 3 (2001): 1–21.

Office of Migration Policy and Refugee Policy. 1998. "Liberians Redesignated for Temporary Protected Status." National Conference of Catholic Bishops, *Policy Notes* (1998): 1.1.

Orloff, Leslye. "Women Immigrants and Domestic Violence." In *Women Immigrants in the United States*, ed. Philippa Strum and Danielle Tarantolo. Washington, D.C.: Woodrow Wilson International Center for Scholars, 2003. 49–57. http://www.wilsoncenter.org/index.cfm?topic_id=1427&fuseaction=topics.publications&group_id=21754 (accessed December 15, 2008).

214 Cassandra R. Veney

Parker, Allison. "Can Human-Rights Law Help to End U.S. Mistreatment of Noncitizens?" *Inalienable Rights* (Human Rights Watch), January 10, 2004. http://hrw.org/english/docs/2004/10/01/usdom10493.htm (accessed October 20, 2006).

Pojmann, Karen. "Refugees Stuck in Red Tape." Pacific News Service, 2003. http://www.alternet.org/rogjts/16103 (accessed October 15, 2006).

Ryan, J. Kelly. "The U.S. Refugee Resettlement Program: Trends and Possibilities." U.S. Department of State, Remarks to the ECDC National Conference on Africa Refugees, Arlington, Virginia, May 24, 2004. http://www.state.gov/g/prm/rls/37910.htm (accessed October 15, 2006).

Strum, Philippa. "Afterword." In *Women Immigrants in the United States*, ed. Philippa Strum and Danielle Tarantolo. Washington, D.C.: Woodrow Wilson International Center for Scholars, 2003. 181–182. http://www.wilsoncenter .org/index.cfm?topic_id=1427&fuseaction=topics.publications&group_id=21754 (accessed December 15, 2008).

United Nations High Commissioner for Refugees. "UNHCR Concerned about U.S. Detention of Asylum Seekers." UNHCR News Service, March 21, 2003. http://www.unhcr.org/news/NEWS/3e7b42547.html (accessed October 21, 2006).

U.S. Department of State. 2002. "Refugee Admissions for Africa." Fact Sheet, Bureau of Population, Refugees and Migration, Washington, D.C., November 19, 2002, http://www/state.gov/g/prm/rls/fs/15351.htm. Accessed April 12, 2005.

U.S. Immigration and Customs Enforcement. "ICE Removes 758 Criminal Aliens from 5-State Area during July." Press release, August 15, 2006. http://www .ice.gov/pi/news/newsrelease/articles/060815neworleans.htm (accessed September 15, 2006).

———. "National Fugitive Operations Program." http://www.ice.gov/pi/dro/nfop .htm (accessed November 24, 2008).

U.S. Office of Refugee Resettlement. "Eligibility for Refugee Assistance and Services through the Office of Refugee Resettlement." U.S. Department of Health and Human Services, Administration for Children and Families, 2003. http://www.acf.hhs.gov/programs/orr/geninfo/index.htm (accessed October 20, 2006).

Veney, Cassandra R. *Forced Migration in Eastern Africa: Democratization, Structural Adjustment, and Refugees.* New York: Palgrave-Macmillan, 2007.

The White House. "Fact Sheet: Basic Pilot: A Clear and Reliable Way to Verify Employment Eligibility." Press release, July 5, 2006. http://www.whitehouse.gov/news/releases/2006/07/20060705-6.html (accessed November 24, 2008).

———. "Fact Sheet: Operation Liberty Shield." Press release, March 17, 2003. http://www.whitehouse.gov/news/releases/2003/03/20030317-9.html (accessed August 15, 2006).

Woldemikael, Tekle M. "Ethiopioans and Eritreans." In *Refugees in America in the 1990s*, ed. David W. Haines. Westport, Conn.: Greenwood, 1996. 147–169.

Young, Wendy. "Women Asylum Seekers." *Frontiers: A Journal of Women's Studies* 24, nos. 2–3 (2003): 113–116.

11 IMMIGRANTS AND THE AMERICAN SYSTEM OF JUSTICE: PERSPECTIVES OF AFRICAN AND CARIBBEAN BLACKS

John A. Arthur

Public sentiments and opinions about crime, the criminal justice system, and the punishment of offenders are as varied as the American public. Americans' reactions to and perceptions about the justice system in general are shaped by several factors. Notable among these factors are individual attributes such as social class, age, gender, religion, political orientation, region of the country, experience of criminal victimization, and racial and ethnic membership. Structural determinants of public sentiments toward the administration of justice include community characteristics such as mass media portrayal or representations of crime (the overdramatization of crime news), local and national crime rates, politicization of crime, population density, perceived sense of fear and safety, ethnic composition, quality of housing, and community labor force attributes (Bohm, "American Death Penalty Attitudes"; Tyler and Weber; Biderman et al.; Warr et al.).

For years, social scientists have examined how individual and community attributes converge to influence public perceptions and attitudes about the criminal justice system in particular, and the administration of justice in general. In his contribution to the literature, Wilbanks noted that whites and blacks are sharply at odds over whether the system of justice is fair or discriminatory. He reported that blacks have persistently voiced concern that the courts and the justice system in general discriminate against them. Wilbanks's findings were corroborated by Lynch and Patterson, who also reported that non-whites are more likely to be sent to prison than their white counterparts. In a related study, Young found that blacks persistently believe that the system of justice is biased, unfair, and inequitable against them when it comes to the imposition of sentences and police arrests. According to Young, this perception may explain in part the lack of trust and confidence that blacks and non-whites have toward the system of justice. The perception among blacks of unfairness in the justice system is also reflected in blacks' lack of support for the death penalty and other forms of social sanctions. Barkan and Cohn; Arthur ("Proximate Correlates"); and Bohm (*The Death Penalty in America*) have reported that antipathy toward blacks, racial stereotyping, prejudice, and discrimination account for the lack of black support for the death penalty specifically, and for the institutions of justice in general.

The above studies and others collectively point to a pattern that Americans are divided by race and class in their beliefs about the effectiveness of the justice system in the fulfillment of its core missions and objectives: the apprehension of law violators, the prosecution of the criminally accused, the protection of citizens from crime, and the imposition and application of penal sanctions to punish those who are adjudicated to have violated the laws of society. The varied attitudes and opinions about crime and justice suggest that the formulation of public policies to deal with crime has become highly fractious and contentious. To confront the country's crime problem, most Americans demand that legislators pass tougher laws, that the police act proactively rather than reactively in the enforcement of the law, and that the courts impose longer prison terms.

The public agitation for punitive sentencing is a reflection of the public's perceptions about the insecurities produced by the fear of crime. Whether the public focus is on the death penalty, police use of force, or harsher and long-term imprisonment for offenders, citizens' racial and ethnic backgrounds repeatedly confirm the racial chasm in public sentiments and judgment regarding the American system of justice. As a minority group with considerably less economic, political, and cultural capital, the majority of blacks in the country have come to accept the reality of the dominance of the justice system in their communities and in all walks of life. This dominance instills a sense of fear, mistrust, apprehension, and loathing on the part of black Americans. In this regard, the agents and agencies of justice are seen as representing the massive power of white-controlled institutions that could alter or block the progress of blacks in the United States.

The purpose of this study is to identify the determinants of black African and Caribbean immigrants' attitudes and perceptions about the American system of justice. The goal is to investigate how notions of racial and ethnic identity associated with the immigrants help shape or define the contours of their relationship with the justice system. Structural and individual factors associated with a broad range of crime and criminal justice issues, including police behavior and practices, the prosecution and adjudication of criminal defendants by the courts, and the imposition of punishments, are assessed in terms of their efficacies in predicting how the immigrants view the criminal justice system. Public attitudes and perceptions regarding the administration of justice are pivotal in the formulation of public policies regarding crime and the administration of justice. The philosophical foundations of the institution of justice and its administration in any democratic culture will be eroded and threatened by a lack of citizen confidence and trust in the ability of the system to offer the public protection. For the segment of society which believes that its views are not incorporated into the shaping of public policy regarding crime and the administration of justice, there is a prevailing sense of marginalization, disillusionment, and alienation. This uneasiness may affect the willingness of specific groups to support the ideas and ideals behind the administration of justice.

BLACK AFRICAN AND CARIBBEAN MIGRATION TO THE UNITED STATES

The past four decades have witnessed significant increases in the voluntary migration of black Africans to the U.S. This increase occurred during the last three to four decades of the twentieth century. During the 1980s, the total number of Africans who migrated to the U.S. was nearly two hundred thousand (176,893). Over the next ten years, during the 1990s, the number of Africans legally admitted into the country increased by 100 percent to 354,939 immigrants. Estimates from the U.S. Census for the year 2000 reveal that the total number of African immigrants legally living in the U.S. grew to reach 701,000 (Arthur, *Invisible Sojourners*; Gordon; Konadu-Agyemang and Takyi). Though their numbers are small relative to the migratory stream of people coming to the U.S. from Asia and Latin America, the African immigrants have established a presence in major urban centers in the U.S. such as New York City, Dallas, Washington, D.C., Northern Virginia–Maryland, Atlanta, Houston, Chicago–Northern Indiana, Charlotte, Los Angeles, and Minneapolis–St. Paul.

The majority of the African immigrants are attracted to the U.S. because of the better economic and cultural opportunities America has to offer. Coming from societies in Africa where civil, economic, and political institutions are threatened by wars, conflicts, dictatorships, and failed regimes, many of the African immigrants view the U.S. as a land of opportunity, and a chance to change their economic fortunes for the betterment of their extended family members. Economic, political, cultural, and sometimes man-made and natural disasters culminate to serve as push factors compelling thousands of Africans to flee the continent in search of greener pastures in the West. Conversely, prevailing higher standards of living, the demand for cheap and abundant supply of labor, and configurations in immigration policies have converged to pull and attract some of Africa's best and brightest to the advanced industrial countries.

African and Caribbean migration to the West started before World War I. Many students from these regions were sponsored by their home countries or by family members to go to the U.S., Britain, and Canada to

pursue tertiary education. The expectation was that upon their graduation, many of these students would return home and play a role in the development of their countries.

Once in the U.S., the immigrants focus their energies in building on
the human capital that the majority of them brought with them. In pursuing cultural (education) and economic (labor force participation) goals, the
immigrants are able to carve niches for themselves in both the public and
private sectors of the economy. Part of the new global migration of skilled
and unskilled persons to the U.S., the movement of blacks from Africa and
the Caribbean is sponsored by vast networks of extended family relatives
and associates who have undertaken the journey to the U.S. Whether newcomers migrate alone or are sponsored by relatives to come to the U.S., the
opportunity to come and live in the West is viewed as an investment in
the future economic well-being of the entire family. The decision to migrate is oftentimes not made by isolated individuals. Rather, larger units
comprising familial networks and household members cooperate by combining their resources to assist those family members who are best qualified to provide the family with the maximum return on its investment.
Like their African counterparts who have settled in the U.S., blacks from
the Caribbean are driven to America by economic factors: the need to improve upon their quality of life and to flee from persistent economic and
political downturns. For the majority of immigrants who come from Africa and the Caribbean, a common factor is that their respective governments have yet to fulfill the economic needs of their people.

Migration to the U.S., the U.K., and Canada has become the principal means of achieving social mobility, pursuing cultural goals in the
form of higher education, finding gainful employment, and sending remittances home to support family members left behind. As with their black
African immigrant counterparts living in the U.S., the migration of Caribbean blacks has been facilitated by changes in U.S. immigration policies during the last three decades. Both groups have benefited from the
Hart-Cellar Immigration Act of 1965. This Act shifted U.S. immigration
policy from national origins and quotas to family reunification. By the
time this Act was enacted, several of the African and Caribbean countries
had won political independence from colonial Europe. This made it possible for countries in the two regions to send large numbers of their citizens abroad. Blacks in the two regions of the world also benefited from
the passage of the Immigration Reform and Control Act of 1986 (IRCA).
Under the IRCA, laws were enacted by Congress to slow or stop illegal
immigration to the U.S. mainly from Mexico and other Central American countries. Africans and Caribbeans benefited from this law because
it provided an amnesty to undocumented foreigners already living in the
country to apply to become permanent residents. The Act sought to impose penalties on employers who knowingly hire illegal foreigners and

required that employers check the citizenship status of all their work-ers (Martin, "Good Intentions"; Martin and Midgley, "Immigration to the United States"). Four years after IRCA passed, Congress enacted the 1990 immigration reforms aimed at making it easier for persons with skills deemed to be in short supply by American employers to become perma-nent residents. The intent of the law also included the need to diversify the pool of immigrants who were coming to the U.S. by increasing the number of immigrants from countries with low representation of immi-grants in the country. Like their counterparts from black Africa, the Ca-ribbean blacks who enter the U.S. tend to settle in the large and densely populated cities, particularly New York City, Philadelphia, and Washing-ton, D.C., and surrounding suburbs in Richmond, Chicago, Miami, At-lanta, Boston, Los Angeles, and Houston.

As they pursue their American dream and seek upward mobility, many of the African and Caribbean immigrants find that they must also nego-tiate the complex terrain of race and ethnic identity in a race- and class-conscious American society. Being black continues to have a deleterious impact on the consciousness of both native- and foreign-born blacks. More than with other ethnic groups in the country, the cultural images associ-ated with blacks are that they tend to be crime-prone, living in poverty, faced with high numbers in school dropouts, welfare dependent, and con-fined to the inner cities, where they face chronic unemployment. As with native-born blacks living in the U.S., having a black identity takes on a powerful force and meaning in black-white relations. Whether they come to the U.S. as immigrants or are born here, blacks in the American dias-pora find themselves having to confront prejudice, racism, and institu-tionalized forms of discrimination.

For these black immigrants, race connotes a salient marker and an important determinant of access to economic and social mobility. Com-ing from countries where their blackness was not considered a major is-sue, some of the immigrants are faced with the denigration and margin-alization of peoples of black African ancestry in the U.S. In their countries of origin, their blackness was not a hindrance to their social mobility or to their class advancement; neither did it thwart their full incorporation and integration into society. Upon arriving in the U.S. from countries where the vast majority is black, these immigrants come to be identified as part of black America. Any differences and cultural traits they possess (positive or negative) are subsumed into a collective black American iden-tity. Identification with black America comes with the stigmatization, prejudice, and de facto discrimination usually associated with native-born black Americans. The comparison with American-born blacks was also made by Bryce-Laporte ("Black Immigrants"; "The New Immigration"; "Caribbean Migration"). Black African and Caribbean immigrants are pigeonholed into accepting a black identity that is based on negative racial

constructs associated with centuries of racial discrimination and prejudice emanating from the legacies of slavery and Jim Crow.

As indicated, for a majority of these immigrants, the awareness of
their blackness became an issue only upon arriving in the U.S. Anger,
frustration, and sometimes outright hostilities define how the immigrants
confront and deal with the daily vicissitudes of discrimination and racism. Cast into a subordinate racial group in the U.S. and having accepted
the deleterious effects of the insidiousness of racism in America, the immigrants develop coping strategies to reduce the harmful effects of discrimination and the generalized denigration of blackness in America. The
immigrants stress the social and human capital that the majority of them
have imported or brought with them from home: a good education, a
strong work ethic, deferred gratification, and commitment to family. Most
of them do not accept or subscribe to the negative images and labels associated with their blackness. The racial and ethnic identities that they
seek to negotiate in the U.S. are based upon a Pan-Caribbean or African
identity, an identity that recognizes their distinctness and difference from
America. This identity enables them to be selective in terms of which aspects of the American body polity they will engage. The saliency of race
as a social marker in America has come to mean that at times, to ensure
their economic and cultural survival in America, the black immigrants
have to limit their interactions to those aspects of American society that
are critical to the achievement of their economic and cultural goals. This
means having to segment and structure their lives in such a way as to protect the qualities that define their uniqueness as a people.

DATA AND METHODS

Data from a random sample of black African and Caribbean immigrants
residing in Minneapolis–St. Paul, Charlotte, and Toronto were gathered
via face-to-face structured interviews carried out between 2000 and 2004.
The interviews were designed to collect baseline demographic or classificatory data about the immigrants. Respondents were asked questions
about educational attainment, occupation, income, family size, age, respondents' subjective class and political identification, region of country,
year of immigration to the U.S., citizenship status, and gender. To gauge
the immigrants' attitudes about the criminal justice system, a number
of questions reflecting opinions about crime and justice were included
in the interview items. Among these were fear of crime, courts' punishment of offenders (efficacies of criminal sanctions), and rating of the immigrants' encounters with the police, police brutality, and criminal victimization. A community integration variable measured by a composite
of four variables was included in the independent variables. The list of respondents was obtained from immigrant ethnic and national associations

represented in the three cities. The structured interviews were supplemented with focus-group sessions of immigrant representatives who self-elected to participate in focused group sessions. These sessions were designed to collect in-depth information about the perceptions and attitudes of the immigrants about a broad range of issues, including attitudes toward social institutions such as the police, courts, and prisons system. The data were analyzed using multiple regression techniques. This strategy allows for an estimate to be calculated that represents the effects of the independent variables in predicting the attitudes of the black immigrants toward the justice system. Standard beta coefficients are reported, and to assess statistical significance, we use a significance level of .05.[1]

PRESENTATION OF FINDINGS

The results shed light on the factors related to the perceptions of black immigrants regarding the American system of justice. The results indicate that immigrants' age, gender, educational attainment, income, and year of migration to the U.S. are statistically significant in explaining immigrant attitudes toward and perceptions of the American system of justice. In general, younger immigrants (under thirty years old) hold a less than favorable opinion about the justice system than their older counterparts. The most favorable attitude toward the criminal justice system came from older immigrants (sixty years old and above). Black immigrant women tend to hold a more favorable opinion of the justice system than their male counterparts. In general, the women immigrants in the sample are in support of a wide range of issues regarding crime and the administration of justice in the U.S. A majority of the women (60 percent) are in favor of legislation requiring a permit for the purchase of a handgun, support a waiting period before the purchasing of handguns to allow the police to conduct criminal background checks of gun purchasers, advocate longer sentences for those convicted of violent crimes, and are also favorable to the idea of establishing neighborhood crime watches, including the formation of citizen-police associations to assist communities to detect crime and provide more details of crimes to the police. Though there is some support among immigrant men for the criminal justice system, the support is not as strong as it is among females. A majority of the black immigrant men view the criminal justice system as discriminatory and designed to enforce those normative standards that pertain to white hegemony and control over minorities and underrepresented, powerless groups in America.

The findings show that among black immigrants, subjective class background and degree of community integration are statistically significant in predicting perceptions about the justice system. The most favorable impression of the justice system was found among black immigrants in the upper class. These immigrants tend to emphasize a conservative view of crime and social control by stressing the retributive as opposed to rehabilitative function of the criminal justice system. From their perspective, the role of the criminal justice system is to preserve the established order by ensuring that antisocial behaviors are punished, irrespective of extralegal attributes of offenders such as age, race, or home environment. Among this group, the institution of policing is seen as an important aspect of maintaining social order and preserving the status quo. This means that the police will have to be equipped with the resources to detect, apprehend, and deter criminal conduct. Equally, these immigrants see the function of the courts in the same manner: the need to impose severe sanctions on those who are adjudicated by the courts to be guilty of wrongful and illegal conduct. A majority of these immigrants (65 percent) perceived that although structural factors (unemployment, poor housing, incomplete schooling, drug abuse) are significant in predicting the etiology of crime, by far the most salient causes of criminality can be linked to the inability of some Americans to take advantage of the tremendous economic (work) and cultural (education) opportunities the country has to offer. They attribute the problem of crime in the urban centers of the country to cultural factors such as gang behavior, proliferation of drugs, the decline in parental authority regarding the socialization of children, and the inability of some communities to foster community integration and a sense of belonging. In such an environment, the immigrants perceive the role of the police as peace brokers, assisting in balancing the imperatives of protecting the community and at the same time ensuring that those they apprehend are treated fairly and judiciously.

In general, black immigrants who affirmed a strong sense of bonding with their communities reported more favorable perceptions of the criminal justice system than their counterparts who perceived a lack of community spirit as well as marginalization and alienation. For those who reported strong community bonds, there is a tendency to engage in civic and cultural activities to promote better relationships with various agencies of government, including law enforcement. Most of them frequently report criminal incidences to the police and are supportive of measures put in place by the community to reduce or prevent criminal behavior. For the immigrants who reported having weak ties with the community, the results reveal that not only is support for the institutions of justice weak, but more significantly, there is a perception of individual or group powerlessness in working with the criminal justice system to provide better services for their communities. Although they decried the high crime rates in their neighborhoods, they nonetheless are afraid of the police and a vast majority indicated that they did not intend to cooperate with the police for fear of reprisal or retaliation by criminal elements in their community. As a powerless and marginalized group, these immigrants may perceive that they do not have any input in the formulation of policies about crime and punishment. Most reasoned that their low sub-ordinate status, coupled with their immigrant status, does not provide them with the social capital to engage the police in finding solutions to the crime problem. This may account for their apparent cynicism, apathy, lack of trust, and continued erosion of confidence in the social system as a whole.

The results show that an experience of criminal victimization and the resulting fear of crime correlate with how the immigrants perceive the justice system. As expected, those immigrants who indicated that they have been victims of crime, particularly violent crime (robbery, assault, rape, and murder), tend to hold an unfavorable perception of the justice system. The immigrants in this group favor strict and retributive punish-ment for all crimes, irrespective of the degree of harm or injury suffered by the victim. Their perception is that the justice system, notably the courts, is too lenient in its punishment of violent criminals convicted for law violation. They will call for longer periods of incarceration followed by the granting of parole or early release for good behavior. However, early release for good conduct should be reserved for those incarcerated offend-ers who show remorse, accept responsibility for their malfeasance, and demonstrate good citizenship. For those offenders who become chronic recidivists, the preferred path is to incarcerate for longer periods of time without any eligibility for early release in the form of parole or commu-nity service. Immigrants who reported being victims of property crime (burglary, larceny-theft, auto theft, and arson) also perceive that the jus-tice system as a whole should impose longer terms of incarceration to be followed by supervised periods of parole aimed at eventual integration of offenders back into the community. In addition, their preference is for the courts to require offenders to provide restitution and reparation to the vic-tims of the crimes as well as pay punitive damages to remedy the harm that the victims suffered.

Overall, the immigrants perceive that the criminal justice system puts too much emphasis on the rights of the offenders, almost always to the exclusion of the rights of the crime victims and the harm they have suffered. Victims become peripheral to the process of justice and in some cases are made to suffer revictimization by the justice system by having essential services such as healthcare and counseling withheld from them while the offenders' needs are met by the state. This finding is in line with previous studies that have reported that criminal victimization is related to how citizens perceive the justice system. Stinchcombe et al. found that the demand for harsher and more punitive sentencing seems to be stronger among those Americans who persistently report being afraid of crime or have experienced criminal victimization.

The concern about and fear of crime also predicts how the immigrants perceive the system of justice. The public's concern and fear about crime is rooted in the notion that no one wants to be a victim of crime. Like other Americans, the immigrants worry about crime and find its effects devastating, at times even life-threatening. The public's fear of crime is revealed in actions people take to ensure that they do not fall prey to crime. This may include not going out late at night, avoiding neighborhoods and communities with high rates of criminality, locking their doors, not offering to assist strangers or people they do not know, or carrying a gun. Some citizens install electronic and mechanical crime deterrent devices to ward off attempted crime. Media overdramatization of crime (particularly violent crimes) may also influence the public's fear of crime. But more importantly, the fear of crime is also predicated upon attitudinal beliefs about whether citizens perceive that the justice system is able to protect them from criminal predators. Poor and unfavorable rating of the criminal justice system was identified as a more problematic issue among immigrants who perceive a greater fear of crime than among those immigrants who are less fearful and afraid of crime. Among urban immigrants and those respondents residing in densely populated areas, concern about and fear of crime was higher than among immigrants residing in suburban communities. According to Warr ("Dangerous Situations"), people who live in big cities discern a higher risk of crime and are more afraid of criminal victimization than those who live in rural or suburban communities. This risk may account, in part, for the fear urban residents have of crime and their feelings that the institutions of criminal and social control are ineffective in providing them with protection.

Structural factors also influence the low favorability rating given to the institutions of justice by the urban immigrants. The fear of crime and the less favorable impression of the institution of justice by the urbanite immigrants stems from the fact that many of these immigrants live with the reality of neighborhood crimes that often go undetected by the police. This fear is heightened by the perceived sense of poor and weak social integration and the lack of a sense of community in some of the nation's major urban centers. For those immigrants residing in big cities, the fear and concern about crime is related to the racial and ethnic composition of urban centers in the U.S. Living in areas where the racial and ethnic mix is predominantly African American and Hispanic further heightens the immigrants' anxieties about crime. As Taylor and Covington found, the fear of crime is higher in urban centers with a disproportionately high number of blacks than in areas where whites are in the majority.

As a group, blacks persistently report being more afraid of crime because of their residential proximity to urban centers, where criminal offenses are common and the probability of becoming a victim of crime remains very high. Living in close proximity to places with high crime rates may have the unintended consequence of increasing feelings associated with anomie, or the perception that the social system has lost its ability to offer people protection, hope, and institutional confidence. Feelings of anomie are also associated with marginalization, social isolation, and a general lack of trust. Immigrants who expressed fear and concern about crime reported lower ratings and approval of the institutions of justice, particularly the police and the courts. This is indicative of feelings of vulnerability sometimes culminating in staying away from open and public spaces and not relying on or trusting strangers. For those blacks who have to confront the daily rituals and perils associated with crime, life can be tough as people have to make decisions to enhance their security and well-being. These security measures include the hardening of criminal targets through such measures as installing mechanical and non-mechanical crime deterrent devices to ward off criminal elements. In some instances, citizens may resort to carrying guns to ensure additional protection. Improvements in police patrols and the establishment of police-community relations in such high-crime areas may provide the panacea to assure the community that the police and law enforcement agents are going to vigorously and proactively confront the crime problem.

Support for the criminal justice system is correlated with immigrant educational attainment and total household income. More educated immigrants from Africa and the Caribbean show strong support for the justice system. Black immigrants who possess baccalaureate and postbaccalaureate degrees express more positive attitudes toward the criminal justice system than their counterparts who hold associate degrees or high school credentials. In general, better-educated immigrants tend to emphasize the need for agents and institutions of justice to be tough with criminals and for the courts to impose severe penalties for those who are convicted of crime. This group of immigrants supports legislative initiatives that will impose severe and long-term sentences for those who commit violent crimes and use or deal in drugs and have gang affiliation. Their level of satisfaction with the police is higher than among immigrants with high school education. They affirm the ability of the courts and judges to apply the law fairly, without showing any bias toward any group or groups in society. Their support for harsher and more punitive sentencing of offenders is based partly on their fear of crime, increasing gang activities, and proliferation of drugs in the urban and suburban communities, and partly on their desire to be safe in their neighborhoods. This class of black immigrants also believes that the police treat everyone fairly and that race, class, and age have little to do with how the police deal with those they arrest.

Satisfaction with the police and the judiciary is lower among black immigrants who have low levels of education and those who do not have a college education. The immigrants in this group reported being stopped by the police frequently and often treated in a condescending or disrespectful manner because of their race and where they live. The majority of them reside in lower-class neighborhoods where crime is a major public issue. As Weitzer and Tuch point out, police-citizen interactions in high-crime areas and areas that are predominantly minority tend to be contentious and sometimes volatile. Most of these immigrants view police behavior in their neighborhoods as a form of harassment and a targeted differential enforcement of the law. These negative encounters often translate into less than favorable attitudes toward the police. This selectivity and bias against poor blacks is viewed as one of the reasons behind the dispropor-tionate representation of blacks in official police arrests data. The nega-tive feelings toward the police among immigrants are a reflection of the general antiblack sentiments that prevail in the U.S. The immigrants per-ceive that there are entrenched racial stereotypes held by agents and agen-cies of criminal justice which predispose them to display a bias against blacks as a whole.

Immigrants' political identification and citizenship status were used to gauge immigrants' beliefs about crime and criminal justice. To a large degree, these two variables provide a measurement of civic and status in-tegration into American society. Becoming a citizen through naturaliza-tion is a manifestation of immigrants' willingness to forge integration and ties with the host society and to embrace its norms and institutional arrangements. It also provides the means for engagement in the political process, such as the right to vote in national and local elections. Both vari-ables measure the immigrants' identification and institutional affiliation with, as well as desire to become incorporated and/or assimilated into, American society.

The results reveal that a majority of the immigrants (54%) consid-ered their political identification or affiliation as Democratic, liberal, and leaning to the left. Another 41 percent self-identified as Republican, con-servative, and leaning to the right, while the remaining immigrants (5%) identified their political views as independent (neither Republican nor Democratic). Liberal respondents rated police performance and the activi-ties of the justice system in their communities as favorable. This favor-able rating does not indicate an approval of police use of force against innocent citizens or police disrespect for minority citizens. The respon-dents recognized the social and economic impact of crime in their neigh-borhoods (gangs, drive-by shootings, abandoned houses, unemployment, white flight, and poor delivery of social services), but perceived that more law enforcement or policing was not a panacea. Several of these liberal black immigrants emphasized job training for youth, after-school pro-grams, better schools, employment for youths in the inner cities, better access to affordable housing, and programs to encourage ethnic entrepre-neurships.

Immigrants who described their political orientation as conservative also held a favorable perception of the justice system in their communities, though their overall level of support was higher than that of their liberal counterparts. The main differences between the two main political orientations associated with the immigrants are their attribution of the causes of crime and their views of how the criminal justice system or the community-at-large responds to crime. Among the politically conservative immigrants, there is a prevailing ethos that solutions to the crime problem should involve the granting of more powers and resources to the agents of law enforcement. These immigrants feel that decades of government investments in various social and economic programs have failed to lift some Americans out of poverty due to lack of a work ethic and a commitment to individual or self-empowerment. Erosion of moral values and disintegration of the family are cited as the major causes of criminality. Among black conservative immigrants, there is also the perception that the imposition of longer and harsher sentences, while costly for taxpayers, fulfills an important role in society: protecting the public by ensuring that offenders who are incarcerated for longer periods of time will not be around to re-offend or to re-victimize others. This is the social isolation or social incapacitation function of punishment.

The study revealed that generalized support or non-support for the institutions of justice among black immigrants is also influenced by their total family income. High-income immigrant families hold more favorable views about the institutions of justice. Immigrant families who earn over $60,000 per year rated police performance in aspects such as the detection of crime, apprehension of offenders, and relationship with the public as satisfactory and positive. While these immigrants deplore unnecessary police brutality and use of force, often in targeting poor people and blacks in general, they nonetheless perceive that the police in their respective communities behave in a professional manner and are less likely to use force against them or treat them disrespectfully because of their race and ethnicity. This group of immigrants reported having less contact with the police. In instances where they have interacted with the police or the courts, they have found the treatment they received to be fair, judicious, and professional. Those with total family incomes ranging between $39,000 and $59,000 also tend to be supportive of the justice system, but their level of support is not as high as among those immigrants who earn $60,000 and above. They feel that the police and the courts in their districts tend to treat citizens fairly, without regard for race and ethnicity. Concerning the sentencing of those who are convicted by the courts, the immigrants perceive that the punishments handed down by the courts are not "harsh enough" and, in most cases, are "less punitive" than they should be. Despite their favorable rating of the institutions of justice, they nonetheless perceive that police officers who violate citizens by assaulting or disrespecting them should be sanctioned and ultimately removed from the force.

Immigrants' confidence in and support for the police and the courts tends to be lower among black immigrants who earn $30,000 or less. These immigrants reported negative encounters with the police; among those who have appeared before the courts, whether as victims or as persons charged with committing a crime, there is mistrust and apprehension about the justice system. A majority of these immigrants (58 percent) reported being treated as criminals even when they had not been formally charged with law violation. They also reported being mistreated by police, prosecution, and judge when charged with law violation and summoned to appear before the courts. Nearly one-third of immigrants in this group reported being "pushed and shoved" several times and in other instances verbally assaulted by the police for committing minor traffic violations. Many of them (two-thirds) fear being arrested by the police even when they have not committed any crimes, and they consider police patrols in their communities as vigorous and purposive, designed to ferret out crime and other forms of antisocial behavior. Nearly 70 percent of these immigrants believe that the visible presence of the police in their community is based on a police stereotype of blacks as more prone to sell and use illicit or controlled substances, particularly cocaine. Their perception is that the police deem them guilty by association because they happen to be black and live in communities with relatively higher crime rates than the white suburban communities nearby.

The low favorability ratings and perceptions held by the immigrants regarding the criminal justice system are also reflected in the results of the focus group interviews with the black immigrant youths who were included in the study. The findings revealed an interesting dynamic involving how the imposition of labels by power and authority brokers (agents of the criminal justice system) can lead to conflicts and disharmony in group relations. The majority of the immigrant youth hold an unfavorable view of the criminal justice system, particularly the police. Youth relationship to this system is marked by mistrust, fear, anger, and suspicion. Immigrant teenagers describe their relationship with the police as volatile, contentious, and based on negative group contact. They perceive that they are under constant surveillance by the police. Whether they live in urban or suburban areas, the youth feel the police target them more than they do their white counterparts. Culturally, they think that in the eyes of agents of the criminal justice system, black teenagers are perceived as "troublemakers," "aggressive," gang-prone, and a law enforcement problem which every effort must be made to contain. The youth expressed concerns about having to interact with the police while in the company of their peers, particularly when driving a car. Frequently, they indicated being stopped and frisked and having search-and-seizure methods applied to them by the police. This experience was also described by female immigrant youth, though their level of frustration in dealing with the police is not as deep as the level of mistrust held for the police by black male immigrant youth. The overarching theme that resonates in the attitudes of the vast majority of the immigrant youth toward the police is the youths' perception that the police ascribe and apply pro-gang definitions to nearly every aspect of their interactions with the youth. This often leads to the police having to search the youths' vehicles, often targeting drug use and consumption. This finding holds irrespective of the socioeconomic class background of the immigrant youth or whether they reside in an area with high crime rates.

*   *   *

The purpose of this study has been to identify and discuss the factors that predict the attitudes and perceptions of black immigrants toward the American system of justice. A number of conclusions can be drawn from the study. First, racial and ethnic attributes are important social constructs in American society. In an American society that is increasingly characterized by diversity and internal differentiation, race and ethnicity not only shape and define life chances, membership in society, and access to economic and cultural opportunities, but, more centrally, determine the social or human capital that ultimately impinges upon the unraveling of subordinate and superordinate inter-group rivalries and schisms. Second, the American experience of the vast majority of black immigrants in the U.S. is defined by a continual struggle to become an integral part of the shaping and formulation of institutional policies in every domain of social life. Race colors public attitudes and sentiments not only about police behavior but about every component of the justice system. Third, an objective feature that the immigrants have come to associate with the criminal justice system in particular, and the administration of justice in general, is a feeling of negativity teetering toward despair about the fact that the system, for the most part, does not offer minority and racially powerless groups the same protection and quality service that it offers to powerful white and privileged Americans. The continued sentiment of negativity that blacks in general associate with the administration of justice may persist, as long as racial stereotypes and prejudices about minorities and criminality remain entrenched. Images of the 1991 Rodney King police beating incident in Los Angeles, the subsequent police killing of the unarmed West African immigrant Amadou Diallo in 1999, and the shooting of Sean Bell in 2006 are etched on the minds of young black males, creating an atmosphere characterized by simmering conflicts between the police and blacks.

This study found that class and socioeconomic status are significant factors in depicting the public rating of the criminal justice system. Among the black immigrants who were studied, class, income, and educational status were all crucial in predicting how the immigrants perceived the system of justice. In addition, support for the police and the courts are also strong among those black immigrants who identified their political orientation as conservative. These findings are in line with previous studies that have reported that political conservatives and Americans who are middle-class, earn a high income, and have a college education generally tend to be more supportive of the justice system (Arthur and Case). The notion that the police and other agencies of the criminal justice system serve the interests of those with moderate-to-high socioeconomic status is reflected in this finding. High socioeconomic groups tend to emphasize the functional role of the criminal justice system in society: to preserve the social order and protect the citizenry. In this regard, they tend to be highly supportive of granting the police and other agencies of criminal justice wider latitude in the fight to prevent and control criminal conduct. These citizens are generally not the ones who are typically processed by the justice system; as indicated earlier, blacks, minorities, youth, and people living in the urban areas are the ones who are frequently processed by the justice system.

Conversely, whites, middle-class citizens, suburbanites, high-income earners, and college-educated Americans tend to have a favorable perception of the criminal justice system. Criminal justice policies and legislation related to crime are usually formulated with the values and perceptions of the middle class in mind. The political imperative to appease this class of citizens is so strong that crime control policies are crafted to reflect the demand for harsher sanctions and proactive policing by this segment of society. Class, race, and socioeconomic status converge to influence the political processes involved in framing the public debate about criminal justice policies. As Steve Barkan aptly notes, "Certain racial and ethnic differences in public beliefs about crime and criminal justice are so strong that it might not be exaggerating to say that racial and ethnic cleavages exist in American society on these beliefs" (51). In essence, groups with greater power, status, and advantages (whites, males, the more educated, and the wealthy) are more likely than are less privileged groups to favor and support the criminal justice system, particularly the police use of force.

Issues of procedural fairness and the equal treatment of all persons accused of committing crimes dominate the consciousness of blacks. When they have perceived that the justice system is fair and equitable, the immigrants have tended to show support for the justice system. Conversely, their perceptions of arbitrariness, unfairness, and judicial disparity have come to underlie the apparent reluctance on their part to support the aims and objectives of the criminal justice system. The weak support for the criminal justice system among those black immigrants who identified themselves as poor or lower-class, without college education, is not hard to explain. This is the group that reported the most negative contacts with the police and the judicial system. Their perception of unequal justice is rationalized from the conflict-coercion perspective. This perspective acknowledges that the primary objective of the criminal justice system is to enforce and apply the laws of the dominant and powerful superordinate groups in society; the goal is to control the less powerful, subordinate, low-status groups. As Richard Quinney has noted, "Through the legal system, then, the state forcefully protects its interests and those of the capitalist class. Crime control becomes the coercive means for checking threats to the social and economic order; threats that result from a system of oppression and exploitation" (53).

Irrespective of their sentiments regarding the American system of justice, a plurality of the black immigrants believe that concerted efforts must be initiated to countervail the tension between police and minority communities across the nation. While they acknowledge that racism is ubiquitous and blacks continue to feel its deleterious effects when it comes to the administration of justice, many of the immigrants contend that media portrayal of crime involving blacks and other minorities has created a chasm of fear and loathing on the part of white society toward blacks and other minorities. The result is that many blacks become targeted by agents of the criminal justice system not because they have a proclivity for criminality, but merely because of their skin color. And sometimes, irrespective of their class, level of education, residence, or income, skin color as a social marker is sufficient justification for blacks to be linked to crime, or to be stopped for questioning by the police without cause.

What has emerged from this study is that a large segment of the black immigrant population, just like their native-born black counterparts, believe that the system of justice is oppressive, capricious, and designed to maintain white and advantaged-group hegemony over less advantaged subgroups such as blacks and other minorities. For black immigrants who have settled in the U.S., the opportunity to live, work, or attend school in the U.S. is welcome. And a large number of the immigrants recognize that these opportunities are not readily available to them in their respective countries of origin. However, while they strive to improve upon their economic and cultural status in the U.S., they also remain aware that they are outsiders, foreign, alien. Above all, their identity as blacks marks them as second- and third-class citizens who will never achieve racial equality in the white-dominant society.

Coming from outside the U.S., where class and not race was the marker of access to mobility and status, the majority of the black immigrants find it difficult to seek full integration into society because of their recognition that they will never become full members of it. Despite the social and human capital attributes (good work ethic, strong family networks, commitment to higher education, positive self-esteem, and confidence in their black identity) that the majority of the black immigrants brought with them to the U.S., most of them perceive that their black identity marks them and assigns them to a subordinate class, which makes it easier for the agencies of criminal justice to mistreat them and get away with it. The vigorous arrests for and prosecutions of street-level urban crimes where the majority of blacks reside mean that blacks often come into contact with police and law enforcement agencies more than any other group(s) in the country. Often, when politicians have made an issue of crime control and paraded under the banner of "law and order" as the rallying point of their campaigns, the results have translated into higher arrest rates for blacks and poor immigrants in the inner cities. Such attention and focus gives an unfortunate impression that the crime problem in the U.S. is a black problem and has the potential to cause hysteria and fright among suburban and middle-class whites. The result is that most Americans come to identify crime as a black problem, to be dealt with by the established authorities through the imposition of tougher and stiffer penalties such as "three strikes" laws. Over time, blacks come to perceive the justice system as heavily weighted against them and designed to keep them powerless to alter its course and direction. As the data from the focus group reveals, the justice system is seen by many black immigrants as a mechanism for enforcing laws and applying sanctions to those who violate these laws, without any effort on the part of the government to change the circumstances responsible for driving people to break the law. The immigrants find it daunting that a well-entrenched system of social control, with political muscle and immense resources at its disposal, has the power to influence and affect the lives of so many people, particularly blacks and minorities.

The immigrants feel that the system of justice lacks the political will and resources to invest in the prevention and reduction of criminal acts. However, the resources of the system are put in place when it comes to the punishment of those who are adjudicated to have breached the law. The system of justice lacks a coordinated approach to eradicate the perceptions of racism and discrimination or to put in place a seamless regimen to deter illegal racial practices which for decades have impacted how blacks and racial minorities in general perceive the system of justice. The perception that the justice system is heavily tilted against them forms the background to the determination of many blacks not to assist the police in fighting crime.

The unfavorable attitudes and perceptions that blacks in general have come to hold toward the system of justice are a microcosm of a larger picture of generalized lack of confidence in major social institutions in the

U.S. In every aspect of social well-being, peoples of black African ancestry living in the U.S. lag behind their white counterparts. The gap of inequality still persists when blacks are compared to other minority groups, particularly Asians, Hispanics, and newly arriving immigrants. Mainly confined to the permanent underclass in the U.S., blacks continue to face the vestiges of exclusionary racial practices that have lingered from the days of slavery into the post–civil rights era. Despite the moderate economic and cultural gains that blacks have made in the U.S., there is ample evidence that these gains have been confined to a small segment of black society, particularly those in the middle class with college degrees, living in dual-income households. The majority of blacks have not fared well economically. Blacks living in the inner sections of large American cities continue to experience a downward spiraling as jobs leave for suburbia or relocate entirely outside the U.S. The decline in manufacturing employment and the continued restructuring of the country's economy have had a deleterious impact on the economic circumstances of black Americans. The result is that wherever they live, blacks in general continue to face structural impediments toward full integration into every aspect of American society. And as a group, blacks routinely continue to bear a heavy burden and pay a high price for internal and international economic restructuring.

In every facet of American society, the gap of inequality between blacks and whites, as well as between blacks and other groups such as new immigrants from Latin America and Asia, continues to widen. Chronic unemployment and underemployment among inner-city black youths, mounting discrimination in housing and education, and the inability of black teenagers or school leavers to find gainful employment in their communities have created doubts as to whether the American dream is still attainable for a large segment of America's black population. Peoples of African descent in the country continue to experience subpar education, discrimination in housing, dwindling employment opportunities (particularly among blacks who live in the urban centers and who have not completed high school), healthcare inequities, and a growing political disenfranchisement. These problems lie at the root of the racial hostility, and sometimes anger and frustration, felt by a majority of blacks. For the vast majority of the blacks who were the focus of this study, the general concern is that institutionalized prejudice remains an important part of the negative perception that native-born blacks and black immigrants alike have come to have of the system of justice in the U.S. The discrimination encountered by blacks is at the root of the alienation and marginalization that blacks in general have come to associate with social institutions in the country. Over half a century of public policy debates and government programs have failed to lessen the gap of inequality and the discrimination that most blacks perceive and experience on a daily basis in the U.S. The lack of confidence among blacks in key institutions thwarts efforts to achieve social justice and equality in the country's body polity.

Finally, it bears stating that perceptions or attitudes about crime and the criminal justice system are not fixed or static. They are always in a state of flux and are affected by micro and macro factors in the social environment. Increased access to information, technological changes, and alterations in norms and mores as well as institutional changes all converge to cause shifts in public attitudes and opinions. Shifts in social class membership and inter- and intra-community group relations are significant sites for changes in attitudes to occur. So are changes in social identity, and more broadly, changes in the institutional components of society. Making causal inferences about citizens' attitudes on pressing social issues such as crime is very complex and fraught with methodological and theoretical shortcomings. The process is not linear, and causal inferences that are made about attitudes and opinions are at best tenuous and tentative. The politico-legal and social contexts involved in the formulation of criminal justice ideologies and philosophies as well as shifts in the rationalization of penal/criminal justice structures will ultimately affect public attitudinal behaviors and perceptions regarding the place of crime and justice in society.

NOTE

1. For the sake of brevity, detailed summary statistics are not reported but may be obtained from the author.

REFERENCES

Arthur, J. *Invisible Sojourners: African Immigrant Diaspora in the United States.* Westport, Conn.: Greenwood/Praeger, 2000.
———. "Proximate Correlates of Blacks' Support for the Death Penalty." *Journal of Crime and Justice* 21, no. 1 (1996): 159–172.
Arthur, J., and C. Case. "Race, Class and Support for Police Use of Force." *Crime, Law, and Social Change* 21 (1994): 167–182.
Barkan, Steven. *Criminology: A Sociological Understanding.* New Jersey: Prentice Hall, 2006.
Barkan, Steven, and Steven Cohn. "Racial Prejudice and Support for the Death Penalty by Whites." *Journal of Research in Crime and Delinquency* 31 (1994): 202–209.
Biderman, A., L. Johnson, J. McIntyre, and A. Weir. *Report and Pilot Study in the District of Columbia on Victimization and Attitudes towards Law Enforcement. Field Survey One. President's Commission on Law Enforcement and Administration of Justice.* Washington, D.C.: U.S. Government Printing Office, 1967.

Bohm, R. "American Death Penalty Attitudes: A Critical Examination of Recent Evidence." *Criminal Justice and Behavior* 14, no. 3 (1987): 380–396.

———. *The Death Penalty in America: Current Research.* Cincinnati: Anderson, 1991.

Bryce-Laporte, R. "Black Immigrants: The Experience of Invisibility and Inequality." *Journal of Black Studies* 3, no. 1 (1972): 29–56.

———. "Caribbean Migration to the United States: Some Tentative Conclusions." In *Caribbean Immigration to the United States,* ed. R. Bryce-Laporte and Delores Mortimer. Washington, D.C.: Research Institute on Immigration and Ethnic Studies, Smithsonian Institution, 1983.

———. "The New Immigration: A Challenge to Our Sociological Imagination." In *Sourcebook on the New Immigration: Implications for the United States and International Community,* ed. R. Bryce-Laporte. New Brunswick, N.J.: Transaction Books, 1980.

Gordon, A. "The New Diaspora: African Immigration to the United States." *Journal of Third World Studies* 15, no. 1 (1998): 79–103.

Konadu-Agyemang, K., and Baffour Takyi. "An Overview of African Immigration to U.S. and Canada." In *The New African Diaspora in North America: Trends, Community Building, and Adaptation,* ed. K. Konadu-Agyemang, B. Takyi, and John Arthur. Lanham, Md.: Lexington Books, 2006.

Lynch, M., and E. Patterson. "Racial Discrimination in the Criminal Justice System: Evidence from Four Jurisdictions." In *Racism, Empiricism, and Criminal Justice,* ed. B. Maclean and D. Milovanovic. Vancouver, B.C.: Collective, 1990.

Martin, P. "Good Intentions Gone Awry: IRCA and U.S. Agriculture." *Annals of the American Academy of Political and Social Science* 534 (1994): 44–57.

Martin, P., and E. Midgley. "Immigration to the United States: Journey to an Uncertain Destination." *Population Bulletin* 49, no. 2 (1994): 2–47.

Quinney, R. *Class, State and Crime.* 2nd ed. New York: Longman, 1980.

Stinchcombe, A., R. Adams, C. Heimer, K. Schepple, T. Smith, and D. Taylor. *Crime and Punishment: Changing Attitudes in America.* San Francisco: Jossey-Bass, 1980.

Taylor, R., and J. Covington. "Community Structural Change and Fear of Crime." *Social Problems* 40 (1993): 374–397.

Tyler, T., and R. Weber. "Support for the Death Penalty: Instrumental Response to Crime, or Symbolic Attitude?" *Law and Society* 17, no. 1 (1982): 21–45.

Vickerman, Milton. *Crosscurrents: West Indian Immigrants and Race.* New York: Oxford University Press, 1999.

Warr, M. "Dangerous Situations: Social Context and Fear of Criminal Victimization." *Social Forces* 68 (1990): 891–907.

Warr, M., J. Gibbs, and M. Erickson. "Contending Theories of Criminal Law: Statutory Penalties Versus Public Preferences." *Journal of Research in Crime and Delinquency* 19 (1982): 25–46.

Weitzer, R., and S. Tuch. "Race and Perceptions of Police Misconduct." *Social Problems* 51 (2004): 305–325.

Wilbanks, W. *The Myth of a Racist Criminal Justice System.* Pacific Grove, Calif.: Brooks and Cole, 1987.

Young, R. L. "Race, Conceptions of Crime and Justice, and Support for the Death Penalty." *Social Psychology Quarterly* 54, no. 1 (1991): 67–75.

12 AFRICANS ABROAD: COMPARATIVE PERSPECTIVES ON AMERICA'S POSTCOLONIAL WEST AFRICANS

Baffour K. Takyi

I n the past thirty years, the United States (America) has witnessed a surge in immigration unseen since the turn of the last century. The Census Bureau has reported that the foreign-born population (documented and undocumented) has been growing rapidly, from 9.6 million people in 1970 to 14.1 million by 1980. This number increased further to 19.8 million in 1990 and 31.1 million around the end of the century (Gibson and Jung). As a result of the growth, immigrants now constitute over 10 percent of America's population.

In contrast to previous waves of immigration to America, the majority of these new immigrants are from non-Western societies, including Africa (Massey, "Economic Development"). Students of postcolonial African social history may have also noticed some new developments in recent international migration of Africans. Because European powers had colonized the Africa region, Europe had traditionally been the destination of African emigrants. These earlier African migrants, especially of the pre-independence period, saw their trip or stay as "temporary." Among those who left Africa for Europe in those early days were the intelligentsia or the few educated elites from their countries. In contrast, the destinations and composition of postcolonial African emigrants have become quite diverse. Unlike the historically developed patterns—America, Canada, Australia—the Middle East and other non-Western regions have increasingly become major destinations for African emigrants.

In addition, these new emigrants include the highly educated, those with no or limited education, as well as those with highly demanded skills and those without these skills. More importantly, it seems that these migrants are increasingly becoming permanent fixtures in their new destinations. Thanks to contemporary advances in communications technology, African migrants have become more transnational, with many shuttling regularly between their countries and their new homes in the "diaspora."

In the case of America, its appeal as a destination for African migrants is a recent phenomenon. Researchers attribute this change to a number of factors,[1] including the country's shift to a worldwide immigration quota in the mid-1960s that abolished the previous country-of-origin quota put in place in the 1920s. Even though the true impact of these policy changes has become a subject of debate in some quarters, some scholars have pointed to the abolition of the previous restrictions as a cause of the recent surge in Third World immigration to America (Massey, "The New Immigration," "Economic Development"; Portes and Rumbaut). Beginning in the 1990s, and due in large part to the 1986 Immigration Reform and Control Act (IRCA) and the Immigration Reform Act of 1990, there has also been a steady and gradual increase in the number of Africans who have been arriving in the cities and towns of America. Indeed, it has been pointed out that Africa has benefited immensely as a result of the diversity provisions in the 1990 immigration reforms (Konadu-Agyeman, Takyi, and Arthur).[2] Besides these policy changes, Africans have been drawn in large numbers to America by its many educational institutions that offer professional and other higher-level degrees, not to mention the availability of jobs for those with skills, especially in academic and medical institutions (Zeleza; Takyi; Dodoo and Takyi, "Race and Earnings").

Although hard numbers on Africans who now call America home are difficult to come by, and the African flow to America is still low compared to immigrant waves from other world regions such as Asia, Latin America, and the Caribbean, some researchers have noted significant inflows from Africa in recent years. Accounting for less than 1 percent of America's total foreign-born population for most of the twentieth century, Africa's share of America's foreign-born people had increased to about 3 percent in 2000, and 4 percent as of 2004. Rumbaut has estimated that of all the world regions, Asia and Africa accounted for the fastest growth rates in immigration to America during the 1980s. According to Parillo, Africa has averaged about 43,000 legal immigrants per year since the 1990s. Logan and Deane have also pointed out that between 1980 and 1990, the number of Africans in America increased by 6 percent per year.[3] Furthermore, they have argued that the number of black Americans with recent roots in sub-Saharan Africa nearly tripled during the 1990s.[4] Analyzing data from the 2000 U.S. decennial census, Takyi has also observed that the growth in the African immigrant community was more pronounced among black Africans (11 percent versus 4 percent for white Africans).

Despite the increased migration from Africa, and the abundant scholarly literature that currently exists with respect to recent immigrants to America, the extant literature on African immigrants is rather limited. Indeed, missing for the most part from the recent discourse on post-1960s immigrants are studies that examine the experiences of the emerging African immigrant community in several American cities over the past two decades. It is only recently that a new crop of Africanist scholars have begun to focus their research on recent African immigrants (see, for example, Pierre; Takyi; Dodoo and Takyi; Arthur; Akyeampong; Takyi, "The African Diaspora"; Elabor-Idemudia; Kamya; Perry; Takougang). For instance, Takyi ("The Making"), Gordon ("The New Diaspora"), Kamya ("African Immigrants"), Takougang ("Black Immigrants"), and Apraku (*African Émigrés*) have all used data from the 1980s and 1990s to describe some aspects of the African immigration. Dodoo and Takyi have also examined race differences in earnings between black and white Africans in America and reported sizeable differences among these immigrants who have relatively similar human capital profiles. In yet another study of black migrants, Dodoo ("Assimilation") has noted that despite their higher levels of education, African immigrants fare worse than other black immigrants in America, and attributes this observation to what he suggests are the "negative Western notions about Africa" (528). More recently, Read and Emerson have used health data to investigate the health of native and foreign-born blacks (defined in terms of their geographic origins: Africa, South America, the West Indies, and Europe).

Admittedly, these recent studies have offered some significant insights into the African community in America, but there is still much that is unknown about these immigrants. For example, very little is known about their family structures, adaptive responses, and living arrangements while in America. Of note also is the fact that the recent discourse on African migrants tends to be plagued more by the debate on the "brain drain," or the reported loss of Africa's skilled and professional workers to emigration (see, e.g., Dodoo, Takyi and Mann; Ozden and Schiff; *Carrington and Detragiache*). Also, it is not quite clear how the presence of a group of African-descended people, whose cultural backgrounds and immigration experiences are different from those of the African immigrants who arrived in this country centuries ago, may be shaping the whole idea of "African or black identity" in America.[5] These new migrations are more transnational and transcultural in nature, with some migrants having multiple ties and identities, attributes that could help fuel tensions between the various African-descended peoples. The extent to which African immigrants who have been coming to America over the past decade are quietly changing the dynamics of intra-racial relations in many American cities that are home to the nation's largest share of African Americans is unknown at best (for some exceptions, see Austin).

The present essay is an attempt at extending the ongoing theoretical and empirical analysis of what is known about the new African diaspora, by examining migration from postcolonial Africa to America. This chapter departs from existing studies especially in its emphasis on postcolonial West Africans. In attempting to look at this group of African immigrants, the essay does not compare them to other black groups in America (such as those created from the historical diaspora); rather, it examines the pattern of migration from West Africa, focusing on the composition as well as characteristics of this immigrant group. In addition, the essay offers insights into some of the intra-group variations among the major sending nations in the region.

Why is a discussion of West African immigrants important? The first reason is that, even though African immigrants are a diverse group, the extant literature tends to view them as a homogenous group, making it difficult to tease out any intra-group differences that may exist among these new waves of African immigrants. As Zeleza; Takyi; and Dodoo and Takyi have all suggested, this analytical approach to the study of Africans is at best limited in many respects, overlooking, for instance, differences in the internal and external relations of various African groups, in terms of their racial and ethnic identity, social class, gender, generation, political ideology, and religious backgrounds. Given these considerations, there is need of research that takes into account this heterogeneity and thus allows for the examination of how different African groups do in their new country: the United States.

Second, the West African experience in America is significant in its own way with respect to the overall discourse on the black (African) diaspora, especially when we focus on the "historic" or "established" Atlantic diaspora (Zeleza). Indeed, it was this region of Africa alone (particularly the areas of modern Ghana, the Senegambia region, Nigeria, Benin, and the Congo and Angolan Basin) that served as the source of the "Black Atlantic." Not surprisingly, many native-born Americans of African descent trace their ancestry to parts of this region. Because of this historical link, West African institutions and culture have also had some influence on the Atlantic diaspora, with several scholars explaining the situation of African Americans from the point of view of their cultural ties to the region (see, e.g., Simpson; Apter).

Third, in the recent waves of Africans who have come to America, about two out of every five immigrants is West African. In addition, unlike Africans from, say, Northern and Southern Africa, who are more likely to racially identify as non-black Africans, West Africans immigrants are overwhelmingly of "black" (Negro) ancestry. In this sense, then, a study of the West African experience can be situated as part of the overall discourse on black Africans, as well as the larger black community in America (see, for example, Bryce-Laporte, "Black Immigrants" and "Black Immigrants . . . Reintroduced").

As the pendulum of history swings once more to the source of the original black diaspora, and because postcolonial Africans have increasingly embraced America as they escape from outdated and obsolete institutions, poverty, and political repression in their own homelands, the need to document the experiences of these largely black immigrants cannot be underestimated in our increasingly racialized and multicultural society. To a large extent, the objectives behind this study are primarily descriptive, since the essay does not test any theories about the West African experience in America. It is, however, hoped that the findings could serve as a basis for future research (theoretical and empirical) that test ideas and assumptions about observed patterns and trends with respect to this group of contemporary Africans in America.

For the sake of clarity, when we speak of West Africans, we are referring to immigrants from the nations that are part of the current Economic Community of West African States (ECOWAS).[6] One of the strengths of this essay is that, unlike existing data (including those produced by the U.S. Census Bureau itself), we include immigrants from Cape Verde, a West African island nation with a long history of emigration, in the analyses.[7] Drawing on the fact that West Africans are from diverse countries with different historical and colonial experiences, we distinguish between the main sending nations and use them in the comparisons. As stated earlier, and to the best of my knowledge, there are very few studies that explore the unique experiences of the various West Africans in America in terms of their national origins.

METHODOLOGY

The data used in this analysis of West African immigrants come primarily from the Integrated Public Use Microdata Series (IPUMS)[8] of the 1980, 1990, and 2000 United States decennial censuses. These data were supplemented, where possible, with aggregate data from Summary Tape Files (STFs) of the census as well.[9] For these three census years, we relied on the 5 percent IPUMS microdata that have detailed information on all those who were sampled in those years, including a question on place of birth that permits the identification of all people born in this country and elsewhere.[10]

To help with the comparisons, as very few Africans (because of their relatively small numbers) were captured in the earlier censuses, prior to the 1980s, these three IPUMS datasets were merged to create a single file of Africans in America. Africans were first identified using the responses to the census question on birthplace.[11] After identifying all Africans, we then selected those who reported a West African country of birth, using their specific country of birth for this assignment. Since by West Africa we mean those countries that are part of the Economic Community of West African States (ECOWAS), a collection of sixteen countries that borders

North Africa in the north, Central Africa (Middle Africa) in the east, and the Atlantic Ocean in the south and west, we excluded from our sample countries in the Congo and the Angolan basin which are at times included as part of the historical West African region and also were one of the main sources for the development of the historical or Atlantic diaspora.

As with many secondary data, we should point out the possibility that the official statistics we are using may underestimate the true size of the community of West Africans. This is especially because the data may have excluded West Africans immigrants who entered the country without legal documents. Also, the data may be affected by the reported undercount of some ethnic minorities (e.g., blacks) and immigrants in previous censuses. Hirschman, for example, notes that counts of the foreign-born (immigrant) population at times underestimate the influence of the immigrant community, as their age structure and geographic location have a tendency to accentuate their presence. Moreover, the second generation (native-born children of these immigrants) are not counted even though they are often reared in the social and cultural milieu of their immigrant families or parents.

SIZE, TRENDS, PATTERNS, AND COMPOSITION OF WEST AFRICAN IMMIGRATION TO AMERICA

Since the late 1960s, more and more Africans have immigrated to America in search of their "American" dream. According to Census Bureau reports, about a million or more Africans currently call America home. Of this number, nearly 40 percent are from the West African region alone, making the region an important source of recent African immigrants. The growing number of Africans in general is due to high levels of immigration during the past three decades.

With respect to West Africans as a whole, table 12.1 shows that about a half-million were residents of America at the turn of the new century. Of this number, 65 percent are from two main countries: Nigeria and Ghana. These two countries have consistently been the primary source of West African immigration to America over the last three decades for which data are available. In 1980, these two countries accounted for slightly more than half of all West Africans in America (58 percent). By 2000, this figure had increased to 67 percent. By far, Nigeria continues to be the major source of West African immigrants in America.

Although Nigeria is the main source of West African immigrants, its share of America's West Africans during the period was stable and flat (changing about 1 percent between 1980 and 2000). The slight decline in migration from Nigeria was compensated for by increased migration from countries such as Ghana, which saw its share of West Africans increase by 8 percent, followed by Liberia (7.7 percent) and Sierra Leone (3.6 percent).

Table 12.1. The Size and Composition of West African Immigration in America, 1980–2000

	Census year				Total Change 1980–2000	Percent Change 1980–2000
	2000	1990	1980	All		
Panel I (Number)[a]						
Country of Birth						
Ghana	68,122	20,863	8,343	97,328	59,779	717
Liberia	42,754	12,356	3,701	58,811	39,053	1,055
Nigeria	140,929	60,423	27,024	228,376	113,905	421
Sierra Leone	21,944	7,193	2,101	31,238	19,843	944
Cape Verde	27,059	15,948	10,452	53,459	16,607	159
Other W-Africans	10,215	11,179	9,787	31,181	428	4
Total	311,023	127,962	61,408	500,393	249,615	
% of Overall Total	62.2	25.6	12.3	100.0		

						Percent Change 1980–2000 as a share of West Africans
Panel II (% of Total)[b]						
Country of Birth						
Ghana	21.9	16.3	13.6	19.5	8.3	61
Liberia	13.7	9.7	6.0	11.8	7.7	128
Nigeria	45.3	47.2	44.0	45.6	1.3	3
Sierra Leone	7.1	5.6	3.4	6.2	3.6	106
Cape Verde	8.7	12.5	17.0	10.7	(8.3)	(49)
Other W-Africans	3.3	8.7	15.9	6.2	(12.7)	(79)
Total	100.0	100.0	100.0	100.0		

a: Refers to changes over time for each country
b: This figure was computed as the country's share of all West African immigrants for that census year

An interesting observation about the West African community is that it is dominated by the anglophone countries in the region (except for Cape Verde), indicating the possibility of linguistic experience in these countries as a key reason for emigration.

In explaining the growth in migration from West Africa, and particularly Ghana, Sierra Leone, and Liberia, one cannot ignore the way changing U.S. immigration policies have benefited people from these countries. For example, the influx from Nigeria and Ghana may have something to do with the 1986 IRCA and 1990 immigration changes. These two legislations either legalized the undocumented here, making it possible for them to bring in their family members under U.S. immigration preferences, or allowed them to immigrate to America under diversification of source countries provisions. Also, Shillington and many others (see, e.g., Takyi) have pointed to the political and civil unrest, human rights abuses, intimidation, harassment, and imprisonment without trial in the region, particularly Ghana (during the 1980s), Sierra Leone, Liberia, and more recently Cote d'Ivoire, in explaining some of the increases in emigration from the region.

SOCIO-DEMOGRAPHIC CHARACTERISTICS

What is the profile of West Africans in America? One of the main assumptions about international migration is that it is quite selective, with the young more likely to move than the old (Lee). Indeed, there are striking similarities between the composition of the West Africans and what the existing literature suggests. As a whole, the typical West African immigrant is, relatively speaking, a young person in his or her thirties, with the average age hovering around thirty-four years. This pattern is true of the major sending countries. However, West African immigrants from the islands of Cape Verde tend to be older, averaging about five more years than the typical West African. Also, over 20 percent of Cape Verdeans and about 10 percent of those from Liberia are over fifty-five years (table 12.2).

Consistent with what has been observed with respect to contemporary international migrations (see, e.g., Zlotnick), our analysis suggests that women (42 percent) feature prominently in migration from West Africa to America. While women are a significant part of the emigration from Africa generally, for Liberia and Cape Verde the ratio of female to male immigrants is the same slight majority (50.5 percent). Racially, the majority of West Africans self-identify as black Africans (83 percent), while 17 percent consider themselves as non-black West African. Nearly half of non-black West Africans are from Cape Verde; 77 percent of Cape Verdean immigrants identify as non-black.

Given the pro-family ideology that is common among Africans, it is not surprising that we find that half of all West Africans in America are married. Among the married couples, considerably more are in this country with both parents resident (43 percent) than with only one resident (7 percent). Families without a resident spouse range from a low of 4.2 percent for Cape Verdeans to a high of 8.7 percent reported among Ghanaians. Liberia (43.5 percent) had the highest rate of single immigrants, followed closely by Cape Verde (37.9 percent), then other West Africa (37.8) and Sierra Leone (37.6).

GEOGRAPHIC AND RESIDENTIAL PATTERNS

The geographic distribution of West African immigrants in America as reported in table 12.3 shows that they are more likely to be found in the

Table 12.2. The Socio-Demographic Characteristics of America's West Africans

	Country of Birth						All West Africans
	Ghana	Liberia	Nigeria	Sierra Leone	Cape Verde	Others	
Age (Mean)	34.5	33.6	33.1	34.2	38.7	34.2	34.2
Age Cohort							
Under19	11.2	18.2	12.3	16.0	16.7	13.0	13.5
19–34	38.0	35.3	40.6	34.0	30.0	44.2	38.2
35–54	45.4	36.6	43.1	43.4	31.7	32.8	41.0
55 and over	5.4	9.9	4.0	6.6	21.6	10.0	7.4
Gender							
Female	40.5	50.5	38.8	46.9	50.5	36.6	42.1
Male	59.5	49.5	61.2	53.1	49.5	63.4	57.9
Ethnic Group							
White African	1.9	5.1	3.3	6.0	16.0	27.0	6.3
Black African	93.2	89.8	93.0	89.2	23.0	66.9	83.3
Other African[a]	4.9	5.1	3.7	4.8	61.0	6.1	10.4
Marital Status							
Married, spouse present	43.0	34.9	46.2	37.8	41.9	41.7	43.0
Married, spouse absent	8.7	5.5	8.1	6.6	4.2	8.3	7.4
Separated	5.5	5.4	5.2	7.5	3.4	3.1	5.1
Divorced	7.5	6.7	6.3	7.6	7.1	5.4	6.7
Widowed	1.1	3.9	1.8	2.9	5.5	3.7	2.5
Never married/ (N/A)	34.2	43.5	32.4	37.6	37.9	37.8	35.3
N	97,328	58,811	228,376	31,238	53,459	31,181	500,393

a: Other African are those who identify themselves as neither black or white African

Northeastern and Southern regions. The proportion of these West Africans is over 70 percent, with the Northeast recording 38 percent and the South 37.4. With respect to the major sending nations, we find some interesting patterns. Despite the fact that the Northeast and the South are where most West Africans are found, there are some important differences when we consider the specific sending countries. For example, almost all immigrants from Cape Verde (90 percent) are to be found in the Northeast, followed by about half of all Ghanaians (44.6 percent). In contrast, slightly more than half (53.2 percent) of immigrants from the country of Sierra Leone and nearly half of Nigerians (46.5 percent) are to be found in the Southern states.

Beyond the regional level, it appears that West Africans are quite cosmopolitan in terms of their residence, with about 70 percent living in metropolitan regions of the country (this includes those who reside in-

Table 12.3. The Geographic and Metropolitan Region of Residence of West African Immigrants in America

			Country of Birth				All West
	Ghana	Liberia	Nigeria	Sierra Leone	Cape Verde	Others	Africans
Panel A							
Region of Residence							
Northeast	44.6	38.9	24.3	25.7	90.2	39.5	38.0
Midwest	13.7	20.2	15.8	9.6	2.0	17.2	14.1
South	33.8	33.0	46.5	53.2	5.1	29.5	37.4
West	8.0	7.9	13.4	11.6	2.8	13.8	10.5
Metropolitan Residence							
Not applicable	22.5	22.2	27.7	23.5	31.4	37.9	26.8
Not in metro area	1.3	2.1	2.1	1.0	0.9	4.0	1.8
In metro area, central city	34.6	29.9	29.8	21.9	24.4	28.7	29.6
In metro, area, outside central city	30.1	32.2	26.2	41.3	10.9	19.5	26.6
Central city status unknown	11.4	13.7	14.3	12.3	32.4	9.8	15.2
Total	100	100	100	100	100	100	100
Panel B: Metropolitan Statistical Areas (MSAs)							
NA	3.9	4.8	5.3	2.6	10.2	10.0	5.6
Atlanta, Ga.	3.4	4.7	5.8	4.0	0.1	2.9	4.3
Boston, Mass.-N.H.	1.4	2.4	2.0	3.4	32.0	1.9	5.2
Worcester, Mass.	2.2	0.5	0.0		0.0	0.1	0.5
Chicago, Ill.	6.0	1.9	4.9	0.7	0.6	2.7	3.9
Charlotte-Gastonia–Rock Hill, N.C.-S.C.	0.6	1.4	0.4	1.2	na	0.7	0.6

Continued on the next page

Table 12.3. Continued

	Country of Birth						All West Africans
	Ghana	Liberia	Nigeria	Sierra Leone	Cape Verde	Others	
Cleveland, Ohio	0.3	0.8	0.5	0.2	0.1	1.1	0.5
Dallas–Fort Worth, Tex.	2.1	2.3	5.2	3.2	0.2	0.9	3.3
Houston-Brazoria, Tex.	1.9	1.6	8.6	1.8	0.1	1.3	4.7
Los Angeles–Long Beach, Calif.	2.9	1.8	5.3	3.9	0.8	4.1	3.8
Minneapolis–St. Paul, Minn.	1.3	9.1	1.5	0.4	0.1	1.0	2.1
New York–Northeastern N.J.	32.6	18.6	16.2	15.1	2.6	27.2	18.8
Philadelphia, Pa.-N.J.	2.1	8.0	1.9	3.5	0.6	1.2	2.6
Brockton, Mass.	0.2	0.3	0.0		17.5	0.3	2.0
Raleigh-Durham, N.C.	0.4	0.9	1.1	1.1	na	0.3	0.8
Richmond-Petersburg, Va.	0.3	0.5	0.3	1.4	na	0.1	0.3
San Francisco-Oakland-Vallejo, Calif.	0.8	2.4	2.2	1.1	0.5	2.6	1.7
Trenton, N.J.	0.2	2.1	0.2	0.1	na	0.3	0.4
Washington, D.C.-Md.-Va.	16.1	10.6	9.5	32.2	0.9	11.4	11.5
Baltimore, Md.	2.1	2.3	2.3	1.9	0.2	0.6	1.9
All other MSAs in the U.S.*	19.2	23.1	26.6	22.2	33.3	29.2	25.4

* This includes the many MSAs that are not listed above.

side and outside of the major central cities). Among West Africans, Ghanaians are concentrated more in central cities (34.5 percent) than what we observe for the other immigrant groups (panel A). Overall, it appears that two metropolitan regions have the highest concentration of West Africans: the New York/New Jersey (18.8 percent) and the Washington, D.C./Northern Virginia metropolitan statistical area (MSA) regions (the Census Bureau defines a Metropolitan Statistical Area as an area containing a recognized population nucleus and adjacent communities that have a high degree of integration with that nucleus). However, the concentration in these MSAs varies by country of origin. Indeed, about a third of all Ghanaian immigrants (32.6 percent) are found in the New York/New Jersey MSA, while the Washington, D.C., region has been the preferred destination for Sierra Leonean immigrants (32.3 percent). The Nigerian concentration, accounting for 31.5 percent of all Nigerian immigrants, is in the following MSAs: New York/New Jersey, Washington, D.C., and Atlanta. Other sizable pockets of Nigerian immigrants are to be found in the Dallas/Houston (5 percent) and Chicago (5 percent) areas. Together, these MSAs have over 40 percent of all Nigerians in America.

SOCIOECONOMIC CHARACTERISTICS OF WEST AFRICAN IMMIGRANTS

The characteristics of America's West Africans are typical of the African community as a whole. One of the consistent findings within the recent research on African immigrants in America is that they tend to have high levels of human capital as measured by educational attainment (Konadu-Agyeman, Takyi, and Arthur; Dodoo and Takyi; Takyi; Gibson and Jung), an observation that is contrary to what has been reported with respect to the foreign-born population as a whole. For example, Borjas has argued that the preference America has given to family-reunification and refugee immigrations since the mid-1960s has meant that immigration flows from developing countries have been of lower quality. Our analysis of IPUMS data for the past three decades provides some confirmatory evidence about what has been reported about Africans in America. While some West African groups are more highly educated than others, slightly more than a third (34.4 percent) of all West Africans report a bachelor's degree or higher. This figure is about ten percentage points higher than the national average of 24 percent reported for the entire U.S. (table 12.4).

Among the leading migrant-sending West African countries, Nigeria sends the highest percentage of people with bachelor's or higher degrees (47.9 percent). It is followed next by Ghana (29.8 percent), and not so closely by Sierra Leone and Liberia. Cape Verde (5.1 percent) accounts for the lowest percentage of college-educated West Africans.

Table 12.4. Educational Attainment and Work Characteristics of West African Immigrants in America

			Country of Birth				All West Africans
	Ghana	Liberia	Nigeria	Sierra Leone	Cape Verde	Others	
Education							
≤ High School	41.6	47.1	25.4	44.9	84.0	52.0	40.2
Some College	28.6	27.9	26.8	27.9	10.9	23.1	25.4
BA or more	29.8	25.0	47.9	27.2	5.1	25.0	34.4
Mean years of Education	7.3	6.8	7.6	7.0	5.0	6.5	7.1
Labor Force Participation							
Percent in Labor Force	78.0	74.7	76.1	77.4	63.8	64.8	74.4
Usual hours worked per week	29.6	26.4	28.5	28.2	22.7	23.5	27.5
Occupational Category							
Not in occupation	31.7	37.2	32.1	36.0	44.3	38.7	34.6
Managerial, Professional/Technical	14.6	12.2	19.6	13.6	4.6	15.4	15.5
Technical, Sales, and Administrative	20.7	21.4	24.3	22.6	8.5	15.0	20.9
Service	11.5	11.7	8.9	11.4	10.9	11.1	10.2
Farming, Forestry and Fishing	3.0	2.4	2.8	2.7	1.0	3.5	2.6
Precision Production, Crafts and Repairs	9.5	8.6	6.0	8.0	10.1	6.9	7.6
Fabricators and Operators	9.0	6.5	6.3	5.6	20.5	9.4	8.5
N	97328	58811	228376	31238	53459	31181	500393

As one would expect among immigrants, these new arrivals exhibit a high level of labor force participation, with over 70 percent reporting some form of work. Labor force participation rates range from a high of 78 percent for Ghanaians to a low of 63.8 percent found among Cape Verdean immigrants. On the other hand, despite their high labor force participation rates, West Africans, on average, tend to work less than the typical forty hours per week. Moreover, the types of work they normally do (judging by their occupational profiles) seem to be inconsistent with their high levels of education. In fact, only about 16 percent of West Africans work in managerial and professional settings, as our data show. Nigerians (19.6 percent) have a higher proportion of professionals than any other West African group. Almost a third of all West Africans are employed in technical, sales, administrative, and service jobs.

ADAPTIVE STRATEGIES AND MECHANISMS

Are West Africans becoming Americans? Researchers on assimilation and immigrant incorporation into American society often point to various processes by which immigrants become integrated into the U.S. Among some of the commonly studied indicators of integration are the acquisition of citizenship, homeownership patterns, and businesses ownership. For instance, owning rather than renting a home, some have argued, is a signal statement of success, security, stability, and social mobility in the U.S. (Adams). Although these three processes of incorporation are driven in large part by a number of factors, including length of time spent in the U.S., we must bear in mind that how individuals fare in American society is often a function of their citizenship status. Some jobs are dependent on one's immigrant status, and citizenship offers immigrants a piece of the proverbial pie, not the least part of which is the ability to participate in the political process.

In our study, we explored some of the above issues by examining the proportion of West Africans who owned their own homes, were citizens, or owned their own businesses (table 12.5). Self-employment rates for West Africans are quite high: 31 percent. Also, immigrants from Cape Verde include a higher percentage of self-employed people (41.4 percent) than any other West African group in America. The correlation between this high rate of self-employment among them and their poor English language skills was not explored in the study. Given that most African immigrants are recent migrants, with the majority having been here for less than ten years, it is not surprising that very few are naturalized citizens. Once more, Cape Verdeans appear to defy this norm, as slightly more than 40 percent of them are naturalized American citizens. Given that there is a strong correlation between citizenship and home ownership, it is not

Table 12.5. Adaptive and Incorporative Strategies of West African Immigrants in America

	Country of Birth						
	Ghana	Liberia	Nigeria	Sierra Leone	Cape Verde	Others	All
Adaptive Mechanisms							
Percent Self-Employed	27.5	31.3	29.4	28.8	41.4	39.9	31.1
Percent Naturalized	28.2	23.5	27.4	23.3	40.8	27.8	28.3
Percent More than 10 years in U.S.	36.9	39.3	38.0	39.9	57.9	35.6	40.0
Percent Homeowners	30.7	37.8	35.7	32.7	52.1	29.9	36.2
English Language Skills							
N/A (Blank)	1.0	1.5	1.8	1.2	1.2	1.8	1.5
Does not speak English	0.3	0.5	0.4	0.7	8.6	0.7	1.3
Yes, speaks only English	18.5	67.8	23.2	29.8	10.0	24.4	26.6
Yes, speaks very well	62.7	21.9	62.5	51.0	34.0	40.2	52.6
Yes, speaks well	14.9	6.6	10.2	14.0	26.1	23.5	13.4
Yes, but not well	2.5	1.7	1.8	3.4	20.1	9.3	4.5
Total	100.0	100.0	100.0	100.0	100.0	100.0	100.0

surprising that more than half of all Cape Verdeans report owning their own homes.

* * *

Increased immigration from Africa and other parts of the "black world," at a time of declining birth rates among the native-born Americans of African ancestry, is helping to increase the diversity of the black community in the U.S. Stimulated by these new developments, research interests have in recent years focused on the experiences of non-native-born blacks in America. Unfortunately, there is one group of blacks that has become "invisible" in the discourse on blacks: Africans, and particularly West Africans. Given the role West Africa played in the creation of the "Black Atlantic" diaspora, the recent emigration from the region to the Americas raises some interesting policy questions and debates in post–civil rights America. This chapter is not about such a debate. Rather, it has used pooled data to offer some insights into the situation of immigrants from West Africa. While a few of these immigrants are non-black, the majority are of black ancestry. These immigrants are mostly recent migrants, and in large part come from either Nigeria or Ghana. They tend to be highly educated, and to live in metropolitan or residentially segregated areas.

To explore further the experiences of these immigrant groups, other kinds of studies are needed. For instance, studies are needed that examine the comparative experiences of recent and not-so-recent West African immigrants. It would also be interesting to compare the experiences of English-speaking and non-English-speaking West Africans and to raise the question: how do their different historical and linguistic skills affect their integration into American society? Also, how does the presence of West Africans in metropolitan areas impact other American blacks in the local community? Such studies would give us a better understanding of the place of the postcolonial West African in American society.

NOTES

1. The typical reasons that have been alluded to here include push and pull factors (economic dislocations in the region, political unrest, availability of jobs in the U.S., and also the ease of movement as a result of changing patterns of technology and communication). See, for example, Konadu-Agyeman, Takyi and Arthur; Adepoju.

2. African counties have been major beneficiaries of the diversity lottery immigrant awards since 1990.

3. Recent data from the American Community Surveys (ACS) suggests that more than a million Africans now call America home.

4. Even though Europe, especially Britain, France, and Portugal—all former colonists—was the preferred destination for African migrants, restrictive Euro-

pean immigration policies and anti-immigrant sentiments in these countries, at a time of changing U.S. immigration, have all been cited as reasons for America becoming a favorable attraction for Africans wanting to leave their countries of origins in search of a better life or refuge against political, social, and civil unrests (see, e.g., Takyi).

5. This point draws more on recent reports that the children of black immigrants represent a sizable proportion of black or minority students in several Ivy League Schools. See also Austin.

6. Because of the focus on the ECOWAS region, the Congo basin (West-Central Africa), which also provided significant numbers of Africans to the Americas during the peak period of Atlantic slavery, is not included in this study.

7. Given that the Census Bureau's code that allows one to identify Cape Verdeans is classified under the Atlantic Islands, it is not surprising that existing studies that rely on IPUMS codes 6000 to 6099 for Africa will exclude these West Africans (see, e.g., Takyi). We are grateful to the Census Bureau staff for pointing out this error in classification.

8. The Integrated Public USE Microdata Series (IPUMS) is housed at the University of Minnesota. It consists of thirty-eight high-precision samples of the American population drawn from fifteen federal censuses and from the American Community Surveys of 2000–2004. The thirty-eight samples draw on every surviving census from 1850 to 2000 and provide a rich source of quantitative information on long-term changes in the American population. To facilitate analysis of changes over time, the IPUMS assigns uniform codes across all the samples and brings relevant documentation to help researchers in their study. For more information about this data, visit http://usa.ipums.org/usa/.

9. This is especially the case with our analysis on size and immigration trends.

10. The 5 percent IPUMS samples are based on responses provided by a representative sample of households and persons in them that received the Census's long form.

11. According to Gibson and Jung, since 1890, all individuals who have been born in a foreign country, but who have had at least one parent who was an American citizen, have been classified as native rather than foreign-born.

REFERENCES

Adams, John S. "The Meaning of Housing in America." *Annals of the Association of American Geographers* 74 (1984): 515–526.

Adepoju, Adereji. "South-North Migration: The African Experience." *International Migration* 29 (1991): 205–221.

Akyeampong, Emmanuel. 2000. "Africans in the Diaspora: The Diaspora and Africa." *African Affairs* 99, no. 395 (2000): 183–215.

Apraku, Kofi. *African Émigrés in the United States*. New York: Praeger, 1991.

Apter, A. "Herskovits's Heritage: Rethinking Syncretism in the African Diaspora." *Diaspora* 1 (1991): 235–260.

Arthur, John A. *Invisible Sojourners: African Immigrant Diaspora in the United States*. Westport: Praeger, 2000.

Austin, A. "Are Africans in America African Americans?" *Black Directions* 2, no. 2 (2006): 1–7.

Borjas, George J. "Assimilation, Changes in Cohort Quality, and the Earnings of Immigrants." *Journal of Labor Economics* 3 (1985): 463–489.

Bryce-Laporte, Roy Simon. "Black Immigrants: The Experience of Invisibility." *Journal of Black Studies* 3 (1972): 29–56.

———. "Black Immigrants: The Experience of Invisibility and Inequality, Reintroduced." In *2001 Race Odyssey: African Americans and Sociology*, ed. Bruce R. Hare. New York: Syracuse University Press, 2002. 203–235.

Carrington, W. J., and Enrica Detragiache. "How Extensive Is the Brain Drain?" *Finance and Development* 36 (1999): 46–49.

Djamba, Y. K. *"African Immigrants in the United States: A Socio-Demographic Profile in Comparison to Native Blacks."* *Journal of Asian and African Studies* 34 (1999): 210–215.

Dodoo, Francis Nii-Amoo. "Assimilation Differences among Africans in America." *Social Forces* 76 (1997): 527–546.

———. "Earnings Differences among Blacks in America." *Social Science Research* 20 (1991): 93–108.

Dodoo, Francis Nii-Amoo, and Baffour K. Takyi. "Africans in the Diaspora: Black-White Earnings Differences among America's Africans." *Ethnic and Racial Studies* 25 (2002): 913–941.

Dodoo, Francis Nii-Amoo, Baffour K. Takyi, and Jesse R. Mann. "On the Brain Drain of Africans to America: Some Methodological Observations." *Perspectives on Global Development and Technology* 5 (2006): 155–162.

Elabor-Idemudia, Patience. "Gender and the New African Diaspora: African Immigrant Women in the Canadian Labor Market." In *The African Diaspora: African Origins and New World Identities*, ed. Isidore Okpewho, Carole Boyce Davies, and Ali Mazrui. Bloomington: Indiana University Press, 1999. 234–253.

Gibson, Campbell, and Kay Jung. "Historical Statistics on the Foreign-Born Population of the United State: 1850–2000." U.S. Census Bureau Working Paper no. 81. Washington, D.C., 2006.

Gordon, April. "The New Diaspora: African Immigration to the United States." *Journal of Third World Studies* 15 (1998): 79–103.

Hirschman, Charles. "Immigration and the American Century." *Demography* 42 (2005): 595–620.

Kamya, H. "African Immigrants in the United States: The Challenges for Research and Practice." *Social Work* 42 (1997): 154–165.

Kilson, Martin L., and Robert I. Rotberg. *The African Diaspora: Interpretive Essays.* Cambridge, Mass.: Harvard University Press, 1976.

Konadu-Agyeman, K., Baffour K. Takyi, and John Arthur. *The Neo-Diaspora: The African Community in the United States.* Lanham, Md.: Lexington Books, 2006.

Lee, E. "A Theory of Migration." *Demography* 3 (1966): 47–57.

Logan, John R., and Glenn Deane. *Black Diversity in Metropolitan America.* Lewis Mumford Center for Comparative Urban and Regional Research, University at Albany, August 2003.

Massey, Douglas S. "Economic Development and International Migration in Comparative Perspective." *Population and Development Review* 14 (1988): 383–413.

———. "The New Immigration and Ethnicity in the United States." *Population and Development Review* 21 (1995): 631–652.

Okpewho, Isidore, Carole Boyce Davies, and Ali A. Mazuri, eds. *The African Diaspora: African Origins and New World Identities.* Bloomington: Indiana University Press, 1999.

Ozden, Caglar, and Maurice Schiff, eds. *International Migration, Remittances and the Brain Drain.* New York: The International Bank for Reconstruction and Development/World Bank/Palgrave Macmillan, 2006.

Parillo, Vincent N. *Strangers to these Shores.* 7th ed. Boston: Allyn and Bacon, 2003.

Perry, D. "Rural Ideologies and Urban Imaginations: Wolof Immigrants in New York City." *Africa Today* 44 (1997): 229–260.

Pierre, Jemima. "Black Immigrants in the United States and the Cultural Narratives of Ethnicity." *Identities: Global Studies in Culture and Power* 11 (2004): 141–170.

Portes, Alejandro, and Ruben G. Rumbaut. *Immigrant America: A Portrait.* Berkeley: University of California Press, 1990.

Read, J. Ghazal, and Michael O. Emerson. "Racial Context, Black Immigration and the U.S.: Black/White Health Disparity." *Social Forces* 84 (2005): 181–199.

Rumbaut, Ruben. "Origins and Destinies: Immigration to the United States since World War II." *Sociological Forum* 9 (1994): 583–621.

Shillington, Kevin. *Ghana and the Rawlings Factor.* London: Macmillan, 1992.

Simpson, G. "Haiti's Social Structure." *American Sociological Review* 6 (1941): 642–649.

Takougang, Joseph. "Black Immigrants to the United States." *Western Journal of Black Studies* 19 (1995): 50–57.

Takyi, Baffour K. "The African Diaspora: A Socio-Demographic Portrait of the Ghanian Migrant Community in America." *Ghana Studies Journal* 2 (2000): 35–56.

———. "The Making of the Second Diaspora: Emigration from Africa to the United States and Its Policy Implications." *Western Journal of Black Studies* 26 (2002): 32–43.

Zeleza, Paul T. "Rewriting the African Diaspora: Beyond the Black Atlantic." *African Affairs* 104, no. 414 (2005): 35–68.

Zlotnik, Hania. "International Migration 1965–96: An Overview." *Population and Development Review* 24 (1998): 429–468.

13 QUESTIONS OF IDENTITY AMONG AFRICAN IMMIGRANTS IN AMERICA

Msia Kibona Clark

Immigrating to the U.S. from Tanzania at a very young age and landing in middle America was devastating to a young girl who spoke with an African accent and was the only African for miles. I grew up in Cleveland, Ohio, and the group I was supposed to gravitate toward was the one that rejected me the most. Facing rejection from African Americans in my early years and having no African immigrant community to turn to, growing up in Cleveland would forever shape my identity. The city today has a small African population, but in the 1980s the African presence was almost nonexistent, with the exception of small Nigerian, Liberian, and Ethiopian communities. It also seemed that since the death of the era of the Black Power movement in the 1960s, the African American community in Cleveland, as in the much of the country, had lost a good deal of its diversity and connections with Africa, leaving only a small number who had kept Pan-African activism and sentiments alive (Joseph 296–305; Ogbar 199).

This meant that a young African girl-child like me was forced to conform or be marginalized. Unlike for many of today's newly arriving Africans, there was no African community within which to take refuge. I therefore suppressed my accent and assimilated as much as possible, often keeping feelings of not belonging to myself, all the way through college. During this same time, I went through a swing of sentiments, from absolutely hating African Americans to desiring nothing else but acceptance by them.

To my mother's family, I was their African cousin; to my father's, I was a Kibona who had been lost to America. Outside of my family, my identity has been held hostage by the attitudes and perceptions of anyone with their own idea of who and what is an African and/or an African American. There has been no continuity in how others perceive me. There are those who insist on saying I'm no longer African as well as those who are just as insistent that I am Tanzanian, and shame on me for not speaking my mother tongue with the same ease as my fellow countrymen. In the end I straddle the identity rope, never feeling completely African American nor completely Tanzanian.

Identity is always a tricky subject. One's identity is very personal but can also be very political. This is especially the case for peoples of African descent living in America. As more and more Africans are coming to the United States, questions surrounding Black identity are becoming more complex. Debates between whether one drop of Black blood made a person Black and whether biracial persons could claim both identities have dominated discussions on Black identity in the Black communities for generations. The new debates surrounding the identity of bicultural children will take the Black identity dialogue in a whole new direction. When one talked about being biracial there was often conflict, both internal and external, especially in a world determined to label one as Black but just as determined to point out the physical indicators that signaled one's biracial status to the rest of the world. Today, in Black America, it's all about being bicultural. That term can be defined in many ways: it can mean the product of African American and Caribbean parentage, Caribbean and African parentage, African parentage from different countries on the continent, African and African American parentage, or, more interestingly, born and raised in the United States but of African parentage. This essay deals with the latter two, as these seem to bring about the most debate in both the African and African American communities.

As a product of a bicultural union, my own identity, like that of others of similar backgrounds, depends on my environment. With a Tanzanian father and an African American mother, my paternal culture (Ndali) dictates that I am what my father is. This means I am expected to follow the traditions and customs of my Ndali patrilineage. When I fail to meet these expectations, depending on the severity of my infraction, I am either dismissed as ignorant because of my American upbringing or thoroughly lectured on what is expected of me as a Kibona. In America, however, my identity is no longer simply a matter of cultural and traditional expectations; it becomes political. My racial background comes with a new set of expectations and obligations. Not identifying as an African American would in itself be a political statement of where my perceived alliances lay.

Several Africans, such as Phillipe Wamba, Manthia Diawara, Olufemi Taiwo, and Lydia Omolola Okutoro, have talked of arriving in America and becoming African first and Tanzanian, Guinean, or Nigerian second. Many have described their surprise over the seemingly intractable racial divisions in the country. For those Africans who were born in the U.S. or who are bicultural, however, racial politics in America is familiar and easier to navigate, and they occupy a unique position in the tensions brewing within Black America. When they are among Africans, especially in

Africa, they are often reminded of their Americanness, whether it is in the clumsy way they pronounce words in the unfamiliar African language of their parents or in the inevitably uncomfortable moment of deciding whether to join or to correct those Africans who subscribe to stereotypes used in mocking African Americans. In America, however, this group of Africans often find themselves in the position of educating African Americans—whether friends or others who innocently make stereotypical remarks about Africans—about the African reality.

What is interesting about this group is that they can and do claim either identity or both simultaneously. Legally they are African Americans, but in reality they are neither fully African nor fully African American. At different times, and depending on the context, they may be considered members of both the African and African American communities; depending on their upbringing, they are often just as comfortable in an all-African as in an all–African American environment. The ambivalence of their position can thus be appreciated.

IDENTITY

"Race" is defined as the categorization of human beings based on specific physical or genetic traits or characteristics (Davis 18; Marable 186). "Culture" is a product of a people's shared history, beliefs, values, traditions, rituals, language, arts, and kinship structure, and it is transmitted through "social communication" (Davis 18; Marable 185). An "ethnic group" is constituted from a people with a shared culture (Davis 18; Marable 185). "Race" has emerged, however, to become a critical factor in American society, and, except for Black Americans, there has been a recognition and validation of the various ethnicities and cultures that make up individual racial groups in the United States. Until recently, when African immigration to America increased in the 1980s, there had not been a serious need for Blacks in America to reevaluate their identities. African immigrants are still steadily increasing their presence in America, so much so that they are referred to as the "new African diaspora" or even the "new African Americans." If one accepts the popular estimate that ten million Africans were brought to the Americas during the transatlantic slave trade, and that only 5–6 percent of those ten million arrived in the United States, then scholars are right in claiming that more Africans have arrived in the U.S. in the past twenty years than throughout the entire period of the transatlantic slave trade (Klein and Schwartz 17; Manning 37; McMillan 15; Raboteau 4). Not only are Africans coming to the U.S., but they are establishing communities in America and setting up roots here, thus indicating that their presence will forever change power dynamics both in Africa and in America. Table 13.1 shows the dramatic increase in sub-Saharan African immigration to the United States,

Table 13.1. Number of Africans Coming to the United States on Immigrant Visas

Years	Numbers of Immigrants
1821–1940	26,059
1941–1970	50,413
1971–1980	80,779
1981–1990	176,893
1991–2000*	305,608
2001–2004*	214,494

*Includes only sub-Saharan Africa
Source: United States Citizenship and Immigrations Services, "Table 2: Immigration by Region and Selected Country of Last Residence: Fiscal Years 1820–2004," January 2006.

with the 1980s as the decade in which this immigration began to significantly increase.

Table 13.2 gives a comparative view of the composition of Black America, where Africans are clearly showing the largest growth rate at almost 167 percent. While African immigrants are still less than 5 percent of the total Black U.S. population, their increasing numbers are necessitating a discussion of race and ethnicity in Black America.

RACE IN AMERICA

In America's highly racialized society, racial and ethnic group identities are very significant, and membership in a racial group often means "a cultural or ideological uniformity associated with group membership" (Sowell 118). This is especially the case with minority groups, and has meant the "homogenization of distinctions among racial minority groups" (Winant 43). Racial identity also necessitates minimizing ethnic differences to a great extent, in order to form a racial identity based on common cultural characteristics, goals, and histories.

Asian Americans, for example, are considered to be a racial group. Among Asian Americans there exists ethnic, linguistic, and cultural diversity. While many non-Asians may not acknowledge the distinctions in the Asian American community, within the Asian American community, ethnic and cultural differences are recognized. Asians in America, however, have managed to minimize the cultural and linguistic differences among themselves and as a result have collective political and economic bargaining power (Winant 60). One important example is the lobbying of President Ronald Reagan for reparations for survivors of the internment of over 110,000 Japanese Americans between 1941 and 1945. It was not until President Reagan was up for reelection that the lobbying efforts of Asian

Table 13.2. The Composition of Black America

	Population in Numbers		Percent of the Black Population in America		
	1990	2000	1990	2000	Growth Rate
African Americans	28,024,275	33,048,095	96%	93.9%	17.9%
Caribbean Immigrants	924,693	1,542,895	3.2%	4.4%	66.9%
Africans	229,488	612,548	.8%	1.7%	166.9%

Source: Glenn Deane and John Logan, "Black Diversity in Metropolitan America," Lewis Mumford Center for Comparative Urban and Regional Research, University at Albany, August 15, 2003.

Americans, who constitute about 3 percent of the U.S. population, prevailed. In the end the United States government agreed to pay $20,000 to each of 60,000 survivors of the internment camps (Maga 606; O'Connor and Willis). This is not to say there are no internal issues within the Asian American community. Asian Americans have, however, managed to form a collective Asian identity that has served the needs of each of its diverse cultures and is inclusive of the needs of its diverse groups.

Nowhere, however, is the pressure to conform to a group ideology and worldview felt more than in the Black community in America, where few distinctions are made between race and ethnicity (Marable 185). There are in fact criticisms over the perception that the Black community in America is a homogeneous group (Foner 164; Sowell 118). This leaves little room for the diversity that Black immigration has brought to the country.

Because of the relationship between black and white in America, African Americans are often perceived, even by themselves, as a racial group, not as an ethnic group (Marable 185). Most scholars treat African Americans or Black Americans as a racial rather than an ethnic group. This is significant because scholars speaking of African Americans as a race apply all the ethnic, historical, and cultural characteristics of an African American ethnicity to the Black race in America. This becomes problematic when foreign-born Blacks are factored into the equation.

African Americans, as they are perceived today, are not a race, but an ethnic group within the Black/African race. The unique characteristic of the African American community is that African Americans started out as a racial group. African Americans were a blend of the different ethnic groups that were brought to the United States during the transatlantic slave trade. Because of the circumstances of slavery and the nature of the American slave system, Africans were stripped of their names, languages, and identities early. This perhaps speeded up the African Americanization process. Through the years and the generations, memories of Africa progressively faded and a new group emerged, based on both an African past and an American reality. During this process, African Americans were transformed from a racial group with memories of distinct African identities to an ethnic group whose plural identity had given birth to a distinctive and unique culture.

If one, therefore, examines African Americans (as currently perceived) as an ethnic group, one can better understand the multiple identities among Black Americans. Black immigrants, whether from Africa or the Caribbean, constitute different ethnic groups within a Black racial identity. Hence, Blacks in America, or Black Americans, often embrace multiple identities and should not be forced into embracing a rigid African American identity that is based only on the values and experiences of one ethnic group. If successive generations of African immigrants are to become African Americans, as some scholars suggest, then either the definition of what it means to be African American must change, or a new term must emerge that reflects the experiences of those Black Americans of *recent* African descent.

As things stand today, African Americans are perceived to be a group whose ancestors arrived in the United States involuntarily via the transatlantic slave trade, whose history is rooted in the American South but consolidated by a series of encounters culminating in the Civil Rights Movement (Akbar and Sanders Thompson; Butterfield; Davis 18; Swarns). Because the experiences of African Americans resulted in an identity being imposed on them by historical forces, self-definition and self-identification have become part of African American self-determination. However, given the present ethnic composition of the African American community, there is room for Black immigrants under the umbrella of African America. Broadening the definition of "African American" would serve to transform this ethnic identity and change it back into a racial identity. Broadening the definition does not, of course, mean that any African living in the United States becomes automatically African American. Take Chinese Americans: those who have become American citizens or been born and/or raised in America have the option of identifying as Asian Americans, Chinese Americans, or just Chinese. The same should hold true of Africans in America.

CHILDREN OF AFRICAN IMMIGRANTS

I remember when the first African family that I knew of moved into my neighborhood. I was in high school and the family was from Togo. The family had a son my age who rode the school bus with me every day. By this time, my Tanzanian accent had started to give way to an African American accent and I had pretty much assimilated into the African American community. I still recall, however, days of riding the school bus with the new Togolese student sitting in the front and I in the back. This was just after 1987, when *Shaka Zulu* had come on TV and images of Shaka running through the bush, spear in hand, were fresh in everyone's mind. As a result of these images, the Togolese student endured a barrage of Africa jokes on a regular basis, all the way home. The reason this painful memory will remain a part of my childhood is that I did nothing; I just sat and listened, thankful it was not me. I never laughed with the other students, but I never spoke up for fear of being rejected myself. As we grew older and went our separate ways to college, our mothers remained friends. The family finally moved out of the neighborhood; but the shame at what I let happen, and the wish that I had apologized for my own weaknesses, will always remain with me.

Nonetheless, the offspring of Africans in America have been very crucial to the identity debate. Africans and African Americans have been pitted against each other by hundreds of years of damaging propaganda, harmful media images, and destructive school curricula. Jobs, scholarships, grants, and tenure have been resources Africans and African Americans have competed for, leading African Americans to feel threatened by Africans. On the other side, Africans often arrive in the U.S. with warnings that they not socialize with Black Americans. While the tensions between these two groups continue, African immigrants who have come to the U.S. are going to school, working, and starting families. The children of these immigrants are often being raised in African immigrant communities; unlike their parents, however, they are also being raised with MTV/BET and African American cultural images. Considerably weaned off their parents' African accents, these children often grow up with dual identities and an intimate knowledge of both communities. They are educated in the American school system, where they learn of the Civil Rights Movement and other markers of African American cultural history during Black History Month. Although a good number live in suburbia, where they are less exposed to the African American aesthetic, many more live in neighborhoods where they learn the African American vernacular on playgrounds during the day and, at night, the unique rhythms of the language of their ancestors.

To be sure, there is pressure from first-generation Africans for their children to retain their African identities. Indeed, given the numbers of first-generation Africans now living in the United States, it is possible for a second-generation African to find an entire social network of Nigerians in his or her own city. Still, there are many second-generation African immigrants who feel pressured by the wider African American community to become "African Americanized" (Diouf; Martin; Okutoro). Despite these challenges in intra-racial relations, not all Africans and African Americans have kept each other at arm's length. Many have smashed the imaginary boundary each group has built around itself and have dis-

covered elements of a shared culture, shared interests, and shared histories. Out of these friendships have emerged romantic relationships. This
has especially been the case between African men and African American
women.

All over the U.S., African American women in search of partners are
dating African men in increasing numbers. This is especially the case
among professional African American women, who often outnumber their
African American male counterparts and who have a harder time finding suitable mates who share their own professional status. The shortage
of African American men is seen on university campuses, and the fact
that between 25 and 30 percent of African American men between the
ages of 20 and 29 are in jail, on probation, or on parole has driven African
American women to look increasingly to the Black immigrant population
for suitable mates (Amick; Hall; Smith). Africans are the most educated
group in America, surpassing white Americans, Latinos, and Asians. With
the rise in the African professional class, African American women are
finding some success with African immigrants. Another important factor is that among Africans migrating to the U.S., there is a higher percentage of men than women. This means that just as African American
women experience a shortage of African American men, so is it likely that
African men will seek African American women as mates, because the
higher proportion of men than women in the African immigrant community makes it hard for African men to find African women as mates.

The children of these unions further complicate perceptions of Black
identity in the United States. Unlike the children of African immigrants,
these children are often not discouraged from associating with African
Americans, since they have one foot firmly planted in each community.
While they are taught the struggles of the African American community by their African American parent, they learn the importance of traditional African values and practices from their African parent. There are
several distinctions among bicultural children. There are those raised in
the U.S., and there are those who have been raised in Africa and have then
migrated to America later. Those raised in Africa are very likely more in
touch with their African roots than those raised in America. Another distinction is between those born as a result of an African American parent living in Africa and meeting an African, and those born as a result
of an African parent living in America and meeting an African American. These children may have migrated with their parents to America at
a young age, or may have been born in America. It can be said with relative confidence that those African Americans who went to live in Africa, where they found a future mate, had at least some level of African
consciousness and often a distinctly Pan-African outlook. The same is
not necessarily true of the African American mate of an African in the
U.S.; he or she may or may not require any real consciousness of Africa

to marry, or have a child with, an African. Nonetheless, these considerations are relevant to the development of the bicultural child.

Some important distinctions can also be drawn between children of African immigrants and children of bicultural unions. If the parents are active in the African community, this often influences how well the children identify with their African identity. There are, however, cases in which an African parent is not active in his or her African community but has a child who actively cultivates an African identity. This identity is also impacted by how frequently the parents travel to Africa with their child and to what extent language, customs, and food from Africa are part of their lives in America. A similar point may be made about children with one African American and one African parent. The difference is, however, that bicultural children who are raised in the U.S. often have more exposure to the African American community.

The final factor in the way these children achieve their identity is the children themselves. Just as no one knows why children from similar families choose divergent paths, there is no exact science for determining why children of African immigrants and bicultural children gravitate toward their African identity, their African American identity, or a combination of both. There are examples of those who consider themselves African American and completely assimilate into the African American community at the expense of their African identity. In my own experience, I distinctly remember attending college with two African women, one of Liberian immigrant parents and the other of Nigerian immigrant parents. We attended a small historically Black university in the south where there were no other African students on campus, only the occasional Caribbean student. Both of these students claimed African American identities and assimilated into the campus's African American population.

There are also those who have grabbed hold of their African identities and are often more nationalistic than their college classmates who have just arrived from Africa. This group, though familiar with the African American community, often claims only an African identity. In an interview, an administrator of a university's international student office said that a group of students who were second-generation Africans approached her about the possibility of starting a sorority just for second-generation African immigrants. The plan failed for several reasons, not least because of the sheer difficulty of singling out students who do not go through the international student office (Clark 108).

Finally, there are those who have adopted a dual identity. The pendulum may often swing, depending on the situation in which they find themselves; but members of this group find it easier to move effortlessly between both communities because they have a more open-minded attitude to the matter of affiliations.

Table 13.3. Self-Identification Patterns among Africans in the United States

	2nd-generation or bicultural	1st-generation African immigrant
As an African	46%	60%
As an African American	23%	2%
As an American	0%	2%
As a Black Person	8%	25%
Don't Know	8%	0
As a national of their country, e.g., Nigerian	n/a	10%
Other	15%	2%

Source: Msia Kibona Clark, "The Impact of African Immigration on Pan African Relations and Black Identity in the United States," Ph.D. diss., Howard University, 2006.

Scholars and activists refer to all of these African immigrants and their children as the "New Diaspora," the "New African Americans," or the "Other African Americans." Many Africans, especially first-generation African immigrants, are often not enthusiastic in claiming an African American identity (Okome; Diouf; Selassie; Swarns). Many hyphenate their identity to indicate their country of origin—"Nigerian-American," or "Ghanaian-American," etc. These are often Africans who were born and raised in Africa but are now U.S. citizens. There are also Africans like Dean Shaffdeen Amuwo of the University of Illinois, Chicago, who says he identifies himself as a Nigerian, an African, and an African American, in that order (Amuwo). He says he has an African American identity, even though he realizes African Americans may not see him as an African American.

A 2005/2006 survey I conducted of people of African descent in the Washington, D.C., area showed interesting identification patterns. Table 13.3 shows how first-generation African immigrants and those who were born in the U.S. to at least one African parent self-identified. The majority of those born in Africa overwhelmingly self-identified as African. While those born in the U.S. to at least one African parent favored an African identity, a significant number identified themselves as African American. There was also some identity conflict. While none of the first-generation Africans were unsure of their identity, a small number of those born in the U.S. to at least one African parent were unsure of their identity.

My survey also gauged how children of African immigrants are perceived. Table 13.4 shows how survey participants, depending on their ethnic background, viewed the children of African immigrants. Also included in this table are responses from African American survey participants. First-generation African immigrants were split on whether the children of

Table 13.4. Identification Imposed on Children of African Immigrants

	2nd-generation or bicultural	1st-generation African immigrant	African American
As an African	36%	27%	32%
As an African American	43%	27%	46%
As an American	0%	6%	4%
As a Black Person	7%	27%	8%
Don't Know	7%	8%	7%
As a national of their country e.g., Nigerian	n/a	4%	0
Other	7%	0	2%

African immigrants were African or African American. Most of those born in the U.S. to at least one African parent, as well as most African Americans, saw children of African immigrants as African American, with a significant proportion seeing them as African. This is interesting, considering that second-generation African immigrants and bicultural participants identified themselves somewhat differently.

More survey questions dealt with Black identities in general. Half of the African and African American survey participants agreed that someone is African American if their family had been in the U.S. since slavery (Clark 177). The other half of the African and African American respondents were less strict in their definition of who is an African American. Some 40 percent of African Americans and 30 percent of Africans felt that an African American was any Black person who identified as an African American, regardless of where they were born. Self-identification and citizenship seemed to be the key, because only 15 percent of African Americans and 17 percent of Africans felt that Black people who live in America, but are not U.S. citizens, are African American. The interesting difference with the Caribbean participants came when 50 percent of them felt that any Black persons who are American citizens, regardless of where they were born, are African American. This contrasted with the 62 percent of African Americans and 72 percent of Africans who disagreed (Clark 177).

When it came to defining who is African, 58 percent of the African respondents felt anyone of African ancestry, regardless of where he or she was born, is African, compared to 34 percent of African Americans who felt the same way. The majority of African Americans (82%) felt that someone was African if he or she had been born and raised in Africa of African parents (Clark 178). When the issue of bicultural children came up, fewer respondents felt that bicultural children, regardless of where they were born or raised, were African. There was also less tolerance among African Americans as to who could identify as being African. Where 40 percent said someone who self-identified as African American was African American, regardless of where they were born, only 26 percent agreed that someone who identified as African was really African, regardless of where they were born (Clark 178). Blacks from the Caribbean seem to see no contradiction in embracing both their racial and ethnic identities (Clark 178).

Several interesting themes emerged during interviews. On the topic of second-generation African immigrants, everyone who discussed the subject felt that second-generation African immigrants or those who had come to the United States at a young age play an important role in both the visibility of Africans and in the mediation between Africans and African Americans. As for visibility, it seems that there is a need for these African immigrants to prove their "Africanness." One of the biggest fears of African parents is that their children will become Americanized (or worse, African Americanized) to the detriment of their African culture. There is much pressure within the African community for one to retain one's African identity. There is also pressure to distinguish oneself from African Americans. For Africans who either were born in the United States or came to this country at a young age but have lost their African accents, there seems to be an almost constant need to express their identity. This becomes clearer when one compares these Africans to the recent arrivals.

In my research, I have interviewed several Africans; two of these represented the bicultural and second-generation African perspective, respectively. One interviewee, Oni ("Oni" is an alias), is bicultural. One of her parents is Senegalese and the other African American. Oni, who was raised in Senegal but attends college at a historically Black university in America, reluctantly admitted to participating in the ridicule of African Americans. Her choice of friends and her immersion in activities within the African immigrant community all reflect an embrace of an African over an African American identity.

Oni, however, says her identity is subject to external factors. While she is in the United States, she tends to lean toward a Senegalese identity. Interestingly, she does not feel she fits in anywhere completely. Her family has different perceptions of her. Some family members on her mother's side say that Oni is not African American enough, while many on her father's side say she is not African enough. As far as other Africans are concerned, many have made comments about her "impurity" in not being 100 percent African. Oni's self-identification and socialization appeared to be related, to some extent, to the fact that she is often told by Africans that she is not African enough, or that she is impure because of her African American heritage.

The other interviewee is Makeba ("Makeba" is an alias), who was born in Nigeria but has been in the United States since she was six and is a graduate of a historically Black university. Most of her friends come from Nigeria. Until she went to college, she had only dated her fellow countrymen, never an African American. Makeba identifies herself as a Yoruba Nigerian, and says there is tremendous pressure from her family to maintain that identity. In fact, her parents want her to marry not just a Nigerian, but a Yoruba. Makeba holds many of these values herself, and wants her children to also maintain a distinct African identity.

As stated earlier, it is impossible to generalize about all second-generation African immigrants and bicultural persons. In my own case, I have managed to embrace both identities and could never choose one over the other. A bicultural identity was one that I had to grow into. It has meant accepting that others would attempt to define me, that at times my different identities would carry their respective sets of obligations, and that on occasion I would find myself being an official representative of Africans in the midst of African Americans, and vice versa. In marriage, for example, while my mother's family was elated about my engagement, to my father's family I was a Kibona and must follow a traditional (African) protocol before any talk of an engagement. The fact that I was raised in the U.S. meant little. Happy that I had decided to marry a Tanzanian, my family debated quite seriously my husband's ethnic background (Haya), the virtues of his people, and whether his family would accept their son marrying a non-Haya. Negotiations for the bride-wealth, my send-off party and wedding committee, even the new expectations and responsibilities that I now have were not options, but requirements. Embracing a bicultural identity has been personally enriching, ensuring me the best of both worlds.

A critical piece of the identity debate is the importance of one's accent. An accent generally signals one's origin. In the case of African immigrants in the United States, this has played a significant role in how they identify themselves and how other people identify them. Blacks in America who have shed their foreign accents and acquired American accents have in the process simultaneously acquired multiple identities. Regardless of how such persons identify themselves, they will have several identities imposed on them. For instance, a Nigerian who has lost his or her Nigerian accent and acquired an American accent is still a Nigerian. On listening to such a person talk, however, the surrounding (non-African) community would very likely assign him or her an African American identity.

Issues of race, racial identity, and racial politics are important in America, more so perhaps than in any other place on earth. When one examines the different ideas of race found in countries such as South Africa or Brazil, one finds that the rigid definitions surrounding the two major opposing races in the U.S. are peculiar to the country. The ways in which national and ethnic identities have been consolidated into racial identities are also unique to America (Winant 60). Ethnic identity is clearly a worldwide phenomenon, though it assumes a greater seriousness in Africa, where ethnic cleavages have pitted even groups with linguistic and cultural affinities against each other. However, despite the experience of colonialism, the average Black African has few racial complexes in his or her dealings with non-Africans. Southern Africa may be an exception; although Blacks live alongside significant numbers of Asian and European peoples, a prolonged experience of European occupation and repression has made Blacks especially sensitive about their racial identity.

In America it is crucial that Africans, African Americans, and Caribbean peoples open up a dialogue about identity. The political, social, and economic benefits of an all-inclusive African American racial identity would make an enormous difference to the lives of everyone. It would require broadening the agenda of Black America to include the interests of African immigrants. It would especially translate into a stronger stance on American foreign policy on Africa as well as on the relations between the two regions. Integrating African immigrants into American society would also open up a wealth of resources that African immigrants bring with them. Migration by Africans has generally been seen as a "brain drain" by their home countries and greeted by African Americans with some hesitation. It is important that the phenomenon not bring conflictual relations between migrants and the host community, but that the two utilize the best that each can offer in order to advance the welfare of the entire group.

Before the 1980s, when Africans started immigrating to the U.S. in large numbers, they were hardly an issue in the struggle by African Americans to establish an identity for themselves in American society. But things have changed. Black America is increasingly faced with the presence of large populations of first- and second-generation Africans and other "foreign" Blacks. These will unavoidably translate into "African Americans" in the usual American racial configuration—whether the newcomers like it or not—and native African Americans need to deal with that reality. However scholars and everyone else may argue the political and other gains or losses of that reality, one thing remains certain: a lasting legacy of African immigration to the United States will be its contribution to the redefinition of African American identity and many aspects of African American culture.

NOTE

The author prefers to capitalize the word "Black," as it is used in this chapter to refer to a racial and/or ethnic group.

REFERENCES

Akbar, Maysa and Vetta L. Sanders Thompson. "The Understanding of Race and the Construction of African American Identity." *Western Journal of Black Studies* 27, no. 2 (June 2003): 80–88.

Amick, Marcus. "Does Drug War Target Blacks?" *Michigan Chronicle* 63, no. 40 (2000): 2.

Amuwo, Dean Shaffdeen. "Analysis; Africans in America." Interview by Neal Conan. *Talk of the Nation,* National Public Radio, March 3, 2005.

Butterfield, Sherri-Ann. "Challenging American Concepts of Race and Ethnicity: Second Generation West Indian Immigrants." *The International Journal of Sociology and Social Policy* 2, nos. 7–8 (2004): 75–102.

Clark, Msia Kibona. "The Impact of African Immigration on Pan African Relations and Black Identity in the United States." Ph.D. diss., Howard University, 2006.

Davis, James F. *Who Is Black: One Nation's Definition.* University Park: Pennsylvania State University Press, 1991.

Deane, Glenn, and John Logan. "Black Diversity in Metropolitan America." Lewis Mumford Center for Comparative Urban and Regional Research, University at Albany, August 15, 2003. http://mumford1.dyndns.org/cen2000/BlackWhite/ BlackDiversityReport/black-diversity01.htm (accessed March 21, 2005).

Diawara, Manthia. *We Won't Budge: An African Exile in the World.* New York: Basic Civitas, 2003.

Diouf, Sylviane A. "The New African Diaspora." The Schomburg Center for Research in Black Culture. http://www.inmotionaame.org/texts/?migration= 13&topic=99&type=text (accessed March 21, 2005).

Foner, Nancy, ed. *Islands in the City: West Indian Migration to New York.* Los Angeles: University of California Press, 2001.

Hall, Christopher. "Challenging Selective Enforcement of Traffic Regulations after the Disharmonic Convergence: Whren v. United States, United States v. Armstrong, and the Evolution of Police Discretion." *Texas Law Review* 76, no. 5 (1998): 1083–1124.

Joseph, Peniel E. *Waiting 'Til the Midnight Hour: A Narrative History of Black Power in America.* New York: Henry Holt, 2006.

Klein, Herbert S., and Stuart Schwartz. *The Atlantic Slave Trade.* London: Cambridge University Press, 1999.

Maga, Timothy P. "Ronald Reagan and Redress for Japanese-American Internment, 1983–88." *Presidential Studies Quarterly* 28, no. 3 (1998): 606.

Manning, Patrick. *Slavery and African Life: Occidental, Oriental, and African Slave Trades.* London: Cambridge University Press, 1990.

Marable, Manning. *Black Liberation in Conservative America.* Boston: South End, 1997.

Martin, Jazmyn. "The Tug between Heritage, Change." *Philadelphia Tribune,* March 27, 2005.

McMillan, James A. *The Final Victims: Foreign Slave Trade to North America, 1783–1810.* Columbia: University of South Carolina Press, 2004.

O'Connor, Tom, and Amy Karnehm Willis. "Understanding Discrimination against

Asian-Americans." JUS 415/SOC 355: Sociology of Discrimination. Syllabus, North Carolina Wesleyan College, January 6, 2006. http://faculty.ncwc.edu/toconnor/soc/3551ect10.htm (accessed March 2006).

Ogbar, Jeffrey O. G. *Black Power: Radical Politics and African American Identity.* Baltimore, Md.: Johns Hopkins University Press, 2004.

Okome, Mojúbàolú Olúfúnké. "The Antinomies of Globalization: Some Consequences of Contemporary African Immigration to the United States of America." *Ìrìnkèrindò: A Journal of African Migration* 1 (September 2002). http://www.africamigration.com/.

Okutoro, Lydia Omolola. "I Once Was Lost . . . African Identity of Young Woman Born in Lagos, Nigeria, and Living in the United States." *Essence,* August 2003.

Raboteau, Albert J. *Canaan Land: A Religious History of African Americans.* New York: Oxford University Press, 2001.

Selassie, Bereket H. "Washington's New African Immigrants." In *Urban Odyssey: A Multicultural History of Washington D.C.,* ed. Francine Curro Cary. Washington, D.C.: Smithsonian Institution Press, 1996. 264–275.

Smith, Abbe. "Can You Be a Good Person and a Good Prosecutor?" *The Georgetown Journal of Legal Ethics* 14, no. 2 (2001): 355, 366–368.

Sowell, Thomas. *Race and Economics.* New York: David McKay, 1975.

Swarns, Rachel L. "An Issue of Identity: African and Caribbean Immigration to the U.S. Is Spurring a Debate about Who Qualifies as 'African-American.'" *New York Times Upfront,* December 13, 2004.

Taiwo, Olufemi. "This Prison Called My Skin: On Being Black in America." In *Problematizing Blackness: Self Ethnographies by Black Immigrants to the United States,* ed. Jean Muteba Rahier and Percy Hintzen. New York: Routledge, 2002. 35–52.

United States Citizenship and Immigration Services (USCIS). "Table 2: Immigration by Region and Selected Country of Last Residence: Fiscal Years 1820–2004." http://uscis.gov/graphics/shared/statistics/yearbook/YrBk04Im.htm (accessed January 2006).

Wamba, Phillipe. *Kinship: A Family's Journey in Africa and America.* New York: Dutton, 1999.

Winant, Howard. *Racial Conditions: Political Theory Comparisons.* Minneapolis: University of Minnesota Press, 1994.

14 RESISTING "RACE": ORGANIZING AFRICAN TRANSNATIONAL IDENTITIES IN THE UNITED STATES

Jill M. Humphries

We are tired of white American and African American men speaking for us.
—*African immigrant woman*

BLACK TRANSATLANTIC MIGRATION

Increasing transnational migration and immigration of black ethnic groups to the United States is changing the notions of race, ethnicity, and nationality and the ways in which people fundamentally understand themselves in U.S. society as well as relations with their home countries (Rogers 2000; Waters 1999). While the U.S. racial architecture subsumes black ethnic groups within one homogenous racial group, irrespective of history, culture, and nationality, what it means to be black in U.S. society is contested and changing as a result of the inclusion of other black ethnic groups. To be black can no longer be simply equated with a single racial/ethnic group—African American. Rather, African immigrants (Pierre; Bryce-Laporte), Afro-Caribbean immigrants (Rogers), and black Latinos (Greenbaum; Jones-Correa) bring different understandings and interpretations of what it means to be black. The different racial systems that exist in their home countries, and the varying meanings they place on these experiences, fundamentally affect how they see themselves in U.S. society (Greenbaum; Rogers; Waters).

This in turn has implications for political organizing in the African constituency arena. Most studies that examine the African constituency tend to focus on either the African American ethnic lobby as a monolithic entity without examining its heterogeneity, or multiracial coalitions primarily composed of Euro- and African American participants. Few studies examine the process of building multiracial/multinational coalitions that include African immigrants as primary actors in the process. This essay seeks to explore how African immigrants envision themselves in the U.S. racial hierarchy and the implications of that hierarchy for establishing multiracial and black intra-racial alliances. More specifically, I explore the ways in which African immigrants deploy notions of identity and identity politics as a tool for mobilizing collective and oppositional identities in the United States/African constituency arena. I examine these issues in the context of the National Summit on Africa, a nationwide constituency building initiative.[1]

In the first part of this chapter, I briefly discuss the historical context for the National Summit on Africa[2] as an African advocacy initiative and its relationship to U.S. foreign policy toward Africa, given the constraints imposed by the antidemocratic nature of the process and the rationale for such constituency building initiatives. In the second part, I examine the relationship between identity and identity politics, U.S. racial structuring, and the implications for building African American and African immigrant alliances in the African constituency arena. In the final part of the chapter, I provide two examples from the California case study and National Summit that illustrate the complex process of establishing a collective identity with which to mobilize participants, and more specifically the process by which African immigrants mobilized and organized around their immigrant African identities. In the conclusion, I examine the implications for political organizing in the African constituency arena.

CREATING A SPACE FOR DOMESTIC CONSTITUENCIES IN U.S. FOREIGN POLICY MAKING

The end of cold war politics (D. F. Gordon et al.; Clough), the decline of authoritative leadership (D. F. Gordon et al.), and the rise and consolidation of democratic transitions (Walters; Diamond and Plattner) among African states signal a new period for Africa in global affairs and, in particular, for United States–Africa relations. As a result, U.S. policy makers are faced with the challenge of developing a new policy mandate that is mutually beneficial to the fifty-four African states in addressing a wide array of transnational issues such as increasing globalization, sustainable development, economic and trade relations, and health, environmental, and security issues. Previously, U.S. national interests in Africa were defined through a Eurocentric and masculinist bias (Brown), with a focus on resource extraction, and with a priority toward geostrategic concerns (Horne).[3] This myopic approach has contributed to the U.S.'s inability to develop a proactive and comprehensive policy toward Africa.

It was not until the 1970s—as a result of two converging factors: (1) increasing black congressional participation, and (2) grassroots agitation and protests over U.S.–South African investments—that a space was created for citizen input, which ultimately led the United States to begin addressing other issues pertaining to U.S.–Africa relations (Clough). Nevertheless, there is still a pressing need to articulate a "new mode of thinking" about U.S.-Africa relations both within the foreign policy arena and to the general American society. This new framework situates U.S.-Africa relations in a broader context of U.S. foreign policy relations with other nations. From this perspective, U.S. national interests are best served by building viable partnerships with African states that support economic and security issues, thus promoting prosperity at home, preventing crises that threaten security or require costly political-military and/or humanitarian interventions, and working with partners to address common political and security concerns such as international terrorism, drug trafficking, and environmental degradation (D.F. Gordon et al.).

As the U.S. continues scaling back development aid to African countries (Minter), it is important to build institutional linkages with other actors such as nonprofit and business organizations. Gordon et al., in *The United States and Africa,* highlight the emergence of new American voices and interests that are producing new Africa-oriented political forces and alliances that wish to mainstream Africa into U.S. foreign policy and promote mutually beneficial relationships. There have been several efforts by different institutional actors to change U.S.-Africa relations and to influence the policy making process. One such example is the Corporate Council on Africa's (CCA) Attracting Capital to Africa 1997 Summit (D. F. Gordon et al.). The nonprofit sector is another key actor that can play a vital role in this process by bringing a broader range of participants that reflect the diversity of the African constituency into the policy making process.

The question of organizing domestic constituencies plays an increasingly important role, given that many scholars suggest that civic engagement can influence the policy arena to be more democratic by reflecting the interests of a diverse constituency. In the next section, I discuss the link between identity politics, U.S. racial structure, and the African constituency.

IDENTITY POLITICS AND THE AFRICAN CONSTITUENCY

Previous African advocacy initiatives were composed of the African American ethnic lobby (Henry; Dickson; Kilson) and multiracial coalitions (Culverson). This is the first contemporary study that examines the process of building multiracial/transnational coalitions that include African immigrants as primary actors in the process. The National Summit on Africa is one such example that allows us to examine the political participation of African immigrants in organizing efforts.

I draw from the new social movement literature to understand political and economic struggles, as well as the way in which groups construct and articulate new identities and cultural representations (Tarrow). In the case of the National Summit, state leaders must construct universal themes that articulate preexisting cultural or ideological beliefs that resonate with participants to facilitate identity formation and mobilization (Snow and Benford). Friedman and McAdam contend that activists do not craft new collective identities but rather use preexisting organizational roles and/or political identities to fashion new identities.

Klandermans and Goslinga describe the collective identity process as "focus[ing] on the link between the individual and the cultural systems" (328). It also provides a mechanism through which participants coalesce around shared meanings that resonate with their life experiences and ideological positions, signify their affiliation and connection with others (Taylor), and articulate organizational goals (McAdam). Furthermore, members signify their common identity by "adhering to a set of common beliefs, attitudes and rules of behavior" (Taylor 512). Similarly, identity politics involves redefining and affirming historically marginalized identities. It is through this process that individuals become aware of their differences, attach significance to certain aspects of their identity, and contest and reject others (Penrose and Jackson).

Some scholars contend that the breakdown of identity politics and the embracing of multiple identities can undermine the development of coalition politics (Handler). They argue that multiple and competing interests make it extremely difficult to coalesce around a unified mission. It thus becomes increasingly difficult to construct a unified identity that is necessary for collective action. I argue that the coalition building process within the African constituency is heavily tied to people's sense of a racial, ethnic, and transnational identity that influences their political position. Given the diversity of the African constituency arena—which includes the African American lobby, business community, various interest-specific organizations, and multiracial activist organizations—it is extremely difficult to build a unified identity. In turn, coalition building initiatives require a level of flexibility whereby members can construct and coalesce into unified identities ("Advocates for Africa") even while maintaining situated identities based on racial, ethnic, and transnational considerations, and while continuing to act as social justice advocates of specific interests within the coalition (Espiritu). For this reason, the complex and dynamic interaction that we see occurring among the various coalition actors requires us to pay particular attention to how identity politics shapes and informs one's actions. As Ackelsberg states:

> How do we take into account the ways our needs and self-conceptions may
> be fundamentally affected by differing cultural, racial, gender, class and
> other contexts; how do we do so without "freezing" identities in ways that
> both misrepresent their complexities and, at the same time, may make coa-
> litions and alliances impossible? (90)

Identity building and coalition building are interconnected and inseparable; they are conflictual at times, but are mutually reinforcing. The
challenge to coalition building "is to be able to acknowledge differences
among ourselves—and the fluid nature of our identities while still making space not only for connections among people but for productive alliances between them" (Ackelsberg 90).

I argue that in the case of the National Summit, the formation of racial ethnic hierarchies in the U.S. shapes and informs how identities are
formed and coalitions are built, and in turn how participants negotiate
these constraints by deploying alternative constructions of identity. The
next section examines the relationship between the U.S. racial system and
African immigrant racialization.

RACIAL AND ETHNIC FORMATIONS
IN THE UNITED STATES

African immigrants enter into a highly racialized society that shapes and
informs their social location and opportunity structure. While black and
white Americans represent the bottom and top of this racial order, multiple and simultaneous racial projects have emerged to define the racial
structure of the United States (Marable; Winant; Omi and Winant). Given
that antiblack racism is a constitutive part of U.S. society and its institutions, African immigrants who are racially categorized as "black" are
faced with the stigma of being placed at the bottom of the racial order.
The extent to which African immigrants can deploy an immigrant identity may facilitate their ability to negotiate and mediate this racializing
process.

The process of racial and ethnic identity formation for African immigrants is unlike that of their African American counterparts, whose racial identity was imposed on them. African immigrants come with their
national and ethnic identities complete, whereas African Americans' ethnic identity emerged from the creolization of African ethnic groups. As
"black transnationals," immigrant Africans are both black and immigrant. Glick Shiller and Fouron define transnationals as "migrants who
are fully encapsulated neither in the host-society nor in their native land
but who nonetheless remain active participants in the social settings of
both locations. They construct their identities in relation to both societies" (330).

As a result, African immigrants' conception of race is primarily shaped by their home country's experience under European colonialism or black rule. While African Americans and African immigrants are both racially classified as black, the racial category has very different historical meanings in either context. The experience of racial segregation and subordination may not be the primary form of subjugation under black rule. Rather, social groups may be discriminated against on the basis of their religion, ethnicity, class, or gender (Bryce-Laporte). Most African immigrants do not have a collective memory of racial segregation and subordination; hence they do not see themselves through a racial prism. Rather, their immediate experiences as "black immigrants" have shaped their sense of being members of a group seeking greater opportunity and political freedom as a distinct social group. It is precisely these differences in historical meanings in the lives of African Americans and African immigrants that make using "black" as a unitary identity with which to organize problematic. I would argue that U.S. blacks and African immigrants are not part of the same ethnic group but rather should be understood as "black ethnic" (Greenbaum) and "transnational groups" (Schiller et al.; Glick Shiller and Fouron).

In sum, to subsume the racial identity of African immigrants and African Americans under the superordinate racial category of "black" fails to recognize how different sociohistorical processes help shape black diasporic populations in the socioeconomic structure of the U.S. and larger global community. Likewise, class differences between African Americans and immigrant Africans may also affect the agenda setting and coalition building process.

CLASS STRATIFICATION AMONG AFRICAN AMERICAN AND AFRICAN IMMIGRANT GROUPS

In addition to different racial socialization processes, class stratification is a factor that may impede the development of strategic alliances between African Americans and immigrant Africans. As black ethnic and transnational groups, African Americans and immigrant Africans occupy different positions within the U.S. socioeconomic system. It is therefore important to examine the new diaspora of black Africans in the U.S. Takougang ("Contemporary African Immigrants," "Recent African Immigrants") and A. Gordon trace the arrival of the new diaspora as a distinct social group to the 1950s post-independence movements. The first major wave of African nationals came primarily from two countries, South Africa and Egypt, and were later followed by migrants from Ethiopia, Ghana, Kenya, Liberia, Nigeria, Cape Verde, Tanzania, and Uganda (Takougang, "Contemporary African Immigrants"; A. Gordon).

While the first migrants came to the U.S. for educational opportunities, later returning to their home countries (Takougang, "Contemporary African Immigrants," "Recent African Immigrants"; Clausen and Bermingham), successive waves of immigrants migrated for different reasons. Several converging factors led to a shift in global migration patterns of African migrants. First, the rise of anti-immigrant sentiment during the 1970s in European countries, coupled with a shift in labor immigration policies, reduced the number of African immigrants that could legally enter European countries. Second, stagnating economies coupled with low investment and trade (Takougang, "Contemporary," "Recent"), as well as political instability, led to the inability to absorb manpower in Africa (Logan); and civil war created an inhospitable environment for many Africans. As such, only the most educated and skilled classes emigrate to developed countries (Takougang, "Contemporary").

African immigration to the U.S. can be explained in terms of the link between home country economic and political factors and host country immigration policies. As previously discussed, the economic and political instability of African nations creates a set of conditions that hinders the socioeconomic stability of the educated and skilled classes. The immigration policies of developed countries target a more educated and technically skilled group of individuals to fill labor demands. In the case of the U.S., in 1965 the quota system that favored European migration was replaced with a preference system "that favored the entry of immediate relatives of U.S. citizens and permanent residents with skills needed by the economy" (Gordon 82).

When U.S. immigration policy turned toward humanitarian and refugee concerns, migration from "Third World" countries increased. The number of African refugees increased with the passage of the 1980 Refugee Act, which provided greater opportunity for them to resettle in the U.S. Similarly, the Immigration Act of 1990 has provided the greatest potential for African migrants to immigrate to the U.S., through the Diversity Program. This program privileges countries from underrepresented regions, whereby potential immigrants participate in a lottery system to receive visas to the U.S. By 1995, 20,200 visas (37 percent of the lottery) were allocated to Africa (Gordon).

As a result of past stringent and antiblack immigration laws, African immigrants represent a highly skilled, professional (Takougang, "Contemporary"; U.S. Immigration; U.S. Bureau of the Census; Djamba; Speer) or merchant (Stoller) class of immigrants to the U.S. The end result is that African immigrants' educational level and socioeconomic status tend to be higher than the U.S. national average for Americans and particularly those of the majority of African Americans (Austin; U.S. Bureau of the Census).[4]

Unlike African immigrants, African Americans have had their educational attainment and class status hindered by the historical legacy of American segregation and continuing practice of antiblack racism. Although African Americans have made great strides in pursuing higher education, which has increased their class mobility over the past thirty years, the educated class is still relatively small.

The educational and socioeconomic differences that exist between African immigrants and African Americans situate them in different social and class strata within which their interests may diverge. These factors have implications for building black ethnic coalitions, given that each group may have a different set of interests. When African immigrants stress their immigrant status, they are using a situational identity, which may conflict with African Americans' unitary concept of black identity. Furthermore, the way that Africans perceive the U.S. as promising greater economic opportunity and political freedom conflicts with the African American experience of exclusion (Arthur). African Americans are still fighting for their human rights, including economic access and parity with Euro-Americans.

Given the educational and social-class differences (professionals and tradesmen) that exist between African Americans and African immigrants, the latter may find themselves aligning their interests with those of Euro-Americans who are more educated and focused on business and who share similar interests with Africans. Nevertheless, African immigrant racial identity is circumscribed by their blackness within American society; given their identity as "black immigrants," they will experience, interpret, and respond to racial discrimination differently than African Americans.

As previously discussed, the opportunity structures of African Americans and immigrant Africans are shaped by their home country's racial and economic structures (Bryce-Laporte). In the case of immigrant Africans as black transnationals, the way they respond to the U.S. racial order is conditioned by whether race is a fundamental organizing principle of socioeconomic relations in their home countries and by their level of exposure to racial structuring (Waters; Jones-Correa; Glick Shiller and Fouron). For this reason, race may not be a delineating factor for many Africans unless they have had extended contact with or experienced direct subjugation by Europeans, as in South Africa (Arthur).[5] Instead, their discussions may focus on other factors such as ethnic, class, gender, religious, and urban/rural biases (Bryce-Laporte).

In contrast, given the social location of African Americans as a subjugated racial group within the U.S., and the way the racial order structures relations with Euro-Americans, African Americans tend to be more conscious about race (Meriwether; Williams; Bryce-Laporte), although they also experience simultaneous class and gender oppression (Crenshaw). The following section provides a brief overview of the research methodology used for our study.

METHODOLOGY: ENGAGED POLITICAL PEDAGOGY

This essay is part of a larger research project that was conducted over a twenty-four-month period (May 1999–May 2001) in primarily two settings, while I was serving as a California state delegate and southern California policy and legislative officer responsible for tracking, compiling, and reporting U.S.–Africa legislation to the state delegation and attending the National Summit in Washington, D.C. I interviewed a nonrandom sample ("snowball") of 45 respondents (African Americans and white Americans), of which one-third (15) were African immigrants. Supplementary data were collected through participant observation, documentary, and survey data collection to inform the study.

As a participant-observer, I attended weekly organizing meetings in southern California, and regional and national summit activities held in San Francisco, California, and Washington, D.C. Primary observations focused on communication patterns and interactions between state leaders and delegates, among the state leadership, and with the National Secretariat. Likewise, interviews were conducted with state chairs and co-chairs to describe and interpret common day activities, events, and processes (Fontana and Frey). Furthermore, I monitored e-mail and online conference texts, e-groups, group meeting minutes, and correspondence. I should note that I have over eighteen years of experience working in U.S.-African affairs, as well as working in, studying in, and traveling to over fifteen African countries—an experience that, I believe, has deepened my understanding of African American and African immigrant relations and U.S.-African affairs.

THE NATIONAL SUMMIT: A CONTESTED POLITICAL SPACE

In this section, I provide a brief history of the National Summit on Africa.[6] I then present the results from three scenarios: First, I examine the factors that led to the creation and dissolution of the African/African American slate at the Pacific West Regional Summit and its ripple effects across the California delegation. Second, I examine the conflict that arose over who had the legitimate right to speak on behalf of the California delegation. Finally, I explore the emergence of two protest groups that had their early formation within the California delegation, and that acted as catalysts for the micro-mobilization of African immigrants and social justice activists that emerged at the National Summit.

The history of the National Summit on Africa is a story about negotiating personal relationships upon multiple ideological, political, and racial terrains with the intent of building a multiracial U.S.–Africa constituency. The concept of a National Summit on Africa was strongly influenced by the 1994 White House Conference on Africa (Bork interview). The purpose of the conference was, first, to address the declining and changing role of U.S.–Africa relations in foreign policy; second, to broaden the range of actors operating in foreign policy; and third, to reinvigorate an interest in Africa, not only within the government sector, but within U.S. society at large (National Summit staff member 2000). While the National Summit was originally conceived to be a government-led initiative, it was thought to be too costly and time-consuming to be led solely by the government (National Summit staff member 2000). It was envisioned that the National Summit would become a private-sector initiative in order to leverage the necessary resources. According to Walters, this shift in U.S. policy toward Africa signaled a major change "from an emphasis upon public sector–sponsored development assistance to private sector–driven trade and investment" (288).

Timothy Bork, who was a program officer for the African and Middle East Division at the Ford Foundation and who attended the White House Conference on Africa, promoted the idea of the National Summit on Africa (Bork interview).[7] While Mr. Bork is credited with being the "Father" of the National Summit, its birth is actually attributed to several individuals who were involved in the initial planning process. The initial concept paper, "The African and Middle East Strategy Concept Paper: Improving the United States Policy Environment for Africa's Renewed Development," was co-authored by Cherrie Waters and Salih Booker, two longtime African activists who envisioned the National Summit "to be a catalytic vehicle to facilitate the process . . . to allow other NGOs, African Americans, and women to voice interest in Africa" (National Summit board member).[8]

The Ford Foundation and Carnegie Corporation funded the National Summit initiative for eight million dollars over a three-year period from 1996 through 1999 (Foundation program officer interview). The shape of the National Summit would forever reflect the competing conceptions and interests of the initial players.

The conceptual framework for the National Summit was modeled after the United Nations World Summits. It was envisioned to be a national convening body of U.S.-Africa-specific constituencies, mandated to develop a comprehensive policy plan-of-action to help guide United States foreign policy toward Africa; to educate the American public about Africa; and to broaden and strengthen the network of Africa's supporters in the United States:

The creation of this initiative aims to improve the policy environment for
Africa by strengthening the key Africa-specific institutions in the U.S, and
launching a three-pronged communications effort that would raise Africa's
visibility among the U.S. public and policy-makers alike. (Waters and
Booker 1)

The Summit was designed to include key stakeholders from various
sectors of society, including politicians, representatives from Africa-
specific organizations, those in private business, and citizens. Each individual would have an equal opportunity to participate as a state delegate,
inform the deliberative process, and shape the national policy plan-of-
action.[9] The National Summit was organized geographically along six regions: Southeast, Midwest, Pacific Coast, New England, East Coast, and
Mountain West. The regions were composed of fifty states and four U.S.
territories. Six regional summits, whereby state delegates crafted individual regional policy plans-of-action, were held over a two-year period.[10]

The deliberative process was structured so that state delegates participated in five thematic working groups[11] and were tasked with the responsibility of revising and editing the original draft policy plan-of-action.
This iterative process occurred throughout the entire National Summit at
the local, state, regional, and national levels. The five draft regional policy
plan-of-action documents were synthesized into a working draft national
policy plan-of-action document that culminated in the final document,
the "National Policy Plan-of-Action for U.S.-Africa Relations in the 21st
Century."

The elected state leadership was responsible for organizing and mobilizing delegates and redrafting the regional policy plan-of-action, as well
as raising money to facilitate delegate participation at the National Summit. The next section examines the formation of the California state delegation and the inherent difficulties associated with organizing a multi-
diverse constituency.

FORMATION OF THE CALIFORNIA DELEGATION

People were jockeying for positions as if this were really important . . .
—Group facilitator, 2000

In California, the first event in the organizing process was a mini–policy
summit hosted by the African Studies Center at the University of California, Los Angeles, in May 1999. The purpose of this mini-summit was
to bring together a diverse group of individuals representative of the constituencies from the academic, business, and general communities who
worked in the U.S.-Africa arena or who had some general interest in Af-

rica. A second goal was to introduce participants to the mission and goals
of the National Summit on Africa, with the intent of stimulating the regional and National Summit deliberative process to develop initial recommendations for the national policy plan-of-action. The third was to
prepare them to participate as delegates to the regional summit in San
Francisco.

Participants were assigned to one of the five thematic working groups,
and were given the responsibility of modifying the draft national policy
plan-of-action. Immediately following the mini-policy summit, subgroups
began to form around particular interests. For example, a group of African
immigrants from northern California formed a working group with the
intent of developing their own policy recommendations. In addition, a regional schism started to develop. A majority of participants were from
southern California; consequently, when the entire state convened at the
regional summit, some participants from northern California felt that
they had been excluded from the process.

The next month, the Pacific Coast Regional Summit was held June
5–6 in San Francisco.[12] The purpose of the regional summit was to con-
vene the nine western states and Guam together to develop the western
regional policy plan-of-action, and to select state leadership to represent
the formal state delegations to the National Summit on Africa's Washington, D.C., conference. It was at this summit meeting that the California delegation was selected. At the regional summit, it was also decided to partition the governance structure of the state delegation along
state regional lines—northern, central, and southern California. The objective was to maximize regional representation, ensure inclusiveness and
diversity of delegate perspectives, and achieve full participation in the formation of the delegation and policy positions. The state leadership team
would be composed of a chair and three co-chairs, each of whom represented one of the three regions.[13]

STATE LEADERSHIP SELECTION PROCESS

The tension between African immigrants and others first became evident
in the leadership, and reflected the level of importance they placed on selection for and holding a leadership position. Four camps immediately
arose, each of which had a different conception of who should constitute
the leadership and the key functionaries of the event: (1) African immigrants; (2) a coalition of African Americans and African immigrants; (3)
a multiracial business group; and (4) and a multiracial social justice activist group. A number of state delegates in the audience stated that the
majority of leadership positions should be held by African immigrants, because they were directly from African countries. As one African immigrant woman stated in an interview, "We are tired of having white Ameri-

can and African American men speaking for us." Others felt that it was important that policy makers understand the summit to be an American-led initiative, which would argue that leaders be American citizens. It was felt that representatives would respond to "voting constituents," not foreign nationals.

Two major slates developed to run candidates both in southern and northern California. First, the EZ/Turner southern California coalition was spearheaded by a cooperation between African Americans and African immigrants. EZ and Turner agreed to run respectively for chair and co-chair, but not against each other. It was envisioned that Agrippa Ezozo ("EZ"), who worked for UCLA Campus Human Resources, would rally support from the African immigrant community while Paul Turner, a project manager for Southern California Edison, would leverage corporate resources to help finance the activities of the California delegation. There was a competing northern California coalition, with Dr. Ramona Tascoe, internationally known physician and cofounder of Friends of Africa, running for chair and Nunu Kidane, Africa Program Director for International Development Exchange, for co-chair. John Oriji, history professor at California Polytechnic State University in San Luis Obispo, ran as the sole candidate for the central California co-chair position.

Candidates presented their credentials to the delegation. In a vote of the delegates, Dr. Tascoe was selected as state chair over Ezozo Agrippa, while Nunu Kidane was elected as northern co-chair. John Oriji was elected as central co-chair. The election of the southern California co-chair should have been relatively straightforward; however, at the urging of northern California delegates, Ezozo decided to run against Paul Turner. This led to a run-off between EZ and Turner for the southern California co-chair position. The vote was split, with Turner losing in a relatively close run-off with EZ.

In an attempt to flaunt his institutional resources, Paul Turner highlighted his corporate affiliation with Southern California Edison. As a result, the crowd began to boo him off the stage. In retrospect, Paul Turner failed to understand the regional politics of northern and southern California. The majority of delegates resided in the north, which is historically more liberal and oriented toward social justice activism than southern California, which tends to be more conservative and business-focused. A California delegate described the situation in an interview:

> I was sitting with Paul Turner, who had made an agreement with EZ that [they would not run against each other]. EZ changed his mind and won. Paul had negative feelings about it. Paul, with his corporate background and resources, would have been more instrumental. EZ did it for the wrong reasons. EZ broke the gentlemen's agreement. EZ shouldn't have been in charge. He has strong

opinions but he didn't have the resources and experience. Paul is a
"schmoozer"; he's the type of person you want at the top.

The first significant event, then, was the demise of the agreement to
run an African American and African immigrant leadership slate. Identity, political autonomy, and regionalism played a major role in the demise of the slate. The political strategy to run two southern California
delegates in leadership positions was predicated on the reality that northern California participants outnumbered southern California participants,
giving northern California a clear advantage in the delegation. The only
way to ensure that southern California was adequately represented was
to solidify the African immigrant vote, across regional boundaries, with
southern California representatives. The African American and African
immigrant leadership agreed that in exchange for supporting a black slate,
African leadership would be represented throughout the state.

Although the African immigrant leadership initially supported a black
slate, they clearly expressed a desire to select their own leadership without
African American participation. This was illustrated by African immigrants in northern California aligning their interests behind EZ, which
ultimately led to the demise of the slate and the creation of a central California co-chair position held by an immigrant African. When EZ lost the
state chair position to Dr. Tascoe, a multiracial coalition composed of African immigrants and Euro-American activists from northern California
urged EZ to run against Paul, thus breaking the agreement. As one participant reported:

> *The African block from northern and southern California supported*
> *the slate until northern California delegates knew they had the*
> *numbers to vote in a candidate . . . They voted their prejudices in-*
> *stead of in their political interest.*

In this instance, African American and immigrant African interests
diverged, and it was politically more expedient for African immigrants
to align their interests with white Americans, thus breaking the "agreement" and accomplishing their goal to represent themselves rather than
be represented by an African American candidate. Here, then, we can
see the deployment of an African immigrant identity as a separate and
distinct political act privileging their position as "immigrant Africans."
In this case, African nationality and immigration status were more important than pan-racial unity.

Similarly, some white Americans saw this as an opportunity to influence the process by aligning their interests with African immigrants
rather than supporting a unified black slate. Although the Summit attempted to portray itself as a multiracial initiative, the key national lead-

ership positions were held primarily by African Americans. As a result, a number of white academics and foreign policy experts boycotted the event because they perceived the Summit "to be geared towards the African American community . . . and as an African American initiative primarily catering to blacks," while others felt excluded from the process and displaced from their traditional leadership and policy making roles (Anonymous interview). Thus it was easier for some white Americans to align their interests with immigrant Africans rather than with African Americans who espoused a pan-black ideology. The tension exhibited between white and black Americans can be traced to the relative position that white and African Americans hold in U.S. society and particularly within the African constituency arena. For African Americans to assert Pan-African unity is an inherently political act of resistance against a racist society (Woodard). Furthermore, the racial fault lines exhibited in the coalition building process among African Americans, immigrant Africans, and white Americans are directly related to the relative position that each group holds in the racial order.

The legacy of the broken slate agreement and regional division had implications for the rest of the summit process. Key African American players from southern California chose not to play an active role in the organizing process due to the rift at the regional summit. They believed that African immigrants had violated an unspoken code by aligning their interests with white American interests at the expense of pan-black unity (Anonymous interview). Therefore they were now responsible for their actions and should not expect support from African Americans. Unfortunately, these African American elites had more experience with the system, and had access to and controlled a variety of resources that the delegation needed in order to be effective.[14]

NEGOTIATING BLACK
TRANSATLANTIC POLITICS

When the California delegation converged with other state delegations, the fragile coalition began to dissolve once again over the issues of identity and leadership that had been prevalent throughout the summit coalition process. African American and African immigrant relations were further strained when Dr. Tascoe announced that the California delegation would host Daniel arap Moi, President of Kenya (see figure 14.2). Despite an invitation from the Secretariat to all African heads of state, the sole appearance by President Moi sparked a protest in front of the convention and a public walkout from a sponsored luncheon. Additionally, the Secretariat's pro–trade and investment position and its endorsement of the African Growth and Opportunity Act (AGOA) further balkanized the fragile agreement between coalition groups. I argue that the state leader-

FIGURE 14.1.
Southern California working group: Ezozo Agrippa, Ramona Tascoe, Carolyn Fowler, and unknown participant. Southern California delegation meeting, Cal Poly Pomona, December 18, 1999. Photo by Jill M. Humphries.

ship's inability to resolve these conflicts led to the micro-mobilization of two protest groups at the National Summit.

A further incident highlights these issues and the emergence of these two groups, the All African Organization and the Social Justice Coalition. Murmuring broke out among the California delegates, who inquired, "When did we decide to host President Moi?" Dr. Tascoe's relationship with President Moi emerged from her providing humanitarian and medical assistance to the Kenyan victims of the U.S. embassy bombings. Although she disclosed her professional affiliation with the Kenyan government at the first southern California delegate meeting, Dr. Tascoe failed to consult the delegation about hosting President Moi at the National Summit. As it was, hosting President Moi positioned the California delegation against African civil society actors, global social justice advocates, and the African immigrant community, who had been at the forefront in challenging U.S. support of authoritarian African leaders. One African immigrant declared:

> *Ramona's position was that we needed to work with Moi. Kenyans'*
> *position was that they wanted to protest instead of follow the pro-*

```
┌─────────────────────────────────────────┐
│          The California Delegation        │
│                   of                      │
│       The National Summit on Africa       │
│                                           │
│         invite you to a reception with    │
│                                           │
│           The President of Kenya          │
│                                           │
│       The Honorable Daniel Arap Moi       │
│                                           │
│          Friday, February 18, 2000        │
│                                           │
│          5:00 p.m. – 7:00 p.m.            │
│                                           │
│       The Rayburn Building, Capitol Hill  │
│                                           │
│          Rooms B-338 and B-399            │
│                                           │
│         Hors D'oeuvres and Tonic          │
└─────────────────────────────────────────┘
```

FIGURE 14.2.
California delegation's President Moi invitation.

*cess. Ramona didn't find out about people at the bottom and work
with them. She should [have ignored] Moi and [made] alliances
with the bottom.*

However, not all delegates expressed this sentiment toward Dr. Tascoe.
As one northern California delegated lamented, "Ramona was victimized
over the Moi issue [when she was attempting to take advantage of the]
confluence of opportunity."

As discussed previously, the way in which African Americans and African immigrants understand and interpret domestic politics in African
nations is shaped by their social location within their home country (Waters; Bryce-Laporte). African Americans primarily view politics through a
racial prism, given their experiences as a racial group in the U.S. Dr. Tascoe's action in hosting President Moi can thus be interpreted as an expression of black nationalism (Woodard), no matter how misguided the effort.

In contrast, first-generation African immigrants approach African politics as nationals whose responses are guided by lived experiences rather than by imagined realities. They therefore have a more nuanced understanding of the multiplicity of factors, such as ethnicity, religion, and rural/urban bias, that may shape political events. By the same token, how they choose to initiate change in their countries of origin is influenced by opportunities that have opened to them as African immigrants living in the U.S.

Consequently, many African immigrants interpreted Dr. Tascoe's actions to be indicative of many black Americans' lack of awareness and understanding of African politics. Furthermore, African immigrants felt that the way in which African Americans privilege race over other factors such as ethnicity, class, and urban/rural tensions prevents them from understanding political struggles occurring in Africa. As a result of this bias, many African Americans are unable to construct a nuanced critique of authoritative African leadership and continue to support African leaders simply because they are "black." This, in turn, positions African Americans against immigrant Africans as well as emergent democratic movements occurring across the African continent. As one Botswana national protested,

> Look at the Zimbabwe issue: African Americans need to understand the picture, what is right, kicking out white people is not right. Stop making decisions based on feelings. African leaders, Southern African leadership haven't criticized Zimbabwe. African American leaders need to take a position [and not] think [that] they are selling out. [They need to] look at things in a logical way; [there are] procedures to follow [and] don't behave barbarically. [We need to learn how to] criticize ourselves and [taking] criticism is very difficult.

Similarly, an African American scholar recounting an incident that occurred at a Nigerian conference commented:

> The big issue that came up at dinner we got into was Carol Moseley Braun. That was a very interesting discussion because Nigerians, except maybe one or two brothers, they were like, they wanted to get her, they would have backed Republicans or anyone else to get her. She had, as far as they were concerned [been misguided]. [By] her having this relationship with Abacha, . . . her boyfriend walked her into it, they were absolutely unforgiving, they would have contributed money to a Republican campaign to have her defeated. They were unequivocal in whatever it takes to get her out of office, they wanted her, and they were not at all sensitive to her relationship to the African American community, the first black woman senator. . . .

> *Furthermore the problem with African Americans and race in Africa has been ethnicity. African Americans see themselves primarily through a racial prism because they went through a process of "de-ethnicization" in the U.S. So they turn back to Africa with a de-ethnicized view. As a result, the big foil has been ethnic conflict because through ethnic conflict you have intra-racial conflict.*

Some African immigrants commented that of all the people in the U.S., they expected African Americans to take an interest in the democratic and social justice struggles occurring on the continent, precisely because of the kinship links that bind African people together and the social justice struggles African Americans spearheaded in the U.S. In this case, African immigrants used "kinship" as the organizing principle with which to establish a common bond with African Americans, and they felt hurt that the majority of African Americans were unfamiliar with African social justice struggles.

Furthermore, the example of Dr. Tascoe illustrates how African Americans privilege racial identity as a means to establish a collective identity with African immigrants. Using a pan-black identity as a strategy for unifying coalition groups under a common agenda obscures differences that may exist among them. In this case, Dr. Tascoe thought she was exhibiting pan-black solidarity by honoring President Moi. However, her position conflicted with that of Kenyan nationals who were protesting against his twenty-year regime.

The Kenyan nationals' actions illustrate how transnational identities are deployed to link home country politics with U.S. lobbying tactics to protest against U.S. support of President Moi and his regime. The previous scenario demonstrates that pan-black positions alone do not promote solidarity nor resolve underlying tensions that exist among the various coalition actors. On the contrary, relationships should be forged on the pragmatic political, economic, and cultural realities of the actors to build solidarity between African American activists and African immigrants (Horne).

These contrasting and conflicting views illustrate how different racial processes experienced by African Americans and immigrant Africans shape their sense of identity and their political positions. The examples cited above illustrate how the social location of African Americans as a U.S. racial group, in contrast to immigrant Africans as black transnationals, helps shape their understanding of racial politics in the U.S. and the global context as well as their interpretation of African politics. Mobilizing African Americans around issues not primarily related to race is thus a very difficult task (Meriwether; Williams). Rather, building black ethnic/transnational alliances is a complex process that entails exploring the link between identity and group location.

FORMATION OF NATIONAL SUMMIT
PROTEST GROUPS

The second major event at the National Summit was the formation of two protest groups, the All African Organization and the Social Justice Coalition. The emergence of these bodies illustrates how identity is inherently a political factor. African immigrant activists used this opportunity to organize the African immigrant community by hosting two successive meetings during the Summit in Washington, D.C., to discuss the formation of the All African Organization Committee. For the first time, African immigrants were provided with a venue to discuss the formation of an African political action committee.

Simultaneously, a multiracial coalition primarily composed of social justice activist organizations—e.g., African Policy Information Center, Africa Fund, American Friends Service Committee, and the Association of Concerned African Scholars—convened to discuss a countermovement against the National Summit. Both groups identified and articulated problems with the Summit process, such as the exclusive nature of the deliberative process, lack of accountability, and marginalization of African immigrants and more "progressive" elements within the African constituency. However, they organized around different collective identities as African immigrants and social justice activists. These socially constructed and organic identities emerged from historically specific circumstances that had different cultural and political meanings for the actors. Thus these examples illustrate how the positionality of coalition actors informs identity and how identity shapes political positions.

All African Organization Formation

The All African Organization was spearheaded by two California African graduate students, Thierry Ngoufan and Julius Ujeh, "who felt the pulse of the African immigrant community and capitalized on the opportunity" (California delegate interview). Throughout the entire Summit process, some African immigrants expressed concerns that their voices were not being heard. As illustrated in scenario two, some African immigrants believed that they were more authentic and credible than their American counterparts because they were born in Africa. Likewise, they privileged a collective sense of knowledge about African society, claiming that the aspirations of their country-folk made them more legitimate than their American counterparts to speak on behalf of Africa. The formation of the All African Organization may thus be understood as a collective expression of political action to advance a uniform agenda on behalf of immigrant Africans.

However, not all Americans agreed with the position espoused by African immigrants, that they were more authentic and should therefore be the primary voice at the Summit. Indeed, one white American participant stated that "[financial] scholarships [to participate in Summit activities] should be provided to anyone who supports Africa in a positive way." When asked why a side meeting was convened for African immigrants, the response by an African immigrant was, "[I] have a different agenda." Clearly, some Americans felt as if African immigrants failed to understand the political process and the importance of "voter representation." Rather, "Africans [were living] in a field of dreams as if we go to D.C. all will be ok."

On the contrary, some African immigrants understood the nuances of the American political system and the importance of American involvement: "This had to be an American thing. White, black Americans had to push this. The Summit is organiz[ed] by Americans trying to put Africa on [the] agenda. We who are interested in Africa can help Africa [by voting] to push issues." The contrasting and varying perspectives expressed by the Summit participants illustrate how their social location in the local, national, and international structure informs their perception as to who should lead the political organizing initiative.

Despite the concern over a lack of inclusion in the Summit process, some Africans boycotted the all-Africa meeting because they felt that it was divisive and "shortsighted and impeded the broader goal." Some African delegates challenged the special claim of a unique "African identity," since many Africans were married to Euro- and African Americans. Furthermore, they pointed out that African immigrants have a relative lack of knowledge and political sophistication with the American political system, let alone U.S. foreign policy. Finally, it was stated that African immigrants needed African Americans to assist them with negotiating the political system, precisely because they were black themselves and were operating in a system that had historically discriminated against their black American cousins.

In sum, African immigrants coalesced around transnational identities. As African immigrants and nationals, they felt they had a unique perspective and insight on what types of policies would facilitate sustainable economic and social development. Immigrant Africans believed that it was precisely these shared lived experiences that made them more authentic and legitimate spokespersons for African affairs than their American counterparts. Immigrant Africans articulated a second narrative that expressed a traditional U.S. value of self-representation and political empowerment. In order for the policy plan-of-action to be a legitimate document, it had to reflect the interests of African immigrants.

The National Summit on Africa (NSA) has brought together thousands of individuals and hundreds of organizations to move forward the dialogue on US-Africa relations. We recognize the efforts of all those involved. However, we are extremely concerned that the process has been organized in violation of many of the core values that motivate and drive our efforts to promote social, economic, environmental and political justice in Africa. We protest the use of our names and the reputations of our organizations in ways that violate the following fundamental principles of democracy, transparency and accountability. (Protest statement read at the final plenary of the National Summit on Africa by Mojubaolu Olufunke Okome)

Social Justice Coalition

In contrast, the Social Justice Coalition coalesced into a politics of solidarity. This group was composed primarily of U.S. civil society organizations such as religious, trade union, nonprofit, and community-based organizations traditionally engaged in the anti-colonial and anti-imperial struggles of the sixties and seventies and now engaged in social justice, anti-globalization, and human rights struggles. This multiracial and multinational U.S. network of constituent groups had long-established social relationships and partnerships with African civil society organizations.

Like the All African Organization, the Social Justice Coalition also expressed concern about having limited influence throughout the Summit process. Additionally, they felt the lack of representation by civil society organizations from Africa or their U.S. counterparts limited their ability to provide a countervailing force to the National Summit evolving into an "elite-driven" and pro-corporate organization rather than a neutral convening body. By publicly supporting the African Growth and Opportunity Act (AGOA)—a trade legislation—and urging delegates to do likewise, the National Summit leadership further enraged the social justice community, who felt that they had been misled and used to legitimate its corporate agenda (Lobe and Cason) and that the original mandate of the National Summit had been violated.[15]

The tension between the Secretariat and the Social Justice Coalition involved issues of identity and struggles over material conditions as well as the path for development in African nations. The identity of the social justice advocates was forged out of a history of creating shared meanings engaged in anti-colonial, anti-apartheid, anti-globalization, and democratic struggles. Issues of fair versus free trade, establishing labor and environmental protection laws, and corporate responsibility policies were not just ideological differences but had real life consequences for the material conditions of African people. To continue participating with the Secretariat without challenging the direction of the initiative would appear as if they sanctioned the AGOA, and these actions would jeopardize preexisting relationships and solidarity with African civil society organizations that were at the forefront of these struggles in their home countries.

What effect did this countermovement have on the Summit process and post-Summit activities? African immigrant mobilization efforts were hindered by the lack of institutionalized organizational networks. Thus, it was difficult to organize in such a spontaneous manner. In contrast, the social justice activist coalition was able to micro-mobilize a counter-movement at the National Summit, given their extensive preexisting social relationships and the dense organizational networks of Africa-specific organizations, trade unions, and church-based groups.

Given its incipient origins, the All African Organization had very little impact on the Summit's continuance. On the other hand, the Social Justice Coalition sparked several protests, a delegate petition statement, and a protest letter from NSA ex–board member Salih Booker, who apologized for promoting the Summit and encouraging organizations to be involved with its activities. Furthermore, social justice representatives who resided on the National Summit Board orchestrated a mass resignation, calling into question the legitimacy of the Secretariat's existence. What effect these protests had on the National Summit's decision to withdraw from the advocacy arena and focus on public education cannot yet be determined. To date, the National Summit on Africa has evolved into the Africa Society, which is designed "to educate all Americans about Africa and its people, to build bridges of understanding and partnership, and to facilitate the Continent's social development and political transition to more open, democratic societies" (http://www.africasummit.org).

* * *

In this chapter, I have examined the importance of identity and identity politics in the African constituency arena in the United States. As the case study illustrates, with the participation of African immigrants, organizing domestic constituencies to influence U.S. foreign policy toward Africa has become a more dynamic and complex process. Many African immigrants organized around pan-ethnic/national identities to distinguish themselves from their American counterparts. The deployment of a collective identity as "African immigrants" or the "neo-diaspora" was used to underscore cleavages along ethnic/national, class, urban/rural, and gender lines so as to facilitate mobilization. The California case study further illustrates that African immigrants viewed the National Summit as an opportunity not to engage in antiracist struggles or to displace white Americans from their dominant position in African affairs, as their African American counterparts did, but rather to displace "Americans" from being the dominant actors in influencing African affairs. Although African immigrants recognized the salience of race in American society and in the marginalization of African affairs, they did not interpret this as an opportunity to challenge the racial order.

While race may be the primary organizing principle of socioeconomic relations in the U.S., it is not necessarily so in other national contexts. African immigrants may use selection criteria other than race to build coalitions. As illustrated in scenario one, attempts to deploy a universal "black" identity for mobilizing both African Americans and African immigrants under a unified political slate failed. Immigrant Africans did not respond to calls for "black" racial unity; given their status as black immigrants, they responded instead to calls for African immigrant unity. The failure of the slate can be attributed to two primary but related issues. First, the leadership assumed that race could unify the different subgroups; they believed that African immigrants and African Americans attached the same meaning and significance to racial unity, despite the fact that black diaspora populations have experienced race differently and have followed different paths of identity formation. Finally, African Americans underestimated the desire of African immigrants to represent themselves as a distinct and separate sociopolitical group.

A related issue that I examined in scenario two involved identity, legitimacy, and leadership issues and how they affected the ability of the leadership to organize and mobilize the California delegation. As witnessed, the inability of the state leadership to resolve the distribution of power affected the political organizing process. How state delegates interpreted these events was influenced by several interlocking factors including one's race and nationality. Thus the state delegation was never able to resolve these tensions that led to the micro-mobilization of two groups, the All African Organization and the Social Justice Coalition. Scenario three explored the emergence of these two groups and the deployment of identity as a means to galvanize participants against the National Summit activities.

What these scenarios illustrate is the inherent difficulty in building a unified identity to mobilize the diverse constituencies that compose the African constituency arena. I argue that given the new cast of actors, ranging from the middle/professional class and the pro-business lobby to the African immigrant community, there is need of coalition leaders who can articulate multiple collective action frames that resonate with the values of coalition members, in the hope of establishing a flexible identity that will facilitate mobilization. Certainly, the African immigrant community offers a new dynamic given their transnational identity and formation into distinct social and political groups. Further investigation is needed to explore African immigrant organizing and the effects of these new social and political formations on the balance of power within the African constituency arena.

NOTES

1. For a more in-depth discussion about the National Summit on Africa see Humphries, "Cyberorganizing United States Constituencies for Africa," and "The Role of Race, Ethnicity, and Nationality in United States–Africa Coalition Building."
2. The National Summit on Africa has evolved into the Africa Society, a

Washington-based public education organization with six regional affiliates: Arizona, Boston, Georgia, Maryland, Virginia, and Washington. http://www .africasummit.org.

3. For a more detailed conversation on these issues see Hochschild; Booker ("Thinking Regionally: Priorities," "Thinking Regionally: A Framework"); Krenn; Dumbrell (1990); Jeffreys-Jones; and Schraeder ("Speaking," *United States*, "Removing").

4. For a more in-depth discussion on the socioeconomic profile of African immigrants in the United States see Austin.

5. In the case of Rwanda, the Catholic Church constructed separate racial identities for the Tutsi and Hutu social groups (Mamdani).

6. For a more in-depth discussion about the National Summit on Africa see Humphries, "The Role of Race, Ethnicity, and Nationality in United States–Africa Coalition Building."

7. Timothy Bork is currently a resident associate with the Carnegie Endowment.

8. See Booker (*A Review of Public Education*) for a more detailed discussion about public education and constituency building programs for Africa.

9. The original draft policy plan-of-action was developed by five expert working groups composed of academics, professionals, and other African experts.

10. The six regional summits spanned from May 1998 to September 1999, culminating with the National Summit in Washington, D.C., in February 2000.

11. To facilitate the deliberative process, the Summit is composed of five thematic working groups that include: (1) Economic Development, Trade and Investment, and Job Creation; (2) Democracy and Human Rights; (3) Sustainable Development, Quality of Life, and the Environment; (4) Peace and Security; (5) Education and Culture.

12. The Pacific Coast Regional Summit, composed of Alaska, Arizona, California, Hawaii, Idaho, Nevada, Oregon, Utah, Washington, and Guam, convened in San Francisco June 5–6, 1999.

13. Dr. Ramona Tascoe was elected as California chair; Nunu Kidane, northern California co-chair, who resigned and was replaced by Francisco Da Costa; John Oriji, central California co-chair; and Agrippa Ezozo, southern California co-chair.

14. The general meeting became the battleground whereby delegates challenged Dr. Tascoe's leadership and sole decision making behavior. As a result, the convener of the meeting dismissed the delegation from the premises of the building (see figure 14.1). For a more in-depth discussion about the National Summit on Africa see Humphries, "The Role of Race, Ethnicity, and Nationality in United States–Africa Coalition Building." Dissertation. University Southern California, 2003. Ann Arbor: UMI Services, 2003. 3103906.

15. Available at http://www.fpif.org/pdf/reports/africa_activism.pdf.

REFERENCES

Ackelsberg, M. A. "Identity Politics, Political Identities: Thoughts toward a Multicultural Politics." *Frontiers* 116, no. 1 (1996): 87–101.

Anonymous. Personal interview. Los Angeles, 1999.

Arthur, John. *Invisible Sojourners: African Immigrant Diaspora in the United States.* Westport, Conn.: Praeger, 2000.

Austin, A. "Are Africans in America African American?" *Black Directions* 2, no. 2 (2006): 1–7. http://www.blackdirections.com/2006_04_01_blackdirections_archive.html#Africans%20Issue (accessed December 16, 2008).

Booker, Salih. *A Review of Public Education and Constituency Building Programs for Africa.* New York: Ford Foundation, 1993.

———. "Thinking Regionally: A Framework for U.S. Policy toward Africa." Unpublished manuscript, 1999.

———. "Thinking Regionally: Priorities for U.S. Policy toward Africa. Background Paper." Washington, D.C.: African Policy Information Center, 1996.

Bork, Timothy. Personal interview. Washington, D.C., November 15, 2000.

Brown, W. *Manhood and Politics.* Totowa, N.J.: Rowman and Littlefield, 1991.

Bryce-Laporte, R. S. "Black Immigrants: The Experiences of Invisibility and Inequality." *Journal of Black Studies* 3, no. 2 (1972): 29–56.

California delegate. Personal interview, 2000.

Clausen, E., and J. Bermingham. *Chinese and African Professionals in California.* Washington, D.C.: University Press of America, 1982.

Clough, Michael. *Free at Last: U.S. Policy toward Africa and the End of the Cold War.* Washington, D.C.: Council on Foreign Relations Press, 1992.

Crenshaw, Kimberly. "The Intersection of Race and Gender." In *Critical Race Theory*, ed. K. Crenshaw, N. Gotanda, G. Peller, and K. Thomas. New York: Free Press, 1995.

Creswell, J. W. *Qualitative Inquiry and Research Design: Choosing among Five Traditions.* Thousand Oaks, Calif.: Sage, 1998.

Culverson, D. R. "The Politics of the Anti-Apartheid Movement in the United States, 1969–1986." *Political Science Quarterly* 11, no. 1 (1996): 127–149.

Diamond, L. J., and M. F. Plattner. *Democratization in Africa.* Baltimore, Md.: Johns Hopkins University Press, 1999.

Dickson, D. A. "American Society and the African American Foreign Policy Lobby: Constraints and Opportunities." *Journal of Black Studies* 27, no. 2 (1996): 139–151.

Djamba, Y. K. "African Immigrants in the United States: A Socio-Demographic Profile in Comparison to Native Blacks." *Journal of Asian and African Studies* 34, no. 2 (1999): 210–216.

Dumbrell, J. *The Making of U.S. Foreign Policy. American Ethnologist* 17, no. 2 (1990): 329–347.

Espiritu, Y. L. *Asian American Panethnicity.* Philadelphia: Temple University Press, 1992.

Fontana, A., and J. Frey. "Interviewing the Art of Science." In *Handbook of Qualitative Research*, ed. Yvonna Lincoln and Norman Denzin. Newbury Park, Calif.: Sage, 1994. 361–376.

Foundation program officer. Telephone interview, 2000.

Friedman, D., and D. McAdam. "Collective Identity and Activism: Networks, Choices and the Life of a Social Movement." In *Frontiers in Social Movement Theory*, ed. A. D. Morris and C. M. Mueller. New Haven, Conn.: Yale University Press, 1992. 156–173.

Glick Shiller, N., and G. Fouron. "'Everywhere We Go, We Are in Danger': Ti Manno and the Emergence of a Haitian Transnational Identity." *American Ethnologist* 17, no. 2 (1990): 329–347.

Gordon, April. "The New Diaspora: African Immigration to the United States." *Journal of Third World Studies* 15, no. 1 (1998): 79–103.

Gordon, D. F., D. C. Miller, and H. Wolpe. *The United States and Africa: A Post–Cold War Perspective.* New York: Norton, 1998.

Greenbaum, S. D. *More than Black: Afro-Cubans in Tampa.* Gainesville: University Press of Florida, 2002.

Handler, J. "Postmodernism, Protest, and the New Social Movements." *Law and Society Review* 26 (1992): 697–731.

Henry, C., ed. *Foreign Policy and the Black (Inter)National Interest.* Albany: State University of New York Press, 2000.

Hochschild, A. *King Leopold's Ghost: A Story of Greed, Terror and Heroism in Colonial Africa.* New York: Houghton Mifflin, 1999.

Horne, G. "Race for Power: U.S. Foreign Power and the General Crisis of White Supremacy." *Diplomatic History* 23, no. 3 (1999): 437–461.

Humphries, Jill Marie. "Cyberorganizing United States Constituencies for Africa." *Perspectives on Global Development and Technology* 5, no. 3 (2006): 163–195.

———. "The Role of Race, Ethnicity, and Nationality in United States–Africa Coalition Building." PhD diss., University of Southern California, 2003.

Jeffreys-Jones, R. *Changing Differences: Women and the Shaping of American Foreign Policy, 1917–1994.* New Brunswick, N.J.: Rutgers University Press, 1995.

Jones-Correa, M. *Between Two Nations.* Ithaca, N.Y.: Cornell University Press, 1998.

Kilson, M. "African Americans and Africa: A Critical Nexus." *Dissent* 39, no. 3 (1992): 361–369.

Klandermans, B., and S. Goslinga. "Media Discourse, Movement Publicity, and the Generation of Collective Action Frames: Theoretical and Empirical Exercises in Meaning Construction." In *Comparative Perspectives on Social Movements: Political Opportunities, Mobilizing Structures, and Cultural Framings,* ed. Doug McAdam, John D. McCarthy, and Mayer N. Zald. Cambridge, England: Cambridge University Press, 1996. 312–337.

Krenn, Michael, ed. *The Impact of Race on U.S. Foreign Policy: A Reader.* New York: Garland, 1999.

Lobe, J., and J. Cason. "Africa Activism: What Direction Now?" Foreign Policy in Focus Policy Report, February 25, 2000. http://www.fpif.org/papers/africapr/index.html (accessed 2002).

Logan, B. "The Reverse Transfer of Technology from Sub-Saharan Africa to the United States." *Journal of Modern African Studies* 25 (1987): 598.

Mamdani, M. *When Victims Become Killers: Colonialism, Nativism, and the Genocide in Rwanda.* Princeton, N.J.: Princeton University Press, 2001.

Marable, M. *The Great Wells of Democracy: The Meaning of Race in American Life.* New York: BasicCivitas, 2002.

McAdam, D. "Building a Constituency for Africa: Implications of Social Movement Theory." In *Making Connections for Africa: Report from a Constitu-*

ency Builder's Dialogue, ed. I. Countess, L. Hobbs, D. McAdam, W. Minter, and L. Williams. Washington, D.C.: Africa Policy Information Center, 1997. 7–22.

Meriwether, J. *Proudly We Can Be AFRICANS: Black Americans and Africa, 1935–1961.* Chapel Hill: University of North Carolina Press, 2002.

Minter, William. "Reflections on Africa Policy." *Foreign Policy in Focus* 4, no. 7 (February 18, 2000). http://www.fpif.org/progresp/volume4/v4n07.html (accessed December 16, 2008).

National Summit on Africa board member. Personal interview. Los Angeles, 2000.

National Summit on Africa staff member. Personal interview. 2000.

Omi, W., and M. Winant. *Racial Formation in the United States from the 1960s to the 1990s.* New York: Routledge, 1994.

Penrose, J., and P. Jackson. *Construction of Race, Place, and Nation.* Minneapolis: University of Minnesota Press, 1994.

Pierre, Jemima. "Black Immigrants in the United States and the 'Cultural Narratives' of Ethnicity." *Identities: Global Studies in Culture and Power* 11 (2004): 141–170.

Rogers, R. "Afro-Caribbean Immigrants, African-Americans, and the Politics of Group Identity." In *Black and Multiracial Politics in America,* ed. Y. Alex-Assensoh and L. Hanks. New York: New York University Press, 2000. 15–59.

Schiller, G. N., L. Basch, and C. Blanc-Szanton, eds. *Towards a Transnational Perspective on Migration: Race, Class, Ethnicity, and Nationalism Reconsidered.* New York: New York Academy of Sciences, 1992.

Schraeder, P. J. "Removing the Shackles? U.S. Foreign Policy toward Africa after the End of the Cold War." In *Africa in the New International Order,* ed. Edmond J. Keller and Donald Rothchild. Boulder, Colo.: Lynne Rienner, 1996. 187–205.

———. "Speaking with Many Voices: Continuity and Change in U.S. Africa Policies." *The Journal of Modern African Studies* 29, no. 3 (1991): 373–412.

———. *United States Foreign Policy toward Africa, Incrementalism, Crisis and Changes.* Cambridge, England: Cambridge University Press, 1994.

Snow, D., and R. Benford. "Master Frames and Cycles of Protest." In *Frontiers in Social Movement Theory,* ed. A. D. Morris and C. McClurg-Mueller. New Haven, Conn.: Yale University Press, 1992. 133–135.

Speer, T. "The Newest African Americans Aren't Black." *American Demographics* 16, no. 1 (1994): 1–3.

State Chair. Personal interview. 2000.

Stoller, P. *Money Has No Smell: The Africanization of New York City.* Chicago: University of Chicago Press, 2002.

Takougang, J. "Contemporary African Immigrants to the United States." *Ìrìnkèrindò: A Journal of African Migration* 2 (2003). http://africamigration.com.

———. "Recent African Immigrants to the United States: A Historical Perspective." *The Western Journal of Black Studies* 19, no. 1 (1995): 50–57.

Tarrow, S. "Mentalities, Political Cultures, and Collective Action Frames: Constructing Meanings through Action." In *Frontiers in Social Movement Theory,* ed. A. D. Morris and C. McClurg-Mueller. New Haven, Conn.: Yale University, 1992. 174–202.

Taylor, D. "The Rise of the Environmental Justice Paradigm." *American Behavioral Scientist* 43, no. 4 (2000): 508–580.

U.S. Bureau of the Census. *Profile of the Foreign-Born Population in the United States: 2000.* Current Population Reports, Series P23-206. Washington, D.C.: Government Printing Office, 2001.

U.S. Immigration and Naturalization Service. *Yearbook of Immigration Statistics.* Washington, D.C.: Government Printing Office, 2003.

Walters, R. "The African Growth and Opportunity Act: Changing Foreign Policy Priorities toward Africa in a Conservative Political Culture." In *Diversity and U.S. Foreign Policy: A Reader,* ed. Ernest J. Wilson III. New York: Routledge, 2004. 288–304.

Waters, Cherrie, and Salih Booker. "The African and Middle East Strategy Concept Paper: Improving the United States Policy Environment for Africa's Renewed Development." Washington, D.C.: Ford Foundation, 1996.

Waters, M. C. *Black Identities: West Indian Immigrant Dreams and American Realities.* Cambridge, Mass.: Russell Sage Foundation at Harvard University Press, 1999.

Williams, L. "American Interest Group Research: Implications for Africa Constituency-Building." In *Making Connections for Africa: Report from a Constituency Builder's Dialogue,* ed. I. Countess, L. Hobbs, D. McAdams, W. Minter, and L. Williams. Washington, D.C.: Africa Policy Information Center, 1997.

Winant, H. *The World Is a Ghetto: Race and Democracy since World War II.* New York: Basic, 2001.

Woodard, K. *A Nation within a Nation.* Chapel Hill: University of North Carolina Press, 1999.

PART FOUR
A MEASURE OF SUCCESS

15 IMMIGRATION AND AFRICAN DIASPORA WOMEN ARTISTS

Nkiru Nzegwu

The literature on women, art, and immigration is thin. Hardly any literature exists on the impact of immigration on women artists in the African Diaspora world. This is not to say that no books have been written on African American women artists, or on a mixed selection of African and Caribbean women artists in Britain and Europe.[1] The focus of those books lies elsewhere. Whatever their claims they do not explore the conditions, processes, and rationale of emigration on the work of these women artists, nor do they examine the choices the artists may have made at the pre-migration phase of their lives, or what were the consequences of those choices on their careers. The point is that there is a wide analytical gap between the pre- and post-immigrant experiences of African Diasporan women artists and what critics and art historians take them to be doing.

This essay attempts to fill this lacuna by focusing on three African Diaspora (two African and one Caribbean) women artists from three different countries, residing in three different geographical spaces. The first is an Ethiopian, Kebedech Tekleab (b. 1958), a painter who has lived in Washington, D.C., since emigrating to the United States from a Somalian concentration camp; the second is Hërsza Barjon (b. 1958), a Haitian wife, mother, and mambo-in-training from Port-au-Prince who now lives in Miami, Florida; and the last is Ebele Okoye (b. 1969), a Nigerian painter and animator who lives in Cologne, Germany. The essay explores who they were prior to their emigration to their new homes as well as what are the central themes of their art in their new environments. It strives to understand what their works say about their personal experiences and the larger social reality around them. How have their paintings or animations been shaped by their personal and social experiences at home and in their new spaces? What do the paintings and animations say about how they imagined the world and are imagining change? What theories of home, displacement, and integration are expressed in their works? What do these say about their hopes and desires, and how do these impact on issues of identity and power in their new homes? Lastly, in what ways are they redrawing the artistic landscapes of the countries—United States and Germany—in which they have settled, and reshaping the idea of global culture?

Before proceeding to analyze the works of these artists, I should state that owing to space constraints I will address only a few of the questions I have raised. Also, it is important to state that these women were not selected at random. They were chosen because of their distinctive visual language, and more importantly, because they are exemplars of new and exciting trends going on in African and women's immigration. These three artists represent three different types of women migrants: the war survivor, the mother-wife and priestess, and the young single pursuer of dreams. The common bond that holds them together in this essay is their search for a better life, their tenacity of will, their agency, and the fact that they are remarkably successful artists.

NEW AFRICAN DIASPORA WOMEN AND MIGRATION

A common assumption in African immigration discourses is that men are the key migrants, with women following behind as dependent spouses.[2] This picture is increasingly being falsified at British, American, French, and Canadian Consulate visa offices in Lagos, Accra, Dakar, Nairobi, and other African cities; and in Kingston, Port-au-Prince, Port-of-Spain, and other cities in the Caribbean. There are as many women as men seeking visas to travel or to emigrate, given the dire economic trends and general insecurity in diverse parts of Africa. Conflicts in Ethiopia, Somalia, Rwanda, Congo, Sierra Leone, and Liberia, for example, have contributed a significantly large pool of women to the immigration and refugee resettlement programs of the United States, Canada, France, Germany, and the Nordic countries. For instance, from 1983 to the present, Somali, Sudanese, Liberian, and Ethiopian refugees make up the majority of admissions in the United States (Singer and Wilson).[3] The numerous local and regional wars that have devastated many African communities and killed off husbands, fathers, and sons have turned high numbers of women and children into refugees and migrants. For these women, emigration is a matter not of choice but of necessity. They seek safe and stable countries to relocate to in order to raise their children.

This mobility of African women is a relatively recent phenomenon.[4] In the past, only African men received immigration permits and African women emigrated as wives and fiancées to Britain, Europe, Canada, Australia, and the United States; they are now emigrating on their own cognizance. The experiences of African women contrast sharply with the experiences of Caribbean women, who have had a much longer history of emigration to the United States, Britain, Canada, and France in the twentieth century. These had migrated usually as single and unmarried domestics. Makeda Silvera, a Canadian cultural activist, discusses how many Caribbean women came to Canada in 1955 and again in the 1970s as part of bilateral agreements Canada had negotiated to transfer cheap domestic labor from stagnant Caribbean economies to the expanding Canadian economy (vi). Other countries, such as Britain, France, and the United States, had similar agreements with Caribbean countries. In the case of Africa, single and married women only began to leave their countries in high numbers in the last two and a half decades. It was not that they were less adventurous than their Caribbean cousins; the political and economic conditions in their countries after independence made such migrations unnecessary. However, following the drastic economic downturn in many African countries from the mid-1980s, the rapid collapse of tertiary education in those countries, and the prevalence of regional wars in vast sections of the continent, single women like Tekleab and Okoye are making the necessary decision to seek educational and professional opportunities in foreign countries.

Other, newer models of African women's emigration began to emerge in the early 1970s. Upper- and middle-class parents were gradually beginning to support their daughters' life goals and sending them overseas for their university education. By the 1980s, a high number of young, educated African women, like Okoye, were traveling abroad for their education and were boldly making moves to pursue their career goals in Europe, Canada, Australia, or the United States. In 1986, many African women in the United States took advantage of the Immigration Reform and Control Act and regularized their stays. By the end of the 1980s, the occupation-based model of immigration was firmly in place. Under this model, professional African women, notably nurses and teachers, began emigrating to Europe and the United States in response to the high demand for their professional skills in these regions. Another occupation-based trend emerged in the mid-1990s as hair braiders and sex workers began migrating to Europe and the United States. This trend was most noticeable among French-speaking Senegalese, Malian, Guinean, and Ivorian women who moved to the United States and set up hair-braiding salons in Harlem, Brooklyn, and Queens in New York City. Meanwhile, a large contingent of semi-educated Nigerian and Ghanaian women migrated to different parts of Europe, especially Italy and the Netherlands, to work in the world's oldest profession. They turned to prostitution because it offered them a route to earn foreign currency and, in so doing, escape the grinding poverty of their lives.

It is noteworthy that these new trends did not eliminate the long-standing pattern of young women accepting marriage proposals from African students and immigrants in Europe and North America. This remains the most common way African women migrated to the U.S., Canada, and Britain.[5] The next largest group of women immigrants came as a result of the Diversity Visa Lottery instituted by the United States government to admit a large percentage of people from underrepresented parts of the world, including Africa and the Caribbean. The next highest number of African women immigrants came from the refugee resettlement programs that focused on casualties of war.[6] While we acknowledge the tremendously positive aspects of all these immigration programs, it is important to note that they have created shortages of skilled human resources in some economically weak African nations. The local economies lose their highly skilled citizens to economically vibrant regions of the world, further widening the gap between their old countries and their new homes.

KEBEDECH TEKLEAB: ESCAPING THE CONFLICT OF THE HORN

Wars are the bane of Africa. They have created tremendous upheaval and agony on the continent and led to massive movement and displacement of people from their homes and communities. Kebedech Tekleab was one such victim of displacement. Currently living in Washington, D.C., Tekleab belongs to the large group of Ethiopian and Eritrean women who, in 1989, emigrated to the United States through the refugee settlement program. She has produced a significant collection of memorable paintings that reflect on Africa's traumatic militarized history. Her work is interesting because it teaches about life under harrowing conditions that everyone should pledge to eliminate.

Tekleab was born and raised in Addis Ababa, Ethiopia. She began her art training at the Addis Ababa Art School, which was founded in 1957. During the period from the late 1960s to the mid-1970s, neither she nor her family contemplated emigration even though there was growing public dissatisfaction with the imperial government of Emperor Haile Selassie I. This attitude changed soon after the 1974 revolution that overthrew Selassie, when the ruling Supreme Military Council, known as the Derg, unveiled its policies.

Resistance to the rule of Emperor Selassie had begun in earnest in 1965, as Ethiopian students demonstrated against the government's corruption and rising food and commodities prices. By 1974, these demonstrations had escalated into full-scale street protests as students and other members of the opposition clashed with the police and called for sweeping political reforms of the feudal structure and for radical land restructuring. Functioning as the third estate of the realm, the students also demanded that the eighty-year-old emperor step down. Growing public disenchantment with Selassie's rule provided the necessary cover for a group of army officers, led by majors Mengistu Haile Mariam and Atnafu Abate, to over-throw the emperor. The new military regime made its radical mark with its 1977 Land Reform Proclamation, which nationalized all rural land, abolished tenancy, and put peasants in charge of enforcement.[7] Members of the Ethiopian aristocracy whose power was threatened by the dramatic changes launched an urban guerrilla campaign, known as the "White Terror." In response, the Derg launched its brutal campaign of terror, referred to as the "Red Terror," that targeted opposition forces composed of students, labor leaders, leftist intellectuals, members of the aristocracy, and others. All suspected members of the opposition were rounded up, jailed, and tortured, and many were killed on the grounds that they were plotting against the government.

Life under the fratricidal madness of the Red Terror was unbearable. From 1977 to 1984, while the reign of terror lasted, members of the student resistance movement who had eluded arrest, including the nineteen-year-old Tekleab, lived in fear. They knew that parents of arrested students desperately searched for their sons and daughters, and that most times these searches ended agonizingly at the piles of tortured corpses the government dumped daily at specific road intersections (Tekleab 8).[8] Families with financial means fled the country with their children to diverse parts of the world—Europe, the United States, and Canada. Those without means sought refuge in neighboring African countries, excluding Somalia. Tekleab knew she had to leave, but many escape routes had closed and a few open ones were perilously close to the region where the Somalian government had unleashed a proxy war against Ethiopia in 1977. Somali irredentism and the desire of General Muhammad Siad Barre to annex the Ogaden region of Ethiopia, during the latter's politically vulnerable moment, resulted in a war that was fought by guerrillas of the Western Somali Liberation Front (WSLF).

After extensive planning, Tekleab secretly left Ethiopia on foot in 1978 with a group of family and friends. The traumatic journey took them through difficult geographical terrain and the Ogaden conflict region, where they were caught by Somali guerrillas. They were detained for close to ten years in one of the most brutal concentration camps of Somalia. Initially, the captured prisoners were sent to a women's prison in Hargesa in northern Somalia, but later Tekleab and others were transferred to Hawaii camp, in southern Somalia, where she stayed for about eight years until her release in 1989. The geographical area of the camp was hot and dry, and infested with mosquitoes, scorpions, and flies. Malaria and schisto-somiasis were endemic and scorpion bites were common, and in winter, everything turned black from the swarms of flies and insects that covered it. Tekleab knew that to survive in this harsh geographical environment and brutal prisoners' camp, she had to draw on her inner reserve and live by the sheer power of her will. Everyone in that concentration camp except those who were terminally ill, or the very old, and children under twelve years of age, was subjected to hard labor, daily. Even children between the ages of seven and twelve were forced to knit *kofias*, small knitted hats with intricate designs worn by Muslims who had gone to Mecca.

On relocating to the United States in 1989, and after enrolling in the art program of Howard University, where one of the teachers was her Ethiopian compatriot Skunder Boghossian, Tekleab began to process long-suppressed memories and to purge her emotions through art. To do this successfully, she undertook a retrospective review of her life in the Hargesa and Hawaii concentration camps and began to portray aspects of her grueling experiences and the atrocities she had witnessed. The purgative process was healing, but it also served to convey to the wider world the terrible, destructive impact of wars on the human psyche. Speaking truth to history, Tekleab drew attention to the rarely portrayed horrors of war and the tragic impact of these on families in the conflict zones. Africa's regional wars are much more than about bad governance and territorial disputes. They call attention to the wholesale slaughter of lives in serving inhumane global politics, and to the dangers of arming or militarizing weak states that inevitably turn these weapons on the very citizens they claim to protect. At the same time, Tekleab's paintings draw attention to the courageous feats of ordinary people struggling to survive the conflicts and doing their very best to remove themselves from harm's way. By highlighting the psychological damage children, women, and noncombatant men endured, her hope is to mobilize against the use of coups d'état and wars in addressing conflicts.

In the first phase of her art career, Tekleab's painting style recalled that of Afewerk Tekle, a critically acclaimed Ethiopian artist, and one of the country's post–World War II generation of professional artists. It recalls Tekle's realistic painting style that was more poetic than literal. Tekleab restrained her emotions in order to produce images and moods that also seem to evoke the illusionistic style of Ethiopian traditional painting. As her skill deepened, her style changed and, like Gebre Kristo Desta's *Green Abstract*, became non-narrative. The parallel with Desta's work continued as she dispensed with linear perspective and its three-dimensional depth, and transformed her paintings into pictures of emotions. These pictures are fundamentally visual equations, condensed emotional formulae of human actions. To create the complex, sophisticated forms that became her distinctive style, she treated equally the background and foreground of her paintings so that they could be viewed together. Although these paintings lacked perspectival depth, they were not as flat as one would expect. This was because Tekleab had placed her forms in an atmospheric soup and expressed volume with lines, rather than with light and shadow.

The paintings described below utilize this volumetric technique to deliberate on life behind the barbed wires of the concentration camp. Its textures and suggested lines create a richer-quality picture with interesting gaps for viewers to fill, and by so doing, participate in the imaginative act of creation. *Shackled* is one such picture. It is a cathartic, deep response to the suffering of incarcerated women, children, and men who were tortured and subjected to mass killings. It depicts a vulnerable moment in the life of prisoners, a moment of inactivity when everyone is asleep. Still shackled, the sleeping bodies lie haphazardly in the overcrowded little room. Because they lack the space to perform one of life's basic functions, prisoners sleep on top of one another, very much like dead bodies lying where they have fallen. The painting makes the point that there is a very thin line between life and death. This thin line also separates the weak, exhausted bodies of sleeping prisoners from the dead, emaciated bodies of fellow prisoners who died at the camp. That same line also separates the students cowering in their little secret hideouts, and the tortured broken bodies the Derg's police tossed out at road intersections in Addis Ababa after nights of brutal interrogation. In memorable ways, the visceral nature of what it means to be asleep and to be dead is captured in the painting.

To be shackled *and* imprisoned transcends the usual banality of prison life. To be shackled in prison is to be allotted a fate of nonexistence. It is to be placed beyond the very meaning of humanity and life. A shackled prisoner is a wild person, one who has passed beyond the visible barriers of normalcy. In the Somali camp where Tekleab lived for years, there was no normal prison life.[9] Few knew the camps existed. The prisoners lived in hell. There was no affirming the life of living prisoners, let alone departed inmates. There were no rituals of mourning, no proper burial ceremonies to validate a deceased prisoner's presence on earth. It was as if one had never lived. Corpses were hastily and silently dumped into shallow ditches beside the garbage dump and quickly covered up with dirt. Not wanting to distract her viewers from the painting's message of anonymity and alienation, Tekleab chose for *Shackled* a limited palette of monochromatic colors that evoke emotional responses of alienation. She used thin, ephemeral washes and stains and textures to heighten the mood of displacement and to give a dash of ambiguity to the battered and swollen anonymous bodies.

Although the horrors Tekleab experienced in Hawaii prison were geographically localized, she did not Africanize this brutality; the stylized bodies in her paintings could be from anywhere. She rightly treated brutality as universal, as an unconscionable universal act that unleashes terrible suffering on people. She makes this powerful point by linking brutality to all other conflict regions in our recent past: from East Timor, to Bosnia-Herzegovina, Somalia, Angola, Rwanda, Armenia, Abu Ghraib,

Darfur and many other such places around the world. Brutality is the common denominator of all wars, including just wars, so it behooves everyone to repudiate rather than promote wars.

Thematically and aesthetically, the next painting, *Degradation*, is related to and continues the theme of *Shackled*. It depicts the shame and humiliation that occurs within a prison following incarceration. The long, horizontal 30 × 69" canvas portrays seven or more embarrassed adult women lined up against a wall in a slightly hunched position, averting their eyes from themselves and the viewers. They furtively seek to cover their nakedness with their hands. Their emaciated, skeletal bodies fill the canvas, forcing the viewer to confront their actions. Tekleab grappled with the harrowing fact that being a prisoner offers no protection from the boorishness of guards who delight in physically abusing, humiliating, and traumatizing inmates. Myriad acts of humiliation eat into and eventually corrode human dignity, ensuring that prisons become a place where the very worst in people emerges. They are the cesspool for bad human behavior. Regular social norms are breached and moral frameworks are inverted. As a site of human misery, alienation, and debasement, prisons ensure that self-esteem and personal dignity rarely remain intact after incarceration. Prison conditions are structurally designed to break down human will. This occurs all the more in the overcrowded conditions at Hawaii and Hargesa, where members of the Ethiopian aristocracy were inmates with lower-class women, and old ladies in their seventies and eighties shared living space with very young girls, including orphans and newborn babies. The dignity of everyone was stripped away, literally. Old ladies, middle-aged women, young women, and girls were stripped of their clothes and herded together. Raised in a culture where nakedness is frowned upon, the older women were doubly traumatized and frantically sought to shield themselves from prying eyes.

The consistent and unrelenting message that Tekleab pushes in these paintings is that physical torture, mental torture, and humiliation are practices that destroy the very properties of what it means to be human. The destructive impact of these acts highlights the fragility of the human psyche. No one is emotionally invincible by nature. Everyone can easily be pushed to their breaking points. The next painting, *Solitary Confinement* (1994), focuses on this point. It theorizes and visually highlights the error of the misguided theory of individualism and its thesis of wholly individualistic, wholly self-sufficient, autonomous individuals.[10] It depicts four individual figures seated in four separate compartments with their backs to the viewer. We do not see their faces since the point of solitary confinement is isolation, anonymity, and invisibility. Here, Tekleab paints the conditions of the Lantabur prison, reserved exclusively for Ethiopian soldiers. High-ranking officers were held in solitary confinement for eleven years. According to her, they were allowed to exercise in the open air for only ten minutes a day, and they "were not allowed to contact their fellow prisoners. By the time the International Red Cross took over the camps in 1988 after the peace negotiations between Ethiopia and Somalia, most of the officers who had been in solitary confinement for such a long time were unable to speak and walk. Some had completely lost their sanity" (Tekleab 11).

At the emotional level, the painting captures hopelessness, loneliness, and despair in the crouching forms of the four figures. The four long coffin-like rectangles within which each of the figures is isolated graphically convey that they are technically dead, even though they are still individuals and still alive. In their isolation and loneliness, life has frozen. Because they are forbidden to communicate with anyone, they have lost the power of speech. Living as individual isolates as enunciated by the theory of individualism, these individuals have stepped into the land of the living dead, barely existing in the long stillness of aloneness. The longevity of their stay, and the failure of the guards to abide by the Geneva Conventions on the treatment of war prisoners, convinces them that no one cared. Once hope has gone, they lose the will to either die or live. Understanding the deep, destructive impact of isolation on the human psyche moves us to see that individuals are basically social beings. Because Tekleab understands what solitude means and how it differs from isolation, she chose very light, pastel, cold colors and rough textures that mimic the harshness and frostiness of isolation. These are the colors that best express the cold, lonely feeling of abandonment.

Wire Series #3 (1994) is another painting that represents imprisonment as the land of the living dead. Within the dark, brackish space enclosed by the wire, ghostly silhouettes appear, suggesting a depersonalized and dehumanized existence. These erect, immobile human forms are superimposed on dense, crisscrossed, double-barbed wires that give the piece an ominous feel of foreboding. It is true that isolated from the outside world, prisoners lose their social identity and become anonymous beings; the same is true of the guards who have to work and live in the same environment. Although concentration camp guards may believe that they are radically different from the prisoners, given that they have power over them, they are subject to the same corrupting influences of prison life as the inmates. Their acts of brutality continually diminish their worth as humans, coarsening their personalities and transforming them into callous beings. The only prisoners who survived the crushing conditions of prison life were those who mentally resisted them. They did so by believing quietly and most ardently that "It is the oppressors who are insane / Consumed by the wounds of their conscience / The victims do not have blood on their hands / They are as pure as the black sky / As clear as the myriad white stars / Vividly showing the scab of a wounded life" (Tekleab, trans. Tadessa Adera). Inmates have to think this way to ward off despair and to survive. Resistance awakens resilience, which, in turn, strengthens the will and opens the pathway to vast reserves of strength. Tekleab chose somber colors—green, brown, dark green—to express the corrupting conditions of prison life and to link them to the decay, the smell, and the putrid conditions of a stagnant pool. Such a still body of water has lost its freshness, is filled with algae and dead weeds, and has a dank odor. The dark, brackish color evokes lack of movement and physical and mental stagnation.

Following emigration to and reunification with her family in Washington, D.C., Tekleab was able to heal and secured a new lease on life. The last two paintings discussed below speak about rebirth, hope, and the resilience of the human spirit. The hot, vibrant colors of *The Power, Pow-Wow Series* #2, speak to uplift and triumph. The painting proclaims that Tekleab has been made whole. Tekleab painted this message after a trip to Fargo, North Dakota, and participation in a Sioux purification rite in the sweat lodge and performance of the Pow-Wow. This trip enabled her to see firsthand the beauty of the Sioux culture, but more importantly, she learned the secret of the strength of a people who had been much-derided and considered to be doomed to extinction. In Fargo, the Sioux invited her to participate in two of the sacred healing rites that fortify and heal them. The people she met did not smile easily, but when they did, "the smiles are like deep pigments that do not fade away soon. I saw eyes that penetrate deep behind the objective body. I heard conversations which are not light and flowery splashes thrown at random, but limited and selected like marble engravings only to serve a purpose" (Tekleab 53). Among the Sioux, Tekleab's soul awakened to life, and her senses were sharpened, allowing her to see the brilliantly intense colors of life.

The activity in the sweat lodge was a forgiveness rite that required her to forgive herself by praying "for the whole world: the red people, the yellow people, the black people and the white people" (59). This prayer bore no trace of malice or bitterness, since it operated at the depersonalized transcendental level that neutralized whatever bitter experiences one may have had. Tekleab discovered from participation in the Pow-Wow that it was a deeply spiritual dance ceremony. It uplifted and purged bitter experiences, particularly her experience of the Somali concentration camp. The first thing that caught her attention about the Pow-Wow was the similarity of the dance to Eritrean and Tigrayian dances. It was very smooth. The smooth circular movements removed blockages, and amplified and channeled energy. It was a dance of life. The dancers, in a full spectrum of the seasonal colors—fall, winter, spring, and summer—danced the seasons of life. Because of the vibrancy of life they exuded, she selected hot colors—alizarin crimson, cadmium red, ocher, and yellow—

with a slight touch of cooler colors—blue and green—to celebrate life and to offer thanks for this wonderful gift of healing.

Thanksgiving, another painting in the Pow-Wow series, gives gratitude to the Sioux and the powerful force of their healing institutions. The painting depicts four nebulous forms in fluid dance movements symbolizing the spirit of dance. The painting resolves questions that go to the heart of life. It states that traumatized people overcome their pain and fears when they let go of these experiences, move into the spirit, and permit themselves to heal. The lesson Tekleab learned from the Sioux sweat lodge is that instead of being paralyzed by the massacres they endured in their history and the destruction of their families, the Sioux have sublimated their rage to love themselves. This deep principle of sublimation and transmutation is the only way to heal deep psychological trauma. It does not mean that the perpetrator of crimes goes unpunished. It means that the victim separates himself or herself from the dead, corrosive weight the perpetrator carries until the expiration of the latter's dastardly actions. Taking this path to healing gave Tekleab back her life, her laughter, and her self.

HËRSZA BARJON: BOHIO (DESCENT OF THE LWA) IN AMERICA

Moving on to Haiti and to Hërsza Barjon, also known as "Hëza," allows us to examine the new role of wives and mothers in their new immigrant spaces as well as the deep spiritual beliefs that sustain them. Like Tekleab, Hërsza was born in 1958 in Port-au-Prince, the eldest of two daughters of Rudolphe Antoine Ligondé and Jeanne Castera. At age eleven, she recalls, she was doing automatic writing that her mother and close family members could not understand. When asked what she was doing, she declared that she was writing letters to "friends." At other times she would respond that she was replying to her friends' queries. The problem was that nobody knew or saw these friends. Her mother privately wondered whether the fact that Hërsza had had to be resuscitated on the pedestal of a Mambo shortly after her birth had anything to do with the behavior. She wondered privately, because publicly, mulattos of the social class of the Rigardés are averse to acknowledging any connection to the African-based religion of Vodou. Any admission of having consulted a Mambo would establish her belief in a religion that members of her class denigrate as the religion of ignorant, poor blacks who make up eighty percent of the population. The hypocritical nature of this stance looms large when, outside of Haiti, these very same mulattos proudly claim Vodou as their cultural heritage. In fact, important mulatto artists, namely Philippe Dodard and Edouard Duval-Carrié, have done just that, Dodard during remarks at his exhibition in Fort Lauderdale (on November 2, 2006), and Duval-Carrié when he insisted that "Vodou has been the soul of Haiti, the backbone of that country, the essence that permitted these people to emancipate themselves and at the same time it is a religion" (75).

Hërsza's family's anxiety about her automatic writing drew an equally determined response from them to help her get over it. Generally, unaware of her encounter with the Mambo and the circumstances surrounding it, they underscored the nonexistence of her "friends," making it seem that she was mad. This harsh, though understandable strategy forced Hërsza to either close the open doorway to the other realm through which forces were intruding into her imagination, or clam up about her friends. The psychological pressure she endured seems to have prevented her from remembering precisely when her automatic writing ability ceased. It seems to have flowed seamlessly into the next artistic phase of her life, when she created patchworks, painted on decorative fabrics, and fabricated crafts. This move into the "normal" arts was a welcome relief to the family. Hërsza's mother then decided that her daughter's artistic skills should be properly trained and channeled. At eighteen years old, Hërsza was encouraged to study with two of Haiti's internationally renowned artists—Bernard Séjourné (1954–1994) and Jean-Claude Legagneur. The hope was that proper training and guidance would refine Hërsza's skill. Still, it is unclear why her parents did not send her straight to an art school to receive the sort of training that Séjourné and Legagneur did.

The classes in the artists' studios began in 1976. At this time, Séjourné and Legagneur had become notable artists in Port-au-Prince and were famed for their use of colors, their artistic attention to human forms, particularly women, their production of intensely personal forms of women in pensive moods and with haunting colors, and their celebration of spirituality, women's beauty and grace (Quincy Troupe, quoted in Lewis and Hewitt 138). Interestingly, Hërsza did not find the training and the style of her art teachers satisfying, though she learned from them their bold use and superb handling of colors, and their sophisticated grasp of symbolism as well as the techniques for bringing symbols to life.

To fully come into her own as an artist, Hërsza had to formulate her own visual language of forms. She had to resist social pressures that tried to enforce conformity on what constitutes good art. Naturally, this social pressure dimmed her vision, rendering her works limp and lacking the vitality they gained in later years. Although this period was marked by uninspired artistic production, it was also an important period of learning about major Haitian artists, and the role of the Centre d'Art in the Haitian art scene.

Between 1979 and 2002, when she moved to the United States, Hërsza got married to Richard Barjon, had two children, and had her first exhibition at the Art Deco in Port-au-Prince in 1990. She followed it up in 1992 with another exhibition at the Festival Art Gallery in Port-au-Prince. Her first exhibition in the United States was in 1994, at Miami's Florida Museum of Latin and Spanish Art. From 1994 to 2001, Hërsza had five exhibitions in Haiti preceding her major show in 2004, The Descent of the Lwas, held at Gallery Six of the Broward County Main Library in Fort Lauderdale. It consisted of 109 paintings on the principal Lwas of the Vodun pantheon. This portrayal of the Lwas was a major accomplishment, since this was the first time any Haitian artist, let alone a female, had painted all the Lwas. The project on the Lwas began after Hërsza read Déita's *La Légende des Loa-Vodou Häitien*, in which Déita claimed the legendary Boukman Dutty, of the Bois Cayman ceremony, took her on a spectacular, mystical journey to see the Lwas. In an interview by Jean Willy Gerdes, Hërsza acknowledged that she was profoundly affected by the book: "I did not know that there was so much passion in Vodou that could ignite that much passion in me" (Gerdes). The book transformed her art, as it seemed to burst open the fragile mental doors she had erected in childhood to close off her visions. The Lwas poured in. She began to see some of the very forms that had filled her childhood imagination and inspired her automatic writing.

The Lwas are divinities or energy forces and ancestors, most of which are from Lan Guiné, primarily from West and Central Africa. Houngan Patrick Bellgarde-Smith, president of the Congress of Santa Barbara, or KOSANBA, an association of scholars for the study of Haitian Vodou, describes them as electromagnetic forces with specific vibratory pattern. He explains that when a person's vibration reaches that of the deity he or she goes into a trance, and becomes possessed by the deity. This act of taking over the bodies of their worshippers is described as "mounting" the *cheval,* or horse. Scholars of Vodou agree that Lwas preside over definite areas of life and serve as intermediaries between humans and the Gran Mèt, the Supreme Force of the universe. When called upon, they intervene in people's lives to guide, chastise, reward, or punish them. They do this by removing blockages, opening channels, and facilitating the continuous flow of energy (Michel, *Ancestral Rays* 39).

Marc A. Christophe, professor of Romance languages and member of the board of KOSANBA, also reviewed Hërsza's collection The Descent of the Lwa. He describes her paintings of the Lwas as nothing less than revolutionary, since one of "the most archaic aspects of Vodou and Haitian mythology is the virtual absence of pictorial representation of the Vodou '*mystères*'" ("Epiphany" 15). In his view, her paintings represent a monumental departure from the traditional Haitian artistic iconography of referencing the Lwas in paintings ("Epiphany" 15). He states that a few pioneer Haitian artists—Hector Hyppolite, Gerard Valcin, Prefete Duffaut, André Pierre, Robert Saint Brice, and Louisianne Saint-Fleurant—had attempted in various paintings to represent their visions of the Lwas, but these efforts failed because they represented them by means of abstract stylistic equations of the Lwas' personalities, known as *vèvès*. Or, they accorded them similar qualities that Christian artists have granted to the Christ, even though such a framework is both inappropriate and inadequate for depicting the Lwas. Indeed, it seems that rather than painting the Lwas' portraits as Hërsza did, they were sidetracked into painting stories in which the Lwa may be a hero but not exclusively the central subject. For example, Duval-Carrié's 1979 oil portrait of Lwa Azaka, a magnificent 48 × 108" triptych titled *Azaka, Agro Rex* (Azaka, King of Agriculture), is not exactly a portrait. It lacks a deep sense of what Lwas are and has the feel of a contrived, imaginative rendition of a consubstantializing intangible form. Duval-Carrié's effort is unconvincing because, as he admits, "I had studied very little Vodou, and I had never seen anything like a portrayal of the deities. I know that all the people who serve the Vodou spirits do is draw these *veve* . . . and stuff like that. So I decided why don't . . . I give them their final, full, flesh-type of pictures so that people would readily recognize the *lwa* from their attributes. I just wanted to bring that personification" (75).

A portrait of a Lwa is more about mystery, otherworldliness, and magnetic force than about personification. One cannot approach or hope to depict the Lwa from a superficial, disengaged stance. To paint a Lwa, one has to be madly inspired to see and be possessed. Christophe correctly points out that though these paintings of the Lwas display beauty, artistry, and colors, they do not "convey the intrinsic personality of the Lwa and the intense drama that emanates from their majestic presence" ("Epiphany" 15). One only needs to see the *cheval* under possession to know that spiritual fortitude and a clarified vision are required to behold the Vodou *mystères* and to paint the Lwas. Perhaps this is why none of the earlier paintings captures the essences of the Lwas as one finds in Hërsza's portraits of *Quebiesou Danieh (Kevye Zo), La Grand Ibolele (Oudoudoua),* or *Oumgan Ican Legba,* or even *Dambalah Wedo.* Her approach is different from other artists' work. Her paintings tell tales of strange encounters, as does the spectacular portrait of *Quebiesou Danieh (Kevye Zo),* who appears in dazzling golden light, streaked with yellow and red and framing her impassive, beautiful face. There is no doubt that Hërsza beheld the Lwas. She seems to have engaged the awesome, majestic Lwas frontally and directly. She captures them in powerful portraits that present their awesomeness and power. Just in case viewers' level of apprehension is too low to recognize the Lwa, she removes any traces of ambiguity by displaying their *vèvès,* and utilizing the correct colors and symbolism of the Lwas.

The haunting, otherworldly intensity of the Lwas is captured in huge forms that fill the canvasses. In this encounter between the two worlds—the physical and the spiritual—it is as if each Lwa has appeared in full glory and posed for his or her portrait. The Lwas' magnetism and power radiates through their eyes in *Dambalah Wedo, Ogoun Balendjo, Luciani Baron*

*Lacroix, Lenglenssou Bassen Sang, Oumgan Ican Legba, Guede Carre-
four, Ogou Shango, IFE, Les Trois Egypte,* and *Les Six Elements (Le Bois/
La Terre/L'Eau/Le Feu/Le Souffle).* In the portrait of *Ezili Dantò,* the Lwa
of motherhood, protection, and wisdom, and Haiti's matron saint, Hërsza
provides an occasion to reflect on Haitian history that is not often found
in Eurocentric accounts of that history. In the Kreyol counter-narrative of
Haitian history, Ezili Dantò fought with her children to ensure their triumph during the revolution. She is credited with protecting Haiti and her
people from the physical and psychic attacks they endured from the time
of Haiti's independence in 1804 till now. For many, Haiti would not exist
were it not for Ezili Dantò's unconditional love and protection. She and
Ogou were known for their brilliance, courage, and fierce defense of the
Africans during the Wars of Emancipation against the French, and they
continue that defense now. She led the uprising that freed all the enslaved,
and the blistering defeat of Napoleon's army under General Leclerc. She
rallied hundreds of men and women to battle, and her colors of blue, red,
and black were finally chosen to become the colors of the Haitian flag.
Once the revolution began, Ezili Dantò's tongue was cut out so that no
enemy would ever gain knowledge of the battle plans.

In Hërsza's painting, Ezili Dantò is a beautiful dark-skinned mother
who loves her children intensely and fiercely. Her form dominates the
entire vertical canvas. She stares directly and impassively at the viewer.
Her face is framed by a shoulder-length scarf with deep, volumetric folds.
It is held in place at the top of her head by a circular, rust-colored head-
band. Her oval face, with large, piercing almond eyes and thick, full lips, is
striking. Dark, parallel, vertical scarification marks run down her cheeks,
a reference to her West African heritage. Her orange-pink robe falls from
her shoulders, revealing outlines of her chocolate brown breasts. In her
left hand she holds a short, slim, slightly curved dagger used to ward off
any danger. With her right she unveils the lower section of her orange-
pink robe, exposing a small, pint-sized, fully grown male, clothed in long
white kaftan and white hat. Situated to her right is her *vèvè,* written in
red, a direct reference to her warrior personality.

Hërsza's work on the Lwas began before her emigration to the United
States with her family in 2002. She first painted the central work of the
series, the 9-foot-long tableau of fruits, or *Table of Deliverance,* in Haiti
after reading Déita's book. Christophe describes this magnificent painting
as "a glorious ode to abundance and prosperity." He argues that it could
be "viewed at once as an offering to the gods and as an admonition to humans to come together in a spirit of sharing and fellowship" ("Epiphany"
22). The painting is organized around a central precept of African religion, which is the propitiatory concept of ritual offerings by which worshippers connect to specific Lwas who, in turn, are nourished and renew

their energy. *Table of Deliverance* is inscribed with sacred meanings and symbolism that transform it from a "still life with Vodun artifacts" to an invocation to the forces that rule human destiny. Only the trained or knowledgeable eye could see the pictorial clues that lie in the work, beginning with Lwa Azaka Mede's richly woven *alfor*, or shoulder bag, the two white water cups used in *sèvis* (ceremony), the two blue figurines that symbolize the Marassa, or the sacred twins, or the reference to Ogou Ferraille by means of his Barbancourt rum. Damballa's presence is acknowledged by the two eggs that symbolize wisdom and knowledge, and a fragrance bottle for Ezili, the Lwa of love and earthly riches. The symbolism and vibrant, vivid colors of the paintings in this series belie the poor lighting conditions under which they were painted in the middle of the night.

Painting is a sacred process of creating, and the deeply inspired Hërsza paints at night to better channel the energy of the Lwas. For her, this is the optimal time for creativity, because "at night the world reveals itself to me; the day is the window into the ugliness of earthly life. So the night is not the night but the day. The night is the day, because that is when my spirit is free. I find myself in reality. I am in harmony with the emptiness of a reality that is not empty" (personal communication, October 25, 2005, trans. Babacar M'Bow). At the rational critical level, Hërsza is aware that painting at night imposes its own special challenges, since the yellowish incandescent light under which she works rules out the pristine nature of the colors. She acknowledges that "physically at that moment, I cannot make any distinction of the colors. All the colors are the same." However, this physical limitation does not impair her ability to select and mix vibrant colors for her paintings. She is able to select the right colors as if she were working in daylight. Reflecting on the physical challenges of night painting, she admits that "I do not control myself. I pick up colors according to the vibration the colors present to me." And wondrously, the colors are the correct ones for the task at hand. Painting under this inspired framework says a lot about how Hërsza conceptualizes reality. To the question, who are you? She responds, "I am a spirit." And to the question, which spirit? She answers, "El. El is the spirit of life; she is the spirit of light" (personal communication, October 25, 2005).

Hërsza confesses that when she paints at night she is aware that her vision changes and she apprehends the colors by their vibration. The vibrant intensity of colors in this state of heightened consciousness is far beyond anything she has ever seen during daylight. She suspects she must be in a trance, since she ordinarily cannot explain how she senses the right colors and is able to distinguish the vibration of the right colors. This is really not different from how people see during the day. If the truth be told, the way the eye and the brain coordinate to determine the exact color is not different from the way Hërsza's inner senses determine the vibration of the colors.

In migrating to the United States, Hërsza brings the visual images of the Lwas to a culture in which the visual is everything. Because this migration is inseparable from the economic and political insecurity in Haiti, Hërsza did not leave Haiti behind. She became a transnational citizen, shuttling back and forth between Miami and Port-au-Prince. Prior to her immigration, violence and poverty had forced many Haitians to flee to the United States, but the latter refused to give them asylum as is done for Cubans. More than 40,000 fled Haiti in rickety boats in 1991 and 1992 during the violent and corrupt military government of Lt. Col. Raul Cedras, but most ended up at the U.S. Navy base in Guantánamo Bay, Cuba, a makeshift refugee camp. The U.S. immigration policy under the Clinton administration was to send them back to Haiti even though they feared persecution by the brutal regime of Cedras. In October 1994, President Jean-Bertrand Aristide returned to Haiti accompanied by 20,000 United States troops, but security and political stability deteriorated once the troops withdrew.

International economic reports list Haiti as the poorest country in the Americas, given that at least 90 percent of its residents live on less than a dollar a day. Although the Barjons do not belong to this class, this is not to say that the family is affluent. Life in Haiti was difficult when the family lived there. Unemployment was close to 80 percent, and Hërsza did not have a viable market for her art. The root of the problem is the huge wealth gap between the predominantly Kreyol-speaking blacks who make up 95 percent of the population of 8.7 million and the French-speaking mulattos who own the bulk of the country's wealth. Wealthy Haitians would not buy works of art that depict or glorify Vodou themes, and those who would appreciate them cannot afford the works. In frustration, the Barjon family emigrated to the United States in order for Hërsza to have a market for her art.

What this means is that Hërsza effectively became the primary breadwinner of the Barjon family. This dependence of her family on her art income says a lot about new migration patterns for women from the Caribbean. In the past, domestics, nursing aids, and nurses were the main migrating professions, but Caribbean women in different professions are increasingly immigrating to the United States. Hërsza has been able to create a niche for her art in Miami. Following her critically acclaimed exhibition in 2004, she has become a significant force in the African Diaspora community of south Florida. Her art defines another African-based reality as well as highlights the extensive reach of this culture in south Florida, a reach that heralds the beginning of a new era of the study of African Diasporic religions and cultures in the Americas.

EBELE OKOYE: GOING FOR DREAMS/MAKING
NEW FAMILIES

Ebele Okoye's emigration to Germany most closely mirrors that of a new
breed of young, unmarried, independent African women intent on defining their lives on the global stage. Well-educated, articulate, and mobile,
they have no qualms about traveling to any country to achieve their professional objectives. Unlike Tekleab, these women are not fleeing armed
conflict; rather, they are fleeing restrictions that are inimical to attaining
their career goals. In a way, their emigration objectives seem to converge
with Hërsza's, except that they do not have husbands, fiancés, or lovers to
expedite their moves to the new African Diaspora locations. What is remarkable about this generation of independent single African women is
their single-mindedness as well as the major social and political implications of their migration plans. These will be discussed later.

    Okoye was born in Onitsha in 1967, in the middle of the Nigerian civil
war. Her family relocated to their hometown of Igbo-Ukwu to escape the
relentless bombing of the city of Onitsha. At the end of the war, her father went back to his job in the city while she stayed with her mother in
Igbo-Ukwu to complete her primary and secondary education. Okoye recalls that her fascination with art began when, at ten years old, she saw
Charlie Brown comics and loved them. She loved the illustrative art of
cartooning, and the narrative-strip style of comic books that allowed her
to visually follow the story. She learned from her parents that "whenever I told stories, which occurs frequently, I have a tendency of resort-
ing to visual portrayals" (Okoye). According to her father, she drew her
"stories on any material she could lay her hands on, from the sand in the
courtyard to the family's nice Sunday table cloth!" Because she was the
last child, her parents were indulgent of her creative efforts and tolerant
of her inquisitiveness. But they drew the line when she began cutting up
her clothes to make new ones and when she tried to dismantle the radio
to see how it functioned. Unlike some parents, who are unappreciative of
their children's artistic proclivities, Okoye's were very understanding and
supportive parents who took pride in her explorations of her talent and
gave her every opportunity to excel. In fact, her mother still has her first
drawing.

    Okoye's penchant for illustration continued during secondary school,
until she came across an article on animations that changed her life. From
then on, all she wanted to do was animation. This quest to learn animation led her to enroll in a technical art school, the Institute of Management and Technology (IMT), Enugu, Nigeria, that had a Fine and Applied
Arts and Graphic Design Department. She had reasoned that that was the
best place to learn animation, but unfortunately, none of the technical art

schools in Nigeria offered the subject. She decided to specialize in graphic art illustration and to sharpen her drawing skills, because she understood the importance of drawing to illustration, and the relationship of art illustration to animation. After completing the two-year program and receiving her Ordinary National Diploma (OND) in fine and applied arts, she enrolled for the Higher National Diploma (HND) in graphic design and illustration. Among her teachers were some of Nigeria's most exciting artists of the 1990s—Nsikak Essien, Chris Afuba, and Chris Echeta. According to Essien, Okoye was one of four very talented art students (three men and a woman) who initiated an art revival that "turned the Institute of Management and Technology, Enugu, Nigeria upside down" (Essien). Their works were so exciting and challenging that he took every opportunity to visit their drawing classes to see what they were doing. "Listen, something was occurring and I didn't want to miss any bit of it" (Essien).

Essien contends that there was "a lot more freedom . . . more adventure" in Okoye's work (Essien). Some of this freedom and sense of adventure came from the confidence she had developed in her freelance work, from the themes of the cartoon strips she produced for newspapers and magazines, and from the storyboards she had made for advertising agencies. Because she did these projects while still in school, she was able to enrich her school work with experiences from work and, in turn, deepen her freelance work with what she learned in school. Upon graduating in 1989, Okoye worked for a number of advertising agencies in Lagos, Aba, and Enugu—specifically Web Creations, Goldmark Advertising, and Hammerhead Interiors—while continuing her freelance work as a cartoonist for different newspapers and magazines. Her preferred medium was pen, brush, and ink. In 1990, she illustrated Nigeria's first soccer comic, *Kickas' World*, now defunct. In a soccer-obsessed country like Nigeria, this comic was a major phenomenon, and the fact that a woman was the illustrator was a newsworthy event. It earned her prized internships in printing presses, publishing houses, advertising agencies, and design and architecture studios. From 1990 to 1992, Okoye produced a body of satirical works for such Nigerian women's magazines as *Classique, Poise,* and *Today's Choice*. In 1995, she had her first solo exhibition—*Storms of the Heart*—at the National Museum, and followed this up with other exhibitions in 1996 and 1998—*Realities I* and *New Culture*, respectively—at Didi Museum. These exhibitions—*New Culture, Realities,* and *Storms of the Heart*—were all critically reviewed in major Nigerian newspapers including *The Guardian, This Day, Daily Times* and *Sunday Times,* and *Champion*.

A testament to Okoye's hard work is that she had a solo exhibition every year from 1995 to 2003, even while studying in Germany. For her, a "day in praxis is worth more than ten years in training." She acknowledges that she is "driven everyday by the urge to learn more, and she is curious and open to new challenges and criticism with a view to finding the best possible solution to any given task" (Okoye, "Biography"). While producing works for her solo exhibitions, Okoye also participated in a number of group exhibitions. The last group show she participated in before her departure to Germany—*Woman to Woman*—featured only the works of women artists and opened at the Goethe Institute in Lagos in July 2000. It was conceived to examine women's relationship to the sociopolitical issues of the day as well as to issues that affect their lives as women. Some of the works addressed the simple complexities of being a woman, or environmental themes, and others focused on issues of women's reproductive health, such as the prevalent problem of high maternal mortality. No doubt, the frank and brutal character of some of the works generated intense controversy in the art community in Lagos.

The paintings Okoye produced for this exhibition addressed the plight of the "other woman," particularly the relationship of the latter to "Mrs. Wife." Over the years, *Lagos Weekend*, Nigeria's infamous, racy tabloid, had made this a worthwhile and respectable topic of analysis for numerous Nigerians. Who are in *ménage-à-trois* relationships? Who is sleeping with whom and where? And what did madams or misters do? These are some of the juicy items of gossip that readers looked forward to on Fridays. Okoye simply transported that salacious theme to the visual arts. Her paintings engaged the issues, not in cartoon-mode illustrative style but as formal paintings. However, she borrowed the cartoon production style of producing numerous frames to tell the story. Thus, her paintings were grouped in strips, consisting of three or four paintings per theme.

In *The Other Woman* series, portraits of other women pictorially depict "stories I'd heard . . . stories that touched, fascinated and affected me. . . . Unanswered questions . . . and relationships as mundane as being the other woman" (personal communication). The frames or paintings numbered one, two, and three in *The Other Woman* series focus on mood portraits of the other women. By means of these portraits of their moods, Okoye enters into a visual discussion of the perennial problem and relationship of wives and the other woman, as depicted in the *Dance of the Chameleon*, one of the paintings in the series. The Other Woman always lurking in the background of many marriages is often a shadowy figure, many times younger than the balding, middle-aged man who professes his love for her. He declares his love and respect but does everything possible to conceal her identity from family and friends. "No, I am not seeing any woman!" he lies to his wife. "God is my witness; I do not have another woman. What makes you think that I do?" he puffs in righteous indignation. Yet hidden in the shadowy background, away from the prying eyes of Mrs. Wife and Mrs. Wife's friends, he enjoys a young, succulent body, oblivious that God is a witness to the tryst. When he is sufficiently in over his head, having promised heaven and earth to the chick, the squeeze begins. It is time to deliver on the promises. "When do we get married?" she asks sweetly. If he is to continue to get the sultry, passionate embrace of his newfound love, he must get rid of madam, the Mrs. Wife (Nzegwu).

The story is just heating up. The next painting in the series, *The Other Woman 3*, highlights what happens as the relationship becomes increasingly complicated. Viewers fill in the blank spaces with their own storyboard. The philandering husband stomps around his home looking for an excuse to get rid of Mrs. Wife, whom he had solemnly sworn "to love and to cherish until death do us part." His bad behavior attracts comments to which he responds uncaringly, "If you don't like it you can leave. If you can't take it somebody else will." Sometimes, to expedite the departure of Mrs. Wife, the Other Woman storms into the home. She discomforts the wife with her saucy presence, demanding insolently, "So what are you still doing here? When will you leave? Can't you see he has no use for you!" Should the wife adopt the "sit tight" strategy of most Nigerian Mrs. Wives and proclaim, "I am the wife. I've got the ring! And I am staying put!"? The Other Woman retorts, crushingly, "Okay, you keep the ring, I'll keep the man" (Nzegwu). For the Lagos art audience, Okoye's strategy of addressing salacious issues in an art exhibition was a scream, given that they were accustomed to seeing only tame and uninteresting paintings of *Fulani Milkmaids*, *African Dancers*, *Mother and Child*, or *Durbar Horses*. The risqué topic and paintings, such as *A First-of-April Morning Kiss*, provided the necessary jolt that got the Lagos audience re-engaged in animated discussions on the role of art and artists.

Although Okoye was at the top of her game as a professional artist, having attracted critical attention to her work, she still yearned for an opportunity to attend an animation school. She applied to several colleges and universities in Germany and finally gained admission to the University of Cologne to study African studies. She accepted the admission for African studies so as to enter the German university system. Never for one moment did she abandon her hopes of studying animation.

But why Germany? Okoye had visited Germany for three weeks in 1996 and in 2000, and loved it. At first glance, her choice of country is unusual because most young, unmarried women prefer to travel to the United States, Britain, or other countries—typically Canada, Ireland, or Northern Ireland—where English is the main language of communication, and where there are a critical number of Nigerians in the professional class. In fact, prior to the 1970s most Nigerians preferred to receive a British education, but that is no longer the case. Because of the language barrier, Nigerians who ended up in Germany were usually recipients of German scholarships, and these Nigerians have usually been men. While there, some of these men have married German women, and, prior to the economic downturn in several African countries, quite a few settled in the country.

Okoye's profile defied this pattern. She was not a recipient of a German scholarship; and she was not a man. But she had compelling family reasons to want to go to Germany. She had earlier developed her fascination for the country with help from her older brother's German wife. Okoye began learning the language after her brother recruited her to be a guide-cum-translator and companion for his wife during their visits to Nigeria. This task resulted in Okoye learning German, which she consolidated after a six-month intensive language course at the Goethe Institute in Lagos. Her single-minded tenacity paid off. By 1996, she had become sufficiently fluent in the language to hold conversations with German speakers. By the time she left for Germany in 2002, she was fluent in three languages: Igbo, English, and German.

On arrival at the University of Cologne in 2001, she enrolled in another language course in order to deepen her language fluency for academic study. A year later, in 2002, she moved on to the University of Applied Sciences in Düsseldorf to study design. Her arrival in Düsseldorf was the first time she used a computer for design purposes. This was new and exciting territory, but one that was immensely challenging. In fact, in just the same way that she was able to learn German in a short period, and to work as a translator by her second year in Germany, Okoye took to computers as a duck to water. She embraced computer arts with great enthusiasm, and in a few months had proficiently learned numerous software applications, notably the Adobe bundle—Photoshop, Illustrator, InDesign, After Effects, and Premiere—and Macromedia's Flash, Director, and Dreamweaver. Her first animation, a 1:02-minute-long work in Flash, took just a few weeks to complete, and six months after learning Director, she produced an interactive Flash project about life in Lagos, titled "A Few Minutes on the Streets of Lagos." After an internship at the West Deutscher Rundfunk (WDR) studios in Cologne, she added Quantel Paintbox to her tools portfolio. On returning to her program in Düsseldorf after her WDR internship, Okoye chose animation as a subject but was completely surprised at the dull, unchallenging nature of the course. The search for greater challenges led her, in 2003, to apply and gain admission to the renowned International Film School, Cologne (IFS), for a further training in animation. At the film school, she trained intensively under well-known figures in animation such as Michael Dudok de Wit, Larry Lauria, Jimi Murakami, and Sylvain Chomet, with courses in storyboarding under Marcie Begleiter. The training ended in 2004 with an end-of-year collaborative film project, *Tag Attack* (5:00 minutes), with three other students. Since graduating from the school, Okoye has worked as an animator at the Trickstudio Lutterbeck in Cologne (known for *Die*

Sendung mit der Maus) in a 26-minute Christmas special produced by Ted Sieger and Alexandra Schatz.

Life in Germany suited Okoye's work ethic and temperament. She was doing what she had always dreamed of, and she loved the challenge that was coming her way. Early in 2006, Okoye screened her self-directed 4:03-minute 2-D animation, *The Lunatic,* at Europe in Motion's eighteenth film festival in Dresden. Its next screening was at Sofia, Bulgaria, in a joint project for animators organized by the Filmfest Dresden and the Goethe Institut Sofia. *The Lunatic* is based on the short story "Die Verrueckte" by Simone Kanter. There are nine frames to this animation. It begins with what Nigerians would call a luxury bus, filled with passengers and zooming across the screen. The bus dominates the entire frame, making it difficult to see the background scenery. Next a saloon car rolls by, set against a background of towering high-rises. A cyclist and a large, pot-bellied male pedestrian move in the opposite direction to the car, and then a red-haired woman appears in a billowing red cape, a huge sly smile plastered on her face. The next two frames zoom in on her face, and we see her drawing deeply on a cigarette. Still puffing away, she silently takes off her cape, and hangs it on some railing. A close-up shot of her torso reveals her breasts, firm and perky, then droopy and sagged in the final shot. According to Okoye, this animation addresses the fact that people who are assumed mad are always being either ridiculed or totally ignored, according to the normative behavioral pattern of the society in which they exist. Okoye dedicated this project to her cousin, Eunice, who in her words, "derailed" at sixteen years old, and eventually died at age thirty-three. Okoye's first designated 2-D animated film for television, "Ten Past Ten," is in five episodes of three minutes each, tailored for children. Her ultimate goal is to begin producing 3-D animations of Igbo folktales for television and DVD.

As if life as a budding animator and filmmaker was not hectic enough, Okoye continued to gain as much professional experience as possible to diversify her portfolio. Parallel to this work on animation, she continued her art and has had numerous solo exhibitions of her work as well as participating in group exhibitions, such as Globalia, which took place in 2004 at the Frauenmuseum in Bonn, Germany, and Annecy 2004, an animation festival at the International Film School, Cologne, that were important highlights to her professional life as an animator. For the Globalia, she submitted a class assignment from the International Film School, *The Fight,* her first ever animation, set to an arbitrary sound which the professor had assigned. She had to find a compelling storyline for this arbitrary sound. Okoye developed the narrative using the principles of key frames and in-betweens to produce a 20-second animation, featuring the crossing of paths between a science fiction–obsessed kid and a monster. The kid emerges from the right margin on his vehicle, manually pushing the lever back and forth to roll the vehicle along. As the vehicle emerges fully from the side to the center of the screen, the kid suddenly gasps in terror, quickly throws his vehicle into reverse, and begins pulling furiously in fast retreat. A massive monster appears from the left margin; its large flipper arm flips across the screen, grabs the kid, and tosses him from his vehicle into the distance. The monster then picks up the kid's vehicle and stomps away from the scene, twirling the vehicle around its massive flipper hand as if it were a slingshot. The animation fades.

Okoye described Annecy 2004 as a wonderful experience. It was her very first time at the festival, and it was as if she had died and gone to animation heaven. She found it "awesome, that so many people from different backgrounds were brought together by animation. Sometimes, one reads reports about events, and/or places and gets that feeling that it was either not well represented or discovers some missing Information" (Okoye, "Biography"). Currently, Okoye is preparing for an upcoming painting/performance/video art show in 2007 at Galerie am Liegleweg, Neulengbach, Austria, which hosted her very successful exhibition Nomadic Diaries in the summer of 2002. This touring no-sales exhibition started in Munich and went through Halle, Neulengbach, and then to Cologne in 2003. Its sequel was Between Territories, shown at Galerie Haus 23 in Cottbus.

Okoye continues to challenge herself in illustration, storyboarding (for live-action films, animated films, and advertisements), and creative animations in the area of narrative and abstract storytelling as well as storytelling as important to advertising. But the choices she has made for her career present a peculiar set of sociopolitical challenges, and hence her mother persistently reminds her of her civic and social duties: "So when are you going to get married? When will you give me grandchildren?" These queries from home obviously invade her privacy and seem to suggest that procreation is the defining role of womanhood. But since the personal is also political, the questions actually raise complicated issues that confront many young unmarried African women in the Diaspora. For anyone persuaded by the feminist argument that motherhood is overrated, the question is, what is the point of a successful career when the benefits are not passed on to progeny for advancement? How would the Diaspora survive and replenish itself if everyone abdicated their procreative responsibilities?

However, for those women who would like to settle down and have children the issue of where to find compatible partners is a pressing one. The problem is compounded by parents' hostility to the idea of daughters marrying outside their ethnic group. Where do they find such partners in the Diaspora? And how do they start families when suitable African men are scarce? The issue is of concern to women like Okoye who leave for the Diaspora at the very moment they should be settling down and having children. In Okoye's case, she chose a country with a small population of

Nigerian professionals, and the steps she has taken so far to advance her career goals have not made things exactly easy. Indeed, she could follow the path of some women and submit to an arranged marriage, or she could import a person of her liking and take her chances that such a marriage would work. But as these two options have been tried and found unsuccessful by many women, others have resorted to redefining the scope of personal relationships and marriage to include men of all races. Where in the past they might have gone along with their parents' desires and ended up in miserable marriages, many are now taking charge of their lives.

In fact, Okoye seems to have begun to think about these issues way back in 1999, when she produced two paintings titled *Amour sans Frontiers I* and *Amour sans Frontiers II*. These paintings explored the issue of mixed marriages. What is interesting about them is that they were produced long before she knew she would be going to Germany. Was it a prophetic fantasy? The two works offer resolutions to the choices the young women will be making in the future. *Amour sans Frontiers I* focuses on a family that is a reflection of Okoye's elder brother's: the father is black, the mother is white, and the child is mixed. In *Amour sans Frontiers II*, however, the mother is black, the father is white, and the baby is mixed. Had Okoye already made up her mind?

THE IMPACT OF THESE MIGRATIONS ON GLOBALIZATIONS

Scholars such as Peter L. Berger have written about cultural globalization as if it were the Americanization of the world ("Four Faces" 419–427). In their reader on globalization, Patrick O'Meara, Howard D. Mehlinger, and Matthew Krain argue that the spread of technology, easy access to the international media, availability of standardized foods and products, and the pervasive influence of American popular culture are changing how people in different parts of the world think and act (417). While there is some truth in these assertions of American cultural self-esteem, the underlying attempt to represent American popular culture as distinct and pure, and as the only globalizing culture, is misguided. It ignores the fact that American culture is an amalgam of ideas and products assimilated from other cultures. Our exploration above of the art of African Diaspora women artists makes it clear that African cultures, among others, are now part of American popular culture.

In a certain sense, this essay is fundamentally a discourse on global and globalizing African cultural realities. The idea of African cultural globalization may provoke amusement in one who thinks of Africa as a village, but it is clear that this process has been going on for centuries with the migration of Africans. As is evident to any serious scholar, these newer migrations of Africans and people of African descent are resulting in the spread of African cultural values and visual art forms to different parts of the world, especially to countries of the First World. What these migrations show is that utilizing what may be called the "covering law thesis of American culture" to think about globalization is wrong. It would be better to reconceptualize the world to think of it as a linked, networked system of intersecting and overlapping circles. Within this system, ideas emerge from a mixture of worlds and diffuse through others. These globalizing ideas influence or impact various cultures in much the same way that countries in the Western hemisphere were shaped by African, European, and Native American cultures. There is a certain sense in which the values of American popular culture are extensions of the African Diaspora.

However, unlike the old African Diaspora, whose members were forced to abandon their language and culture, members of the new African Diaspora do not have to experience this cultural and linguistic alienation. The current rules of global migration allow them to retain a very clear sense of who they are and their culture. This new African Diaspora of the last twenty-five years has created its own cultural distinctiveness by drawing from old cultures to simultaneously reshape and expand the visual language of its new homes. Like other Ethiopian immigrant artists in the United States before her, Tekleab carried over to her new American environment visual imageries, stylistics, and techniques of centuries-old Ethiopian cultural and artistic practices. Hërsza's work, by contrast, retains a very definite Afro-Haitian value scheme. The issues she deals with in her art have African resonances even though they are pitched at a universal level and engage American cultural life. As a channeler of forces of the Lwas, she is engaged in an evangelical mission of disseminating Vodou cosmogony and cosmology in ways that visually expand the religious repertory of the United States. Okoye's commitment to animate Igbo folk tales and to bring them to the screen indicates that she intends to inscribe her values in the global environment. Seeing herself as a Nigerian artist in Cologne is crucial to achieving this, since she required those folktales to speak the right idiolect.

Technically strong and accomplished, these three African Diaspora women artists are agents of a networked world and harbingers of greater cross-cultural understanding. They are breaking down rigid barriers at both the personal and the cultural level. Their newness and "outsider" status has sometimes gained them positive attention, especially among open-minded curators, art organizers, and institutions that are committed to cultural diversity. Such people and organizations are aware of the importance of inclusion in creating a stable diverse society. However, it is still crucial to note that they also face social obstacles and barriers because of their outsider status. They do not often have easy access to exhibition spaces or find gallery representation. The common expectation is that they should quietly take their place at the back of the line.

NOTES

1. A few of these texts in the United States are Arnett, Friis-Hansen, and Arnett; Steward et al.; Herzog; Shaw; Farrington; Robinson; Collins; Henkes; Hall; Wilson; and Bontemps and Fonvielle-Bontemps.

2. Immigration data does show that men still make up a larger proportion of the African-born emigrants than do women. However, only 55 percent of the African-born were men, and while the rest of the data are not disaggregated in terms of women and children, we can safely assume that a significant proportion are women. Although many recent African-born immigrants are economic migrants and tend to be men of working age, there is also a growing number of women migrants. The groups with the highest percentage of men were Mauritania (87.0 percent), Gambia (66.8 percent), Togo (65.7 percent), and Senegal (65.3 percent). The groups with the highest percentage of women were Mauritius (56.7 percent), Liberia (53.1 percent), and Cape Verde (50.9 percent). See Dixon (http://www.migrationinformation.org/USFocus/display.cfm?ID=366#2).

3. The numbers are: Somalia, 47,753; Ethiopia, 35,144; Sudan, 22,647; Liberia, 20,925; Sierra Leone, 6,028; Democratic Republic of Congo, 3,191; Nigeria, 1,249; Rwanda, 1,238; Togo, 1,038; and Burundi, 908. Source of Wilson and Singer's data is the U.S. Office of Refugee Resettlement, Report to the Congress FY 2004, 585.

4. It is important to note that the median earnings of African-born women ($27,508) were 9 percent higher than those for all foreign-born women ($25,260). The African-born groups with the highest female median earnings were from Malawi ($36,736), South Africa ($35,451), Egypt ($35,434), and Mauritius ($35,089). Those with the lowest female median earnings were from Togo ($16,034), Somalia ($19,077), Cape Verde ($21,426), Gambia ($21,605), and the Ivory Coast ($21,658). See http://www.migrationinformation.org/USFocus/display.cfm?ID=366#2.

5. Data from Migration Information Source show that the number of African-born in the United States increased 142 percent between 1990 and 2000. In 2000, there were about 880,000 African-born residing in the United States, while there were only 363,819 African-born in 1990 (Dixon, http://www.migrationinformation.org/USFocus/display.cfm?ID=366#2).

6. These data show that the refugee category is the third-largest in number. According to U.S. immigration data, the African-born groups with the largest numbers who entered between 1990 and 2000 were from Nigeria (71,285), Egypt (46,425), and Ethiopia (43,295). All in all, West Africans (326,507) accounted for 37.0 percent of the overall African-born population in 2000. The main sending countries from this region were Nigeria (134,940), Ghana (65,570), and Liberia (39,030).

7. The new administrative Coordinating Committee of the Armed Forces, Police, and Territorial Army was called the Derg, Amharic for "committee" or "council."

8. The number of people killed in the period between 1977 and 1979 was conservatively placed at 250,000.

9. Imprisonment also draws attention to the parallels between home and prison. Both are based on the principle of inclusion through exclusion. Both provide a living, eating, and sleeping space where people are bound together by the same fate to become a family. The primary difference between this family and the normal one is that prison takes away any protection from brutality, while home offers protection from brutality. It is not in all cases that the latter is true. Sometimes home offers no protection from brutality because the home is the brutal space. In any case, the condition of imprisonment highlights the provisional nature of home. The very boundary that defines the safe haven we know as home is the same boundary that prisons deploy to create a non-home. It keeps others out, and that boundary—whatever it is—can become the impregnable barrier of the prison wall.

10. In fact, scores of psychological studies as well as real-life cases of solitary confinement in prison prove that individuals are rarely autonomous, self-sufficient beings.

REFERENCES

Arnett, Paul, Dana Friis-Hansen, and Matt Arnett, eds. *Mary Lee Bendolph, Gee's Bend Quilts, and Beyond*. Tinwood Books 2007.

Berger, Peter L. "The Cultural Dynamics of Globalization." In *Many Globalizations: Cultural Diversity in the Contemporary World*, ed. Peter L. Berger and Samuel P. Huntington. New York: Oxford University Press, 2002. 1–16.

———. "Four Faces of Global Culture." In *Globalization and the Challenges of a New Century: A Reader*, ed. Patrick O'Meara, Howard D. Mehlinger, and Matthew Krain. Bloomington: Indiana University Press, 2000. 419–427.

Bontemps, Arna A., and Jacqueline Fonvielle-Bontemps. *Forever Free: Art by African-American Women, 1862–1980*. College Park: University of Maryland Art Gallery, 1981.

Brown, Karen McCarthy. *Tracing the Spirit: Ethnographic Essays on Haitian Art*. Davenport, Iowa: Davenport Museum of Art, 1995.

Christophe, Marc A. "A Sacred Space for the Resolution for Haiti's Age Old Antinomies." In *Ancestral Rays: Journey through Haitian History and Culture*, ed. Claudine Michel. Santa Barbara: Center for Black Studies, University of California, Santa Barbara, 2005. 22–24.

———. "Epiphany of the Vodou Lwa in Hërsza Barjon's Paintings." In *The Descent of the Lwa: Journey through Haitian Mythology: The Works of Hërsza Barjon*, ed. Claudine Michel. Fort Lauderdale, Fla.: Broward County Libraries Division, 2004. 15.

Collins, Lisa Gail. *The Art of History: African American Women Artists Engage the Past*. New Brunswick, N.J.: Rutgers University Press, 2002.

Dixon, David. "Characteristics of the African Born in the United States." Migration Policy Institute, January 2006. http://www.migrationinformation.org/USFocus/display.cfm?ID=366#2.

Duval-Carrié, Edouard. Interview by Karen McCarthy Brown. In *Tracing the Spirit: Ethnographic Essays on Haitian Art*. Davenport, Iowa: Davenport Museum of Art, 1995. 75–77.

Essien, Nsikak. Foreword to *Storms of the Heart.* July 1995. Published in conjunction with the exhibition *Storms of the Heart,* by Ebele Okoye, at the National Museum, Onikan, Lagos, Nigeria.

"Ethiopian Refugee Artist." *Common Ground: Radio's Weekly Program on World Affairs,* week of June 17, 2003, program 0324. http://www.commongroundradio .org/shows/03/0324.shtml.

Farrington, Lisa E. *Creating Their Own Image: The History of African-American Women Artists.* New York: Oxford University Press, 2004.

Gerdes, Jean Willy. *Bohio (Descent of the Lwas): A Painting Collection by Hersza Barjon.* DVD, 2004.

Hall, Robert L. *Gathered Visions: Selected Works by African American Women Artists.* Washington, D.C.: Smithsonian Institution: Anacostia Museum, 1992.

Henkes, Robert. *The Art of Black American Women: Works of Twenty-Four Artists of the Twentieth Century.* Jefferson, N.C.: McFarland, 1993.

Herzog, Melanie Anne. *Elizabeth Catlett: An American Artist in Mexico.* Seattle: University of Washington Press, 2005.

Lewis, Samella, and Mary Jane Hewitt, eds. *Caribbean Visions: Contemporary Painting and Sculpture.* Alexandria, Va.: Art Services International, 1995.

Michel, Claudine, ed. *Ancestral Rays: Journey through Haitian History and Culture.* Santa Barbara: Center for Black Studies, University of California, Santa Barbara, 2005.

———. *The Descent of the Lwa: Journey through Haitian Mythology: The Works of Hersza Barjon.* Fort Lauderdale, Fla.: Broward County Libraries Division, 2004.

Migration Policy Institute. http://www.migrationpolicy.org/.

Nzegwu, Nkiru. "Making a Statement: Two Female Artists—Ebele Okoye and Nkechi Nwosu-Igbo." *Ijele: Art eJournal of the African World* 1, no. 2 (2000). http://www.ijele.com/vol11.2/okoye-igbo.htm.

Okoye, Ebele. "Biography." www.redsands.de (accessed March 2007).

O'Meara, Patrick, Howard D. Mehlinger, and Matthew Krain. "An Emerging Global Culture?" In *Globalization and the Challenges of a New Century: A Reader,* ed. Patrick O'Meara, Howard D. Mehlinger, and Matthew Krain. Bloomington: Indiana University Press, 2000. 417.

Robinson, Jontyle Theresa. *Bearing Witness: Contemporary Works by African American Women Artists.* New York: Rizzoli, 1996.

Shaw, Gwendolyn DuBois. *Seeing the Unspeakable: The Art of Kara Walker.* Durham, N.C.: Duke University Press, 2005.

Silvera, Makeda. *Silenced.* Toronto: Sister Visions, 1983.

Singer, Audrey, and Jill H. Wilson. "Refugee Resettlement in Metropolitan America." The Brookings Institution, March 1, 2007. http://www.migrationinformation .org/Feature/display.cfm?id=585.

Steward, James Christen, Deborah Willis, James Steward, Lowery Stokes Sims, Smith Richard Cándida. *Betye Saar: Extending the Frozen Moment.* Los Angeles: University of California Press, 2005.

Tekleab, Kebedech. "Humanity in Descent: Visual Images of Human Suffering." MA thesis, Howard University, 1994.

Turner, John. "Historical Setting." *A Country Study: Ethiopia.* Library of Congress. http://lcweb2.loc.gov/frd/cs/ettoc.html.

U.S. Office of Refugee Resettlement. Report to the Congress for Fiscal Year 2004. Washington, D.C., 2004.

Wilson, James Lee. *Clementine Hunter: American Folk Artist.* Gretna, La.: Pelican, 1988.

16

EMERGING COMMUNITIES: THE RELIGIOUS LIFE OF NEW AFRICAN IMMIGRANTS IN THE UNITED STATES

Jacob K. Olupona and Regina Gemignani

This chapter describes some of the findings of our ongoing study of African immigrant religious communities in urban America. We initiated this project several years ago with the central purpose of examining the role of African-led faith communities in the United States, including the significance of these communities in the lives of immigrants and their broader impact on the American social and religious landscape. In addition to research, the project has also been closely involved in a number of other areas such as organizing a working group of scholars, investigating policy implications, recommending strategies for civic engagement, and facilitating interactions among African religious leaders and other stakeholders.

The African Immigrant Religious Communities project began largely as a response to the frequent inquiries we were receiving about the nature of the African religious organizations that were rapidly proliferating across America. At the start of our work, these groups—and indeed African immigrants in general—were for the most part invisible in terms of scholarship and popular knowledge. Misrepresentation and stereotypes were common in the media and elsewhere, as little accurate information was available. The project's primary aim was to reverse this trend—shedding light on the interests, goals, and growing impact of these nascent communities.

In order to achieve this aim, we have conducted ethnographic research across a wide range of African faith traditions, including Islam, African indigenous religion, and the various Christian traditions including evangelicalism, African Initiated Churches, and mainline Christianity. This involved extensive interviews and observations that originally took place in seven major urban centers, including Atlanta, Chicago, Los Angeles,

Miami, New York City, the San Francisco Bay Area, and Washington, D.C. We then expanded this work to include other significant sites of activity such as Boston, Newark, New Haven, Philadelphia, and Sacramento. A thematic analysis was used to interpret and explain the sizeable body of data which resulted from this work. A number of themes have emerged from these data and are central in framing our ongoing investigation and analysis. These include identity formation, transnationalism, gender dynamics, and civic engagement. Subtopics that we have investigated in some detail include the "reverse mission" of African Christian leaders, relations with other ethnic and religious communities in America, styles of worship, organizational structures and hierarchies, political participation, women's leadership opportunities, and the gender division of labor in the household and places of worship.

The major portion of this essay will be devoted to a discussion of our findings as related to several key themes—identity formation, civic engagement, and gender—drawing upon the three main faith traditions. Before moving on, however, we will briefly describe these diverse religious communities.

THREE AFRICAN RELIGIOUS TRADITIONS AND THEIR GROWING SIGNIFICANCE IN THE UNITED STATES

For this study, African immigrant religious communities were defined as those groups in which the members include a significant number of people who have recently migrated from the continent of Africa and who define themselves as African (e.g., versus Arab/Middle Eastern). In most but not all cases, African immigrants also lead the groups (examples to the contrary include African American mosques with African members, white- or Latino-led evangelical churches with a large African membership, etc.). Our study addresses three African faith traditions—Christianity, Islam, and indigenous African religion. Within these varied traditions there is further diversity stemming from the rich religious heritage of the African continent and the different paths that the groups take in America. There are evangelical churches that primarily serve Liberian, Nigerian, Ghanaian, or Ethiopian communities, and Catholic churches composed of members from Nigeria, Cameroon, Ghana, Sudan, Senegal, Zaire, Ethiopia, or Eritrea—each with their own styles of liturgy and worship. Aladura churches that are active in America include the Celestial Church of Christ, Cherubim and Seraphim, Church of the Lord (Aladura), and the Christ Apostolic Church. Congregations also include Nigerian Anglicans, Liberian and Ethiopian Lutherans, and Ghanaian Methodists. There are mosques that are primarily composed of a single ethnic or national group (e.g., the Nigerian Muslim Association), or a broad mix of West African immigrants. A multitude of churches, mosques, and temples have multi-ethnic congregations that are not dominated by a single cultural or language group.

Christianity

Among African immigrant religious associations in the U.S., Christian communities are notable in terms of size, rate of growth, level of social engagement, and distinctiveness within their wider faith tradition. Within the Christian communities themselves there are varied traditions, including Pentecostal and charismatic churches, African Independent Churches, and specialized African ministries within mainline denominations. Churches and denominations such as Deeper Christian Life Ministry, the Redeemed Christian Church of God, the Holy Order of Cherubim and Seraphim, the Ethiopian Orthodox Church, the Celestial Church of Christ, and the Church of the Lord (Aladura) represent distinct and unique expressions of world Christianity that are making significant inroads in America. The leaders of these groups are resolute both in terms of their own personal faith and in respect to their vision for community development. Their churches have been instrumental in renewing values of family and community in the lives of immigrants, and providing avenues for civic involvement. Their growing success in the U.S. is likely to influence public views of immigrant religion, persuading Americans to take more seriously the spiritual and social significance of these communities.

Islam

At the start of our research, many of these groups were just a few years old in America. They were engaged in the initial processes of purchasing a mosque, establishing leadership, and other tasks related to their establishment. Prior to that, as individual members of the Muslim community, most Africans had worshipped with fellow Muslims from the Middle East and from Asian and African American communities. Like the Christian groups, African Muslim communities have exhibited a great deal of growth and development in recent years. Due to their distinct style of dress, African Muslims are the most visible Muslim immigrant groups in many of these cities, and we also find that they are developing a more substantial social and economic presence than many of those groups. Important topics of investigation include the increasing level and forms of social engagement, the relationship between religion and expanding economic enterprises, and issues of self- and communal identity. Also of central significance is the response of African Muslims to the current sociopolitical situation of the U.S., encompassing issues such as racism, immigration matters, and terrorism—for example, the hostile attitude of some Americans toward Muslims in the September 11 aftermath.

African Indigenous Religion

The study of African indigenous religion in America is also of great concern to this project. African traditions, such as Yoruba and Kongo religions, provide a space for refashioning indigenous spirituality and a cultural and social meeting place between immigrant communities, African Americans, and European Americans. As observed in our current work, African indigenous religion is not widely practiced by Africans. However, the leadership is mainly African. Devotees of African indigenous religion tend to be African Americans, Latinos, and to a lesser extent, European Americans. Ironically, African indigenous priests seem to be much more successful in converting non-Africans than are Christian leaders, although it is the latter who emphasize their internationalism and their engagement in a mission to the West. We are highly interested in the way in which the African immigrant priests are influencing the spiritual and material life of their host communities. This seems to be happening quite spontaneously, and one is led to think of these individuals as natural missionaries. Few African priests have tried to convince us of their ability to gain converts. Their success in this area speaks for itself. For example, in many towns and cities we visited, such as Atlanta and Sacramento, we came across a sizable number of orisha devotees that cut across race and class; they held allegiances to a myriad of African traditions and they served under many priests and mentors from West and Central Africa.

RELIGION AND IDENTITY

As often pointed out in recent studies of immigration, ideals of cultural and religious pluralism have created a context in which immigrants are no longer expected to assimilate to an external norm. As a result, religious communities become less the isolated "ethnic enclave" of the past, instead emerging as sites for a vital expression and agency which aims to establish one's place in a multicultural America. Through their religious affiliations, African immigrants are actively redefining themselves and creating a distinct social identity. As communicated by so many of our study participants, religion is central to immigrants' search for community and belonging.

An important example is found in the African Muslim communities that are proliferating in cities such as New York, Philadelphia, Boston, Miami, and Washington, D.C. As a response to the profound loss of identity that affects African Muslims living in the U.S., African mosques are evolving into community centers. Many members cite the desire to bring together "the brothers and sisters from West Africa" as a key reason for their existence. They also emphasized to us that the mosque is much more than a religious site, representing a space in which multiple aspects of life intersect. As centers of community life, the mosques provide a sense of continuity with the past as well as avenues for change and growth—such as increased participation in U.S. social and cultural life.

One of the greatest concerns of African immigrant religious communities is the welfare of the younger generation. A number of leaders strongly believe that the youth are out of touch with the cultural knowledge and values that are critical to their well-being and successful integration into U.S. society. As a result, the transmission of cultural and religious values to the youth has emerged as a central priority among virtually all African immigrant religious communities. Various approaches to youth development are found, including programs and seminars that are more formal as well as informal support for parents grappling with decisions about how to strengthen cultural identities and values in the context of intergenerational conflicts, youth ambivalence, and widespread negative media images and stereotypes of Africa.

African Muslims are very active in setting up Islamic educational programs for the youth. During public functions at the mosques, there is often a display of Islamic knowledge by the youth. As they successfully recite the Qur'an they signify the continuity of the community, demonstrating the religious and cultural understanding of their generation despite being raised in the U.S. Most mosques run Islamic classes on weekends and during the summer break. A *masjid* president from Philadelphia states, "We have a school that runs every weekend where we teach our children those Islamic and African values that we hold dearly. We do not want our children to become Americans in their thinking . . . Therefore, to close the gap, we organized this school for them. We teach them French and Mandingo, which is our language, alongside other values such as respect for elders." A mosque member in New York describes how it is important for children to be "grounded in our history, where we came from and where we will eventually go back to settle." An imam from New York describes the importance of the Islamic school held in the basement of their mosque, and the need for parents and others to contribute as much as possible to complement the teachings, in order to balance what the children are "hearing at school five days a week." He states,

> I go to the basement to complement what the teachers are teaching. I tell them stories about Africa and its different cultures. I make them understand that they might be in the U.S. or might even have American passports but that they are not Americans. I always tell them they are Africans and Muslims and that their cultures are different in many ways from the American culture and

that when they go to school to learn, they must also be able to rec-
oncile what they learn from [the religious leaders] and their parents
and what they learn in school.

The imam describes his goal of developing a school where "African languages, history, and thought will be in the curriculum."

Within Christian communities there is a similar emphasis on cultural and religious values, and on special programs to aid in the development of the youth. Interestingly, in the Pentecostal communities we are
finding very diverse expressions of identity. Pastors range from those who
would rather not be associated with anything "African," to others who
argue for the growth of a "culturally based African church" in America.
In reality there is a great deal of fluidity, as church leaders and members express the complex identities of their transnational lives. In any one
church, ethnic cell groups may coexist with prominent markers of pan-
African identity and with symbols of a global "internationalism." There
is a strong desire to maintain traditional values of family and community
while also embracing American ideals of freedom and individualism.

Like other African faith communities in the United States, those that
practice African indigenous religion offer much more than a place of worship, representing instead "a way of life." Temples or "houses" (*ile*) are
being established across many U.S. cities such as Oakland, Atlanta, Chicago, and New York. These temples serve as centers for community life,
offering spiritual guidance, education, fellowship, social services, and recreation. Education is a major focus, and a significant part of the program
are the lecture series which cover a range of subjects such as knowledge
of the orisha, community health concerns, and African customs and traditions (e.g., the role of elders, upbringing of children and youth). At times
the lectures are given by visiting priests. Educational programs also include classes in African languages, dance, and drumming. The groups
have developed a strong network of devotees and priests. Orisha worship
is viewed as a "way of life" that encompasses many aspects of an individual's existence.

Religious affiliation shapes African immigrant identities in multiple
and profound ways, through commonly held beliefs and values, through
forms of social interaction, and through religious performance. In many
African immigrant congregations, music and dance are integral to this
religious experience and to the understanding and experience of community. Without over-generalizing, our findings suggest that across the three
major faith traditions, African religious communities share a vibrant mode
of worship. Worship is often cited as the most important factor differen-
tiating their communities from others. As stated by one church member
in Sacramento, "In a Nigerian church, the style and the zeal and the commitment make the difference . . . I doubt if I could get that in any culture
anywhere."

In relating their community histories to an audience, religious leaders often emphasize this aspect of their churches. For example, one pastor describes renting church space during the early history of their church and being asked to "turn down the volume." Another recounts attending a church when he first came to the U.S. and asking, at the end of the one-hour service, "Are we ready to do the dancing yet?" Music and dance also play an important role in a number of African mosques. Stokes states that in the context of immigration, music defines "a moral and political community in relation to the world in which they find themselves." Music is a significant contributor to identity formation, as it "evokes and organizes collective memories and present experience of place with an intensity, power and simplicity unmatched by any other social activity" (Stokes 3).

Any discussion of identity in the African religious communities in America must be attentive to issues of race. African immigrants are the newest wave of immigrants to enter the United States with inadequate institutions of support. African immigrants must also contend with significant issues of racism and tension within the larger American society. Like earlier waves of immigrants, they compete for scarce resources, often leading to social tension and division. These challenges are apparent in questions of identity emerging among African and Caribbean immigrants and African American communities.

Parents who emigrated to provide their children with better opportunities in education and employment find themselves enrolling their children in inner-city or substandard schools across the United States, a phenomenon seen in all of our sample cities. In many public schools, immigrant children are exposed to apathy, high dropout rates, large class sizes, and institutionalized forms of segregation and inequality. The response of many African immigrants when faced with this dilemma is to establish religious schools or to encourage youth and Sunday school programs in their churches. It is all an attempt to develop a separate identity quite different from those of the African American and Caucasian communities in an effort to protect their children from the stereotypes and racism present in American society. The result of this dilemma is a growing tension between African Americans and the African immigrants.

An example of tension between African immigrants and African Americans may be seen in a Washington, D.C., interview with a pastor of a Baptist church. Arguing that there are few communities in the United States that open their arms to African immigrants, he observes, "Africans are expected to integrate and 'melt into the pot.'" He cites recent examples of Africans refused by white churches and suggests that African American churches have also alienated Africans because members of these churches feel threatened that Africans might take away the little opportunity for upward mobility that African Americans have gained. African immigrants in this case are viewed as economic competitors with African Americans.

As a result, African immigrant respondents express difficulty in dealing with questions of their identity. One pastor and church founder states, "As Africans in the United States, we have two strikes against us: first we are black, and then we are African." Many African immigrant religious communities also wrestle with the question, "How can the United States be both a Christian and a racist nation?" As a result of American racism, African immigrants tend to have mixed and contradictory feelings toward their African American associates. They share a common goal in fighting racism, but at the same time, African immigrants also tend to separate themselves from African American culture for fear of greater discrimination.

Currently, within the religious communities leaders express a growing concern about these divisions, and there are some important efforts under way to improve relationships. For example, Beck points out that ties are increasingly forged within the Muslim community through shared religious practices (e.g., African Americans converting to Muridism), and some religious associations, such as the Harlem Islamic Leadership, are playing an important role in working toward greater unity. African indigenous religion seems to have been particularly successful in establishing a space for positive relations between Africans and African Americans. Our findings suggest that the African temples offer an important context for promoting mutual understanding between these communities. African-born priests are not only leaders and teachers for African Americans in their spiritual quest; they also integrate African American perspectives, beliefs, and traditions into their spiritual practices. An example is found in forms of the orisha tradition, a Yoruba religious system, that have been filtered through the lens of Santería and are best understood as religious expressions of black nationalism.

The transnational practices, understandings, and orientations of African immigrant religious communities are also highly relevant to identity formation. As is increasingly true for immigrant populations, Africans in the U.S. lead transnational lives. Their economic ventures, political interests and activities, social ties, and cultural beliefs and practices span across the Atlantic, linking them not only with their home countries but also with African immigrants in European nations such as France, Great Britain, and Germany. Religion plays a central role here, especially through transnational practices such as the continuous movement of leaders, ideas, musical styles, and liturgical genres in which new religious approaches and practices are continuously exchanged across the Atlantic. Tettey has suggested that such processes play a key role in carving out a space for African immigrants and helping them to overcome the dissonance of their transnational lives ("Transnationalism"). Thus, religion is central in addressing the alienated and conflicted nature of diasporic existence.

It is important to point out that many immigrants—especially African Christians—define and construct *global* identities that reflect their perceived role as missionaries to the West and to the entire world. Pastor Gbenga Talabi of Victory Life Bible Church in Sacramento describes this global mission:

> *Today, Africans have joined the league of voices bringing the new wave of evangelism in a great prophetic dimension to the Western world. It is important to examine the causes, the benefits, and the impact on a world that is distressed, riddled with crisis, and looking for urgent answers to global problems.*

This ideal of spiritual agency provides not only purpose to these movements but a global sense of "home" that transcends fixed notions of place and identity. Such findings can be viewed as evidence for the "new awareness and vitality manifested in immigrant identities" (Rapport 79) as immigrants creatively address and adapt to a world characterized by movement and dislocation.

CIVIC LIFE AND POLITICAL INCORPORATION

Over the past several years, African immigrant religious groups have become increasingly engaged in addressing crucial social, cultural, economic, and political issues and problems facing their community. They work in areas such as substance abuse, domestic violence, prison outreach, youth services, mentoring, community-police relations, and education and employment programs. They are unusual among U.S. faith-based groups in the wide range of services they offer, often going beyond the traditional emphasis on food, clothing, and housing assistance.

Our research findings have identified the deep sense of trust that pervades relationships within (but often not between) religious communities as an important part of their efficacy in improving immigrants' lives. Many of the issues that are most commonly addressed, such as substance abuse, mental health, finances, and marital/family conflict, are often considered highly personal and not something that one easily shares with others either inside or outside the African community. One member describes how marital problems originally led her to an African church, where she received assistance from her pastor, the woman's fellowship, and other support networks in her church. She states,

> *We need a support system and the church definitely provides that. And especially what we now call the Pentecostal movement, which is a more active movement and the whole thing is centered on love, just being Christ-like . . . I was married before and had issues that I really couldn't go to what the Western world calls counseling. The*

way we were brought up, you have a support system, you have fami-
lies. Even if your direct parents are not around, you have aunties
and uncles that you can bond with, that you can easily go to and
say, "Listen, here it is. I have hit a rock regarding this issue. I need
your advice, I need your suggestions . . . " Because we're here in a
family, I can address [these issues] . . . We are more receptive be-
cause of the work Christ is doing in our lives. There is the humility
that comes with knowing Christ. We are humble; we're open to one
another. . . . One of the very, very, primary issues—there is love for
one another. When you love somebody, you're willing to meet the
person halfway. So to speak, you're willing to lay your life down to
accommodate that person. And when you are in that state, you can
work with the person.

Almost all of our respondents describe the importance of a community
that understands their concerns and provides support for their struggles.
One member of a Pentecostal church explains,

The messages will give you strength. They know the needs of the
community. They know there are a lot of people there who don't
have their papers to stay, who are still expecting the government
to legalize their stay. And when you're in that kind of a situation,
you don't have a good job, you don't have any stability. So those
prayers are ongoing support. Sometimes you get a call from another
Christian brother or sister sharing his or her own experience with
you. And then you'll find out that what you are passing through is
not strange to [others], just in accordance to what the Bible says:
"No temptation that falls on man is strange, that any man has not
passed through." So you get strengthened by the counseling, the
support and the care and concern of the church community.

At the same time that there is a strong focus on providing support for
African immigrants, the religious groups are becoming more involved in
social issues affecting their wider neighborhoods, towns, and cities. Some
of their activities include food and clothing drives, youth seminars, substance abuse counseling, and material and spiritual outreach to various
groups such as the homeless, migrant laborers, and the incarcerated.

In the African religious communities, there is also substantial involvement in the political sphere. Much of the involvement is oriented toward issues on the African continent, and churches and mosques are lively
centers for debate about African social, economic, and political issues, for
promulgating particular views and agendas, and for disseminating written
materials. Political expression is also expanding to encompass a number
of political debates within the U.S., including immigration policy, citizenship, race relations, affirmative action, abortion, and gay marriage. As
stated by one of our conference participants, Sister MaryPaul Asoegwu,

"in these communities, [members] take stock, organize themselves, take a stand on issues and are able to dialogue with other groups." The communities act "as a springboard to connect to the larger society from a position of strength."

Sermons of religious leaders, while not overtly political, often contain political messages. Most leaders describe their desire to keep politics and religion separate, and especially their reluctance to "tell people who to vote for." At the same time, some relate how, during the time of the election, they will lecture on particular topics that deeply concern them and will hope to sway the membership toward their viewpoint.

Interestingly, we are finding African Christian leaders to be quite heterogeneous in their political views. Some pastors feel that the church should not be overtly involved in politics. However, others feel very differently. Okome, for instance, tells us that many of the pastors believe their role is to support particular Christian views and values, though not a particular candidate or party (Okome, "African Immigrant Churches").

Leaders of African religious communities cite several obstacles as constraints to their ability to pursue their community development goals, especially a lack of material and informational resources, and the need for greater unity among African religious leaders. The lack of unity is especially troublesome to many of the leaders. Citing problems of trust and competition, they have described the need for greater efforts to unite the communities to work collectively toward positive social change.

SOCIAL TRANSFORMATION, RELIGION, AND THE NEGOTIATION OF GENDER

Gender relations are a final but not least important theme in our evolving research on African immigrant religion. Recent studies on gender, religion, and immigration highlight the opportunities for women to develop their autonomy through their leadership experiences in the religious communities (Ebaugh and Chafetz). In the African religious congregations, one finds wide variation in the degree of women's involvement and leadership. But even in those communities where gender hierarchies exist in the leadership, it is common to find women actively pressing for, and gaining, a more influential voice. For example, Nida reports that transformations in Ethiopian Orthodox religious practice in the American context have meant that in some places women may now chant mass and are beginning to assume greater leadership roles ("African Religious Beliefs"). We have found similar changes in a number of African mosques. In some African Pentecostal churches in the United States, women have begun to serve as head pastors, something which is quite rare at home.

Generally, in the African Pentecostal communities, women play a very prominent role. In most cases, they comprise more than two-thirds of the membership. And women's participation in these churches goes beyond their mere numbers, as they play a key role in leadership and in the maintenance and expansion of these religious institutions. Women also are highly involved in transnational religious networks. Women leaders travel worldwide to plant churches, present sermons, and hold seminars. They are also leaders of missionary and development efforts on the African continent.

Despite the substantial evidence for women's leadership opportunities in the religious communities, few of the churches ordain women as pastors, and, as is true for all Muslim communities in America, there are no women *imams*. In addition, as reported by Crumbley and Cline-Smythe, the voices of women may not be heard despite their formal leadership roles. In the Church of the Lord Aladura, women are ordained as ministers and hold a great degree of political power as the church leadership structure at all levels is characterized by gender parity. Yet, based on cultural beliefs, women leaders are expected to show deference to men—in their interactions with other church leaders, for example. Also, Crumbley and Cline-Smythe's findings suggest that women leaders' ceremonial power in some AICs may be constrained through menstrual rites that segregate them from holy spaces and objects ("Gender and Change").

As religious communities aim to assist and guide immigrants in their social integration, marriage and the family arises as a critical arena in the study of religion and gender. In the African immigrant communities, an important factor influencing the family is the increasing work opportunities and incomes of wives in relation to their husbands. Women are becoming major wage earners in African immigrant households—due to their opportunities in the skilled professions, especially nursing. This has helped to elevate their status in the home and community, and strengthened their position in decision making. At the same time, men are faced with the reality that their participation in childcare and homemaking is necessary for the household to function. As a result of these transformations, a certain level of conflict has arisen. For example, one woman states,

> You'll find a change that starts affecting the relationships in the family. This is more common with people who are outside the church. When I say church, I mean a relationship with God. Those who don't have any relationship with God, they find it so hard. A lot of homes are broken, a lot of relationships torn because the wives make more money than the husbands.

A number of respondents feel that these factors are contributing to a sharp rise in divorce rates among Africans in America.

We are finding that religious communities are emerging as a key context for the negotiation of gender relations, as members reconcile more conservative cultural and religious gender ideals with transformations in women's income, autonomy, and status. In some ways, African immigrant religious communities reproduce gender divisions, promoting men's role as the household head and redirecting women toward the sphere of home-making and childcare. However, the religious community also serves as a site for the reinterpretation of gender ideologies and relations. Religious leaders have taken a lead role here, offering counseling services, marriage seminars, and study groups that aim to help ease the transition for men and women. Moreover, women themselves draw on the rich symbolic and social resources of their church communities in order to reconstitute relations of gender and the family.

One of the ways in which women negotiate gender relations is through the creation of a multitude of women's associations that offer mutual support in areas such as employment and marriage relations. Also of great importance, especially in the African Pentecostal churches, is the value assigned to the private sphere. In many of these communities, the private realm of home and family is placed at the center of both women's and men's lives. The private realm is made public through community events that make the private goals of family harmony and youth socialization the central aspect of the church's public agenda. An important focus of our research with Pentecostal communities has also been the interpretation of religious teachings about gender relations. We have found that women use religious teachings to reinterpret patriarchal authority, providing evidence for Shibley's thesis that evangelicalism serves as a "flexible ideological resource" for reconstituting relations of gender and the family ("Contemporary Evangelicals" 74).

The dual role of immigrant churches as both patriarchal and liberating is highly evident in the context of African immigration, and the construction of gender in these arenas is a particularly complex and dynamic process. Our research efforts are focusing on these processes in order to better understand the challenges faced by women immigrants and the ways in which they have been able to improve their status and opportunities through their participation in religious community life.

*   *   *

Although several studies have contributed significantly to our understanding of new immigrant religious communities in the United States, very little scholarship has explored African immigrant religions comprehensively, perhaps because these communities remain largely "invisible" to mainstream culture and society. Our study has begun to draw scholarly attention to the cultural and religious distinction of African religious immigrant communities. It also offers comparative materials which inform the emerging discourse on the interface of religion and immigration.

This ongoing work has provided an understanding of the scope, range, and variety of African religious practices in the United States. Particularly significant are the religious practices and cultural norms which enable African children and youth to define their identities as Africans living in the United States. These religious and cultural norms serve as a buffer between home and community on the one hand and, on the other, the apparently hostile and racialized world in which refugees and immigrants now find themselves. African religious communities continue to participate as American organizations, as citizens in the political economy of the nation. Their upward mobility is a sign of their success, just as their civic engagement indicates their desire to be integrated into the larger American society. As transnational citizens, members of African communities can be loyal U.S. citizens and yet maintain their relationship with their native countries. Religion plays a central role in ensuring the resiliency of this significant and evolving sector of American society.

REFERENCES

Crumbley, Deidre Helen, and Gloria Melake Cline-Smythe. "Gender and Change in the African Immigrant Church." In *African Immigrant Religious Communities in America*, ed. Jacob Olupona and Regina Gemignani. New York: New York University Press, 2007. 158–181.

Ebaugh, Helen Rose, and Janet Saltzman Chafetz, eds. *Religion and the New Immigrants: Continuities and Adaptations in Immigrant Congregations*. Walnut Creek, Calif.: AltaMira, 2000.

Nida, Worku. "African Religious Beliefs and Practices in Diaspora." In *African Immigrant Religious Communities in America*, ed. Jacob Olupona and Regina Gemignani. New York: New York University Press, 2007. 207–226.

Okome, Mojubaolu. "African Immigrant Churches and the New Christian Right." In *African Immigrant Religious Communities in America*, ed. Jacob Olupona and Regina Gemignani. New York: New York University Press, 2007. 279–305.

Olupona, Jacob, and Regina Gemignani, eds. *African Immigrant Religious Communities in America*. New York: New York University Press, 2007.

Rapport, Nigel. "Coming Home to a Dream: A Study of the Immigrant Discourse of 'Anglo-Saxons' in Israel." In *Migrants in Identity: Perceptions of Home in a World of Movement*, ed. Nigel Rapport and Andrew Dawson. New York: Berg, 1998. 61–83.

Shibley, Mark A. "Contemporary Evangelicals: Born-Again and World Affirming." *Annals of the American Academy of Political and Social Science* 558 (1998): 67–87.

Stokes, Martin, ed. *Ethnicity, Identity, and Music: The Musical Construction of Place*. Providence, R.I.: Berg, 1994.

Tettey, Wisdom J. "Transnationalism, Religion, and the African Diaspora in Canada: An Examination of Ghanaians and Ghanaian Churches." In *African Immigrant Religious Communities in America*, ed. Jacob Olupona and Regina Gemignani. New York: New York University Press, 2007. 229–258.

17

THE ORISHA RESCUE MISSION

Donald Cosentino

A LA RECHERCHE DES DIEUX PERDUS

Let me begin with an interchange I had with Isidore Okpewho about the relevance of my research to the symposium giving rise to this book. Re-acting to the description which states (inter alia), "the symposium will give us the opportunity to reflect on the migration of 3rd World black peoples to the developed societies of the United States and Europe," I wrote, "I can't fit my research into those parameters. Granted even the most generous post-modern indulgences, Charley Guelperin, the subject of my research, is still a white man appropriating Yoruba mythologies for the benefit of his Latino/Hollywood clientele . . ." To which Isidore replied, "If you substitute 'cultures' for 'peoples' you will find the state-ment is perfectly true. When last I looked, it was clear to me that some of the more avid adherents of transplanted African life ways, e.g., Pentecos-tal worshippers, are hardly African immigrants themselves, or even Black Americans; they are white people like your good self!" So indeed, with Isidore's salubrious reminder that African cultures, including art and re-ligion, are on a journey sometimes unaccompanied by African peoples, I heartily agreed to participate in the distinguished proceedings.

Charley Guelperin was born in Buenos Aires in 1947. He began his training there as a Spiritist medium in his teenage years, and through a series of providential encounters in Los Angeles was crowned a child of Obatala, the senior *orisha* or *ocha* (divinity)[1] within the Yoruba-Cuban religion of Santería.[2] Charley's service to these adopted gods defines his life. In a series of conversations I have had with him over the last de-cade, Charley has revealed a mission not merely to serve the orisha, but to rescue those of them in danger of being forgotten in the backwaters of Cuba. Implicit in Charley's rescue plans is the extraordinary and ex-panding role the orisha play in the *imaginaire* of worlds far removed from Ile-Ife.

While we were traveling together in Cuba, Charley introduced me to

Ignacio, an old Cuban *santero* (priest), and laid out the rescue plan they had jointly devised. As he explained it,

> *A quarter of the Yoruba pantheon is lost forever. Ignacio finds the remaining orisha and brings them here. He gives me their information because otherwise we will never remember them. Not just their names but their ceremonies, how to carve their* angolanes *(images) in special woods, their particular food sacrifices, their* patakis *(exemplary tales of the orisha). A lot of people say Ignacio's orisha are bullshit because other santeros aren't talking about them. They don't even know of their existence. Like Akweyi, the two guards who were stationed by the cross of Jesus, who are the ocha of Atonement.*

I interrupted this remarkable revelation to ask whether the Akweyi included St. Longinus, whom pious Christian legend identifies as the Roman soldier converted under the cross. Charley affirmed that indeed Longinus was an Akweyi, but most people would never invoke him since he is not the kind of orisha you can profit from. Only people who are truly religious would bother to keep such orisha.[3] As he affirmed in our conversation:

> *These are truly obscure orishas. I have twenty such orisha equally obscure. And they will die if nobody feeds them. Or go dormant. If they don't find followers, eventually some of them will die or disappear.*

Sounds to me like the orisha experience the same sort of samsara as Homo sapiens. That the orisha pantheon is evolving?

> *That's why I always say there are four hundred plus one orisha. No, four hundred* and *one. Because still a new orisha can be created. Nothing is static, not on this plane or any other plane. The other day we were talking about AIDS being a new disease, or least we didn't know about it before now. So that means there are new pains and sufferings coming. Certainly we have new diseases as a result of pollution, and of the atmospheric problems we've been having. So that means there are new things forming. Things are on the move with spirits and with people, constantly.*

So the orisha are growing, dying, and being born again! Perhaps that four hundred and first orisha will replace another who is not being fed? An orisha who has grown dormant?

> *There is probably a hundred of those dormant orisha in a different plane. They finished their conscience on this plane. They are not safely needed any longer.*

Are these orishas you're rescuing in Cuba also dormant? Or nearly dormant, like a language that has only three remaining speakers?

> *They nearly dormant, exactly. Why? Because these are orishas*

who come from small groups of people in Africa. They were most likely village orishas. They wasn't national orisha like Chango or Yemaya. Maybe there was a village who made aspirins, so they needed an orisha who could help in the manufacture of aspirin. But that orisha wasn't important to another village who manufacture furniture or tables. These local orisha who belong to a particular village probably belong to the court of Chango or Osun: but they were familiar orishas. And where this familiar orisha most likely to come from? Most probably this miniature kind of orisha was at one point a relative of one of the kings or obasis of that village. And after his death, he became an orisha. When those same villagers came to Cuba, they brought not only Chango and Ogun, but also the orishas of furniture and aspirins with them. These are the disappearing ones I rescue.

But there might be hundreds or thousands of such miniature orishas. No matter how much you do, it's still a drop in the ocean.

Absolutely! But it's better a drop in the ocean, than no water at all.

When we say there are four hundred orisha, we really mean there might be four billion?

Indeed. Maybe when we say four hundred orisha, we mean four hundred true stars of the orisha. And under these stars there's this spiritual pyramid built with billions of orisha. We talking all the time about Isis and Osiris, but who knows that in little towns on the Nile, there wasn't other orishas? But peoples only remember Isis and Osiris.[4]

How do you keep count of these rescued orisha? Do you memorize them or write down their names in lists?

I write them down. I keep files. I number the rescued Orishas because I have so many. I now have close to a hundred. It's hard to remember all those names!

Do you feed the rescued orishas? Do you run a divine soup kitchen?

Yeah. But there are orishas who won't tell you what they want to eat. Eleggua is their messenger and eventually he will say, "Yemolu wants this, or Jimagua wants this."[5]

What happens when you die? Will you try to pass your orisha on before you die? Can you give them to your children?

No. The orisha decide for themselves. When we do the readings, if it comes in fives, they pass to your blood relatives. If it comes in the sixes, they pass to religious relatives. If the shells come in any other number, they exit.[6] *So some stay, some go. They decide!*

A second conversation about the Orisha Rescue Mission took place several months later at Casa Obatala, the house Charley maintains in Las Vegas as a kind of country retreat for his rescued orisha. It may be significant to note that Casa Obatala is just up the road from University of Nevada, Las Vegas, where Wole Soyinka runs a parallel institute for refugee artists.

Sitting by his pool, I asked Charley: Where do you get the energy and dedication to do this?

Charley replied: Santería is not just my religion . . . it also became like a work of an anthropologist for me. I'm trying to recover the knowledge of a society and a culture and a background and ancestry. I'm trying to reconcile the true African with the Afro-Cuban and Afro-American. The orishas are pretty much the weaving that keeps them together and keeps them who they are.

I'm recovering these orishas from vanishing. But I also rescue the memory and the ancestry of people who are followers of those particular orishas. People who in Africa were followers of that particular orisha who now become their mojo. *It's my way to pay homage to all of those ancestors before me, who were able to bring this to Cuba. Through terrible ways.*

One of the stories is the blacks used to be swallow the shells— the stones—of the orishas, before they boarded the ships. And then they would defecate them. And eat it again, till they reach Cuba. To build a shrine for them again. I mean people who is willing to go through so much, even so we have people doing it today for diamonds and cocaine. You know, they swallow condoms full of cocaine or heroin, just to smuggle it. Those people did it for a spiritual belief. Anybody who put their life at risk, the way these people were doing it—it's to be respected and to be honored.

Why can't you do what Pope Paul VI did: he went through the list of the saints and struck out those who no longer seemed to be relevant, or historical. Aren't there some orisha who have outlived their services? If they're being forgotten, there must be a reason.

My mother outlived her services too! She's eighty-five years old and outlived her services. Should I crate her and put her in the basement with the other things at UCLA? Keep her at the proper temperature? I mean, who's to say orishas outlive their services? Maybe they don't have practicality anymore. But they will never outlive their services. They are angels of God. How is it possible they can outlive their services? Orisha are eternal. That's why Olofi chose a stone to be the embodiment of the orisha. The stone is something that for millions of years remains the same. Not that stone doesn't have a life, because stones do have life. But stones can remain dormant. Like zombies. Cathartic, but not dead. But if we feed them the right salt they can come back to life.[7] Maybe they will be blubb'ing idiots, because they been poisoned by all these concoctions, but they're alive. And god forbid, somebody feeds them salt; they will go after the person who made them a zombie. They come out of their sleep and go after the person who mistreats them and disrespects them. The fact that they are sitting here in the yard, on the side, doesn't mean that they are no loved

*or respected or no cared for it. As a matter of fact, I must get two
new coconuts for orisha Oko. They cracked. Throw away those and
make new coconuts for the orisha.*

When you say you are going to reclaim orisha what EXACTLY
does that mean? How does that work?

*It works by going to old-timers who have these particular
orishas, and know their ceremonies, their beginnings, how they
been passed from family to family. We need to know ancestry;
who were the people originally involved in Africa and how did
they reach Cuba? Who were the families that kept them and what
rituals they perform? What animals does this orisha like to eat?
Why do they like those animals? What elements, or accoutrements,
reinforce that orisha and in which* odu *were they born? And then
they will even give you the songs of that particular orisha. And
prayers for that particular kind of orisha we call* Adimu.

*Adimu orisha don't go to the heads. The original orisha go to
the head when you crowned. These go to the hands. It is through
the hands that you receive these Adimu orishas. What happened
is we lost a lot of the ceremonies how to put Adimu orisha in the
head. If you don't put it correctly into the head, you can ruin the
life of that individual. We don't know any farther how to perform
that ceremony, how to do it directly. We don't do it out of fear, or
out of no enough knowledge. For example, Olokun: nobody crowns
in the United States. Or even in Cuba any longer. But we do it in
Brazil. So they kept some secrets.*

*The consequences of mistakes in this religion are terrifying. It's
dangerous when you play, because these are astral forces we don't
completely understand. Or control. A lot of santeros believe that
when they crown they become saints. No, we only santeros. Orisha
are saints. We are not. We only practitioners of the orisha cult. We
are NOT orishas. But a lot of people, for gain or for vanity, they
start acting like they are walking orishas. And that can be disas-
trous in the results. I play with people. I fuck with peoples' head.
I* WILL NEVER FUCK WITH AN ORISHA. *Because they fuck back. And
it hurts. So I will never try. Never. I don't even want to take the
chances to see if it works or if it doesn't. That's why I have to be
anal retentive and ritualistic about it.*

*They have their own rituals. They have their peculiar ways.
They have their peculiar animals that they like. They have their
own way that they like to be fed. Or be done when they are created. Don't go away from that. That's who they are, and that's what
they want. Each orisha has a menu. Respect their menu. At the beginning, all orishas ate everything. Every animal. Male, female,
any animal. Then they choose their favorite animals. Not because
of what it tasted like, because blood is blood. But because of their
relationship with those kinds of animals. And the orisha had a
relationship with the animals. As much as they had a relationship
with the plants. Because a lot of the orishas were in the animal*

*world or the plant world before they became orishas. Like Orula.
Orula was mineral, animal, and vegetable, and also was orisha. So
one of the wives of Orula was the leaf of the* malanga. *That's why
the babalawo, when they do an ebo, wrap it in a malanga leaf.*[8] *As a
respect for the first wife of Orula. The rooster was his godson. And
one of the first babalawos. That's why the rooster has a crown over
the head. Because it was a babalawo. And the wife of the rooster,
meaning the hen, disrespected Orula. And that's why Orula eats
hens. Out of the disrespect that the female have, and the contempt
that the female felt for Orula.*[9]

Why do your stories about the orisha sound so much more
elaborate than those I heard in Nigeria?[10] Have orisha myths grown
more elaborate in Cuba because whites have appropriated and elaborated them?

*Africans were the owners of these traditions, and because it
was an oral society, they didn't felt that things had to be written
down. They did a lot of ceremonies to the heads to have that type
of memory. For example,* rogation *of the heads with dried fish for
empowerment of the head. Then the anthropologists got involved.
People like Bascom.*[11] *I believe they rescue a lot of these traditions
in many ways. So I believe whites did a tremendous amount of
damage to the blacks physically, and mentally, but they also rescue
religiously a lot of the elements of the blacks. And kept it alive.
Rescued, elaborated, and enlarged.*

Let's go back to your orisha salvage job. Tell me how many
orisha you think in Cuba still have some existence?

Two hundred eleven.

How many have you reclaimed?

One hundred eight.

What's your intentions?

Keep going.

How far?

To two hundred eleven.

How can you be sure it's two hundred eleven? Is that your best
estimate?

*That's my best estimate. So, I will keep going as far as I can af-
ford to keep going with this quest. It's just like any other quest.
It takes time, dedication, commitment, money. I have the time.
I have the dedication. I have the commitment. I don't have the
money. So as I get the money, I keep going on. And getting more
and more. Not because I became a collector of orishas, an anthropologist who want to keep 'em. But because I became a true santero
who wants to save everything that has to do with the African tradition. And I want it for my own empowerment. I want it for my own
peace of mind and for the future generations of the religion.*

But your discoveries get shared with the community, right?

*You know one thing? I discovered that the community is not in-
terested. Some of them prefer to block their minds as if they don't*

exist. They [think the rescued orisha] are the creation of some-
body who wants to make money. It's ignorance. Lack of commit-
ment. Too much responsibility. Another one you have to take care
at home: check if the water is there, the coconut is there, the doll
is correct, or the implements that the orisha needs to work are
there . . . I give you one very specific example: I receive Odua. All
the implements of Odua supposed to be done in sterling silver. Be-
cause silver is what Odua exchange gold for—silver. Because he
felt gold was a destruction of his plane. So he cast gold away from
him. Ochun took it, and says "I'm keeping it." And he change it
for silver. So silver became his metal, and the implements of Odua
should be that silver. When I receive Odua, the coffer, where he
lives on—I done it on pure silver. And all the implements inside,
I actually took the job to find out what they look like. And make
drawings of those. Then I call my godson who is a jeweler, and
made cast molds of those drawings, and then with those molds I
cast in silver all the implements of Odua.

It cost me close to three thousand dollars to go through that
process. I didn't do because I could afford it—because I wasn't
able to afford it. I took money off a credit card to do it. Two credit
cards, one for twelve thousand dollars, one for eleven thousand dol-
lars that belongs to the orishas. And both credit cards are up to
the limit. Twenty one thousand dollars I owe. I always at the limit
because I always keep borrowing from them: paying-borrowing,
paying-borrowing—to do more orishas. Is not a matter if I can af-
ford it or not. No, I cannot afford it. Somebody has to be ritualistic.
And do it according to the way they supposed to be do.

These orisha that you've been busy salvaging—the vast majority
of them—you're not busy working with them? I mean you're honoring them, or preserving them, but you don't use them?

I don't necessarily use them, but just the fact that I have them
empowers me. They still have the radiation, the spiritual radiation.
It affects me, independently, if I work with them or not. A lot of
these orishas have been lost because the people cannot go through
the expenses of the work, or find the artisans that are capable to
do this. So when I go to Cuba I have to find myself an artisan who
sculpts in wood. I have to find the woods they have to be used
for these particular orishas sometimes. Or cast in silver through
my jeweler here, because in Cuba they can't do it anymore. Or in
Cuba, you know, they don't have the necklaces of the orishas no
more because they don't have the beads. So I do it in here; so some-
times I bring stuff from Cuba to do it here.

LES DIEUX RETROUVÉS

I do not present these comments by Charley Guelperin about his Orisha
Rescue Mission because they are representative of orisha worship in the

United States or elsewhere in the New World. They are not. Charley is a white magus who finds in Yoruba cosmology the perfect completion of his own complex spiritual history. The orisha he rescues emigrated from West Africa to Cuba in the heads and bowels of captive Africans, where in various fashions and to varying degrees they have been remembered and served by descendents of African slaves. His appropriation of "lost" orisha is only a singular (if extraordinary) example of a more general secondary migration of African divinities into the white and mulatto populations of Cuba. This process has accelerated over the last century, advancing to such a degree that "crowning the orisha" is now an attractive alternative to joining the Communist Party for many white Cubans.[12] But this induction of African divinities into a creolized Afro-Cuban culture has come at the cost of historical memory. The orisha have now become *ocha:* naturalized Cuban citizens whose historical origins are relegated to a fantasized Africa as remote from any present reality as the ancient Egyptian magi are from their dramatic representations in the contemporary rituals of Freemasonry or Rosicrucianism.[13] When I was myself inducted into the neo-Yoruba ancestral cult of Oro in Havana, the presiding babalawo showed me a statue of Chango, explaining that the Orisha of Thunder and Lightning had been abused in his homeland, and was now a permanent Cuban resident.[14]

The immigration status of the orisha varies across American cultures. Prevailing "roots" scholarship (Herskovits, Bastide, et al.) asserts a unilinear movement from West and Central Africa to the New World, where immigrant divinities were re-dressed in Catholic images and Masonic robes. But there are dissenters from this model, notably J. Lorand Matory, whose research on Brazilian Candomblé discerns not *roots* but *rhizomes* running in all directions between the Americas, the Caribbean, and Africa.[15] Matory returns agency not to surreptitious peasants, but to a complex "ethno-class" of Afro-Brazilians acting out of enlightened self-interest:

> I have identified international merchants as the foremost agents of the trans-Atlantic nations of the African diaspora. The case of the diasporic Yoruba nation suggests the further importance of musicians, literati, translators, and priests, including alienated Christian missionaries and leading Freemasons of the oppressed group . . . [diasporas] do not simply exist but, on the contrary, must first be profitably "imagined" by interested classes in order for *populations*, periodically, to become *communities.* These diverse units of collective self-construction—not to mention what is nowadays called the "global community"—are interpretive frames that require *nothing but* imagination to make them real. (102–103)

Matory describes this process of religious self-fashioning as *"Anagonization,"* from the term *Nago,* widely used to describe Yoruba people in

Brazil and elsewhere in the Americas. For Matory, it is a case of *Anago-nizing* diverse Afro-Brazilian populations. For Charley Guelperin, it is a mission to bring the orisha to a globalized community of Central American immigrants, NBA stars, Hollywood hangers-on, Israeli businessmen, gypsies, and curious college students who frequent Botanica El Congo Manuel in East Hollywood. In either direction, as Charley tells it, the orisha have won:

> *You know, Orula told the Africans a hundred years before the di-aspora begun, that they will go to different lands and conquer. And a hundred years later came the slavery trade, and they came to America as slaves. And a lot of them rebelled and said, "Orula lied to us. He told us that we would conquer lands, and we are in chains. Screw Orula! And screw the Orishas! Let's become Catholics or Christians or whatever." But they didn't understood that it weren't them physically that would conquer, but it was the religion that would conquer. The Knowledge. The Tradition. And now, five hundred years later, and still the Tradition is pretty much alive and flourishing around the globe. Out of that group. So Orula didn't lie. They conquered. They really conquered.*

NOTES

1. Divinities within Santería are identified alternately as *orisha* (from the Yoruba), or as *ocha* (from the Creolized Cuban liturgical Yoruba called *Lucumi*), or simply as *santo,* in recognition of the correspondence between the creolized Yoruba divinities and Catholic saints.

2. See Cosentino, "Travels with Charley and Manuel," for a more detailed account of Guelperin's religious background, including "Spiritism" (*Espiritismo*), memorably described by V. S. Naipaul:

> The Argentine middle-class . . . is swept by the new enthusiastic cult of espiritismo, a purely native affair of mediums and mass trances and miraculous cures, which claims the patronage of Jesus Christ and Mahatma Gandhi. The espiritista mediums heal by passing on intangible beneficent "fluids." They believe in reincarnation and the perfectability of the spirit. They say that purgatory and hell exist now, on earth, and that man's only hope is to be born on a more evolved planet. Their goal is that life, in a "definitive" disembodied world, where only superior spirits congregate. (*The Return of Eva Peron* 111)

3. In the course of my own field research, I have noted that this same pseudo-saint Longinus is understood to be a *zonbi* master by some Haitian Vodouists, since he was witness to the first (Christ's) resurrection of the Dead; while the post-Pascal peregrinations of Longinus are now celebrated in Màntova, Italy, where legend says he deposited balls of mud, soaked with the blood of Christ, which are still preserved in twin reliquaries kept under the high altar of the city's Cathedral. The

Christian gospels and pseudo-gospels thus continue to inspire many and diverse ecumenical elaborations, e.g., Dan Brown's *Da Vinci Code*, or Mel Gibson's *Passion of the Christ*.

4. Charley's reference to Osiris and Isis adumbrates the work of many Yoruba and neo-Yoruba historians who for more than a century have attempted to parallel the orisha with the divinities of Pharaonic Egypt. See especially the foundational text by Samuel Johnson, *The History of the Yorubas*.

5. Eleggua (a.k.a. Eshu, Legba, Eshu Elegbara, Exu) is the trickster divinity of Yoruba and neo-Yoruba religions throughout the Black Atlantic. See Donald Cosentino, "Who Is That Fellow in the Many-Colored Cap?"

6. Charley is describing *itutu*, the divination performed at the death of a santero.

7. Charley is referencing the Haitian belief that *zonbi* (zombies) can be reanimated by feeding them salt. Knowledge of *zonbi* folkways (except in celluloid forms) is not general in Cuba or the United States.

8. Babalawos (Yoruba, "father of secrets") are a fraternity of diviners within the Santería tradition, as they are among the Yoruba of Nigeria and Benin. Charley is a santero, but not a babalawo.

9. Orula is the Cuban name for the orisha Orunmila in Yoruba tradition. He is the master of Ifa divination, and thus the divine prototype for all babalawo.

10. I was a Peace Corps volunteer in Annang Province, Eastern Nigeria, from 1964 to 1966; and a Lecturer at Ahmadu Bello University in Zaria, Northern Nigeria, from 1976 to 1978.

11. William Bascom (1921–1981), the American anthropologist who first transcribed and translated the divination verses (*odu*) of the Ifa tradition: see *Ifa Divination: Communication between Gods and Men in West Africa*

12. Not even Fidel Castro is exempt from the process of orisha assimilation: The January 1 anniversary of the 1959 Communist Revolution is also celebrated as the feast day for Odua, just as the red and black colors of the Revolutionary Army are used to celebrate Eleggua. Even Castro's fabled womanizing is popularly attributed to Chango, stud of the Yoruba pantheon, as his attendance at seaside events links him with Yemaya, divine mother of the oceans. Christine Ayorinde explains: "The readiness to claim Castro as an initiate of Santeria is both an indication of his enormous charisma and a reflection of the long-standing popular belief that all Cuban leaders practice either Afro-Cuban religions or Spiritism" (134).

13. For a darker description of such white co-option, note the comments of Afro-Cuban intellectual Waterio Carbonnell: "Another symptom of the debility of (Cuban white) bourgeois culture was the way in which it allowed itself to be contaminated [*sic*] by the religious beliefs of the Blacks. The savage gods, the gods which ate children, civilized themselves and took possession of the spirits of the wealthy. Not in order to take them in completely, nor to cohabit with them but to try to resolve their amorous problems, their wish to occupy high government positions, or to get them out of difficulty in their businesses" (quoted in Ayorinde 61).

14. I use such terms as "white," "black" or "mulatto" descriptively, without necessarily referencing U.S. or Cuban class/color stratifications. They order things differently in the Caribbean. For instance, the babalawo who showed me the statue of Chango had blue eyes and fair skin, but traced his ancestry to black Africans in the Canary Islands. As Puerto Rican santero and scholar Ysamur Flores says of

pan-Caribbean DNA, "Que no tiene Dinka, tiene Mandinka" (Those who don't descend from the Dinka, descend from the Mandinka). Personal communication.

15. See *Black Atlantic Religion: Tradition, Transnationalism, and Matriarchy in the Afro-Brazilian Candomblé* (Princeton, N.J.: Princeton University Press, 2005).

REFERENCES

Ayorinde, Christine. *Afro-Cuban Religiosity, Revolution, and National Identity.* Gainesville: University Press of Florida, 2005.

Bascom, William. *Ifa Divination: Communication between Gods and Men in West Africa.* Bloomington: Indiana University Press, 1969.

Cosentino, Donald. "Travels with Charley and Manuel." In *Botanica Los Angeles: Latino Popular Religious Art in the City of Angels,* ed. Patrick Polk. Los Angeles: UCLA Fowler Museum of Cultural History, 2004. 74–87.

———. "Who Is That Fellow in the Many-Colored Cap? Transformations of Eshu in the Mythology of Haitian Vodoun." *Journal of American Folklore* 100, no. 3 (July–September 1987): 261–275.

Johnson, Rev. Samuel. *The History of the Yorubas.* 1897. Reprint, Lagos: C.S.S. Bookshops, 1921.

Matory, J. Lorand. *Black Atlantic Religion: Tradition, Transnationalism, and Matriarchy in the Afro-Brazilian Candomblé.* Princeton, N.J.: Princeton University Press, 2005.

Naipaul, V. S. *The Return of Eva Peron, with the Killings in Trinidad.* New York: Knopf, 1980.

18 REDEFINING "AFRICA" IN THE DIASPORA WITH NEW MEDIA TECHNOLOGIES: THE MAKING OF AFRICARESOURCE.COM

Azuka Nzegwu

Although African immigrant experiences have been widely documented in numerous formats—writing, video, and audio narratives—little has been done with new media technology. Two basic questions of interest are: How is this technology being used to tell the stories of immigrants? And, is the use of these technologies changing how Africa is perceived and understood?

This essay examines how new African immigrants in the United States are using web-based open-source technology to challenge the dominant narratives and dominant structures of knowledge production *on* Africa and *about* Africans. In particular, the essay looks at the construction of online portals that seek to highlight the experiences, scholarly viewpoints, and critical analyses of African scholars and immigrants. It documents the ways new African immigrants have used web-based technologies to create their own communities that challenge constructed knowledges about their personhood. It analyzes one new medium and its processes of knowledge expansion as well as its correction of erroneous data and generalizations. This essay will highlight how the internet is revolutionizing knowledge through the creation of new online voices and repositories of knowledge that challenge old orthodoxies, and provide open and easy access[1] to anyone engaged in such efforts.

THE EUROCENTRIC BACKGROUND OF THE U.S. ACADEMY

The standard Euro-American format of producing knowledge about "Others," especially those from developing countries, is an intricate web of fictitious and true assertions that are bound by colonial and imperial objec-

358

tives. Ironically, the site for this kind of knowledge production is academic institutions. Carole Boyce Davies, a new African Diaspora immigrant from Trinidad now living in the United States, asserts in "Decolonizing the Academy" that "the academy is the most colonized space" (ix). Despite its declared principles of intellectual objectivity and the creation of area studies programs such as Africana, Latin American, Caribbean, and Asian Studies on most college campuses, some of these problems have not been mitigated. Davies's statements imply that Euro-American intellectual production, which centers on colonial issues, serves to maintain European and American hegemony not only within the academic institution but also in the larger world. She states that academic institutions "privilege knowledge emanating from European thinkers, to legitimate European belief systems, histories, ideologies, principles, and literatures"[2] (ix). In essence, this model of knowledge that privileges white male scholars and enables them to propagate their ideas is Eurocentrism. The model also benefits the academic careers of Third World scholars who subscribe to its rules.

Eurocentrism is anchored by Anglo-Saxon beliefs and works by devaluing and rejecting the histories, cultures, and languages of those outside the axis of power. To achieve its mission, it recognizes scholars whose scholarship promotes its notion of knowledge by publishing their ideas and upholding them as "experts." According to Trask, in "The Politics of Academic Freedom," white men "assume the mantle of authority, deciding what is taught, who can teach, even what can be said, written, and published" (222). Essentially, this discursive practice excludes the participation of Hawaiians and all those (including African immigrants) whose histories are being constructed. Over time, this practice of exclusivity has been represented as the model of knowledge for all to accept, whether or not it applies. This creates all sorts of problems, particularly the problem of knowledge constriction that triggers resistance when new immigrants and colonized people begin challenging and interrogating their colonial education, their use of former colonial languages, and their relationship with the dominant white class (Trask, "Women's *Mana*" 115).

Africans and Third World scholars in the United States have challenged the historical and cultural inaccuracies of the hegemonic knowledge system propagated in the academy, especially its attempt to situate them as subordinate beings.[3] Usually, when these scholars resist, it is done through publications and presentations at conferences. Because of their choice and venue of resistance, they are sometimes forced to utilize the very tools, ideas, canonical figures, and knowledge assumptions of this Eurocentric system. But insofar as they limit themselves to the traditional modes of knowledge production, they are unable to go beyond the parameters of the Eurocentric system and its problems of knowledge dominance. Thus, there is a need to explore alternative methodologies and forms of knowledge production to effectively challenge and restructure our knowledge scheme and the sort of data it privileges.

INTERNET AND THE PUBLIC SPHERE

A decade ago, the internet was seen as the new frontier, with few participants in that domain, but today it has become the most powerful and dominant public sphere of information and knowledge dissemination. Pierre Lévy, a French philosopher and media theorist, eloquently describes "cyberspace" as "A site that harbors unimagined language galaxies, enables unknown social temporalities to blossom, reinvents the social bond, perfects democracy, and forges unknown paths of knowledge among men" (Lévy 337). For him, "cyberspace"

> refers less to the new media of information transmission than to original modes of creation and navigation within knowledge, and the social relations they bring about. These would include, in no particular order: hypertext, the World Wide Web, interactive multimedia, video games, simulations, virtual reality, telepresence, augmented reality (whereby our physical environment is enhanced with networks of sensors and intelligent modules), groupware (collaborative activities), neuromimetic programs, artificial life, expert systems, etc. All of these tools are combined in exploiting the molecular character of digitized information. (Lévy 337)

Levy's definition cogently shows that cyberspace represents many untapped possibilities in which languages and modes of communication can take all forms, instead of monolithic rigidity. Elsewhere, I have discussed the extent to which technological innovations and progress have impacted our lives and changed our interaction with others, to the extent that our communications have become driven more by electronics than by traditional social etiquettes and norms. I have argued that the introduction of new and affordable devices, such as digital cameras, camcorders, and improved video production software, has not only changed how stories are being told, but is changing *who* is telling these stories (A. Nzegwu 226). The ubiquitous spread of the internet and the ubiquitous connection to the Web have created a new environment that is challenging the notion of inclusivity and of who can speak. Anyone who has access to the internet can have their say on this global soapbox. In fact, the billions of interactions on the internet are partially fueled by our human need to belong, which nurtures dialogues and relations spurred by these incessant engagements. I term these engagements "bytepera," a never-ending modern-day soap opera whose language of communication includes text, video, pictures, sounds, etc. Thus, not only has the internet affected our lives, but many of our daily operations, such as banking and commerce, have seen a seamless integration, so that even a simple task such as paying bills is now electronic, and with Paypal, Google Checkout, MoneyBooker, Storm-Pay, and other merchant gateway protocols,[4] our transactions can take place over vast expanses of geographical space. Now, whether this integration is unavoidable in that one has no choice but to adapt to the changing times, or whether one positively welcomes it, has become a moot point. The fact of the matter is that the sustainability of most of our routines is now largely dependent on the services and goods produced by the internet, new media technologies, and software.

Interestingly, advances in the internet are creating a new type of global kinship that is independent of traditional processes of relation and linkage formation. The Web has become a dominant force that enables different levels of engagement among unlikely participants, resulting in the rampant development of central-specific knowledge by unlikely producers and distributors. As Lévy notes, "The emerging technocultural environment, however, will encourage the development of new kinds of art, ignoring the separation between transmission and reception, composition and interpretation" (340). Whether one is using different types of Web services, such as video and photo sharing, communities, groups, portals, or banks, there is a plethora of choice that caters to varied needs. These global groups are positing special kinds of kinships and identities that are allowing contemporary global migrants to be both in Diaspora and at home. This global form of instantaneous communication is creating a new kind of identity. In the words of a member of an online Eritrean message board,

> But identity is not a constant and is something that is renegotiated on regular basis, be it at the individual or at the national level. This is especially problematic for those of us living in the Diaspora, we deal with so many identities and our existence is literally schizophrenic. We want to remain actively interested in the affairs of the homeland, at the same time we live in countries that could careless about our internal struggles and hence our miserable dependence on mediums like Dehai for a sense of belonging and for the illusion of home that it creates. I would even venture and say that the various cyber shoutings and negative exchanges that we are accustomed to in dehai are a necessary and unavoidable aspect of being a part of such a community. (Ghebru)

Elsewhere in the spectrum, a professor who started an online African-focused resource website addresses the personal and social possibilities and benefits of the internet as a medium for information delivery. She states that

> Those who see emigration as brain drain tend not to see the benefits of African emigration. They underplay the fact that it has enabled a large pool of Africans to be employed and to support a significant number of rela-

tives at home. Moreover, it has placed Africans in strategic positions around the world from which they could effectively represent and influence policies for Africa. But we cannot deny that there are no high personal costs to emigration. The permanent separation from families at home and the raising of culturally alienated children who are disavowing their African heritage to avoid the embarrassing stereotypes and negative images of Africa in the North represent significant externalities. It is at this juncture that africaresource.com comes in as a content provider of the sort of educational materials that represent Africa positively. The goal is to offer materials that critically challenge the negative stereotypes of Africa seen on the internet. (N. Nzegwu, "Africaresource.com" 82)

It is critical to further explore the relationship between these two ideas of new global identities and the social possibilities of the internet, since they speak to the general nature of online sites of knowledge production. Dehai.org is a bare-bones message board where users can post messages. It is a tool for community building, information sharing, knowledge generation, and outreach for Eritreans in Diaspora. Dehai.org binds all Eritreans together, regardless of their geographic locations, political affiliations, and social values. Established in 1993, the virtual meeting place encouraged users' needs for cultural, social, and political connection in order to exchange ideas about their histories and contemporary identities, and discuss their culture, language, values, and shared collective memory and experiences under Ethiopian rule (Bernal 172–173). In her exploration of the knowledge-producing value of new technologies, Victoria Bernal notes that the role of the internet in mobilizing Diasporic Eritreans has enabled them to create new public spheres for participating in national politics in their homeland (162). Ironically, these Diasporic Eritreans would have faced great difficulties if they had been in Eritrea trying to effect political changes in their national government. But the global reach and power of the internet has not only made it possible for them to come together, it has also enabled them to become a political force in ways that bypass official censorship (Bernal 166). Bernal argues that the impact of the internet is that it presents new ways for communicating histories, ideas, and expectations while enabling the creation of online communities (163). Far more important is the rapid and audacious way in which this online message board has facilitated action-oriented research, and brought about radical change from a geographic distance. Dehai.org illustrates users' voluntary action to become researchers of their sociopolitical institutions and participants in nationalist discourses of their country. It is important to stress that the considerable political pressures Dehai.org brought to bear on the Eritrean government forced it to offer national identity cards, institute proper tax systems, and solicit financial and political support from Diasporic Eritreans (Bernal 164). In fact, the success of Dehai.org has spurred the development of other Eritrean groups.

The point here is that the internet provides a powerful form of knowledge generation and knowledge construction that falls outside of the currently legitimized parameters for talking about and producing knowledge in the academy. This message-boarding method of knowledge generation has both intended and unintended effects that have encouraged disparate voices to flourish, introduced new ideas, and created new authorities. Bernal points out that because the internet is "decentralized, participatory, unregulated, and egalitarian in operation" (165), it fosters multiple and diverse voices which subsequently produce knowledge (Bernal 176). This model radically differs from the traditional model operative in the United States academy, where information is hierarchically structured, communicated in a unilinear direction and anonymously, and does not allow immediate and direct response and participation from users.

By virtue of its anonymity, the internet dismantles this hierarchy that is often used oppressively to deny legitimacy and voice to anyone who does not propagate Eurocentered norms and uphold Europe's canonical figures. The World Wide Web accomplishes this in the following way. It conceals the identity of both speakers and users and it gives voice to those who are not normally seen as authorities. It forces us to question what we are taught, and it de-emphasizes the socioeconomic inequalities of participants. It is important to note that the most prolific writers on Dehai.org are taxi drivers and parking lot attendants who have substantive information to impart, regardless of their jobs (Bernal 165). Although it is not apparent, these new producers of knowledge often are well-educated Eritreans who are unable to get jobs commensurate with their level of education in the societies of Europe, the United States, and Canada, where they presently live. Access to the internet, however, gives them a singular opportunity to contest and present their society's history as they know and experience it. Dehai.org does not just serve as an online community; it is also a "cultural outlet for intellectual and creative talents" and functions as a site for cultural production and political expression (Bernal 170–171). For the purposes of this discussion, what is most important is that Dehai.org constructs a shared national and virtual historical library and calls for greater cultural attachment to immigrants' homelands (Bernal 175).

A comparable website is AfricaResource.com, an educational portal[5] that produces and distributes research materials and products on Africa and African Diaspora. AfricaResource.com was founded in 1999 by Nkiru Nzegwu, a philosopher, artist, and university professor, with *no* funding from *any* institutions. I stress this fact because the initiative began during the dot-com era, when dubious startups were bankrolled by venture capitalists more interested in returns than in high-quality research content on Africa. The only way that AfricaResource.com could operate without compromising its ideals, as well as its scholarly integrity in producing and publishing research materials on Africa and African Diaspora, would be to self-finance. Nkiru Nzegwu's witty observation in "Africaresource.com: Bridging the Digital Divide," on the link between marginalized communities (content producers) and financial bankers (venture capitalists) in respect of prospective projects like AfricaResource.com, is very telling:

> In a certain sense, africaresource.com is an experiment on how to avoid such control even as we strive to bridge the digital divide. Autonomy and organizational control are necessary in these matters if the founding vision and goals are to be realized. Goals can be achieved when the vision is clearly defined; forces will then realign to ensure its realization. These may be compromised if in the formative years providers of funding can dictate their wishes. Africaresource.com began three years ago in 1999 with no funding from any institution. During the boom years of the dot-com industry, both program officers of nonprofit agencies and fund managers of investment firms used a set of physiological traits to gauge the potential success of an Internet scheme. The traits are: male body, white skin, youth, and recent degree from a prestigious school. It seemed not to matter that many of the proposed schemes were ill conceived. In the euphoria of the time, fund managers never asked the hard questions they reserved for women, making it seem as if they had already formed an opinion of who can generate and control wealth. The bottom line is that in their reference scheme, an over-the-hill immigrant African woman of the wrong color with an unpronounceable name, doctoral degree in the humanities, and teaching in some lackluster public university does not fit the bill. Everyone *knows* that such people are not Internet savvy, imaginative and resourceful. (N. Nzegwu, "Africaresource.com" 81)

I have quoted this at length to show the types of problems and concerns that many marginalized communities are having starting new ventures that strongly localize and place their cultures and histories at the center. Nzegwu's comment on the physiological traits also reveals the unwritten and unspoken criteria reserved for minorities and women, a codified institutional process in investment firms, corporations, and foundations. So, it is not surprising that the only way Nkiru Nzegwu could retain complete control of AfricaResource.com, and to ensure the highest standard of publishing, was to develop it on her own terms. AfricaResource.com became an independent, online institution that places Africa and the African Diaspora histories, cultures, and experiences at the center of knowledge production processes.

AfricaResource.com is not only a project of knowledge transformation; it is also a project of technical knowledge acquisition that demonstrates how to use new technologies as a tool for engagement with and rapid deconstruction of colonial knowledge on Africa. At its inception, AfricaResource.com was developed to serve as an authoritative academic content provider on Africa,[6] in contrast to the conventional African websites of "safari travelogues, tribal/primitive art and craft retail outfits, news portals, two web directories, and U.S. government information sites" (N. Nzegwu, "Africaresource.com" 82). AfricaResource.com achieves it goals by developing, publishing, and distributing academic content on Africa and African disapora. It is fulfilling the role of content provider and distributor by challenging dominant knowledge production on Africa while reconstructing its *true* histories, cultures, and identities.

According to Nkiru Nzegwu, the goal of AfricaResource.com is "to promote strong, independent, challenging theorizing and to become an arena in which scholarly discussions and academic research on Africa by Africans, peoples of African descent, and non-Africans can easily be conducted or obtained" ("Africaresource.com" 83). In producing AfricaResource .com, the underlying objective is to provide materials for secondary and higher education teachers, including college professors, to increase their awareness of Africa. As Nzegwu notes, "it is important to control one's self-definition in the borderless world of the Internet, africaresource.com undertook to become a mini memory bank of evidence-based, Africa-centered knowledge" ("Africaresource.com" 82). In expanding the available knowledge with authoritative materials from leading African scholars in the Diaspora and in Africa, the hope is to revolutionize knowledge by producing evidence-based knowledge on Africa so that users will be adequately prepared for the challenges of the future (N. Nzegwu, "Africaresource .com" 82). Specifically, AfricaResource.com is concerned with broadening the parameters of knowledge, expanding the pool of authoritative experts, deflating the ideas and powers of canonical Euro-American experts, and forcing them to engage the evidence-based knowledge of African scholars. In effect, the goal of AfricaResource.com is to combat Eurocentrism and to change educational institutions' priorities and views on Africa.

Unlike Dehai.org, AfricaResource.com utilizes the hierarchical model that recognizes scholar-citizens of African societies as purveyors of knowledge. It favors academically produced research and knowledge rather than the action-oriented research preferred by activists. In the last ten years, many new sites and portals on Africa have emerged from older and younger populations. Examples of these communities and portals are Nigeria (Nigeria.com), an eminent Nigerian portal; Naija Ryders (Naijaryders.com), a forum for Nigerian-American youth; African Hip-Hop (Africanhiphop .com), a portal on hip-hop and African cultures; Kenyan Diaspora Network (Kenyandiaspora.org), a community for connecting organizations in Diaspora to government agencies in Kenya; African Events (africanevents .com), an online magazine dedicated to African culture; Black Television

Online (Blacktvonline.com), which distributes videos that focus on the black perspective; and Ethiopian Students Association International (esai .org), a forum that promotes the advancement of Ethiopians globally. These newer Africa projects use the internet to engage their constituents and to create active online communities. The relevant issue here is that AfricaResource.com, unlike the other websites, is critically aware of the politics of knowledge production and is building a globally accessible re-pository to counteract the myths and fictions of Eurocentric knowledge. Because it is education-focused, it rejects the normative, privileged sta-tus of the white male scholars who remain the canonical voices for most scholars.

THEORETICAL VALUE OF THE INTERNET AND THE SUCCESS OF AFRICARESOURCE.COM

Today, AfricaResource.com's offerings include five peer-reviewed aca-demic electronic journals, two of which have won awards (*West Africa Review; JENdA: A Journal of Culture and African Women Studies; Ijele: Art eJournal of the African World; African Philosophy;* and *ProudFlesh: A New Afrikan Journal of Culture, Politics and Consciousness*), a con-ference system, a bibliographic list, stories (poetry, autobiographies, fic-tion, etc.), topical scholarly essays, a blog on Rastafarianism, a direc-tory of leading personalities, a glossary on hip-hop, specialized resources (e.g., Orishas, Gender, Fela), an art gallery, and more. I chose to analyze AfricaResource.com, also known as ARC, for three main reasons. It of-fered a cogent alternative model of knowledge production on Africa at a time when the World Wide Web was gripped by the euphoria of unreal-istic business dreams. Secondly, unlike the websites that collapsed dur-ing the dot-com bust era, AfricaResource has continued to steadily grow and expand its resources. And thirdly, it is a site I am very familiar with, having worked extensively on it.

Users' responses to the electronic journals of AfricaResource.com, as well as its resources, have been very positive and amazing. A published poet on AfricaResource.com, Yusuf Adamu, says: "I have been published and widely read on your website. I wish to thank you very much for the opportunity offered" (May 2006). Agunbiade Ojo, a new user, confirms the relevance of the resource website: "This is a good resource site for many Africans. How I wish many African students would avail them-selves the great resources available in this site" (June 2006). Another en-thusiastic user who discovered the website, Randee I-Morphe, marveled at the resource, "Africaresource—this is just great stuff, perhaps turning out to be one of the best kept secrets of the African heritage! Keep up the good work!" (October 2006). And an Indian scholar, Ipshita Chanda (2002), writes,

> I teach in a Comparative Literature dept. in an Indian University, and have worked on African literatures in English. For the last four years, I've also been teaching it to very enthusiastic students, many of whom are women and are fascinated by the gender ideologies of the different African nationalities. We have followed *WAR*, especially the gender issue, and used it in our work, and I actively recommend *JENdA* as well. (Quoted in N. Nzegwu, "Africaresource.com" 82)

She then goes on to say:

> I worked on anglophone African drama (Ama Ata Aidoo was one of the dramatists I considered, the others being Soyinka and Ngugi) and decided early on that there were very few non-African critics of African literatures whom I could stomach. From then on I have developed the firm if rather extreme idea that we need to be in touch with African scholars more than state-of-the-art western theorists about our cultures, however famous the latter are in world academia. That was why I was thrilled with *West Africa Review*, *JENdA*, and *Ijele*. (Quoted in N. Nzegwu, "Africaresoure.com" 82)[7]

Chanda's critical observation is very pertinent because it allows us to see the impact of new technologies in addressing Eurocentric hegemonic discourses. The new media alternatives I am proposing are overturning older structures of intellectual work and are instituting new models of theoretical engagement. They are creating new authorities and enlarging the audiences as well as actively engaging them in theoretical discourse. They are allowing a new wave of scholars and knowledge activists to give and gain a deeper sense of histories, cultures, and societies. Essentially, the internet and new media technologies are creating new globally accessible repositories of information and libraries of knowledge where possibilities of linking and linkages are limitless. Thus, their greatest impact is their ability to influence and shape intellectual ideas, political policies, and discourses of students and professors in far-flung regions of the world.

DIGITAL DIVIDE AND RACISM

It is not unusual to find scholars and critics who question why communities of the Third World should be concerned about the internet since they lack the means to access the information on it. The critic Subbiah Arunachalam shares a similar view when he states,

> To access information in cyberspace, one first needs access to the corresponding electronic technology. Often technology diffuses rather slowly, and even today most scientists and scholars in developing countries do not have access to the new information and communication technologies. As a result, the performance of researchers can be (and is) affected, not because

they are poor physicists or chemists but because they are not connected to
electronic information networks. (Arunachalam 22)

This comment is definitely important, since we need to ensure that no
digital divide exists between the First and Third worlds. Nevertheless, the
fact that a large segment of the African population does not have internet
connection should not deter us from realizing and ensuring that the internet can be used to deconstruct Eurocentric knowledge. Emphasis should
always be on the fact that there are capable Africans with relevant skills
who understand the politics of knowledge production and are working toward using the internet to preserve Africa-centered knowledge. We should
not be deterred in our task because not all Africans have access to, or can
use, the internet.

We should be aware that too often, comments on the digital divide between the First World and Africa are covert suggestions that Africans lack
relevant skills in new media technologies. Such comments are implicitly
racist in that they ignore the existence of African scientists and computer
engineers. Philip Emeagwali, Thomas Mensah, Chinedu Echeruo, and
Folashade Wisdom have been crucial in developing diverse elements instrumental on the Web. Dr. Emeagwali, Nigerian-born computer scientist
and civil engineer, is among the early innovators pivotal in creating and
defining the structures of what is understood today as the internet. The
pioneering work with supercomputers by Dr. Emeagwali laid the ground-
work for new innovations and development in modern computing technology and networks. CNN Student News dubbed him "one of the fathers
of the Internet and a trailblazer in petroleum extraction."[8] Emeagwali won
the prestigious Gordon Bell Prize in 1989 for performing the fastest computer calculations—3.1 billion per second—in world history. Surprisingly,
his work is not a result of a collaborative effort, as is the case for many
Bell winners. Information on his website states that his

> discovery of a formula that enables supercomputers powered by 65,000 elec-
> tronic brains called "processors" to perform the world's fastest calcula-
> tions inspired the reinvention of supercomputers—from the size and shape
> of a loveseat to a thousand-fold faster machine that occupies the space of
> four tennis courts, costs 400 million dollars a piece, powered by 65,000
> processors and that can perform a billion billion calculations per second.
> Emeagwali solved the most difficult problem in supercomputing by re-
> formulating Newton's Second Law of Motion as 18 equations and algo-
> rithms; then as 24 million algebraic equations; and finally he programmed
> 65,000 processors to solve those 24 million equations at a speed of 3.1 bil-
> lion calculations per second. Emeagwali's 65,000 processors, 24 million
> equations and 3.1 billion calculations were three world records that gar-
> nered international headlines, made mathematicians rejoice, and caused

his fellow Africans to beam with pride. The New African magazine readers ranked him as history's greatest scientist of African descent. (http://
emeagwali.com)

I have quoted this material at length to make the crucial point that
African scientists are able to compete with the best and brightest of other
societies, even though the continent currently lags behind in computer
use. In my view, this is a matter of economics and education rather than
of technical capacity. The relevance of Emeagwali's theory is that it shows
us the importance of thinking outside the box. Instead of using expensive processors for calculation, linking up 65,000 processors was more
effective and faster in doing calculations. This is very important as the
underlying framework of the internet is its ability to link up different networks, and the speed of the network is based on how quickly processors
can speak to each other. Without this invention, it would have been difficult for the likes of Tim Berners-Lee, who is credited as the father of the
World Wide Web, or Google, celebrated for having the fastest search en-
gine, to have *any* impact.

Another African innovator, Thomas Mensah, Ghanaian-born, is a
chemical engineer and an expert in the field of advanced materials. He
holds a patent for his pioneering work in fiber optics for applications including guided missiles and supersonic fighter aircraft such as the F-22,
the fastest jet in the world.[9] New and upcoming African engineers and
computer scientists include Chinedu Echeruo, Folashade Wisdom, Nwabu
Nwanne, and Bomi Olamijulo-Oki. Linux professional Folashade Wisdom,
a Nigerian woman, aced Novell's Certified Linux Engineer examination
in Accra, Ghana, in 2005. She scored the highest-ever mark (99.25 percent) for anyone on the continent on the exam. According to the managing director of Novell Africa Limited, Graham Hallworth, Wisdom is "the
first Lady CLE [Certified Linux Engineer] in Africa and the first CLE in
Nigeria—you have the highest mark so far amongst the other CLE's in Africa including South Africa." He goes on to say, "This is a great achievement as it is a difficult examination with a low pass rate."[10] Another great
initiative out of Nigeria is headed by Nwabu Nwanne, who is currently
the lead administrator for the Igbo Open Source Translation, a free web-
hosting repository for open-source projects.[11] The aim of this project is to
translate open-source programs such as OpenOffice (software suite similar
to Microsoft Office), Mozilla FireFox (Web browser), and Linux KDE (operating system) into the Igbo language.[12] This project expands the meaning
of "open-source" because it localizes these free software applications into
the language of the people, and enhances their experience. Continuing
with translation is another exciting project by Bomi Olamijulo-Oki of
africanportal.net. Bomi created the ABDYoruba Keyboard, which is actu-

ally a downloadable application that works like a virtual keyboard. With this application, people can digitally switch to the ABDYoruba Keyboard to write in Yoruba.[13]

Chinedu Echeruo is the Nigerian-born founder of Hopstop.com, a navigational website that helps New Yorkers find directions to locations. Hopstop.com also functions as the city's guide to entertainment, restaurants, shopping, etc. The interactive website works by using the mass-transit system (metro and bus) as the blueprint for mobile walking directions for residents to navigate around New York City. What he did was an important milestone, because he created a map-like navigation system and provided the module so users can feed their information to hopstop .com using their computers, cell phones, and personal digital assistants (PDAs).[14] In addition to directions, hopstop.com gives users best routes for getting to their destinations. Unlike Emeagwali and Mensah, Echeruo, a Harvard business graduate, is among the new breed of savvy immigrants who have used their experience to create business ventures. Hopstop.com, which was created in 2001 and targeted primarily to New Yorkers, has expanded to include other cities such as Boston, Washington, D.C., San Francisco, and Chicago.[15] The service it offers is similar to Google's Google Maps and Google Mobile and it actually made its debut *before* Google added a version of this tool to its roster of services. Echeruo's work allows one to think of the website as a personal directory assistant, or fly-by-concierge, always available to perform its duty.[16]

TECHNICAL PRAXIS OF DEVELOPMENT AND NEW FORMS OF KNOWLEDGE DOMAINS

In the following, I discuss the importance of open-source free software for developing and managing portals, not only because of the relevance of technical knowledge in deconstructing old orthodoxies and transforming knowledge, but to show that there are Africans who possess the prerequisite skills. The following analysis defines the technical requirement for creating the prototype design and conducting the actual development during the creation of new knowledge structures for the public common. I include it to make the point that the structures of the internet are not Eurocentric; that these are the knowledge issues that concern web developers and content producers; and that this is the kind of knowledge these experts produce. While the internet is a phenomenon of modern technologies, it is not intrinsically a Eurocentric tool, nor can it be perceived as a product of Western culture, despite the proverbial claims. The internet can be seen as a modern-day common to which no one has or should have exclusive rights and claims of ownership.[17]

The "open-source" phenomenon of the internet is a social movement that is based on the idea of the common. It shares two principles for the distribution of software: cooperation and collaboration. Examples of free open-source software are Mozilla Firefox (browser for viewing Web pages), OpenOffice (suite similar to Microsoft Office),[18] and Joomla (content management system, or CMS, for managing dynamic websites). These free applications are released under the GNU General Public License (GPL) and are placed in the public domain. This placement removes any copyright restrictions or possible violations, allowing users to alter the source codes as long as their contributions are released back to the public so they can be freely redistributed. Most of the Web open-source software has dedicated websites and project forums for developers and users to communicate and share ideas. Volunteers who are members of the common and who come from different parts of the world take on roles such as moderators, document writers (of software documentation), support, third-party developers, etc.

The implication of using free open-source software and working in a collaborative model is to transform knowledge. This transformation is crucial in an environment where multinational Euro-American corporations including Microsoft, Apple, IBM, Oracle, and Adobe dominate and monopolize all public outreach media, and the cost for software purchase is extremely high. For example, the full version of Microsoft Office Professional Edition 2003 is $499, but individual programs such as Word, PowerPoint, and Access 2003 are $229 each. Meanwhile, the open-source version, OpenOffice suite, is *free* and *robust.* The tables below show the prices of commercial and open-source software, and indicate whether the software is cross-platform and will work on Windows and Macintosh computers. The applications include word processors and other office-use applications, operating systems (Windows—Microsoft has a monopoly on the market), Web production suites (for creating Web pages and graphics), video editors (for making films, documentaries, animation, etc.), Web browsers (for viewing websites), and post-production tools (for creating special effects in films, documentaries, etc.).

At the basic level, these types of free, open-source software are cost-effective and enable anyone on a low budget to use them in achieving their goals instead of buying prohibitive proprietary software.[19] It is important to stress that "low budget" does not indicate lack of quality. Joomla, which is a Swahili word (*Jumla*),[20] is open-source software that is used by commercial and nonprofit organizations, government agencies, universities and colleges, and publishers to build and manage dynamic websites. The level of tweaking required to achieve desired results is dependent on the technical proficiency of the administrator and her or his enthusiasm in learning the software. Though the learning curve might be steep, knowledge of this CMS is absolutely crucial for the management of a web-

Table 18.1. Prices of Commercial Software

Name of Software	Type of Software	Cost of Software
Microsoft Word, Access, and PowerPoint 2003	Office Suite—Professional Edition (Cross-platform)*	$299 for each, $499 for the entire package
Windows XP Professional	Operating System (Cross-platform)	$299
Mac OS X Tiger	Operating System (Macintosh-only)	$129 (single pack)
Macromedia Studio 8	Website Authoring (Cross-platform)	$999
Final Cut Studio 5.1	Video Editor (Industry Standard) (Macintosh-only)	$1,299
Adobe Premiere Pro 2.0	Video Editor (Industry Standard) (Cross-platform)	$849
Internet Explorer**	Web Browser (Cross-platform)	Free
Safari**	Web Browser (Macintosh-only)	Free
Adobe After Effects	Post-Production (Industry Standard) (Cross-platform)	$999

All prices were current as of May 2006.
* The platform indicates whether the software is for specific platform or cross-platform. In this case, I am looking exclusively at Windows (PC) and Macintosh (Mac).
** Some of the free programs, such as Web browsers, are bundled with new computers, but can also be downloaded online at their respective corporate websites.

site and *can* be learned by anyone. The beauty of Joomla is that it is scalable, in that it allows third-party developers to create add-ons known as modules and components. These add-ons enable administrators to perform special tasks that are not part of the standard Joomla package. Some of these extensions (add-ons) include: dynamic form creation, document manager, subscription services, e-commerce (online store), website directory, gallery, forums, event calendar, and much more. A CMS such as Joomla aids in knowledge building only if one acquires the technical knowledge or is prepared to pay for it. The availability of free software helps facilitate the production of knowledge, as it enables populations that have been marginalized to have the opportunity to author their history, one that truly reflects their experiences. As a result of these engagements, new bodies of knowledge are produced and are accessible to Web users in ways that the traditional mode cannot capture.

Table 18.2. Prices of Open-Source Software
Much of the open-source software listed in the table below also works on Linux, an open-source operating system similar to Microsoft Windows but far more secure.

Name of Software	Type of Software	Cost of Software
OpenOffice 2.0 (word processor, presentation, spreadsheet, etc.)	Office Suite (Cross-platform)*	Free
Linux	Operating System (Web Standard) (Cross-platform)	Free
Nvu	Web Authoring (Cross-platform)	Free
Vivia	Video Editor (Windows and Linux)	Free
Jahshaka	Video Editor/Effects (Cross-platform)	Free
Mozilla FireFox 2.0	Web Browser (Cross-platform)	Free
Apache	Web Server[1] (Web Standard) (Cross-platform)	Free

* The platform information indicates whether the software is for specific platform or operates cross-platform. In this case, I am looking exclusively at Windows (PC) and Macintosh (Mac).
** Some of the free programs, such as Web browsers, are bundled with new computers, but can also be downloaded online at their respective corporate websites.
1. A Web server is online storage for displaying websites. Normally, when you create a website, you need to put it online if you want the website to be publicly accessible. In this case, putting the web pages on the server will allow the public to view the materials.

DEVELOPMENT PROCESS:
BUILDING THE PORTAL

Contrary to assumptions that one cannot necessarily use "the master's tools to deconstruct the master's house," acquisition of the technical skills of the multicultural open-source software enables one to deconstruct Eurocentrism in a variety of ways. AfricaResource.com did this by providing a forum for airing ideas that challenge Eurocentrism. The strength of this website is that it is outside the control of forces of Eurocentrism. Africa Resource Center, Inc., began as a small static Web page, which is a basic page that was created to present information online. The design of the page included a logo, graphics, links to internal and external resources, and text. The design and functionality worked in tandem in relaying information to website visitors. During that time, updating did not pose a problem since the website was growing at a manageable pace, but by 2002, problems began to surface. The major problem was updating and maintenance. When a static website grows fast, it is time-consuming to update and maintain it. In most cases, when something changes or a new feature is implemented, it has to be changed site-wide manually, and that can become a major task if one has hundreds of pages, because each of the pages will need to be edited to reflect the new changes. By 2003, I began researching open-source software to come up with an alternative solution for managing AfricaResource.com. After spending much time learning a great deal about GPL software and content management systems, I knew that it was time for a major redevelopment of the website. The project objectives for revamping AfricaResource.com into a dynamic website were to improve website efficiency, maintenance, and performance, to stabilize timely content delivery, to incorporate effective search and retrieval site-wide, to increase site materials offerings, and to boost traffic.

During this time, I began learning about PHP (popular Web-based scripting language) and mySQL (popular open-source database). By the middle of 2004, I had created a design document, and the technical specification of the project workflow to guide development. After the requirement was finalized, I designed six possible prototypes for what would eventually become the database-driven website known as AfricaResource .com. The development focused on three main areas: information architecture, design, and usability. In general, information architecture refers to the structure or the organization of information online. Usability is concerned with the user-friendly nature of a website, the ease of navigation, and the rate of information retrieval. Design addresses the visual appeal, and the graphical components needed to develop the prototype. Developing AfricaResource.com required a high level of technical proficiency because of the many modifications required, including balancing the aesthetics, usability, and functionality.

The images below illustrate the transformation of AfricaResource.com. It depicts the visual representation of the website from 2000 to 2006. During the period highlighted, the first image is the static HTML website while the second is dynamic mySQL/PHP (database-driven). The screen capture visually shows the progression of AfricaResource in terms of design, usability, and functionality.

This figure represents the beginning phase of AfricaResource.com. When the website was started, I had limited technical experience; but that obstacle did not hinder my quest of realizing this project that became known as AfricaResource.com. Neither the lack of technical proficiency nor the constant struggle I knew would come outweighed the objective of this project, which was to publish and distribute cutting-edge

FIGURE 18.1, a, b, and c. Website screen capture (2000 to 2002). Source: Internet Archive (http://www.archive.org).

research and critical insights on Africa and African Diaspora. Suddenly, the prospect of AfricaResource.com becoming real, with its own domain name, or internet address, dwarfed any limitations. Though the Web pages were vibrant and colorful, they represented a mergence of varied design and technical background with the actual content generation, or knowledge production. The static HTML website moved from a two-column to a three-column structure, as reflected in the third image of figure 18.1. Each new design represented our need to update "the look," organize the content, and visually re-present the website. Those, as well as timely update and maintenance of the website, were some of the issues that had to be addressed. With abundant technical expertise, proficiency, and renewed energy, the website is approaching *new* and different horizons that are not bound by hierarchical and traditional modalities of representation.

After extensive design and development, the website was reborn using the free content management system (CMS) Joomla. Besides the home-page, which employs the three-column structure, many of the internal pages are two-column, with many of the navigation links on the left panel. Also noticeable is the use of colors; more muted organic colors were used to complement the design and create a welcoming ambiance. In that sense, there was less dependency on images and hot-spot navigation sys-tems. Following the organic nature of the website, it was necessary to re-duce its weight (that is, the size of the file) by decreasing the quantity of elements comprising the website. This was done to ensure that the pages would load quickly on a visitor's Web browser. The idea is that when an image is used, it has to serve a purpose; it must be optimized for the web and should only be used for directing internal resources inside the net-worked information system.

In comparison with the attention a published book garners, the rate of growth of AfricaResource.com within the last six years has been as-tonishing, even though current statistics have not been compiled. Previ-ous statistics, collected in 2000, were the result of extensive search and analysis of how website resources were used and by whom. There are over 130 universities and institutions worldwide that are presently linked to our resource and electronic journals, and the readership sample is from eighty-five countries including Botswana, Belize, Fiji, Malaysia, Iceland, Japan, Uruguay, Ireland, China, Rwanda, Israel, Korea, India, Saudi Arabia, Croa-tia, Turkey, Brazil, Jamaica, Tanzania, and Iran. By 2002, AfricaResource .com was linked to universities and colleges including Adam Mickie-wicz University, Poland; Adelaide University, Australia; Can Tho Univer-sity, Vietnam; Columbia University; Emory University; Goethe-University Frankfurt, Germany; Harvard University; Indiana University; University of Iowa; McGill University, Canada; Sarah Lawrence College; Rutgers University; Stanford University; Università di Napoli Federico II, Italy; Université Paris, France; University of Basel, Switzerland; University of Cambridge, United Kingdom; University of Cape Town, South Africa; Uni-versity of Copenhagen, Denmark; University of Helsinki, Finland; Uni-versity of Hong Kong; University of Leiden, Netherlands; University of Southern California; University of the Witwatersrand, South Africa; Uni-versity of Tromso, Norway; University of Waterloo, Canada; University of Wyoming; Victoria University of Wellington, New Zealand; Vander-bilt University; and Yale University.[21] Also, the website has served as a re-source for organizations and institutions such as UNICEF, IMF, United Nations, National Geographic, PBS, American Library Association, Pren-tice Hall, National Library of the Netherlands, Nordic-Africa Institute, and others. Users include colleges and universities, libraries, corporations

FIGURE 17.2, a, b, and c.
Website screen capture (2006 to present). Source:
Africa Resource (http://www.africaresource.com).

and organizations, research institutes and think tanks, students, and general Web users. In 2001, AfricaResource.com was recognized by PBS as *Best of the Web*; the BBC has favorably reviewed the content; and the site is part of Google's human-edited directory (N. Nzegwu, "Africaresource.com" 85). In addition, AfricaResource.com e-journals have been recognized. For example, *JENdA: A Journal of Culture and African Women Studies*, with all African women editors, won the 2002 ICAAP Award for Excellence in Electronic Publication. This annual award by ICAAP (International Consortium for the Advancement of Academic Publication) goes to the best and most successful electronic journal that is advancing the art and science of electronic publication.[22] And both *West Africa Review* (July 6, 2001) and *JENdA: A Journal of Culture and African Women Studies* (March 3, 2001) were selected by the University of Wisconsin–Madison for the NSF-funded Scout Report.

In late 1999 when the website began, the user rate climbed to 300 visitors a week within one month. As the website began to expand, the traffic jumped from 7,000 to 11,000, and then to 14,000 visitors a day. A new issue of a journal normally yields 80,000 visitors per day. This trend was achieved by the bold decisions of the editors. For instance, *West Africa Review* was the only place online that provided critical analysis of Henry Louis Gates's travelogue *Wonders of the African World*. This issue highlighted the responses of prominent African scholars to the documentary. As a result, because of its historical and intellectual prominence, *Black Scholar* asked to reprint the entire issue in its print journal. Also, the visitors have a peculiar level of interest, as the longest recorded stay is 322 minutes, the shortest stay is 5 minutes, and an average user statistic is 20 minutes. All this indicates that our website use is not comprised of random hits (N. Nzegwu, "Africaresource.com" 85).

FUTURE OF PRODUCTION FOR AFRICA-FOCUSED CONTENT

Rethinking Africa in the Diaspora with available new technologies involves thinking about the type of knowledge produced for Africa. N. Nzegwu notes the importance of the review process of journals. This is highly crucial, since it is where one gets to ascertain that the author's data are socially and culturally sound. It is not enough to say that an essay about Africa is theoretically sound, if by that we mean that it references dutifully the works of white male scholars. She states,

> Our review process is exacting. Relevant reviewers are selected with the additional qualification of having fairly extensive knowledge of the cultural phenomena and of the historical, political, and social issues informing the thesis of the particular article. Because they are all committed to

excellence in scholarship on Africa, our reviewers are especially attentive to originality of thesis, theoretical sophistication of the arguments, relevant social and historical events, and clarity of purpose. (N. Nzegwu, "Africaresource.com" 83)

We need to take our bearing from the recently deceased distinguished African historian Adu A. Boahen, who contended that if animals accept that the lion should tell the history of the animal kingdom, they should expect that the history will be the lion's own story. The need for attending to the review criteria cannot be overemphasized, since it ensures that only those with relevant qualifications and language proficiency can evaluate a work on Africa. In that sense, Africa Resource Center as the publisher guarantees that the knowledge meets the requirement of being Africa-specific, rather than offering dubious and unsubstantiated generalizations.

An Igbo folktale retold by the renowned author of *Things Fall Apart*, Chinua Achebe, of the tortoise's battle with the lion is equally instructive here. Knowing that it would lose the fight, the tortoise requested permission from the lion to perform a death ritual. It scratched and pawed the earth, uprooted shrubs and the tall elephant grass, effectively creating a scene of utter chaos. It then told the lion that now it was ready to die, since that chaotic scene would clearly prove that two *equally* matched animals fought to the death there. The point of this tale is not that AfricaResoure.com is engaged in a futile contest with Eurocentrism that it will lose, and so is trying to create an impression of having fought a good fight. Rather, the point is that it is unrealistic to think that one cannot wage a battle from a disadvantaged position. One can and should do this, since a well-prepared underdog with a plan can triumph in the biblical manner of David against Goliath.

* * *

In "Producing Knowledge in Africa Today: The Second Bashorun M. K. O. Abiola Distinguished Lecture," Paulin Hountondji contends that it is urgent "to set up devices and procedures for retrieving, recollecting and critically reappropriating all that can be useful and relevant to present-day problems in our age-old heritage" (8). As a specialist in this area of endeavor, I can substantiate that the internet provides this avenue for circumventing historical repression and the authoritative voice of conventional white scholarship as well as the invidious roles of some publishing houses in maintaining the privileged status of Eurocentrism. New media technologies and the internet provide a model of knowledge that is outside the control of Eurocentrism's structure of knowledge. In many ways, the internet does play an important role in that the more the work produced by it is shared, accessed, and disseminated, the more the value of the knowledge structures in it will increase.

This is the kind of venture that would greatly advance knowledge and research on Africa while challenging the dominant Euro-American hegemonic model of knowledge production. The scholarship it fosters will prove enlightening for those who consult it. The possibility of utilizing free, open-source software gives scholars the opportunity to increase African-oriented intellectual materials, to enable authors to easily speak on the internet, to allow different voices to participate, and to offer alternative ways of publishing. AfricaResource.com has the ability to question, challenge, and change perceived notions and bias. The power of the internet is that it enables people to interact and to transcend national, social, and cultural boundaries. Ideas become part of the global repository that can be searched and linked to by individuals in any part of the world. Whereas in the past certain ideas remained in obscurity because publishers would not publish them, in the world of the internet, they can be accessed, influence other ideas, and define new paths of research.

NOTES

All links were valid as of November 2006.

1. "Open access" refers to online content that is free and can be accessed by anyone on the internet. The idea behind open access is that if scholarly materials are more freely available online, they will increase our knowledge. The basis of open access is exposure; through it, the author(s) of the free content will gain more visibility while increasing their rate of citation.

2. Davis has paraphrased the *CASS Report* 16, no. 1 (2000): 25.

3. The works of Carole Boyce Davies; Nkiru Nzegwu ("Colonial Racism," "O Africa," *Family Matters*); Haunani-Kay Trask; Paul Tyiambe Zeleza; Oyèrónké Oyêwùmi; and Olufemi Taiwo ("Colonialism," "Exorcism") provide insight on this point. As well, extensive bibliographic reference can be found on AfricaResource .com.

4. A gateway processor is an online company that acts as a third-party merchant in assisting internet users to make purchases online. Since products are paid for online with a credit card, these third-party merchants are needed, depending on the configuration of a particular store, to complete these transactions. I will use a fictional e-commerce setup, Haile Store, to illustrate the point. Haile Stores sells books online with different payment options. Clients can pay by credit card or use a third-party payment processor such as Google Checkout or Paypal. If the client pays using Paypal, they do not have to use their credit card at Haile Stores. Since their credit card information is stored on Paypal's secure server, they only need to log in to Paypal and pay their bill. This is especially useful for people who do not want to disclose their credit card number to make payments everywhere they shop online.

5. Portals are like a gateway to information or resource centers. Essentially, a portal contains avenues to further resources and information which, for the most part, make links and networks to others parts of the portal, including external resources.

6. The mission of AfricaResource.com is discussed online in the "About Us" section at http://www.africaresource.com.

7. Users' praises are online in the "About Us" section: http://www.africaresource.com/content/view/29/88/.

8. The link is http://cnnstudentnews.cnn.com/fyi/interactive/specials/bhm/story/black.innovators.html.

9. A profile of Dr. Thomas Mensah can be found under "Profiles" in the Lifestyle section at AfricaResource.

10. This is referenced from Nigerian Linux Users Group (NGLUG): http://www.nglug.org/node/48. This website is operated by a group of Linux professionals in Nigeria as a response to the increasing use of open-source solutions in businesses and universities across the country. Part of their objective is to share their knowledge and contribute their work to the global village. Given the argument about access in Africa, it is important to note how individuals in Nigeria are propagating this idea of open-source in their own environment.

11. More information on Igbo Linux Project: http://www.igbolinux.org/.

12. Project at http://sourceforge.net/projects/igbo/.

13. ABDYoruba Keyboard: http://www.africanportal.net/Publications/ABD/mktut1.htm.

14. See Levack , "Mastering the Mass Transit."

15. Information about other cities can be found on the homepage of Hopstop, http://www.hopstop.com.

16. Hopstop assists New Yorkers by enabling them to enter their request through their cell phones or mobile devices, to be fed through the website. Once the information is processed, the system will find out the quickest route and the fastest way to get there. A profile of Chinedu Echeruo can be found on AfricaResource.com.

17. Commons can include "aspects of life that had been accepted . . . as collective property, or the common heritage of all peoples and communities, existing for everyone to share" (International Forum on Globalization 81).

18. This is an alternative to the expensive Microsoft Office suite. OpenOffice is powerful and open-source and, arguably, offers the best word processor.

19. Microsoft Word is an example of proprietary software. Proprietary means that it is commercial, requiring payment before anyone can use the product. In a large environment, an organization would have to purchase licenses that would authenticate its members as valid users.

20. The Africanization of open-source projects is an interesting trend in the industry. For example, *Ubuntu* is a Zulu (South Africa) word that describes humanity and the relation a person has with another person in that space. In 2004, Mark Shuttleworth, a white South African multimillionaire and venture capitalist, chose Ubuntu as the name of his open-source Linux-based operating system. Ironically, searching for "Ubuntu" online usually yields results from the Ubuntu project and all the affiliated websites, blogs, etc. It is interesting to note how reappropriation by the establishment, especially by projects that have gained significant prominence, is actually diminishing the cultural history of such African-based ideologies.

21. The full Web statistic is online under the "About Us" section: http://www.africaresource.com/.

22. See *JENdA* journal online: http://www.jendajournal.com.

REFERENCES

Arunachalam, Subbiah. "Information Technology: What Does It Mean for Scientists and Scholars in the Developing World?" *Bulletin of the American Society for Information Science* 25, no. 4 (April/May 1999): 21–24.

Bernal, Victoria. "Diaspora, Cyberspace and Political Imagination: the Eritrean Diaspora Online." *Global Networks* 6, no. 2 (2006): 161–179.

Boahen, Adu A. *African Perspectives on Colonialism.* Baltimore, Md.: Johns Hopkins University Press, 1987.

"Computer Scientist Philip Emeagwali." AfricaResource.com, 2006. http://www.africaresource.com/content/view/146/181/ (accessed November 21, 2006).

Davies, Carol. "Decolonizing the Academy: Advancing the Process." In *Decolonizing the Academy: Diaspora Theory and African–New World Studies*, ed. Carole Boyce Davies, Meredith Gadsby, Charles Peterson, and Henrietta Williams. Trenton, N.J.: Africa World Press, 2003. ix–xvi.

Ghebru. Posting to Dehai Eritrean News and Eritrea News Online Archives. May 2, 1997. http://www.dehai.org.

Hountondji, Paulin J. "Producing Knowledge in Africa Today: The Second Bashorun M. K. O. Abiola Distinguished Lecture." *African Studies Review* 38, no. 3 (1995): 1.

"Innovator Dr. Thomas Menash." AfricaResource.com, 2006. http://www.africaresource.com/content/view/154/181/ (accessed November 21, 2006).

International Forum on Globalization. *Alternatives to Economic Globalization: A Better World Is Possible.* San Francisco: Berrett-Koehler, 2002.

Levack, Kinley. "Mastering the Mass Transit." *EContent*, June 2005. www.econtentmag.com/Articles/ArticleReader.aspx?ArticleID=8072 (accessed November 20, 2006).

Lévy, Pierre. "The Art and Architecture of Cyberspace." In *Multimedia: From Wagner to Virtual Reality*, ed. Randall Packer and Ken Jordan. New York: Norton, 2001.

Nzegwu, Azuka. "Digital Narrative: Exploration of New Media Production of Form and Content." MA thesis, Indiana University, 2003.

Nzegwu, Nkiru. "Africaresource.com: Bridging the Digital Divide." *African Issues* 30, no. 1 (2002): 81–85.

———. "Colonial Racism: Sweeping Out Africa with Europe's Broom." In *Philosophy and Racism*, ed. Susan Babbitt and Sue Campbell. Ithaca, N.Y.: Cornell University Press, 1999. 124–156.

———. *Family Matters.* Albany: State University of New York Press, 2006.

———. "O Africa: Gender Imperialism in Academia." In *African Women and Feminism: Understanding the Complexity of Sisterhood*, ed. Oyèrónké Oyéwùmi. Trenton, N.J.: Africa World Press, 2001. 99–158.

Oglesby, Christy. "Innovators Who Break Barriers." CNN Student News, February 9, 2001. http://cnnstudentnews.cnn.com/fyi/interactive/specials/bhm/story/black.innovators.html (accessed November 2, 2006).

Okeke, Philomina E. "Postmodern Feminism and Knowledge Production: The African Context." *Africa Today* 43, no. 3 (1996): 223–234.

Oyêwùmi, Oyèrónké. *The Invention of Women: Making an African Sense of Western Gender Discourses*. Minnesota: University of Minnesota Press, 1997.

Screen Capture of AfricaResource.com (Dynamic). AfricaResource.com. http://www.africaresource.com (accessed May 1, 2006).

Screen Capture of AfricaResource.com (Static). Internet Archive. http://www.archive.org (accessed May 1, 2006).

Taiwo, Olufemi. "Colonialism and Its Aftermath: The Crisis of Knowledge Production." *Callaloo: A Journal of African American and African Arts and Letters* 16, no. 4 (1993): 891–908.

——. "Exorcising Hegel's Ghost: Africa's Challenge to Philosophy." *African Studies Quarterly* 1, no. 4 (1998). http://www.africa.ufl.edu/asq/v1/4/2.htm.

Trask, Haunani-Kay. "The Politics of Academic Freedom as the Politics of White Racism." In *From a Native Daughter: Colonialism and Sovereignty in Hawai'i*. Monroe, Me.: Common Courage, 1993. 225–246.

——. "Women's *Mana* and Hawaiian Sovereignty." In *From a Native Daughter: Colonialism and Sovereignty in Hawai'i*. Monroe, Me.: Common Courage, 1993. 110–125.

Zeleza, Tyiambe Paul. *Manufacturing African Studies and Crises*. Dakar: CODESRIA, 1997.

PART FIVE
TRANSNATIONAL PERSPECTIVES

19

AFRICAN VIDEO, FILM CINEMA, AND CULTURAL REPACKAGING IN THE DIASPORA

Folu F. Ogundimu

The globalization of communications and culture at the end of the cold war in the late twentieth century has had at least three unintended effects on African diaspora populations worldwide. Firstly, the rapid diffusion of new and improved communications technology—such as Direct Broadcast Satellite (DBS) systems, the internet, and wireless telephony—has enabled previously remote areas of many African countries to become instantly accessible to a global metropolis, with far less restricted controls from authoritarian political institutions. Secondly, access to global markets and the need for African states to partake in the new globalizing arena has resulted in reforms of political and economic structures in many countries. One aspect of these reforms has been the implementation of painful structural adjustment programs of cutback management in various sectors; the end of state subsidies; and the privatization of vast areas of the domestic economy. When these changes have been coupled with the liberalization of currency exchange rules, import and export controls, and also travel, we have seen the emergence of a new, vibrant entrepreneurial merchant class that engages in transborder and transnational trade in goods and services. Thirdly, the revolution in the globalization of communications and culture has enabled African producers of cinematic culture to actively incorporate, reappropriate, and domesticate global culture in such a way that the African cultural imagination is finding resonance with global audiences, especially those in the African diaspora.

Domesticating global culture is partly expressed by the fusion that enables Nigerian, Ghanaian, or Senegalese musical artists to produce local hip-hop music videos featuring rap music in local languages, Pidgin, English, or French with local beats but with all of the iconographic symbols of urban black American hip-hop culture, as seen on Black Entertainment Television (BET) or Music Television (MTV). Similarly, local stories, folk drama, and newer tales of urban and contemporary life in Africa are increasingly repackaged for cinematic audiences in both Africa and the diaspora. These types of fusion of the global and local, as well as depictions of African traditional cinematic genres, are, not surprisingly, finding much resonance among diaspora African communities, especially recent migrants to the global metropolis.

Using the case of African video and film cinema, this chapter explores how contemporary discussions of globalization and transborder flows of communications and culture underreport, ignore, and misunderstand the dimensions and relevance of African film and video cinema representation in the global environment. The chapter will also show the limitations of explanations that still portray Africans as victims of cultural imperialism. Although the persuasive arguments by theorists of cultural reproduction and cultural imperialism cannot be easily dismissed, a case can just as plausibly be made that today's African audiences and cultural entrepreneurs are not entirely passive consumers of alien cultural products. Indeed, it is far more likely that, given the robust and dynamic platforms for diffusing the global culture so easily available today, both vendors and consumers of culture are constantly negotiating the spaces for cultural diffusion in a complex market that makes Africans not just consumers of alien cultural artifacts but producers and exporters of African culture as well.

CULTURAL REPRODUCTION AND CULTURAL IMPERIALISM

Most cultural reproduction theorists assume there is a dependency relationship between foreign producers of mass media content and audiences in developing countries. This assumption holds that because the major producers of global culture are based in major industrialized countries of North America and Europe—Disney, Viacom, Warner, MTV, Paramount, CBS, Sony, Bertelsmann, Vivendi, and Pearson, to name a few—audiences in consuming nations (periphery countries) are essentially socialized "into a knowledge system or frame of mind that will make them more compatible or sympathetic to foreign ideas and consumer values."[1] Flowing from this argument is the notion of cultural imperialism, the thinking that only powerful nations have the capacity not only choose the type of information society most compatible with their cultural institutions but also to foster their alien cultural values onto unsuspecting citizens of periphery nations.[2]

This thinking is not new. The concern about cultural imperialism was first articulated by Third World scholars at the historic summit of non-aligned nations in Algiers in 1973. The Algiers summit is remarkable for two reasons. It issued a formal call for a restructuring of global economic relations, with a call for a New International Economic Order (NIEO). It also placed on the agenda, for the first time, the issue of cultural imperialism with a statement in the Economic Declaration that was adopted at Algiers. This statement describes the "activities of imperialism" as covering "cultural and social fields, thus imposing an alien ideological domination over the peoples of the developing world."[3]

Arguments for a new world order of information and communication speak to attempts to redefine the hegemonic relations of nation-states. J. Herbert Altschull observes that "Attempts by the advancing (developing) countries to correct the global imbalance both in economic power and in control over information are two parts of the same struggle; they are inseparable."[4] Historically, such attempts had economic and military implications. The formation of the French news agency, HAVAS (later AFP), and the U.S.–owned Associated Press (AP), in competition with the British-owned Reuters are illustrative cases. The call for a New World Information and Communication Order (NWICO) met with stiff resistance by the West, partly because the opposition was led by a coalition of corporations, media advocates, and scholars who saw no reason for a fundamental restructuring of the world economic or information system. They called the proposal a sneaky attempt by the Soviet side to impose state controls over the free flow of information. Nevertheless, the call for a New World Information and Communication Order was taken up by UNESCO and assigned to a sixteen-member International Commission for the Study of Communication Problems, chaired by former Irish minister and Nobel laureate Sean MacBride. The task of the MacBride Commission was to see how best to address the core complaints of developing countries over imbalances in the world communication order. Two of the imbalances they spoke of concerned the monopoly on international communication resources by a few developed countries; and poor coverage of developing societies by the world's news organizations.

The attempt by the MacBride commission to deal with the NWICO issue was ensnarled, unfortunately, in the polarizing ideological politics of the cold war. The MacBride report was adopted by UNESCO as Resolution 4/19 at the 1980 Belgrade Conference, and released in October 1980.[5] The 312-page report contained eighty-two recommendations organized into four main areas: (1) the status of communication and information; (2) the problem of free and balanced flow; (3) measures for a new world information order; and (4) the role of communication in public opinion making. One of these recognized that imbalances in the flow of information and communication go beyond imbalance in the flow of news. The commission thought the imbalances included every facet of cultural life: technology, entertainment, books, films, equipment, training, finance. It also thought that failure to redress the problem ensured consolidation of control over the "facilities of cultural development," with the negative effect of promoting "alien attitudes across cultural frontiers."[6] Some critics have cited this reference to cultural imperialism as acknowledgment of the position of the non-aligned group as first articulated at the 1973 Algiers summit. Although UNESCO survived as an international and multilateral organization, the bloodletting over NWICO and the work of the MacBride Commission almost undid the organization, culminating in the suspension of membership by the United States, Britain, and Japan from the organization for a few years, and the ouster of its long-term Senegalese Secretary-General, Ahmadou Mahtar M'Bow.

In the post–cold war era, the demand for a New World Information and Communication Order has far less resonance, although the same contentions about the poor representation of the image of Africans and African countries in the global communications arena remain. The difference today is that unlike in the pre-1990s era, Africans are increasingly gaining mastery of the technical capacity to produce information and communication about themselves; they have greater flexibility in choosing from among a competing set of global vendors who seek to gain markets in Africa; and above all, they now possess the ability to diffuse their own image of themselves to a global audience, in direct competition with the dominant Western agencies of global culture. This capacity to appropriate cultural production and reinterpret themselves to global audiences is increasingly being exploited, not just by the traditional mass media such as newspapers, radio, and television. More importantly, image diffusion is taking place in real time on the internet; by direct satellite broadcasting; by cellular transmission of text, still photography, and video; by electronic mail and fax machines; by download; and by video and film cinema.

VIDEO AND FILM CINEMA DIFFUSION

Although there is growing evidence that large numbers of African video and cinematic productions are circulating in several countries within Africa and increasingly in the African diaspora, it is difficult to estimate either the exact scale of the productions or the volume that reaches audiences outside Africa. In the absence of formal, systematic studies to determine both the volume of the productions and how large the traffic is, best-guess estimates of the significance of the industry can be inferred only from anecdotal data. Formal institutional data are incomplete, hopelessly outdated, or nonexistent for the Africa sector. A 2003 survey of current business published by the U.S. Bureau of Economic Analysis of film and tape rentals in sub-Saharan Africa records $91 million for the region, with South Africa accounting for $82 million of the volume. The survey does not identify the origin of production for the films and tapes. The last data released by UNESCO on film production showed that Africans were the largest importers of films from the U.S.A. proportionately, compared to any other region. But the finding dates to 1997, when the survey of national cinematography was conducted. The report also shows that the largest film-producer countries of film features were India (839), China and Hong Kong (469), Philippines (456), the U.S. (385), and Japan (238). In Africa only Egypt, with 72 productions, and Nigeria, with 20, made the UNESCO list of top producers.[7]

Although the 1997 UNESCO data specifically deal with film features, the emergence of a large burgeoning market for video cinema, alongside other formats such as feature films in digital and downloadable or streaming formats, appears to have effectively blurred the lines demarcating what counts as feature films or video productions in Africa. For audiences thirsting for culturally proximate content in cinematic forms, the choice of format is largely irrelevant for dictating consumption. Acknowledging the video boom phenomenon in anglophone Africa, Frank Ukadike writes that the "explosion of video production and its popular appeal . . . attests to the manifestation of what might be called a real 'first' cinema, a cinema which competes with the so-called 'First Cinema' of the West on its own terms."[8] He argues further that "Video has changed the industry's outlook not because of its merit but because of the manner in which the producers negotiate the parameters of the hybrid spaces in the popular imagination in conjunction with the question of marketability and reception, marketing strategies hitherto not attempted by its predecessor, the celluloid film."[9]

Although the boom in the videofilm industry was a response to the fiscal austerity arising from the structural adjustment programs (SAPs) imposed by the International Monetary Fund and other financial institutions during the 1980s, the new cinematic form in Nigeria, and Ghana, has quickly become widely accessible to a new generation of cinematic producers who found in video productions an effective way to assure economic viability with low-cost investments in production and marketing. As a result, the new genre essentially challenged, if not displaced, the filmed genre of indigenous theatrical traditions. Although the video boom has made significant inroads by way of eroding the traditional audience base of the indigenous theater tradition, the Yoruba theater tradition itself has proven resilient as it exploits the new technology in transforming itself as an integral component of the new industry. Newer theater troupes adopt the video format as well as the popular traveling theater tradition of the modernist era, made famous by such troupes as those of Hubert Ogunde, Duro Ladipo, Moses Olaiya, and Kola Ogunmola in Nigeria's post-independence era. The latter-day traveling theater tradition itself incorporated significant elements of the *Alarinjo* performance theater genre most commonly associated with the precolonial era. As Biodun Jeyifo observes, the *Alarinjo* tradition may be in decline but it "is still extant today and involves a variety form of theatrical expression. The performers are masked and their theatrical fare combines dramatized satirical sketches drawn from a corpus of stock character types, instrumental and vocal music, mimetic dancing, acrobatics and visual spectacle."[10] As with the transformation of the *Alarinjo* Theatre into its popular conception in the form of Yoruba traveling theater, one sees in some of today's filmed genre of Yoruba theater on Nollywood video a continuity of what Jeyifo captured earlier as a similarity to the normative structure of earlier traditions. This is because the traditions derive their essence from the "structure of performance idioms of traditional Yoruba art forms like the *Alarinjo* Theatre and the *Ewi* poetic chants of the *Egungun* society."[11] Clearly, these forms have gained commercial appeal among a highly segmented audience, if not translated as yet to a much wider non-Yoruba-speaking audience.

The trail blazed by Nigerian and Ghanaian entrepreneurs is spurring new entrants into the market, including Hollywood genre producers looking to strike co-production deals with African cinema producers. For example, at the 2005 Sithezi Film and TV market held in Cape Town, South Africa, several producers showed up to promote co-production initiatives between African filmmakers and foreign vendors. Additionally, 233 buyers representing 60 companies in 20 countries registered for the event, which saw 18,115 visitors.[12]

Clearly, success of the videofilm industry is fueling optimism everywhere in Africa, causing the Nigerian Information Minister, Frank Nweke, to proclaim effusively that African films are poised to dominate the global market.[13] Although such optimism might be premature, there is no doubt that there is great potential for the industry. Besides the South African film industry reporting gross revenue of $30 million in 2004, other data about the size and economic viability of the other national videofilm industries are highly speculative, and the estimates by industry sources vary wildly. For example, a report by the *Economist* in 2006 states that Nigeria's Nollywood film industry releases over two thousand productions a year, about two-thirds of them in English, netting gross sales of $200–300 million a year.[14] The two thousand production figure exceeds the combined releases of Hollywood and India's Bollywood film industries; and not only does the $100 million range in revenue estimate sound unrealistic, but the variance in revenue figures is also unacceptably high. Another estimate provided by a filmmaker associated with Nollywood, Paul Obazela, said there were over two thousand cinema outlets in Lagos alone, and he put the total worth of the industry at more than $250 million.[15] To buttress the argument that Nollywood was gaining international acceptance, Obazela said the presence of African American film stars Vivica Fox and Danny Glover at the African Film Awards in Nigeria in 2005 was proof enough.

But critics of Nigeria's video cinema industry are dismissive of these claims by Nollywood boosters. For example, film scholar Ola Balogun says that Nollywood video productions are conceptually nonequivalent to film productions; that the statistics produced by the industry are both unreliable and fantastic; and that "Nigerian home videos are of such atrociously poor quality in terms of filmmaking skills that they cannot be taken seriously by film professionals."[16] Similar criticisms have been made by others, that Nollywood is "a populist industry, with plots that have been affectionately dubbed voodoo soap operas, full of witchcraft, voodoo and the occasional cannibal."[17] Even Martin Loh, director of Ghana's National Film and Television Institute, was quoted in one news report as saying there was a need for a shift in production emphasis from materials that emphasize superstition, ethnicity, civil strife, fear, and violence.

Such criticisms might well be valid, but one might also argue that from an artistic point of view, videofilm producers should be allowed the freedom to pursue their creative passions as they best see their own lived experiences of the African reality. Even critics who acknowledge the poor aesthetic quality of the productions concede that the lively stories portrayed in the African video cinema "appeal to the public who shape popular culture" as well as "growing African populations resident in Europe, the USA, and Canada."[18] Moreover, Ukadike notes, as the videos reach classrooms and non-African audiences, they gain an added measure of importance in ways celluloid film never did because the video productions portray the local African experience in a variety of genres: comedy, satire, musical, adventure, and horror movies. Also, the technology of video has enabled social mobility within African cultures, with women fully participating in the production and marketing processes, and female video producers "exploring cultural conventions and innovative strategies that challenge Eurocentric and male chauvinistic assumptions/readings of black female subjectivity."[19]

AUDIENCE RECEPTIVITY AND NEW DIRECTIONS

For years, the popularity of the Nigerian video cinema and its Ghanaian counterpart has partly stemmed from the fact that the productions are culturally proximate to the experiences of their audiences. Audiences can relate to the characters, their representation of the African personality, their mannerisms, traditions, speech forms, and dress, and the spatial environments that serve as locations for the productions. One report about the popularity of African movies on Zimbabwe Television (ZTV) notes that the most popular ones are those from Nigeria, "which hundreds of thousands of Zimbabweans have fallen in love with, including their fabulous actors."[20] According to one viewer quoted in the report, "The Nigerian movies no doubt appeal to almost everyone. They talk of our lives as

Africans. And that's what we want in film, something we can understand and easily relate to." She also said Zimbabweans want to watch a film that teaches them something. And that is what "the Nigerians have been popular for . . . bringing to life issues affecting people not just in Nigeria but in other African countries as well." One consequence of the popularity of the Nigerian videos is that Zimbabwean men and women could be seen donning the flowing West African robes, the report said. Expressions such as "Please my sistao I beg of you" or "Does love fill my stomach" and the very popular "God forbid, I won't allow it, over my dead body" were said to be common expressions not only in Nigeria but also now in Zimbabwe.[21]

Although the Nigerian video productions and their Ghanaian counterparts touch on a wide range of subjects, their themes are relatively simple, dealing with problems of relationships, especially domestic relationships; motherhood; the triumph of good over evil; religion and myth; and a reflection of the African cosmological system, where human affairs are mediated by the visible and invisible. The trend of productions in Ghanaian video in the 2000s is to deal with what Amoah Larbi calls the "Sankofa" genre. This deals with the need to return to the beginning to produce epic narratives and simplified stories of cultural revival and cultural nationalism. Examples of such productions include those on Yar Asantewa, using historical records to revisit Ghanaian history, as in the story of Yar Asantewa's attempt to rally the Asante in rebellion against the British.[22] Larbi says Ghanaian producers are also experimenting with new genres that deal with the crisis of émigrés from Ghana and Ghanaian returnees from abroad. These include productions like *Police Officer 1* and *2*, and *The Scent of Danger*. The newer-generation videos are increasingly more sophisticated in production techniques, with subtitles if produced in local languages. Increasingly, the releases are co-produced with Nigerian partners and they frequently include cross-cultural themes, especially knowledge of Nigerian cultures.

Besides films with universalized themes, some of the productions have simple narratives that explore complex issues facing several societies in Africa. This is the case with the South African–produced *Yesterday*, which explores the impact of AIDS on a family unit and community relations. The film exposes the vulnerability of gender relations in local settings that have inbuilt structural dislocations, as in the case of migrant labor. Issues of powerlessness, ethnic prejudice, domestic violence, and the politics of spatial asymmetry between urban and rural folk are all explored in this gripping yet simple narrative. Throughout Africa, local and national television stations are finding that these narratives provide valuable and cost-effective means of providing twenty-four-hour programming on stations that previously relied largely on foreign vendors for their programming content.

Apart from the Nigerian and Ghanaian productions, a wave of co-productions involving large South African, African American, and Hollywood financial backing is beginning to make inroads into the African film scene marketed globally. These co-productions include films such as *God's Bits of Wood* by Senegalese author Sembene Ousmane, featuring African American actor Danny Glover. The story is based on the 1947 strike of the Senegal-Niger railway workers, which was the seed of the struggle for independence in francophone West Africa. There is also the success of South African filmmaker Zola Maseko's film *Drum*, winner of a 2004 Pan African Film Festival award. The film is about a jazz club in Johannesburg of the 1950s, in which jazz is presented as music that helped break race barriers. Backed by American financiers, the director was pressured to cast African American actor Taye Diggs in the lead role. Maseko says that although U.S. funding helped the film's commercial success, such funding is not helping Africans to tell their own stories.[23] The commercial viability of these co-productions and of the Oscar-winning South African–produced *Tsotsi* is leading to a flood of interest in African films on the international film festival circuit, according to a Hollywood industry source.

Whereas the commercial appeal of many of these co-productions is for a wider audience, not just diaspora Africans, they nevertheless command the interest of Africans living outside Africa. These films include *Hotel Rwanda* (2004), which explores the horrific massacre of Tutsis during the Rwanda crisis; *The Last King of Scotland* (2006), about the rule of Ugandan strongman Idi Amin; and *Catch a Fire* (2006), chronicling Patrick Chamusso's transformation from oil refinery worker to radical of the African National Congress during the apartheid era.[24] In 2007, *Rwanda Rising*, a film that documents changes now taking place in Rwanda, was scheduled for release at the Pan African Film Festival; and *Primeval* (2007), which features an eighty-minute musical score of over one hundred African musical instruments, was also scheduled for release.[25] Additionally, some multinational corporations, including Warner International, are striking partnership deals with South African and Nigerian entrepreneurs, including Lagos-based Johnnic Communications (Johncom) Africa, to play major roles in the Nigerian film and music business.[26]

Other recent breakthroughs in bringing African video and film cinema to diaspora audiences have included the launching of a Pan-African Movie Channel for download subscription on the internet. The channel offers popular African movies, dramas, and documentaries as subscription video on demand at its website, www.africast.tv. It was backed by an initial investment of $1.5 million by Internet Marketing Consortium. Its offerings have included *The Campus Queen* (2004), a story of college life and rival organizations in an African university; *Dole* (2001), which offers a perspective on crises facing today's African youth; *La petite vendeuse de*

Soleil (The Little Girl Who Sold the Sun, 1999), featuring the story of a handicapped girl reinventing herself as Senegal's first female newspaper vendor; and *Sango Malo* (The Village Teacher, 1991), featuring an intimate portrait of social and economic changes to village life in Cameroon.[27]

Without going into much detail, it is noteworthy that the growth of videofilm productions in Africa has also spurred ancillary industries in entertainment publishing, film festivals, and awards shows—all of which feed the growing appetite for celebrity news and information about the nouveau stars of African videofilm entertainment. Perhaps the best-known of the African film festivals is the annual FESPACO Film Festival, which takes place in the capital of Burkina Faso, Ouagadougou. Other festivals are mushrooming across the continent, many of them a direct response to the popularity of the videofilm industry. They include the African Movie Academy Awards, which were held in Nigeria in 2005 with a total of 150 entries,[28] and the African Students Film and Television Festival held in 2005 in Ghana,[29] which had 48 entries.

*   *   *

Although there is a need for formal studies on the breadth, volume, and impact of African cinematic productions in the diaspora, there is sufficient evidence to suggest that Africans are taking advantage of the many opportunities offered by globalization to repackage their own stories and market them to a ready consumer audience in the global metropolis. Contrary to assumptions that Africans are passive consumers of global culture, powerless against the onslaught of alien culture, as envisaged by cultural reproduction theorists and cultural imperialism advocates, this chapter argues that African cinema artists and entrepreneurs are in fact major actors in the export of their culture to the world. Unlike in the pre-1990s era, they have seized upon the advantages offered by the fiscal austerity imposed by structural adjustment programs to evolve a whole new industry that has effectively captured economic surpluses by trading on the dreams and fantasies of African audiences who thirst for cinematic representations of realities that resonate with their lives. In the process, the video cinema industry has created a nouveau celebrity class that enjoys social prestige and economic comfort where previously many belonged to the marginalized, unemployed, urban underclass.

The success pioneered by the Nigerian and Ghanaian video industry has not only spurred a continent-wide imitation, but gradually elevated the visibility of African cinema on the international stage. The search for partnership and co-production agreements with African entrepreneurs by well-financed filmmaking and media multinational corporations, and wealthy independent producers from industrialized countries, shows that Africa is one of the epicenters of opportunity for the movie industry today. A report in the *Hollywood Reporter* in December 2006 says $300 million was spent at the cinema box office in Africa in 2005, most of it in South Africa. The figure is expected to rise remarkably by 2010. This chapter has shown that data about the movie production industry in sub-Saharan Africa is notoriously unreliable. Clearly, data that are bandied about by Nigeria's Nollywood spokespersons are no more credible. But the activity in the Nigerian market and the popularity of Nigerian videos in overseas markets suggest that this is obviously a profitable sector of activity.

The lack of reliable data on the industry has to be taken as a tempo-rary inconvenience. Soon, we expect independent monitoring and evalua-tion agencies, spurred by the need for external investments in the market, to result in the evolution of data reporting agencies that will ensure the accurate keeping of records. Such a development will almost certainly as-sist in elevating the technical quality of productions, something that is already beginning to happen. It will also enable the emergence of viable public-private partnerships that could truly lead to the establishment of sophisticated movie production sets and theaters, with governments using tax incentives, investments in infrastructure development, promotional subsidies for marketing, etc., to spur the further growth of the industry and speed the appeal of African films in the global export market.

Another issue that deserves some commentary relates to the narrative themes of the video and film cinema productions that are presently com-ing out of Africa. Leaving aside matters pertaining to technical quality and aesthetics, a close attention to the productions shows that it will be unfair to pigeonhole the African output in particular slots. Both the genres of the representations and the story themes featured have shown some fluidity, representing attempts by producers to accommodate the dy-namic changes in the lives of most ordinary Africans. Regardless of how crudely the producers and artistes may have produced these representa-tions, the fact of the matter is that they are wildly popular with a wide swath of African audiences, both within Africa and in the African dias-pora. One might suspect that Africa's image in the global sphere would be better off if video and film cinema producers from Africa studiously avoided images that fitted into the stereotypical roles and representations that Africans have historically been identified with by colonial prejudice. But this is a sensitive issue. If we dictate to the artist, we are effectively infringing on the freedom and poetic license the artist has to paint a pic-ture of the world as he sees it. I would rather err on the side of giving un-restrained poetic license to the artist than legislating, dictating, or advis-ing how best to forge story narratives on video. It is clear that our artists are learning from their own errors, their own crudity. They are forced to improve their products when audiences fail to buy them, or when they fail to win nominations or awards from any of the video cinema festivals now proliferating in Africa.

With the advent of streaming video on the internet, and video-on-demand, the future of African video and film cinema is indeed very rosy. Already, large numbers of diaspora Africans in Europe and North America are showing that they are willing to spend their hard currency and disposable income on subscriptions to video-on-demand if the productions both meet aesthetic and technical proficiency standards and feature story themes they can identify with, in terms of enhancing their self-worth and personhood as Africans living in non-African societies. The opportunity to earn tremendous amounts of money by way of subscriptions from institutional vendors including university libraries, schools, museums, and others is also limitless.

It is instructive, though, that as African entrepreneurs open this next frontier for their businesses, they have yet to learn much of what is required in capturing these types of institutional sources of revenue. For example, when Africast.tv launched, it made no provision for institutional subscribers. At the time of writing, it was still to respond to an inquiry for subscription information from my own university library, which was willing to take up institutional subscription, more than one month after we first posed the inquiry. Similarly, businesses that offer online services of this kind must be able to respond immediately to subscribers who seek clarification about interruptions of their services, even when they continue to make regular subscription payments. Not attending to such customer inquiries and complaints will most certain ly damage the credibility of African vendors and render them liable to lose market access in the global metropolis.

NOTES

1. See McPhail, *Global Communication*, 36–37n14.

2. Hedley, "Technological Diffusion or Cultural Imperialism?"

3. See Roach, "The Western World and the NWICO" 94.

4. See Altschull, *Agents of Power* 306.

5. MacBride Commission, *Many Voices, One World*.

6. MacBride Commission; Altschull 319.

7. http://www.unesco.org/culture/industries/cinema/html_eng/prod.shtml (accessed November 24, 2008).

8. See Ukadike, "Video Booms and the Manifestations of 'First' Cinema in Anglophone Africa" 127.

9. Ibid.

10. See Jeyifo, *The Yoruba Popular Travelling Theatre of Nigeria* 34. Also, see Adedeji, *The Alarinjo Theatre*.

11. Jeyifo 11.

12. Vallie, "An African Marketplace Trading in Fantasy."

13. "African Films to Dominate Global Market," *Weekly Trust*, November 5, 2006.

14. "Nollywood Dreams: Nigeria Film Industry," *Economist*, July 29, 2006.

15. Vallie, "African Stories Told by Africans."

16. Balogun, "Does Nigeria Indeed Have a Film Industry?"

17. Vallie, "African Stories."

18. Ukadike 127.

19. Ukadike 130.

20. "Zim Falls in Love with Nollywood." *The Herald* (Zimbabwe), August 13, 2005.

21. Ibid.

22. Amoah Larbi, "African Video Narratives," talk delivered at the Michigan State University Ghana Multidisciplinary Studies Program, Legon, Ghana, May 2006.

23. Kariuki, "African Films Gaining on the International Scene."

24. Galloway, "South Africa: Catching a Fire."

25. Frizzel, "Primeval."

26. Coetzer, "Into Africa."

27. "Africast Launches America's First Pan-African Movie Channel," *Canada Newswire*, August 9, 2005.

28. "Nigerian, S/African Films Dominate AMAA Nominees," *This Day* (Nigeria), April 21, 2005.

29. "Ghana and Nigeria Share Laurels at African Film Festival." *Public Agenda* (Ghana), September 12, 2005.

REFERENCES

Adedeji, Joel. *The Alarinjo Theatre: A Study of Yoruba Theatrical Art from Its Earliest Beginnings to the Present Times.* PhD diss., University of Ibadan, 1969.

Altschull, Herbert J. *Agents of Power: The Media and Public Policy.* White Plains, N.Y.: Longman, 1995.

Balogun, Ola. "Does Nigeria Indeed Have a Film Industry?" *This Day* (Nigeria), June 11, 2005.

Coetzer, Diane. "Into Africa: African Biz Pushes North to Take on Pirates." Billboard.com, September 2, 2006.

Frizzel, John. "Primeval." In "Keeping Score: Top Film and TV Composers Discuss Their Latest Projects," compiled by Ada Guerin. *The Hollywood Reporter*, January 5, 2007.

Galloway, Stephen. "South Africa: Catching a Fire." *The Hollywood Reporter*, October 31, 2006.

Hedley, Alan. "Technological Diffusion or Cultural Imperialism? Measuring the Information Revolution." *International Journal of Comparative Sociology* 39, no. 2 (1998): 198–213.

Jeyifo, 'Biodun. *The Yoruba Popular Travelling Theatre of Nigeria.* Lagos, Nigeria: Department of Culture, Federal Ministry of Social Development, Youth, Sports and Culture, 1984.

Kariuki, John. "African Films Gaining on the International Scene." *The Nation* (Kenya), April 3, 2005.

MacBride Commission. *Many Voices, One World: Towards a New More Just and*

More Efficient World Information and Communication Order. London: Kagan Press, 1980.

McPhail, Thomas L. *Global Communication: Theories, Stakeholders, and Trends.* Malden, Mass.: Blackwell, 2006.

Roach, Colleen. "The Western World and the NWICO: United They Stand?" In *Beyond Cultural Imperialism: Globalization, Communication and the New International Order,* ed. Peter Golding and Phil Harris. Thousand Oaks, Calif.: Sage, 1997. 94–116.

Ukadike, Frank N. "Video Booms and the Manifestations of 'First' Cinema in Anglophone Africa." *In Rethinking Third Cinema,* ed. Anthony Guneratne and Wimal Dissanayake. New York: Routledge, 2003. 126–143

Vallie, Annaleigh. "An African Marketplace Trading in Fantasy." *Business Day* (South Africa), November 25, 2006.

——. "African Stories Told by Africans." *Business Day* (South Africa), November 25, 2006.

20 EXCESS LUGGAGE: NIGERIAN FILMS AND THE WORLD OF IMMIGRANTS

Akin Adesokan

In the spring of 2005, a number of African films were featured in a traveling series in different parts of the United States, mostly in university towns. One of these films was *Agogo Eewo* (The Sacred Gong), a political allegory by the Nigerian filmmaker Tunde Kelani, which was released in 2002.[1] Actually a sequel to another political allegory, *Saworoide* (Brass Bells, 1999), this film has been widely viewed in Nigeria as a critique of the Oputa Panel, the country's halfhearted attempt to reproduce South Africa's Truth and Reconciliation Commission at the end of a fifteen-year brutal military interregnum. But the audience at the Cornell Cinema in Ithaca, New York, needed to be told this, preferably through a contextual introduction, since allegorical works are not always explicit about the realities they allegorize. To the average filmgoer, *Agogo Eewo* appeared as a conventional drama of a monarch trying to rid his polity of corruption by invoking some traditional institutions of checks and control.

But there was something else about the film for which an introduction could not have prepared the audience. The screening was prefaced with a five-minute solo *bata* dance, now taken from its religious context as the music of Sango, the Yoruba god of thunder, and executed by a colorfully dressed dancer. The performance was an impressive intro which the poor lighting of the scene did not compromise. As the story raced to its climax, it became clear that, probably for the purpose of this U.S. traveling series, the film had been cut in several places. The general sense of the film was preserved, but to someone who had seen the 2002 version, these cuts were obvious and rather beguiling. Was the earlier version too significantly Nigerian for an American audience? There was nothing particularly abstruse or obscure about the missing parts. How could the introducer's claim that *Agogo Eewo* was censored make sense when the scenes that unsettled the ideologically motivated censors were no longer on view?

This observation regarding the challenges of contextualization, and the questions arising from it, provide a useful basis for advancing the argument of this essay about the relevance of Nigerian films to the experiences of Nigerians and Africans living outside the continent. The argument is that the vitality of these films is proportionate to the degree to which they engage the lived reality of the context of their existence, and this explains their popularity with viewers within other African countries and among Nigerian immigrant communities in North America and Western Europe, the spaces of diversity where the coalescence of technological and demographic changes ensures the world-readability of certain cultural forms.[2] However, it is this very vitality or particularity, the magnet for the increasing attention from journalists, scholars, and policy makers, which circumscribes the films' standing in the politics of global cultural translation. To state it baldly: Nigerian films appeal to local and immigrant audiences for the same reasons that they cannot be easily world-readable; but existing in this global context can aid the films in transcending the economic specificity of their origins. The strong editing of the Cornell version of *Agogo Eewo* might have been a realistic attempt at standardization in terms of running time, but even its most comical scenes did not elicit the same reactions as they did in the Exhibition Hall of the National Theater in Lagos.

Is there a connection between the character of the films produced in Nigeria and the preoccupations of African immigrants in Western countries inhabiting different but simultaneous cultural contexts? Indeed, does the specificity, the "cultural code" of the films mirror the degree to which relocated Africans are prepared to assimilate into their new societies? This essay will address these questions in the broader context of the reception of African and other non-Hollywood films (particularly Indian and Chinese/Asian) which have a longer history of being inserted into the process of standardization in global cultural markets. Perhaps it is necessary to note here that the difference between cultural translation and standardization, as the two terms are used here, parallels the difference between quantity and quality—that, if well managed, the one can become the other. The relevant example would be Chinese food, which retains its peculiarity to the extent that it has been globally commercialized, and to a lesser degree reggae music and *kente* cloth.[3] Apart from examining a number of theoretical issues about commodification either as technological or ethnographic reality, and looking at two films as examples of Nigerian cinema's presence in this circumscribed international scene, we will also describe the cultural-economic conditions specific to West Africa that can be understood as catalysts in the emergence of the videofilm tradition.

The films under discussion, *Osuofia in London* and *Dangerous Twins*, are produced in Nigeria, not in or by the immigrant communities, although they use the experience of immigration as partial or whole template for the stories.[4] The choice of these films is informed by the strong awareness of the claims of "the homeland" (to use the terminology of the classical conception of diaspora) on the relocated, claims equally weighted between realism and moralism.[5] There is also the fact that the production of Nigerian films through immigrant networks in North America and Western Europe is an integral part of the interdependency of simultaneous locations. Yinka Smart-Babalola's 2002 political drama *Akobi Gomina* (The Governor's Heir) was also filmed in London, and the filmmaker himself recently moved back to Nigeria to work full-time. The two films under discussion came out in 2004. Although produced in Nigeria, they were filmed both in that country and in foreign locations, with *Dangerous Twins* pressing the fact of its multiple locations—"filmed in London, France, Holland, Belgium, Switzerland, Nigeria, and USA"—into marketing service. They are very different films—*Osuofia in London* is a comedy while *Dangerous Twins* is closer in genre to a family melodrama—but each bases its appeal on the presence of a star, not so much on the renown of the director. The two lead actors are among the most sought-after in Nigeria—Nkem Owoh (Osuofia) and Ramsey Nouah.[6]

The cinematic phenomenon in Nigeria has caught global attention in recent years, as the films are featured in festivals, television documentaries, and innumerable newspaper and magazine feature articles, from the *New York Times* and *Christian Science Monitor* to the *International Herald Tribune* and *Economist*. In this respect, the label "Nollywood" is routinely employed by those who intend to grade it next to the two prior "woods": in the estimation of both journalists and Nigerian filmmakers, it is the third-largest film industry in the world, after the United States (Hollywood) and India (Bollywood). As this essay will show, this is a valid comparison as far as the scale of production goes. About one thousand titles are released in Nigeria every year, and are sold in venues that range from the roadside tuck shop to immigrant "African markets" in England, the United States, and elsewhere. They are also made for home screening—hence the die-hard classification of the films as "straight-to-video"—but some are also screened in theaters. An increasing number are broadcast on television channels across the continent—for example, on the twice-weekly program *African Magic*, on the South Africa cable network MNET. There is a growing body of commentaries dedicated to a scholarly treatment of the films.[7]

Yet, in terms of its history, the cinematic development in Nigeria requires a greater deal of specification than has been attempted for a meaningful comparison to the economic formations which structure the developments in the U.S. and India. Not all of this differentiation can be reduced to the recognition that Nollywood is still in its infancy, compared to Hollywood and Bollywood, which have been in existence since the second decade of the twentieth century. A brief review of this history may shed a light on the phenomenon of unprecedented emigration of Nigerians and other Africans that the genre of films under discussion indirectly thematizes.

This new cinema began in the late 1980s as an economic necessity. The word "new" is deliberately chosen; before the development which Nollywood references, there was a tradition of filmmaking in Nigeria, one that turned on an axis of "national" cinema, although again this was more by presumption than by actual practice. Filmmakers in Nigeria and Ghana, countries formerly colonized by the British, belonged in this *national-auteurish* sense in the same rank as those in former French colonies such as Senegal, Mali, and Burkina Faso. It was in this sense (the common factor between the national and the auteur models being filmmaking in the chemical-based celluloid form) that Ola Balogun (*Ajani Ogun, Ija Ominira, Money Power*) was featured in Ferid Boughedir's important documentary *Camera d'Afrique*, and in Francoise Pfaff's early anthology *Twenty-Five African Filmmakers*. In the same sense, Eddie Ugbomah (*The Death of a Black President, Apalara*) and Brendan Shehu (*Kulba na Barna*) could still make the list of interviewees in Frank Ukadike's more recent book of interviews. This is in spite of the fact that these Nigerian filmmakers were no longer as active either locally or internationally as their counterparts to the west whose work, given the coalescence of the institutional support of the French government's Ministry of Cooperation and their interest in questions of political and cultural identity, bulks large as African cinema, especially in classrooms, art house exhibitions, and film festivals outside of the continent.[8]

In 1995, when the critic Jonathan Haynes conducted what now amounts to a postmortem of this national cinema in Nigeria, the filmmakers discussed were not exactly of the tendency one might call *auteurish*, even when they still filmed in the celluloid 35mm format, but were already grafting their aesthetics onto the technology of video. This would explain the structural and aesthetic problems identified by Haynes in the films he discussed, and visibly displayed in the title of the essay (Haynes, "Nigerian Cinema: Structural Adjustments"). Although the growth of the videofilm form as an economic necessity has been discussed enough not to warrant a recapitulation here,[9] the combination of globalized media and accelerated migration which this essay addresses suggests a close connection with economic condition, hence the account that follows. The economic factor entered the discourse of filmmaking through the introduction of the regime of economic deregulation that went by the name of the structural adjustment program, or SAP, its telling acronym. It was part of the vast neoliberal economic reforms administered by the International Monetary Fund, the World Bank, and foreign bilateral donors, all agents, as Leslie Sklair has usefully noted, of the transnational corporate capital complex (5).

In different parts of the so-called developing world, there were variations in this reform package, but in the main it involved the restructuring of the fiscal systems of the countries concerned through the privatization of the banking system and debt alleviation to ensure balanced budgets; the scrapping of price control and marketing boards and other regulatory mechanisms; and the removal of government subsidies from public corporations. In Nigeria, where the devalued currency is still on a downward slide after almost two decades, as in the rest of the developing world, SAP continues to be viewed as a punitive tool of economic domination. It is that, to be sure, but we also need a nuanced presentation of its career in the African context, such as Beatrice Hibou attempts in a discussion of the position of the bureaucratic state in relation to what she terms the ruses of economic intelligence.

At any rate, this economic phenomenon and the political milieu of military dictatorship in which it unfolded have introduced a pervasive social dislocation into Nigerian society which has not been fully accounted for. It would, of course, be incorrect to ascribe all of Nigeria's social and economic problems to the structural adjustment policy of the Bretton Woods agencies, whose undertaker's reasoning was partly encouraged by earlier policy decisions, imposed and self-inflicted, that led a country awash with oil money soon after its political independence to the economic impasse of the mid-1980s.[10] The phenomenon of brain drain, that large-scale relocation of skilled and unskilled labor mainly to Western Europe and North America, is one of its many effects. In the realm of commercial activity, SAP led to the collapse of the entire system of cultural production—music, live theater, book publishing, and so on—which used to be organized, or at least perceived, as parts of the Nigerian "national" culture.

Benedict Anderson, among others, has characterized globalization quite succinctly as a process of "enormous disintegration, which is also a process of liberation [in which the world has been] integrated into a single capitalist economy" (59). This is to say that the same forces of transnational capital are responsible for the global disintegration of the nation-state (or the national cinema of the celluloid mode) and the ascendancy of new media of communication such as the video and, more tellingly, digital technology. It was in this context that the new Nigerian cinema came into its own, with antecedents in the Yoruba traveling theater, vibrant in West Africa from the 1940s through the 1980s; television drama; soap operas from North and South America; popular magazine strips; musical videos; Hindi films; and the rump of the Nigeria cinema up to the early 1990s. This last item, framed against the deliberate delineation of the "new" cinema above, indicates a central impulse in this essay: namely, that the fact of the videofilms being made in Nigeria is not necessarily to be taken in the conventional sense of a national idea. Instead, a more productive attitude would be to relate their aesthetics and their thematic preoccupations to a large-scale reconfiguration of social relations beyond the political geography of the nation-state. It is in this sense that talking about the extra-Nigerian audiences of the films in African and Western countries, especially in immigrant communities, can be meaningful.

Video technology was the cheapest mode in which this adaptation first manifested itself, and it led to these films being variously labeled as home videos, videodramas, and latterly videofilms. Although *Living in Bondage* (1992), produced by the electronic merchant Kenneth Nnebue, remains the breakthrough work in this form, Kelani (the director of *Agogo Eewo*) was one of the first to produce a film with distinct cinematic qualities, decisively transcending the residual suspicion of established filmmakers who continued to think of cinema in none other than celluloid terms. Although Kelani's works are not the focus of this essay, they provide here an example of the kind of practice that has a rich and productive basis for engaging in the politics of cultural translation on an international level, bearing in mind the director's misgivings about the exportability of Nigerian films based on the economic conditions of their emergence (Désir 107).

Emerging out of the shuttle between the economic and the cultural, the Nigerian films are a good example of the commodity form that Fredric Jameson postulates as the content and vehicle of the communicational idea widely known as globalization. Jameson is quite clear about the ideological underpinnings of globalization, especially with regard to information (or, his preferred term, communicational) technologies which exist to underline the incomplete character of modernity. Indeed, he contends that the "modernization" of the world, a differentiated phenomenon, is unthinkable without a sense of the implantation of these technologies, and that the graduated manner in which the different communicational forms—radio, film, television, and print—spread in the twentieth century has obvious cultural consequences. This is to the extent that technology in this later stage of capital supersedes the informational content of the earlier forms through practices such as advertisement, publicity, and disseminated television programs which carry with them cultural signs. Yet, as Jameson argues, this transaction is not without an economic aspect. He writes:

> We begin remembering that the newly flexible production was made possible precisely by computerization . . . and we also remember that computers and their programs and the like are among the most hotly exchanged goods among nations today. In this variant, then, the ostensibly communi-

cational concept has secretly been transformed into a vision of the world market and its newfound interdependence, a global division of labor on an extraordinary scale, new electronic trade routes tirelessly plied by commerce and finance alike. (56)

It ought to be noted that this development is also what Arjun Appadurai has described as "cultural flows" in five distinct forms, each given the evocative suffix of "scape." The shuttle between the cultural and the economic aspects of the communicational concept manifests itself in a broader sense. The cultural content displays itself as "a postmodern celebration of difference and differentiation [whereby] all the cultures around the world are placed in tolerant contact with each other in a kind of immense cultural pluralism on a global level" (Jameson 56–57). On an economic level, the manifestation is that of "the rapid assimilation of hitherto autonomous national markets and productive zones into a single sphere, the disappearance of national subsistence [and] the forced integration of countries all over the globe into [a] new global division of labor" (57).

This is very much the sense of Anderson's formulation cited above. Difference and standardization are the twin results of this phenomenon, but Jameson, who thinks of the impact of American media forms on foreign contexts in terms of "co-option," "wiping out," or "breaking up," casts a political glance at what is basically an economic force. With the semi-hypothetical Americanization of the world through the economic instruments of GATT and NAFTA, a sort of post–cold war Marshall Plan— which Jameson documents as destructive of European national cinemas with the exception of the French—Hollywood cinema would now become a transferable model. It is an economic model, but also a political one, since its formal and generic constants also ensure that those radical experimentations in cinema in which spaces for political filmmaking were once imagined are now limited.

One may wish to counter this view of the circumscription of generic possibilities in cinema by pointing to the vitality of Nigerian films as an ironic justification of the call by the proponents of Third Cinema for filmmaking practices "that the System cannot assimilate and which are foreign to its needs" (Solanas and Getino 52), but Jameson's argument is extremely nuanced and cannot be critiqued simply as a celebration of American exceptionalism. For example, it is a fact that no other country has the kind of access that ideas and products from the United States enjoy in different parts of the globe, and that this access exists principally at the economic realm. Also, the degrees may vary but the example Jameson provides of the imitation of the gestures of American television personalities by an Indian youth may be replicated in the tonal properties of daily speech heard on Lagos streets, this time largely influenced by the distinct culture of the internet.

However, it remains a debatable point whether this economically driven culture supersedes the pluralism of world cultures, because the uncanny texture of the internet can hardly be subsumed to the economic or cultural habits of a particular nation. For this Jamesonian shuttle is SAP writ large. The dis/integration of national markets under the force of the reform package is the economic dimension of the process that also let diversity loose through the aesthetic possibilities partly resulting from the implantation of technology. The difference lies in the degree to which the aesthetic forms thus liberated can compete with those of Hollywood films—to retain our earlier example. This is a factor of both market policies such as tariffs and the conglomeration of distribution networks, as well as of the dominance of Hollywood as a formal paradigm.

Jameson notes the limit set to the importation (into the American or Western context) of foreign perspectives by the spreading technologies of the two epochs. This condition is probably the one responsible for the widely held notion of despondency that goes by the term "cultural imperialism." Thus, difference is sustained, but its content, as film or novel, calls for translation if some cultures must survive in an economic sense. This is the thrust of the other set of theoretical reflections on the nature of translatability of film as a kind of ethnographic reception, provided in the writings of Rey Chow, who debunks the assumptions of originality implicit in the discourse of cultural imperialism. But first, we will look at the two films, *Osuofia in London* and *Dangerous Twins*.

The opening sequence of Part I of *Osuofia in London* has the texture of a documentary.[11] In fact, the images are not original; the seamless shots of a duiker, elephants, mountain ranges, and waterfalls are most likely archival images that are open for purchase, and this is obvious from their tone of a Discovery Channel documentary. The particular if unintended jump cut between the shot of the duiker staring at the camera and of Osuofia on top of the palm tree propped up by his daughters is further distanced by the diegetic sound of the gunshot which has missed its target. The director's interest lies not so much in this scene as in the documentary film–style narration that precedes it. The discourse of difference between the two worlds poignantly underscores the discussion above regarding the circulation of images under the communicational regime of globalization. The voice-over speaks of the "small and peaceful village" that "big cities and their fast lifestyles can never enter in their wildest dreams" and where "politics and confusion remain unknown." This statement is definitely not addressed to the attention of a Nigerian listener, who does *know* politics and confusion most intimately, however distant she may be from Lagos or Abuja, respectively the economic and political capitals of the country.

The opposition of the hardy but natural ambience of Osuofia's village to the vertical steel-and-mortar of metropolitan London activates all the prejudices and binarisms that the discipline of cultural studies in the last two decades has thrown into sharp relief.[12] More crucially, the rest of the film, especially the second half of Part I (set in London), is an elaborate acting-out of the negative perceptions of the uncouth villager bungling all encounters in the city to brilliant comic effect, a process at once muted and advertised by the fact of its location in England, with all the chords this strikes in the context of the historical relations between that country and Nigeria. Osuofia's enactment of this set piece is framed by a complex demonstration of his stock character, for the screen name itself is carried over from a previous film in which this character first emerged. The comic, indeed clownish, aspects of this figure are distilled from the folk attributes of the scrooge, the village charlatan equally menaced by and menacing to the rest of the community.[13]

Yet, there is a subtext at work. The explicit narrativeness characteristic of the videofilms is brought into focus early in the story. Osuofia is in London to claim the money that his late brother, Donatus, has bequeathed to him in his will. But it becomes clear, as Part I progresses, that he has been set up for an elaborate scam by Donatus's widow and her associates. Notably, the film does not specify one dimension to the plot: the reversal of the order of criminality in which a citizen of Nigeria, a country with an international notoriety as the originating point for acts of Advance Fee Fraud, or "419," is now the potential victim! Donatus's widow, Samantha, now Osuofia's wife, returns to the village with him, and we know from her frequent soliloquies ("What do I do? What do I do?") that she retains a quiet resolve to seize the money which he has been lured to London to sign away but which is now firmly in his hands.

Meanwhile, Osuofia celebrates his novel status as a white woman's husband, acting the native informant to the point of crude presentation of racial difference in which Trafalgar Square and Piccadilly Circus are constant reference points, and members of his family are routinely accused of jealousy if they voice their suspicion of his English wife. In the sequence dwelling on his return to the village, the negative image of Nigerians as veteran scammers is reversed as Samantha attempts to poison Osuofia so she can steal his passbook, failing which she has to confess that her action is motivated by the stories she has heard about Nigerians!

Dangerous Twins plays this terrain in another register. The differences in cultural attitudes between Nigeria and England form the basis of the opposition in the characters of the Thomas twins: Lagos-based Kehinde swaps places with his twin brother, Taiwo, who is having difficulty starting off a family in London. They are so identical that their wives cannot tell them apart; Kehinde will "help" his brother's British wife, Judy, conceive, while Taiwo relocates to Lagos to manage his brother's business. Early in the film, when the brothers meet in the Lagos home of Kehinde,[14] the viewer is treated to a long-drawn-out set piece during which they argue and joke about their old pranks, resulting in very distinctive characterization enabled by editing techniques. Although the ploy serves a basically narrative purpose, it develops the paradoxical edge of slowing down the pace, and the doubling becomes the "point" of the story. The familiar trope of good and bad twins is played up so spectacularly that a comparison with David Cronenberg's 1988 film about identical twins, *Dead Ringers*, would be hyperbolic, not to say ridiculous. Indeed, the impossibility of a productive comparison between the films may well be one way of suggesting the aesthetic distance between art films (the old "Second Cinema") and Nigerian films as a cinematic novelty. Cronenberg's film avoids the cliché of melodrama in favor of something more complex: Beverly and Elliot Mantle are one soul divided into two bodies and two mutually dependent minds at the point of conception.

Taiwo's cool and "English" demeanor contrasts sharply with the mood of Lagos, with its failing electricity, noisy parties, and tardy employees. He imports austerity measures from London, decades after SAP has supplanted that older regime of economic self-discipline; his constant invocation of "downsizing" and the injunction that "modern-day business relies on technology and e-commerce" represent a cultural attitude and a well-aimed critique of corruption in Nigeria. His stern refusal to engage in the micropolitics of resource management—buying one's own generator, running private security—leads to the degeneration of the family and business he is charged with managing.

In these sequences when the Lagos-based wife (Kehinde's own wife) expresses her frustrations with this transformed "husband" (the real Kehinde is a reputable spendthrift, a self-confessed "bad boy"), the Lagos leg of the story takes a tragic (or melodramatic) turn. Taiwo's confrontation with the shady Kaska—his brother's ally—results in the latter sending armed robbers after him, and the director, Tade Ogidan, known for such thrillers as *Hostages* and *Owo Blow*, executes a meaty sequence of crosscuttings from the scene of the robbery to Taiwo's futile effort at convincing the police to come to his family's aid. The viewer here encounters an effusive commentary on social dislocation—the dystopia called Nigeria—borne out in the personal crisis of Taiwo Thomas's life, the head of the family maintaining an upright attitude supposedly unbecoming in a Nigerian, leaving his wife, employees, and the police completely surprised.

Meanwhile, Kehinde's loud style impresses Judy—as far as she can tell, he has merely changed, and for the better. The degree to which the film's primary interest lies in the Nigerian scenes—which could also be due to the contingencies of production—can be seen in the infrequency of Kehinde's circulation within London. There is an extravagant "treat" for Judy in Switzerland and Holland, and a London version of the employer-employees face-off, except that Kehinde substitutes a spending spree for

Taiwo's astringent rules. The irony is that it is precisely this uprightness that ruins the business in Nigeria; Taiwo's refusal to play the Lagos game is sure to alienate everyone. Having traded his British passport for his brother's, proper and decent Taiwo is constrained to agree to serve as a drug courier with a fake passport in order to reenter England. The London sequence, shorn of the infrastructural turbulence of Lagos, lacks dramatic poignancy. Even when Judy becomes pregnant and has a baby, the designed peace of the family comes across as facile, as if the characters are engaged in a premeditated act of hide-and-seek.

Far from a commentary on the shortcomings of the nuclear family and the self-absorption of the European—the Lagos family is no less nuclear—this is an effect of the thinness of the plot at this point. The schematic template of duplicitous twins has to break down at some stage. In spite of this limitation, *Dangerous Twins* assumes a striking kind of symmetry between Lagos and London. Witness, for example, the defamiliarized way that both Taiwo and Kehinde relate to their respective employees: the latter making unaccountable demands on the company's resources, the former driving workers all too familiar with Nigeria's "ethics" of compromise to distraction. Whether in Lagos or in London, the brothers' different attitudes represent a meta-commentary on cultural mores—British seriousness and rectitude versus Nigerian recklessness—that are nonetheless versions of the stereotypes that *Osuofia in London* presents with fewer nuances. On the other hand, the constant change in focus of dramatic action in *Osuofia in London* does not slacken the tension. Due largely to the comic thrill in Owoh's frisky relationship with Samantha, the need to sustain the ruse around the value of Donatus's bequest keeps the story in focus, even without the involvement of villagers that makes the first half of Part I such a delightful set piece of real comic force.

There is an uncanny strategy in both films—the interpellation of a global audience through conscious dialogues and characterizations. It is uncanny because, in spite of the extra-Nigerian locations for the films, they remain Nigerian, and distinctly so. Osuofia's statements in Igbo are directed *sotto voce* to his trusted daughter, Nkechi, and constitute the only subtitles in this notably "English-language" film. Speaking of language, Nigerian English and pidgin coexist with British English and Igbo in the films. Ramsey Nouah, who plays the two brothers in *Dangerous Twins*, speaks in two distinct voices, but when he wishes to confuse his British assistants he resorts to pidgin, which is then transcribed in English subtitles. The specifically Nigerian character of this linguistic dexterity may seem to challenge our earlier proposition that the videofilm practice is not scored on a national scale, but this is only apparently so. Indeed, the linguistic deployment suggests an audience that goes beyond Nigeria in a manner rare even in U.S. cinema, with its closed circuit of recyclable stars, as does the very inclusion of British actors who then become part of a vast imaginary as aspiring personalities in a cinematic tradition inconceivable on the old national model.[15]

The world of migrants that these films address may be visibly and largely the Euro-American one of their addressees' physical residency, but this essay argues for something more expansive and spatially promiscuous: the condition of expatriation that comes with a sense of simultaneous cultural affiliation that is increasingly the lot of many people in the world today, whether mobile or sedentary. Nigerian films appeal to other Africans partly because of their approach to the question of artistic representation. The most generically obvious way to talk about this approach is the so-called melodramatic mode, but—and this is the interesting aspect of the choice—the history of its systematization is, first, the history of the encounters between Nigerian cinema and television and American and Hindi films, and second, the aesthetic dimension of affect. The first is the one sense in which comparing Nollywood to Hollywood and Bollywood may be difficult to impeach; the second is conceptually deducible from the old, much-abused notion of African communalism, with its assumption of altruism as a moral imperative.

The point here is not that the two films we are discussing embody a communal ethic—far from it!—but that the conceptual grasp of the melodramatic pattern in Nigerian videofilms which the films display is partly a result of an inclusive morality that philosophically grew out of what is defined as communalism.[16] The fact that immigration—or, broadly speaking, migration—happens within the wider context of other changes, such as the transnationalization of capital and the ongoing democratization of technologies, ought to suggest to us that the assumption of comparative advantage often associated with metropolitan residency, while still valid, is being undermined by the no less valid diffusion of metropolises. To that extent, the interest of a Nigerian immigrant based in Houston, Texas, in the social reality of Lagos is not simply a moral imperative; it is also a function of realism in a world where Houston is not the only guarantor of opportunities for self-improvement.

Yet, the commercial character of the videofilm form positions it in a relationship to Hollywood and other traditions of commercialized filmmaking that is just as uncanny. The conventions of classical American television drama—establishing shot, continuity editing, shot-reverse-shot —that the videofilms deploy so unselfconsciously sit awkwardly next to trenchant claims of "telling our own stories," often in the same way that oral-traditional narrative styles are sublimated to melodramatic modes. On another level, the use of flashback, which is as old as television drama, has now acquired a particularly imaginative force, as the monotony of a village scene is relieved by constant recourse to encounters in London, usually in the guise of different characters remembering the past. What is at stake in these acts of simultaneous distancing from and rapport with the powerful ideological apparatus of filmmaking?

In a densely analytical discussion of the reception of Chinese films outside of their primary context of reference, Rey Chow argues that artistic forms circulating within the frame of cross-cultural exchange are caught in the "deadlock of the anthropological situation" (176). This is the practice linked to colonialism whereby even the supposedly objective or progressive program represented by the "Western" anthropologist engages (results in) the transformation of cultures thus encountered. The classic anthropological scene is a premise of inequality, and, Chow continues, "it is in response to this fundamentally unequal and unfair situation of knowledge organization and distribution of the postcolonial world that criticisms of contemporary Chinese films' 'betrayal' of 'China' have been made" (178). She makes the interesting point—resonant with the Nigerian injunction of telling our own stories—that charges of "betrayal" and cultural "infidelity" presumed in such criticisms merely reinforce the deadlock of the anthropological situation. Focusing on visuality, "the state of to-be looked-at-ness" (as she phrases it, leaning on Laura Mulvey), represents a way out of the deadlock, especially since the grounding of film on surfaces rather than in depth draws attention to the subjective origins of ethnography. This move is integral to Chow's argument for a new ethnography which destroys the operational premises of classical anthropology, when the distinction between "us" and "them" is no longer sustainable.

Staged secondarily to debunk such conventional notions as "original," "derivations," and "intention" that have shaped translation as a profession, Chow's discussion of cultural translation draws on and critiques theoretical ideas about translation (Benjamin, De Man, Tejaswini Niranjana) that establish this profession's link with nineteenth-century anthropology. The present essay will not pursue this secondary critique. Also, her shift of focus from elite scholastic culture to mass culture seems like an ironic reproduction of the polarization that her critique sets out to dismantle, just as the suggestion that East and West are "equally decadent participants in contemporary world culture" (195) could do with more finessing. Nonetheless, the central concern in her essay with visuality's strategic power in the dissemination of cultural forms across geographical boundaries complements the impulse to aesthetic pluralism contained in Jameson's argument. The loaded word "commodification" makes an appearance in this regard, for it holds out the promise of weakening that the culture of philosophical profundity requires to transcend the myopic discourses of origin and naturalization undergirding classical anthropology. The analysis is instructive for our discussion of the career of Nigerian films in the plural context of relocation, for the precise reason that the profanity of commodification is an opportunity for survival, assuming that the false claims of originality and purity of cultures are compromised in the process.

For the Nigerian films have not quite begun to engage the global audience with any rigor, even if the kind of transnational imagining which puts British actors on the screen in roles that go beyond the exotic in Nigerian productions is hardly contemplated in the better-canonized African cinema. Within the same move, the particularity or limited world-readability of videofilms suggests conformity to one of the stipulated features of Third Cinema, which is the latter's ability to deal with subjects for which the "System" has no use. The reality is that since global inter-mediation has displaced the segmentation of cinematic practices along the cold war model of ideologically incommensurate "worlds," an active or emergent "market" like Nollywood faces issues of translatability, standardization, and access in contexts that are no longer discrete. Two prior formations—traveling African films and Bollywood diasporic productions —remain relevant in working out the terms of this negotiation. These two formations define the path that Nigerian films have to tread, even if not in exactly the same ways.

The foreign market was part of the context of reception of African films right from inception. Indeed, the fact that an adversarial form is funded and distributed by the cultural-ideological forces it was designed to undermine is one of the curious paradoxes of this cinematic tradition. In the mid-1980s, this global circulation coincided historically with the institutionalization of a multicultural curriculum in the U.S. and the cultural politics of the French Ministry of Cooperation. This has produced the powerful result of positing the critique of institutions—economic, cultural, religious—as the dominant tendency in African cinema, especially when received, as they often are, within the metropolitan frame, where such critiques resonate with old and actually existing anticolonial politics of Marxist and other persuasions. In cases where this trend is, in its turn, subject to critique (for example as a way of addressing the commercial viability of African films), the tendency on the part of some articulate directors has been to attack *politicalness*, narrowly defined, as the great disabler of popular success, and then resort to the comic or the allegorical mode as the aesthetic alternative.[17]

After forty years of sustained existence, African films continue to circulate mostly through festivals both outside and inside the continent. The individual careers of filmmakers such as Ousmane Sembène, Souleymane Cissé, and Gaston Kabore are well established, but with the possible exception of Sembène, this is largely in scholarly terms. As any teacher of African films will testify, there is little problem in accessing francophone African films for classroom instruction. The problem lies in their adaptability to current technology, the fact that the films still exist in video format, thus making teaching them more arduous than if they were to be in digital format. This is a question of their viability as commercial products: if they had such market appeal and existed in a wider network of cultural circulation, it would be far less difficult to market them as DVDs. After the 2005 FESPACO, it was announced that all of Sembène's films would be available in digital form; those who are interested are still waiting to see this happen. Meanwhile, the film *Tsotsi*, winner of the 2006 Academy Award for the Best Foreign Language Film, was immediately available for theatrical release, and later on DVD.

Some years ago, attempting to examine the career of African films in the circumscribed context of festival screenings, Manthia Diawara wrote that "for international cinema, the Lincoln Center [in New York City] has been a sure passageway to commercial theaters; a testing ground for cinephiles and distributors with their eyes open for foreign films that would go over well with American spectators" (394). The point is not so much what the American public wants; the success of a foreign film is not guaranteed in the commercial quantity that Diawara had in mind. The point has to do with something a little more complex: how the presence of Africans in much of Western Europe and North America can guarantee a space of translation for an aesthetically incremental form like the Nigerian cinema. Even if the Nigerian producers and directors do not wish to travel the exact road of well-known African cineastes, this example remains a reference point in terms of how to access this international arena. Their reputation so far points to yet another possibility of cultural eclecticism, the combination of popular success and the existence of the kind of diasporic audience that sustains Bollywood films outside of the Indian subcontinent.

Even as far back as the 1980s, when the global economy was barely recovering from the slump of the previous decade, the cinema of India was the country's sixth largest industry, grossing $600 million annually and employing 300,000 people. It had begun in 1913, long before the invention of the television; by the beginning of the seventies over 15,000 titles had been produced (Mishra 1), and the generic conventions by which Hindi films are now universally known were already stabilized. Indian cinema went through the silent era alongside the rest of the filmmaking world, although the country did not become politically self-governing until 1947. It was not an economic necessity in the manner of the Nigerian phenomenon. India as a country may share postcolonial status with African, South American, and Caribbean countries; in the area of filmmaking, it ranks closer to the United States.

It is also the case that the South Asian diaspora, dating back to the nineteenth century formation of indentured labor migration and supplemented by the post-1960 expatriation of skilled labor to the U.S., Canada, England, and other places, is more coherent (even if internally differentiated) in terms of historical memory than the African immigrant communities in all their segmentations. Vijay Mishra argues that the diaspora of the 1960s—what he calls the "diaspora of late capital"—is very different from the nineteenth-century labor migration, which was peasant-based and connected to the plantation system.[18] There is a close connection between this diasporic tradition and Bollywood as a cultural form, especially the later formation connected with skilled labor in the computer sector. The existence of the Indian or South Asian diaspora, according to Mishra, has always been constitutive of the different aesthetic practices imaginable within Bollywood cinema. In other words, the themes, ideas, and narrative patterns that have become characteristic of this cinematic tradition draw their inspiration from the projections of the audiences that exist in the diaspora, especially in North America. Anthony Alessandrini is emphatic in stating that "members of the [South Asian] diaspora have increasingly formed an important part of the primary audience for the Indian popular film industry" (317).

Alessandrini is fascinated by the example of *Hum Aapke Hain Koun!* (Who Am I to You, retitled *Yours Forever*), a successful Bollywood film that rids itself of the classical features of the form, and celebrates India's policy of liberalization in moves that could also be perceived as simultaneously playing to the desires of diasporic audiences for whom the results of such liberalization have long been a fact of life. There is also the example of *Dilwale Dulhania Le Jayenge* (Lovers Win Brides, 1995), a film that Mishra describes as "the seminal text about diasporic representation and consumption of Indian popular culture" (250). In their different ways, these films insinuate themselves into the complex relations "between the fantasies of the homeland and the self-legitimacy that underpins diasporic lives." More recently, there is the spectacular *Lagaan* (nominated for Best Foreign Language Film in the U.S. in 2003), a work that plays consciously for a diasporic audience—its narrative technique and use of the conceit of cricket is linguistically Hollywood, and in this it reminds the viewer of the genre of sports film—even though its principal theme is the unity of India. Add to these the works of diasporic Indians/South Asians, such as Mira Nair's *Mississippi Masala* (1992), Gurinder Chadha's *Bend It like Beckham* (2003) and *Bride and Prejudice* (2005), and Deepa Mehta's *Bollywood/Hollywood* (2002), and one has the distinct sense of different films having little in common outside of their being figured as belonging to a diasporic community broadly conceived.

At any rate, there is something at stake: the films' interpellation of a vast and eclectic community, a spectatorship for which, in the words of Mishra, Bollywood cinema is "one of the key translatable signs in the diasporic production and reproduction of India" (237).[19] Apart from its extensive use of Bollywood song-and-dance sequences, Chadha's *Bride and Prejudice* contains a poignant scene parodying Bollywood through the superimposition of characters against a theater screen image of a Hindi film. Instructively, Mishra concludes his discussion with the following words: "a study of Bombay cinema will no longer be complete without a theory of diasporic desire because this cinema is now global in a specifically diasporic sense" (269).

*   *   *

In the *New York Times* issue of April 7, 2004, the Critic's Notebook column devoted two-thirds of the broadsheet's page to five films from Africa (Mitchell 3). It was a feature piece on the year's edition of the New York African Film Festival, organized by Mahen Bonetti since 1993, and the 2004 edition had presented a mid-career retrospective on the career of the Nigerian producer-director Kelani. Of the five, only Kelani's *Agogo Eewo*, with which the article opened, was a feature; some of the documentaries were part of the package in the traveling series referred to at the beginning of this essay. The writer allotted three paragraphs to each film, commenting generally on their plots with no attempt at contextualization or even the suggestion of a common purpose framed in the continental address of the title. But there was this sentence, following the review of the drama from Nigeria: "The most captivating films in this year's African Film Festival build on tribal traditions and add a gleaming spire of modernism," the reviewer noted, and moved on to summarize Craig and Damon Foster's *Cosmic Africa*. What makes this feature article beguiling, apart from its liberal use of the word "tribal," is its fixation on the video format of the films, proof that for even the most sympathetic viewers the politics of formatting is inseparable from aesthetical issues.

There is another subtle point—that of a common frame of reception, the liberal, educated interest of elitist New York, which speaks of a documentary about a dreamy astrophysicist in the same breath as the routine of mural paintings in Burkina Faso (*Traces: Women's Imprint*) and the tragedy of racial entitlement in East Germany (*Dirt for Dinner*). In this context, savvy and potentially homogenizing, it is legitimate to wonder about the impact of these films outside of the Lincoln Center, although the fact that the traveling package made it to Cornell within a year reflects the complications of the commercial theater scene Diawara envisaged the previous decade.

Whatever future is imagined for the films currently being made by and for Nigerians, it seems that they cannot avoid an interest in the sense of self projected by the communities currently developing outside the continent and retaining, in whatever form, a sense of familiarity with an increasingly nebulous but still imaginable diaspora. Indeed, borrowing a leaf from the book of the Indian diaspora, it is very likely that the cinema, whether of the distinctly Nigerian or "African" variety, will constitute the tool for enduringly working this imagination. It may be a long time before a Nollywood film comes to theaters everywhere in the continental U.S., should that constitute a point of interest for a filmmaker. Nor is there any guarantee that the Nigerian model is exportable right from Lagos. Indeed, more imaginative use of the cinema than is currently attempted by Nigerian filmmakers is required for presenting stories that go beyond mere curiosity or local interest, and neither *Osuofia in London* nor *Dangerous Twins* is the correct model for such a cinema. Not yet, or not quite yet.

It is, however, not beyond imagination that the preoccupations of Nigerian films—their interest in real life issues, however extraordinary the circumstances; their eclectic appeal to emergent global consciousnesses; their exhortatory signification of ethical issues—find identification among Nigerian, African, and other human populations at home in a world no longer conceived in strictly "national" terms. The historic coalescence of technological forms suited to affordability, portability, and instantaneity on the one hand, and large-scale movement or dispersal of peoples on the other hand, should make the idea of cultural translation, rather than simple standardization, particularly attractive. It is easy enough to overstate the relevance of the films coming out of Nigeria, but the extravagance is entirely justified by the current appeal of the phenomenon.

NOTES

1. Other films in the traveling series included *Madame Brouette* by the Senegalese filmmaker Sene Musa Absa, *Cosmic Africa* by Craig and Damon Foster (from South Africa), and *Dirt for Dinner* by Branwen Okpako, a Nigerian-born filmmaker based in Germany.

2. Although no empirical study of the reception of these films exists as yet, this assertion is based on two recent developments, among others: the formation of the Filmmakers Association of Nigeria in Washington, D.C., in 2003, and a listeners' survey carried out by the British Broadcasting Corporation. See http://news .bbc.co.uk/go/em/fr/-/1/hi/world/africa/4524458.stm . The phrase "world-readable" is taken from James English (*The Economy of Prestige,* 319). Although English is speaking specifically about how a text grounded in the identity of a "subnational" culture (Maori out of New Zealand) transcends the national literary culture, there are implications in his argument for the cultural translation of artistic forms within the global economy of prizing and conferment of prestige.

3. Certainly, expressions such as "standardization" and "commodification" raise immediate questions about what pass for standards, especially in terms of cultural productions and the notions of difference and valuation that attend them. The Frankfurt School tendency, set forth in the works of Max Horkheimer and Theodor Adorno, is well known for its valuation of high art, against which mass culture is perceived as a betrayal. This powerful critique continues to be sustained in different ways, most recently by David Harvey (*Spaces of Capital*). On the other hand, Huyssen (*After the Great Divide*) posits a more nuanced view of the division from the standpoint of postmodernism. This essay occupies the middle ground between dismissals and celebrations of commodification for rea-

sons that will become clearer in the writing. The sense in which standardization is used here relates rather to formal or presentational aspects of cinematic works—running time, date, visual packaging, and other descriptive data—which do not usually figure in the production designs of Nigerian films.

4. There is something close to a genre in films dealing with this theme, including *One Dollar, Olowo America* (The Moneybag from America), and *Dollar from Germany*. Sola Osofisan's *Missing in America* (2004) explores the theme from the perspective of a Nigerian woman determined to locate her husband in the U.S.

5. Citing a certain Olga Maitland of IAMTN [International Association Money Transfer in Nigeria?], the online daily bulletin *Nigeria Today Online* reported that "Nigerians in the diaspora have remitted at least US$28 billion over the last eight years. Experts have estimated that the true amount including money moving through informal channels is probably four times that amount, i.e. US$112 billion over the same period. Remittance flows to Nigeria account for approximately 5% of Nigeria's GDP, according to Maitland." (*Nigeria Today Online*, February 22, 2006).

6. One of the features of the films is based on this trend, the structuring of the template of a film on the attraction of an actor, in three distinct formations: the glamorous individual, the performer of known idiolects, and the physically incongruous. The two first formations apply to the films at hand. For detailed discussion of these features, see Adesokan, "Worlds That Flourish," chapter 2.

7. See Haynes, *Nigerian Videofilms*; Okome, "Writing the Anxious City"; and McCall, "Juju and Justice," "Nollywood Confidential."

8. The subject of the subsistence of Africa films on foreign patronage is an important one, but it can also become over-flogged. For insightful discussions, see Diawara, "On Tracking African Cinema"; Ukadike, "New Developments"; Mermin, "A Window on Whose Reality?"; and Akudinobi, "Survival Instincts."

9. See Haynes and Okome, especially 24–26; Ukadike, "Video Boom" 128.

10. See Belasco, *The Entrepreneur as Culture Hero*; Falola and Ihonvbere, *The Rise and Fall*; Osaghae, *The Crippled Giant*.

11. Both films are in two parts, a trend of sequels that has been traced to the partial origin of the videofilm phenomenon in television soap operas. See Adesokan, "How *They* See It" 195.

12. In this respect, the soundtrack that accompanies Osuofia's arrival in London is telling, because the tune, "Englishman in New York," originally by the British pop star Sting, was re-dubbed into a Nigerian version in the late 1980s by Ms. Esse Agesse, who later married Kingsley Ogoro, the film's producer-director, when he was a music video producer. By this move, the producer positions the tune and the scene in this metropolitan context, while avoiding the possible copyright issues attached to the use of the song, which now purportedly belongs to his wife.

13. The actor first formalized the screen name as "Osuofiasn" in *Ikuku: The Wind* (1995), Part I of which he directed. In this film, he is one of two brothers, and he plays the role of a village drunk who styles himself "Osuofiasn." Before this film, Owoh's screen-name was Markus.

14. For purposes of consistency, the essay will refer to the characters by their identities before the swap.

15. In this respect, the experience of a British producer, Nick Moran, and his misbegotten attempt to shoot a documentary of Nollywood is instructive. For an account of his saga, see http://film.guardian.co.uk/features/featurepages/0,4120,1126184,00.html (accessed June 14, 2006).

16. The philosopher Kwasi Wiredu has written: "A communalist society is one in which an individual is brought up to cultivate an intimate sense of obligation and belonging to quite large groups of people on the basis of kinship affiliations. This inculcation of an extensive sense of the human bonds provides a natural school for the enlargement of sympathies, which stretches out beyond the limits of kinship to the wider community" (185).

17. In this sense, it may not be simple coincidence that two films which represent either tendency, Ngangura Mweze's *La Vie est Belle* and Souleymane Cisse's *Yeelen* (Brightness) both came out in 1987.

18. See Mishra 235 for useful statistics.

19. One might also recall the featuring of some Bollywood classics on the American network channel Turner Classic Movies over three weeks in the summer of 2003, the entire series introduced by the late Ismail Merchant.

FILMOGRAPHY

Agogo Eewo (The Sacred Gong). Dir. Tunde Kelani. Mainframe Productions, Yoruba (with English subtitles), 1 hr. 40 mins., PAL, 2002.
Dangerous Twins I and *II*. Dir. Tade Ogidan. Ogali Productions, English, approx. 3 hrs. 45 mins., VCD/DVD, 2004.
Dead Ringers. Dir. David Cronenberg. Media Home Entertainment, 117 mins., VHS, color, 1989.
Ikuku (The Wind I and II). Dir. Nkem Owoh, Zeb Ejiro. Andy Best Productions, English/Igbo (with English subtitles), VCD/DVD, 1995.
Living in Bondage I and *II*. Dir. Kenneth Nnebue. NEK Video Link, Igbo and English (with subtitles), approx. 4 hrs., PAL, 1992.
Madame Brouette. Dir. Moussa Sene Absa. Senegal, 104 mins., 2002.
Missing in America. Dir. Sola Osofisan. Creative Chronicles and Concepts Inc., U.S./Nigeria, 109 mins., DVD, color, 2004.
Osuofia in London (I and II). Dir. Kingsley Ogoro. Kingsley Ogoro Productions, English, approx. 3 hrs. 12 mins., VCD, 2004.
Saworoide (Brass Bells). Dir. Tunde Kelani. Mainframe Productions, Yoruba (with English subtitles), 1 hr. 35 mins., PAL, 1999.

REFERENCES

Adesokan, Akin. "'How *They* See It': The Politics and Aesthetics of Nigerian Video Films." In *African Drama and Performance*, ed. John Conteh-Morgan and Tejumola Olaniyan. Bloomington: Indiana University Press, 2004. 189–197.
——. "Worlds That Flourish: Postnational Aesthetics in Nigerian Videofilms, African Cinema, and Diasporic Black Writings." PhD diss., Cornell University, 2005.

Akudinobi, Jude G. "Survival Instincts: Resistance, Accommodation and Contemporary African Cinema." *Social Identities* 3, no. 1 (1997): 91–121.

Alessandrini, Anthony C. "'My Heart's Indian for All That': Bollywood Film between Home and Diaspora." *Diaspora* 10, no. 3 (2001): 315–340.

Anderson, Benedict. *Specter of Comparison.* London: Verso, 1998.

Appadurai, Arjun. *Modernity at Large: Cultural Dimensions of Globalization.* Minneapolis: University of Minnesota Press, 1996.

Belasco, Bernard. *The Entrepreneur as Culture Hero: Preadaptation in Nigerian Economic Development.* New York: Praeger, 1980.

Chow, Rey. *Primitive Passions: Visuality, Sexuality, Ethnography, and Contemporary Chinese Cinema.* New York: Columbia University Press, 1995.

Désir, Dorothy. "In Spite of Modernity: Interview with Tunde Kelani." In *Through African Eyes: Dialogues with the Directors,* ed. Mahen Bonetti and Prerana Reddy. New York: NYAFF, 2003. 105–110.

Diawara, Manthia. "On Tracking African Cinema at World Film Festivals." *Public Culture* 6 (1994): 385–396.

English, James. *The Economy of Prestige.* Cambridge, Mass.: Harvard University Press, 2005.

Falola, Toyin, and Julius Ihonvbere. *The Rise and Fall of Nigeria's Second Republic.* London: Zed, 1985.

Harvey, David. *Spaces of Capital: Towards a Critical Geography.* New York: Routledge, 2001.

Haynes, Jonathan. "Nigerian Cinema: Structural Adjustments." *Research in African Literatures* 26, no. 3 (1995): 97–119.

Haynes, Jonathan, and Onookome Okome. "Evolving Popular Media: Nigerian Video Films." In *Nigerian Videofilms,* ed. Jonathan Haynes. Jos, Nigeria: Nigerian Film Corp., 1997.

Hibou, Beatrice. "The 'Social Capital' of the State as an Agent of Deception: Or the Ruses of Economic Intelligence." *The Criminalization of the State in Africa,* ed. Jean-Francois Bayart, Beatrice Hibou, and Stephen Ellis. Bloomington: Indiana University Press, 1999. 69–113.

Horkheimer, Max, and Theodor Adorno. "The Culture Industry: Enlightenment as Mass Deception." In *Dialectics of Enlightenment,* trans. John Cumming. New York: Continuum, 1989. 120–167.

Huyssen, Andreas. *After the Great Divide: Modernism, Mass Culture, and Postmodernism.* Bloomington: Indiana University Press, 1986.

Jameson, Fredric. "Globalization as a Philosophical Issue." In *The Cultures of Globalization,* ed. Fredric Jameson and Masao Miyoshi. Durham, N.C.: Duke University Press, 1994. 54–77.

McCall, John C. "Juju and Justice at the Movies: Vigilantes in Nigerian Popular Videos." *African Studies Review* 47, no. 3 (2004): 51–67.

———. "Nollywood Confidential: The Unlikely Rise of Nigerian Video Films." *Transition* 95 (2004): 98–109.

Mermin, Elizabeth. "A Window on Whose Reality? The Emerging Industry of Senegalese Cinema." *Research in African Literatures* 26, no. 3 (1995): 120–133.

Mishra, Vijay. *Bollywood Cinema: Temples of Desire.* New York: Routledge, 2002.

Mitchell, Elvis. "From Village Huts to the Cosmos: Filmmakers on Africa." *New York Times,* April 7, 2004, E3.

Moran, Nick. "Nollywood or Bust: Lock, Stock Star." *Guardian* (UK), January 19, 2004. http://film.guardian.co.uk/features/featurepages/0,4120,1126184,00.html (accessed June 14, 2006).

Okome, Onookome. "Writing the Anxious City: Images of Lagos in Nigerian Home Video Films." *Black Renaissance/Renaissance Noire* 5, no. 2 (2003): 65–75.

Osaghae, Eghosa. *The Crippled Giant: Nigeria since Independence.* Bloomington: Indiana University Press, 1998.

Sklair, Leslie. *The Sociology of the Global System.* Baltimore, Md.: Johns Hopkins University Press, 1991.

Solanas, Fernando, and Octavio Getino. "Towards a Third Cinema." In *Movies and Methods,* ed. Bill Nichols. Los Angeles: University of California Press, 1976. 44–64.

Ukadike, N. Frank. "New Developments in Black African Cinema." In *Reading the Contemporary: African Art from Theory to the Marketplace,* ed. Olu Oguibe and Okwui Enwezor. London and Cambridge, Mass.: Iniva and MIT Press, 1999. 166–213.

———. *Questioning African Cinema: Conversations with Filmmakers.* Minneapolis: University of Minnesota Press, 2002.

———."Video Boom and the Manifestations of 'First' Cinema in Anglophone Africa." In *Rethinking Third Cinema,* ed. Anthony R. Guneratne and Wimal Dissanayake. New York: Routledge, 2003. 126–143.

Wiredu, Kwasi. "Our Problem of Knowledge: Brief Reflections on Knowledge and Development in Africa." In *African Philosophy as Cultural Inquiry,* ed. Ivan Karp and D. A. Masolo. Bloomington: Indiana University Press, 2000. 181–186.

21 FROM THE NEW DIASPORA AND THE CONTINENT: AFRICAN AMERICAN RETURN FIGURATIONS

Joseph McLaren

African writers who have resided in the diaspora have been faced with the challenge of writing about their nations from the distance of the Atlantic, and some of these writers have also engaged the diaspora, creating images and characters drawn from old diaspora representations often relating to "return to the motherland" motifs. Certain African fiction writers from the classic foundational period, writers who have had a long residence in the West, such as Chinua Achebe and Ngugi wa Thiong'o, have yet to fully configure in a novelistic work diaspora representations, whether of the "old" or "new" categorizations. For the most part, Achebe and Ngugi have continued to address national concerns or continental ones from their positions in the diaspora. In contrast, well-known writers such as Ama Ata Aidoo, Ayi Kwei Armah, and Buchi Emecheta have drawn diaspora representations.

Although Nigerians represent the greatest number of new diasporans in the United States, Ghanaian writers pioneered treatments of old diasporan returnees. Aidoo's play *The Dilemma of a Ghost* (1964) is a seminal work in a unique genre of diaspora representation, treatment of the African American returning to the continent. Armah, who earned a degree in sociology from Harvard and an MFA from Columbia, and who taught at the University of Massachusetts and the University of Wisconsin, ultimately returned to the continent. From his current vantage point in Popenguine, Senegal—some 45 kilometers from Dakar—his new "African" home, Armah has in his later works charted, like Kofi Awoonor, the old diasporan returnee. A variation of this figure can be found in Armah's earlier novel *Fragments*, which focuses on the "been-to" character—a continental African who visits the West and returns to the homeland—but also develops a Puerto Rican woman doctor. The novel is a continuation of Armah's neocolonial criticism found in *The Beautyful Ones Are Not Yet Born* (1968), which addresses national issues and the spoiled fruits of independence. In *Fragments*, the "been-to" Baako fails to achieve a harmonious reintegration. Armah's novel *Osiris Rising* (1995) shows a diaspora-influenced inclination, as does Awoonor's *Comes the Voyager at Last: A Tale of Return to Africa* (1992), which represents Ghana as a primary site of return. Ghanaian poet Kofi Anyidoho, in *Ancestrallogic and Caribbean-blues* (1993), also addresses the diaspora through imagery and metaphor.

Complementing Ghanaian authors, Nigerian writers have also portrayed migration themes. Buchi Emecheta's *Second-Class Citizen* (1974), *Gwendolyn* (1989; also published as *The Family*, 1990), and *Kehinde* (1994) suggest diaspora engagement through depictions of England and Jamaica. Ike Oguine, of the emerging generation of Nigerian writers, has in *A Squatter's Tale* (2000) met the challenge of depicting new diasporans in the United States. Most important, the publication of Isidore Okpewho's *Call Me by My Rightful Name* (2004) suggests that a Nigerian writer using perspectives of Yoruba culture can offer a complex rendering of the "return motif" through characterizations of African Americans.

In addition to the more well-known African writers residing in the West, there is a group that can be categorized as academic-creative writers because they are literary scholars and university professors in addition to being creative artists. Like Okpewho, many in this group are Nigerian and have resided in the United States for a decade or more.[1] Their reasons for migrating vary, from educational opportunity to family necessities to political causes, the latter influencing novelist Phanuel Egejuru's exile (Egejuru, Survey). Okpewho left Nigeria in order to secure a "better climate for working and raising [his] family" (Okpewho, Survey). F. Odun Balogun identified family reasons and the structural adjustment programs in Nigeria as the causes for remaining in the United States following a fellowship, and the pursuit of higher education was the motivation for Anthonia Kalu and Chimalum Nwankwo. Dramatist Tess Onwueme, whose play *The Broken Calabash* was successfully produced at Wayne State University in Detroit, won a Martin Luther King, Jr., Distinguished Writers/Scholars Fellowship (surveys from Balogun; Kalu; Nwankwo; Onwueme). In contrast, poet Niyi Osundare, whose "scholarly articles are read as though possessed by the poetic muse" and who was caught in the Katrina catastrophe in New Orleans, has not made a permanent migration to the United States: "I have never 'migrated', and so do not see myself as belonging to any 'New Diaspora'" (Na'Allah xxv; Osundare, Survey). Another Nigerian poet, Tanure Ojaide, writes about his "immediate reality and . . . on happenings in the US" (Ojaide, Survey).

Balogun's experience in the United States motivated his as-yet-unpublished novel, "The Call of the West." His goal is to "chronicle the experience of the new diaspora such that its universal human essence is captured and held out for viewing by both the people I now live among and those I left behind in the old home" (Balogun, Survey). Balogun's short story collection, *Adjusted Lives* (1995), contains pieces that explore diaspora spaces, such as "The Hyde Park Preacher," in which the central character Ogunmola, having been in London for five years, is heartened and challenged by the words of a Nigerian preaching at Hyde Park. The preacher urges the return to Nigeria and questions the presence of Africans in the West but also considers the merits of acquiring Western technology: "These are three millions of the best sons and daughters of Africa!" (Balogun, *Adjusted Lives* 65).

Onwueme, whose residence in the diaspora "provoked [her] to write two plays," *Riot in Heaven* (1996) and *The Missing Face* (2000), notes, "America and my Africa broaden, nurture each other as they share a symbiotic relationship and cross-fertilize each other" (Onwueme, Survey). Similarly, Okey Ndibe's *Arrows of Rain* (2000) "would have been a different novel (and almost certainly weaker)" had it been written in Nigeria (Ndibe, Survey).

Okpewho, who remarked in an interview, "it is difficult to show if I am primarily a creative writer or scholar. . . . I find myself more at home with creative writing than scholarship" (Ohaeto 129), also acknowledges the effects of diaspora experience: "my imagination has been broadened, so that I see the events in my country of origin within a larger cultural context" (Okpewho, Survey). Political, social, and cultural realities of the diaspora can influence writers who consider it a "temporary perch" and Nigeria as "home," as with Osundare, who has imbibed African American cultural elements; some of these can be found in his poem "The Weeping Book" and are suggested as well in his poem "For Tom Dent," a tribute to the deceased African American poet, activist, and director of the New Orleans Jazz and Heritage Foundation: "Who will heal the tall sadness of your absence / the silences which astonish my ears" (Osundare, *Pages from the Book* 51). As Osundare has observed, "my contact with African American culture at close quarters has deepened my understanding of Black culture and my appreciation of its complexity" (Osundare, Survey). Nigerian poet Nwankwo uses African American political motifs, a sign of his Pan-African "inclinations," as in his poem "When the Soul Train Parks (Song for Rosa Parks)": "The last soul train has parked smoothly / And the roses are there now for Rosa Parks" (Nwankwo, Survey; "When the Soul Train").

OSIRIS RISING: AFROCENTRICITY AND RETURN

Migration and residence in the West, whether permanent or temporary, can expand a writer's choice of literary themes and characterizations beyond those representing continental Africa. This can be observed in the work of certain African fiction writers who have portrayed "been-to's" or, less frequently, old diasporans who return to the motherland. Among the academic–creative writers in the diaspora, Okpewho can be paralleled to Armah because they both employ specific cultural or mythological paradigms in framing diaspora consciousness and return motifs. How do these two authors, representing different decisions of residency and selections of African cultural sources, configure African American characterizations? In framing diasporans, African writers face the challenge of authenticating black voices and of representing "New World" cultural and political elements such as jazz, racial identity, black vernaculars, and Afrocentricity.

Armah's *Osiris Rising* (1995), his sixth novel, raises important questions about return narratives—the treatment of collective memory of the slave trade, the adaptation to traditional culture, Pan-African politics, and neocolonialism. In dealing with political issues and characters who represent these issues, Armah has been faulted by certain critics who claim that "the artistic integrity of the novel is compromised by the need to tell a political tale" (Perrin 249). However, this kind of criticism does not take into account the mythmaking intentions of Armah, his mining of Afrocentric sources, and the importance of political concerns throughout Armah's work. *Osiris Rising* can be linked to *Two Thousand Seasons* and *The Healers* in that "it moves backward to the African past to borrow a myth to reconstruct the history of Africa and make projections about its present and future" (Agho, book cover, *Osiris Rising*). In *Osiris Rising*, Armah's portrayal of an African American woman's journey uses "Africa's oldest source" of Isis and Osiris, part of the Afrocentric canon, to craft a work that can be paralleled to narrative structures of other return narratives; as in *Fragments*, the returning character is a woman. One central issue is the adaptation to traditional culture by those who have been separated by time and other factors from African indigenous languages and rituals, those in the diaspora who have developed identities that are, in part, distinctly diasporic. Also, contemporary African political concerns resulting from neocolonialism and cultural imperialism provide an underlying context for measuring romanticized versus realistic depictions of the return trope. Armah's narrative considers the political cohesion of Africa and its relationship to global dilemmas. Another aspect of the novel is its mode of production. It was published in Popenguine by Per Ankh publishers, a group of Armah's associates "committed to the emergence of a quality African book industry" (book cover, *Osiris Rising*).

Osiris Rising develops the return motif by dealing with contemporary issues, and although no specific time frame is given, nor is an African country designated in the opening, the general impression is that of a return to a contemporary West African state. Like *Two Thousand Seasons* and *The Healers*, *Osiris Rising* is also concerned with the way Africa has lost a historical legacy that existed prior to European contact. The earlier Armah novels, produced in the seventies during his stay in Tanzania, are ironic reflections of Nyerere's *Ujamaa*, though Armah was critical of Ujamaa, and may also project "traditional heroism" as in Thomas Mofolo's *Chaka* (Ogede 440, 441). *Osiris Rising* is also similar to certain political analyses of Africa, in that it focuses on the external and internal factors that have resulted in state and societal predicaments. In this way, the novel can be viewed as a political text that mirrors the kind of analysis found in Ghanaian George B. N. Ayittey's *Africa in Chaos* (1998), in which neocolonial states and their leaders are targeted as causes for dilemmas in contemporary Africa. Ayittey views late twentieth-century Africa as affected by the powerful few: "Modern Africa, by contrast, is the abode of the elites, the parasitic minority group. This sector is a meretricious burlesque, operating by an assortment of imported or borrowed institutions" (Ayittey 16). In *Osiris Rising*, Armah's targeting of certain university intellectuals as the source of the new cultural transition mirrors in part Ayittey's "internalist" thesis.[2]

Osiris Rising functions on a number of levels. The chapters are named after figures in ancient Egyptian culture and religion, such as Nwt or Nut, the sky-goddess. At once, Armah offers a love story, a narrative of ideas, a political statement against neocolonial regimes, a satire of the legacy of colonial education, a parable based on the Isis-Osiris story of Egyptian religion, and, as in *The Healers*, a historical parable. For Armah, "A sense of the past is an essential guide to the present and the future, and is best enhanced by knowledge of African languages." His study of both Kiswahili and Egyptian hieroglyphics are signs of this interest (Ogede 443).

In certain respects, *Osiris Rising* mirrors Armah himself—the disaffection with neocolonial Ghana and the rejection of a university career in the West to pursue an activist role on the continent. Like Asar, the revolutionary-intellectual of the novel, Armah also connected with liberation movements, evidenced by his work in 1963 in Algeria as a translator for *Revolution Africaine*. Also, like the principal female character Ast, Armah pursued a study of Egyptian hieroglyphics and history. His fictional legacy shows a "deepening suspicion of all conceptual systems derived from Europe and their concomitant literary styles and techniques" (Wright 4–5).

The theme of internal state repression and the struggle by African intellectuals and university professors to turn the tide of corruption is the main thrust of the novel. The characters are representations of various positions in this conflict of forces and wills. The main character Ast journeys to Africa primarily because of her disappointment with the cultural life in the United States. Although her mission appears idealistic, she is practical in her wish to teach in a rural area, where she can make a contribution.

Furthermore, Armah presents the state as rapacious and paranoid. The character who represents the security forces is called SSS, an abbreviation for State Security Service, and the character's name, Seth Spencer Soja, plays on the Isis-Osiris figure Set as well as the pidgin word "soja," meaning soldier. SSS, who attempts to rape Ast on her first night of arrival, is bent on thwarting what he perceives as subversive activities. These activities are connected with the teaching role of Asar, who is framed in a romantic and sexual relationship with Ast. Asar, a former revolutionary who has been involved in liberation movements in Zimbabwe, Mozambique, and Angola, is considered a threat. His activities are clearly documented in security directives that identify potential revolutionaries and subversives.

Armah's portrayal of African Americans includes a somewhat satirical development of a would-be messiah, who introduces returning African Americans to the continent. Given a compound name that contains symbolic icons—Ras, Jomo, Cinque, Equiano—he was formerly an activist named Sheldon Tubman (87). Each of the Africans implied in the compound name could be associated with betrayal, and the name Tubman also echoes that of the former Liberian president. Another satiric treatment is in the naming of Sheldon's assistant as the Fake Ethiopian, Prince Wossen of Ethiopia, who is portrayed as a former African American street hustler. (The satirical treatment of African Americans can also be found in the work of Caryl Phillips.) On the other hand, another of his African American characters, artist Don Bailey, is a realist who understands the fakery of Cinque. Bailey's observations point to the realities of African American adjustment and relocation, a negotiation of the complex realities of returning. At one point in the novel, a dentist family is mentioned, a family that relocated with practical goals in mind and achieved a successful expatriate experience, a valorization of certain professional African American expatriates in Ghana and a possible allusion to Dr. Robert "Uncle Bobby" E. Lee, a member of the African American Association of Ghana.

Although the portrayal of Cinque in *Osiris Rising* can be perceived as a satire of African American return, the novel also projects Afrocentricity through ancient African systems signified by teaching activities at Manda and Bara, where the secret society of the ankh is based. The ankh, symbolizing life and infinite continuity, has been associated primarily with Egypt or Kemet. The ankh has also been attributed to Nubians as well as the Twa, the so-called Pygmies of Central Africa in the region of the Great Lakes who, it has been argued, invented the symbol, predating Nubia and Kemet (Ben-Jochannan 294).

In focusing on the ankh as symbol, the novel replicates Afrocentrists such as Molefi Asante and Egyptologists such as Cheikh Anta Diop and Yosef Ben-Jochannan, who have emphasized that Egypt was originally a black land, being obviously part of the African continent. Armah is sup-

portive of Diop's efforts, celebrating his ability to "look at 'the Western intellectual monument,' without being overwhelmed" (Ogede 440). Armah's
voicing of this link to ancient Egypt is a rare affirmation from a West African (anglophone) academic-intellectual, many of whom have challenged
the Afrocentric perspective in its emphasis on Kemetic roots. Afrocentric
ideas are developed in a long section of the novel that details a position
paper of the progressive intellectuals led by Asar. The imbedding of the
position paper within the novel's plot structure suggests Armah's political
agenda, a radical commitment signified by the case for reforming the history department to include the teaching of Egyptian history. Armah also
uses this portion of the novel to project a black revolutionary goal, as seen
in his satirical portrait of white expatriate professors in West African universities.

The satire uses three representative characters, each from a particular
department: African Studies, History, and Literature. Wright Woolley, a
former District Commissioner and head of African Studies, sees the new
curriculum as "the destruction of everything he had worked so hard to
build in this God-forsaken place" (225). The transformation in the English
Department separated English from Literature, thus marginalizing the
Eurocentric curriculum in English, similar to the actual transformations
at Makerere and the University of Nairobi. The new curriculum proposal
sets forth principles to revise the old approaches to African studies that
have been identified as "an ancillary branch of colonial military, administrative and missionary intelligence gathering" (214).

> In place of the old anti-historical approach, we advocate a dynamic con-
> sciousness of history as process. We are for the inclusive use of all sources,
> written and oral.
>   We advocate the reinstatement of Ancient Egypt at the center of Af-
> rican history and culture. We think African Studies programs should em-
> brace the intellectual universe of our entire continent, including Ancient
> Egypt. (215)

In addition to curricular issues, Armah is also concerned with presenting African American characters using black vernacular. Rare among
African novelists, Armah uses both idiomatic and syntactical patterns associated with African American English. Although there are occasional
usages that do not ring true—such as "smuch" for "as much" and the
use of "brang" for the past tense of "bring" ("Folks who brang that head
on us," a remark by the Fake Ethiopian)—for the most part, Armah is familiar with the oral features of African American vernacular (126–127).

Complementing the representation of African Americans is the use
of Egyptian mythology. By evoking the name Osiris in the title, Armah
overtly uses the story of the god Osiris as a mythological parallel to re-

forming the nation-state. Osiris has been termed the son of the sun-god Ra
(Bernal 115), one of four children, the "offspring of an intrigue between the
earth-god Seb . . . and the sky-goddess Nut." Osiris is credited with having brought Egyptian society to a state of enlightenment and the adoration
of gods (Frazer 421), and is also known for having carried out a "civilizing
mission" (Bernal 116). Responsible for spreading methods of cultivation
discovered by his wife and sister Isis, he was captured and dismembered
by his brother Set (Typhon in Greek mythology). Osiris, whose remains
were divided into fourteen pieces and scattered in various places, was res-
urrected by Isis, who found the parts of his body except for his genitals.
The supplement credited to Plutarch suggests resurrection, the reassem-
bling of the pieces of the body: "In the resurrection of Osiris the Egyptians saw the pledge of a life everlasting for themselves beyond the grave"
(Frazer 425–426). Ben-Jochannan argues that the significance of the Osiris
story is in the resemblance of the Madonna and child of Christianity to
Isis and her son Horus (Ben-Jochannan 126).

In the novel, Ast is a parallel to Isis and Asar to Osiris. Ast envisions
Asar as "off on the first of humanizing journeys, carrying not weapons of
destruction but ideas to support new life, images to feed love of universe"
(8). This closely parallels the story of Osiris and his journey throughout
the world to spread civilization and knowledge of agriculture. The character Seth, the security officer, is a replica of Set of the Osiris story, who
kills his brother. The fact that the murder in the novel takes place on a
boat may relate as well to the original story, in which Osiris's body is sent
floating down the Nile, where it becomes encased in a tree.

In his presentation of African American characters, Armah uses Ast
as the ancestral link with the unbroken ankh, that part of the diaspora
legacy that is not implicated in the Atlantic slave trade. She is part of the
unification that can be achieved by the joining of the intellectuals of the
diaspora and those of the continent. On the other hand, Armah's treatment of Cinque and the Fake Ethiopian can be related to the complicity
of Africans in the slave trade. Cinque's attempt to find the source of his
broken ankh is a parallel to Ast's search for the origins of her symbol. Although Cinque and Ast trace their ankh family symbols to African roots,
the significance of their journeys is quite opposite.

As in *Two Thousand Seasons* and *The Healers*, *Osiris Rising* develops the theme of betrayal, signified by connections to the slave trade. This
issue complicates the return narrative inasmuch as the African American or diasporan, like the character Ast or the other African Americans
in *Osiris Rising*, may not necessarily experience the embrace of ancestors but the reality that certain familial linkages may lead to genealogical
ties to slavery rather than resistance. Armah's work shows "individuals
as having personal histories which unfold in ways interconnected with

the processes through which their communities and societies attain self-knowledge" (Osei-Nyame 149).

Armah uses characters to embody history and political positions. Another of his women characters, Tete, is the griot whose extended statement on the secret society of the ankh and the legacy of Cinque's ancestry forms the author's total statement on Africa's past and slavery. Tete's remarks are incantatory, much like the prose of *Two Thousand Seasons*. In her sweeping history, she implies an Afrocentric theory of diffusion in which the ankh symbol, as a sign of Egyptian culture, reaches West Africa and through time emerges in various forms and patterns in parts of the continent. The development of the society of the ankh is linked to retention of ancient values.

> The friendship of the ankh wanted to preserve only the best of our values. We had a civilization. It was prosperous then, but these far seers saw it falling apart, our people degenerating from builders to consumers of gifts they no longer knew how to create, things handed down by more vigorous ancestors. (261)

There are possible allusions here to *Things Fall Apart* (1958) and perhaps Sembene's film and novel *Guelwaar* (1992). The other part of Tete's narrative involves transatlantic slavery and the way Africans were involved with Europeans in capture and trade. This kind of portrait, a major element of *Two Thousand Seasons*, is also developed by Caryl Phillips in the "Heartland" section of *Higher Ground* (1989) and by the African American author Charles Johnson in *Middle Passage* (1990).

As in *The Beautyful Ones Are Not Yet Born* (1968), *Osiris Rising* uses the motif of water and escape. In the earlier novel, the narrator helps a friend associated with the Nkrumah regime escape capture by the coup forces. However, in *Osiris Rising*, a boat is used by Asar to make contact with the town of Bara. The boat is also the site of execution of the progressive forces symbolized by Asar, who is unable to escape capture. The pessimism of the ending of the novel is a direct reversal of the utopian transitions suggested by the position paper of the university intellectuals, which seemed to have effectively transformed the university curriculum. *Osiris Rising* resolves the fate of Asar with his murder by Set, replicating the text of the ancient Egyptian Osiris story. Because the novel ends in an ambiguous way—the state, represented by the security forces, appearing to be victorious—one wonders whether the pessimism reflected in *The Beautyful Ones* resurfaces in *Osiris Rising*. On the other hand, Armah might very well be suggesting that Asar, like Osiris, will achieve a resurrection at some undetermined point in the future and, with the assistance of an Isis figure, mount yet another ascendancy and humanizing mission.

Interestingly, Armah's later novel *Kmt: In the House of Life* (2002), called an "epistemic novel," shows the influences of Afrocentricity in its recognition of Maat and ancient Egypt as a touchstone.

Armah's message to African Americans is complex, in that although it supports an Afrocentric interest in Egypt, it points to a realistic confrontation with certain African regimes that are examples of repression and elitism. Furthermore, the search for self in an African homeland may force diasporans to confront a history of slavery that involves ancestors on both sides of the cataclysm.

CALL ME BY MY RIGHTFUL NAME AND DIASPORA CONSCIOUSNESS

The dilemma of problematic African ancestors connected to the Atlantic slave trade can also be found in Okpewho's *Call Me by My Rightful Name*, which, like Armah's *Osiris Rising*, develops African American characters in the theme of a return to the continent. Okpewho, a scholar of African oral literature and mythology, has said of Armah's writing that it offers "something a little more than traditional myths do: the potential for victory over the forces of destruction is actually realized" (Okpewho, "Myth" 292). In *Call Me by My Rightful Name* Okpewho, a member of the academic–creative writer group of new diasporan Nigerians and author of *The Victims* (1971), *The Last Duty* (1976), and *Tides* (1993), has moved beyond the traditional African novel situated primarily on the continent and addressing ethnic or national concerns. In his first novel, *The Victims*, the context is primarily the village, and his second, *The Last Duty*, although different in form and concerned more with national issues, is still framed by the African homeland. Overlooked perhaps and needing reexamination is Okpewho's *Tides*, which in its exploration of ethnicity and oil may have significant prophetic reminders and ironic echoes of current issues surrounding black gold in West Africa.

Bridging the African diaspora, *Call Me by My Rightful Name*, which focuses on the African American character Otis Hampton, is set in both the United States and Nigeria. Although a good portion of the novel concerns the sojourn of the main character in Nigeria, the opening demonstrates Okpewho's rendering of African American life. This achievement is rare in novels produced by writers born in Africa but now part of the new African diaspora. In fashioning the central character, a collegiate basketball player who develops a physical reaction akin to spirit possession whenever he hears an African language or drumming, Okpewho suggests a model of diaspora consciousness and adds another layer to the African-authored "roots" or "return" narrative. *Call Me by My Rightful Name*, which offers a paradigm derived from Nigerian sites and a Yoruba worldview and cosmology, can be divided into essentially two parts dealing with elements of diaspora characterization: the representation of black Americans in North America and their portrayal in Yorubaland. Officially, however, Okpewho divides it into three. The first part, titled "Tiger," is prefaced with an epigraph from a "Traditional Spiritual" containing the lines "Somebody's calling my name." Part 2, "Son of Itayemi," referring to the founding ancestor of Otis's family, has as its epigraph lines from jazz poet Jay Wright's *The Homecoming Singer* ("This necessary chaos follows me," 76). Part 3, "Akimbowale," is titled from the name of Otis's enslaved ancestor and the name finally given to Otis. The epigraph is from Nigerian poet Christopher Okigbo's *Distances* ("I was the sole witness to my homecoming," 154).

Okpewho configures various African American spaces, certain parts set in New England and others in Georgia, as he portrays a variety of African Americans, such as Otis's mother, father, and aunt Ella Pearl, who, "as president of the Daughters of Africa, led the association's delegation of three to welcome" Marcus Garvey when he visited Augusta, Georgia. Recognizing the importance of Otis's return to Africa, Ella Pearl is given detailed characterization as a churchgoing African American woman who has an interest in African culture and "artifacts" (83). The New England sections depict a university environment, where the crisis of the main character is first revealed. Tensions in diaspora-continental African relationships are first established when Otis attempts to make contact with African students after he hears the rhythms of their language, which trigger "a seesaw of emotions, from uneasiness to calm" (25). These are the initial stages of reactions also caused by hearing African drums. The effects of hearing an African language are part of the motivation for his journey: "Something . . . a connection is growing within him . . . those Africans . . . their words . . . their language . . . the music, *that* music. He can't link these things" (27).

In addition to shaping Otis as a middle-class African American who speaks mostly in standard English, Okpewho also creates Caribbean characters. Otis's love interest, Norma, is of Jamaican ancestry and exhibits strong elements of sixties black nationalism. As perceived by Otis, she is "Always talking about the great kingdoms of old Africa, and that we're all proud princes and princesses," notions that can be connected to Afrocentric ideas of ancient Egypt (5). Norma interviews Guinea Man, a local Jamaican cultural figure, as part of her field work. His voice is represented in Jamaican patois, and his remarks show his closeness to a roots experience and his understanding of historical issues regarding race: "Is a pity dem white man bring us heah in slave ship. Dat be trick dem white man make fe catch we fe come from Africa and work in dem plantation" (35–36). The slave trade is portrayed in racial terms, uncomplicated by internal issues of African culpability raised later in the novel.

As author, Okpewho effectively demonstrates diaspora consciousness and is able to transfer such consciousness to his main character. Diaspora consciousness is a psychic-cultural-political level of awareness that allows one to relate African cultural realities to diasporan ones. In Otis's search for the cure to his spasms, he finds in an almost Haleyesque way the village of his ancestral roots and the lineage represented by twin sisters, Taiwo and Kehinde, who saw their brother sold off into slavery. Their memory of the last moment of seeing their brother is part of a web of recollection that leads to the healing ritual dance of Otis, where he recites the text chanted generations ago but "instead of the words I used to say, calling for help" (220). (The use of the healing ritual dance of reunification can be found as well in the novel of return that predates Okpewho's work, Awoonor's *Comes the Voyager at Last,* where the village is used as the space of reclamation.) Had Okpewho closed the novel with the reunification performance ritual, it would have been a mere romanticized treatment of Otis's healing and roots realization. By detailing village politics, the resurfacing of the age-old oppositions that led to Otis's ancestors' enslavement, he offers a more realistic resolution.

For Otis, the ritual of realization and reunification follows months of acculturation and language acquisition. It is in stark contrast to Otis's moment of arrival, of first seeing African space, a moment that resembles Langston Hughes's commentaries in *The Big Sea* (1940) or, ironically, a Southern African American's first sight of Harlem as seen in the 1925 Rudolph Fisher short story, "The City of Refuge." In *Call Me by My Rightful Name,* Otis displays a sense of wonder clarified by the narrator's remarks on his lack of familiarity with a seemingly total black world.

> Wow, so this is Africa! . . . He's never been in a situation where there wasn't even a sprinkling of white people in a predominantly black community.
>
> He remembers the story of Africans living on trees; he actually looks to see if he will find anything of the kind. (105)

This stereotypical reaction, mirroring that of whites from the West who view Africans as either savage or primitive, is perhaps a reflection of black middle class adoption of such stereotypes. What is most interesting about Okpewho's work is the complication of the arrival and the achievement of the cure after the acquisition of Yoruba language. The importance of African languages can be related to issues voiced by such advocates as Ngugi, who question the dominance of European languages in creative African writing. Otis's acculturation in Ijoko-Odo is based primarily on his immersion into the Yoruba language, his initiation into a secret society, and his understanding of the Ifa divination system.

However, this acculturation does not provide the linkage necessary to complete his acquisition of diaspora consciousness. Although Otis comes to a thorough understanding of his Yoruba ancestry, he needs to resolve the problematic connection to the transatlantic slave trade of certain descendants in Ijoko-Odo. Reconciliation or justice for those involved in the internal trade forms the closing sections of the novel. In the use of exile as punishment, the novel indirectly offers a commentary on reparations initiatives. Perhaps the novel suggests that such moments of retributive justice are applicable to specific situations such as that of Otis, who literally finds his roots and identifies the descendants of those responsible for the enslavement of his ancestor. The implication is that those who participated in the internal trade are primarily responsible for the separation of Otis from his ancestors. The novel does not necessarily investigate the larger connections to the Atlantic slave trade, slave routes to the coast, and the primary reason for generating internal strife through capture—the European involvement in the global commercial enterprise of slavery in the Western hemisphere.

Regarding stylistics and structure in *Call Me by My Rightful Name*, Okpewho uses the epistolary format in part 3, reflecting his technique in earlier works. In *The Victims* and *The Last Duty*, the latter of which contains multiple first-person voices, Okpewho employs traditional and innovative novelistic patterns especially relating to multivoiced narratives. The decision to use the epistolary format in *Call Me by My Rightful Name*—building on its use in Okpewho's third novel, *Tides*—and to present the majority of the correspondences from the perspective of Otis/Akimbowale allows for differing narrative articulations which place Otis in the position of commentator. Alice Walker in *The Color Purple* (1983) also uses the epistolary form, but the vernacular usage of Celie contrasts with the standard English of Otis. In *Call Me by My Rightful Name*, Otis's voice does not differ substantially from that of the original third-person narrator. The epistolary effect through Otis creates an imaginative space for the reader, who is still faced with placing the characters in a linear time framework. Okpewho also varies the traditional novel verb tenses in the first two parts by using the present tense in the third.

Aside from stylistics, the important African diaspora art form, jazz, is used effectively in *Call Me by My Rightful Name* to show the reshaping of Otis's consciousness. In fact, the title of the novel echoes a composition found on the Archie Shepp–John Coltrane recording *New Thing at Newport* (1965). In order for Otis to fully understand the implications of his immersion into Yoruba culture, he needs a bridge between it and the African American experience. Through the character Chip McAdoo, an African American who was in Nigeria prior to Otis's arrival, Okpewho not only presents the civil rights/black protest politics of the sixties but the African elements in jazz. Chip introduces Otis to such jazz artists as Miles Davis, Billie Holiday, John Coltrane, and Duke Ellington. The connection between jazz and African music is expressed in musical and cultural terms, and the extended summary of the "music lesson" that Chip gives Otis is restated in a letter to Norma. Chip is used to show the differences in European classical music, African music, and jazz through a sequence of differentiations leading to a joining of jazz and African music.

However, Okpewho does not focus on the rhythmic basis of a linkage between jazz and African music, which is certainly a musicological way to show transference. Instead, he uses the concept of chord changes played in the jazz format to show a similarity between jazz and African music as it relates to complementarity with difference. It is also significant that certain of the jazz references are to differing styles, compositions, and recordings, such as a Count Basie recording of Ray Noble's "Cherokee" or the Charlie "Bird" Parker rendering "Ko-Ko," which uses the same "changes" as in "Cherokee." Chip acts as jazz instructor and griot. "Jazz music is like African music generally, he said, in operating on the basis of chords or a block of notes that can be lifted from one context and transferred to another context where it takes on a life of its own" (209). This can refer as well to "quoting" in a jazz improvisation, using parts or passages from a different jazz composition, while improvising on another. It would have been musicologically sound to have paralleled this device to a specific piece of African music, since there are direct references to compositions from the jazz canon.

Further developments of Otis's understanding of music involve a rhythmic transference, a Negritude-like realization expressing a linkage to his ancestry, which is also founded on the principle of reincarnation.

> In other words, since Africans moved from here to America, taking their drums along with them, some of these peculiar codes have a chance of cropping up whenever drums are played. If I am a reincarnation of my enslaved ancestor, as everyone seems convinced I am, I can see why some drum sounds, buried deep in memory since the traumatic moment of his capture, might excite certain sensations in me every time I heard drums play. And it may make no difference whether the music is from the U.S. or the Caribbean. (211–212)

This is a diaspora argument for transference of African musical cultural elements, for the conjoining of African American and Caribbean rhythms shows the underlying African root.

In addition to locating Otis's African American consciousness in jazz and African music—ironic, in that it is in Africa that Otis discovers the significance of an African American art form—Okpewho also identifies the political issues of the 1960s as part of Otis's political awakening. Otis is in Nigeria during a year of political turmoil in the United States, when there are "civil rights riots, people burning their draft cards over the war in Vietnam, etc." These occurrences are juxtaposed to social upheavals taking place in Nigeria, where "There are rumors of the military stepping in to take over power" (237). The sharpening of Otis's political aware-ness while in Nigeria parallels the way new diasporan writers have refined their continental understandings as a result of diaspora residence.

Otis's acquisition of black consciousness is expressed in the episto-lary format. The last letters of the novel are written back to Nigeria and offer a summation of Otis's sojourn; one of them clarifies his new political consciousness and cultural identity. He acknowledges that he might have dismissed black studies as a project of "troublemakers" and might have pursued the individualism of profit through professional basketball, but "What I learnt there has made it difficult for me to fold my arms while other people continue with the same tactics that caused our people to lose a sense of themselves" (251). This is an important statement from a for-merly apolitical character, who begins to accept black nationalism; how-ever, this understanding is joined with the experience of African politics, not only within the village setting but in relation to national politics in Nigeria.

Otis's ultimate realization brings him closer to Nigerian contexts. He objects to there not being *"one* [course] devoted specifically to Af-rica" in his college curriculum, but is aware that there are references to such Nigerian writers as Clark, Soyinka, and Okigbo. At the same time, he recognizes that "it's time to overhaul the American higher education system" and include courses exploring the history of "black peoples and the contributions they've made to the growth of American society in par-ticular" (249). This interest in university curricula is similar to that found in *Osiris Rising,* which is also concerned with renewing higher educa-tional agendas, this time on the continent.

*   *   *

Novelists such as Okpewho and Armah have characterized African Americans using the return motif and have addressed such issues as lan-guage, slavery, and university curricula. Armah locates the return expe-rience using figures from ancient Egyptian religion and culture and, like Okpewho, addresses the problematic question of ancestry, genealogy, slav-ery, and culpability. Both writers employ diaspora consciousness and cer-tain "mythologies," but not necessarily in the sense of imagined narra-tives deriving from specific cultural realities. Okpewho focuses precisely on a West African ethnicity, and in using the Yoruba worldview shows that cultural emersion by a diasporan can lead to political and cultural awareness of one's past as well as to spiritual healing and a sharper un-derstanding of contemporary internal political issues in African ethnic communities. In Armah's work, the genealogical distance between Afri-can Americans and ancient Egyptian culture needs to be bridged through broader mythological and symbolic representations, such as in the figure of Osiris. The unraveling of a Yoruba genealogical tree with its entanglements in the Atlantic slave trade is perhaps a more empirical cultural project.

Because Otis completes his circle of connection and eventually returns to the United States better equipped to confront the challenges of the sixties, Okpewho's envisioning of diaspora return is ultimately optimistic, whereas the Osiris-like fragmentation of Asar, who in the end of *Osiris Rising* "exploded silently in fourteen starry fragments, and the pieces plunged into the peaceful water," suggests the continuation of the struggle of reunification with African mythological sources and also the internal struggle between the neocolonial state and progressive Pan-Africanist thought (305).

Armah's Afrocentric and Pan-Africanist approach contrasts with the more ethnically specific genealogical orientation of Okpewho, and this contrast is indicative of the earlier debate over Afrocentricity by certain African Americans and continental Africans, some of whom view the location of ancestry in Egypt as imaginary and less viable as compared to West African sources of homeland. Even the West African notion of homeland can be problematic, because of the erasure of specific ethnic roots for the old diasporans in general, who, for the most part, will not achieve the Otis-like return. To effectively articulate the return motif both positions are central, given that the particularity of ethnicity is an inescapable reality of contemporary African politics and that the broad historical vision claiming Egyptian sources can help link West Africa to the North and East of the continent, providing an extended basis for joining a Pan-African sentiment with an Afrocentric vision. By grounding Otis's understanding of the Yoruba world in language emersion, Okpewho demonstrates the importance of indigenous systems in the process of cross-diaspora consciousness. Similarly, in the African American context, jazz, with its complexity as a musical language, offers those from the continent a body of information and a musical system with which to link African and African American cultures, a bridge across the Middle Passage.

Writing about the African nation of origin and diaspora spaces is not a process of mutual exclusion, and the articulation of both suggests the fulfillment to a degree of a Pan-African or perhaps diaspora-conscious agenda, where ethnicity is not erased, where experiences of the old diasporans and their cultural heritage born of slavery become the material for literary works of new diaspora writers. These new literary works produced by academic-creative writers may continue to address the home nation but may also construct characterizations of the first, second, and successive generations of the new diaspora. Although separated from their homelands by forces that differ from those of the Atlantic slave trade, the new diaspora migrants in the United States and especially their descendants may likely become "African Americanized" if they engage the historical legacy of race, which continues as a defining marker of identity. Certain writers have been influenced by diaspora residency and have developed diaspora consciousness in ways that channel homeland issues into clearer perspectives and which provide the literary raw materials for fashioning diasporan characterizations of both the old and new configurations.

NOTES

1. South African poet Amelia Blossom Pegram, poet Rashida Ismaili, influenced by numerous African American writers, and aspiring novelist Sarah Manyika have had extended residence in the diaspora. Their reasons for migrating are consistent with those of the other writers interviewed.

2. See the review of Ayittey's book by Jeremy Harding, "Scapegoating History," *New York Times Book Review*, March 8, 1998, 7, in which Ayittey is described as a "writer who takes no prisoners," indicating his willingness to critique African leaders. Ayittey compares himself to African American Keith Richburg, whose *Out of America: A Black Man Confronts Africa* (1997) resulted in a critical firestorm initiated by certain black intellectuals. In its portrayal of negative images of Africa, Richburg's book exemplifies a serious identity conflict (Ayittey xii–xiii).

REFERENCES

Achebe, Chinua. *Things Fall Apart.* London: Heinemann, 1958.
Agho, Jude A. "Ayi Kwei Armah's *Osiris Rising:* New Wine in an Old Wine Skin." *Ariel* 33, no. 2 (April 2002): 57–70.
Aidoo, Ama Ata. *The Dilemma of a Ghost.* New York: Collier, 1971.
Anyidoho, Kofi. *Ancestrallogic and Caribbeanblues.* Trenton, N.J.: Africa World Press, 1993.
Armah, Ayi Kwei. *The Beautyful Ones Are Not Yet Born.* 1968. Reprint, London: Heinemann, 1969.
———. *Fragments.* Boston: Houghton Mifflin, 1970.
———. *The Healers.* Portsmouth, N.H.: Heinemann, 1978.
———. *Kmt: In the House of Life: An Epistemic Novel.* Popenguine, Senegal: Per Ankh, 2002.
———. *Osiris Rising: A Novel of Africa Past, Present and Future.* Popenguine, Senegal: Per Ankh, 1995.
———. *Two Thousand Seasons.* 1973. Reprint, Portsmouth, N.H.: Heinemann, 1979.
Awoonor, Kofi. *Comes the Voyager at Last: A Tale of Return to Africa.* Trenton, N.J.: Africa World Press, 1992.
Ayittey, George B. N. *Africa in Chaos.* New York: St. Martin's, 1998.
Balogun, F. Odun. *Adjusted Lives: Stories of Structural Adjustments.* Trenton, N.J.: Africa World Press, 1995.
———. E-mail survey response to author. October 8, 2006.
Ben-Jochannan, Yosef A. A. *Africa: Mother of Western Civilization.* Baltimore, Md.: Black Classic Press, 1988.
Bernal, Martin. *Black Athena: The Afroasiatic Roots of Classical Civilization,*

Vol. 1: The Fabrications of Ancient Greece, 1785–1985. New Brunswick, N.J.:
    Rutgers University Press, 1987.

Budge, E. A. Wallis. *The Egyptian Book of the Dead.* 1895. Reprint, New York:
    Dover, 1967.

Egejuru, Phanuel. E-mail survey response to author. October 11, 2006.

Emecheta, Buchi. *The Family.* New York: Braziller, 1990.

——. *Kehinde.* Portsmouth, N.H.: Heinemann, 1994.

——. *Second-Class Citizen.* London: Allison and Busby, 1974.

Fisher, Rudolph. "The City of Refuge." *Atlantic Monthly,* February 1925, 178–187.

Frazer, James George. *The Golden Bough: A Study in Magic and Religion.* New
    York: Macmillan, 1951.

Guelwaar. Dir. Ousmane Sembene. New Yorker Films, 1992.

Hughes, Langston. *The Big Sea.* New York: Knopf, 1940.

Ismaili, Rashida. E-mail survey response to author. October 9, 2006.

Johnson, Charles. *Middle Passage.* New York: Atheneum, 1990.

Kalu, Anthonia. E-mail survey response to author. October 18, 2006.

Manyika, Sarah. E-mail survey response to author. November 5, 2006.

Na'Allah, Abdul-Rasheed. Introduction to *The People's Poet: Emerging Perspec-
    tives on Niyi Osundare,* ed. Abdul-Rasheed Na'Allah. Trenton, N.J.: Africa
    World Press, 2003. xxiii–xxxv.

Ndibe, Okey. *Arrows of Rain.* Portsmouth, N.H.: Heinemann, 2000.

——. E-mail survey response to author. October 9, 2006.

Nwankwo, Chimalum. Letter survey response to author. October 8, 2006.

——. "When the Soul Train Parks." In *Prisons of Fire* (forthcoming).

Ogede, Ode S. "Angled Shots and Reflections: On the Literary Essays of Ayi Kwei
    Armah." *World Literature Today* 66, no. 3 (Summer 1992): 439–444.

Oguine, Ike. *A Squatter's Tale.* Portsmouth, N.H.: Heinemann, 2000.

Ohaeto, Ezenwa. *Winging Words: Interviews with Nigerian Writers and Critics.*
    Ibadan, Nigeria: Kraft Books, 2003.

Ojaide, Tanure. E-mail survey response to author. October 11, 2006.

Okpewho, Isidore. *Call Me by My Rightful Name.* Trenton, N.J.: Africa World
    Press, 2004.

——. E-mail survey response to author. October 15, 2006.

——. *The Last Duty.* Essex, UK: Longman, 1976.

——. "Myth and Modern Fiction: Armah's *Two Thousand Seasons.*" In *Critical
    Perspectives on Ayi Kwei Armah,* ed. Derek Wright. Washington, D.C.: Three
    Continents Press, 1992. 278–297.

——. *Tides.* 1993. Reprint, Lagos, Nigeria: Longman, 2003.

——. *The Victims.* Garden City, N.Y.: Doubleday, 1971.

Onwueme, Tess. *The Broken Calabash.* Owerri, Nigeria: Totan, 1984.

——. E-mail survey response to author. November 7, 2006, and November 9,
    2006.

——. *The Missing Face.* New York: Africana Legacy Press, 1997.

——. *Riot in Heaven.* New York: Africana Legacy Press, 1996.

Osei-Nyame, Kwadwo. "Pan-Africanist Ideology and the African Historical Novel
    of Self-Discovery: The Examples of Kobina Sekyi and J. E. Casely Hayford."
    Journal of African Cultural Studies 12, no. 2 (December 1999): 137–153.

Osundare, Niyi. E-mail survey response to author. October 9, 2006.

———. *Pages from the Book of the Sun: New and Selected Poems*. Trenton, N.J.: Africa World Press, 2002.

Pegram, Amelia Blossom. E-mail survey response to author. October 9, 2006.

Perrin, Andrew J. "What Is African?" Review of *Osiris Rising* by Ayi Kwei Armah. *Callaloo* 22, no. 1 (1999): 247–249.

Phillips, Caryl. *Higher Ground*. New York: Viking, 1989.

Richburg, Keith. *Out of America: A Black Man Confronts Africa*. New York: Basic, 1997.

Shepp, Archie, and John Coltrane. "Call Me by My Rightful Name." *New Thing at Newport*. Impulse, 1965.

Walker, Alice. *The Color Purple*. New York: Washington Square, 1983.

Wright, Jay. *The Homecoming Singer*. New York: Corinth, 1971.

22

SELF, PLACE, AND IDENTITY IN TWO GENERATIONS OF WEST AFRICAN IMMIGRANT WOMEN MEMOIRS: EMECHETA'S *HEAD ABOVE WATER* AND DANQUAH'S *WILLOW WEEP FOR ME*

F. Odun Balogun

> . . . maybe not too late
> For having first to civilize a space
> Wherein to play your violin with grace
> —*Gwendolyn Brooks, "Children of the Poor"*

Given the history of land alienation, geographic and social space has enormous significance for black peoples. Slaves were violently uprooted and transplanted into alien spaces, and colonized Africans were forced to yield power over their lands to foreigners. As exiles, whether voluntary or circumstance-compelled, members of the new African diaspora also intimately know the psychological anxiety of land alienation, which, in any case, is a common experience for all immigrants irrespective of where they come from. In a sense, the central theme of black history and literature has been how black peoples have coped in the last three centuries with the trauma of land alienation. Thus, my interest in the past few years has concerned how African and African American writers depict the problematic relationship of the black self to the self's place of habitation as a factor of identity formation. Here my limited objective is to examine from a comparative perspective the depiction of the self-place-identity relationship with particular reference to two West African immigrant women memoirs, namely, Buchi Emecheta's *Head above Water* and Meri Nana-Ama Danquah's *Willow Weep for Me*. I wish to explore, from these examples of two distinct generations of African women immigrants, the extent to which the autobiographical female self is a product of the self's relationship to her place of physical location. In other words, what is the relational role of the concepts of *self* and *place* in identity formation in these two works? Before proceeding, however, I wish to clarify the meaning of these concepts.

The term "self," often called "mind" or "soul," is a problematic category in metaphysics, where, depending on the philosopher's intellectual orientation and methodological/analytical approach, it can be said to be an abstraction that really does not exist, a mere illusion. However, as Richard Taylor insists in his book *Metaphysics,* the nihilistic answer to the question about the existence of the self yields place to affirmation whenever the philosopher approaches the question not with an outward-inward focus that moves from nature to the self, but with an inward-outward mode that seeks the self in nature. It is then that the metaphysical search for the self ends, not in the discovery of nothingness, but in the realization that the self is one with nature (124–126). Whether or not one shares Taylor's transcendentalist philosophical view, there is no denying that the self can be apprehended only in reference to the non-self, beginning with the mix of biological and psychological shell that the self inhabits and including the geographical, racial, cultural, and social locales of the self. Hence, sociologically, the "self" can be seen as the identity one fashions out for oneself based on both the perception one has of one's place in society and the character of one's identification with the society's cultural values. In other words, "self" as self-identity is the sum of how one regards oneself in the context of other selves and the cultural and moral principles by which one chooses to live.

One of the most crucial determinants (advocates of metaphysical determinism would say, the *only* determinant) of self-identity is the relationship of the self to the self's place in time, the two latter categories, "place" and "time," being almost indistinguishable in metaphysics (Richard Taylor 72–80). Pragmatically defined, the term "place" is the geographical setting located in a specific chronological time that is characterized by a certain intellectual or philosophical atmosphere and within which the self is situated and functions. Indeed, as Charles Taylor puts it in *Sources of the Self: The Making of the Modern Identity,* "To know who you are is to be oriented in moral space, a space in which questions arise about what is good or bad, what is worth doing and what not, what has meaning and importance for you and what is trivial and secondary" (28).

The concepts "self" and "place" have always operated in literature in a symbiotic relationship, and the weight of importance attached to each concept in relation to the other depends on the philosophy of the literary school of thought passing judgment. At the end of the nineteenth and beginning of the twentieth century, for instance, environmental and biological determinism was the philosophy embraced by the naturalist school, which believed that the self is overdetermined by biology as well as by the place, environment, that the self inhabits. While critics agree that there is a mutual influence, that identity is implicated in place (Alexander 379, de Jongh 575), my study of African and African American literatures, however, suggests that the more active ingredient in this relationship is the self, because it determines the character of place/environment.

PARALLELS

Buchi Emecheta and Meri Nana-Ama Danquah have very obvious differences. Born in 1944, Emecheta is almost twice as old as Danquah, who was born twenty-three years later in 1967. Emecheta's first published novel, *In the Ditch*, appeared in 1972, and since then she has produced close to two dozen works, mostly novels. Danquah's first work, *Willow Weep for Me*, was published in 1998, and to date she has added two edited books, and all of her three publications are nonfiction. Emecheta emigrated from Nigeria in 1962 as an adult at the age of eighteen to the U.K., a country renowned for its conservatism, while Danquah was brought from Ghana in 1973 at the age of six to the U.S., whose culture is known for its permissiveness.

With these generational and experiential gaps and with differences in their cultural exposures, as well as the generic distinctions in their literary tastes as writers, one would expect few or no commonalities between the two women. In fact, however, there are amazing parallels, similarities, and coincidences in their circumstances as individuals and as writers. These parallels, similarities, and coincidences occur primarily because of their position as black African immigrant women writers, living within two Western societies (U.K. and U.S.) that are male-dominated and are still struggling to overcome racism. Directly related to this major factor are secondary factors that include experiences of a poverty-stricken existence as struggling black artists who are, at the same time, teenage mothers and single parents. This, for instance, explains why the two women subsequently embraced the ideologies of feminism as well as antiracism, both of which have become enduring themes in their works.

Another significant source of the similarities that appear in the lives and writing of the two women is their shared history of childhood and adolescent years that were traumatized by family tragedies, loss, and abuse. A direct consequence of this history, for instance, is the development of each of them into a withdrawn, shy personality, lacking confidence and a sense of self-worth, despite being independent-minded, strong-willed, even stubborn. The negative backgrounds will condition them to respond in the future in similar ways to similar incidents that will occur in their adult lives. For instance, a powerful factor that shapes the women's lives as well as their narratives is their highly critical attitude toward society and adult authority. The values of the traditional African society, especially those that regulate gender relationships, come under severe scrutiny and criticism and both women make determined efforts to become the ideal parents that their own parents had not been for them.

All of these primary and secondary factors combine to engender in the women an overwhelmingly powerful motivation to tell their stories in order to illuminate for others the great odds against which they have struggled and also to highlight the reasons why they have prevailed in their struggles. Since, in spite of generational differences, the history and experiences of Emecheta and Danquah as individuals are similar, their writings inevitably reflect a number of similarities. Likewise, because of the urge to educate the world about themselves, the difference in generic patronage between the two writers has turned out to be inconsequential. Danquah prefers the direct mode of literary composition (nonfiction), but as anyone who reads her memoir soon discovers, she approaches her narrative with the fastidiousness of a stylistically conscious artist, one whose prose is frequently rhythmic and imagistic. On the other hand, even though Emecheta predominantly writes fiction, her novels, as she herself attests in *Head above Water*, are for the most part not just autobiographical fiction but also unapologetic social histories, what she calls "documentary novels" (1–2, 58–60, 104, 147). The profusion of autobiographical details and social histories in Emecheta's novels makes her fiction and nonfiction almost indistinguishable. This perhaps explains why the critic Ezenwa-Ohaeto, in his insightful analysis of *Head above Water*, often subconsciously referred to it as a "novel" and to Emecheta as "protagonist" even though he was consciously analyzing the work as a memoir (350, 351, 352, 356, 360, 365).

STORIES OF BECOMING

The story that Emecheta shares with the reader in the memoir *Head above Water*, published in 1986, is the story of a becoming—ultimately a heroic tale of how a fatherless and motherless child from Ibuza, a village in Nigeria, overcomes great obstacles to become a world-renowned writer living in a lofty world capital, London, where she is courted by autograph and interview hunters. The obstacles she has overcome are such as would daunt the faint-hearted. Rather than surrender to the poverty into which orphanage plunged her, or be discouraged by the beating and callous neglect of her supervising relatives, the child not only works harder, but also secretly sits for an examination and wins a scholarship to study in a secondary school. Barely seventeen when she completes her secondary education, she marries and goes abroad to join her husband, only for her marriage to fail as soon as she arrives in London. She subsequently becomes a teenage single parent, battling poverty and racism in London. Still she remains undaunted and continues to struggle, taking care of children, who

soon number five, while holding down various poorly compensated employments. At the same time, she still manages to continue her studies
for her degrees and also works on her ambition to become a writer. She
is stretched beyond her limits, but she pushes on, and in the end, she triumphs over the odds and realizes dreams that would have seemed impossible for most people in her situation. The hopelessly disadvantaged or-
phaned girl of Ibuza becomes a well-educated and famed writer in a world
capital, London.

Meri Nana-Ama Danquah's memoir, *Willow Weep for Me*, is another
story of becoming in the face of great odds. Danquah, too, experiences the
trauma of loss quite early in her life, although this loss, unlike Emecheta's,
is not associated with death. At the age of three, she confronts the first
in a series of abandonments by family and friends—abandonments that
not only wound her as deeply as if she has sustained loss through the
death of loved ones, but also eventually incapacitate her into a clinical
depressive. Her mother leaves her with her maternal grandmother in Accra, Ghana, and goes away to the U.S. to study at Howard University in
Washington, D.C. Three years later at age six, she is brought to join her
mother in Washington, D.C., but soon the abandonment from which she
has hardly recovered is tragically compounded when her parents divorce.
Since she is very close to her father, she is deeply hurt by the divorce, especially as she daily witnesses the agony that her mother suffers after the divorce but tries unsuccessfully to hide from the daughter. Because of this,
Danquah develops a strong resentment, verging on dislike and hatred, of
her father. And as if all these were not enough, her first experience of sex
with a schoolmate, an experience which qualifies as rape, is soon followed
by the perfidy of repeated sexual abuse by her mother's boyfriend. This
too is rapidly followed by yet other losses or abandonments. For instance,
a beloved relation whom she calls Uncle Paul and with whom she has a
good substitute daughter-father relationship suddenly relocates to Africa,
going from Washington, D.C., to Morocco. Her grandmother, whom she
loves and who has been visiting, also returns to Ghana. About the same
time, she witnesses the accidental death of a schoolmate who is killed by
a school bus. Her longtime school friend, David, becomes frustrated with
her and drops their friendship. Traumatized by all these painful losses,
she seeks escape in school truancy, alcohol, and casual sex which soon
results in pregnancy and abortion. At this point, afraid that the need to
alleviate her pain might again push her to attempt suicide, as she unsuccessfully did while in the ninth grade, she packs and flees Washington,
D.C., and goes to Los Angeles at the age of eighteen, the same age as when
Emecheta leaves Nigeria for England.

In Los Angeles, Danquah has a brief taste of romance and marriage
to a Ghanaian with whose child she has become pregnant. Soon, however, the marriage fails, and like Buchi Emecheta, Meri Nana-Ama Dan-

quah becomes an immigrant teenage single parent, living in poverty in a sprawling, indifferent urban city. When her life in Los Angeles becomes unbearable, she flees back to her mother in D.C., but this turns out to be a temporary stay as she soon returns to Los Angeles. The rest of her story provides details of how, as a result of good advice and help from friends, she finally acknowledges the truth of her condition as a depressive, seeks psychotherapy and medicament, and begins the process of healing that owes a lot to her conscious decision to embrace and deploy the power of positive thinking. Gradually, Danquah metamorphoses from a depressed, self-hating, and suicidal individual to a confident, self-assured person who, having taken control of her life, also starts enjoying professional success as a writer.

IDEOLOGICAL STRATEGIES

Danquah's *Willow Weep for Me,* then, is not merely an account of the experience of overcoming depression, but more the story of a growing self-awareness, self-discovery. It is this self-discovery that helps Danquah to avoid the ultimate tragedy of succumbing to her disease. Her memoir therefore is clearly a story of a personal triumph through self-discovery. A masterful narrator, Danquah deftly emphasizes, using strategic repetitions throughout her story, the extreme nature and severity of her disease in order for the reader to better recognize the heroic level of the endurance, perseverance, and psychological power it took for her to be able to overcome it. Equally strategic is the manner in which she structures her memoir so that it also functions simultaneously as an intellectual argument that is substantiated by her own personal experience as well as the experiences of her friends, among whom were highly respectable social elites. The argument that Danquah carefully makes, and by and large successfully proves, is this: it is erroneous to think that depression is a symptom of laziness, sloth, and weak-mindedness on the part of irresponsible individuals who cannot face up to the often difficult task of living. On the contrary, she insists, depression is a serious disease provoked by a combination of complex social, psychological, and biochemical causations, one that also manifests itself through a multiplicity of debilitating symptoms.

Danquah's objective in providing education about the nature of her disease is to help dispel the false notion that depression exclusively affects white women. Black women, she consistently emphasizes, are equally, if not more, susceptible to the disease. She believes that the sooner this knowledge is shared and generally acknowledged, the earlier and the more easily black women who suffer from depression will come out of the closet to seek treatment and share information. To make her points convincing, Danquah employs several of the devices of classical argument, including making claims, providing evidential proofs, stating counterclaims and disproving them, and using repetition, reiteration, and strategic sequencing or placement of chapters. The narration is also constructed in the cyclical mode in order to reinforce its thesis by returning to the idea with which it started. As a result of these stylistic strategies, Danquah's memoir in a number of places reads like a scholarly essay instead of a personal story. Thus, similar to Emecheta's *Head above Water*, which in general highlights the plight of disadvantaged poor women on social welfare in London and in particular emphasizes the inequity suffered in the UK by the black, immigrant, single-parent mother, Danquah's *Willow Weep for Me* promotes a feminist agenda in general and black feminism in particular.

The feminist ideological orientation of the two memoirs is heavily colored by their authors' personal experiences of marriage to husbands portrayed as abusive; as a result, it raises the old question regarding the authenticity of the content of autobiographies. For instance, there is clearly in both narratives a negative appraisal of male domination and women's relegation in the traditional society as well as in the modern. While Emecheta roundly condemns male chauvinism in London, representative capital of the modern West, she becomes particularly stringent in her criticism of the traditional African society, portraying it as a society that enslaves wives to their husbands (*Head* 3–5). Both writers uniformly reiterate the view that the primary cause of today's failed or unhappy marriages in African families, including their own and those of their parents, is the perpetuation, in modern times, of the obsolete philosophy of the traditional African male who dictatorially treated the African woman as a subordinate, if not as a slave, rather than as an equal. In Emecheta's biography, there is an unforgiving bitterness against her ex-husband and a pervasive suspicion of men in general, and this suspicion includes even her best male friend, Chidi, who consistently comes through for her whenever she needs help or a shoulder to cry on. Danquah does not exhibit a similar comprehensive cynicism about men; she reserves her suspicion and scorn for only the men she perceives as having hurt her. These include her ex-husband, her mother's boyfriend who sexually abused her as a teenager, and, to some extent, her father at the time he abandoned her and her mother. Danquah otherwise generally enjoys a mutually respecting and nourishing friendship and relationship with people of the opposite sex, as her story amply demonstrates.

The explanation for this difference, of course, goes beyond the possibility that Emecheta has extended her suspicion of the ex-husband and her father, "who was a violent person although a good Christian," to all men in general (13). Caring alone for five children while working and studying for a degree probably drained Emecheta of all energies, leaving her little for paying attention to any man. Also, giving one of her reasons for rejecting the repeated marriage proposal of Chidi, a man with whom she shared "a very, very long friendship, spanning more than twenty years," Emecheta says: "And of course, with our people, marriage means more children. I did not want any more" (222–223). Since, however, all writing is subjective and memoirs are notoriously unreliable, we will never know the whole truth of either the account Emecheta gives of her ex-husband, Sylvester Onwordi, or the image Danquah paints of her ex-husband, Justin Armah.

PLACE AND SELF/IDENTITY

The significance of space or place as cultural location cannot be missed in either of the two narratives, because each memoir is in fact the account of the autobiographical narrator's relationship with her places of location. The consciousness of place is made evident early in both memoirs, because emphasis is placed on the permanent impact that the spaces of childhood and teenage education had on the impressionable young girls, especially during their years in high school.

Perhaps as an instance of a direct literary influence of the older writer on the younger, the narrated experiences of Danquah while at Foxcroft High School in Middleburg, Va., bear remarkable resemblances to the earlier experiences of Emecheta at the Methodist Girls' High School in Lagos, Nigeria. Though located apart in time and space in two continents, the two high schools are practically the same, being run as private female institutions, employing the traditional strict regimen of the boarding school, complete with uniform, regular assembly, and prayer. They are also taught exclusively by white women, even in the one in Lagos, deep in black Africa, except that here one or two black African women teachers are permitted in the list of the white female faculty. Like Emecheta at the Methodist high school, Danquah at Foxcroft is a shy, self-effacing though brilliant teenager, lacking in confidence and self-acceptance. Both girls believe that they are ugly, behave as outsiders, and regularly come late and poorly clothed to the school assembly, thus creating scenes and notice.

It is also at their schools that both teenagers discover a passionate love for literature and writing—Emecheta for prose, Danquah for poetry. Similarly, a school teacher plays a memorable role in each girl's developing literary aspiration. In Danquah's case, the young female teacher who shares and nurtures her love of poetry disappoints her by not informing her that she will not be returning after the school break, thus adding to Danquah's already lengthy list of painful losses and abandonments. Emecheta similarly experiences her first episode of racism, blatant and public, right at home in her classroom in Africa. Her white teacher, Ms. Humble, who asks the students in her class to share their aspirations for post-graduation professions, treats Emecheta's declaration of her dream to become a writer with a humiliating public disgrace and dismissal, believing Emecheta to be presumptuous in wishing to become what, in her opinion, only white people are entitled to aspire to. It is also at her high school that Danquah faces the crudest and most blatantly cruel racism that she has yet experienced when, at a school mixer, a white boy declines her invitation to dance on the unapologetic excuse that "I don't dance with niggers" (43). It is obvious then that the high school, as a social and educational space, left a sour taste on the tongues of each of the future writers before they moved out—Emecheta to earn a degree, Danquah on account of her mother's inability to continue paying fees that were too high.

At any rate, in these two memoirs, places as a rule frequently experience change. Danquah, for instance, perceptively remarks toward the end of her narration that "change continues to be a major signifier for my life" (264). The place of habitation is sometimes externally imposed, as, for instance, when Emecheta is allocated London City Council housing that is not to her liking, or when Danquah as a child gets transported from Ghana across the Atlantic to join her mother in the U.S. More often, however, in these two memoirs, locational changes are self-motivated; in other words, place is a matter of choice, even when the choice is relative, being invariably influenced by the factor of the chooser's circumstance. Another way to state this is to say that the autobiographers are always on the move, always beginning, continuing, or ending a journey, one that at times is reversed, as when Danquah, for instance, repeats the pattern of her going from Washington, D.C., to Los Angeles, and vice versa.

Each specific individual journey is a statement of the self's relationship of satisfaction or disaffection with both the locations of departure and of destination, as well as with the transient space in between. As a rule, one moves from a location permanently or temporarily because the location from which one is moving can no longer meet all of one's needs, regardless of how important or minor the needs may be. In other words, every self-motivated move is a journey in search of greater self-fulfillment. This is the case, either when Emecheta seeks and accomplishes the fundamentally important journey of emigration on a boat from Nigeria to the United Kingdom, or when Danquah relocates for the first time from Washington, D.C., to Los Angeles. It is equally true when the trip is minor or temporary, such as when the writer leaves home to perform routine duties such as going to work or buying groceries. Not having food at home, or endangering one's livelihood by not going to work, for instance, makes home, however luxurious, less appealing and the temporary trip away from it a necessary journey for greater fulfillment.

If it is true, then, that every voluntary relocation indicates an appetite for greater satisfaction, it logically means that every journey is an implied statement of some level of dissatisfaction with the previous place of location. This is clearly the case with each of the fundamentally important journeys of relocation cited above as undertaken by Emecheta and Danquah. Emecheta, for instance, seeks to leave Nigeria for the UK because Nigeria is the site of the woes from which she wishes to distant herself. These woes include her orphan status and her neglect and frequent beating by a supervising relative, her uncle. The most important, however, is the limited opportunity for self-actualization that Nigeria offers to a disadvantaged female teenager as bright and ambitious as Emecheta. When Danquah first moves to Los Angeles, it is also because she wants to put a distance between herself and all that Washington, D.C., symbolizes for her. Too much for her is the pain of an endless stream of abandonments by loved ones whose cumulative outcome is the reckless teenage lifestyle she embraces in Washington, D.C., as an escape, but which only leads her into greater unhappiness and ultimately into depression. The immediate fear that her constant thoughts of suicide might lead her to taking her own life is what prompts the radical decision to relocate from Washington, D.C., which for her is the site of pain.

It should be noted, however, that although the two women share strong reservations regarding the male chauvinist character of traditional African culture, they do not treat the culture with a wholesale rejection. They both equally value traditional African communal folk culture, which they perceive as inspiring to artistic creativity, and which Emecheta, additionally, admires for its communal, humanist ideals:

> I could deliberate, chew over and repeat the works of Rupert Brooke, Keats and Shakespeare, yet I was the daughter of scantily educated parents who came right out of their innocent and yet sophisticated bush culture, ignorant of the so-called civilized world. Yet in communal caring, and mutual sharing, and language gestures and music-making, they are unsurpassed in their sheer sophistication. (16)

Another point of similarity is that both writers symbolically associate the creative inspiration of the traditional African culture with elderly women relatives, both of whom initiated the writers, while the latter were still children, into the culture by regaling them with beautifully rendered folktales and family histories. For this reason, the writers deeply appreciate and love the elderly women. Danquah, for instance, lovingly nicknames her grandmother "Auntie C," while Emecheta feels particularly indebted to her aunt, whom she calls "Big Mother." Emecheta believes that she derived the inspiration to become a writer from "Big Mother" and that even after her death "Big Mother" has remained her muse.

The outcome of each of the physical journeys undertaken by the two women autobiographers is often the same. An immediate but temporary satisfaction is achieved, but only for this to be supplanted by ultimate dis-appointment. "As usual," remarked Ezenwa-Oheato, who analyzes *Head above Water* as a trope of survival, "dreams differ from reality, and the experience in England turns out different from the expectations for she [Emecheta] confesses: 'England gave me a cold welcome'." (353). After the initial joy of arriving in London, Emecheta soon confronts the harsh reality of a failed marriage, the hardship of poverty, and caring as a single parent for five children in the inhospitable, racist environment of London. This reality is obviously far from the dream that had lured her to the UK. Danquah's experience in Los Angeles is similar to Emecheta's in London. Soon following the brief honeymoon of romance and marriage are the bitterness of separation, the agony of coping with poverty as a pregnant single woman, and the return to depression. This drastically painful dif-ference between expectation and reality soon sends Danquah packing to return to Washington, D.C.

The pattern of disappointment with both major and minor journeys having become recurrent for both writers, and seeing the dream of self-improvement that they associate with physical relocations go down the drain, reality becomes cruelly bitter for them. The writers' dreams of achieving happiness through relocation have obviously been fostered by the mistaken belief that happiness is location-bound, a matter of place. This sort of thinking, for instance, is clearly obvious in the response that Danquah gives her parents when they express doubts regarding the effi-cacy of relocation as the solution to her problems: "It's my life, Mummy. I'm not happy here. And if I go to L.A. and I'm not happy there, I'll go somewhere else" (*Willow* 154). The common association or equation of happiness with a specific place by both Danquah and Emecheta is what prevents the two writers for a long time from embarking on the one jour-ney that they have needed to make to find happiness.

This needed journey does not involve physical relocation of the self from one place to another; rather, it is a journey inward into the self through self-reflection, self-reevaluation, and self-reconstitution. Aside from the fact that it takes a while before either writer individually rec-ognizes the need for this kind of journey, it is also not an easy journey for either of them to make. This is because the ticket for this journey is self-acceptance, a trait that neither writer seems to possess. In fact, as noted earlier, they both think themselves ugly; consequently, they lack self-confidence, self-assurance, and inner peace. Additionally, they battle constantly with "feelings of failure and worthlessness" (*Willow* 223). Emecheta, who describes herself as suffering from "chronic inferi-ority complex" (95) as a high school girl, for instance, derogatorily says this of herself: "There was nothing to like about me anyway" (*Head* 20). Danquah, when she is about the same age, also suffers from acute inferi-ority complex, and considers herself ugly, with "my round face and dark brown complexion, those thick lips and chunky legs" (106). She so intensely loathes herself that she often thinks of suicide, and her depressive condition constantly predisposes her to negative self-evaluation:

> Depression is a very "me" disease. There is an enormous amount of self-criticism, self-loathing, and low self-esteem. Everything revolves around the perception of self. Most depressives find themselves—as much to their own disgust as to everybody else's—annoyingly and negatively self-obsessed. (31)

Thanks, on the one hand, to their fighting spirit, their resilience, and their determination not to quit until they triumph over their problems, and thanks, on the other hand, to the steadfast commitment of their friends, who are constantly supporting them with empathy and advice, the time finally arrives when the writers individually come to recognize the necessity of the inward journey. Another crucial element that predisposes the writers to contemplate the option of the journey within is their undiluted maternal love for their children. They are both determined to leave no stone unturned in their search for what would make them ideal parents so that their children will not experience the handicaps that they faced as children. What Emecheta, for instance, wishes to have people say of her after her death is how committed she was to the well-being of her children: "The worst that could happen to me was to die by the wayside with everybody saying: 'To think she gave all her life for her children'." (225). Danquah, on her part, acknowledges that there are two things uppermost in her life. While one is "to build a career as a writer," the other is her daughter, Korama:

> I least expected or appreciated the power that her presence would hold. I didn't know I had it in me to deliver something so beautiful to the world . . . as the person who was chosen to facilitate her development, I wanted to learn how to trust my instincts; I wanted to know when to utilize my skills and when to let go so her story could write itself. Simply put, I wanted to honor the person that she was by being a positive force in her life. (229–230)

What both women writers finally come to realize is that they cannot be the kind of mothers they want to be if they turn out to be failures. To avoid such a fate, each woman decides to positively rechannel her energies. Emecheta, for instance, though sick and on medication, consciously chooses to deny her condition and, through an act of willpower, succeeds in concentrating on the multiple tasks of providing for her children, completing her degrees, and working to become a successful writer. While studying for the extremely rigorous, seven-part sociology examinations, for example, Emecheta develops what she humorously calls "my Sociology

and graduation syndrome" (102). Because she is acutely sleep-deprived—
"I completely forgot how to sleep" (96)—she becomes weak-kneed and
often falls in the streets. On one such occasion of her embarrassing falls,
a woman friend who has helped her up explains to inquisitive passers-by:
"She has been doing too much studying" (101). Since she has no option but
to study that hard, she psychologically works on getting rid of the health
problem, and soon she succeeds: "I no longer fall in the street, I simply
willed it away and somehow it went" (102). As to why she has to study so
hard, she explains:

> I could not say that I had read Sociology for pleasure's sake or to make me a
> better and more cultivated woman. Who wants cultivation when you have
> five children to feed? All these worries had made me put too much into my
> revision [review of the course material]. (97)

Danquah also realizes that if she remains depressive, staying helplessly in bed all day and incapable of meeting her and her daughter's basic needs for food or a clean house, it will be impossible to realize her
dreams for her daughter. Consequently, on many occasions, even when
she is most clinically depressed, thoughts of her child force Danquah to
will herself out of helplessness into action. During one of her frequent
bouts of depression, Danquah helplessly goes into the "eating and sleeping habit" (68), and at a point when she wakes up, she observes:

> The last time I woke up, I stared at her [daughter] holding a doll with one
> hand and greedily sucking the thumb on her other hand. I felt ashamed and
> selfish. She needed to be fed, bathed, and taken to nursery school. As I pre-
> pared myself to get up, the phone started ringing . . . It was way too late to
> take Korama to nursery school . . . She would have to stay home with me
> the entire day. I looked over at her. She was still sitting quietly on the bed.
> She looked like a wounded puppy—sad, pained, waiting for help. I wanted so
> badly to be a good mother to her. All she had was me, and the sight of that
> responsibility was almost as heavy as the burden of my depression. I didn't
> want to take care of anybody else. I didn't even know how to take care of
> myself. All I wanted to do was crank up the heat and get back under the
> covers. (71–72)

But Danquah does not go back under the covers, and her thoughts at a
later occasion also show that her maternal concerns for her daughter play
a major role in her decision to go into treatment for her depression:

> This made me think about Korama. As she got older, what would her
> thoughts be on my mothering? Would this illness block her vision of my
> attempts to do right by her? Would she see it as an illness, or assume it was
> just part of my character, and allow it to negatively define our relationship?
> I didn't want my depression to be the only thing that defined or distin-

guished me and my life. This was something I wanted to work on, by myself and in therapy. (246–247)

Circumstances including the recurrent negative outcomes of outward
journeys, the unwavering positive support from friends, and the feelings of
maternal love like those just cited constitute the factors that combine to
finally motivate Danquah into embarking on her inward journey. The outcome of the new journey, the journey within, is that she finally chooses
to stop being in denial, to acknowledge her depressive state, and to heed
friends' advice to go into therapy. Her narrative makes it obvious that her
therapy works only because she now has the right disposition of mind.
Combined, this disposition and the therapy change her into a new person,
one who has finally discovered herself, her inner strength and how beautiful a person she is. Not surprisingly, self-discovery leads her to a new
revelation. At the end of her narrative, and for the first time, she is capable of truthfully declaring: "I love who I am" (*Willow* 265). Experiences
similar to Danquah's also lead Emecheta to the same positive conviction
at the end of her own memoir, where she says: "Suddenly, I found that I
was becoming a new person" (*Head* 228).

The success the two women subsequently begin to experience in their
writing—as their works increasingly get published and they win fame and
become more financially solvent, if not yet comfortable—is another factor
that further predisposes them to a more positive self-appraisal and the development of confidence, assurance, pride, and a sense of self-worth. This
is a more crucial factor for Emecheta, whose problems have everything to
do with the poverty of a single mother raising five children, than for Danquah, whose situation is compounded by the psychological and biochemical problems of depression.

The physical journeys and relocations to new places and sites, no
doubt, also play their own role in each writer's journey of becoming, for
they function as the nuisance factors, the obstacles that must first be overcome for the writer's quest to be successful. The journeys and relocations
provide the social circumstances and the challenges—e.g., poverty, racism, male chauvinism, divorce, separation, abandonment, and aspiration
to social success—which, in their complex combinations, ultimately motivate the writers by compelling them to search for solutions to their problems. Emecheta, for instance, is aware of this dialectical relationship between her failures and her final success. She recalls the insightful remark
of a professor friend she had met in Chicago, who said to her: "I bet if
your ol man did not give you a kick in the ass, you probably would not
have written" (61). However, despite the significance of the outward journey, what the two memoirs make abundantly clear is that the road to self-
discovery and self-identity is through the inward, rather than the physical
outward, journey.

It is important to note that the period that marks the writers' inward journey toward self-discovery also coincides with the onset of the women writers' interest in exploring and identifying with geographic nature. For instance, what constitutes a special attraction and a selling point for Emecheta in the new house in Briston Grove which she wants and eventually purchases, and into which she moves with her children at the end of the narrative, is the fact that the house is not located in the urban concrete jungle of the London City Council flats where they have lived until then, but in a quiet wooded area, complete with its own yard and back garden. In addition, the house is also close to a park; in other words, close to greenery, trees, shrubs, flowers—nature. Danquah's passion for indoor plants also begins with the start of her self-discovery, and the language with which she articulates this new passion is particularly informing:

> I went out and bought plants because I thought that they would be easy to take care of. They all died. I bought more. Those died, too. One after the other, I kept bringing plants into my home until, at last, I learned how to tend to them. That was a major coup. *It probably sounds ridiculous, but I saw my plants as an extension of myself. If they thrived, I thrived, my daughter thrived.* (254; emphasis added)

No one, except perhaps mid-nineteenth-century American transcendentalist writers such as Emerson and Thoreau, could have stated a more complete identification with nature than does Danquah in this passage. Nearness to nature, according to the romantics, connotes nearness to God, to purity, wholeness, goodness. The positiveness and optimism in this declaration by Danquah is another affirmation of her self-discovery.

* * *

It is ironical that had Emecheta and Danquah been living in, writing for, and publishing in their respective African countries—Nigeria and Ghana—they would probably have found it impossible to locate publishers for their memoirs. Their feminist, anti–male chauvinist ideology would have been the first hindrance in societies such as theirs, dominated, as is the West, by males, but unlike the West, lacking the diversity of publishing opportunities as well as the comparatively long cultural tradition of female public expression and democratic participation, won through generations of women's liberation struggles. For this reason, Buchi Emecheta's remark, made in reference to another situation, is also a most pertinent observation in matters of the noted irony: "What I think saved me was coming to England when I did" (155–156). Aside from male resistance, Danquah's memoir would have confronted an additional problem in Africa. Depression is still a poorly understood medical condition even in the West—with all its sophistication in the science and technology of modern medical practice—let alone in Africa, poorly equipped as it has long been for the diagnosis, treatment, and societal accommodation of unfamiliar pathologies.

As is already evident, however, what most pertinently unites the two memoirs is their reaffirmation of the traditional concerns of black peoples, whose relationship with the space of location in modern times has been problematic, especially so when they live as resident aliens or naturalized citizens in the diaspora. What emerges while reading the memoirs is the disconcerting realization that, despite the years between Emecheta's generation and that of Danquah, little has changed for the black people residing in the West, be it in Europe or America. This lack of significant progress is made evident by the common nature of the racial, social, and gender challenges that both women faced as black and female immigrants in London and Washington, D.C., two representative capitals of the West.

As fighters, however, both writers rejected the negative societal values that sought to define and confine them; instead they sought to positively impact and transform those values so that society might be more livable for their kind. In other words, in Charles Taylor's expression, each writer aspired to transform the society in which she lived into a "moral space" (28). Nonetheless, as long as they labored under the influence of what Richard Taylor identifies as the "outward-inward" philosophical approach to self-actualization, believing that happiness resided in a place and that all it took to achieve this happiness was relocation to the right place, their struggles yielded no positive outcome. When they reversed their philosophical outlook and embraced the "inward-outward" approach, their lives changed for the better.

Having through the inward journey recovered their true identities, they not only discovered inner happiness, they also found themselves empowered to effectively impact their environments. Danquah's memoir, for instance, marked not only a personal triumph over depression but also the beginning of her power to influence her space with the purpose of making life better for all women suffering from depression, especially black women depressives who had been intimidated by racial stereotypes from admitting to their disease, and therefore from seeking therapy. Similarly, Emecheta's undergraduate and graduate educational triumphs not only brought her happiness but also fueled the success of her writing, income from which augmented her family's finances as well as made her crusade against racism, sexism, and the neglect of the poor urban white women on welfare in London far more visible and potent. By these outcomes, the two women's memoirs seem to suggest the dominance of the influence of the *self* within the mutually transforming relationship between *self* and *place,* as is often the case in black literatures.

REFERENCES

Alexander, Sandra Carlton. "Identity." In *The Oxford Companion to African American Literature*, ed. William L. Andrews, Frances Smith Forster, and Trudier Harris. New York: Oxford University Press, 1997. 379–383.

Danquah, Meri Nana-Ama. *Willow Weep for Me: A Black Woman's Journey through Depression*. New York: Ballantine, 1999.

de Jongh, James. "Places." In *The Oxford Companion to African American Literature*, ed. William L. Andrews, Frances Smith Forster, and Trudier Harris. New York: Oxford University Press, 1997. 575–579.

Emecheta, Buchi. *Head above Water: An Autobiography*. London: Heinemann, 1994. First published 1986 by Ogwugwu Afo, and Fontana.

———. *In the Ditch*. London: Barrie and Jenkins, 1972.

Ezenwa-Ohaeto. "Tropes of Survival and Affirmation in Buchi Emecheta's Autobiography, *Head above Water*." In *Emerging Perspectives on Buchi Emecheta*, ed. Marie Umeh. Trenton, N.J.: Africa World Press, 1996. 349–366.

Taylor, Charles. *Sources of the Self: The Making of the Modern Identity*. Cambridge, Mass.: Harvard University Press, 1989.

Taylor, Richard. *Metaphysics*. Englewood Cliffs, N.J.: Prentice-Hall, 1974.

23 LANGUAGE, MEMORY, AND THE TRANSNATIONAL: ART OF WOSENE WORKE KOSROF

Andrea E. Frohne

The first volume, *The African Diaspora: African Origins and New World Identities*, focused largely on the diaspora as a historical view back to the transatlantic slave trade. The current volume illustrates that it is becoming increasingly necessary in this globalized era to differentiate between the African diaspora of the slave trade on the one hand, and the new African diaspora concerning postcolonial migration on the other. In organizing a symposium on the new African diaspora, Isidore Okpewho and Nkiru Nzegwu focused on dynamics and experiences shaping the lives of African and African-descendant peoples in the U.S. and Europe. Paul Tiyambe Zeleza has equally supported this, suggesting an exploration of links between the two: "it is important to distinguish between dispersal and diaspora and the historic and contemporary diasporas and the connections between them" (Zeleza 261). Ali Mazrui has also called for a recognition of contemporary diasporas by famously coining the term "American African" to refer to first- or second-generation immigrants from Africa to the Americas who are "products of the Diaspora of Colonization" and postcolonial migration.[1]

This essay considers multidirectional flows and influences of ideas, nations, traditions, memories, spaces, economies, and language in contemporary art by Wosene Worke Kosrof.[2] A transnational approach is explored because an exploration of the new African diaspora necessitates a recognition of multifaceted flows and influences between Africa, the United States, and spaces traveled around the world.

As an aspect of the new African diaspora, transnationalism allows for such multidirectional relationships between multiple nation-states. Basch, Glick Schiller, and Blanc conceive of transnationalism as "the processes by which immigrants forge and sustain multi-stranded social relations that link together their societies of origin and settlement . . . [to] build social fields that cross geographic, cultural, and political borders"

(Basch et al. 7). Within this context, one simultaneously relates, using both real and imagined processes, to two or more nation-states through actions, decisions, memories, and realities immersed in such networks of relationships (Basch et al. 7). Edward Said offers the rich concept of the contrapuntal in considering overlapping communities and histories of both the metropole and formerly colonized societies (*Culture and Imperialism* 18). He writes that "habits of life, [and] expression or activity in the new environment inevitably occur against the memory of these things in another environment. Thus both the new and the old environments are vivid, actual, occurring together contrapuntally" ("Reflections on Exile" 366).

The notion of the transnational replaces static models of center/periphery and self/Other (Low and Lawrence-Zuniga 27) to allow for interconnections of identities and cultures. Before moving to Wosene Kosrof, a brief consideration of the Alada-Ulm divination tray circa 1650 illustrates the importance of recognizing influences crossing the Atlantic in both directions. Such an approach is quintessential in African art history, and proves more viable than employing a solely unidirectional look back to a culturally bounded homeland. The production and circulation of the divination tray includes a Fon artist, Yoruba divination system, Yoruba and Fon cosmologies, Ewe iconography from present-day Togo and possibly present-day Ghana, European Christianity, Fon royalty (King Tezifon), Spanish royalty (King Felipe IV), German merchants, and the Ulmer Museum in Germany. In considering the Alada-Ulm divination tray in terms of a Yoruba world-system, Olabiyi Yai writes that *itàn*, or history, is conceived as a chronology as well as a geographic dimension of history that includes expansion, so that "Yoruba have always conceived of their history as diaspora" (108).[3] To tell a story (*pa itàn*) "is to 'de-riddle' history, to shed light on human existence through time *and* space" (Yai 109; emphasis added). Therefore, an understanding of the Alada-Ulm tray from this perspective is inherently and already transcultural and transnational. Or, consider Yinka Shonibare's art works with African/Indonesian/Dutch/Brixton/British/Nigerian textiles because they are batiks based on an Indonesian technique that are manufactured in the Netherlands and Britain and exported to Africa. Complicated colonial networks of economics, culture, and commodification ensure that Shonibare's pieces categorically refuse to be situated in any one culture, geographic space, or nation.[4] Stuart Hall's consideration of cultural identity is appropriate for such multidirectional flows, "as a 'production' which is never complete, always in process, and always constituted within, not outside, representation" (222).

Just as cultures continue to interpenetrate and interconnect, nations too expand beyond their political borders. This is particularly evident in the continuing aftermath of colonialism, as well as our era of globalization, defined by Anthony Giddens as "the intensification of world-wide so-

cial relations which link distant localities in such a way that local happenings are shaped by events occurring many miles away and vice versa"
(64). Donald Levine builds on the notion of deterritorialization to suggest that the referent for nationhood is more and more detached from its
physical space (Levine 12). Because of the multiplicity of African diasporas extending beyond national borders (e.g., Atlantic, Pacific, circum-
Mediterranean, Middle Eastern, diasporas within Africa), Allen Roberts
ponders the obsolescence of "Africa" as defined by geographic location,
suggesting instead a focus upon process geographies, which consider the
"becoming" of social, political, and economic relations between people
and places. Nonetheless, these aspects of globalization that may speak to
the new African diaspora do not reflect neocolonial realities of economic
imbalance, civil war, citizenship policies, etc., faced by many in Africa.

Continued migration to the metropole or new home has resulted in
an implosion of the peripheries and former margins (Kearney 550). Postcolonial realities thus necessitate an increased realization of the disintegration of a once-imagined purity. Salah Hassan and Iftikhar Dadi's exhibition and co-edited work *Unpacking Europe* interrogate this with the
question "How European is Europe?" where an imagined homogeneity
conflicts with heterogeneous, cross-cultural influences of lived experience (Hassan and Dadi 12).

ART OF WOSENE WORKE KOSROF

How do discourses of transnationalism, globalization, and the new African diaspora impact the contemporary art world? The above issues can
be considered in relation to art by Wosene Worke Kosrof. Wosene (as he is
called professionally) was born in Ethiopia and came to the U.S. following the 1974 revolution and the ensuing Red Terror, during which Haile
Selassie was overthrown, a Marxist government took over, and thousands
were killed and persecuted. The artist earned his BFA in 1972 from the
School of Fine Arts in Addis Ababa and an MFA from Howard University in Washington, D.C.[5] As an artist who has returned to Ethiopia since
1995, traveled all over the world, and lived in the United States for at least
half of his life, how does Wosene merge, interrelate, and move within and
without the borders of the U.S. and Ethiopia? He finds the term "artist of
the African diaspora" fixed, a pigeonholing into a specific identity that
does not consider him to be an American citizen who has traveled extensively. Wosene resists being located in a specific culture or assigned one
label such as diasporic, Ethiopian, or American. His art comprises a reflection, representation, and creation of transnational flows, national identities, and personal memories. Similarly, South African artist Moshekwa
Langa in the Netherlands responded to Kobena Mercer's question, "What
does 'diaspora' mean for you?" in an interview, "Oh, but I didn't know I

was in the diaspora. It's very uncomfortable to think of myself in such a setup, because 'diaspora' is very definite . . . I resist the kind of total description that doesn't allow for other, additional parts of myself" (Mercer 106). Thus, by locating Wosene in a discussion of the transnational or a new African diaspora, I run the risk of applying yet another label to him or framing his art in another confining lens. For instance, the pieces I have selected for this essay speak to specific themes; however, as a prolific artist, Wosene explores a wide range of subject matter extending beyond my arguments offered here. Wosene in fact envisions his art as international contemporary abstract fine art, to be engaged by any audience.

My hope is that a consideration of the transnational comfortably allows one to move in and out of spaces, nations, memories, and identities. It is precisely the confinement within a category of identity that I hope the transnational can reconfigure by insisting upon multistranded flows. I would also advocate that notions of transnationalism and new diasporas apply to any people in any part of the world, and are not restricted to the colonized or marginalized. This is not to say however that issues of power are absent.

The notion of the transnational should not be confined to a simplistic conceptualization of duality between the place of origin and the new living space. Rather, Benton and Gomez usefully conceive of the transnational as a triadic relationship between the globally dispersed self, inhabited states, and the ancestral homeland (254). Such a conceptualization allows for a more realistic worldview that includes international travel and cross-cultural influences. For instance, Wosene has painted such pieces as *The French Quarter* (2003) and *Venezia* (2004) when he has been inspired by certain experiences, scenes, and memories while traveling in New Orleans and Venice and has created dialogues with the spaces afterward. *House of the Dogon* (2004) speaks to a pan-African dimension of Wosene's works, although he did not formally belong to such a group. The artist maintains a strong interest in African arts beyond the borders of Ethiopia and has incorporated Kuba textiles, Bamana mud cloths, and African masks into his works. *Roots of Jazz III* (2005) celebrates an extremely important muse for Wosene. Jazz music both inspires and becomes visual in his paintings with its rhythms, syncopation, and improvisations. *Monterey Bay II* (2005) is an excerpt of Wosene's home life in California. It represents the flurry of activity including fishermen of an earlier era catching sardines, former fish processors working the canneries of Cannery Row, cafes, restaurants, and paths on land, as well as seals, jellyfish, and orcas in the waters of the bay. The abstracted characters show "where families and friends gather by the water, to connect with one another as well as with the spirits of the Pacific."[6] This myriad of subject matter offers a rich case in point of the multidimensional and multidirectional global experiences and influences that Wosene expresses dynamically through art. If he were known only as an Ethiopian artist, would *Monterey Bay* or *The French Quarter* be explored as part of his repertoire? In fact, Ikem Okoye has pointed out that such is the case with Sokari Douglas Camp's works, in which her Kalabari-based pieces are highlighted while London-oriented ones are typically excluded from museum exhibitions.

The basis for Wosene's art is formed of characters from Amharic, the national language of Ethiopia. He has continued to develop his signature style of disassembling, distorting, and aestheticizing Amharic as he harnesses the power of text and language, transforming it into art, as in *WordPlay* (figure 23.1). His aesthetics of language is in keeping with Amharic itself, because, as Ayele Bekerie writes in *Ethiopic: An African Writing System*, the language system is "a representation of a system of knowledge," a holistic system creating a structure of knowledge comprised of philosophy, aesthetics, astronomy, ideography, musicology, numerology, and so on (Bekerie 7, 125). However, Wosene insists that we do not need to know the Amharic language or read the alphabet to access his art. In fact, the Amharic characters in Wosene's art rarely spell a word or a phrase. Wosene is, instead, interested in the concept of language as art and art as language—the possibilities of language characters in general as a source of communication, education, and connection. The characters and their forms cut across cultures for all people in a global, transnational sense. Color, art, and aesthetics are key to basking in the energy, dynamism, and multisensory beauty of the works. On a personal level, painting Amharic characters becomes a negotiation of space and place by recalling national landscapes, classic Ethiopian art, Berkeley experiences, and the many places the artist has traveled.

Wosene explores the energy and vibrancy of the Amharic alphabet in *WordPlay* (2002).[7] Characters are subtly divided into quadrants, where they are turned upside down, sideways, and right side up. As in riddles, puns, and games, language can be amusing, fascinating, or difficult to interpret. He continues the play by signing his name in Roman letters right side up, and then moving his Amharic signature to the right into the next quadrant, where it is turned sideways and reads from the top down. What are the possibilities of language symbols, which, when combined, can create grammar, and when systematized, can facilitate communication? The characters are free to float, flow, dance, wait, or extend themselves into different aspects of life, education, and communication. Wosene illustrates both the simplicity and the complexity of language as visual text and visual communication. The suggestion of the quadrants urges one to think about space and visuality. The orality of language coalesces with the domain of the visual and the three-dimensional. How does text create and interpenetrate space? How can alphabets construct and create communication and community?

Wosene explores these questions through a word play within the frame

FIGURE 23.1.
WordPlay, 2002. Acrylic on canvas, 18.25 × 18. Wosene Worke Kosrof.
Collection of the artist. Wosene Worke Kosrof.

of the art itself. Obscured within *WordPlay* several times are the words
"wax and gold," or *sem na werk*. The term refers to an art of language,
comprised of a literal and an alternative, hidden meaning, that has been
articulated at least since the fifth century. It stems from goldsmiths who
mold their work in wax and then pour in molten gold, with the wax melting away. The outer mold of wax represents the obvious meaning while
the inner gold is the hidden, enigmatic alternative. Because the alphabet
does not include symbols for accents and syllable stress, one word can
mean more than one thing depending on its pronunciation. To find the

gold or hidden meaning, the text or poetry has to be thought about and de-riddled. To this effect, the artist writes, "If we spend time looking at art, art changes us, just as the practice of meditating on an icon painting changes us. To spend time meditating shows us who we are and shows us all the complexities enfolded within us."[8] *WordPlay* is both a play of words and a work of art, a rich blending of literature, orature, and visual art offering us the opportunity to look and think beyond the surface of the composition.

Dancing Spirit (1996) is painted on goatskin in order to emulate traditional Ethiopian manuscripts (figure 23.2).[9] The roughly cut leather along the top accentuates this. Also, there are holes around the perimeter of *Dancing Spirit*, such as would be found on manuscripts, through which the pages would be threaded and bound. As well as manuscripts, *Dancing Spirit* also references protective talismanic scrolls. For the artist, "scrolls have long been an important influence in my work."[10] These traditional protective scrolls are also made of leather and are created when a client visits a *dabtara* (cleric), a healer who can remedy an illness or problem of a client. The scrolls, which are long, thin strips of goatskin, cut to the height of the client in need, are filled with protective words and imagery. In the painting *Dancing Spirit*, there is a small cross so central to healing scrolls, but it is off-center. This cross references the Seal of Solomon that can be found on healing scrolls, a particularly powerful image consisting of an eight-pointed star with a face in its center that is either divine, or the trapped face of a demon or negative spirit. The eight-pointed star becomes the Cross of Jesus, and represents victory over enemies of the client, Satan, and death (Mercier 50). The text on healing scrolls typically consists of a multitude of Names of God and prayers to combat afflictions. This written text is the powerful component to the scroll because it commands the negative spirit, destroys a demon, and has the power to resolve a problem. Demons flee upon hearing a Name of God. In naming something through text, the invisible is rendered visible and therefore disempowered.

In *Dancing Spirit*, a jumble of distorted Amharic characters tumble from the center. After distorting the characters, cutting them up, and not forming words, some of the text is unreadable and unknowable, just as a prayer scroll is not wholly understood or legible to the user populace. Toward the left, Wosene writes, "He is conquered/defeated by name," because through the act of naming the negativity on a healing scroll, the affliction is commanded and prevented from perpetuating harm. This work recalls the time, perhaps nostalgically, when scrolls were used more, as the words *fiedel mota* or "The days of the alphabet" appear above the grey *X* at bottom.

The spirits are alive in other religious traditions as well. The pre-Christian, pan-Ethiopian god Wookabi is referenced at the top. Above that, the Islamic moon and crescent can be identified in black. Finally, the hori-

FIGURE 23.2.
Dancing Spirit, 1996. Mixed media on goatskin, 24 × 28. Wosene
Worke Kosrof. Collection of David and Laura Mohr, San Francisco,
Calif. Wosene Worke Kosrof.

zontal and vertical checkerboard motifs remind us of traditional Ethiopian manuscripts, where checkerboards can operate as artistic borders, or
designs on angels' and saints' clothing.

Toward the left is the Amharic for "OK." The artist advocates tolerance for and celebration of spiritual traditions in his rendering of various
belief systems. Moreover, the combined belief systems contribute to the

national identity of Ethiopia. Old traditions are honored on the one hand, and brought into the realm of modern art on the other, as the talismanic characters of scrolls are rechoreographed by the artist. The characters are dancing spirits, freed from any fixed system of language or belief. Imbued with power and healing, the characters are alive and dancing in celebration of spiritualities that have existed throughout time.

Along the left-hand side of *Dancing Spirit* are cut-up credit cards and soda cans collected from different countries, which Wosene began working with as mixed media in the mid-1990s. Located literally on the border of the artwork, the multinational companies such as Coca-Cola and Visa are corporations that in reality cross over borders into multiple nation-states. The symbols reference the potentially destructive effects of globalization, with one culture's icons impacting another.[11] Technology, knowledge, and economy are sources of change that societies face, but at the risk of destroying or homogenizing cultures. As icons of U.S. culture and society, the soda cans and credit cards are juxtaposed against Ethiopian spirituality. However, the juxtaposition also creates a bridge between cultures and knowledge so that dialogues arise between the classic and contemporary of differing nation-states. Thus, Wosene brings popular culture, an economic critique, and the reality of globalization into Ethiopian traditions. The artist explains, "the [goat] skin is me, the credit card is who I've become . . . Most of the time I created these mixed media works as healing scrolls, with lots of credit cards and soda cans to exaggerate color where the characters should be if it were a scroll" (Purpura and Martinez-Ruíz 15).

Wosene's knowledge and memory of Ethiopia constitute the formal aspect of his work while global experiences comprise his subject matter. Similarly, the nation within the transnational is not blurred or generalized to the point of eradication, but is necessarily a component to the transnational (Angele-Ajani 295). Certain spaces, national monuments, and historic events are intertwined with collective memories in such a way that they are tied to a nation, becoming symbolic of that nation (Featherstone 53). The Amharic language, references to traditional manuscripts and healing scrolls, Coke cans, and Visa cards speak to icons of specific nations as well as transnational flows. For Wosene, they simultaneously speak to personal experiences.

Wosene again incorporates the cross from healing scrolls into *Coming Home III* (2005). The Amharic in this piece is chaotic and unorganized; however, there are broken vertical lines suggested on the canvas to mimic the verticality of talismanic scrolls. The cross and scrolls literally become modes of healing to assist Wosene, or those who have been away from home for an extended period, as reminders of the natural splendor of their country, of the spirituality embedded in their cultures, as well as of memories of their personal histories.[12] Words and invocations read aloud from scrolls can provide healing for nostalgia and homesickness, as well

as lessen feelings of loneliness or longing for the past. His scrolls seem to
have proved efficacious as the painting is bathed in a happy, light-hearted
yellow and graced by a rising sun at the top. As well as the scrolls, language itself is part of the process of "coming home." It carries the potential to speak of the rich history and culture of Ethiopia. *Coming Home III*
is evidence of a healing process that involves transnational life, travel,
and identity.

Migrations II (2006) is a powerful work that speaks to our global era
of living both within a nation-state and transnationally through constant
border-crossing and interactions with others (figure 23.3). The painting ab-
stractly illustrates the transnational that "signals the fluidity with which
ideas, objects, capital, and people now move across borders and boundaries" (Basch et al. 27). Therefore, some of the Amharic characters are
within the squares of a grid found in traditional manuscripts. Other characters are tilting, leaning, and moving over and through the grid lines to
demonstrate the fluidity of crossing borders as they emerge or converge.
Some of the Amharic characters are disjointed and broken, others extend
over the square grid into another square, some are thin and faint, and others blend with or contrast against varying colors. In the tension between
their chaos and superficial order, the characters bump into each other,
some blend together and some are divided from each other, some move en
masse while others remain alone or independent.

The extreme outer edges of *Migrations II* contain evenly spaced lines
of the sort that would serve as guidelines for scribes and parchment makers producing manuscripts. Wosene then paints his own uneven black
frame or border inside of these lines. Sometimes the lines are extended
to create quadrants within the painting, but it is evident that in other
sections, the grids have been painted over so that they are only slightly
visible or not at all. We see here implications of the construction of borders as well as the absence of them. All of this constant flux, coupled
with stationary positioning, locates us in space, but can never pinpoint
us exactly not only because we are constantly moving, but because those
around us are also. What are the implications of migration, and how are
we defined in space and as people because of border crossings? For Wosene,
the answer lies in the complexity and versatility of visual language, and
all the many narratives his visual "texts" explore. Language transcends
the nation-state, evades geographic space, and negotiates communication
and identity. Interestingly, Wosene's birth name was Woseneweleh, which
means "borderless." His grandmother shortened it to Wosene, meaning
"borderline."[13] Just as his name fluctuates, Wosene negotiates space and
place through a transnational lens in which world experiences and life
in the U.S. inform memories and lived experience of Ethiopia and vice
versa.

Night of the Red Sky (2003) was painted in Berkeley upon the artist's

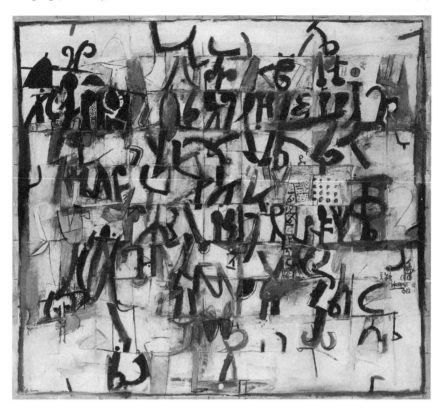

FIGURE 23.3.
Migrations II, 2006. Acrylic on linen, 46 × 51. Wosene Worke Kosrof.
Courtesy of Color of Words, Inc., Berkeley, Calif. Wosene Worke Kosrof.

return from a visit to Ethiopia and deals with painful memories of the
Red Terror, when thousands were persecuted and killed under the emerging dictatorial regime (figure 23.4). In Wosene's work, the red of bloodshed
is visible above ground, suggesting the death, fighting, and suffering in-
stigated by the Derg, the military regime. Below the green, perhaps grass,
lies a flurry of underground resistance. Each Amharic character attempts
to free itself—as if voices are struggling to speak out. These characters
represent students, philosophers, and writers printing materials underground.[14]

Amid the Red Terror above is a brilliant sun and the character "Ah,"
for hope. Wosene reflects this on the far left with a block of yellow-orange
light that flows upward in order to offer hope that the underground dissi-

FIGURE 23.4.
Night of the Red Sky, 2003. Acrylic on linen, 36 × 30.75. Wosene Worke
Kosrof. Collection of Jolene Tritt and Paul Herzog, Mt. Lakes, N.J.
Wosene Worke Kosrof.

dent movement will rise up.[15] He explains that although people's struggles
are not over, and as they work to free themselves, they endeavor to create
a new social structure. With rebuilding comes healing and understanding. Because Wosene understands healing power to emerge from society
and community, a coffee cup and an urn for brewing Ethiopian coffee
are found in the third register. This coffee cup is also significant to his
life in Berkeley when he visits coffee shops, engaging in conversation.
When meeting for coffee, barriers are broken, hope is raised, and knowledge is shared through communication. The fourth register spells "wax
and gold" to identify yet another form of communication recalling Ethiopian artistry, creativity, and history in the face of destruction and suppres-
sion. It attests to the power of language and perhaps Ethiopian identity.
Finally, ancient, long-lasting knowledge is intimated by the three Egyptian pyramids[16] still standing and dimly visible on the bloody horizon.
The pyramids fittingly occupy the horizon of death, as they once marked
underground tombs for pharaohs. However, excavations of the tombs led
to discoveries of wealth and knowledge, and here, the underground resistance lies literally beneath the pyramids. Much more overtly political
than other works, *Night of the Red Sky* concerns issues of knowledge,
memory, and history.

Wosene's ties to Ethiopia are expressed on a national level as well as
through the personal. *Words of Memory* (2002) depicts the artist's childhood home, filled with memories of his mother's storytelling, which
"filled us with our culture."[17] Here, the focus is on only a few Amharic
characters (figure 23.5). They are freed, standing on their own, and now
virtually devoid of color except for the red and black of traditional Ethiopian texts. Characters, or parts of words, *become* the structure and foundation of the house. The oral histories that filled his childhood therefore define an architecture of memory. This work was produced in the
U.S. after Wosene returned from a visit to Ethiopia, so it becomes a work
about memory created in a different geographic and temporal location.
Both memory and the imagined are integral to these multifarious, transnational flows that include not only space, but time as well for the new
African diaspora.

Nonetheless, Wosene would not confine his works to a diaspora. Although Amharic is the cultural base, it "breaks out of its borders" to become art with aesthetics, energy, taste, smell, and sound. He adds that
the characters are not limited to one people—"Who the hell knows Amharic?!"[18] For this reason, Wosene commands a transnational audience
that engages his pieces from multidirectional points of entry, including
those in and from the Horn of Africa or those who appreciate contemporary abstract art without knowledge of an African or Ethiopian context. Wosene's art circulates in contrapuntal realms. The ubiquitous language characters signify communication, education, and healing through

FIGURE 23.5.
Words of Memory, 2002. Acrylic on linen, 20 × 20. Wosene Worke Kosrof. Collection of Christa Clarke, Westfield, N.J. Wosene Worke Kosrof.

oral communication and written traditions. Wosene's art is a reflection of transnational flows, personal memories, and interpenetrating spaces and cultures.

NOTES

1. Ali Mazrui, "Africans and African Americans in Changing World Trends."
2. I would like to thank Patricia L. DiRubbo and Wosene Worke Kosrof for offering invaluable suggestions and clarifications after their detailed reading of

an earlier version comprising largely the second half of this essay. I also thank Ayele Bekerie at Cornell University for assisting me with the Amharic, particularly in *Dancing Spirit*. Research for this project was made possible by a Research and Development Scholarly Project Award from Dickinson College, Pa., in spring 2004.

3. For an additional contribution concerning the divination tray, see Ezio Bassani's essay in *The Yoruba Artist: New Theoretical Perspectives on African Arts*, ed. Rowland Abiodun, Henry Drewal, and John Pemberton III (Washington, D.C.: Smithsonian, 1994).

4. For Shonibare, see Andrea Frohne, "Review of Yinka Shonibare Exhibitions in New York City," *Nka: Journal of Contemporary African Art* 21 (2007).

5. The artist has exhibited nationally and internationally in shows that include *Seven Stories about Modern Art in Africa* at London's Whitechapel Gallery, curated by Salah Hassan (1995); *New Visions: Recent Works by Six African Artists*, curated by Salah Hassan and Okwui Enwezor (1995); *Ethiopian Passages: Dialogues in the Diaspora* at the National Museum of African Art of the Smithsonian in Washington, D.C., curated by Elizabeth Harney (2003); and *African Art, African Voices* at the Philadelphia Museum of Art, curated by John Zarobell (2004). The artist's solo exhibitions include *Words: From Spoken to Seen—The Art of Wosene Worke Kosrof* at the Mexican Heritage Plaza in San José, Calif., curated by Bárbaro Martínez-Ruiz and Allyson Purpura (2006); *My Ethiopia: Recent Paintings by Wosene Worke Kosrof* at the Neuberger Museum and the Newark Museum, curated by Christa Clarke (2003–2004); as well as exhibitions at the Skoto Gallery in New York City, Stella Jones Gallery in New Orleans, Norman Parish Gallery in Washington, D.C., and shows in Ethiopia, Japan, Puerto Rico, Germany, and Sweden.

6. *Spirits in Stone*, http://www.spiritsinstone (accessed August 8, 2006).

7. The Amharic character is referred to as a syllable because it is a consonant and vowel put together, and it is this grouping, represented by a single character, that is called "fiedel." Amharic uses the characters of the ancient liturgical language known as Ge'ez.

8. Excerpt from wall text and label copy for the exhibition *Objects of Devotion: Traditional Art of Ethiopia* in conjunction with *My Ethiopia: Recent Paintings by Wosene Worke Kosrof* at the Newark Museum of Art (2003–2004). Thank you to curator Christa Clarke for this material.

9. Interview with author, Carlisle, Pa., February 2004.

10. Excerpt from wall text and label copy for the exhibition *Objects of Devotion: Traditional Art of Ethiopia* in conjunction with *My Ethiopia: Recent Paintings by Wosene Worke Kosrof* at the Newark Museum of Art (2003–2004).

11. Interview with author, Carlisle, Pa., February 2004.

12. E-mail communication with artist, August 2006.

13. Telephone interview with author, November 7, 2005.

14. Interview with author, Carlisle, Pa., February 2004.

15. Telephone interview with author, November 7, 2005.

16. Interview with author, Carlisle, Pa., February 2004.

17. College-wide artist lecture given by Wosene Kosrof for the annual Weiner Lecture at Dickinson College, 2004.

18. Telephone interview with author, November 7, 2005.

REFERENCES

Angele-Ajani, Asale. "Displacing Diaspora: Trafficking, African Women, and Transnational Practices." In *Diasporic Africa: A Reader*, ed. Michael A. Gomez. New York: New York University Press, 2006.

Basch, Linda, Nina Glick Schiller, and Cristina Szanton Blanc. *Nations Unbound: Transnational Projects, Postcolonial Predicaments, and Deterritorialized Nation-States.* Amsterdam: Gordon and Breach, 1994.

Bekerie, Ayelie. *Ethiopic, An African Writing System: Its History and Principles.* Lawrenceville, N.J.: Red Sea Press, 1997.

Benton, George, and Edmund Terence Gomez. "Essentializing Chinese Identity: Transnationalism and the Chinese in Europe and Southeast Asia." In *Approaching Transnationalisms: Studies on Transnational Societies, Multicultural Contacts, and Imaginings of Home*, ed. Brenda Yeoh, Michael Charney, and Tong Chee Kiong. Norwell, Mass.: Kluwer, 2003. 251–300.

Clarke, Christa. *My Ethiopia: Recent Painting by Wosene Worke Kosrof.* New York: Neuberger Museum of Art, 2004.

Featherstone, Mike. "Localism, Globalism, and Cultural Identity." In *Global/Local: Cultural Production and the Transnational Imaginary*, ed. Rob Wilson and Wimal Dissanayake. Durham: Duke University Press, 1996.

Giddens, Anthony. *The Consequences of Modernity.* Stanford: Stanford University Press, 1990.

Hall, Stuart. "Cultural Identity and Diaspora." In *Identity: Community, Culture, Difference*, ed. J. Rutherford. London: Lawrence and Wishart, 1990. 222–237.

Harney, Elizabeth. *Ethiopian Passages: Dialogues in the Diaspora.* Washington, D.C.: National Museum of African Art, Smithsonian Institution, 2003.

Hassan, Salah, and Iftikhar Dadi, eds. *Unpacking Europe: Towards a Critical Reading.* Rotterdam: Museum Boijmans Van Beuingen and NAi Publishers, 2001.

Jackson, Peter, Philip Crang, and Claire Dwyer, eds. *Transnational Spaces.* London: Routledge, 2004.

Kearney, M. "The Local and the Global: The Anthropology of Globalization and Transnationalism." *Annual Review of Anthropology* 24 (1995): 547–565.

Koser, Khalid. *New African Diasporas.* New York: Routledge, 2003.

Levine, Donald. "Reconfiguring the Ethiopian Nation in a Global Era." *The International Journal of Ethiopian Studies* 1, no. 2 (1994): 1–14.

Low, Setha M., and Denise Lawrence-Zuniga, eds. *The Anthropology of Space and Place: Locating Culture.* Malden, Mass.: Blackwell, 2004.

Matsuoka, Atsuko, and John Sorenson. *Ghosts and Shadows: Construction of Identity and Community in an African Diaspora.* Toronto: University of Toronto Press, 2001.

Mazrui, Ali. "Africans and African Americans in Changing World Trends: Globalizing the Black Experience." In *Issues in Africa and the African Diaspora in the 21st Century*, ed. Seth N. Asuman and Ibipo Johnston-Anumonwo. Binghamton, N.Y.: Binghamton University Global Publications, 2001. 3–20.

Mercer, Kobena. "Moshekwa Langa: In Conversation." In *Looking Both Ways: Art of the Contemporary African Diaspora,* ed. Laurie Ann Farrell. New York: Museum for African Art, 2003.

Mercier, Jacques. *Art That Heals: The Image as Medicine in Ethiopia.* New York: The Museum for African Art, 1997.

Okoye, Ikem. *"Ajuju Azu Ndu II:* (or Fishy Questions) on the Body of Contemporary Izhon and Igbo Sculpture: Sokari Douglas Camp and Chris Afuba." In *Issues in Contemporary African Art,* ed. Nkiru Nzegwu. Binghamton, N.Y.: International Society for the Study of Africa, 1998. 19–46.

Purpura, Allyson, and Bárbaro Martinez-Ruíz. *Words: From Spoken to Seen: The Art of Wosene Worke Kosrof.* San Jose, Calif.: Mexican Heritage Corp., 2006.

Roberts, Allen. "Is 'Africa' Obsolete?" *African Arts* 33, no. 1 (Spring 2000): 1, 4–9.

Said, Edward. *Culture and Imperialism.* New York: Knopf, 1994.

———. "Reflections on Exile." In *Out There: Marginalization and Contemporary Culture,* ed. Russell Ferguson et al. Cambridge, Mass.: MIT Press, 1990. 357–366.

Yai, Olabiyi. "In Praise of Metonymy: The Concepts of 'Tradition' and 'Creativity' in the Transmission of Yoruba Artistry over Time and Space." In *The Yoruba Artist: New Theoretical Perspectives on African Arts,* ed. Rowland Abiodun, Henry Drewal, and John Pemberton III. Washington, D.C.: Smithsonian, 1994. 107–115.

Zeleza, Paul Tiyambe. "The African Academic Diaspora in the United States and Africa: The Challenges of Productive Engagement." *Comparative Studies of South Asia, Africa and the Middle East* 24, no. 1 (2004): 261–275.

24 OUT BEYOND OUR BORDERS: LITERARY TRAVELERS OF THE TRANSDIASPORA

Sandra Jackson-Opoku

Africa as an original home, exists at the limits of the imagination.
—*Kadiatu Kenneh, African Identities: Race, Nation and Culture in
Ethnography, Pan-Africanism, and Black Literature, 122*

When you write, it's like braiding your hair. Taking a handful of
coarse unruly strands and attempting to bring them unity.
—*Edwidge Danticat, "Women like Us," 220*

A rt, with its universal artifacts of human expression, also travels on webs of limitless imagination. It decodes the world and its events through images, movement, music, and words.

Consider the trickster Kwaku Ananse of Akan orature, the spider who was a man, the man who was a spider, spinning stories in a web that spans the globe. From his African embarkation he has traveled the diaspora in the voices of black people, changing names and shapes and languages as he accompanies their migrations to the Americas, Europe, back to Africa, and out again. Ananse is an oral storyteller, occupying the contact zones where diasporic communities meet and interact. Some of the characters that came along in written stories would follow the same trajectory.

In classic Ananse tradition, I come to this project as a working, wandering storyteller as well as a student of Africana literature. By no means a definitive study, this essay represents my initial attempts to identify some of the literary archetypes that inform my own work. I am interested here in fiction writers and texts that not only chronicle the particular, but consciously span the diverse cultures of African diasporas, old and new.

"Some people," says the fictional Elizabeth Osei Esubonteng, a prospective diaspora traveler, "are meant to move out beyond our borders" (Jackson-Opoku, *River* 390).

Paul Gilroy's notion of the Black Atlantic is a vast sea that locates black cultures around the Atlantic basin in degrees of cultural, historical, and political proximity.

> I have settled on the image of ships in motion across the spaces between Europe, America, Africa, and the Caribbean as a central organising symbol for this enterprise and as my starting point. . . . Ships immediately focus attention on the middle passage, on the various projects for redemptive return to an African homeland, on the circulation of ideas and activists as well as the movement of key cultural and political artefacts . . . (Gilroy 4)

Those voyages were guided by Atlantic currents: the Guinea, the Gulfstream, the Benguela, the Brazilian. There are physical and philosophical currents circulating a cultural literacy that transcends distinctions of language and nation. Vévé Clark identifies this "Diaspora literacy" as "the ability to read and comprehend the discourse of Africa, Afro-America, and the Caribbean from an informed, indigenous perspective" (Clark 40). As writers are sometimes known to mix metaphors, along with that of the ocean current I shamelessly borrow both Edwidge Danticat's and Carole Boyce Davies's symbol of the braid in attempting to define this deliberate intertwining of Africa, her generational diasporas, and the currents that flow between them (Danticat, Davies).

For purposes of discussion and the attempt to locate my work within this tradition, I define the "transDiapora" as an intersecting current of ideas that attempts to braid borderlands of nation, language, culture, and community.

If the old diaspora derives from the transatlantic slave trade and the new diaspora the movements of more recent migrants, then the transDiaspora is a deliberate attempt to connect these strands of experience. TransDiaspora art often interrogates and interprets the moments that inform the movements of black people—slavery, abolition, the colonization movement, the travels of Christian missionaries, Ethiopianism, independence and postcolonialism, the Black Power movement, Afrocentricism, etc.

Hybridity and multiple identity are central elements of the transDiaspora. Writers migrate along with our subjects. Indeed, cultural distinctions can sometimes be hard to pin down, even for producers of expressive culture. I still recall an argument with a colleague over two decades ago about whether Claude McKay was a Jamaican or African American writer. While not all writers who migrate write the transDiaspora, many inevitably document the fluid, dynamic contact zones of which they are a part.

Speculative fiction writer Nalo Hopkinson, for example, a child of a Jamaican father and a Trinidadian mother, lived all over the Caribbean, finally settling in Canada. Along with the speculative cultures of imagined realms, Hopkinson uses these lived experiences as a canvas in her writing. Both Paule Marshall and her literary daughter Edwidge Danticat identify with their Caribbean heritage and American experience. The Afropean diaspora has been represented by contemporary fiction writers including Buchi Emecheta, Helen Oyeyemi, and German-Ghanaian Amma Darko.

How is the transDiaspora imagined in the pages of fiction? A unique angle of examination is the archetype of the transDiasporan traveler. Langston Hughes saw the African diaspora as a journey of rivers.

> I bathed in the Euphrates when dawns were young.
> I built my hut near the Congo and it lulled me to sleep.
> I looked upon the Nile and raised the pyramids above it.
> I heard the singing of the Mississippi when Abe Lincoln went
>   down to New Orleans, and I've seen its muddy bosom turn
>   all golden in the sunset. (Hughes ll. 4–7)

Where rivers meet, they may flow separately within the same body of water for a time: the confluence of the blue Ohio along the muddy Mississippi, the black Rio Negro flowing alongside the clear Amazon. TransDiaspora travelers, as in the lyrics of an African American spiritual, deliberately "trouble the waters." They do not only cross borders, they lift up the edges and braid the strands of diverse cultures; traversing, transferring, and transforming as they travel.

Incarnations of this archetype include the exile, the one who migrates from his or her homeland, either through choice or involuntary circumstance; the pilgrim, a traveler of spiritual purpose; the "omobowale" (a term taken from a Yoruba expression for "the child has returned home"), a repatriated diasporan exile; and the "bintu" (a mildly derisive Pidgin English term), a first-generation exile returnee from abroad, usually one who has "been to" the industrialized West and come back with an altered persona. A brief survey of contemporary transDiasporan novels reveals a number of such figures.

An exile is the protagonist of *Hottentot Venus*, a fictional biography of Sarah Baartman, the most well-known of several South African migrants whose steatopygic features were displayed in circuses and side shows throughout nineteenth-century Europe. Her transDiaporan experience is illustrated by her troubled interactions with Reverend Wedderburn, a black British abolitionist attempting to rescue her from her exploitation: "Inhuman is what is happening to you, Sarah. You are the unwitting collaborator of your own exploitation, agent of your own dehumanization!" (Chase-Riboud 132). *The Second Life of Samuel Tyne* casts a family of exiles from colonial Gold Coast into a small town in Canada, where they interact with the resident white and black communities (Edugyan).

Buchi Emecheta's subjects have mirrored her own peregrinations. Though earlier novels were set in Nigeria, more recent works chronicle the travels of exiles of various nationalities who strike out for foreign lands, as well as bintus who return home with the alterations of exile. These include *The Family, Second Class Citizen*, and *Kehinde*.

An "omobowale" is the protagonist of Guadeloupean novelist Maryse Condé's first two novels, which tell the story of a francophone West Indian woman searching for her roots in Africa. The pilgrim is featured in Alice Walker's *The Color Purple* in the person of Nettie, an African American missionary to a fictional Olinka village.

Many of these texts combine archetypes. Akosua Busia, Hollywood actor and daughter of a former Ghanaian prime minister, authored *The Seasons of Beentu Blackbird*. Despite its title, the African American protagonist is not a returned exile, but an omobowale and sexual pilgrim, a polygamist whose visits to lovers in the U.S., Caribbean, and Africa are governed by seasons of the year. In the same tradition, the omobowale-pilgrim protagonist of Isidore Okpewho's coming-of-age novel, *Call Me by My Rightful Name*, is an African American whose sudden ability to recite chants in corrupted Yoruba leads him to Africa in a search for ancestral connections. The biracial central character of British Nigerian writer Helen Oyeyemi's first novel is a child born in the West and returned to Africa for psychic healing.

The figure of the transDiaspora traveler populates my small body of work. *The River Where Blood Is Born* is a sweeping historical saga charting the journeys of eight generations of African women across multiple continents, cultures, and realms. In *Hot Johnny (and the Women Who Loved Him)*, the transDiaspora is represented by the experiences of the protagonist's Afro-Mexican great-grandmother, as well as a trio of African women he encounters while stationed as a U.S. airman in Somalia and Kenya. A third novel in progress tells the aftermath of a white world-beat musician's death and its influence on a cast of transnational characters.

TransDiaspora fiction sets about the ambitious projects of illuminating certain historical moments, giving voice to silenced characters and experiences, conjuring ancestral memories, and fostering linkages among diverse communities of African descent.

An inevitable struggle to achieve cultural authenticity and authority are challenges diasporan writers face creating stories that may be distant or disconnected from their immediate experience. Indeed, writers stepping outside their cultural comfort zones might well be seen as violating the conventional wisdom of creative writing: "write what you know."

There are the political considerations of agency and appropriation—

i.e., does someone outside a culture, even one of African descent, have a right to tell another's story? How much research must be undertaken before a writer achieves the authority to "get it right"? How much can be left to creative license when one portrays real people and events? Does the writer owe primary allegiance to the story or to the culture of origin? Are writers in North America or Europe guilty of cultural imperialism when interpreting the African or Caribbean experience through the lens of literature?

Nalo Hopkinson admits that in the project of accessing transDiasporan stories, mistakes are unfortunate but almost inevitable. Alice Walker has been both celebrated and excoriated for tackling the controversial topic of female circumcision in several of her works. Emecheta has been criticized for flubbing Jamaican patois in *The Family*. Chase-Riboud constructs a peasant protagonist with unexpected sophistication. The young Sarah Baartman engages in philosophical debates with European men, and even conjures orangutan references in a South African landscape where "wolves and coyotes howl in the valley," though such animals are not native to that part of the world (Chase-Riboud 42).

Literary scholar Henry Louis Gates traces the trope of the talking book to the eighteenth century, when the perception among enslaved Africans held that books spoke to the literate and withheld their secrets from the unlettered. He offers as evidence this reference from the slave narrative *A Narrative of the Most Remarkable Particulars in the Life of James Albert Ukawsaw Gronniosaw:*

> As soon as my master had done reading I follow'd him to the place where he put the book, being mightily delighted with it, and when nobody saw me, I open'd it and put my ear down close upon it, in great hope that it would say something to me; but was very sorry and greatly disappointed when I found it would not speak, this thought immediately presented itself to me, that every body and every thing despised me because I was black. (Gates 136)

Gates claims the trope of the talking book as an intertextual discourse that was referenced and revised in other narratives that followed it. Indeed, Chase-Riboud uses this trope to express the unlettered Sarah Baartman's fascination with the written word, as well as her frustration at being unable to master it. Problematic, though, is that she lifts the text almost verbatim from Gronniosaw's narrative.

> As soon as Reverend Freehouseland had finished reading, I followed him to the place where he put the book, and when nobody was looking, I opened it and put my ear down close upon it, in the hope that it would say something to me. But I was heartbrokenly disappointed when I found it would not speak to me, and the thought immediately came to me that the book wouldn't speak to me because I was black. (Chase-Riboud 18)

While Chase-Riboud credits several research sources in her acknowledgments, the origin of that important passage remains uncited.

Despite challenges represented by the aforementioned works (and others unmentioned), these are texts that attempt to leap the fences of language and lived experiences, community and culture, politics and place in an attempt to recognize, as Janie Starks says in *Their Eyes Were Watching God:* "You have tuh go there to know there" (Hurston 230). Those of us who shrug aside the limits of "writing what you know" embrace the mission of attempting and sometimes failing to construct, in the words of writer and literary scholar Lynda Hill, "a bridge across transnational borders" (Hill).

> Maybe I'll get in touch with all my different relatives in Chicago, California, Cairo [Illinois], even Africa. We'll have a great big family reunion. And we'll all tell our stories of what happened when we were away from each other. (Sandra Jackson-Opoku, *The River Where Blood Is Born* 184)

REFERENCES

Busia, Akosua. *The Seasons of Beentu Blackbird.* New York: Washington Square, 1997.

Chase-Riboud, Barbara. *Hottentot Venus.* New York: Doubleday, 2003.

Clark, Vévé. "Developing Diaspora Literacy and Marasa Consciousness." In *Comparative American Identities: Race, Sex, and Nationality in the Modern Text,* ed. Hortense Spillers. New York: Routledge, 1991.

Condé, Marysé. *Hérémakhonon.* Washington, D.C.: Three Continents, 1982.

———. *A Season in Rihata.* Portsmouth, N.H.: Heinemann, 1988.

Danticat, Edwidge. "Women like Us." In *Krik? Krak!* New York: Soho, 1995.

Davies, Carole Boyce. *Black Women, Writing and Identity: Migrations of the Subject.* London: Routledge, 1994.

Edugyan, Esi. *The Second Life of Samuel Tyne.* New York: Amistad, 2004.

Emecheta, Buchi. *The Family.* New York: George Braziller, 1990.

———. *Kehinde.* Portsmouth, N.H.: Heinemann, 1994.

———. *Second Class Citizen.* New York: George Braziller, 1983.

Gates, Henry Louis. *The Signifying Monkey: A Theory of African-American Literary Criticism.* New York: Oxford University Press, 1989.

Gilroy, Paul. *The Black Atlantic: Modernity and Double Consciousness.* Cambridge, Mass.: Harvard University Press, 1992.

Hill, Lynda. "Seeing the Mirage: African American Narrative and Change." Paper presented at the Sixth Annual African Studies Consortium Workshop, October 2, 1998. http://www.Africa.upenn.edu/Workshop/linda98.html (accessed December 18, 2008).

Hopkinson, Nalo. Keynote address to the Fourteenth Annual Gwendolyn Brooks Writers Conference of Black Literature and Creative Writing, October 2004.

Hughes, Langston. "The Negro Speaks of Rivers." In *The Norton Anthology of African American Literature,* 1st ed., ed. Henry Louis Gates and Nellie McKay. New York: Norton, 1997.

Hurston, Zora Neale. *Their Eyes Were Watching God*. New York: Harper Perennial Modern Classics, 1998.

Jackson-Opoku, Sandra. *Hot Johnny (and the Women Who Loved Him)*. New York: Ballantine, 2001.

———. *The River Where Blood Is Born*. New York: Ballantine, 1997.

Kenneh, Kadiatu. *African Identities: Race, Nation and Culture in Ethnography, Pan-Africanism, and Black Literature*. London: Routledge, 1998.

Okpewho, Isidore. *Call Me by My Rightful Name*. Trenton, N.J.: Africa World Press, 2004.

Oyeyemi, Helen. *The Icarus Girl*. New York: Nan A. Talese, 2005.

Walker, Alice. *The Color Purple*. New York: Harvest Books, 2003.

———. *Possessing the Secret of Joy*. New York: Pocket, 1993.

25

THE GUYANA DIASPORA AND HOMELAND CONFLICT RESOLUTION

Perry Mars

The Guyana diaspora can best be viewed as a subset of the Caribbean diaspora overseas, although it demonstrates some peculiar features. It is part of the reverse migration trend from the colonies to the metropolitan centers in Europe and North America, which had its main beginnings in the twentieth century following several centuries of forced migration of various peoples, mainly from Africa and Asia, as slaves or indentured servants for colonial plantations throughout the region. The critical peculiarity of the Guyana diaspora resides in the fact that while for the Caribbean as a whole the descendants of African slaves constitute the overwhelming bulk of the population (about 90 percent), Guyana is the only Caribbean country with a majority of Asians, who constitute about 50 percent of its population. This means that, contrary to the suggestion of the main literature on Caribbean migrations or transnationalism (Goulbourne; Harvard University), the Guyana diaspora is not a culturally homogeneous one, but one that seriously reflects the history and contours of the ethnic, cultural, and political bifurcation and conflict that pervade the Guyana scene at home.

Yet, because Guyana itself is striving to become "one people, one nation" and with "one destiny," as the Guyana official motto itself stipulates, it is important to view the Guyana diaspora as at least potentially integrated, with unified aspirations toward peace and progressive development for the original home country. Indeed the diaspora is not home, but mainly a place to expand one's horizons and seek better opportunities for the life one wishes to have at home (see Gordon). For that reason most Guyana diasporan individuals keep returning constantly to their homeland, and investing (mainly through remittances) in the private development of the families they left behind.

This chapter, however, looks beyond recognition of the Guyana diaspora strictly as a source of monetary and material contributions (remittances and financial investments), and reconsiders this albeit loose overseas grouping primarily as a fount of knowledge and expertise relevant to the management and organization of development strategies, including the resolution of political and ethnic conflict, in the homeland. The concept of development here is viewed in terms of a particular relationship between government and people which fosters expansions in the range of freedom and opportunities for all the people of that particular society (see Sen, *Development*). It is further recognized here that a major facilitating condition for the flourishing of such development as freedom is the establishment or realization of a relatively stable and manageable political environment. Thus the existence or persistence of domestic political and ethnic instability is recognized here as at least complicating, if not directly impeding or negating, the development process.

Authoritative efforts toward resolution of political and ethnic conflicts are therefore necessary for establishing basic conditions for political and economic development in the particular society. Contributions toward conflict resolution are approached both indirectly, via the possible reduction of poverty levels which feed criminalized violence and political conflicts within Guyanese communities, and directly, through the actual role of prominent overseas Guyanese individuals and organizations in mediating the conflict situation at higher national political levels in Guyana, or actively supporting the domestic forces that conduce toward the reduction of violent political conflicts in the society.

More specifically, this chapter examines the actual and potential contributions of the Guyanese diaspora abroad, particularly in North America, to the resolution of serious national crises, particularly violent political and ethnic conflicts, at home in Guyana. The focus is on the post-1992 period, when Guyana returned to a democratic phase with free and fair elections, in contrast to the earlier, more authoritarian phase (1964–1985), which was characterized by harsh state repressive practices and the stymieing of democracy through blatant tinkering and rigging of the electoral process to maintain the then People's National Congress (PNC) party rule. At the same time, however, the post-1992 period of rule by the People's Progressive Party (PPP) represented a phase when political conflict in Guyana degenerated into both criminalized and armed guerrilla activities combined with selective ethnic targeting, deadly dimensions of narco-gangsterism, and routinized military and police violence complemented by the operation of politicized death squads.

THE CONFLICT PROBLEM

The problem to be addressed is the persistence and escalation of political and ethnic conflict and the frustrating efforts to reorient the contending domestic forces toward peace and political reconciliation in the country. This chapter attempts to identify one of the possible sources of help toward conflict resolution in Guyana as the Guyana diaspora, and to evaluate its potential for successful intervention in this regard. The argument here is that the Guyana diaspora overseas is in a most advantageous position to contribute to homeland conflict resolution because of its potentially objective distancing from the fray, its obvious concerns for family security back home, and its access to greater resources and high-level political and international influences in the U.S. and North America. For these reasons Guyana diaspora interventions can make a difference in transforming persistent and divisive conflicts rooted in economic disadvantages and inequality into viable cooperation and reconciliation between the two main contending forces.

Historically, the various political conflicts in Guyana can be specifically characterized as follows: electoral/political strife in the 1950s; racial/political violence with foreign instigation during the 1960s; violent political repression during the 1970s; a brief uneasy period of peaceful overtures between government and opposition during the 1980s; a return to electoral violence and ethnic conflict in the 1990s; and what could be called a degeneration into politicized criminal gangsterism, with ethnic targeting attended by excessive police/military and death squad operations, particularly since 2000.

The significance of the post-1992 period is that it represented a series of escalation phases ranging from what could be called "limited violent conflict" (1992–1998), when the political protests primarily against the results of the 1992 and 1997 elections erupted into a combination of street riots, violent ethnic targeting, and coercive state/police interventions to quell the disturbances, to "increasing militarization of the conflict" (1999–2005), with the increased use of the joint forces (military and police) to surgically put down what the government perceived to be criminal violence, located primarily in one village, Buxton, on the east coast of the Demerara region. Events beyond 2005 have seen a further, more intense escalation of the violence to reach what many regard as a phase of insurgency, particularly in light of the January 2008 massacre by masked gunmen of several families, including men, women and children, in an ethnic village, Lusignan, that is a known "electoral stronghold" of the ruling party (PPP/C) and government (see *Kaieteur News*, January 27, 2008; *Stabroek News*, January 27, 2008; *Guyana Chronicle*, January 27, 2008).

Sometimes massive, sometimes sporadic interethnic violence between supporters of both PPP and PNC, particularly following the 1997 elections, threatened to escalate the violence into even greater levels of intensity. Thus, the post-1999 phase combined armed attacks on the police, the politicization of criminal and narco-gangsterism, further ethnic targeting and violence, joint police and army operation against suspected village guerillas, and the extensive use of paramilitary death squads in support of police operations. More specifically, this third phase saw turmoil within the labor movement, and an escalation of the bellicose rhetoric between the two major parties: the then opposition (PNC) leader, Desmond Hoyte, calling for massive "civil disobedience," and the PPP/C president, Bharat Jagdeo, likening opposition activism to "terrorism" (see *Guyana Chronicle*, April 19, 2002; Amnesty International). It was within this escalatory context that a storming of the Presidential Secretariat by opposition supporters took place, resulting in two protestors being killed by the police, and two of the protest leaders charged with treason (see *Guyana Chronicle*, July 18, 2002).

What could be called "the Buxton case" came after 2000 to represent par excellence the organized armed (or more militarized) phase of political and civil conflict. Buxton, a predominantly Afro-Guyanese village about 12 miles outside of Georgetown, the capital city, with high levels of unemployment among youths, provided a convenient milieu for escaped prisoners, drug traffickers, and other deadly criminal elements. Police killings of several armed youths in Buxton led to retaliatory killings of several policemen by gangs, giving rise to President Jagdeo's call to the armed forces in May 2003 to "clean out Buxton" (see PNC, press release, May 8, 2003). Two of the main political characteristics of these Buxton events were (a) the overt politicization of gangster activities when gangsters defined themselves as "freedom fighters" and appeared to have gained tacit opposition political support (see *Guyana Chronicle*, August 27, 2002, and May 3, 2002), and (b) the target killing of East Indians in apparent vengeance attacks against the PPP/C government, which was heavily supported by this particular ethnic group (see *Guyana Chronicle*, July 19, 2002, and January 27, 2008; GHRA, press release, June 10, 2003).

It was also during this post-2000 period of heightened politicized violence that the rise of the notorious death squad became most evident, and itself contributed to the level of intensity of overall violence of this period. The death squad has often been referred to as the "phantom squad" because of its shadowy, secretive, and deadly character. It was said to be born in response to the deteriorating security situation in the country, characterized by the precipitous rise in violent crime following the prison breakout of some notorious criminals in 2002, and the deportation of drug and other criminal offenders from the United States back to Guyana (see *Stabroek News*, January 10, 2004). Opposition charges that the death squad was nurtured by the Guyana government (managed by the then Minister of Home Affairs) and financed by wealthy businessmen (see *Stabroek News*, January 10, 2004, and January 16, 2004) were, however, not borne out by a government-imposed Commission of Inquiry in 2004, particularly after key witnesses either were suddenly killed (execution-style) by unknown assailants, or otherwise failed to show up at the proceedings (see *Caribbean Net News*, June 25, 2004). Many killings of youths in the country, for which no arrests or charges have so far been made, have been attributed to operatives of the phantom squad (ibid.).

The main causal source of the conflict situation in Guyana could be summarized in terms of the skewed or imbalanced distribution of resources and rewards throughout the Guyanese society. From this main source spring the other causal factors such as ethnic divisiveness, political power competition, biased electoral manipulations, class poverty, and the like. Thus the Guyana conflict situation is basically resource-driven, although it combines significantly interest-based and identity-based conflicts in its definitional characteristics (see Mars, "Ethnic Politics"). The relationship between ethnic divisiveness, poverty, and political violence in Guyana is evidenced by three basic factors: (a) the concentration of criminal and political violence in highly impoverished areas such as Buxton and the east coast of the Demerara county, Agricola on the east bank of the Demerara river, and certain impoverished areas (such as Albouystown) in the city of Georgetown; (b) the concentration of African Guyanese in these particular impoverished regions; (c) the association of the people in theses areas with opposition politics and a notion of freedom fighting; and (d) the high unemployment rates, particularly among the youths, within this African-based section of the Guyanese society, as evidenced by the consistent downsizing of employment within the public sector and the mining industry where Afro-Guyanese predominate.

The failure of several international mediation efforts to significantly contain the explosive conflict levels in Guyana has led to an interest in new types of interventions which might better grasp the nuances of the Guyana situation, particularly the peculiar linkages between national economic and social development and the capacity to resolve violent and divisive conflicts as a precondition toward developmental change. The Carter Center, which successfully helped in negotiating the return of free democratic elections in Guyana in 1992, had only limited successes in its subsequent efforts to mediate the expanding electoral violence following both the 1997 and 2001 elections (see Carter Center). Similarly, both the Commonwealth Secretariat and Caricom attempted to mediate the Guyana political conflict situation without much success either (see Caricom, "Caribbean," "Guyana"). Above all, the failure of these international mediation efforts would seem to represent a failure of the will to persevere in what could be defined as a protracted conflict situation in a small country with very low international prestige. To succeed in this context, mediation efforts must be sustained and continuous, and only those who have a direct stake in the welfare and future of the country will be able to muster the will to sustain such an indefinite, possibly infinite, almost sacrificial commitment.

At this juncture the UNDP intervention through what it called the

Social Cohesion Program for Guyana becomes relevant (United Nations Development Program). The UNDP works closely with governmental institutions (particularly the Ethnic Relations Commission) and non-governmental organizations (such as the Guyana Human Rights Association) to bring together a variety of civil society groupings in what they call a national conversation on the conflict situation to flesh out common grounds that might conduce toward political and ethnic reconciliation and conflict resolution in the country. However, this approach has so far not benefited from Guyanese expertise in the areas of either conflict resolution or poverty reduction, and relies almost wholly on individual foreign contracted experts to undertake a task which calls for more grounded information and knowledge of the Guyanese historical experience in a protracted conflict situation.

Indeed, three basic ingredients are required to sustain protracted mediation efforts. These are (a) stakeholder interest, which implies having, for instance, roots, property, or family living in the area of conflict; (b) resources, in the sense of being part of the capability to provide significant material and economic help to the nation as a whole; and (c) leverage, in the sense of being in a position to significantly influence the decisions and policies of the political elites and decision makers in the particular society. While the foreign contractors, ranging from the Carter Center and Caricom to the UNDP, might have either the resources or possibly some leverage in the Guyana conflict equation, only the Guyana diaspora can muster capabilities in all three of these requirements for protracted mediation efforts in the Guyana conflict situation.

THE GUYANA DIASPORA

The basic characteristics of the Caribbean diaspora, of which the Guyana diaspora is a constituent part, are (a) the establishment of settled communities abroad in metropolitan centers of North America and Europe, mainly in New York, Toronto, and London, (b) retention and promotion of Caribbean culture, particularly in the arts, entertainment, and cuisine, (c) maintenance of a position of what in Guyanese parlance could be called "in-betweenity," that is, retaining the concept of home for their home countries while permanently residing abroad with frequent travels to and lengthy stays in their home country—the concept of dual citizenship; and (d) contributing materially and significantly to homeland economy and family welfare via remittances and some economic investments.

The Guyana diaspora abroad is one neglected source of possible mediation capabilities that can have a positive impact on the reduction or resolution of both poverty and political conflict levels back home. A significant proportion of the Guyana population—equivalent to more than half of the current population at home—resides in the United States alone. The

Guyana diaspora population in New York City alone numbers between 130,000 and 140,000 (see New York City Department of City Planning; Kershaw). Statistics indicate that 89 percent of Guyana's most educated population (most at the tertiary levels and postgraduate levels) are living in the most developed (OECD) countries abroad (*Economist*, November 3, 2005). And this percentage is among the very highest in the world.

The Guyana diaspora's contribution to economic development (and implicitly to poverty reduction) is recognized in the high volume of remittances to the homeland. The total volume of gross diaspora remittances from the United States alone to Guyana was about US$230 million in 2003–2004 (Orozco, "Distant but Close" 31), reflecting a significant increase from US$54 million in 1997 (Orozco, "Remittances"). These remittances are said to equate to 83 percent of official development assistance and 134 percent of foreign direct investments, and to represent 13 percent of overall GDP (Orozco, "Remittances"). In addition, gross remittances from the Guyana diaspora constitute 80 percent of the personal income of recipients, and 50 percent of per capita GDP (Orozco, "Distant but Close" 35). However, these remittances generally support livelihoods, rather than business investments (Orozco, "Distant but Close" 6).

The significance of this Guyana diaspora, as far as leverage in relation to the peace processes back home is concerned, lies in the fact that both major political parties directly engaged in the ethnic and power conflict (PPP and PNC) rely heavily on the diaspora for funding of their political campaigns, particularly during national elections (Holder). Remittances from this diaspora alone amount to 83 percent of all official development assistance (ODA) abroad, and are sent to relatives and friends who constitute the backbone supports of these competing parties back home (see Orozco, "Remittances"). Thus, the Guyana diaspora, if properly organized on the basis of its multiethnic appeal, can muster the necessary leverage to influence the direction of party policies in their homeland.

However, the Guyana diaspora must first overcome its own intrinsic problems if it is to become relevant and instrumental to the resolution of the security and development needs of the homeland society. First, the Guyana diaspora lacks any systematic overarching organization. The more than two hundred different and separate groupings of Guyanese associations scattered around the U.S. and North America—inclusive of alumni associations, cultural and festive organizations, and family and kinship networks—need to be brought together under a single umbrella association. This will be a first step toward bridging the serious ethnic divide which attends these Guyanese organizations and communities abroad.

Second, it is necessary to get beyond the essentially celebratory activities of these organizations toward a more consciously organized overarching body which places nationalist political objectives above racially divisive interests in order to influence the peaceful democratic and political processes in the homeland. The Guyana diaspora in North America, for instance, is steeped in ethnic divisions, very much reflecting the politically organized ethnic divisions back home. The Toronto chapter of the University of Guyana alumni, not unlike the New York grouping that surrounds the *Guyana Journal,* is overwhelmingly East Indian in composition, while the leadership of the Guyana Folk Festival in New York tends to be overwhelmingly Afro-Guyanese. Indeed, a recent Harvard University study suggests that the lack of trust between the two major contending parties back home is reproduced similarly within the Guyana diaspora in the United States, with equally divisive results (see Harvard).

Third, the Guyana diaspora, in order to create a better and more relevant and unified association, should emulate the best models of nationalist diaspora associations abroad. Among the Caribbean diaspora organizational efforts the Jamaican approach represents perhaps the best example of any such model. Jamaicans in the United States have always been far ahead of the others as far as these diaspora organizational efforts are concerned. Historically, the creation of the Jamaica Progressive League (JPL) in Harlem in the 1930s influenced the creation and development of the first organized political party (the PNP in 1942) and other movement toward political democracy and independence in Jamaica and the Caribbean generally. In fact, the development of the PPP in Guyana owed much of its founding in 1947 to the influence and example of the early PNP in Jamaica (see Mars, *Ideology*). Today, the Jamaican government is still ahead with its creation of a ministry to systematically engage and involve the participation of its diaspora overseas in homeland developmental efforts.

A primary objective of the proposed overarching Guyana diaspora organization is to foster intercommunication and mutuality of interchanges or interactions between these ethnically polarized groups representing the various Guyanese communities in the United States and Canada. This accommodation must be accomplished for the more important objective of contributing to ethnic and political conflict resolution or mitigation back home. Further, a deliberate attempt must be made to organize Guyanese representing all sides of the ethnic divide to build an organized body that must not only be essentially multiethnic, but be able to simultaneously understand and transcend the different entrenched political positions back home.

Much, however, depends on whether the potential of the Guyana diaspora for overcoming its organizational and divisive problems tends to be greater than the prospects of the two divided ethno-political forces back home overcoming their divisive conflict problems by themselves. It is reasonable to assume that the Guyana diaspora is in a better position compared to the entrenched parties back home to accomplish this difficult leap, since it constitutes the most educated and skilled component of the Guyanese population. The challenge is to transform the brain drain into a brain gain. Migrants leave their homelands essentially to develop themselves—through advanced education, development of skills, or better and more lucrative employment opportunities—and so provide the necessary human capital that is beneficial for the further development of both host and homeland countries.

PUSH-PULL DIMENSIONS

In the Guyana context, the primary factors pushing Guyanese away from their homeland relate to both political instability and economic hardships. Economic push factors include concentrated poverty, lack of job opportunities, deprivation, and inequalities at home. What is most plausible is that while poverty could be said to provide fertile conditions for popular mobilization and recruitment toward criminality and public protest, it is the addition of political grievances and discontent (or even propaganda) to the equation that transforms protest and unrest into political or communal violence and politicized criminal gangsterism.

A major part of the political violence syndrome in Guyana, which propels a significant proportion of out-migration from the country, is the vicious cycle of crime upsurge, police impunity, and violent unrest. Orozco, for example, contends that it is this "continuous violence" which is a major push factor in the out-migration of both Guyana and Jamaican populations, which are major constituents of the Caribbean diaspora (see Orozco, "Distant but Close").

Guyana is, indeed, at serious risk of escalation of political conflict into larger-scale insurrectionary political violence. The underlying risk factors include the persistence or increase of sharp racial, ethnic, and class inequalities, seriously skewed resource distribution along ethnic lines, precarious political legitimacy of successive governing regimes, highly polarized ethnic politics, dislocations among the black peasantry, and what could be called "lumpen development," characterized by entrenched poverty, unemployment, and criminal gangsterism and situated mainly among black youths, particularly in the urban and outlying areas.

Ethnic polarization along the two main party lines (PPP/East Indians, and PNC/blacks) followed the introduction of Westminster electoral democracy in the early 1950s, and would seem to have increased in violent intensity with every national election since then. The main causal location of the increasing strife and violent conflict seems to be the recurrent legitimacy crises which succeeding governments have experienced since independence in 1966. This continual crisis of political legitimacy could be summed up in terms of opposition frustrations in the wake of regime intransigence, lack of inclusiveness in governance, and coercive state response to popular demand. Spoilers of the peace and protagonists of violent conflict include, historically, the two major antagonistic parties and foreign destabilizing interventions, and currently, sporadic urban youth gangs and others closely associated with narcotics traffickers, and a notorious but illusive death squad.

As regards the pull factors that propel the need of the diaspora individuals and groups to make contributions toward conflict resolution in the Guyana homeland, it is worth considering Guyana ambassador Odeen Ishmael's statement to the Guyana diaspora communities in North America. Speaking to University of Guyana (UG) alumni in Toronto in 1999, and again at a Guyanese Diaspora Conference in Washington, D.C., in 2002, Ishmael contended that the Guyana diaspora can be mobilized to successfully mediate to conflict hiatus between the contending parties and groups at home (Ishmael, "Speech," "Remarks"). The Harvard University study also suggests that three-quarters of respondents in their survey feel that contributions in skills and knowledge are the most effective way to impact their home countries. However, while most (47 percent) of the responses see education as the most crucial development priority for their contributions, a much smaller proportion chose security (18 percent) or stability (17 percent) as important (Harvard). But, with the recent escalation of political violence into criminalized ethnic targeting and narco-gangsterism, with widespread and reckless armed robberies and execution killings throughout the country, Guyanese abroad are naturally anxious about the security of their kinfolk and friends at home, and would wish to make efforts to ease or mitigate the downward security spiral.

The failure of the political elite in Guyana to more systematically involve the knowledge/expertise base of this group in mediating the conflict process is so far a serious omission in the way of national contributions to homeland conflict resolution. Most probably, the biggest obstacle to engaging the Guyana diaspora in these efforts is the government's ambiguity about diaspora involvement coupled with its reluctance to admit that there is a serious ethnic problem in the country. Although the PPP elections manifesto of 2006 indicated that the former PNC regime was characterized by Afro-Guyanese political domination and discrimination against other minorities, leading to the outward migration of "hundreds of thousands of Guyanese" fleeing "tyranny and poverty" (PPP/C, "A Brighter Future" 1), intellectual pundits within the PPP government, reinforced by a South African "expert" on conflict resolution, are today adamant that the perception of ethnic conflict in the country either does not exist or is an exaggeration to say the least (see *Guyana Chronicle,* May 9, 2005; *Kaieteur News,* April 20, 2005). Presumably, ethnic conflict suddenly disappeared with the coming of the new PPP government in 1992, in the same way as the PNC government before it claimed the PNC government in 1964 immediately brought "peace not conflict." Presumably also, by this reasoning, the Ethnic Relations Commission officially established by the PPP government in 2003 is intended to mediate a nonexistent ethnic conflict situation in the country.

Compared to the Jamaican government, which set up a ministry for the systematic incorporation of the Jamaican diaspora overseas, the PPP/C government reserved only a single short paragraph in its 2006 elections manifesto to outline its Guyana diaspora policy: "Greater cooperation with the Diaspora as a source of technical expertise and capital for Guyana's development" (PPP/C 29). Also, the PNCR as a possible alternative government did not go very far beyond the PPP/C in perceiving of the Guyana diaspora mainly as a source of capital and economic expertise. In its 2006 elections manifesto the PNCR targets what it terms "Direct Diaspora Investment (DDI)—the largest pool of disposable income held by Guyanese in the Diaspora" (PNCR-1G, "Move Forward " 10).

Another probable discouragement to diaspora involvement in conflict resolution is the view articulated by a small vocal section of the Afro-Guyanese community that the focus on conflict resolution is a disguised attempt at the pacification of Afro-Guyanese militancy and protest. However, this perception is far from accurate. Rather, conflict resolution is to be perceived in much broader and more positive terms to mean not pacification, in the sense of termination of conflict or the squelching of political demand or protest, but reconciliation of the various forces and interests, each with its own autonomous agenda which might in some critical respects conflict with that of the other. Conflict resolution in our sense attempts to balance the governmental penchant for using coercive force with the establishment of a political system characterized by equitable and distributive justice for all. Thus in conflict processes the military/repressive approaches give way to negotiated political solutions.

DIASPORA IMPACT

Past mediations efforts have so far not been sufficiently sustained, and need to be further buttressed by the input of other committed stakeholders such as the transnational communities comprising the Guyana diaspora abroad. Apart from its demonstrated family and political-economic commitments to the country, and notwithstanding its own limitations involving ethnic divisiveness within this group, the Guyana diaspora indeed possesses the necessary educational expertise and skills which can collectively contribute to the ongoing processes of peaceful negotiations between the two major parties and eventually toward the mitigation or transformation of ethnic and political conflicts at home. Combining this expertise with the leverage they already possess through making monetary contributions to political party programs, campaigns, and mobilization efforts, a properly organized Guyana diaspora could undoubtedly influence political policies and decisions back home.

Among the Guyana diaspora initiatives in mediating the conflict resolution processes back home are the two major conferences on conflict resolution jointly mounted by Clark Atlanta University in Atlanta and the University of Guyana in 2002 in Washington, D.C., and in 2005 in Guyana, and also a Memorandum of Understanding (MOU) signed between Wayne State University in Detroit and the University of Guyana in 2004 regarding postgraduate training in dispute resolution for University of Guyana faculty. However, while the conferences either fell into disarray or were slighted or rebuffed by the Guyana government (see Sukhdeo), the MOU has been limited by its production of only three Master of Arts graduates in dispute resolution so far, while one of the colleges (College of Urban Labor and Metropolitan Affairs) that helped in initiating the program was discontinued by Wayne State University in 2006.

Nevertheless, given its qualifications, the Guyana diaspora can impact the conflict situation in Guyana in the following ways:

(a) Promoting Greater Democracy

The Guyana diaspora can help in community education aimed toward understanding the community's role in peaceful outreaches across ethnic borders to control crime and mitigate conflicts, as an alternative to the standard use of military impunity and state coerciveness to address crime and protest. The diaspora's contribution is also important in helping to persuade or pressure the parties to come together—to cooperate more meaningfully with each other. It can be instrumental in providing memoranda useful to the rewriting of the Guyana constitution to make for more inclusive government, and to introduce meaningful changes in the electoral system.

(b) Facilitating Continuous Dialogue between the Major Parties

The Guyana diaspora has the necessary leverage to press for the resuscitation of the Herdmanston Accords brokered by Caricom, and for the Constructive Engagement processes between the PPP and PNC back home in Guyana. The leverage the Guyana diaspora possesses relates to the campaign contributions demanded from diaspora communities by the various political parties back home, the remittances they send to their families, and the educational expertise they command. Properly organized, the Guyana diaspora can use this leverage to pressure or bargain with the domestic political elite toward reconciliation. Previous studies suggest the importance of outside, impartial mediation from expert groups in the Guyana conflict situation (see Mars, "Ethnic Politics"). A properly organized Guyana diaspora can provide a more sustained and committed expertise here, particularly since the mediation efforts of other third parties, such as the Carter Center, the Commonwealth Secretariat, and Caricom, have tended to be short-lived and as yet limited in their impact. The Guyana diaspora might have greater legitimacy and acceptability if country ownership or leadership of the domestic peace process is made a priority by the contending parties.

(c) Alleviating Poverty, and Building up Communities

Although the Guyana conflict situation demonstrates no necessary one-to-one correspondence between economic growth (or poverty) indicators and levels of political violence/instability, it does suggest a possible indirect long-term mutuality of influences between these two spheres (see Mars, "Crisis"). While, therefore, poor economic conditions facilitate political mobilization among the economically disadvantaged, it is political discontent that moves such mobilization toward political violence, depending on the nature of regime response. Diaspora contribution here can take the form of organizing investment initiatives, creating better opportunities for coastland youths by concentrating investments in depressed communities on the coast and in the hinterland regions. The Guyana government should facilitate this by streamlining diaspora investments into areas of maximum job creation in such industries as ecotourism, small- and medium-scale gold and diamond mining, stone and laterite quarrying, food processing manufacturing, and so on.

(d) Furthering Localized Concentrations of Antipoverty Initiatives

Another important consideration stems essentially from (c) above: that is, that it is not so much the overall level of poverty in general that is significant in igniting conflict in Guyana, but particular geographic or localized concentrations of poverty in communities and areas that already harbor significant levels of political discontent and ethnic alienation. Kinship networks extending abroad could be constructive in directing diaspora investments to local depressed and interior communities in the homeland—to create better job and skills training opportunities, and recreational facilities.

(e) Lobbying International Institutions

International assistance is significant in the mitigation of political conflict and violence—particularly those involving crime and the underground economy—at the domestic level. Among the many international agencies that have so far made definitive contributions to peaceful processes in Guyana, the UN aid agencies would seem to be most relevant (or specific) to conflict resolution issues in Guyana. One important route for diaspora engagement would be contacting and pressuring the international donors and humanitarian organizations to get

involved—particularly Caricom, where it is important to work
for the establishment of a permanent desk for conflict and crisis
interventions in the region, similar to what is prescribed in the
Charter of the Organization of American States (OAS). The diaspora could also work on the major political parties at home to be
more open and tolerant toward outside mediation, which must be
seen as an extension of globalization processes.

What then are the conditions for realizing a multiethnic capacity
for mediating the Guyana crisis from the diaspora? In sum, the following conditions must be met: First, a multiethnic overarching organization needs to be instituted, by bringing together Guyana diaspora alumni
and other associations under one umbrella organization. The example of
Joslyn Small's initiative in putting together a multiracial panel on the
WBAI radio broadcast, from New York, of the 2006 Guyana elections, is an
indication that the possibility exists for amicable and helpful interethnic
collaborative exchanges among Guyanese nationals in North America at
least. Second, the resource base of this institution must be ensured by
identifying committed sponsors and reliable funding sources from within
the diaspora, particularly in Europe and North America. These resources
can also be buttressed by subscriptions to the umbrella organization from
its diaspora members and interested others.

Third, it is also necessary to identify expertise in conflict management/
resolution/analysis within this diaspora body, particularly those who have
training in mediation capabilities and/or exposure to mediation experience. In this regard the body will seek collaboration with professional mediation and conflict resolution/analysis centers in the developed societies,
such as the Carter Center in Atlanta, the International Peace Academy of
the United Nations in New York, and relevant university centers. Fourth,
this diaspora body or center needs acceptance and facilitation by Guyana
and Caricom governments. Toward this end, negotiations between these
governments and the diaspora organization bodies might be necessary.
Finally, to establish its credibility, the "Diaspora conflict resolution and
mediation center" to be established within this body needs to maintain a
position of independence or relative autonomy in relation to governments
and international funding institutions.

*   *   *

The Guyana diaspora possesses the capability in expertise, and perhaps in resources, to leverage the conflict resolution and reconciliation
process back home in Guyana. The serial failure of international mediation so far, ranging from the efforts of the Carter Center to those of
Caricom and the Commonwealth, has propelled into the forefront the
need to involve the expertise of the Guyana diaspora, which might be

more committed to the lengthy and sustained participation necessary for the mitigation or resolution of protracted political and ethnic conflicts, as in the case of Guyana. To a significant extent, Guyanese need to own or lead their own political reconciliation processes, and for this reason the Guyana diaspora is closer to home, so to speak, compared to other well-intentioned international agencies. At the very least, the Guyana diaspora can complement these other international agencies by providing further contingency mediation, focusing on specific expertise in areas of poverty reduction and political conflict resolution involving equitable distributive justice for all Guyanese.

However, the diaspora tends to be limited by its own divisiveness along ethnic lines, mirroring similar ethnic divisiveness and conflicts in the homeland. Other significant limitations of the Guyana diaspora reside in its lack of systematic organization and outreaching efforts. But while the Guyana diaspora most probably has the capability through its own higher levels of education and expertise to successfully negotiate the organizational difficulties posed here, there are still significant hurdles to be crossed in the rather ambivalent or even negative attitudes of the Guyana government and political elite, as well as among significant sections of the political opposition, toward the receptivity of Guyana diaspora initiatives.

More clarity is needed on the part of the Guyana government as to where it stands on the issues of involving the diaspora in the internal politics of the nation, its perception of the definability of the ethnic conflict situation, and the extent to which mediation by expatriate Guyanese is legitimate and allowable. Undoubtedly, government's ambiguity about, or denial of, the existence of racial or ethnic conflict in the country is an obstacle to the clarity needed for meaningful third party involvement in the resolution or mitigation of the deadly and violent events and processes already witnessed both historically and within very recent times. Compatible or complementary governmental or state responses, so necessary to make a success of this arrangement, are dependent on this clarification of the situation.

The primary objectives of an organized multiethnic Guyana diaspora are to ensure that the Guyana government first takes responsibility to provide avenues for peaceful protest; second, counterbalances the precipitous use of coercive and deadly force with developing an intelligence gathering capability to more effectively deal with "suspects" in wide ranges of criminal activities; third, takes the initiative or onus to reach out more decisively toward political reconciliation of the forces tending toward ethnic and political divisiveness, and to foster redistributive economics and conciliatory politics as far as possible; and fourth, develops a more comprehensive, systematic, concerted, and unbiased (nonpartisan) program of outreach toward the Guyana diaspora abroad. In fact, furthering the process of democracy and good governance is the key toward reconciliatory politics and the resolution or mitigation of deadly and violent political conflicts in the country.

At the same time, also, the Guyana diaspora should be prepared to frontally address the perception emanating from significant vocal quarters of the Afro-Guyanese population that conflict resolution is synonymous with pacification and the stifling of militant struggle. It should be emphasized that political and ethnic conflicts are resolved not necessarily in the sense of the absolute fusion of all alternatives into one single unit, but in the democratic flowering of distinct and different reconcilable interests and groups. Struggle within this symbiotic pluralistic arrangement is allowed to continue, although struggle does not necessarily have to be violent. Nonviolent struggle to realize unsatisfied or unmet legitimate goals is permissible, although it is recognized that historically nonviolent struggles have often attracted violent responses, particularly from the state or other powerful forces, and so can provoke further violent conflicts in the society at large, as witnessed in the experiences of Gandhi in India and Martin Luther King in America. Thus also, conflict resolution, like struggle, is a continuous process.

REFERENCES

Amnesty International. "Guyana: Security Legislation Threatens Fundamental Rights." Press release, January 13, 2003.
Caricom. "Caribbean Community Mission to Guyana: Measures for Resolving Current Problems." Georgetown: Caricom Secretariat, January 1998.
———. "Guyana: The St. Lucia Statement." Georgetown: Caricom Secretariat, July 1998.
The Carter Center. "Carter Center Completes Guyana Project." Press release, May 21, 2004.
The Economist, "Fruit That Falls from the Tree." November 3, 2005.
Gordon, Monica H. "The Role of Emigration in Caribbean Development." In Caribbean Labor and Politics: Legacies and Cheddi Jagan and Michael Manley, ed. Perry Mars and Alma H. Young. Detroit: Wayne State University Press, 2004. 225–241.
Goulbourne, Harry. Caribbean Transnational Experience. London and Kingston: Pluto and Arawak, 2002.
Guyana Chronicle. Various issues.
Guyana Human Rights Association (GHRA). Press release, June 10, 2003.
Harvard University. "Beyond Money: Diaspora Engagement in Development." Report prepared by Harvard University's Global Equity Initiative for the Canadian International Development Agency (CIDA), Human Rights and Participation Division, Policy Branch. 2005.
Holder, Sheila V. "Political Party and Campaign Financing in Guyana." OAS Unit for the Promotion of Democracy, n.d.
Ishmael, Odeen. "Remarks by Ambassador Odeen Ishmael at the Opening Session

of the Guyana Diaspora Forum on Conflict and Conflict Analysis in Guyana at Howard University." Washington, D.C., December 14, 2002.

———. "Speech by Ambassador Odeen Ishmael at the University of Guyana Guild of Graduates Dinner." Toronto, September 18, 1999.

Kaieteur News. Various issues.

Kershaw, Sarah. "For Schenectady, A Guyanese Strategy." RaceMatters.org, July 26, 2002.

Mars, Perry. "The Crisis of Security and Development." In *Security and Development: Searching for Critical Connections,* ed. Necla Tschirgi, Michael Lund, and Francesco Mancini. Boulder, Colo.: Lynne Rienner (forthcoming).

———. "Ethnic Politics, Mediation, and Conflict Resolution: The Guyana Experience." *Journal of Peace Research* 38, no. 3 (May 2001): 353–372.

———. *Ideology and Change: The Transformation of the Caribbean Left.* Detroit and Kingston: Wayne State University Press, and The Press, University of the West Indies, 1998.

New York City Department of City Planning. "The Newest New Yorkers." 2000.

Orozco, Manuel. "Distant but Close: Guyanese Transnational Communities and Their Remittances from the United States." Draft, report commissioned by the U.S. Agency for International Development. Washington, D.C, January 2004.

———. "Remittances Back Home to Guyana: Issues and Options." *Inter-American Dialogue,* November 7, 2002.

People's National Congress. Press release, May 8, 2003.

People's National Congress Reform–One Guyana (PNCR-1G). "Move Forward with One Guyana." Manifesto. 2006.

People's Progressive Party/Civic (PPP/C). "A Brighter Future for All Guyanese." Manifesto. 2006.

Sen, Amarthya. *Development as Freedom.* New York: Anchor Books. 1999.

Stabroek News. Various issues.

Sukhdeo, Gowkarran. "The Conference at Howard University Conflict Resolution: A Critique." *Guyana Journal,* n.d. www.guyanajournal.com.

United Nations Development Program (UNDP). "Promoting Social Cohesion in Guyana." Georgetown: UNDP, 2006.

26 THE ONTOLOGICAL IMPERATIVE FOR THE NEW AFRICAN DIASPORA

Adeolu Ademoyo

My basic move in this essay is to join the debate, among old and new Africans in the diaspora, on the ontological project of the new African diaspora. The ontological project is best described as how each people imagines the world both in discourse and in practice. Taking into account the multiple experiences of the new African diaspora, this is the critical question I want to explore: in a highly contested global community, what is the most philosophically adequate and defensible method for conceptualizing and representing the intellectual culture of the African diaspora, in both its material and spiritual forms? Two positions are joined in the debate: the "Black Atlanticist" represented by Paul Gilroy, and the "ontologist" represented by Michael Echeruo. I argue against positions such as Gilroy's, which I see as making a non-ontological commitment on the African diaspora. It is the presence of such commitment that has the potential of redeeming the drawbacks of the Black Atlantic theory.

My primary concerns are methodological, conceptual, and practical. While taking the intimacy among cultures as given, the methodological issue is whether a theorization of that cultural intimacy, in a historically determined global context, is without some form of substantive location of the people, the material substance of cultural studies and the theorist. Such location or situated-ness is not merely subjective, where this sense of *subjectivity* is taken as individual choice which transcends identity or as a choice of an identity which is always in the making. Rather such situated-ness is both subjective in an ontological sense and objective. In other words, while each individual may choose her or his location, including his or her identity, it is also the case that the locations of people who are the producers of culture, the material of cultural studies and the theorist, are already historically determined and therefore objectively verifiable. It is from such situated-ness that every group of people imagines the world. This ought to apply to both Africans and the new African diaspora. This methodology allows the new African diasporan to imagine herself/himself and others from her/his own eyes while maintaining cultural intimacy with other cultures. If the diaspora world is truly equitably multicultural, this methodology does not threaten citizenship. Neither does it absolutize cultures; it can only enrich what is taken to be multicultural. This is the sense in which the global can potentially cease to be the local.

My conceptual concern is the question of subjectivity and cultural identity, and how they intersect in cultural discourse with practical cultural issues of the day such as religion, aesthetic forms, citizenship, family matters, etc. The claim that identity is an unfinished process mixes the ever-going cultural intimacy of cultural forms with individual bearers of identity. It also mixes what is a broad historical truth about the process of identity formation with the equally correct concrete nature of identity. Finally, it mixes cultural identity with citizenship. If we conceptually and validly separate citizenship of a nation, which is a legal and political issue, from cultural identity, it seems obvious that we do not *take on* being African or being European the way we may *take on* being citizens of African nations or of European nations. This is because citizenship is portable in a way cultural and racial identity is not. Therefore citizenship does involve choice. It does follow that while cultures and race may not exhaust our subjective resources, they *a priori* define them. Finally, I am concerned with practical issues. First is the possible misinterpretation of a people's cultural resource if, in imagining self and the world, our methodology fails to proceed from self like others do or if our methodology fails to proceed from what Du Bois calls a true self-consciousness. Second is the practical effect of this move on the family in a diaspora context. The following shows the substance of my argument.

NEW AFRICAN DIASPORA, SUBJECTIVITY, AND EPISTEMIC CHOICES

This section considers the foundation of the claims of the "Black Atlanticist." Borrowing from traditional epistemological discourse, I use "foundation" here to mean the sources and criteria of justification of our knowledge claims. In outlining his theoretical claim on the Black Atlantic, Gilroy argues that:

> Striving to be both European and black requires some specific forms of double consciousness. By saying this I do not mean to suggest that taking on either or both of these unfinished identities necessarily exhausts the subjective resources of any particular individual. However, where racist, nationalist, or ethnically absolutist discourses orchestrate political relationships so that these identities appear to be mutually exclusive, occupying the space between them or trying to demonstrate their continuity has been

viewed as a provocative and even oppositional act of political subordination.
(Gilroy 1)

Gilroy shows further how the Black Atlantic stands between two cultural
assemblages which have mutated over time. Making a claim for his approach he argues that:

> in opposition to nationalist and ethnically absolute approaches, I want to
> develop the suggestion that cultural historians could take the Atlantic as
> one single, complex unit of analysis in their discussions of the modern
> world and use it to produce an explicitly transnational and intercultural
> perspective . . . (Gilroy 15)

The analytic integers of this thesis are the Black Atlantic as a unit of
analysis, with transnationality and interculturality as correlative perspectives (Gilroy 15). Applied to the people of African descent in the diaspora,
these perspectives presumably produce a black subject who with some
specific forms of double consciousness strives to be both European and
black. This is sometimes articulated as "creolization." Gilroy states this
in both practical and theoretical terms. His claim is that

> the fractal patterns of cultural and political exchange and transformation
> that we try and specify through manifestly inadequate theoretical terms
> like creolization and syncretism indicate how both ethnicities and political
> cultures have been made anew in ways that are significant not simply for
> the peoples of the Caribbean but for Europe, for Africa, especially Liberia
> and Sierra Leone, and of course for black America . . . (15)

Though not explicitly drawn by Gilroy, a consequence of this is a black/
European creolization of thought-epistemology, metaphysics, ethics, aesthetics, and the language which is the vehicle for that episteme and
thought. Stated differently, in occupying a middle space between two
cultural assemblages the Black Atlantic strives to be both European and
black, a striving that requires a form of double consciousness. (Gilroy 1).
    Given the framing of this thesis, it is either that this "doubleness"
of the Black Atlantic's consciousness and episteme is not a foundation,
or it is a double foundation grounded on nothing. In the latter case, the
starting point of its episteme is double, but in order to maintain its anti-
particularity that double episteme has to be founded on nothing. That
nothing could as well be a nonmaterial subjective state. In other words,
one way out for proponents of the view is to claim that it is a nothingness founded on something, an X and Y—two particulars that are associated with its double parentage. It is problematic, though, how something
can produce nothing or how nothing can be founded on something or how
two particulars would cease to be particulars or "ethnic." This problem

of coherence is further deepened precisely because the subject, who must have proceeded into nothing from something, ought to be conscious of the epistemic choices being made in that progression. The problem of coherence arises because even when philosophically the Black Atlantic as a unit of analysis claims to be anti-particular in its thesis, it is in fact committed to one, which is the subjective state of the creolized and hybridized Black Atlantic subject. However, a subjective state is nonmaterial; it is a psychological state and therefore capable of spawning only the social psychology of the hybridized subject in making a choice. The point, though, is the process of hybridization: it is both self-chosen and perhaps unconscious.

At this juncture, it is pertinent to understand some moments in the global history of peoples of African descent in our account of double consciousness, which the Black Atlantic theory has adopted. First is Du Bois's use of double consciousness as a sensation rooted in an objective material American world which yields the African diaspora no true self-consciousness. Du Bois puts it thus:

> The Negro is a sort of seventh son born with a veil, and gifted with a second sight in this American world,—a world which yields him no true self-consciousness, but only lets him see himself through the revelation of the other world. It is a peculiar sensation, this double consciousness, this sense of always looking at one's self through the eyes of others, of measuring one's soul by the tape of a world that looks on in amused contempt and pity. One feels his two-ness—an American, a Negro; two souls, two thoughts, two unreconciled strivings; two warring ideals in one dark body, whose dogged strength alone keeps it from being torn asunder. The history of the American Negro is the history of this strife,—this longing to attain self-conscious manhood to merge his double self into a better truer self. In this merging he wishes neither of the older selves to be lost. He would not Africanize America for America has too much to teach the world and Africa. He would not bleach his Negro soul in a flood of white Americanism, for he knows that Negro blood has a message for the world. He simply wishes to make it possible for a man to be both Negro and an American, without being cursed and spit upon by his fellows, without having the doors of Opportunity closed roughly in his face. (Du Bois 38–39)

Du Bois's explication of double consciousness is historically marked and therefore differs from Gilroy's use of it; it is also substantively different. A key issue in Du Bois's explication is the relation between true self-consciousnesses, self-conscious manhood, a better and truer self on one hand, and an objective American world which denies this. Under the historical circumstance, while the two-ness of the African diaspora subject— a Negro and an American—represents two unreconciled strivings—he longs to merge this double self into a true self-consciousness. A true self-consciousness in Du Bois therefore cannot be double consciousness, which is compelled. A further explication of a true self-consciousness can only yield a single consciousness that allows one to imagine oneself and the world while embracing its multiple cultures from one's own standpoint just like other peoples do. This is what I think Du Bois correctly and validly gestures toward. Reading from his text, I do not think that Du Bois seeks to occupy a middle ground, for that will be a perpetuation of double consciousness, which, according to the text, detracts from a true self consciousness—and this for Du Bois is a better and a truer self. In Du Bois there is a given self, and a single consciousness which, correctly, in Du Bois does not negate being an African and being an American. On the basis of the distinction Du Bois draws between a compelled double consciousness and the correct true self-consciousness, a better and truer self, Du Bois cannot pass as a defender of the Black Atlantic thesis. This is because Du Bois's double consciousness recognizes its limitation at that point in history, and he actually articulates a counterclaim—a true self-consciousness (what I call an ontological "I" to which other embraced cultures are related by a true self-consciousness) which calls to question double consciousness. In other words, one does not relate oneself to the world; one relates the world to oneself. Thus there are epistemic questions along the line for proponents of the Black Atlantic thesis. The most fundamental of these is the conscious epistemic choice(s) of the black historical subject who operates within its framework. Someone's epistemic choices would either undercut the striving to be both black and white simultaneously or help sustain it. Defenders of the Black Atlantic may wish to pose an inevitable double consciousness as a counterculture of a "modern" diaspora environment, but on the contrary, it seems to me that what modernity is about or ought to be about is the ceaseless engagement of new historical realities without a loss of the "I," a true self-consciousness, to historically hegemonic forces ready to consume it.

Thus, however we may wish to conceptualize it, naturalizing double consciousness in a historically different period as we have it today seems to be a consequence of an epistemic loss, because the representation of one's consciousness is always from an ontological and epistemic point. Otherwise, something is amiss that is presumably a void upon which a subjective state must be foisted. For peoples of African descent, that ontological and epistemic constraint might be historically marked: a first phase could be the twin historical experiences of slavery and colonialism. Given the brutal assault on the material and spiritual/intellectual culture of blacks in the diaspora by the transatlantic enslavement, with very limited opportunities or space for resistance, the epistemic constraint of this first phase is understandable. The legitimate latter-day resistance, in the form of what has been characterized as Afrocentricity, may have come too late in the historical process to correct the damage already done in the first phase.

The second phase is the more contemporary African diaspora. There does not seem to be a rational basis for any claim to epistemic and ontological loss or constraint with respect to the new African diaspora—in the same sense as in the earlier phase of the African diaspora. How could anyone explain such a loss with respect to the new African diaspora? For the more contemporary African in the diaspora, such naturalization of double consciousness could only be understood to be self-imposed and self-inflicted. This is because the historical conditions of the earlier and more contemporary African diasporas are different. For example, the intellectually hostile condition of the earlier African diaspora inevitably created a process of erasure of a foundation. If other diasporans do not exhibit double consciousness, because their engagement of the diaspora is *a priori* rooted in a firm foundation, then there is no contradiction in diaspora subjects of any group engaging their diaspora environment from a non-contingent ontological standpoint or foundation.

Such an engagement of the diaspora environment from a recognizable foundation does not in any way imply a direct reproduction of the ontological and epistemic essences of the homeland. The point in question is a location. Unconstrained by the ontological and epistemic siege of the twin evils of colonialism and slavery, the new diaspora has the conceptual space to operate from a non-contingently derived ontological standpoint in which private and public life is defined by an *a priori* recognition of a critical "I" in both material and spiritual senses—a critical "I" who has a language and an epistemic voice with which to engage *any* environment. As with other diaspora subjects of any identity, there is nothing *double* or *dual* where an epistemic and ontological engagement of one's diaspora environment proceeds from this critical recognition. A critical ontological "I," which in Du Bois is true self-consciousness, is an analytic unit that calls to question the idea of a "naturalized" double consciousness as the black subject's epistemic burden.

It could be argued that, on the contrary, the Black Atlantic as an analytical unit represents a critical "I" even in its dualistic "European" and "African" ontology, and that what is privileged is this duality. But it is not obvious that the proponents of the Black Atlantic as an analytical unit are making such an ontological argument. This is because to strive to be African and European simultaneously is not an ontological move. On the contrary, such striving is a social/subjective move. In a general sense, ontology is a platform *from* which one strives to name the world. That platform includes one's identity. A condition *toward* which one consciously strives cannot be an ontological state. A state *toward* which one strives can only be a *result* of an ontological location. Having imposed on oneself a rootlessness in one's epistemic choices—a rootlessness which, for example, includes an erasure and loss of one's language as a primary source of knowing and naming the world—a defender of the Black Atlantic can only strive without a *prior* voice, an identity, to be both European and African simultaneously. It could as well be argued that language does not always convey ontology or an episteme, especially when it is fossilized, as often happens in the types of contexts we are specifying. This is an open question, and part of that question is, why is it fossilized? But if this is suggested, language, then, must become relevant in relation to its modes out of the diaspora experience, a relation which can be tapped into at various levels of textualizing a collective self-conscious experience. As a conscious epistemic choice by the black diaspora, this would be of immense benefit for the theorizing of the self. But with a choice of the naturalization of double consciousness, that relation as part of a foundation which ought to undercut this choice may not be compatible, perhaps because of its possible reading as "ethnic" and "nationalist" by the Black Atlantic theory.

If, as Echeruo points out in his critique of the position of the Black Atlanticists on the issue of identity, the Atlanticists argue that one's identity is contingent on one's moments of subjectivity (Echeruo 10), then their *a priori* commitment is not toward an ontology but to moments of subjectivity that constantly change. So, if the proponents of the Black Atlantic make a commitment toward an ontology, the minimum that is plausible is that the Black Atlantic as a critical "I" is shaped by moments of subjectivity that constantly change and not by an ontological commitment. Here, what the Atlanticist is making is a choice of her/his own subjectivity, which is entirely acceptable. This may explain the naturalization of double consciousness that is taken to be the natural course of the more contemporary African diaspora by the Atlanticists. But given the possible philosophical arbitrariness of a state of subjectivity that constantly changes, and given that it is a choice consciously made, it is an open question (1) how double consciousness is not a choice but a natural course for the more contemporary African diaspora, and (2) how really transnational the perspective that emerges from that commitment can be in a general sense.

Echeruo correctly puts what I call conscious epistemic choices by subjects in diaspora and non-diaspora situations in a different form when he argues that

> the problem apparently is the striving to be "white" and "black" at the same time, to be simultaneously "European" and "African." Phrased in such equal terms, the problem would become utterly insane. But the very phrasing shows that what is at stake is not the possibility of living as an

African (or a black) in the modern European (or white) world, but in suppos-
ing that both identities are equivalent in ontological terms. For it would not
occur to any European advocate of modernity to phrase the European condition in similar quixotic terms. It certainly would be difficult, if not impossible, for a European to strive to be African and white at the same time in
the sense that Gilroy means it. (Echeruo 5)

What Echeruo's claim suggests is that in an empirical sense if the European or white diaspora does not strive to be African and white simultaneously, then there is a conscious choice being made as to what any diaspora subject today *strives* toward, whether in her daily existence, living,
and family matters or in theorizing our diaspora experience. This is because the element of forced socialization as occurred in the period of enslavement is absent today.

In effect, the hybridization thesis suggests a circular argument that
thrives on some form of empiricism. It exhibits this epistemologically,
precisely because of the naturalized form it takes. In other words, while
ignoring the critical agency of the African diaspora subject which, in engaging the diaspora from a foundational base, undercuts a natural path
to double consciousness, it takes the outward perceptual representation
of the African diaspora as the determining factor of hybridization. Thus,
without asking or seeing why European modernity is a metaphysical condition that is largely European with little mullatoization or circumscribed
hybridity to it, the naturalized double consciousness or naturalized hybridity thesis proceeds to take the project of mullatoization of African and
black intellectual culture without a location as a natural and inevitable
course. In other words, why is hybridization not a natural course for European modernity but a natural course for black and African modernity?

The hybridization thesis appears to accept what is given and justify it
without exploring alternative states that have not been taken and the reasons they have not been taken. For Black Atlanticism, as argued by Gilroy,
those possible alternatives would be "nationalist or ethnically absolute
approaches" (15). But on the contrary, "nationalist or ethnically absolute
approaches" are not the consequences of a rejection of the inevitability
of double consciousness. Rather the issue is what ontological position is
privileged as a foundation in an *approach* to engage our diaspora environment. This is because, contrary to the Black Atlantic, approaches engage concrete material culture, for cultures are "global" in their so called
"particularity" and are "particular" in their so called "transnationality."
Therefore, the issue is what is privileged in each *approach* to undercut the
alienating consequences of effects of enslavement and colonialism. For
example, on Gilroy's reading of the rejection of the inevitability of double
consciousness, while theorizing transnational and intercultural perspec-

tives, Gilroy seems to think that these perspectives preclude a material cultural base as a foundation while what he describes as "ethnic particularity" is limited to a material cultural base.

But according to Echeruo, this way of stating the problem is bewitched by the language deployed to understand the issues (Echeruo 3). And thanks to its empiricist framework, which limits analysis to outward perceptual representations of a reality, the Atlanticist thesis glosses over detail and specific accounts of knowledge forms—epistemology, metaphysics, ethics, gender and family discourse, language, etc.—in the diaspora which are capable of undercutting the alienating effects of enslavement and colonialism and their consequence of a state of double consciousness. It glosses over details of the deployment and propagation of these knowledge forms in the diaspora in ways that contest hegemonic cultural and knowledge forms. Since the Atlanticist paradigm purports to theorize a global African experience, this glossing evidently betrays some form of epistemic limitation with respect to the internal logic and dynamics of the diaspora experience.

KNOWLEDGE FORMS: CONTINUITY AND CONTESTATION

In this section, I examine the implications of the Atlanticist position in some cultural forms, such as music. Subsequently, I will examine how understanding of discourse in other areas might possibly redeem the Black Atlanticist idea of transnationality. Such areas, which are relevant to the lives of the African diaspora in a more salient way, are language, epistemology, and gender, moral, and family discourse.

The Atlanticists focus on discourses such as race, cultural studies (Gilroy, Appiah), and cultural "alienation" (Gilroy 24) between diaspora subjects and their homelands as spaces where transnationality and interculturality (without ontological commitments and foundation) validate the Black Atlantic as an appropriate analytical unit. In his observation on what may be called the transnational expression in music in Britain, Gilroy notes that

> Britain's black settler communities have forged a compound culture from disparate sources. Elements of political sensibility and cultural expression transmitted from black America over a period of time have been reaccentuated in Britain. They are central, though no longer dominant, within the increasingly novel configurations that characterize another black vernacular culture. This is not content to be either dependent upon or simply imitative of the African Diaspora cultures of America and the Caribbean. The rise and rise of Jazzie B and Soul II Soul at the turn of the last decade constituted one valuable sign of this new assertive mood. North London's Funki

Dreds, whose name itself projects a newly hybridized identity, have projected the distinct culture and rhythm of life of Black Britain outwards into the world. Their song "Keep On Moving" was notable for having been produced in England by the children of Caribbean settlers and then remixed in a (Jamaican) dub format in [the] United States by Teddy Riley, an African American. It included segments or samples of music taken from American and Jamaican records by the JBs and Mikey Dread respectively. This formal unity of diverse cultural elements was more than just a powerful symbol. It encapsulated the playful diasporic intimacy that has been a marked feature of transnational black Atlantic creativity . . . (Gilroy 15–16)

Here again, we may be dealing with some form of empiricism. That a cultural form such as music, any musical form, is syncretic seems to be obvious. But the terms of the argument of the Black Atlantic seem to change in the middle, in the course of the defense of naturalized double consciousness, when an appeal is made to black diasporic intimacy in musical forms. Naturalized double consciousness—striving to be black and white simultaneously—is obviously not black diasporic intimacy, which on its own is a sound intimacy and formulation given the history of peoples of African descent. However, striving to be black and white is extrospective intimacy while black diasporic intimacy is introspective. To substitute the legitimate formulation of black diasporic intimacy for double consciousness in order to sustain a theory of Black Atlantic is obviously contradictory. The Black Atlantic as a theory runs into problems whenever it fails to separate the legitimate black diasporic intimacy from striving to be both black and white simultaneously. Given the global geography of race, there cannot be any double consciousness within black diaspora, for double consciousness is a concept applied to striving to be both white and black simultaneously. For example, no Caucasian from French and English cultures is ever seen as having double consciousness. So introspective and extrospective intimacies are different, though given the example of a cultural form such as music, which is used to explain transnationality, the issue for a theory that seeks to naturalize striving to be black and white simultaneously as an inevitable path of the African diaspora is: what is the material and ontological base of such music?

Syncretism goes on in everyday cultural life as a form of creativity. The pertinent issue is: upon what does such syncretic practice rest in undercutting double consciousness or sustaining it for black folks? A theory that seeks to be a grand narrative for salient aspects of African diaspora life ought not to be limited to one aspect of life. It ought to be grand enough to address the burning question upon which the theory rests. And that question is a question of identity: what are the implications of a double consciousness for black folks? "Diasporic intimacy" is a legitimate formulation; I take it to mean "introspective intimacy" within black folks and cultures. But what about "extrospective intimacy" as a factor of black diasporic contact with other cultures, which leads to a striving to be both black and white? Black diasporic intimacy in Gilroy's observation on music theory does not, unfortunately, speak to this. A black diasporic intimacy without ontology or a material culture to support it would be weak in its extrospective relation and intimacy with other cultures; hence it produces a "double consciousness."

When applied to cultural studies, the deployment of cultural forms such as music by Black Atlanticists to show interculturality as perspective ignores the complexity of such forms. It also ignores how, without a material knowledge base, these forms might have been filtered through an aesthetic driven by capital. True, capital "globalizes" and is presumably transnational. But it is a transnationality and globalization that privileges one viewpoint while excluding other viewpoints. The history of the gradual relegation of reggae music in the West from a cultural-resistance outlook to a banal tradition of popular music is a testimony to what happens to transnationality without an ontological foundation. Another example is provided by hip-hop/rap music. In his review titled "The Wrap on Rap: What's Next?" Marcus Reeves observes how "hip hop music became less about mining the creativity of the music than selling stereotypes of Black criminal life and materialism to record companies." He shows how "pro-black rap diminished as its militancy changed over to the ghetto-centric themes of 'gangsta rap' . . . " (Reeves 23). What Reeves does not add is that what we are witnessing here is a triumph of a tradition driven by capital that "globalizes" over a cultural practice (reggae, rap music, etc.) that once spoke to the history and lives of diaspora Africans from a specific ontological standpoint. And the usual justification for this aesthetic violation is the need for such musical forms to appeal to a "larger audience" as a gesture of transnationality. In the process, a commitment is compromised.

Let us move our critical gaze into schools and the relations among black kids, who are some of the consumers of cultural forms such as music that are appropriated by capital and rendered banal by a claim to transnationality. Cultural studies without commitment to ontology and a history underlies the ludicrous, internally destructive, and cannibalistic rivalry that now exists among black kids—from Africa, the Caribbean, and African America—in schools from elementary to college. How does a form of cultural studies based on a "transnationality" devoid of an ontological standpoint address this? The point here is that black kids naturally inherit prejudices and stereotypes created by a system that is mutually destructive of black people wherever they happen to be. The transnational cultural form does not seem to have an answer to the danger; in some situations, in fact, transnational musical forms promote it, no doubt because they inhabit a frame without an ontological base. The most plausible salvation for black kids who are becoming increasingly ignorant of their history is a framework built on an ontological foundation. The Afrocentrists may seem to arouse suspicion in certain intellectual circles by promoting an adoption of a Kemetic (Egyptian) outlook in tandem with a contemporary African American historical consciousness (Asante, *The Afrocentric Idea*). Such a self-consciously elected "doubleness," which is an illustration of black diasporic intimacy, is in the final analysis a healthier ontological option than the sort of dislocated, baseless "transnationality" the Black Atlanticists propose.

Besides cultural studies, there are other contested grounds which are crucial not only because they are spaces where the epistemic voices of other races, and in this case people of African descent, had in the past been proscribed (Taiwo, "Exorcising") by early European thinkers and their cohorts in academia. Their significance lies in the fact that these contested grounds impact the choice of paradigms in cultural studies and are crucial in defining the existential state of peoples of African descent. Olufemi Taiwo, in his "Exorcising Hegel's Ghost: Africa's Challenge to Philosophy," correctly points out two important events in the history of philosophy. First is Hegel's "philosophical" reflection on Africa, which has encouraged the exclusion from academia of anything that goes by the name African philosophy and, by extension, the idea of black philosophy. Second and more important is the complicity, according to Taiwo, of African and (by extension) black scholars generally in willingly sustaining that exclusion both in homeland Africa and in the diaspora. Taiwo's second observation is crucial in calling into question the ontological basis of much black intellectual discourse, which seems to rest on the same analytical frame as pliable musical forms that can be easily debased to a profane tradition.

Cabral's discourse on material and immaterial aspects of culture (Cabral 39–56) is relevant here, especially his brilliant and insightful conclusion in which he states that the conquest of a people proceeds from a successful ontological assault on, and erasure of, the immaterial aspects of their culture: metaphysics, epistemology, religion, language, ethics, aesthetics, etc. To completely robotize a people, all one need do is take away their language and epistemic voice, and the job is done! The human subject may actually become a clone, an active and willing participant in her own epistemic loss. An illustration of this willing participation in that loss and in its perpetuation is further discussed by Taiwo. He argues that modernity consists in nothing but implanting the critical self on the sands of the history of knowledge and mirroring that history after the self—perhaps not in a vacuous transnational sense, for the critical self which Taiwo acknowledges is an ontological self, a foundation. This is the sense, as we may infer from Taiwo, in which the black subject—whether in the homeland or in the diaspora—may not be a willing participant in her own epistemic loss, a loss that is often reconstructed as double consciousness.

As noted, where a theory like Black Atlanticism seeks to be a grand narrative for the African diaspora, it ought to be grand enough to account for other critical discourses and their consequences for the African diaspora experience. These critical fields of discourse include cultural forms such as music but go beyond them. They are fields where the history of peoples of African descent is constantly constructed and shaped. In contention here, as with cultural forms, are critical points of epistemic and cultural intimacies: diasporic-introspective, and diasporic-extrospective. It is therefore pertinent to see how such a theory—Black Atlanticism, with the attendant concept of a naturalized double-consciousness—will work in a critical area of discourse such as ethics. A moral discourse without an ontological foundation both in the homeland and in the diaspora runs the same risk as cultural discourse without ontology, even when cultural and epistemic intimacies are legitimate formulations.

To illustrate the need that Echeruo stresses for ontological persistence in critical discourses at home and in the diaspora, let us take the discourse on how the relation between evil and the twin acts of slavery and colonialism has been conducted. In the history of ideas and the attempt to account for evil in ethical discourse, the European thinker Immanuel Kant represents a major point of departure for European philosophy and episteme. In his theory, following his monocentric conception of God, he constructs an ethics that is disembodied, leading to a rationalization of the concept of good/bad/ evil with a foundation in a singular source: pure reason (Kant, *Practical Philosophy*). Having at one point in his philosophy suspended reason to affirm faith, Kant purged faith and God of their theological substance. He replaced them with a universal law, the categorical imperative, which has its source in "pure" reason. What is taken to be good, bad, or evil is dictated and guided by this "pure" reason, a universal law, a categorical imperative. For instance, moral acts are taken to be a correct or wrong application of this universal law on the basis of a presumably disinterested "pure" reason. This is no doubt a smart move from a philosopher of Enlightenment and modernity, for history has to be fashioned after a critical self. Why? The answer lies in the frequently cited material color of "pure" reason and the "universal" law, which have been unapologetically used to justify evils such as slavery, colonialism, and genocide. To demonstrate the material color of this "pure" reason, diaspora African philosophers such as Emmanuel Eze have shown how Kant marginalizes the African as a mere postulate of the same disinterested "pure" reason in his writings. The purported universality of "pure" reason and universal law stems from a rationalist(?) conception of God.

Let us apply the concept of diasporic intimacy (both introspective and extrospective) to moral discourse and its possible consequence for black history. Perhaps in the spirit of intercultural perspective and some form of epistemic intimacy, some writers on the metaphysics of religion such as Bolaji Idowu have proceeded to present an account of God, morality, and evil in some African intellectual cultures on a European model of a single source of faith (Idowu, *Olódùmarè*). Operating thus on a Judeo-Christian and European model, they unwittingly invest in a moral discourse that justifies evils such as colonialism, slavery, and genocide. In other words, in the process of a cultural and epistemic intimacy with a monocentric conception of God, where a racialized "pure" reason and universal law are used to legitimize slavery and colonialism in the name of God and a "civilizing mission" ordained by that universal law, African scholars both in the diaspora and in the homeland become willing or unwilling participants in their own marginalization (Taiwo). The material conditions and economic quest that led to the evils of slavery and colonialism are ignored, because a universal law and "pure" reason deriving from a universal God justify the misadventure. When African scholars, striving to be both white and black simultaneously in thought and practice, engage in extrospective intimacy without a foundation in their indigenous thought, the logic of their theory and explanation is bound to justify imperialist evils the same way they are justified in the European sources of their discourse.

In contrast, writing from an indigenous ontological perspective, and conscious of the black introspective and extrospective intimacies that Gilroy cites, African diaspora philosophers such as John A. I. Bewaji and Kola Abimbola have shown how implausible it is to transplant the Judeo-Christian God, and consequently the moral concept of evil, onto the African (Yoruba) conception of God (Abimbola 75; Bewaji). Proceeding from this foundation, the correction of an error in thought which amounts to intellectual self-annihilation does not imply a "nationalist and ethnically absolute approach," as the Black Atlanticists might conclude. The accounts of Bewaji and Abimbola, which argue that the Yoruba conception of evil is polycentric rather than monocentric, de-rationalize and de-atomize the conception of evil by situating it in the worldly and material conditions that create it. Unlike the Kantian European model, their accounts cannot legitimize evils such as slavery/colonialism under a divine law, because the sources of evil are not in a misapplication of a universal law (Kant); rather, these sources co-exist with us on an existential plane (Abimbola).

In this discourse, evil is a violation not only of the victims and survivors of evil, but also of a common spiritual and material space; hence the Yoruba say, "*Ko ba oju mu,*" which means evil is a public and perceptual representation of a violation and negation of the normative, the cognitive, the rational, and, the aesthetic. Literally, it means evil is what does not fit (i.e. proper) the normative, cognitive and aesthetic eye. In other words, in conceptual terms, evil violates both a public and private perceptual as well as physical space, since "*oju*" (literally, "eye") has both inner and public dimensions to it. The public aspect is embodied and concrete. In the polycentric conception of evil, the evil agency is multiple and real. They are the *ajoguns* (the evil humans) and their cohorts (Abimbola 75). In this discourse, the account of evil produces a perceptual immediacy that morally mobilizes the commonwealth and community to object to evil. In this embodied and worldly representation, evil goes beyond a failure of the application of a purported universal law of reason, a Kantian categorical imperative. The moral value of such embodiment in its polycentric account is that it leaves no room for a quixotic defense of evil acts under the pretext of carrying out a duty—a universal law or civilizing mission.

Where there is no difference between the slave ships and chains, holding the bible on one hand and raiding a people's resources on the other, and the Nazi death chambers (all of which are vehicles of death); where the world has deemed it fit to apologize for the Nazi genocide and hesitates to do the same for slavery and colonialism—we begin to see the philosophical limit of the Kantian European account of evil upon which Western public morality rests. Given the way it is constructed, this foundational Kantian European account is capable of speaking about evil from both sides of the mouth; subscribing to that account, in the name of extrospective intimacy in remodeling African thought, is thus an intellectual kiss of death. Unlike the Kantian (European) account of evil, which, on the basis of a categorical imperative, engages in an ethical double-talk, to philosophically undercut the African account of evil in its perceptual immediacy one would have to show the difference between the slave ships as symbols of death and the Nazi death chambers. That the world has not elected to apologize for the evils of colonialism and slavery raises serious questions about ontological commitments in the (European?) account of knowledge and shows why it is philosophically indefensible for African and diaspora African scholars to simply conduct critical discourses from a transnational void.

The ontological implications of this are far-reaching. I have examined the discourse on the metaphysics of evil, using scholarship from an African scholar in the homeland (Idowu) and two in the diaspora (Abimbola and Bewaji), to illustrate the epistemic constraints of the Atlanticist position and the dangers of failing to question the constraints. While Idowu may not consciously be operating from transnationalist and interculturalist perspectives, he has supplanted an intellectual culture in the process of extrospective intimacy by using his investment in a Western ontology to explain away an indigenous African intellectual culture. Ultimately, it becomes unclear whether he is striving toward transnationality, or striving to be both black and white in thought. But the outlooks of a scholar such as Idowu writing from the homeland and Black Atlantic scholars such as Gilroy writing in the diaspora are essentially the same. We run the risk of philosophical incoherence when an account of the intellectual cultures of peoples of African descent proceeds from an assumption that a naturalized double consciousness in thought and practice is a natural path for black people. It is not. If it is, it is self-imposed, especially for the more recent African diaspora. Nowhere is this better illustrated than in family matters and gender discourse, to which I now turn.

FAMILY MATTERS: CONTESTING A VOID IN TRANSNATIONALITY

Family matters and gender discourse have both their theoretical and practical value for the African diaspora experience. But first we must clear certain questions. Is it possible in family matters for the African diaspora, or any diaspora at all, to live the way of the family in the homeland? Definitely not, given the harshness of capital, whose first condition is the atomization of the person and family relations. But is it possible to capture the "essence" of family matters in an *African* sense—undercutting patriarchy; restoring stability and control, which help to absorb the shocks and pangs of capital; fighting the atomization of family ties; and shielding our children from the gaping jaws of foster parenting, which often follows the pursuit of capital? I believe that this is possible, provided the family is sustained by an ontology that discourages the urge toward striving to be both black and white simultaneously. This is even more important for the poor in the African diaspora, who may not have the economic strength to resist the crushing effect of capital on the family.

There continues to be a gross misconception of family and gender relations within the family system. Out of some form of epistemic constraint, a colonially inherited form of Christianized, Western, patriarchal gender relations manifests itself in homeland and diaspora theorizations of family matters and gender relations. Consequently, the African family has emerged as basically patriarchal, nuclear, and male-centered. This flawed epistemological filtering is well documented with respect to some Igbo and Yoruba family systems in Africa (Nzegwu, *Family Matters*; Oyewumi, *Invention of Women*). The Western family model has often been used for reading some African family systems, evidently in the light of transnationalist perspectives. Without a clear ontological commitment that disposes us to explore modes of African intellectual culture that existed prior to the colonial intrusion, we run the risk of locating that culture in a false conceptual frame.

This is the problem with the discourse in *In My Father's House* by Kwame Anthony Appiah. The author has obviously given a skewed reading of the constitution of gender relations in the Akan family, in its relation-

ship to the concept *abusua,* matriliny (Appiah 181–192). In the process of
imposing a transnational and intercultural identity on the matrilineal
base of Akan society, Appiah has failed to adequately consult the complex intellectual history of gender relations in the formation of the traditional Akan identity (Nukunya, 1992, Nzegwu, 1996). Against the claims
of a general patrilineal, Judeo-Christian reading of African family relations, which Appiah has uncritically naturalized, a scholar like Nzegwu
has observed:

> It is interesting that Appiah's "informed" gender evaluation is made without
> prior detailed analyses of the complex social history of Asante women and
> gender relations in a matrilineal society. Nor for that matter, any critical
> reference of the variegated history of dominance of Western categories and
> analyses in the production of knowledge about African women. Like many
> feminists, Appiah naturalizes patriarchy in Africa and then takes it for
> granted in explaining the role and status of African women in various so-
> cieties. Intellectual imperialism allows both him and some feminists to en-
> trench the idea that women-orientedness is a European American discovery
> and that African women should follow the path charted by Euro-American
> feminists. ("Questions of Identity" 179)

The reason for ignoring the complex details and dynamics of African
family matters in relation to identity may be a theoretical flight from "essence" in order, again, to entrench a "non-essentialist," transnationalist, intercultural, trans-racial, trans-identity outlook. The problem is that
in doing this, Appiah is foisting a different "essence" on a reality or ontology that is yet to be accounted for or acknowledged. It remains to be
seen, as Nzegwu has cogently pointed out, what the implications are, for
African families and their children in the diaspora, of imposing a Euro-
American woman-centeredness on African family traditions, for the orientation is consistent with a Western nuclear family model and carries its
own cultural baggage and ontology. On the contrary, the African family,
prior to an internalized colonial, Christianized patriarchy, is non-nuclear
and characterized by an internal coherence as well as a gender and ethical
orientation that protects the institution from being crushed by the cold,
impersonal hands of certain social factors and of capital. Unfortunately,
thanks to an extrospective intimacy with a Euro-American family model,
we now witness the disruption of that balance and the destabilization
of black families by the brutal force of capital—a state of affairs curi-
ously being naturalized in the Atlanticist discourse as the "collapse of
black families" in the diaspora. The institutionalization and proliferation
of foster homes and children raised in such depersonalized environments,
without the emotional and spiritual investment of committed family relations, is partly the result of an extrospective intimacy with a Western

nuclear-family model, a consequence the non-nuclear, internally coherent African family model might easily have resisted.

At the practical level of family situations, what we are doing is to un-critically embrace new structures, in the process destabilizing the poten-tialities of time-honored customs and the episteme inherent in African family systems that, in resisting the tyranny of patriarchal authority, are able to guarantee a harmonious context of growth for our children. In their place, we implant a Euro-American outlook with its peculiar meta-physics of individualism in family matters, as a new path for relations that engender corrosive tensions for the black family. This is an especially dan-gerous state of affairs for the new African diaspora families and for poor black families in the old diaspora, for the simple reason that the atom-istic Western metaphysics of the person leaves the individual entirely on her own and at the mercy of an insensitive capital. In effect, family forms constructed in the frame of a transnational void suffer the same fate as musical forms without a firm ontological foundation.

⋆   ⋆   ⋆

In arguing against the Black Atlanticist position on the concept of the African diaspora, I interrogate its fundamental attempt to naturalize "double consciousness" as an inevitable condition of peoples of African descent. In rejecting Gilroy's pivotal idea of "striving to be both black and white simultaneously," I propose that engaging the diaspora from an on-tological base theoretically and practically undercuts the state of double consciousness he seeks to naturalize. In other words, where people of Af-rican descent integrate into the diaspora environment from an ontological location, the result is a single consciousness, an African and black con-sciousness from which the African and black subject can relate to and embrace non-African, non-black diaspora cultures, just as others do. The multicultural setting of the diaspora environment encourages this. And if this is the way others do it, why should it be different for peoples of African descent? If others do not impose on themselves a natural state of double consciousness, why should we? A Black Atlanticist framework only impels us to strive to be who we are not: black and white simulta-neously.

My argument recognizes the twin holocaust of colonialism and slav-ery. In doing so, it nonetheless acknowledges the different historical situa-tions of the earlier African diaspora and the more contemporary African diaspora even when the two are cousins. A recognition of this historical difference is essential. While enslavement in a completely strange spiri-tual and physical environment offered very limited space for ontological resistance against hegemony, the new African diaspora could hardly be seen in these terms; a state of double consciousness for the new immigrants would be entirely self-inflicted and self-imposed, and hardly an inevitable choice. To deny this is to betray ignorance of the facts of history and a failure to implant the "critical African and black I" on the sands of modern history, so as to fashion that history after the African self, just as other races have done on their own terms. Africans and people of African descent can hardly afford to do any less.

REFERENCES

Abimbola, Kola. *Yoruba Culture: A Philosophical Account.* Birmingham, UK: Iroko Academic Publishers, 2006.
Appiah, Kwame Anthony. *In My Father's House: Africa in the Philosophy of Culture.* New York: Oxford University Press, 1992.
Asante, Molefi. *The Afrocentric Idea.* Philadelphia: Temple University Press, 1987.
Bewaji, John A. I. "*Olodumare: God in Yoruba Belief* and the Theistic Problem of Evil." *African Studies Quarterly* 2, no. 1 (1998). http://web.africa.ufl.edu/asq/v2/v2i1a1.htm (accessed November 24, 2008).
Cabral, Amilcar. "National Liberation and Culture." In *Return to Source: Selected Speeches of Amilcar Cabral.* New York: Monthly Review, 1973. 39–56.
Du Bois, W. E. B. *The Souls of Black Folk.* Ed. David W. Blight and Robert Gooding-Williams. New York: Bedford, 1997.
Echeruo, Michael J. C. "An African Diaspora: The Ontological Project." In *The African Diaspora,* ed. I. Okpewho, C. B. Davies, and A. I. Mazrui. Bloomington: Indiana University Press, 1999. 3–19.
Eze, Emmanuel. "The Color of Reason." In *Postcolonial African Philosophy,* ed. Emmanuel Eze. Oxford: Blackwell, 1997.103–140.
Gilroy, Paul. *The Black Atlantic: Modernity and Double Consciousness.* Cambridge, Mass.: Harvard University Press, 2002.
Idowu, Bolaji. *Olódùmarè: God in Yoruba Belief.* London: Longman, 1961.
Kant, Immanuel. *Practical Philosophy.* Cambridge: Cambridge University Press, 1999.
Nukunya, G. K. *Tradition and Change in Ghana.* Accra: Ghana Universities, 1992.
Nzegwu, Nkiru. *Family Matters: Feminist Concepts in African Philosophy of Culture.* Albany: State University of New York Press, 2006.
———. "Questions of Identity and Inheritance: A Critical Review of Kwame Anthony Appiah's *In My Father's House.*" *Hypatia* 11, no. 1 (1996): 175–201.
Oyewumi, Oyeronke. "Conceptualizing Gender: The Eurocentric Foundations of Feminist Concepts and the Challenge of African Epistemologies." *JENdA: A Journal of Culture and African Women Studies* 2, no. 1 (2002).
———. *Invention of Women: Making an African Sense of Western Gender Discourses.* Minneapolis: University of Minnesota Press, 1997.
Reeves, Marcus. "The Wrap on Rap: What's Next?" *Crisis,* May/June 2007, 23–24.
Taiwo, Olufemi. "Exorcising Hegel's Ghost: Africa's Challenge to Philosophy." *African Studies Quarterly* 1, no. 4 (1998). http://www.africa.ufl.edu/asq/v1/4/2.htm (accessed November 24, 2008).

CONTRIBUTORS

Adeolu Ademoyo is Lecturer in African Languages at Cornell University's Africana Studies and Research Center and a doctoral candidate in Philosophy, Interpretation, and Culture at Binghamton University.

Akin Adesokan is Assistant Professor of Comparative Literature at Indiana University, Bloomington, and author of *Roots in the Sky*, a novel. He is currently writing a book about genres and postcolonial cultural forms.

Helen Anin-Boateng obtained an MSc in Health and Social Care from Brunel University, London. A member of the British Association for Counseling and Psychotherapy, she has worked in bereavement and mental health services and is currently employed by the Middlesex University Hospital NHS Trust in London.

John A. Arthur is Professor of Sociology and Criminology at the University of Minnesota, Duluth. He is author of *Invisible Sojourners: African Immigrant Diaspora in the United States* and *The African Diaspora in the United States and Europe: The Ghanaian Experience.*

F. Odun Balogun is Professor of English and Director of the Black Studies Program at Delaware State University. He is author of *Tradition and Modernity in the African Short Story* and *Ngugi and African Postcolonial Narrative: The Novel as Oral Narrative in Multigenre Performance.*

James Burns is Assistant Professor of Music and Africana Studies at Binghamton University. He is author of *Female Voices from an Ewe Dance-Drumming Community in Ghana: Our Music Has Become a Divine Spirit*, which is accompanied by a DVD.

Msia Kibona Clark is Visiting Assistant Professor of African Studies and of Afro-American Studies at Howard University.

Donald Cosentino is Professor of World Arts and Cultures at the University of California, Los Angeles. He is author of *Defiant Maids and Stubborn Farmers* and *The Sacred Arts of Haitian Voodoo.*

Georges E. Fouron is Professor of Education and Social Sciences at the State University of New York at Stony Brook. His latest book, authored with Nina Glick Schiller, is *Georges Woke Up Laughing: Long-Distance Nationalism and the Search for Home*. He is presently working on a manuscript entitled *Globalization and Migration: The Haitian Case*.

ANDREA E. FROHNE is Assistant Professor of African Art History in the School of Interdisciplinary Arts and the School of Art at Ohio University. She has written "Reclaiming Space: The African Burial Ground in New York City," which is included in *African American Place-Making and the Struggle to Claim Space in the U.S.* (2008).

REGINA GEMIGNANI was a postdoctoral scholar in the African American and African Studies Program at the University of California, Davis. She worked with Jacob Olupona on the Ford Foundation–sponsored project "African Immigrant Religious Communities" and co-edited the conference publication *African Immigrants in America*.

JILL M. HUMPHRIES is Adjunct Assistant Professor for the Institute for Research in African American Studies at Columbia University. She is author of *Cyberorganizing United States Constituencies for Africa*. She is editor of *African Brain Circulation: Beyond the Drain-Gain Debate*, and also works as a photo-videographer.

SANDRA JACKSON-OPOKU teaches in the English Department at Chicago State University, where she serves as Fiction Coordinator in the Master of Fine Arts in Writing Program. She is the author of two novels: *The River Where Blood Is Born* and *Hot Johnny (and the Women Who Loved Him)*.

ADZELE K. JONES is an independent researcher. She received her Master of Public Administration degree from Binghamton University.

AMADU JACKY KABA is Assistant Professor in the Graduate Department of Public and Healthcare Administration and a member of the Committee on Africana Studies at Seton Hall University. He is author of dozens of published articles focusing on the economic, social, and political progress of people of African descent across the world.

FLORENCE M. MARGAI is Associate Professor and former Chair of the Geography Department at Binghamton University. She is co-author of two books, *Race and Place* and *Multicultural Geographies*, and has published widely on environmental health disparities, pediatric and immigrant health geographies in the U.S., and geographic targeting of diseases in Africa.

PERRY MARS is Professor of Africana Studies at Wayne State University. He is author of *Ideology and Change: The Transformation of the Caribbean Left*, and editor (with Alma Young) of *Caribbean Politics and Culture: Legacies of Cheddi Jagan and Michael Manley*.

JOSEPH MCLAREN is Professor of English at Hofstra University. He is author of *Langston Hughes: Folk Dramatist in the Protest Tradition, 1921–1943*, co-editor of *Pan-Africanism Updated* and *African Visions*, and editor of two volumes of the *Collected Works of Langston Hughes: The Big Sea* and *I Wonder as I Wander.*

AZUKA NZEGWU is a doctoral candidate in Philosophy, Interpretation, and Culture at Binghamton University. Her research emphasizes theoretical approaches that engage and utilize Web-based technologies.

NKIRU NZEGWU is Professor and Chair of Africana Studies as well as Professor of Philosophy, Interpretation, and Culture at Binghamton University. She is founder of Africa Resource Center, Inc. (africaresource.com), which provides many online educational and scholarly services, including publication of award-winning journals. She is author of *Family Matters: Feminist Concepts in African Philosophy of Culture.*

FOLU F. OGUNDIMU is Associate Professor of Journalism, Communication, and African Studies at Michigan State University. He is co-editor of *Media and Democracy in Africa* and editor of a special issue of *Journal of African Rural and Urban Studies.*

OBIORA CHINEDU OKAFOR is Associate Professor at the Osgoode Hall Law School, York University, Toronto, where he serves as Faculty Associate at the Harriett Tubman Institute for the Study of the African Diaspora and the Centre for Refugee Studies. His publications include *Legitimizing Human Rights NGOs: Lessons from Nigeria* and *The African Human Rights System, Activist Forces,* and *International Institutions.*

ISIDORE OKPEWHO is State University Distinguished Professor of the Humanities and Professor of Africana Studies, English, and Comparative Literature at Binghamton University. He is the author of numerous studies of oral tradition, including *The Epic in Africa; Myth in Africa; African Oral Literature; Once upon a Kingdom;* and scores of scholarly articles. His edited works include *The Oral Performance in Africa* and (with Carole B. Davies and Ali A. Mazrui) *The African Diaspora* (Indiana University Press, 1999). He was president of the International Society for Oral Literature in Africa (2002–2006) and has written four novels, the latest of which is *Call Me by My Rightful Name.*

JACOB K. OLUPONA is Professor of African Religious Traditions, Harvard Divinity School, and Professor of African and African American Studies in the Faculty of Arts and Sciences at Harvard University. He is the author or editor of several works, including *Kingship, Religion and Rituals in a Nigerian Community; Religion and Peace in Multifaith Nigeria; Religious Plurality in Africa;* and (with Regina Gemignani) *African Immigrant Religions in America.* He served as chair and as president of the African Association for the Study of Religions.

BAFFOUR K. TAKYI is Associate Professor of Sociology and Director of the Pan African Studies Program at the University of Akron. He is author (with Kwadwo Konadu-Agyeman and John Arthur) of *The New African*

Diaspora in North America and (with Yaw Oheneba-Sakyi) of *African Families at the Turn of the 21st Century.*

CASSANDRA R. VENEY is Assistant Professor in the Gender and Women's Studies Program and the Department of African American Studies at the University of Illinois at Chicago. She is author of *Forced Migration in Eastern Africa: Democratization, Structural Adjustment, and Refugees.*

PAUL TIYAMBE ZELEZA is Professor of African American Studies and History, the Liberal Arts and Sciences Distinguished Professor, and Head of the Department of African American Studies at the University of Illinois at Chicago. He is an honorary professor at the University of Cape Town. His publications include *A Modern Economic History of Africa,* which won the 1994 NOMA Award, *Manufacturing African Studies and Crises,* which received Special Commendation of the NOMA Award, and *The Encyclopedia of Twentieth-Century African History,* which received honorable mention for the Conover-Porter Award.

INDEX